Prote...
Inve...
Extended Warranty available

Savings to 50% off Dealer's Extended Warranty Prices!

Edmunds Teams up with Warranty Gold to offer You the Best Deal on Peace of Mind when Owning, Buying, or Selling Your Vehicle!

FREE QUOTE

http://www.edmunds.com/warranty
1-800-580-9889

Most people have three things in common when they buy a car.

They pay too much.

They waste time.

They hate the experience.

Which is exactly why you should call the Consumers Car Club, a nationwide auto buying service. We offer the quickest and most convenient way to save time and money when you buy a new car or truck. Simple as that. Just tell us the vehicle and options you want (any make or model-foreign or domestic) and we'll get you a lower price than you can get on your own. Guaranteed in writing. We can factory order any domestic vehicle and usually save you even more. No haggling. No hassles. No games.

Don't forget to ask about our loans, leases and extended service contracts. It's a terrific way to save even more money on the purchase of your new car. For more information, call the Consumers Car Club at 1-800-CAR-CLUB (1-800-227-2582).

The Smart New Way to Buy Your Car™

All new cars arranged for sale are subject to price & availability from the selling franchised new car dealer.

"Edmund's® arms you with more facts. In addition to reviews and specs, new-car buyers will find each car's invoice price, sticker price, destination charge and dealer holdback (profit the dealer makes even if the car sells at invoice)."
— Kristin Davis, **Kiplinger's Personal Finance Magazine,** December, 1997

"Edmund's® ... provides an amazing compilation of facts, details and evaluations about (a) car. You will be able to read honest and direct evaluations of (a) vehicle. You have the information at your fingertips to put together your dream car at invoice price."
— Ron Raisglid, **Buying & Leasing Cars on the Internet** (Los Angeles, CA: Renaissance Books, 1998)

"Edmund's®...is jam-packed with valuable information on virtually every new and used vehicle model as well as tips and safety information."
— Glenn Fannick, **Dow Jones Business Directory** (http://bd.dowjones.com), April 20, 1998

"The Edmund's® car buying guide print version...is an excellent product for consumers to use...(and is) one of the best auto information sources."
— Paul Maghielse, **The Motley Fool** (http://www.fool.com/car/step5car.htm), March 8, 1998

"Another resource of general auto pricing information can be found in bookstores, called the Edmund's® **New Car Price Books.** *Make sure you get their latest quarterly edition..."*
— Darrell Parrish, **The Car Buyer's Art** (Bellflower, CA: Book Express, 1998)

"Edmund's® has built a solid reputation for providing objective, reliable, new and used car and truck prices."
— Ron Raisglid, **Buying & Leasing Cars on the Internet** (Los Angeles, CA: Renaissance Books, 1998)

"Using the percent factor to figure dealer cost is not as accurate as using specific information published in Edmund's® New Car Prices."
— Mark Eskeldson, **What Car Dealers Don't Want You to Know** (Fair Oaks, CA: Technews Publishing, 1997)

"Edmund's® Automobile Buyers Guides are among the most respected new car books around...they're well-written, too, even entertaining. You'll also find detailed pricing information, as well as information about how dealers structure their prices. Ever heard of 'dealer holdback'? You can use this kind of knowledge in bargaining for a great price."
— **Houston Chronicle**, January 23, 1998

"Edmund's® provides engaging descriptions of many models of cars, plus important specifications, (and) a straightforward description of the calculus leading to a fair price for both dealer and consumer."
— **The Wall Street Journal**, April 15, 1999

"If you really want the nitty-gritty, you're going to have to ... (get) ... Edmund's® New Car Prices. This little book is a gold mine for the curious car buyer... It is an automobile fancier's delight, a straightforward, meaty compendium of raw facts. Buy the book, follow the steps outlined ... and you will determine the exact cost of just about any car."
— Remar Sutton, **Don't Get Taken Every Time** (New York, NY: Penguin Books, 1997)

Perfect Partners

USED CARS: PRICES & RATINGS

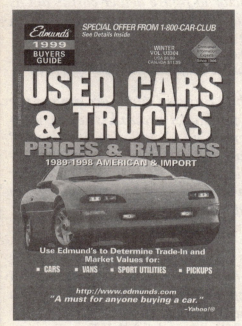

For nearly 35 years, Edmund's® has guided smart consumers through the complex used car marketplace. By providing you with the latest trade-in and market value, you are able to determine a fair price for your car before negotiations begin.

Whether buying, selling, or trading, Edmund's® *Used Cars: Prices & Ratings* gives all the information you need to get your very best deal.

- Prices Most American and Imported Used Cars, Pickup Trucks, Vans, and Sport Utilities

- Shows Summary Ratings for Most Used Vehicles

- Listings Cover Models Over Last 10 Years

- Price any Vehicle Quickly and Accurately

- Adjust Value for Optional Engines, Equipment and Mileage

For information on all Edmund's® Buyer's Guides, call 914-962-6297

2000

NEW CARS

PRICES &
REVIEWS

"THE ORIGINAL CONSUMER PRICE AUTHORITY"

NEW CARS

TABLE OF CONTENTS
WINTER 2000
VOL N3304-0003

Cover photo:
2000 Ford Focus

ISBN: 0-87759-650-6
ISSN: 1086-5470

Library of Congress Catalog
Card No: 71-80100

Editor-in-Chief:
Christian Wardlaw

Data Content Manager:
Alison Cooper

Production Manager:
Lynette Archbold

Managing Editor:
Karl Brauer

Detroit Editor:
John Clor

Senior Features Editor:
Brent Romans

Road Test Editor:
Dan Gardner

Copy Editor:
Deborah Greenbaum

Photography Editor:
Scott Jacobs

New Vehicle Data Editors:
Scott Schapiro
Jeremiah Knight
Wandile Kunene

Used Vehicle Data Editor:
John DiPietro

Senior Layout and Design Artist:
Robert Archbold

Introduction 10
Step-by-Step
   Cost Worksheet 13
How to Buy Your Next
   New Automobile 14
Edmund's® Most Wanted 16
Abbreviations 27
Cover Story:
   Ford Focus 28
Specifications 433
Crash Test Data 467
Warranties and
   Roadside Assistance 491
Dealer Holdbacks 493
Frequently
   Asked Questions 497
Leasing Tips 505
Road Tests:
   '00 Chevrolet Impala 512
   '00 Audi S4 518
Payment Table 524
Customer Assistance
   Numbers 525

ACURA
'99 Integra 34
'99 RL-Series 36
'00 TL-Series 38

AUDI
'00 A4 41
'00 A6 44
'00 S4 48
'00 TT 50

BMW
'00 3-Series 53
'00 5-Series 56

'00 M Coupe/Roadster 61
'00 Z3 63

BUICK
'00 Century 67
'00 LeSabre 72
'00 Park Avenue 77
'00 Regal 82

CADILLAC
'99 Catera 87
'00 DeVille 89
'00 Eldorado 92
'00 Seville 95

CHEVROLET
'00 Camaro 99
'00 Cavalier 103
'00 Corvette 108
'00 Impala 111
'00 Lumina 115
'00 Malibu 118
'00 Metro 121
'00 Monte Carlo 124
'00 Prizm 127

CHRYSLER
'00 300M 131
'00 Cirrus 133
'00 Concorde 136
'00 LHS 139
'00 Sebring Convertible 142
'00 Sebring Coupe 145

DAEWOO
'99 Lanos 148
'00 Leganza 150
'99 Nubira 152

DODGE
'00 Avenger 154
'00 Intrepid 154
'00 Neon 159
'00 Stratus 162

Special offer from 1-800-CAR-CLUB - details on page 3

FORD
- '00 Contour 166
- '00 SVT Contour 168
- '00 Crown Victoria 170
- '99 Escort 173
- '00 Escort ZX2 176
- '00 Focus 178
- '00 Mustang 181
- '00 SVT Mustang Cobra 185
- '00 Taurus 187

HONDA
- '00 Accord 191
- '00 Civic 194
- '99 Prelude 197
- '00 S2000 199

HYUNDAI
- '99 Accent 201
- '00 Elantra 203
- '00 Sonata 205
- '00 Tiburon 208

INFINITI
- '00 G20 211
- '00 I30 213
- '99 Q45 215

JAGUAR
- '00 S-Type 218

KIA
- '00 Sephia 221

LEXUS
- '00 ES 300 224
- '00 GS-Series 226
- '00 LS 400 230
- '00 SC-Series 232

LINCOLN
- '00 Continental 235
- '00 LS 238
- '00 Town Car 241

MAZDA
- '00 626 245
- '00 Miata 248
- '00 Millenia 250
- '00 Protegé 253

MERCEDES-BENZ
- '00 C-Class 256
- '00 C43 259
- '00 CLK 261
- '00 E-Class 264
- '00 SLK230 268

MERCURY
- '00 Cougar 371
- '00 Grand Marquis 273
- '00 Mystique 277
- '00 Sable 380

MITSUBISHI
- '99 Diamante 284
- '00 Eclipse 286
- '00 Galant 289
- '00 Mirage 292

NISSAN
- '00 Altima 295
- '00 Maxima 297
- '99 Sentra 301

OLDSMOBILE
- '00 Alero 304
- '99 Aurora 307
- '00 Intrigue 310

PLYMOUTH
- '00 Breeze 314
- '00 Neon 316
- '99 Prowler 320

PONTIAC
- '00 Bonneville 322
- '00 Firebird 325
- '00 Grand Am 330
- '00 Grand Prix 333
- '00 Sunfire 339

PORSCHE
- '99 Boxster 344

SAAB
- '00 9-3 349
- '00 9-5 352

SATURN
- '00 L-Series 355
- '00 S-Series 358

SUBARU
- '00 Impreza 362
- '00 Impreza Outback 365
- '00 Legacy 368
- '00 Legacy Outback 375

SUZUKI
- '00 Esteem 381
- '00 Swift 383

TOYOTA
- '00 Avalon 385
- '00 Camry 388
- '00 Camry Solara 493
- '00 Celica 396
- '00 Corolla 399
- '00 Echo 402

VOLKSWAGEN
- '00 Cabrio 406
- '00 Golf 408
- '00 Jetta 411
- '00 New Beetle 414
- '00 Passat 416

VOLVO
- '00 40-Series 420
- '00 70-Series 422
- '00 S80 428

© 2000 by Edmund Publications Corporation.
All rights reserved.
No reproduction in whole or in part may be made without explicit written permission from the publisher. Some images copyright www.arttoday.com.

INTRODUCTION

What's with the new name and logo?

"Consumer driven" is our motto. It accompanies our new logo, which was redesigned after we changed our name, and will serve as an advertising tagline. Call us Edmunds.com, your faithful servant since 1966, bringing you the scoop on car and truck pricing for nearly 35 years.

If you've been living without cable TV in an Airstream trailer on the outskirts of Quartzsite, Ariz., for the past couple of years, you might wonder what all this "dot com" stuff is about. In a word, the Internet. It's the future of publishing, of retailing, of banking, of investing, of education, and likely a number of things car hacks like us haven't dreamed of.

We publish a free Web site at http://www.edmunds.com, hence the new name of our company. At this Web site, you car gather all the same facts and figures on mainstream cars and trucks sold in the U.S. that you can by using this book. But there's more than just invoice and retail pricing, reviews, specifications, and how-to-buy articles. The photos are in color. We print the results of full road tests on a weekly basis. Plus, we can direct you to companies that can help you buy or finance a car, obtain an extended warranty, or provide you with aftermarket accessories.

Our free Web site is updated daily. This book you're holding is updated quarterly. That means our Web site can be more accurate if pricing on a vehicle has changed recently. We also publish timely incentive and rebate data on the Web site, required information for anyone looking to buy a new car. Finally, because this book is constrained by size and printing costs and the Web site is not, you get more detail on the vehicle you're considering when you visit the Internet than when you visit the local bookstore.

Why do we give all of the information in this book, and more, away for free on our Web site? Because we're consumer driven. It's our motto.

But I don't have a computer. What does this book provide me?

Not everyone owns a computer or has a desire to surf the Web. Others like to have all the available data gathered in one easy-to-read volume that's small enough to be carried around but large enough to offer thorough coverage. Some even like to collect and archive our printed compendiums of automotive facts and figures. If you fit this description, this edition of our traditional print buyer's guide is for you.

Within these pages, we provide you with pricing and specifications for models currently sold in the U.S. that cost less than $55,000. You'll also find editorial about the vehicles, crash-test data, a list of frequently asked questions about cars and the car-buying process and tutorials that should help you should you decide to haggle with the dealer.

There's also a list of our editorial staff's favorite vehicles in a variety of size and type classes, a full road test of the vehicle on the cover, and customer-assistance phone numbers for the major automakers so you can obtain more information on the models contained in this book.

How do I use this guide?

If you're new to Edmunds.com, or are new to the car-buying experience, here is how to use this guide. Your first step should be to visit a car dealership.

INTRODUCTION

Take a pad of paper with you, and write down all pertinent information from the window sticker of the car you like. Then, go home and snuggle up with this buyer's guide to start figuring out how to get the best deal on the car of your dreams.

Read the articles about **dealer holdbacks**, **buying your next new automobile**, and **leasing tips**. Then study the make and model that you're interested in. You'll find a representative photo of the vehicle, followed by a synopsis of "What's New?" for the model year. Then, a short review provides our opinion of the car. An extensive listing of standard equipment for each trim level comes next, telling you what items are included in the base price of the vehicle. The first paragraph pertains to the base model, and if more than one trim level is available, successive paragraphs will explain what additional features the additional trim levels include over the base model.

Next is the meat of this guide: the pricing data. Each vehicle has base invoice price and base MSRP listed for each trim level, and the destination charge, which is the cost of shipping the vehicle from the factory to the dealer. Don't forget to add the destination charge, which is non-negotiable, when pricing a vehicle. Following the base prices and destination charge is a listing of all the optional equipment available on the vehicle from the factory. Along the left margin you'll find a factory code for each option. The dealer invoice price and the MSRP are listed near the right margin. Some option listings have short descriptions that tell you, for example, what might be included in a particular option package, or what trim level the option is available on, or if there are restrictions and requirements regarding availability.

> "All things considered equal, your target price should include a 3 percent profit to the dealer."

You'll notice that some models do not have option listings. This is because the automaker includes the most popular accessories as standard equipment on a particular trim level, and any additional items that you might like to add to the vehicle will have to be purchased from and installed by the dealer, or are installed at the port of entry. Generally, you can haggle about 25 percent off dealer-installed accessories with little effort.

Looking for the exact specifications of your dream car? Check the back of this book, where you'll find charts displaying the length of the vehicle, the curb weight of the vehicle, and how much horsepower the base engine makes, among others. This format allows you to easily locate and compare specifications between different models and trim levels.

I've followed your advice. Why won't the dealer sell me the car?

Keep in mind that the laws of supply and demand apply to automobiles as much as they apply to any other material commodity. If a vehicle is in great demand and short supply, don't expect to get much of a discount. On the other hand, inflated inventories and tough competition mean that deals are readily available on models that aren't selling well. If a rebate is available on the car or truck you're shopping for, that's an indicator that the dealer will slash the price to the bone to get the car off the lot.

INTRODUCTION

If you've got to be the first on your block with a hot new model, you'll pay for the privilege. In fact, dealers sometimes demand profit above the MSRP on ultra-hot models, and they expect to get it. Meanwhile, it is not uncommon for older, stale models to sell below invoice, thanks to hefty incentive programs and rebates, particularly at year-end clearance time. All things considered equal, your target price should include a 3 percent profit to the dealer. But hot cars will cost more. Sometimes much more.

Contact us.

We strive to give you precise, accurate information so that you can make your very best deal, and we invite your comments. Your best bet for a response is to send email to: editor@edmunds.com. Otherwise, try snail mail to the attention of the Automotive Editors at Edmunds.com, P.O. Box 18827, Beverly Hills, CA, 90209-4827.

NOTE: All information and prices published herein are gathered from sources which, in the editor's opinion, are considered reliable, but under no circumstances is the reader to assume that this information is official or final. All prices are represented as approximations only, in US dollars, and are rounded to the highest whole dollar amount over 50 cents. Unless otherwise noted, all prices are effective as of 10/1/99, but are subject to change without notice. The publisher does not assume responsibility for errors of omission or interpretation. The computerized consumer pricing services advertised herein are not operated by nor are they are the responsibility of the publisher. The publisher assumes no responsibility for claims made by advertisers regarding their products or services.

2000 Honda S2000

STEP-BY-STEP COST WORKSHEET

MAKE: _____ EXTERIOR COLOR: _____
MODEL: _____ INTERIOR COLOR: _____
TRIM LEVEL: _____ ENGINE/TRANSMISSION: _____

ITEMS	INVOICE
Basic Vehicle Price:	
Optional Equipment:	
1.	
2.	
3.	
4.	
5.	
6.	
7.	
8.	
9.	
10.	
11.	
12.	
13.	
14.	
15.	
TOTAL	
SUBTRACT Holdback Amount (if ordering car)	
ADD 3% Fair Profit	
ADD Destination Charge	
ADD Advertising Fees (1.5% of MSRP maximum)	
ADD Documentation and D&H fees ($100 maximum)	
SUBTRACT Trade-In Value or Cash Down Payment	
or, if you own more on your existing car than it is worth,	
ADD Difference Between Trade Value and Loan Balance	
ADD Sales Taxes (and Registration fees, if applicable in your region)	
SUBTRACT Rebates and/or Incentives	
FINAL Price for Purchase or Capitalized Cost for Lease	
TOTAL COST	

EDMUND'S® NEW CARS

HOW TO BUY YOUR NEXT NEW AUTOMOBILE

Every automobile buyer has but one thought in mind — to save money by getting a good deal. Your goal should be to pay 3 percent over the dealer's true cost, not the 10-15 percent the dealer wants you to pay. Use the following guide to help you plan your purchase:

Step 1 Know what type of vehicle you need, and study the different models available.

Step 2 Test-drive, as extensively as possible, each model you're interested in. Pay special attention to safety features, design, comfort, braking, handling, acceleration, ride quality, ease of entry and exit, etc.

Step 3 Check insurance rates on the models you're interested in to make sure the premiums fall within your budget.

Step 4 Contact several financial institutions to obtain loan rate information. Later on, you can compare their arrangement with the dealer's financing plan.

Step 5 Find the exact vehicle you want, and copy all of the contents listed on the window sticker onto a pad of paper. Then, use our pricing information to determine actual dealer cost (if ordering the vehicle from the factory, just use our data to determine what the order will cost when you place it):

a) Total the dealer invoice column for the model and equipment you want using our step-by-step costing form.

b) If ordering the vehicle, determine the value of the holdback and subtract this amount. If the dealer orders the vehicle, he won't pay floorplanning (the charge to stock the vehicle), or advertising (an expected cost of business), which the holdback is designed to subsidize.

c) Add 3 percent fair profit. Keep in mind that hot-selling models in high demand and short supply will command additional profit, sometimes in excess of MSRP in extreme situations.

d) Add the destination charge, which is non-negotiable. Also expect to be charged advertising fees by the auto manufacturer to help pay for those MTV-style TV commercials that got you thinking about a new

HOW TO BUY YOUR NEXT NEW AUTOMOBILE

car in the first place. You should pay no more than 1.5 percent of the vehicle's MSRP.

e) Some dealers charge a delivery and handling (D&H) fee. Negotiate this fee. It's just added profit.

f) Add sales taxes.

g) Deduct any incentives or rebates.

Step 6 Shop this price around to several different dealerships. The dealer who meets or comes closest to your target price should get your business. Be sure that the dealer's price quote will be your final cost. Get it in writing!

Step 7 If your present vehicle will be used as a trade-in, negotiate the highest possible value for it. Try not to accept a value that is less than Edmunds.com's trade-in value for your car. When trading in your vehicle, you should deduct the trade value from the cost of the new vehicle. If you owe the bank more money than the trade-in is worth to the dealer, you are upside-down on your trade and must add the difference between what you owe and the trade value to the cost of the new vehicle. If you're making a cash down payment, either with or without a trade-in, be sure to deduct this amount from the cost of the new vehicle as well.

Step 8 To the final vehicle cost, add documentation fees and, in some areas, license plate charges.

Step 9 When talking to the finance manager as you close the deal, he or she will try to sell you rustproofing, undercoating, protection packages, dealer-added options, and an extended warranty or service contract. Forget about this stuff. Dealers charge a substantial markup on these usually useless items to fatten the profit margin on your deal.

Step 10 Enjoy your new vehicle, knowing that you did everything possible to get the best deal.

EDMUND'S® MOST WANTED

by Automotive Editors, Edmund Publications

Our staff members get the same question over and over: What's the "best" car or truck? There are many ways to answer this question, because there isn't a single "best" car or truck that will meet everyone's needs. When somebody asks us what the "best" of the crop is, we respond by quizzing the inquiring mind about her needs and wants in a vehicle.

Still, readers want to know what cars and trucks we'd buy given the resources. So our editorial staff recently gathered to hash over the roster of 2000 models available to the public. We picked our favorites under $55,000 in a variety of vehicle classes, resulting in a list of cars and trucks we'd want in our own garages.

When reviewing our selections, keep in mind that we're a group of men and women that enjoys driving. Our staff of writers ranges in age from the mid-twenties to the mid-forties. Half of us have kids. We enjoy long road trips. Some of us lead active lifestyles while the rest of us chomp chocolate chip cookie dough and eagerly await "Must See TV" each Thursday night. We need vehicles that fit this kind of lifestyle.

How did we select the Most Wanted? Only 2000 models were eligible, and at least one member of our editorial team had to have driven the vehicle prior to our deadline of October 1, 1999. Nominations were accepted, and votes were counted. Majority rule determined the winner. On some occasions there was unanimous agreement, such as our election of the Mercedes-Benz CLK for best luxury coupe. On others we engaged in heated discussions, such as when deciding if the Toyota Land Cruiser's steep price was worth skipping the redesigned GMC Yukon for best large SUV honors.

Our selections were guided as much by our hearts as our heads. We eat, breathe and dream automobiles, and in many instances, this love for the car overruled common sense during our selection process. But that's the great thing about Edmunds.com's Most Wanted list. It's guided by passion, not science.

Small Coupe: Honda Civic

Hey there, old man. In an amazing display of virility, the Honda Civic once again made the Edmunds.com Most Wanted list. By far the oldest car on our list (the current Civic platform dates back to 1996), the Civic Coupe

EDMUND'S® MOST WANTED

continues to impress us with numerous attributes. Despite a higher initial price than many other cars, the Civic makes up for it with a superior reputation for reliability. The DX and HX are the two entry-level models, the main difference between the two being the HX's more fuel-efficient engine. The Civic Coupe EX features a 127-horsepower VTEC, plus goodies like standard air conditioning, a CD player, and a moonroof. While the coupe's styling is still attractive, the main charge leveled against Civics in general is that they are rather boring. Honda's answer to that is the Civic Si. Available only in the coupe body style, the Si packs a 160-horsepower engine, a stiffer suspension, special 15-inch wheels, and four-wheel disc brakes. With MSRPs ranging from $12,680 for a DX Coupe to $17,545 for the Si, the Civic Coupe continues to be one of the best small cars on the market.

Small Sedan: Ford Focus

Focus? Never heard of it, you say? Don't worry; it's brand-new! Built by Ford, the Focus has performed a giant cannonball dive into the wading pool of small sedans. Not only have our initial impressions been good enough to elevate the Focus to the top of the best Small Sedan category, but we'd also say that it's Ford's best small car ever. What impresses us about the Focus is its intelligent design and how it surpasses expectations. The interior offers considerable room and comfort and the handling and steering actually make the Focus fun to drive. Safety has been addressed with a stiff body structure, standard front airbags, and optional side airbags. Trim levels for the sedan are LX, SE and ZTS. The LX and SE use a 110-horsepower engine for power, while a 130-horsepower engine is optional on the SE and standard on the ZTS. The MSRPs start at $12,125 for the LX Sedan and end up at $15,165 for the ZTS. For the money, you'll be hard pressed to find another sedan that offers as much as the Focus.

Midsize Coupe: Toyota Camry Solara

Torn between your need to have a practical car and your desire to drive something with a bit of pizzazz? One couldn't ask for a more sensible automobile than Toyota's Camry. Offering Toyota's long-standing attributes of reliability and refinement, the Camry quietly and competently goes about its business. The only problem is that it's rather boring in terms of style, both inside and out. Enter the Camry Solara Coupe. Now you can have your cake and eat it too, as the Solara keeps all the goodness of the

EDMUND'S® MOST WANTED

Camry four-door and adds more than a touch of style with its rakish coupe body. And the interior, capable of carrying four adults comfortably, is more attractive as well, with a cockpit feel and faux wood trim that could pass for the real thing. The Solara is available in two trim levels: SE and SLE. SE models come well equipped with A/C, power windows/locks/mirrors, antilock brakes and a four-cylinder engine with 135 horsepower. An ultra-smooth, 200-hp V6 is optional on the SE and standard on the upscale, leather-clad SLE. Transmission choices include a five-speed manual or four-speed automatic on the SEs and auto tranny only on the SLE.

Midsize Sedan: Volkswagen Passat

Yes, you can enjoy driving a family sedan, thanks to the existence of the Volkswagen Passat. Moreover, it comes in an artfully styled wrapper, which helps you stand apart from the crowd. Roomy and comfortable, with top-notch offset crash-test scores, the Passat is well equipped right out of the box. Basic GLS trim includes a torquey 150-hp turbocharged four-cylinder engine and all the creature comforts you'll need. Spend a few extra grand and you can get leather, sunroof, alloy wheels and a substantial V6 engine in zooty GLX trim. A five-speed manual transmission is standard, while a Tiptronic-style automanual is optional. Inside you'll find materials and switchgear that is shared with higher-end Audi products, but you'll have to live with small stereo controls and one of the worst cupholder designs we've seen in years. Nevertheless, this VW will put a smile on your face for miles to come, and is equipped with one of the best powertrain warranties in the business for peace of mind. Carting the family around town isn't a chore anymore.

Large Sedan: Dodge Intrepid

Sedan buyers desiring interior and trunk space need look no further than the affordable Dodge Intrepid. This car is gargantuan, with plenty of room for five adults and much of their luggage. It's a good-looking car too, as long as cab-forward architecture and modern lines appeal to you. There are shortcomings, mainly in terms of refinement, but the low price and high value quotient make it easy to live with cheap interior materials and intrusive road rumble. Choose from base or sporty ES trim levels, and you'll get a well-equipped and comfortable family hauler. A 2.7-liter V6 mated to an automatic transmission is standard on both cars. Base Intrepids include all the usual goodies, but ABS, remote keyless entry and

EDMUND'S® MOST WANTED

a power driver's seat are options. ES has the gimmicky AutoStick automanual standard, and can be equipped with an optional 3.2-liter V6. ES is also your ticket to traction control, aluminum wheels, in-dash CD changer, fog lights and leather upholstery. Either way you go the Intrepid will serve your needs capably if buying a big car is on your "to do" list.

Station Wagon: Audi A4 Avant

Here's a vehicle that truly lets you have it all. Looking for a sporty ride with telepathic steering, minimal body roll and a penchant for dusting sport coupes in the twisties? The A4 Avant handles performance needs in a most un-stationwagon-like manner. But wait, your spouse needs a car that can haul the kids and groceries in a comfortable yet safe environment. The A4 comes standard with air conditioning and climate control. It also gets top marks in crash testing, is equipped with Audi's sure-footed Quattro all-wheel-drive system, and features standard front and side airbags. A 1.8-liter four-cylinder engine makes 150 horsepower while the larger 2.8-liter V6 makes 190 ponies. Check the sport package and cold weather package on your option sheet and you'll have the ultimate family truckster for any and all situations.

Sport Coupe: Ford SVT Mustang Cobra

Sure, the Ford SVT Mustang Cobra was at the center of controversy when some 1999 Cobra motors were found NOT to be making the 320 horsepower they are advertised as having. But Ford had initiated a fix and pushed engine performance higher on the Special Vehicle Team's priority list. With that issued solved, enthusiasts are left reaping the driving-enjoyment benefits of the Cobra's exclusive Independent Rear Suspension system (or IRS). When you add in its five-speed manual, beefy four-wheel discs with ABS and traction control and 17-inch rubber, the Cobra attacks twisty ribbons of pavement like few others in its class. With fresh styling, improved steering and a long list of standard equipment and creature comforts, its surprising that this kind of performance prowess can be this much fun to drive. While other manufacturers are thinking of putting their pony car models out to pasture, Ford's IRS-equipped SVT Mustang Cobra raises the bar on handling while keeping sales at a full gallop. And when it comes to value, where else can you get a 300-odd horse V8 and IRS handling for less than 35,000?

EDMUND'S® MOST WANTED

Sport Sedan: Audi S4

The Audi A4 has always been one of our favorite cars. It's affordable, comfortable, supportive, stealthy, and sexy. Kind of like great underwear, you might say. And now there's a new version of the A4, this time with little blue and yellow rocket ships on it. Ooh, baby! Think of the $37,900 Audi S4 as an A4 2.8 Quattro on massive doses of illegal steroids. Power comes from a 2.7-liter, 30-valve, twin-turbo V6 engine. Horsepower is rated at 250. More impressively, 258 foot-pounds of torque are available as low as 1,850 rpm. Take your choice of either a six-speed manual or five-speed automatic transmission. The S4's suspension is performance-tuned, and the brakes are more powerful than a standard A4's. To visually separate the S4, there are special wheels, larger air-intake openings, different interior materials, and two exclusive colors—Imola Yellow and Nogaro Blue. If you need a four-door sedan that is equally apt at city cruising or back-road roosting, our choice for 2000 is overwhelmingly the S4.

Entry-Luxury Coupe: BMW 3 Series

Last year we were blown away by BMW's redesigned 3 Series sedan. This year the company follows up with its exceptional 3 Series coupe, building them on the same E46 platform. Yet the new 323Ci and 328Ci Coupes are more than just two-door versions of the sedan. They have slightly altered exterior dimensions that make them longer, lower and wider than the four-door cars. A 2.5-liter inline six, creating 170 horsepower, propels the 323Ci while a 2.8-liter six, making 193 horsepower, scoots the 328Ci. These silky-smooth engines can be mated to either a slick-shifting five-speed manual or a new Steptronic five-speed automatic transmission. Of course, the real driving pleasure, when talking BMWs, comes not from straightline blasts but from back-road barnstorming, where the real magic of these ultimate driving machines can be experienced. If you're a performance enthusiast seeking a touch of class at a reasonable price, the sub-$30,000 323Ci deserves a test drive.

Entry-Luxury Sedan: Lincoln LS

The rear-drive LS is a huge departure for Ford's traditionally stodgy Lincoln brand and we've been sufficiently impressed during initial test-drives to name it our pick of the entry-luxury sedan litter. Sharing a platform with Jaguar's impressive S-Type, LS is available with either a strong 210-hp Duratec V6 or a delicious 252-hp V8. The V6 model can be

EDMUND'S® MOST WANTED

equipped with a manual transmission (!), which is bundled with a sport package that includes a tighter suspension and less brightwork on the bumpers. LS V8 Sport models come only with an automanual transmission called SelectShift, and attractive five-spoke 17-inch wheels and tires. As expected, LS comes loaded with luxury accoutrements, and the options list is short. A power sunroof, Alpine sound, traction control and Lincoln's RESCU emergency messaging system are notable extras. Tuned to go head to head with the best from Europe, the LS is fun to drive. It's also a good-looking car, with strongly chiseled flanks and tastefully incorporated Lincoln styling cues. Though unproven, the new Lincoln LS is decidedly different in a market segment awash with overseas nameplates, and represents a dramatic turning point for this American luxury brand. If we had 35 grand burning a hole in our pocket, we'd drive this puppy home.

Luxury Coupe: Mercedes-Benz CLK

Luxury-car buyers demand brand cachet, real wood trim, sumptuous leather, stylish good looks and plenty of doodads to fiddle with during the drive. This Benz meets and exceeds expectations on all fronts. First, you've got the three-pointed star hood ornament, reminding you each and every time you get behind the wheel that you're driving a Mercedes. Burled walnut trim decorates interior surfaces, and high-quality leather is stretched tautly over firm and supportive seats. The exterior of the CLK screams class, with tasteful chrome accents, a traditional grille, trademark round headlamps and ribbed taillights. Loaded with luxury, the CLK comes standard with everything you could want except heated seats, a power sunroof, xenon gas discharge headlamps, CD changer, integrated telephone and rain-sensing windshield wipers. Two models are available: a speedy and sophisticated CLK320 with a smooth-revving 3.2-liter V6, or the beefy V8-powered CLK430 that was seemingly modeled after American muscle cars of yore. With 270 horsepower, 17-inch wheels and stability control, the CLK430 is the rougher-riding and better performing model of the two.

Luxury Sedan: BMW 5 Series

The 5 Series is a favorite of enthusiasts everywhere, and for good reason. Perhaps more than any other carmaker, BMW has the best balance of luxury and performance. Throw in rock-solid build quality, aggressive styling and safety features galore and it's no wonder why this is our

EDMUND'S® MOST WANTED

favorite luxury sedan. Whether gobbling up hundreds of miles of interstate or dispatching decreasing-radius turns on your favorite canyon run, the 5 Series is unflappable. Sharing the same body, the main difference between the two 5 Series models is the powerplant. The 528i comes with a 2.8-liter, inline six making 193 hp, whereas the 540i has a mighty 4.4-liter, 282-horse V8. Either car can be fitted with a manual or automatic transmission and both offer excellent performance in terms of acceleration, braking, handling and ride. For those with deeper pockets and an even greater need for speed, the 540i offers sports car level athleticism, such as a sub-6-second zero-to-60 time.

Luxury Station Wagon: BMW 5 Series

Station wagons are actually cool these days, appealing to the growing contingent of anti-SUV consumers that wants cargo-carrying capability but none of the compromises in performance and ride that come with most truck-based sport-utes. BMW's excellent, but expensive, 5 Series wagon is the antithesis of the sport-utility vehicle. Choose either the 528i with its 193-hp, twin-cam inline six, or the ground pounding 540i for its 282-hp V8. The stiff premium paid for the 540 may be worth it to enthusiasts who can brag that they own the fastest station wagon sold in America. Others will be happy with the smooth, refined and significantly less expensive 528, the only BMW wagon available with either a stick or automatic. By selecting the 5 Series wagon, you get all the benefits of owning a BMW, with none of the detriments of the traditional station wagon. This family truckster behaves just like the 5 Series sedan; the only indication from behind the wheel that you're piloting a vehicle capable of carrying up to 65 cubic feet of cargo is the reflection you find in the rearview mirror. If we were to buy a luxury station wagon, this Bimmer would be ours.

Convertible: Mazda Miata

Introduced as a 1990 model, Mazda's back-to-basics sports car was a smash success right out of the box. With peppy performance from its four-cylinder engine and handling like that of a go-kart, the small two-seater offered all the fun of the old British roadsters, such as Triumphs and MGs, coupled to superior Japanese reliability and build quality. Mazda redesigned the Miata last year, keeping all the car's inherent goodness while still making some worthwhile changes. The most noteworthy improvements are increased engine output (now rated at 140 hp) and a change from a plastic back window to a glass unit. Exposed headlights and more aggressive body contours freshened up the car's

EDMUND'S® MOST WANTED

looks. For a base price of around $20,000, the Miata offers up a fun driving experience unmatched by any other car near its price range.

Sports Car: Chevrolet Corvette

Bet you wish you had a dollar for every time you read some auto scribe blab, "This is the best 'Vette yet!" It seems each time this classic American sports car has gone in for a remake, reviewers come back with that same old saw. But we're here to tell you that (gasp!) this is the best 'Vette yet! Really! Cross-our-hearts, hope-to-die, stick a needle in our eye! Without getting into a discussion of age, let's just say that we're including our experience with big blocks, LT1 small blocks, pace cars, LT5-powered ZR-1s, anniversary editions, second-generation LT1s - you name 'em. And toss in countless hours sampling rides at Bloomington Gold and Corvettes at Carlisle. Granted, the new, 345-horsepower LS1 V8 is not the most awe-inspiring 'Vette engine ever made. But its smoothness almost belies its pushrod architecture. And its delivery of power—when experienced in concert with this car's improved shift action, steering, brakes, suspension, rigidity, comfort, ergonomics and features—positions the Corvette on the top tier of American performance. Its looks might not stoke everybody's fire, but one drive will convince you there's never been a more capable Corvette built than the C5.

Small Pickup: Ford Ranger

Despite a few character flaws, Ford's best-selling Ranger is the truck we'd buy if we needed a small, reliable hauler. We like its rugged good looks, ergonomically correct cabin, and available four-door extended-cab body. A large selection of drivetrains is available to serve a wide variety of needs. You can get your choice of three engines mated to manual or automatic transmissions with two-wheel drive or shift-on-the-fly four-wheel drive. Two trim levels, XL or XLT, are available in regular-cab short- or longbed and extended-cab shortbed configurations. Optional sport appearance and off-road packages dress up a Ranger nicely, and you can even get a stylish FlareSide bed. Rangers work hard and play hard while delivering comfort and convenience in a dependable package. Regardless of what Ranger you choose, you'll be getting one rewarding pickup.

EDMUND'S® MOST WANTED

Full-size Pickup: Ford F-Series

Despite the recent introduction of new full-size GM and Toyota pickups, Ford's versatile F-Series lineup offers pickup-truck buyers superior selection from a wide range of light- and heavy-duty models. F-150 light-duty trucks are the best-selling vehicles in the world. Availability ranges from sturdy work trucks to luxurious four-wheelers with four-door extended cabs to a true 360-hp muscle truck that can spank many sport coupes on the street and at the track. Curvaceous sheetmetal, a carlike interior, comfortable seats and powerful overhead-cam engines are hallmarks of the F-150. Super duty F-250 and F-350 pickups have rugged big-rig styling and an interior with an industrial ambience. Regular-, extended- and crew-cab body styles are available; you can tow as much as 10,000 pounds and benefit from GVWRs reaching above 11,200 pounds. Optional on Super Duty trucks is a torque-pig turbodiesel V8 making 500 ft-lbs. of twist at 1,600 rpm, but to get this added grunt you've gotta spend some big green. Yep, Ford's got everyone's pickup needs covered with the incredibly popular F-Series trucks.

Small Van: Honda Odyssey

Just when it was beginning to look like Chrysler had an unbreakable stranglehold on the minivan market, Honda punts them, and everyone else, into oblivion with its all-new Odyssey. If it were just a matter of having that great 3.5-liter VTEC engine, complete with 210 horsepower and 229 foot-pounds of torque, the Odyssey would not be our choice for this category. And the dual power sliding doors on the EX models, while potentially convenient, didn't sway us immediately to the Honda camp either. But once inside, where we could drop the third-row seat into the floor and remove both second-row seats (all in less than 60 seconds), it became apparent where the future of minivans was going, and that Honda was already there. The Odyssey also offers safety, with top scores in frontal-impact, side-impact, and offset-impact crash testing. A stellar engine, functional and roomy interior, along with benchmark safety and Honda quality at a great price. Sorry Chrysler, your reign has ended.

Large Van: Ford Econoline

For sheer people-hauling ability, it doesn't get any better than a domestically built van/wagon. And although sales of large vans are heavily biased towards commercial use, the Edmunds.com staff would choose Ford's

EDMUND'S® MOST WANTED

Econoline if given the choice. The current lineup is quite extensive. Depending on what version you pick, the Econoline can haul between seven to 15 passengers and tow from 4,700 to 10,000 pounds. For engines, the main gasoline choices are a 5.4-liter V8 with 255 horsepower and 350 foot-pounds of torque, or a 6.8-liter V10 with 305 horsepower and 420 foot-pounds of torque. There's also a myriad of options and configurations to choose from, ensuring that you can find the exact model to match your needs.

Small SUV: Honda CR-V

How can the CR-V be Edmunds.com's Most Wanted small SUV when the hot-selling Nissan Xterra won our recent comparison test? Simple, our editors are willing to deal with a harsh ride, cramped rear seat and "creative" styling elements in return for a truly capable off-road vehicle with plenty of ground clearance and a torquey six-cylinder engine...at least for the duration of a comparison test that involves extensive off-road driving. However, when it's time to drive a small SUV the way most of us really do (on paved roads with multiple passengers), the Xterra fades fast while the CR-V rises to the occasion. The only small SUV currently on the market with a fully functional rear seat, the CR-V also boasts top-notch ergonomics, quality interior materials, and a pleasant, carlike ride. Don't get us wrong, we love Lenny Kravitz and first-aid kits as much as the next guy. But when it comes to how most of us drive our mini-SUVs most of the time, Hondas CR-V leads the way.

Midsize SUV: Jeep Grand Cherokee

Jeep did an amazing job of updating an already great SUV when it redesigned the Grand Cherokee in 1999. For 2000 the JGC continues to rule the midsize SUV field with its powerful engine offerings, luxurious interior appointments, comfortable and confident on-road ride, and class-leading off-road ability. The 4.0-liter, inline six-cylinder engine that comes standard in the Laredo models was refined in 1999 and makes a healthy 195 horsepower. The optional 4.7-liter V8 bumps peak horsepower to a neck snapping 235 with 295 ft-lbs. of torque. Jeep's Quadra-Drive four-wheel-drive system makes quick work of slippery surfaces while its high-travel suspension allows for "billy-goat" class rock climbing. If your demands for a midsize SUV run to the extremes in both on and off-road capabilities, Jeep's Grand Cherokee is simply the only vehicle worth considering.

EDMUND'S® MOST WANTED

Large SUV: GMC Yukon

You've got stuff. You need something to haul your stuff. An '83 Subaru Brat isn't going to cut it. What are you going to get? There are plenty of contestants in the full-size SUV market. All of them are good. But the freshly minted models from GM—the GMC Yukon and Yukon XL, as well as the Chevrolet Tahoe and Suburban—are our top choices. While both the Yukon and Yukon XL are, of course, large, the XL's longer wheelbase endows it with a considerably bigger cargo capacity. Both SUVs can seat up to nine passengers. Visually, the new Yukons don't look considerably different than the ones before. The changes underneath and inside, however, are substantial. GMC has improved both handling and braking. There is more headroom and legroom. The interior design is better. For power, your choices are three different V8s, ranking from 275 to 300 horsepower. Four-wheel drive is available on all models. For most families, we feel the Yukon is plenty big enough. But for those families whose needs and desires exceed a piddly Yukon, the Yukon XL should serve nicely.

Luxury SUV: Lexus LX 470

In the luxury SUV class, excessive is clearly the name of the game. Excessive size, excessive chrome, excessive engine displacement. Interesting then that our pick for the ultimate luxury SUV is a model that is relatively moderate in most respects (except for the excessive price). The Lexus LX 470 is not the biggest, gaudiest or most powerful SUV in the luxury class, but it is easily the most talented. You want a cushy and comfortable on-road ride, plus a palatial interior with high-tech options and you still want it to cross the Rubicon Trail? No problem. Heck, it will even drop down to allow easier entry and egress for passengers, and raise up to offer increased ground clearance during extreme off-road maneuvers. Its adaptive variable suspension can stiffen or loosen up the shock valving in 2.5 milliseconds, depending on road conditions, and its third-row seat is a snap to fold up for additional cargo capacity. We still love Toyota's Land Cruiser and feel it is a better value, but for pure luxury combined with pure utility, see your Lexus dealer today.

8V	8-valve
12V	12-valve
16V	16-valve
24V	24-valve
2WD	two-wheel drive
4WD	four-wheel drive
ABS	antilock braking system
A/C	air conditioning
ALR	automatic locking retractor
Amp	ampere
AS	all-season
ASR	automatic slip regulation
AT	automatic
Auto	automatic
AWD	all-wheel drive
BSW	black sidewall
Cass.	cassette
CD	compact disc
CFC	chloroflourocarbon
Conv.	convertible
Cpe	coupe
Cu. Ft.	cubic foot (feet)
Cyl.	cylinder
DOHC	dual overhead cam
DRL	daytime running light(s)
DRW	dual rear wheels
DSC	dynamic stability control
EDL	electronic differential lock
EFI	electronic fuel injection
ELR	emergency locking retractor
EQ	equalizer
ETR	electronically-tuned radio
Ext.	extended
ft-lbs.	foot-pounds (measurement of torque)
FWD	front-wheel drive
Gal.	gallon(s)
GAWR	gross axle weight rating
GVW	gross vehicle weight
GVWR	gross vehicle weight rating
GPS	global positioning satellite
Hbk.	hatchback
HD	heavy duty
Hp	horsepower
HUD	heads-up display
HVAC	heating, ventilation and air conditioning
I-4	inline four
I-5	inline five
I-6	inline six
L	liter
LB	longbed
lb(s).	pound(s)
LCD	liquid crystal display
LED	light emitting diode
LEV	low emission vehicle
LH	left hand
LWB	long wheelbase
M&S	mud and snow
mpg	miles per gallon
mph	miles per hour
MPI	multi-port injection
MSRP	manufacturer's suggested retail price
N/A	not available OR not applicable
NC	no charge
NHTSA	National Highway and Traffic Safety Administration
NVH	noise, vibration and harshness
OD	overdrive
OHC	overhead cam
OHV	overhead valve
Opt.	option OR optional
OWL	outline white-letter
Pass.	passenger
Pkg.	package
PRNDL	Park, Reverse, Neutral, Drive, Low
RBL	raised black-letter
Reg.	regular
RH	right hand
r/l	right and left
rpm	revolutions per minute
RWD	rear-wheel drive
SB	shortbed
SBR	steel-belted radial
Sdn	sedan
SFI	sequential fuel injection
SLA	short/long arm
SMPI	sequential multi-port injection
SOHC	single overhead cam
SPI	sequential port injection
SRW	single rear wheels
Std.	standard
SUV	sport utility vehicle
SWB	short wheelbase
TDI	turbocharged direct injection
TOD	torque on demand
V6	V-type six
V8	V-type eight
V10	V-type ten
V12	V-type twelve
VR	v-rated
VSC	vehicle skid contrl
VTEC	variable valve timing and lift electronic control
VVT-i	variable valve timing, intelligence
Wgn.	wagon
WOL	white outline-letter
WS	work series
WSW	white sidewall
W/T	work truck
X-cab	extended cab

FOCUS
THE SHARPER IMAGE

Ah yes, the good old days of naming cars. For Ford, it used to be about real-life things, like Mustang, Maverick, and Monarch. But now that we are approaching the new millennium, it seems Ford has run out of nouns. Its latest car is named after a verb. Focus, in fact. Can you name a car after a verb? Is that legal? Really, by this logic, I could name my car the Talk. Or the Burp.

Admittedly, the Focus name isn't as bad as some other small-car names that come to mind. (Top three: 1) Chevy Citation. Physically impossible to get a speeding ticket in it; 2) Toyota Starlet. Sleeping its way to the top didn't help its career; 3) Pontiac Le Mans. "Days of Thunder" had more to do with racing than this thing.) Does the word "focus" have significance for this car? Ford doesn't or won't say, but my guess is that Ford is really *focused* on building a good car. Or maybe it means you're supposed to *focus* on the car itself. Well, whatever. It does make more sense than Pinto, at least.

In a strange way, the Focus needs to thank its antithesis, the truck. Americans have bought so many F-150s, Explorers and Expeditions these past few years that Ford hasn't had a clue about what to do with all the money. It bought Volvo, of course, but it's logical to assume that some of that extra money found its way into the R&D budget for the Focus. We say this because it's Ford's best small car ever.

The Focus is a completely new platform. Going on sale in late September 1999, it's available in three body styles – a three-door hatchback aimed at a younger crowd, a four-door sedan aimed at a grown-up younger crowd, and a wagon for people with too much junk in their lives. For the different body styles, there are four trim levels: ZX3 (3-door); LX (sedan); SE (sedan and wagon); and the high-series ZTS (sedan). Although the front-end structure and design of the Focus is common to all three body styles, Ford hopes that the remaining differences will attract a broad base of paying customers.

BY BRENT ROMANS
PHOTOS COURTESY OF
FORD MOTOR COMPANY

One of the key design elements for the Focus is its intelligent use of space. Ford boasts that the car's overall design started on the inside to provide additional cabin space and comfort. The goal was to have the Focus accommodate humans ranging from a 4-foot-10-inch female weighing 95 pounds to a 6-foot-4-inch male weighing 240 pounds. Arnold Schwarzenegger to George Costanza's mom—Focus designers want to accommodate them both. At the same time!

To achieve this lofty goal, the Focus has a high roofline and a 103-inch wheelbase. The wheels are pushed towards the corners, much like Chrysler did with its LH-series of cars. The high roofline allowed Ford engineers to position the seats higher off the floor, which freed up the positive benefits of easier entry/egress, a better view for the driver, and improved leg comfort for rear-seat passengers.

Besides providing more space and comfort for passengers, the interior also contains thoughtful ergonomics. Though they still spend most of their time drinking Starbucks coffee and talking on cell phones, drivers generally fiddle with the audio controls more than the climate controls. So Ford placed the audio controls higher than the climate controls for easier access. Both feature buttons that can be easily identified by touch alone. The interior itself is attractive, and contains styling elements from both the Escort ZX2 and Mercury Cougar. The ZX3 interior, with its faux-metal highlights, looks sporty. The ZTS Sedan's plood (journalist slang for plastic wood) highlights do not look sporty. They do not look luxurious. They just look like plood.

The seats are comfortable and supportive. All Focus seats can be adjusted in height, and a tilt/telescopic steering wheel is optional. For safety, the Focus utilizes an optimized body structure, standard driver and passenger airbags, seatbelt pre-tensioners and load-limiting retractors, and optional side airbags. A three-point

safety belt for the center rear seat is standard, as are child-safety-seat anchor points.

Once the comfy Mr. Schwarzenegger and Mrs. Costanza finish arguing over whether "Commando" or "Raw Deal" was a better movie, they will focus (Sorry. Won't happen again.) on the improved driving dynamics. By driving dynamics, we refer to the way the car handles, steers, accelerates and brakes. Ford was able to use the latest techniques to produce a lightweight, yet rigid chassis. This in turn enabled Ford engineers to fine-tune the front- and rear-suspension systems to deliver new levels of precision and comfort. Up front, the Focus uses MacPherson struts and new, broad A-arms located by horizontal bushings. A fully independent multi-link suspension has been

top left: Ford Focus wagon, hatchback and sedan
bottom left: front suspension detail
right: Ford Focus hatchback

adopted for the rear. Though more expensive to produce than a twist-beam axle system (such as on the Ford Escort), the multi-link IRS system is more beneficial in ride comfort, steering precision, handling, stability, noise levels and packaging.

The steering system is surprisingly quick, fluid and responsive. Fine-tuning and a careful selection of new materials enabled Ford to reduce the friction within the steering system by 20 percent. All steering components such as the seals, bearings, tie-rod joints and strut top mounts are optimized for low friction. Ford went through this effort because too much friction or resistance in the steering system can make it feel unnatural.

There are two engine choices: a 2.0-liter SOHC four cylinder or a more-fizzy 2.0-liter DOHC Zetec. While both engines can be found in other Ford products, they have been improved for use in the Focus. The 2.0-liter SOHC I4 delivers 110 horsepower at 5,000 rpm. Peak torque is 125 ft-lbs. at 3,750 rpm. The engine has been significantly upgraded to improve NVH by 30 percent and reduce weight. The DOHC Zetec has also been improved in the noise department. Ford says a full 50 percent reduction in perceived engine sound levels has been incorporated for the Focus. Horsepower for this engine is 130 at 5,300 rpm, and maximum torque is 135 at 4,500 rpm. Acceleration is acceptable with the SOHC engine and quite competitive with the DOHC. An automatic or manual transmission is available for either.

While improved steering and handling are all well and good, it's hard to impress the neighbors with them. That job is left to the styling. Whether it succeeds or not is another question. One thing is certain: The styling of the Focus is distinct and functional. Ford says its "appearance is designed to be progressive, adventurous and distinctively different from the softer, more traditional proportions and silhouettes of other small cars." Translation: You won't mistake the three-door for a Volkswagen New Beetle. The hatchback is the most distinctive and European-looking of the bunch, but all versions have an angular shape, with sculpted wheel arches, triangular headlights and taillights, and crisp lines on the body panels. Like it or not, the styling is functional. Ford says the shape provides maximum crash protection and aerodynamics. Drag co-efficient for the sedan is a low 0.31.

The sedan's trunk has an impressive 12.9 cubic feet of capacity. In-frame gas struts—designed to not encroach upon trunk space—are used to shut the trunk instead of traditional mechanical arms that may dent luggage. The

rear speakers are built into the doors to prevent them from hanging down into the trunk. For the wagon, the luggage compartment holds 37.5 cubic feet of cargo and is optimized for access and functionality.

We suspect that the Focus will be a big success for Ford. It's better than the Escort, even though both will continue to sell at dealerships. And it's certainly competitive with the likes of the Dodge Neon or Honda Civic. Base retail prices range from $12,280 for the 3-door hatchback ZX3 to $15,795 MSRP for the SE Wagon. Prices include the destination and delivery charge of $415. For the price, the Focus seems to have all the necessary elements— roominess, comfort, good driving dynamics, safety and functionality. And you can say what you want about the styling. But when you're strapped for cash and can't quite afford an Aston Martin DB7 Vantage to focu…er, attract attention to yourself, something that looks different than every other small econobox on the road can be quite nice. ∎

One 15-minute call
could save you 15% or more
on car insurance.

America's 6th Largest Automobile Insurance Company
1-800-555-2758

ACURA INTEGRA

| CODE | DESCRIPTION | INVOICE | MSRP |

1999 INTEGRA

1999 Acura Integra

What's New?

In a small step up-market, Acura has decided to kill the Integra's entry-level RS trim. The LS gets leather accents and 15-inch wheels, and the sporty GS-R now comes with leather seats.

Review

Honda enjoys the distinction of landing luxury cars in the United States before any other Japanese automaker had even considered the idea. The Legend sedan, marketed under the Acura nameplate, was an interesting choice over domestic luxury sedans, and was an inexpensive and reliable alternative to European luxury marques. However, Honda couldn't expect to sell enough Legends to keep its new Acura franchise afloat, so engineers spruced up the Honda Civic platform and introduced the nimble Integra to complement the bigger sedan in showrooms.

Since 1986, when the Integra debuted, it has garnered praise from a variety of automotive and consumer groups. Integras have always been sporty, practical, fun-to-drive and reliable. They are popular cars with a wide demographic group. The current iteration, which is the third generation of the Integra, is no exception to this rule.

While imminently comfortable for two and even livable for four full-sized adults, the Integra is first and foremost a driver's car. Think of it as a Japanese BMW 3-series and you won't be far off. Sure it's got fewer cylinders and the wrong set of wheels pulling it around, but if you can't afford the price of entry (or maintenance or insurance) for anything from Bavaria, the Integra makes an adequate substitute. With a fully independent four-wheel double wishbone suspension, front and rear stabilizer bars, and a thick steering wheel that gives excellent feedback about what's going on down below, the Integra is one of the best-handling front-drivers in the world.

If competent handling was all the Integra had to offer, it would still be worth considering, even in today's competitive sport compact market. Fortunately, Acura didn't stop there. The base engine, sold on GS and LS trim, is a 1.8-liter four-cylinder unit that makes an adequate 140 horsepower. Step up to the GS-R and you're rewarded with a VTEC-enhanced 1.8-liter inline four that boasts 170 horsepower and 128 foot-pounds of torque.

The Integra sport coupes and sedans are quick and comfortable, with excellent build quality. Since 1994, they've sported swoopy, modern styling, featuring quad, circular headlamps. Seating,

INTEGRA   ACURA

headroom, and overall ergonomics are typical Honda: straightforward and functional. The shifter is one of the best in the industry with a shape that fits the hand perfectly and has a relatively short throw between gears.

Ultimately, however, time and the automotive world wait for no car and the Integra's appearance is showing its age. With cars like the new Mercury Cougar clawing into the potential market, Acura will soon need to prepare the Integra for life in the 21st century.

Standard Equipment

LS COUPE (5M): 1.8L I4 DOHC SMPI 16-valve engine; 5-speed overdrive manual transmission; 90-amp alternator; front wheel drive, 4.27 axle ratio; steel exhaust with chrome tip; front independent double wishbone suspension with anti-roll bar, front coil springs, rear independent double wishbone suspension with anti-roll bar, rear coil springs; power rack-and-pinion steering with engine speed-sensing assist; 4 wheel disc brakes with 4 wheel antilock braking system; 13.2 gal. capacity fuel tank; side impact bars; front power sliding and tilting glass sunroof with sunshade; front and rear body-colored bumpers; body-colored bodyside molding; monotone paint; projector beam halogen headlamps; additional exterior lights include center high mounted stop light; driver's and passenger's power remote body-colored folding outside mirrors; front and rear 15" x 6" silver alloy wheels; P195/55VR15 BSW AS front and rear tires; inside under cargo mounted compact steel spare wheel; air conditioning; AM/FM stereo with seek-scan, single CD, 6 speakers, theft deterrent, and power retractable antenna; cruise control with steering wheel controls; power door locks, remote fuel release; 1 power accessory outlet, front cigar lighter, driver's foot rest; instrumentation display includes tachometer, water temp gauge, in-dash clock, trip odometer; warning indicators include oil pressure, battery, lights on, key in ignition, low fuel, door ajar, trunk ajar; dual airbags; tinted windows, power front windows with driver's 1-touch down, fixed rear windows; fixed interval front windshield wipers, rear window wiper, rear window defroster; seating capacity of 4, front bucket seats with adjustable headrests, center armrest with storage, driver's seat includes 8-way direction control with lumbar support, passenger's seat includes 4-way direction control with easy entry; 50-50 folding rear bench seat with fixed rear headrest; cloth seats, cloth door trim insert, full vinyl headliner, full carpet floor covering, deluxe sound insulation, leather-wrapped gear shift knob; interior lights include dome light, front reading lights; leather-wrapped steering wheel with tilt adjustment; vanity mirrors; day-night rearview mirror; full floor console, locking glove box, front cupholder, instrument panel bin, driver's and passenger's door bins; carpeted cargo floor, plastic trunk lid, cargo cover, cargo light; black side window moldings, black front windshield molding, black rear window molding and body-colored door handles.

LS SEDAN (5M) (in addition to or instead of LS COUPE (5M) equipment): Window grid antenna; child safety rear door locks, remote trunk release; tinted windows; power rear windows; seating capacity of 5, full folding rear bench seat with fixed headrests; front height adjustable seatbelts and chrome side window moldings.

GS COUPE (5M) (in addition to or instead of LS COUPE (5M) equipment): Rear wing spoiler; leather seats and leatherette door trim insert.

GS SEDAN (5M) (in addition to or instead of LS Sedan (5M) equipment): Leather seats, leatherette door trim insert and wood trim.

GS-R COUPE/SEDAN (5M) (in addition to or instead of GS COUPE/SEDAN (5M) equipment): 1.8L I4 DOHC SMPI with variable valve timing 16-valve engine, requires premium unleaded fuel; 4.4 axle ratio.

Base Prices

CODE	DESCRIPTION	INVOICE	MSRP
DC435XMBW	LS Coupe (5M)	17313	19200
DB755XMBW	LS Sedan (5M)	18033	20000
DC436XMBW	GS Coupe (5M)	18798	20850

ACURA

INTEGRA / RL-SERIES

CODE	DESCRIPTION	INVOICE	MSRP
DB756XMBW	GS Sedan (5M)	19294	21400
DC239XMBW	GS-R Coupe (5M)	19924	22100
DB859XMBW	GS-R Sedan (5M)	20194	22400
Destination Charge:		455	455

Accessories

—	Transmission: 4-Speed Automatic (All Except GS-R)	721	800
	Includes 4.36 axle ratio.		

1999 RL-SERIES

1999 Acura RL

What's New?

There are more than 300 changes to the RL this year, so we'll just touch on the important ones: the suspension has been revised for better handling and a firmer ride, brake rotors have added mass, side air bags are standard, styling is more aggressive, the Premium features have been incorporated into one trim level, and, best of all, the price has been slashed.

Review

Acura has decided to take the road more traveled. After suffering at the hands of Lexus for the last several years, Acura has what can truly be described as a flagship sedan. Sporting an extremely solid feel, the 3.5RL carries itself athletically. This year, the suspension has been tuned for a firmer ride and tighter handling. Not quite a sport sedan, the RL is not just a stodgy luxury coach, either.

Which leaves us wondering why the 3.5RL still doesn't offer a V8 engine. Every entrant in the luxo-barge segment has V8 power except for the 3.5RL. In typical Honda Motor Corp. fashion, the RL is equipped with a smallish engine that's supposed to feel big. This works fine on cars like

RL-SERIES   ACURA

| CODE | DESCRIPTION | INVOICE | MSRP |

the Integra or TL-Series where the lightness of a smaller engine can be a benefit to handling, but most people who are plunking down this kind of cash still prefer the comfort and power of a larger engine.

Acura engineers have worked overtime figuring out how to make this car quiet and vibration-free. Innovations like low-friction ball joints in the suspension, Teflon seals on the valves, a liquid-filled rear-trailing arm, foam-filled B- and C-pillars, honeycomb floor panels and vibration absorbing seats are just a few of the things the 3.5RL serves up to make you forget that you are in a car. Indeed, the entire purpose of the 3.5RL is to deliver passengers from point A to point B with minimal fuss and intrusion from the outside world.

Of course, to accomplish that goal, Acura had to make things nice on the inside. The instrumentation and controls are first rate, nothing new for Acura. The effective climate control system even offers rear passengers control over their environment. Seats are not just comfortable; they're feather bed-like. The driver's seat has an eight-way power adjustment that makes finding an exact fit easy. Supple leather and firm but comfortable support make long trips a breeze.

This year, the RL is available in a single level of trim, and compared feature-to-feature with last year's model, the new RL comes in at a considerably lower price. Add to the value equation new safety equipment such as high-intensity headlights, side airbags and bigger brake rotors, and the RL looks even more competent. Then spruce things up with an updated interior and more aerodynamic exterior sheetmetal, tune the suspension for better handling and a more stable ride, and you're looking at the best value in a luxury sedan this side of $45,000.

If all of this doesn't have you reaching for your checkbook, consider Acura's optional Navigation System. This system offers drivers a virtual map that they can use as a real-time guide to finding their way around town. Unlike similar designs, the Acura Navigation System offers verbal commands that allow drivers to keep their eyes on the road. We may never get lost again.

While the lack of a V8 engine is a bit disappointing, take heart when inspecting the car's price. Of rivals from Cadillac, Lexus and BMW, only the Cadillac has a lower base price, and that's without any options. The Acura 3.5RL comes fully equipped in a tasteful package at a price that should make those missing two cylinders seem like a moot point. In fact, we've already forgotten about them.

Standard Equipment

3.5RL (4A): 3.5L V6 SOHC SMPI 24-valve engine, requires premium unleaded fuel; 4-speed electronic overdrive automatic transmission with lock-up; 65-amp battery; 110-amp alternator; front wheel drive, traction control, 3.13 axle ratio; steel exhaust; front independent double wishbone suspension with anti-roll bar, front coil springs, rear independent double wishbone suspension with anti-roll bar, rear coil springs; power rack-and-pinion steering with engine speed-sensing assist; 4 wheel disc brakes with 4 wheel antilock braking system; 18 gal. capacity fuel tank; front power sliding and tilting glass sunroof with sunshade; front and rear body-colored bumpers with chrome bumper insert; body-colored bodyside molding with chrome bodyside insert; monotone paint; aero-composite xenon fully automatic headlamps; additional exterior lights include front fog/driving lights, center high mounted stop light; driver's and passenger's power remote body-colored heated folding outside mirrors; front and rear 16" x 7" silver alloy wheels; P215/60VR16 BSW AS front and rear tires; inside under cargo mounted compact steel spare wheel; air conditioning with climate control, air filter, rear heat ducts; premium AM/FM stereo with seek-scan, cassette, trunk mounted CD changer, 8 premium speakers, amplifier, theft deterrent, and window grid antenna; radio steering wheel controls; cruise control with steering wheel controls; power door locks with 2 stage unlock, remote keyless entry, child safety rear door locks, power remote hatch/trunk release, power remote fuel release; cell phone pre-wiring, 1 power accessory outlet, driver's foot rest, retained accessory power, garage door opener; instrumentation display includes tachometer, water temp gauge, in-dash clock, exterior temp, trip odometer; warning indicators include oil pressure, battery, lights on, key in ignition, low fuel, bulb failure, door ajar, trunk ajar, service interval; dual airbags, seat mounted side airbags; ignition disable, panic alarm, security system; tinted windows, power front windows with driver's 1-touch down, power rear windows; variable intermittent front windshield wipers, rear window defroster; seating capacity of 5, heated front bucket seats with adjustable headrests, center armrest with

RL-SERIES / TL-SERIES

| CODE | DESCRIPTION | INVOICE | MSRP |

storage, driver's seat includes 6-way power seat with lumbar support, passenger's seat includes 4-way power seat; rear bench seat with adjustable headrests, center pass-thru armrest with storage; front height adjustable seatbelts with front pretensioners; leather seats, leather door trim insert, full cloth headliner, full carpet floor covering, wood trim, leather-wrapped gear shift knob; memory on driver's seat with 2 memory setting(s) includes settings for exterior mirrors, steering wheel; interior lights include dome light with fade, front and rear reading lights, 4 door curb lights, illuminated entry; leather-wrapped steering wheel with power tilt and telescopic adjustment; dual illuminated vanity mirrors, driver's side auxiliary visor; auto-dimming day-night rearview mirror; full floor console, mini overhead console with storage, locking glove box with light, front and rear cupholders, 2 seat back storage pockets, driver's and passenger's door bins; carpeted cargo floor, carpeted trunk lid, cargo light; chrome grille, chrome side window moldings, black front windshield molding, black rear window molding and body-colored door handles.

Base Prices

KA965XJTW	3.5RL	36884	41900
Destination Charge:		455	455

Accessories

—	Navigation System	1746	2000

2000 TL-SERIES

What's New?

The real scoop is that the 2000 TL gets a bit faster, thanks to a new five-speed sequential SportShift automatic transmission and free-flowing intake manifold. A side-airbag system becomes standard as does a dual-stage inflator for the front-passenger airbag. The optional navigation system now features a DVD database.

Review

Acura's torch bearer into the rapidly growing near-luxury market is the TL, and it's pitted against some stiff competition in the form of the Audi A4, the Infiniti I30, the Lexus ES 300 and the Mercedes C-Class. Each of these models is already well established in the marketplace, which puts the pressure on Acura not only to meet but to exceed what those cars have to offer. The wildly popular '99 TL, with its promise of luxury, performance and value, had no problem meeting the challenge. It will likely be front and center for 2000 as well.

The TL is based on a Honda global platform, but its wheelbase is 2 inches longer than the Accord's. Unfortunately, for some reason the rear seat pays the price, becoming cramped when a tall driver is at the helm, and there's no underseat room. Storage space, on the other hand, is in abundance, including the deep center console and map pockets in the doors. The driver's seat is quite comfortable, although having only the seating surfaces upholstered in leather is disappointing, and the lack of seat-height adjustability for the front passenger doesn't win points.

The only engine is a peppy 3.2-liter V6 that utilizes VTEC technology to produce 225 horsepower and 216 foot-pounds of torque, while still returning 19/27 mpg in city/highway driving. The V6 remains strong in every gear, and it can scoot from zero to 60 in 8 seconds. This puts the TL ahead of much of its competition in the horsepower race, and we can confirm that it definitely gets out of its own way. The standard SportShift automatic transmission is quite user-friendly.

The TL offers near-luxury equipment without a hefty price, and you get more than just air conditioning and a smattering of leather. You snag a power sunroof, a 180-watt sound system with an in-dash CD, heated front seats, steering-wheel audio controls, rear heat/air vents, micron

TL-SERIES

ACURA

| CODE | DESCRIPTION | INVOICE | MSRP |

air-filtration system, traction control, and four-wheel antilock brakes because it's all standard. The super-simple navigation system is the only option, but this year has been improved by having a matte finish to prevent fingerprints smudges. Its new database has coverage of the entire continental U.S. on only one DVD.

The TL is a car that offers sporty styling and near-luxury features for a price that is well below the class average. The TL continues to deliver performance and value in typical Acura fashion.

2000 Acura TL

Standard Equipment

3.2TL (5A): 3.2L V6 SOHC SMPI with variable valve timing 24-valve engine, requires premium unleaded fuel; 5-speed electronic OD auto-manual transmission with lock-up; 105-amp alternator; front-wheel drive, traction control; steel exhaust with chrome tip; front independent double wishbone suspension with anti-roll bar, front coil springs, gas-pressurized front shocks, rear independent double wishbone suspension with anti-roll bar, rear coil springs, gas-pressurized rear shocks; power rack-and-pinion steering with engine speed-sensing assist; 4 wheel disc brakes with 4 wheel antilock braking system; 17.2 gal. capacity fuel tank; side impact bars; front power sliding and tilting glass sunroof with sunshade; front and rear body-colored bumpers; body-colored bodyside molding; clearcoat monotone paint; aero-composite high intensity auto off headlamps; additional exterior lights include cornering lights, front fog/driving lights; driver's and passenger's power remote body-colored heated folding outside mirrors; front and rear 16" x 6.5" machined alloy wheels; P205/60VR16 A/S BSW front and rear tires; inside under cargo mounted compact steel spare wheel; air conditioning with climate control, air filter, rear heat ducts; premium AM/FM stereo, seek-scan, cassette, single CD, 5 premium speakers, theft deterrent, and window grid antenna, radio steering wheel controls; cruise control with steering wheel controls; power door locks with 2 stage unlock, remote keyless entry, child safety rear door locks, power remote hatch/trunk release, remote fuel release; 2 power accessory outlets, driver's foot rest, retained accessory power, garage door opener; instrumentation display includes tachometer, water temperature gauge, in-dash clock, exterior temp, trip odometer; warning indicators include oil pressure, battery, lights on, key in ignition, low fuel, bulb failure, door ajar, trunk ajar, service interval; driver's and passenger's front airbags, driver's and front passenger's seat mounted side airbags; ignition disable, panic alarm, security system; tinted windows, power front and rear windows with driver's 1-touch down; variable intermittent front windshield wipers, sun visor strip, rear window defroster; seating capacity of 5, heated-cushion front bucket seats, adjustable headrests, center armrest with storage, driver's seat includes 6-way power seat, lumbar support,

TL-SERIES

CODE	DESCRIPTION	INVOICE	MSRP

passenger's seat includes 4-way power seat; rear bench seat with fixed headrests, center pass-thru armrest; front height adjustable seatbelts; leather seats, leather door trim insert, full cloth headliner, full carpet floor covering, leather-wrapped gear shift knob; interior lights include dome light, front reading lights, 4 door curb lights, illuminated entry; leather-wrapped steering wheel with tilt adjustment; dual illuminated vanity mirrors, dual auxiliary visors; auto-dimming day/night rearview mirror; full floor console, mini overhead console with storage, locking glove box with light, front and rear cupholders, 2 seat back storage pockets, driver's and passenger's door bins; carpeted cargo floor, cargo light; chrome grille, chrome side window moldings, black front windshield molding, black rear window molding and chrome door handles.

Base Prices

UA566YJTW	3.2TL	25191	28400
Destination Charge:		455	455

Accessories

NAVIG	Navigation System	1801	2000

Includes 6-inch color touch screen with matte finish mounted high in center dashboard; verbal directions and visual LCD moving map with directional arrow and detailed information on street names, turning instructions and driving distances, information and directions to local restaurants, banks, hospitals, theatres, golf courses, museums and entertainment options; searches by address or phone number; provides audio and visual cues to find proper address; digital video disc database with coverage of the continental United States on 1 DVD. Location and velocity of vehicle are pinpointed using global positioning satellite (GPS) data.

For expert advice in selecting/buying/leasing a new car, call
1-900-AUTOPRO
($2.00 per minute)

2000 A4

2000 Audi A4

What's New?

All A4 models receive minor updates to the interior, exterior and chassis. The front styling has been changed with new headlights, a new grille, new door handles, and new mirror housings. Inside, there's a revised instrument cluster and center console, along with other minor interior changes. The rear seats have been modified to improve comfort. There are now optional head airbags and xenon headlights. The chassis has been reworked for improved ride comfort and responsiveness.

Review

Audi's A4 is sleek, sophisticated, speedy and has won praise from the worldwide automotive media. Small and safe, the A4 has scored well in government crash testing. For U.S. buyers, this translates into a competent alternative to the BMW 3 Series, the Acura TL and the Volvo S40, among others.

For 2000, four versions are available: the A4 1.8T Sedan and 1.8T Avant Wagon, and the A4 2.8 Sedan and 2.8 Avant Wagon. The numerical designations refer to engine size. 1.8T models get a 1.8-liter turbocharged engine that produces 150 horsepower and 155 foot-pounds of torque. Vehicles with a 2.8 designation have a 2.8-liter V6 filling their engine bays. The six-cylinder makes 190 horsepower and 207 foot-pounds of torque. Both engines can be ordered with a five-speed manual or a five-speed Tiptronic automanual transmission. Audi's quattro all-wheel-drive system is standard on Avant wagons and optional on the sedans.

Besides engine selection, The 1.8T vehicles differ from the 2.8 vehicles in only minor trim. The 2.8 Sedan and Avant have bigger wheels and tires, 10-way power seats, aluminum trim on the window frames, and wood interior decor. All cars feature goodies like automatic climate control, remote keyless entry, heated outside mirrors and windshield-wiper nozzles, an eight-speaker CD audio system, and 60/40 split folding rear seats.

Avant wagons have 31.3 cubic feet of cargo room with the rear seat up and 63.7 cubic feet of cargo room with the seat folded down. They also come with a retractable rear luggage cover, a luggage net, and a three-point center seatbelt. Tether anchors for a child seat are now standard.

AUDI A4

Audi buyers can also personalize their cars by choosing from three different interior themes: Ambition, Ambiente and Advance. The three environments, as Audi calls them, differ by the texture and appearance of the seat upholstery and the color and type of genuine wood or aluminum trim. Main options offered by Audi include a Bose premium sound system, a six-disc CD changer, a navigation system, and sport seats. Also new for 2000 are xenon HID headlights.

Dual front airbags, side-impact airbags mounted in the front seats and antilock brakes come standard. Head airbags are optional for 2000. All A4s enjoy free scheduled maintenance for three years, as well as a three-year/50,000 mile warranty.

With prices starting near $24,000, consumers can get a status car that is comfortable and costs less than it does to send your kid to college. Pricing can escalate when heavily equipped, but the A4 is still one of the best entry-luxury sedans on the market.

Standard Equipment

1.8T SEDAN (5M): 1.8L I4 DOHC SMPI intercooled turbo 20-valve engine, requires premium unleaded fuel; 5-speed OD manual transmission; 70-amp battery; engine oil cooler; 90-amp alternator; front-wheel drive, limited slip differential, 3.7 axle ratio; stainless steel exhaust; front independent suspension with anti-roll bar, front coil springs, rear non-independent torsion suspension with anti-roll bar, rear coil springs; power rack-and-pinion steering with engine speed-sensing assist; 4-wheel disc brakes with 4-wheel antilock braking system; 16.4 gal. capacity fuel tank; side impact bars; front and rear body-colored bumpers; body-colored bodyside molding, rocker panel extensions; monotone paint; aero-composite halogen headlamps with washer; additional exterior lights include front fog/driving lights; driver's and passenger's power remote body-colored heated folding outside mirrors; front and rear 15" x 7" silver alloy wheels; P205/60HR15 A/S BSW front and rear tires; inside under cargo mounted compact steel spare wheel; air conditioning with climate control, air filter, rear heat ducts; AM/FM stereo, seek-scan, cassette, CD changer pre-wiring, in-dash CD pre-wiring, 8 speakers, auto equalizer, theft deterrent, and window grid antenna; cruise control; power door locks with 2 stage unlock, remote keyless entry, child safety rear door locks, power remote hatch/trunk release; cell phone pre-wiring, 1 power accessory outlet, driver's foot rest, retained accessory power; instrumentation display includes tachometer, water temperature gauge, volt gauge, clock, exterior temp, trip odometer; warning indicators include oil pressure, battery, lights on, key in ignition, low fuel, service interval; driver's and passenger's front airbags, driver's and front passenger's seat mounted side airbags; ignition disable, security system; tinted windows, power front and rear windows with front and rear 1-touch down; variable intermittent front windshield wipers, sun visor strip, rear window defroster; seating capacity of 5, front bucket seats, adjustable headrests, center armrest with storage, driver's seat includes 6-way direction control, passenger's seat includes 6-way direction control; 60-40 folding rear bench seat with tilt headrests, center armrest with storage; front height adjustable seatbelts with front and rear pretensioners; cloth seats, cloth door trim insert, full cloth headliner, full carpet floor covering with carpeted floor mats, leather-wrapped gear shift knob; interior lights include dome light with fade, front and rear reading lights, illuminated entry; leather-wrapped steering wheel with tilt and telescopic adjustment; dual illuminated vanity mirrors, driver's side auxiliary visor; day/night rearview mirror; full floor console, locking glove box with light, front cupholder, 2 seat back storage pockets, driver's and passenger's door bins; carpeted cargo floor, carpeted trunk lid, cargo net, cargo tie downs, cargo light; chrome grille, black side window moldings, black front windshield molding, black rear window molding and body-colored door handles.

2.8 SEDAN (5M) (in addition to or instead of 1.8T SEDAN (5M) equipment): 120-amp alternator; traction control; front and rear 16" x 7" silver alloy wheels; P205/55HR16 A/S BSW front and rear tires; driver's seat includes 6-way power seat, lumbar support, passenger's seat includes 6-way direction control, lumbar support; genuine wood trim on instrument panel and chrome side window moldings.

AVANT QUATTRO WAGON (5M) (in addition to or instead of SEDAN (5M) equipment): Full-time 4-wheel drive, 3.89 axle ratio; rear independent double wishbone suspension with anti-roll

A4 — AUDI

CODE	DESCRIPTION	INVOICE	MSRP

bar; 15.9 gal. (1.8T)/15.6 gal. (2.8) capacity fuel tank; roof rack; integrated roof antenna; fixed 1/4 vent windows; fixed interval rear wiper; center pass-thru armrest with skibag and storage and cargo cover.

Base Prices

Code	Description	Invoice	MSRP
8D25H4	1.8T Sedan (5M)	21356	23990
8D25U4	2.8 Sedan (5M)	25580	28790
8D55H5	1.8T Avant Quattro Wagon (5M)	23986	26740
8D55U5	2.8 Avant Quattro Wagon (5M)	28210	31540
	Destination Charge:	525	525

Accessories

Code	Description	Invoice	MSRP
—	Cool Shades Paint	405	460
—	Jacquard Satin Upholstery	NC	NC
—	Leather Seat Upholstery (All Except 1.8T Sedan)	1162	1320
—	Perforated Leatherette Upholstery	NC	NC
—	Transmission: 5-Speed Auto with Tiptronic	1047	1075
2PV	Leather-Wrapped Sport Steering Wheel	141	160
4X3	Sideguard Curtain Airbag	264	300
7A2	6-Disc CD Changer	484	550
PAW	Cold Weather Package (Avant)	387	440
	Includes heated front seats and heated driver's door lock.		
PAW	Cold Weather Package (Sedan)	528	600
	Includes ski sack, heated front seats and heated driver's door lock.		
PBS	Bose Premium Sound System	572	650
PCX	Convenience Package	1056	1200
	Includes power tilt and slide glass sunroof, auto-dimming inside rearview mirror, auto dimming outside rearview mirrors and Homelink remote transmitter.		
PMT	Integrated Hands-Free Mobile Phone	431	495
PNL	Audi Navigation System	968	1100
PSQ	Sport Package (1.8T)	660	750
	Includes leather-wrapped sport steering wheel, sport suspension, wheels: 16" 10-spoke alloy and tires: 16" performance.		
PSQ	Sport Package (2.8)	352	400
	Includes leather-wrapped sport steering wheel, sport suspension, wheels: 16" 10-spoke alloy and tires: 16" performance.		
PX3	Xenon High Intensity Headlights	440	500
Q1D	Sport Front Seats	440	500
QTR	Quattro IV All Wheel Drive System (Sedan)	1750	1750

AUDI   A6

| CODE | DESCRIPTION | INVOICE | MSRP |

2000 A6

2000 Audi A6

What's New?

There are two new models joining the A6 2.8 and A6 2.8 Avant. The first is the A6 2.7T powered by a turbocharged V6 engine. The second model is the A6 4.2 powered by a powerful V8.

Review

For 2000, Audi has added two new versions of the A6. Both of them are considerably more powerful than the A6 2.8 and the A6 2.8 Avant Wagon that were previously offered in America. The A6 2.7T Sedan has a twin-turbo 2.7-liter V6 that produces 250 horsepower and 258 foot-pounds of torque. Audi has used two small turbos rather than one large one to make the engine more responsive. In a nice tip of the hat to enthusiasts, the 2.7T comes with a six-speed manual transmission as standard equipment. A five-speed Tiptronic-controlled automatic transmission is a no-cost option.

The Audi A6 4.2 Sedan features the 4.2-liter V8 normally found in the larger A8 Sedan. Obviously Audi's challenge to the V8-powered BMW 540i and Mercedes-Benz E430, this engine produces 300 horsepower and 295 foot-pounds of torque. This engine comes only with a five-speed Tiptronic-controlled automatic transmission. Beyond the engine, the 4.2 also comes with more aggressive styling, bigger wheels and tires, and more standard equipment.

For 2000, the 2.8 and 2.8 Avant get an optional five-speed manual transmission. Audi's quattro all-wheel-drive system is optional on the 2.8 and standard on all of the remaining models. This system constantly monitors the grip of the tires. When one of them starts to lose traction, the quattro system automatically applies power to the tires with the most adhesion to the road surface.

All of the A6 models feature an interior that is one of the best in its class. Audi greets drivers with a generous amount of supple materials and features. As a bonus, A6 buyers can choose from three different types of interiors. The atmospheres — Ambition, Ambiente and Advance — differ in their use of texture and appearance of the seat upholstery, and the color and type of genuine wood and aluminum trim.

The A6's styling is unmistakably Audi, with a swept greenhouse and muscular fenders. However, the A6 isn't a stunner like the A4. The rounded sheetmetal and sharply creased trim detail don't blend well to our eye, and the taillights on the sedan appear to have been lifted from

A6 AUDI

Chevrolet's lowly S-10 pickup. From some angles, the car looks great. From others, it appears somewhat dumpy and jumbled. Front overhang can appear especially out of balance. Fortunately, the gracefully swept greenhouse on both the sedan and wagon lends a touch of class and elegance to an otherwise characterless profile.

Despite nitpicks, we believe the A6 is an enticing choice in the hotly contested entry-level luxury class. If you're looking for a wagon, the A6 Avant should serve nicely. But our personal favorite is the A6 2.7T. This version offers better acceleration than the 2.8 and nearly equals the 4.2. It also doesn't cost much more than the 2.8, and certainly costs less than the 4.2

Standard Equipment

BASE SEDAN (5A): 2.8L V6 DOHC SMPI with variable valve timing 30-valve engine, requires premium unleaded fuel; 5-speed electronic OD auto transmission with lock-up; engine oil cooler; 120-amp alternator; automanual transmission, transmission oil cooler; front-wheel drive, traction control; stainless steel exhaust; front independent suspension with anti-roll bar, front coil springs, gas-pressurized front shocks, rear semi-independent torsion suspension with anti-roll bar, rear coil springs, gas-pressurized rear shocks; power rack-and-pinion steering with vehicle speed-sensing assist; 4-wheel disc brakes with 4-wheel antilock braking system; 18.5 gal. capacity fuel tank; side impact bars; front and rear body-colored bumpers; body-colored bodyside molding, rocker panel extensions; metallic monotone paint; projector beam halogen headlamps with washer; additional exterior lights include front fog/driving lights; driver's and passenger's power remote body-colored heated folding outside mirrors; front and rear 16" x 7" silver alloy wheels; P205/55HR16 A/S BSW front and rear tires; inside under cargo mounted full-size alloy spare wheel; dual zone front air conditioning with climate control, air filter, rear heat ducts; AM/FM stereo, seek-scan, cassette, single CD, 8 speakers, amplifier, auto equalizer, theft deterrent, and fixed antenna; cruise control; power heated door locks with 2 stage unlock, remote keyless entry, child safety rear door locks, power remote hatch/trunk release, power remote fuel release; cell phone pre-wiring, 2 power accessory outlets, driver's foot rest, retained accessory power, smokers' package; instrumentation display includes tachometer, water temperature gauge, volt gauge, in-dash clock, exterior temp, systems monitor, trip computer, trip odometer; warning indicators include oil pressure, battery, low oil level, lights on, key in ignition, low fuel, low washer fluid, bulb failure, door ajar, trunk ajar, service interval; driver's and passenger's front airbags, driver's and front passenger's seat mounted side airbags; ignition disable, panic alarm, security system; tinted windows, power front and rear windows with front and rear 1-touch down; variable intermittent front windshield wipers with heated jets, sun visor strip, rear window defroster; seating capacity of 5, front bucket seats, adjustable tilt headrests, center armrest with storage, driver's seat includes 6-way power seat, power 2-way lumbar support, passenger's seat includes 6-way power seat, power 2-way lumbar support; rear bench seat with tilt headrests, center armrest; front height adjustable seatbelts with front and rear pretensioners; cloth seats, cloth door trim insert, full cloth headliner, full carpet floor covering with carpeted floor mats, genuine wood trim on instrument panel, leather-wrapped gear shift knob; interior lights include dome light with fade, front and rear reading lights, 4 door curb lights, illuminated entry; leather-wrapped steering wheel with tilt and telescopic adjustment; dual illuminated vanity mirrors, driver's side auxiliary visor; day/night rearview mirror; full floor console, locking glove box with light, front and rear cupholders, 2 seat back storage pockets, driver's and passenger's door bins, rear door bins; carpeted cargo floor, carpeted trunk lid, cargo net, cargo tie downs, cargo light; chrome grille, chrome side window moldings, black front windshield molding, black rear window molding and body-colored door handles.

2.7T QUATTRO SEDAN (5A) (in addition to or instead of BASE SEDAN (5A) equipment): 2.7L V6 DOHC SMPI intercooled turbo with variable valve timing 30-valve engine, requires premium unleaded fuel; full-time 4-wheel drive, limited slip differential; rear independent double wishbone suspension with anti-roll bar, rear coil springs, gas-pressurized rear shocks; P215/55HR16 A/S BSW front and rear tires.

AUDI A6

4.2 QUATTRO SEDAN (5A) (in addition to or instead of 2.7T QUATTRO SEDAN (5A) equipment): 4.2L V8 DOHC SMPI with variable valve timing 40-valve engine, requires premium unleaded fuel; 21.7 gal. capacity fuel tank; front express open/close sliding and tilting glass sunroof with sunshade; front and rear 16" x 8" silver alloy wheels; P235/50HR16 A/S BSW front and rear tires; AM/FM stereo, seek-scan, cassette, single CD, 8 premium speakers, premium amplifier, auto equalizer, theft deterrent, and fixed antenna, radio steering wheel controls; garage door opener; overhead airbag; 60-40 folding rear bench seat with tilt headrests, center pass-thru armrest with skibag; leather seats, leather door trim insert; memory on driver's seat with 3 memory setting(s) includes settings for exterior mirrors and leather-wrapped steering wheel with power tilt and telescopic adjustment.

A6 AVANT WAGON (5A) (in addition to or instead of BASE SEDAN (5A) equipment): Full-time 4-wheel drive, limited slip differential, 3.41 axle ratio; roof rack; inside under cargo mounted compact steel spare wheel; AM/FM stereo, seek-scan, cassette, single CD, 8 speakers, amplifier, auto equalizer, theft deterrent, and integrated roof antenna; 3 power accessory outlets, rear window wiper; rear blind; center pass-thru armrest with skibag and storage; interior concealed storage; plastic trunk lid, cargo cover and cargo concealed storage.

Base Prices

Code	Description	Invoice	MSRP
4B24VK	Base Sedan (5A)	30222	33950
4B247Z	2.7T Quattro Sedan (5A)	34480	38550
4B441Z	4.2 Quattro Sedan (5A)	43588	48900
4B54VZ	Avant Wagon (5A)	33028	36900
Destination Charge:		525	525

Accessories

Code	Description	Invoice	MSRP
—	Transmission: 5-Speed Manual (Base) *REQUIRES QUATRO*	NC	NC
—	Transmission: 6-Speed Manual (2.7T)	NC	NC
1AT	Electronic Stability Program (ESP) (4.2)	484	550
4A4	Front and Rear Heated Seats (4.2)	418	475
4X3	Sideguard Curtain Airbag (All Except Base) *NOT AVAILABLE with 4X4.*	264	300
4X4	Rear Side Airbags (4.2)	308	350
4X4	Sideguard Curtain and Rear Side Airbags (All Except 4.2) *NOT AVAILABLE with 4X3.*	440	500
7A2	6-Disc CD Changer	484	550
7X1	Acoustic Rear Parking System	308	350
C4H	Wheels: 17" Polished Alloy (4.2) *NOT AVAILABLE with PSQ.*	660	750
CLOTH	Jacquard Satin Cloth Upholstery (Base/2.7T) *NOT AVAILABLE with LEATHE, LTHR.*	NC	NC
CLOTH	Jacquard Satin Upholstery (Avant) *NOT AVAILABLE with LEATHE, LTHR.*	NC	NC
LEATHE	Leatherette Seat Upholstery (Base/2.7T) *NOT AVAILABLE with LTHR, CLOTH.*	NC	NC
LEATHE	Perforated Leatherette Upholstery (Avant) *NOT AVAILABLE with LTHR, CLOTH.*	NC	NC

A6 — AUDI

CODE	DESCRIPTION	INVOICE	MSRP
LTHR	Leather Seat Upholstery (All Except 4.2)	1364	1550
	NOT AVAILABLE with LEATHE, CLOTH.		
PAW	Cold Weather Package (Avant)	418	475
	Includes heated front and rear seats.		
PAW	Cold Weather Package (Base/2.7T)	550	625
	Includes ski sack and front and rear heated seats.		
PBS	Bose Music System (All Except 4.2)	660	750
PCC	Convenience Package (Base/2.7T)	1452	1650
	Includes power tilt/slide sunroof, driver's seat and exterior mirrors memory, auto-dimming inside rearview mirror, auto dimming outside rearview mirrors, Homelink remote transmitter and steering wheel audio controls. REQUIRES PWX. NOT AVAILABLE with PCX.		
PCC	Convenience Package with PWX (Avant)	1452	1650
	Includes power tilt/slide sunroof, driver's seat and exterior mirrors memory, auto-dimming inside rearview mirror, auto dimming outside rearview mirrors, Homelink remote transmitter and steering wheel audio controls. REQUIRES PWX. NOT AVAILABLE with PCX.		
PCX	Convenience Package (All Except 4.2)	1452	1650
	Includes power tilt and slide glass sunroof, driver's seat and exterior mirrors memory, auto-dimming inside rearview mirror, auto dimming outside rearview mirrors, Homelink remote transmitter and steering wheel audio controls. NOT AVAILABLE with PCC, PWX.		
PGB	Preferred Equipment Package (Base/Avant)	1716	1950
	Includes leather seat upholstery, power tilt and slide glass sunroof and Homelink remote transmitter. NOT AVAILABLE with LEATHE, CLOTH, PCC, PCX, PWX, PX3, 7A2, PNK, 7X1, PMT.		
PKS	Rear Facing Children's Bench Seat (Avant)	616	700
	Includes removable seat.		
PMT	Integrated Hands-Free Mobile Phone	431	495
PNK	Audi Navigation System	968	1100
PSP	Sport Package (2.7T)	660	750
	Includes sport seats, wheels: 16" twin spoke sport alloy and tires: 205/55R16 performance.		
PSQ	Sport Package (4.2)	1320	1500
	Includes sport seats, wheels: 17" forged sport alloy and tires: 17" performance. NOT AVAILABLE with C4H.		
PWX	Warm Weather Package (Avant)	704	800
	Includes sunroof solar panel (replaces glass panel) and rear side window sunshades. REQUIRES PCC. NOT AVAILABLE with PCX.		
PWX	Warm Weather Package (Sedan)	880	1000
	Includes sunroof solar panel (replaces glass panel), power rear window shade and rear side window sunshades. REQUIRES PCC. NOT AVAILABLE with PCX.		
PX3	Xenon High Intensity Headlights	440	500
QUATRO	Quattro IV All Wheel Drive System (Base)	1750	1750
	Includes front and rear electronic differential locks.		

AUDI
S4

| CODE | DESCRIPTION | INVOICE | MSRP |

2000 S4

2000 Audi S4

What's New?

The Audi S4 is a new sport sedan based off the excellent A4 platform. Highlights include a turbocharged engine, all-wheel drive, and improved handling and braking.

Review

The new Audi S4 is the most promising sport sedan for 2000. Although not cheap by any means (base model pricing starts at $37,900), it does offer a mouth-watering array of features and improvements over the regular A4 Sedan that it is modeled after.

Starting things out is a 2.7-liter twin-turbo V6 engine. Sporting twin intercoolers, dual-overhead cams, five valves per cylinder, variable valve timing for the intake camshaft, and optimized combustion chambers, the engine generates 250 horsepower and 258 foot-pounds of torque. Audi has designed the engine to provide much of its power low in the revband. Consequently, the S4 makes quick work of freeway on-ramps and passing maneuvers. Audi gives buyers of the S4 a choice of transmissions; there's a six-speed manual transmission or a five-speed Tiptronic automatic transmission.

All S4s come with Audi's quattro all-wheel-drive system, which constantly monitors the grip of the tires. When one of them starts to lose traction, the quattro system automatically applies power to the tires with the most adhesion to the road surface. Audi says this latest edition of the quattro all-wheel-drive system is capable enough to allow the car to get underway with only one wheel having reasonable traction.

The suspension and braking components have also been improved. Major items of note are bigger and stronger brakes, revised aluminum suspension pieces, performance-tuned shocks and springs, and unique 17-inch wheels with 225/45R17 tires.

The interior retains the same architecture found in the A4, which means an attractive design and a decent number of features. Special leather upholstery covers standard power seats, and contrasting color suede inserts can be had when ordering the sport interior package. Other options to consider include a sunroof, heated front seats, a six-disc CD changer, and a Bose premium audio system. For safety, there are standard front- and head-mounted airbags.

Outside, the S4 differs from regular A4s (not that the A4 is exactly regular, of course) by having the aforementioned 17-inch wheels, larger front air-intake openings, and S4 badging.

S4 — AUDI

Two special colors—Imola Yellow and Nogaro Blue—are available only on the S4.

The S4 driving experience is a pleasure. But what could be considered either a positive or negative, depending on what you want from a sport sedan, the S4 is softer than a '99 BMW M3. Its forgiving nature comes at the expense of pure handling excellence. Taken as a whole, however, we think the 2000 Audi S4 has no equal in the sport-sedan market.

Standard Equipment

2.7 T (5A): 2.7L V6 DOHC SMPI intercooled turbo 30-valve engine, requires premium unleaded fuel; 5-speed electronic OD auto transmission with lock-up; engine oil cooler; 120-amp alternator; full-time 4-wheel drive, limited slip differential; stainless steel exhaust; sport ride suspension, front independent suspension with anti-roll bar, front coil springs, rear independent double wishbone suspension with anti-roll bar, rear coil springs; power rack-and-pinion steering with engine speed-sensing assist; 4-wheel disc brakes with 4-wheel antilock braking system; 16.4 gal. capacity fuel tank; side impact bars; front and rear body-colored bumpers; body-colored bodyside molding, rocker panel extensions; monotone paint; projector beam high intensity headlamps with washer; additional exterior lights include front fog/driving lights; driver's and passenger's power remote body-colored heated folding outside mirrors; front and rear 17" x 7" silver alloy wheels; P225/45YR17 A/S BSW front and rear tires; inside under cargo mounted compact steel spare wheel; air conditioning with climate control, air filter, rear heat ducts; AM/FM stereo, seek-scan, cassette, single CD, 8 speakers, amplifier, auto equalizer, theft deterrent, and window grid antenna; cruise control; power door locks with 2 stage unlock, remote keyless entry, child safety rear door locks, power remote hatch/trunk release; cell phone pre-wiring, 1 power accessory outlet, driver's foot rest, retained accessory power; instrumentation display includes tachometer, water temperature gauge, volt gauge, clock, exterior temp, trip odometer; warning indicators include oil pressure, battery, lights on, key in ignition, low fuel, service interval; driver's and passenger's front airbags, driver's and front passenger's seat mounted side airbags, overhead airbag; ignition disable, panic alarm, security system; tinted windows, power front and rear windows with front and rear 1-touch down; heated jets variable intermittent front windshield wipers, sun visor strip, rear window defroster; seating capacity of 5, front sports seats, adjustable headrests, center armrest with storage, driver's seat includes 6-way power seat, power 2-way lumbar support, passenger's seat includes 6-way power seat, power 2-way lumbar support; 50-50 folding rear bench seat with tilt headrests, center armrest with storage; front height adjustable seatbelts with front and rear pretensioners; leather seats, cloth door trim insert, full cloth headliner, full carpet floor covering with carpeted floor mats, genuine wood trim on instrument panel, leather-wrapped gear shift knob; interior lights include dome light with fade, front and rear reading lights, illuminated entry; leather-wrapped steering wheel with tilt and telescopic adjustment; dual illuminated vanity mirrors, driver's side auxiliary visor; day/night rearview mirror; full floor console, locking glove box with light, front cupholder, 2 seat back storage pockets, driver's and passenger's door bins; carpeted cargo floor, carpeted trunk lid, cargo net, cargo tie downs, cargo light; chrome grille, chrome side window moldings, black front windshield molding, black rear window molding and body-colored door handles.

Base Prices

CODE	DESCRIPTION	INVOICE	MSRP
8D257Z	S4 2.7T (5A)	33908	37900
	Destination Charge:	525	525

Accessories

CODE	DESCRIPTION	INVOICE	MSRP
—	Silk Nappa Leather with Alcantara Inserts	NC	NC
—	Transmission: 6-Speed Manual	NC	NC
7A2	6-Disc CD Changer	484	550
PAW	Cold Weather Package	506	575
	Includes heated front seats and ski sack.		

AUDI   S4 / TT

CODE	DESCRIPTION	INVOICE	MSRP
PBS	Bose Premium Sound System	572	650
PCX	Convenience Package	1056	1200
	Includes glass sunroof, auto dimming outside mirrors, auto dimming interior mirror and Homelink remote transmitter.		
PMT	Integrated Hands-Free Mobile Phone	431	495
PNL	Audi Navigation System	968	1100
WMM	Sport Interior Package	NC	NC
	Includes silk nappa leather with alcantara inserts and silver aluminum belt line trim.		

2000 TT

2000 Audi TT

What's New?

Audi introduces the funky-looking TT Coupe for the 2000 model year.

Review

The 2000 Audi TT Coupe concept car was introduced in 1995, and we hated it. When Audi announced they would build the TT, we scoffed, calling it the automotive equivalent of Miss Piggy. Then we got up close and personal with the TT at various motor shows and driving evaluations. You could say we've developed an acquired taste for the design.

In person, the car just looks right, appearing aggressive and graceful at the same time. The rear boasts rounded flanks and a cleanly arced roofline. Purposeful styling details are executed with ice-cold precision; it is an instant classic—a shape that will be a topic of discussion for years.

The base Audi TT comes with a front-engine, front-drive powertrain layout. Its turbocharged, 1.8-liter, four-cylinder engine makes 180 horsepower and is connected to a standard five-speed manual transmission. Audi's quattro all-wheel-drive system is optional and there is currently no automatic transmission available.

Inside, Audi has created "a visual and tactile feast" of aluminum, leather and stainless steel. The effect is successful, appearing to be expensively outfitted, but not luxurious in the traditional

TT

sense. And, thanks to the hatchback design, the TT offers owners some utility, carrying 13.8 cubic feet of cargo with the rear seat up and 24.2 cubic feet if the rear seat is folded down. Owners might want to keep the rear seats lowered permanently, as they are otherwise useless for hauling people.

Standard equipment includes leather sport seats, cruise control, a tachometer, alloy wheels, a split folding rear seat, and an AM/FM stereo with cassette and speed-sensitive volume control. A six-disc CD changer is optional. Power seats, a sunroof and a full-size spare tire are not available on this car.

To keep passengers safe, Audi installed ABS, traction control and a first-aid kit in the TT. Head and thorax side airbags are also standard. Pre-tensioners and force limiters make seatbelts even more effective than conventional systems and next-generation front airbags deploy at lower speeds.

The TT's styling will make it popular with people who like to impress. However, the horsepower coming from the turbo engine seems to be lacking given the base $30,500 MSRP. True sporting enthusiasts will want to wait until a more powerful version of the TT arrives sometime next year.

Standard Equipment

BASE COUPE (5M): 1.8L I4 DOHC SMPI intercooled turbo 20-valve engine, requires premium unleaded fuel; 5-speed overdrive manual transmission; engine oil cooler; front wheel drive, limited slip differential, traction control; stainless steel exhaust; front independent strut suspension with anti-roll bar, front coil springs, rear non-independent torsion suspension with anti-roll bar, rear coil springs; power rack-and-pinion steering; 4 wheel disc brakes with 4 wheel antilock braking system; 14.5 gal. capacity fuel tank; side impact bars; front and rear body-colored bumpers; monotone paint; projector beam halogen headlamps with washer; additional exterior lights include front fog/driving lights; driver's and passenger's power remote body-colored heated folding outside mirrors; front and rear 16" x 7" silver alloy wheels; P205/55HR16 BSW performance front and rear tires; inside under cargo mounted compact steel spare wheel; air conditioning with climate control, air filter, rear heat ducts; AM/FM stereo with seek-scan, cassette, CD changer pre-wiring, in-dash CD pre-wiring, 6 speakers, automatic equalizer, and window grid diversity antenna; cruise control; power door locks with 2 stage unlock, power remote hatch/trunk release, power remote fuel release; cell phone pre-wiring, 1 power accessory outlet, driver's foot rest, retained accessory power; instrumentation display includes tachometer, water temp gauge, volt gauge, in-dash clock, trip odometer; warning indicators include oil pressure, battery, lights on, key in ignition, low fuel, service interval; dual airbags, seat mounted side airbags; ignition disable, security system; tinted windows, power front windows with driver's and passenger's 1-touch down, fixed rear windows; variable intermittent front windshield wipers with heated jets, sun visor strip, rear window defroster; seating capacity of 4, front sports seats with adjustable tilt headrests, driver's seat includes 6-way direction control, passenger's seat includes 6-way direction control; 50-50 folding rear bench seat; front height adjustable seatbelts with front pretensioners; leather seats, leatherette door trim insert, full cloth headliner, full carpet floor covering with carpeted floor mats, leather-wrapped gear shift knob; interior lights include dome light with fade, front reading lights, illuminated entry; leather-wrapped sport steering wheel with tilt and telescopic adjustment; dual illuminated vanity mirrors; day-night rearview mirror; full floor console, locking glove box with light, front cupholder, instrument panel bin, 2 seat back storage pockets, driver's and passenger's door bins; carpeted cargo floor, carpeted trunk lid, cargo cover, cargo tie downs, cargo light; black grille, black side window moldings and body-colored door handles.

Base Prices

Code	Description	Invoice	MSRP
8N3554	TT Coupe (5M)	27085	30500
	Destination Charge:	525	525

AUDI TT

CODE	DESCRIPTION	INVOICE	MSRP

Accessories

—	**Comfort Package**	616	700
	Includes heated front seats and driver information display with outside temperature display, 5-function trip computer, vehicle auto-check system, radio display and pictrogram for open door and deck lid.		
—	**Performance Package**	880	1000
	Includes xenon HID headlights, wheels: 17" cast alloy and tires: P225/45YR17 summer performance.		
—	**Quattro IV All-Wheel Drive System**	1750	1750
PAS	**Audio Package**	1056	1200
	Includes Bose premium sound system with four speakers is door, two 2-way rear speakers, center speaker in dashboard, 4-channel 175-Watt amplifier and 6 disc CD changer.		
PLH	**Nubbed TT Cloth Seat Insert**	NC	NC
	Includes leather bolsters. Note: Full leather seating is standard.		
PMT	**Motorola Hands-Free Cellular Telephone**	431	495

Edmund's® TOWN HALL

Get answers from our editors, discover smart shopping strategies and share your experiences in our new talk area. Just enter the following address into your web browser:

http://townhall.edmunds.com

Where smart shoppers talk about cars, trucks, and related consumer topics.

3 SERIES — BMW

| CODE | DESCRIPTION | INVOICE | MSRP |

2000 3 SERIES

2000 BMW 3 Series Sedan

What's New?

3 Series coupes are all-new for 2000 and the hatchback has been discontinued. After last year's complete redesign, 2000 sedans see only minor improvements.

Review

BMWs are all about performance. Since the introduction of the 1600-02 in 1966, legions of fans have purchased this Munich-based company's smallest cars in the search for a perfect balance of practicality and power. During the last two decades, the marque has also come to the attention of those looking for prestige. This last group of admirers has had a profound impact on the company's fortunes, making BMW the second-best-selling German manufacturer in the United States.

Things have changed since 1966, though, including the name of BMW's smallest line of cars. Since 1977, BMW has referred to these models as the 3 Series, and for 2000 this lineup of cars is undergoing its fourth major redesign. In typical BMW fashion, the 3 Series lineup is being redesigned at a staggered pace. This means that the first models to change were the sedans in 1999, followed by the coupes, the convertible and all-new wagon, and finally the wicked M3 performance coupe. This allows BMW to extend the life of the design by stretching out introductions over the course of several years. The previous E36 platform had been in production since 1992.

Sedan buyers can choose from the 2.5-liter inline six (323 models) or the 2.8-liter inline six (328 models). A five-speed steptronic automatic transmission is optional this year. Changes to the sedans for the millennium include a new, optional radio-integrated navigation system that is less expensive and less comprehensive than the Onboard Navigation System currently offered by BMW, a climate-control system that automatically switches into recirculation mode when driving through polluted air, and a key memory feature that includes exterior mirror adjustments. Fifteen-inch alloy wheels are now standard on the 323i, and an optional sport-premium package is available.

For the 2000 model year, BMW's coupes steal the spotlight with a complete redesign of their own. Sharing a platform with the 3 Series sedans, the coupes receive a standard five-speed manual transmission, a sport-tuned suspension, and ventilated front and rear disc brakes. Two

BMW 3 SERIES

versions are available: the 323Ci, which has a 2.5-liter inline six that makes 170 horsepower at 5,500 rpm, and the 328Ci with a 2.8-liter inline six making 193 horsepower at 5,500 rpm. Torque output on the 323Ci is 181 foot-pounds at 3,500 rpm. The more powerful 3 Series coupe reaches 60 from zero in just 6.6 seconds and makes 206 foot-pounds of torque at 3,500 rpm. Both engines meet Low-Emissions Vehicle (LEV) standards. Sixteen-inch alloy wheels are standard on the coupes, but 17-inch alloys can be purchased as an option. A five-speed STEPTRONIC automatic transmission is also optional for those who don't want to shift their own gears.

Safety equipment on both coupes and sedans include All-Season Traction (AST) and Dynamic Stability Control (DSC), along with dual front airbags, door-mounted side airbags and BMW's patented Head Protection System (HPS). Rear side airbags and Xenon headlights are optional.

While many things have changed in the past 20 years, some things-luckily-have not. BMW is still recognized as a marque of high quality and affluence. This year, the two- and four-door models available in the manufacturer's 3 Series lineup offer performance and luxury that is likely to win your business, if not your heart.

Standard Equipment

323Ci COUPE (5M): 2.5L I6 DOHC SMPI with variable valve timing 24-valve engine, requires premium unleaded fuel; 5-speed manual transmission; 80-amp alternator; rear-wheel drive, traction control, 3.07 axle ratio; stainless steel exhaust; sport ride suspension, electronic stability, front independent strut suspension with anti-roll bar, front coil springs, gas-pressurized front shocks, rear independent multi-link suspension with anti-roll bar, rear coil springs, gas-pressurized rear shocks; power rack-and-pinion steering with engine speed-sensing assist; 4-wheel disc brakes with 4-wheel antilock braking system; 16.6 gal. capacity fuel tank; rear lip spoiler, side impact bars; front and rear body-colored bumpers; body-colored bodyside molding, rocker panel extensions; monotone paint; sealed beam halogen headlamps with daytime running lights, delay-off feature; additional exterior lights include front fog/driving lights; driver's and passenger's power remote body-colored heated folding outside mirrors; front and rear 16" x 7" silver alloy wheels; P205/55HR16 A/S BSW front and rear tires; inside under cargo mounted full-size alloy spare wheel; air conditioning with climate control, air filter, rear heat ducts, auto air recirculation; premium AM/FM stereo, seek-scan, cassette, CD changer pre-wiring, in-dash CD pre-wiring, 10 speakers, theft deterrent, and window grid diversity antenna, radio steering wheel controls; cruise control with steering wheel controls; power door locks with 2 stage unlock, remote keyless entry, power remote hatch/trunk release; cell phone pre-wiring, 1 power accessory outlet, driver's foot rest, retained accessory power, smokers' package; instrumentation display includes tachometer, water temperature gauge, in-dash clock, exterior temp, systems monitor, check control, trip odometer; warning indicators include oil pressure, water temp, battery, low oil level, low coolant, lights on, key in ignition, low fuel, low washer fluid, bulb failure, door ajar, trunk ajar, service interval, brake fluid; driver's and passenger's front airbags, driver's and front passenger's door mounted side airbags, overhead airbag; ignition disable; tinted windows, power windows with driver's and passenger's 1-touch down, power 1/4 vent windows; variable intermittent front windshield wipers, heated jets, sun visor strip, rear window defroster; seating capacity of 5, front bucket seats, adjustable tilt headrests, center armrest with storage, driver's seat includes 6-way direction control, passenger's seat includes 6-way direction control; 60-40 folding rear bench seat with adjustable headrests, center armrest; front height adjustable seatbelts with front pretensioners; leatherette seats, leatherette door trim insert, full cloth headliner, full carpet floor covering, plastic/rubber gear shift knob; interior lights include dome light with fade, front and rear reading lights, illuminated entry; leather-wrapped steering wheel with tilt and telescopic adjustment; dual illuminated vanity mirrors; day/night rearview mirror; full floor console, mini overhead console, locking glove box with light, front cupholder, 2 seat back storage pockets, driver's and passenger's door bins; carpeted cargo floor, carpeted trunk lid, cargo tie downs, cargo light; chrome grille, chrome side window moldings, black front windshield molding, black rear window molding and body-colored door handles.

328Ci COUPE (5M) (in addition to or instead of 328Ci COUPE (5M) equipment): 2.8L I6 DOHC SMPI with variable valve timing 24-valve engine, requires premium unleaded fuel; 2.93 axle

3 SERIES — BMW

ratio; instrumentation display includes trip computer; driver's seat includes 6-way power seat, passenger's seat includes 6-way power seat; memory on driver's seat with 3 memory setting(s).

323i SEDAN (5M) (in addition to or instead of 323Ci COUPE (5M) equipment): Front and rear body-colored bumpers with black rub strip; black bodyside molding; front and rear 15" x 6.5" silver alloy wheels; P195/65HR15 A/S BSW front and rear tires; child safety rear door locks, power front and rear windows with front and rear 1-touch down; black side window moldings.

328i SEDAN (5M) (in addition to or instead of 328i COUPE (5M) equipment): Front and rear body-colored bumpers with black rub strip; black bodyside molding; child safety rear door locks and power front and rear windows with front and rear 1-touch down.

Base Prices

Code	Description	Invoice	MSRP
0034	323Ci Coupe (5M)	26250	28990
0033	328Ci Coupe (5M)	30750	33990
0044	323i Sedan (5M)	24450	26990
0042	328i Sedan (5M)	30220	33400
	Destination Charge:	570	570

Accessories

Code	Description	Invoice	MSRP
—	Leather Upholstery	1235	1450
—	Metallic Paint	405	475
205	Transmission: 5-Speed Automatic (Sedan) *Includes 3.46 axle ratio.*	1140	1200
205	Transmission: 5-Speed Steptronic Automatic *Includes 3.46 axle ratio.*	1210	1275
261	Rear Seat Side Impact Airbag *Special order.*	325	385
269	Sport-Premium Package (323i) *Includes sports suspension, sport steering wheel, multi-function steering wheel, wheels: 16" sport alloy, tires: 225/50R16 92W performance, power glass moonroof, auto dimming rearview mirror, Myrtle wood trim, power seats with driver's memory, front armrest, interior lighting upgrade, visor mirror lights, sport seats, fog lights, heated mirrors, heated front washer jets and on-board computer. NOT AVAILABLE with 270, 468, 540.*	3655	4300
270	Sport Package (323Ci) *Includes wheels: 17" x 8" sport alloy, tires: 225/45R-17 91W and sport seats.*	850	1000
270	Sport Package (323i) *Includes sports suspension, sport steering wheel, wheels: 16" sport alloy, tires: 225/50R16 92W performance, sport seats, fog lights, heated mirrors and heated front washer jets. NOT AVAILABLE with 269, 468, 540.*	1700	2000
270	Sport Package (328Ci) *Includes wheels: 17" alloy, tires: 225/45ZR17 front and 245/40ZR17 rear and sport seats. NOT AVAILABLE with 468.*	1020	1200
270	Sport Package (328i) *Includes wheels: 17" x 8" sport alloy, tires: 225/45R-17 91W, sport seats, sport suspension and 3-spoke sport leather-wrapped wheel.*	1150	1350
403	Power Glass Moonroof	895	1050

BMW 3 SERIES / 5 SERIES

CODE	DESCRIPTION	INVOICE	MSRP
438	Myrtle Wood Trim	425	500
459	Power Seats with Driver's Memory (323i/323Ci)	805	945
464	Ski Bag (Coupe)	130	150
465	Fold Down Rear Seats (Sedan)	405	475
468	Premium Package (323Ci)	1785	2100
	Includes power glass moonroof, auto dimming rearview mirror, Myrtle wood trim and power seats with driver's memory.		
468	Premium Package (323i)	2975	3500
	Includes wheels: 16" alloy, tires: 205/55R16-91H performance, power glass moonroof, auto dimming rearview mirror, Myrtle wood trim, power seats with driver's memory, front armrest, sport steering wheel and on-board computer. NOT AVAILABLE with 269, 270.		
468	Premium Package (328i/323Ci)	2465	2900
	Includes power glass moonroof, Myrtle wood trim, leather upholstery, 4-way power lumbar support and rain sensing windshield wipers. NOT AVAILABLE with 270.		
494	Heated Front Seats	425	500
508	Park Distance Control (328i)	300	350
520	Fog Lights (323i)	220	260
	Includes heated mirrors and heated front washer jets.		
522	Xenon Headlights (323i/323Ci/328Ci)	425	500
	REQUIRES 520 or 269 or 270.		
522	Xenon Headlights (328i)	425	500
540	Multi-Function Steering Wheel (323i)	405	475
	4-spoke steering wheel. NOT AVAILABLE with 269, 270.		
550	On-Board Computer (323i)	255	300
606	Radio Navigation System	1020	1200
	Includes lower-priced compact version of (609) Onboard Navigation System; does not include color monitor. REQUIRES 550 or 468 or 269. NOT AVAILABLE with 609, 662.		
609	Onboard Navigation System	1530	1800
	REQUIRES 550 or 468 or 269. NOT AVAILABLE with 662, 606.		
662	Radio: AM/FM Stereo with CD	170	200
	Replaces cassette. NOT AVAILABLE with 609, 606.		
674	Harman Kardon Sound System	575	675

2000 5 SERIES

What's New?

The 5 Series cars carryover from last year with small changes and no price increase.

Review

BMWs are famous for the suppleness of their ride and the responsiveness of their steering; "firmness without harshness" is the phrase most often bandied about our offices when discussing these cars' uncanny ability to stay connected to the road while communicating almost telepathically

5 SERIES — BMW

with the driver. The 5 Series is no exception. Available in two flavors, 528i or 540i, drivers can choose a sedan or a sport-wagon bodystyle.

528i models are powered by a 2.8-liter inline 6-cylinder engine that provides excellent midrange torque and makes 193 horsepower. The 528i comes with a standard five-speed manual transmission, or can be optioned with a five-speed Steptronic automatic transmission.

Under the hoods of the 540i sedans and sport wagons sit 4.4-liter, 32-valve V8s that offer zero-to-60 times in the low sixes, make 282 horsepower and can also be mated to five-speed Steptronic automatic transmissions, if desired. The 540i sedan continues to be available with a six-speed manual transmission. If you love to drive, opt for this model and prepare yourself for an invigorating ride. The suspension is pleasantly firm on this lively model, but it is difficult to operate the transmission smoothly.

As one would expect in a top-end, luxury/sport vehicle, equipment levels are first rate. Standard fare includes rear self-leveling suspension, car and key programmable memory, dual zone air conditioning and cruise control with steering wheel controls. All-Season Traction (AST), Dynamic Stability Control (DSC) and Dynamic Brake Control are standard on all 2000 5 Series cars. Rain-sensing windshield wipers and Xenon headlights are standard on 540 models and optional on the 528s this year.

Standard safety equipment includes 9-mph bumpers, dual airbags, door-mounted side-impact airbags, and a front head-protection system. Three-point seatbelts at all seating positions, impact sensors that unlock the doors and activate the hazard lights in the event of a serious accident, remote keyless entry, two-step unlocking, coded drive-away protection, and a vehicle security system are also standard. Rear-passenger side-impact airbags are optional.

To list all of the 5 Series' luxury features would take more space than we have. A few of the more noticeable ones are automatic climate controls, power moonroof, 200-watt stereo, 10-way power front seats with power headrests, heated steering wheel, and a right-hand outside mirror that tilts down when the car is in reverse to help drivers see curbs when parallel parking.

Yes indeed, the 5 Series is a wonderful car. Given all of the inquiries we receive about it, you apparently think so, too. If you can afford to buy one, we recommend that you do. Sure, there are other great cars out there in this price range; we just think this is one of the best.

2000 BMW 5 Series

BMW 5 SERIES

Standard Equipment

528i SEDAN (5M): 2.8L I6 DOHC SMPI with variable valve timing 24-valve engine, requires premium unleaded fuel; 5-speed manual transmission; 120-amp alternator; rear-wheel drive, traction control, 2.93 axle ratio; stainless steel exhaust; electronic stability, front independent strut suspension with anti-roll bar, front coil springs, gas-pressurized front shocks, rear independent multi-link suspension with anti-roll bar, rear coil springs, gas-pressurized rear shocks; power rack-and-pinion steering with engine speed-sensing assist; 4-wheel disc brakes with 4-wheel antilock braking system; 18.5 gal. capacity fuel tank; side impact bars; front and rear body-colored bumpers with black rub strip, chrome bumper insert; black bodyside molding with chrome bodyside insert, rocker panel extensions; metallic monotone paint; sealed beam halogen headlamps, delay-off feature; additional exterior lights include front fog/driving lights; driver's and passenger's power remote body-colored heated folding outside mirrors; front and rear 15" x 7" silver alloy wheels; P225/60HR15 A/S BSW front and rear tires; inside under cargo mounted full-size alloy spare wheel; dual zone front air conditioning with climate control, air filter, rear heat ducts, auto air recirculation; premium AM/FM stereo, seek-scan, cassette, CD changer pre-wiring, in-dash CD pre-wiring, 10 speakers, theft deterrent, and window grid diversity antenna, radio steering wheel controls; cruise control with steering wheel controls; power heated door locks with 2 stage unlock, remote keyless entry, child safety rear door locks, power remote hatch/trunk release; cell phone pre-wiring, 1 power accessory outlet, driver's foot rest, retained accessory power, smokers' package; instrumentation display includes tachometer, water temperature gauge, in-dash clock, exterior temp, systems monitor, trip computer, trip odometer; warning indicators include oil pressure, water temp, battery, low oil level, low coolant, lights on, key in ignition, low fuel, low washer fluid, bulb failure, door ajar, trunk ajar, service interval, brake fluid; driver's and passenger's front airbags, driver's and front passenger's door mounted side airbags, overhead airbag; ignition disable, panic alarm, security system; tinted windows, power front and rear windows with front and rear 1-touch down; variable intermittent front windshield wipers with heated jets, sun visor strip, rear window defroster; seating capacity of 5, front bucket seats, power adjustable headrests, center armrest with storage, driver's seat includes 6-way power seat, passenger's seat includes 6-way power seat; rear bench seat with adjustable headrests, center armrest, with storage; front height adjustable seatbelts with front pretensioners; leatherette seats, leatherette door trim insert, full cloth headliner, full carpet floor covering, plastic/rubber gear shift knob; memory on driver's seat with 3 memory setting(s), includes settings for exterior mirrors, steering wheel, headrests; interior lights include dome light with fade, front and rear reading lights, illuminated entry; steering wheel with power tilt and telescopic adjustment; dual illuminated vanity mirrors; day/night rearview mirror; full floor console, locking glove box with light, front and rear cupholders, 2 seat back storage pockets, driver's and passenger's door bins, rear door bins; carpeted cargo floor, carpeted trunk lid, cargo light; chrome grille, chrome side window moldings, black front windshield molding, black rear window molding and body-colored door handles.

540iA SEDAN (5A) (in addition to or instead of 528i SEDAN (5M) equipment): 4.4L V8 DOHC SMPI with variable valve timing 32-valve engine, requires premium unleaded fuel; 5-speed electronic OD auto transmission with lock-up; 2.81 axle ratio; dual stainless steel exhaust; power re-circulating ball steering with engine speed-sensing assist; front express open sliding and tilting glass sunroof with sunshade; sealed beam high intensity headlamps; front and rear 16" x 7" silver alloy wheels; P225/55HR16 A/S BSW front and rear tires; rain detecting wipers; leather seats, leather door trim insert, genuine wood trim on instrument panel, leather/wood gear shift knob; leather-wrapped steering wheel with power tilt and telescopic adjustment and auto-dimming day/night rearview mirror.

540i SEDAN (6M) (in addition to or instead of 540iA SEDAN (6M) equipment): 6-speed OD manual transmission; sport ride suspension, black bodyside molding with black bodyside insert; front 17" x 8" silver alloy wheels rear 17" x 9" silver alloy wheels; P235/45WR17 performance BSW front tires; 255/40 rear tires; front sports seats, power adjustable headrests, center armrest with storage, driver's seat includes 8-way power seat, passenger's seat includes 8-way

5 SERIES — BMW

power seat; leather-wrapped sport steering wheel with power tilt and telescopic adjustment and black side window moldings.

528iT SPORT WAGON (5M) (in addition to or instead of 528i SEDAN (5M) equipment): Roof rack; trunk pulldown, fixed 1/4 vent windows; flip-up rear window, rear window wiper; 60-40 folding rear bench seat with adjustable headrests, center armrest with storage; cargo cover and cargo concealed storage.

540iT SPORT WAGON (5A) (in addition to or instead of 540iA SEDAN (5A) equipment): Five-speed electronic OD automanual transmission with lock-up;150-amp alternator; 3.15 axle ratio; roof rack; trunk pulldown, fixed 1/4 vent windows; flip-up rear window, rear window wiper; 60-40 folding rear bench seat with adjustable headrests, center armrest with storage; cargo cover and cargo concealed storage.

Base Prices

CODE	DESCRIPTION	INVOICE	MSRP
0050	528i Sedan (5M)	35170	38900
0058	540iA Sedan (5A)	46150	51100
0053	540i Sedan (6M)	48670	53900
0054	528iT Sport Wagon (5M)	36790	40700
0069	540iT Sport Wagon (5A)	48290	53480
	Destination Charge:	570	570

Accessories

CODE	DESCRIPTION	INVOICE	MSRP
—	Metallic Paint	NC	NC
—	Montana Leather Upholstery (528i Sedan)	1235	1450
—	Montana Leather Upholstery (528iT)	1235	1450
—	Transmission: 5-Speed Steptronic Auto (528i)	1210	1275
	Includes 4.10 axle ratio.		
220	Self Leveling Suspension (528iT)	645	760
	NOT AVAILABLE with 269, 270.		
261	Rear Seat Side Impact Airbag	325	385
	Special order.		
269	Sport Premium Package (528i)	3655	4300
	Includes wheels: 17" cross-spoke composite, tires: 235/45R17 93W performance, Shadowline trim, auto dimming interior mirror, rain sensing wipers, sport suspension, multi-function M Sport steering wheel, Vavona wood high gloss trim and Montana leather upholstery. NOT AVAILABLE with 468, 270, 343.		
269	Sport Premium Package (528iT)	4210	4950
	Includes sport self leveling suspension, wheels: 17" cross-spoke composite, tires: 235/45R17 93W performance, Shadowline trim, retractable luggage net, auto dimming interior mirror, rain sensing wipers, multi-function M Sport steering wheel, Vavona wood high gloss trim and Montana leather upholstery. NOT AVAILABLE with 220, 343, 468, 270.		
270	Sport Package (528i)	1675	1970
	Includes sport suspension, wheels: 17" cross-spoke composite, tires: 235/45R17 93W performance, Shadowline trim and multi-function M Sport steering wheel. NOT AVAILABLE with 220, 468, 343, 609. INCLUDED in 269.		

BMW 5 SERIES

CODE	DESCRIPTION	INVOICE	MSRP
270	Sport Package (528iT)	2100	2470

Includes sport self leveling suspension, wheels: 17" cross-spoke composite, tires: 235/45R17 93W performance, Shadowline trim and multi-function M Sport steering wheel. NOT AVAILABLE with 220, 468, 343, 609. INCLUDED in 269.

270	Sport Package (540iT)	3680	4100

Includes sport suspension, self leveling suspension, Shadowline trim, bodyside molding black insert, wheels: 17" radial alloy, tires: 235/45R17 93W performance, sport seats and multi-function M Sport steering wheel. NOT AVAILABLE with 343 or 488. PRICE INCLUDES REQUIRED $1300 Gas Guzzler Tax.

343	Cold Weather Package (All Except 540i)	640	750

Includes heated steering wheel, heated front seats and headlamp cleaning system. NOT AVAILABLE with 270, 494, 269.

403	Power Glass Moonroof (528i/528iT)	895	1050
416	Electric Rear Sunshade (528i)	490	575

Includes manual rear side window shade.

416	Rear Electric Sunshade (540i/540iA)	490	575

Includes manual rear side window shade.

417	Rear Door Window Roller Sun Blinds (Wagon)	155	180
456	Comfort Seats	1020	1200

Includes 16-way adjustable driver's and passenger's power seats with power lumbar suport. REQUIRES Leather Seats (528). NOT AVAILABLE with 270, 481.

465	Fold Down Rear Seats (Sedan)	405	475

Includes ski sack.

468	Premium Package (528i)	2635	3100

Includes wheels: 16" cross-spoke alloy, auto dimming interior mirror, rain sensing wipers, Vavona wood high gloss trim and Montana leather upholstery. NOT AVAILABLE with 269, 270, 481.

468	Premium Package (528iT)	2765	3250

Includes wheels: 16" cross-spoke alloy, retractable luggage net, auto dimming interior mirror, rain sensing wipers, Vavona wood high gloss trim and Montana leather upholstery. NOT AVAILABLE with 481, 269, 270.

481	Electric Sport Seats (528)	405	475

REQUIRES (270 or 26) and Montana Leather Upholstery. NOT AVAILABLE with 456, 468.

488	Driver's and Passenger's Lumbar Support (All Except 540i)	340	400

NOT AVAILABLE with 270, 481. INCLUDED in 456.

494	Heated Front Seats	425	500

NOT AVAILABLE with 270. INCLUDED in 343.

508	Rear Park Distance Control	300	350
522	Xenon Lights (528)	425	500
609	Navigation System (528i)	1690	1990

Includes one geographic disc plus one 6-month update and premium on-board computer. REQUIRES 468 or 269. NOT AVAILABLE with 270.

609	Navigation System (540)	1530	1800

Includes 1 geographic disc plus one 6-month update.

5 SERIES / M COUPE AND ROADSTER — BMW

CODE	DESCRIPTION	INVOICE	MSRP
609	Onboard Navigation System (528iT)	1690	1990
	Includes 1 geographic disc plus one 6-month update and premium on-board computer. REQUIRES 468 or 269. NOT AVAILABLE with 270.		
677	Premium Hi-Fi	1020	1200
	Includes AM/FM stereo cassette and digital signal processor.		
788	Wheels: 17" Mixed Parallel Spoke (540i/540iA)	255	300
	Style 66. REQUIRES 270.		

2000 M COUPE and ROADSTER

2000 BMW M Coupe

What's New?

The M cars carry over for 2000, save for two new exterior colors. Prices remain unchanged.

Review

One thing BMW knows how to do is build sporty cars. The company released its M roadster, a heavily breathed-upon version of the Z3 roadster that was designed to compete head-to-head with the Porsche 911, as an early-1999 model. Then, BMW made headlines with the introduction of its funky-looking M coupe last year. By now, both M cars have established reputations as the cool, good-looking, fast, fun sports cars that everyone wants to have parked in their driveways.

These high-performance versions of the Z3 roadster and coupe make 240 M-power ponies. They are propelled by a potent 3.2-liter inline six, and can reach 60 from zero in less than 5.4 seconds. Developed by BMW's M division and based on the M roadster, the M coupe has an upgraded engine, suspension, brakes, wheels, tires and interior.

BMW launched its M coupe last year with a completely new shape from the A-pillars back. The roof blends into the top of a rear hatch with spoiler, a third brake light and new taillights. With chrome-trimmed gills, four exhaust tips, and a huge rear-end that arches and swells out to house 9-inch wide rear wheels, the M coupe has achieved a modern, beefy look. Just as tasty,

M COUPE AND ROADSTER

however, is the M roadster, with its more conservative yet swoopy styling. Open-air travel is always a pleasure, but few convertibles are as entertaining as the BMW M roadster on a twisty two-lane or a flat stretch of deserted highway.

With stunning thrust and a potent revving capability, the cars exhibit excellent performance and handling. The gear shift lever feels tight, the torque band is wide and the brakes are confidence-inspiring with a progressive feel to the pedal. Rack-and-pinion steering is razor sharp and responds more crisply to inputs than does the Chevrolet Corvette or the Acura NSX, and the BMW's steering wheel is perfectly sized.

The M coupe's suspension is similar to the roadster's, with struts and arc-shaped lower arms in the front and semi-trailing arms in the rear, but the coupe boasts stiffer springs and a larger anti-roll bar. With the coupe's perfectly balanced 50/50-percent weight distribution, its body feels solid-even around the sharpest corners.

Inside, the cars both offer seating for two in comfortable, sporty, two-toned leather bucket seats with integrated headrests. Instrument gauges on the dash and center console are ringed in classy chrome and there are enough of them to tell you what the car is doing at any given moment.

Unlike most two-seaters, the M coupe also provides a practical cargo space behind the seats for luggage or two full-size golf bags. Rear storage areas are accessible through a hatchback rear door and a cargo cover can be rolled back for privacy.

Standard equipment on these sportsters includes alloy wheels, traction control, ABS, limited-slip differential, heated windshield wiper jets, cellular phone pre-wiring, power heated door locks with two-stage unlock, side airbags, a/c and six-way power seats. A stereo with CD player or power sunroof are options. For 2000, consumers can also choose two new colors: Titanium Silver or Oxford Green.

Standard Equipment

M COUPE (5M): 3.2L I6 DOHC SMPI with variable valve timing 24-valve engine, requires premium unleaded fuel; 5-speed manual transmission; 115-amp alternator; rear-wheel drive, limited slip differential, traction control, 3.23 axle ratio; stainless steel exhaust with chrome tip; sport ride suspension, front independent strut suspension with anti-roll bar, front coil springs, gas-pressurized front shocks, independent suspension with anti-roll bar, rear coil springs, gas-pressurized rear shocks; power rack-and-pinion steering with engine speed-sensing assist; 4-wheel disc brakes with 4-wheel antilock braking system; 13.5 gal. capacity fuel tank; rear lip spoiler, side impact bars; front and rear body-colored bumpers; rocker panel extensions; metallic monotone paint; sealed beam halogen headlamps with multiple headlamps; driver's and passenger's power remote body-colored heated folding outside mirrors; front 17" x 7.5" silver alloy wheels rear 17" x 9" silver alloy wheels; P225/45ZR17 performance BSW front tires; 245/40ZR17 performance BSW rear tires; air conditioning; premium AM/FM stereo, seek-scan, cassette, CD changer pre-wiring, in-dash CD pre-wiring, 9 performance speakers, premium amplifier, theft deterrent, and fixed antenna; cruise control; power heated door locks with 2 stage unlock; cell phone pre-wiring, 1 power accessory outlet, driver's foot rest; instrumentation display includes tachometer, water temp gauge, volt gauge, clock, trip odometer; warning indicators include oil pressure, water temp, battery, lights on, key in ignition, low fuel, service interval, brake fluid; driver's and passenger's front airbags, driver's and front passenger's door mounted side airbags; ignition disable; tinted windows, power front windows with driver's and passenger's 1-touch down, fixed rear windows; heated jets, variable intermittent front windshield wipers, sun visor strip, rear window wiper; seating capacity of 2, heated-cushion driver's and passenger's seats, fixed headrests, driver's seat includes 4-way power seat, 6-way direction control, passenger's seat includes 4-way power seat, 6-way direction control; seatbelts with front pretensioners; leather seats, leather door trim insert, full carpet floor covering, leather-wrapped gear shift knob; interior lights include dome light with delay; leather-wrapped sport steering wheel; vanity mirrors; day/night rearview mirror; full floor console, locking glove box with light, front cupholder, driver's and passenger's door bins; carpeted cargo floor, plastic trunk lid, cargo cover, cargo net, cargo light; chrome grille, black side window moldings, black front windshield molding, black rear window molding and black door handles.

BMW
M COUPE AND ROADSTER / Z3

CODE	DESCRIPTION	INVOICE	MSRP

M ROADSTER (5M) (in addition to or instead of COUPE (5M) equipment): Power convertible roof with lining, roll-over protection; premium AM/FM stereo, seek-scan, cassette, CD changer pre-wiring, in-dash CD pre-wiring, 10 performance speakers, premium amplifier, theft deterrent, and fixed antenna and full cloth headliner.

Base Prices

Code	Description	Invoice	MSRP
9926	Coupe (5M)	37780	41800
9924	Roadster (5M)	38590	42700
Destination Charge:		570	570

Accessories

Code	Description	Invoice	MSRP
388	Black Top (Roadster) *REQUIRES 982.*	NC	NC
390	Classic Red Top (Roadster) *REQUIRES 982.*	NC	NC
391	Dark Blue Top (Roadster) *REQUIRES 982.*	NC	NC
403	Tilt Glass Roof Panel (Coupe)	255	300
658	BMW In-Dash CD	170	200
982	Hard Top (Roadster)	1615	1900

2000 Z3

What's New?

Dynamic Stability Control is now standard on all Z3s. The cars also receive freshened exterior and interior appointments.

Review

The Z3, introduced in 1996, has seen unfaltering popularity with young and old alike even as the line has grown to include more models. It seems that wherever we take these cars, a crowd quickly forms to ask questions about performance and to drool over their lovely shapes.

The Z3 lineup consists of three sportsters: the Z3 Roadster 2.3, Z3 Coupe 2.8 and Z3 Roadster 2.8. The Z3 Roadster 2.3 has a 2.5-liter, six-cylinder engine that makes 170 horsepower while meeting Low Emission Vehicle (LEV) standards. Z3s outfitted with larger, 2.8-liter, 193-horsepower, six-cylinder engines are available as coupes or roadsters. These cars also meet LEV standards.

For 2000, Z3 Roadsters receive new L-shaped taillights with clear turn signal lenses, fully lined tops, re-sculpted rear flanks, and a redesigned center console. New colors inside and out spruce up the Z3, as do new alloy-wheel designs. The sound system is actually audible at speed this year, thanks to the addition of two subwoofers. Analog clocks replace digital versions in both the 2.3 and 2.8 models. The 2.3 gets standard four-wheel disc brakes, a limited-slip differential and 16-inch V-rated performance tires. The 2.8 has new chrome grille slats.

All Z3s have a new leather-wrapped M-Technic sport steering wheel and standard Dynamic Stability Control, which senses when the car is veering from its intended path and selectively modulates engine torque and the antilock brakes to bring the car under control. Additional

BMW Z3

changes to the coupe are limited to a new wheel design, which doesn't help it look any less like a high-topped sneaker.

Driving BMW's Z3 cars is a phenomenal experience. Even the most basic Z3 2.3 Roadster, with its powerful inline six and newly ventilated front-disc brakes, is a blast. Only at high speeds does the 2.3 feel winded, but opting for the larger displacement 2.8-liter six in the 2.8 Roadster solves that problem. And for those who must have a rigid structure and protection from the elements, the 2.8 Coupe is a hoot. With superb steering and excellent brakes, any Z3 is fun to drive and own. Despite their prowess, however, pure performance freaks will want to step up to the M Coupe and M Roadster, which offer more power and better handling.

Slotted comfortably between the bargain Mazda Miata and more expensive machines from Mercedes-Benz and Porsche, there is a Z3 to suit anybody's needs. The thrill of open-air motoring in a European two-seater is appealing to any baby boomer who owned a sporty little convertible while in college. The solid coupe, however, makes more sense for Snowbelt dwellers who like a bit of "funk" with their "sport." Thirty-somethings are attracted to Z3s because of their undeniable sex appeal and attainable price. But let's face it: Everybody who loves to drive loves the Z3.

2000 BMW Z3

Standard Equipment

2.3 ROADSTER (5M): 2.5L I6 DOHC SMPI with variable valve timing 24-valve engine, requires premium unleaded fuel; 5-speed manual transmission; 90-amp alternator; rear-wheel drive, limited slip differential, traction control, 3.15 axle ratio; stainless steel exhaust; electronic stability, front independent strut suspension with anti-roll bar, front coil springs, gas-pressurized front shocks, rear independent suspension with anti-roll bar, rear coil springs, gas-pressurized rear shocks; power rack-and-pinion steering with engine speed-sensing assist; 4-wheel disc brakes with 4-wheel antilock braking system; 13.5 gal. capacity fuel tank; side impact bars; manual convertible roof with lining, roll-over protection; front and rear body-colored bumpers; rocker panel extensions; monotone paint; sealed beam halogen headlamps with daytime running lights, multiple headlamps; driver's and passenger's power remote body-colored folding outside mirrors; front and rear 16" x 7" silver alloy wheels; P225/50VR16 performance BSW front and rear tires; inside under cargo mounted compact steel spare wheel; air conditioning; premium AM/FM stereo, seek-scan, cassette, CD changer pre-wiring, in-dash CD pre-wiring, 10 speakers, amplifier, theft deterrent, and fixed antenna; power door locks with 2 stage unlock; cell phone pre-wiring, 1 power accessory outlet, driver's foot rest; instrumentation display includes tachometer,

Z3   BMW

CODE   **DESCRIPTION**   **INVOICE**   **MSRP**

water temp gauge, clock, trip odometer; warning indicators include oil pressure, water temp, battery, lights on, key in ignition, low fuel, service interval, brake fluid; driver's and passenger's front airbags, driver's and front passenger's door mounted side airbags; ignition disable, security system; tinted windows, power front windows with driver's and passenger's 1-touch down; variable intermittent front windshield wipers, sun visor strip; seating capacity of 2, front bucket seats, fixed headrests, driver's seat includes 4-way power seat, 6-way direction control, passenger's seat includes 2-way power seat, 4-way direction control; seatbelts with front pretensioners; leatherette seats, leatherette door trim insert, full cloth headliner, full carpet floor covering, leather-wrapped gear shift knob; interior lights include dome light with delay; leather-wrapped steering wheel; vanity mirrors; day/night rearview mirror; full floor console, locking glove box with light, front cupholder, instrument panel bin, locking interior concealed storage, driver's and passenger's door bins; carpeted cargo floor, cargo light; chrome grille, black side window moldings, black front windshield molding, black rear window molding and black door handles.

2.8 ROADSTER (5M) (in addition to or instead of 2.3 ROADSTER (5M) equipment): 2.8L I6 DOHC SMPI with variable valve timing 24-valve engine, requires premium unleaded fuel; stainless steel exhaust with chrome tip; rear lip spoiler; additional exterior lights include front fog/driving lights; P225/50ZR16 performance BSW front and rear tires; premium AM/FM stereo, seek-scan, cassette, CD changer pre-wiring, in-dash CD pre-wiring, 10 performance speakers, premium amplifier, theft deterrent, and fixed antenna; cruise control; passenger's seat includes 4-way power seat, 6-way direction control and leather seats.

2.8 COUPE (5M) (in addition to or instead of 2.8 ROADSTER (5M) equipment): Premium AM/FM stereo, seek-scan, cassette, CD changer pre-wiring, in-dash CD pre-wiring, 9 performance speakers, premium amplifier, theft deterrent, and fixed antenna; fixed rear windows, rear window wiper; wood gear shift knob; plastic trunk lid and cargo cover.

Base Prices

CODE	DESCRIPTION	INVOICE	MSRP
2899	2.3 Roadster (5M)	28330	31300
2910	2.8 Roadster (5M)	33370	36900
2943	2.8 Coupe (5M)	33055	36550
	Destination Charge:	570	570

Accessories

CODE	DESCRIPTION	INVOICE	MSRP
—	Extended Leather Trim (2.8)	1020	1200
	NOT AVAILABLE with 481.		
—	Leather Upholstery (2.3)	980	1150
—	Metallic Paint	400	475
205	Transmission: 4-Speed Auto with OD	830	975
	Electronically controlled with three shift modes (economy, sport, manual).		
268	Wheels: 17" Radial Alloy (2.8 Coupe)	960	1125
299	Wheels: 17" Cross-Spoke Composite (2.8 Roadster)	960	1125
344	Aluminum Trim (2.8 Coupe)	130	150
	NOT AVAILABLE with 345.		
345	Chrome Trim	130	150
	NOT AVAILABLE with 344.		
396	Premium Package (2.3 Roadster)	1700	2000
	Includes power top, wood trim and leather upholstery. NOT AVAILABLE with 435.		
396	Premium Package (2.8 Roadster)	810	950
	Includes power top and wood trim. NOT AVAILABLE with 435.		

BMW   Z3

CODE	DESCRIPTION	INVOICE	MSRP
398	Power Top (Roadster)	640	750
403	Tilt Glass Roof Panel (2.8 Coupe)	260	300
405	Heated Front Seats	430	500
	Includes heated outside mirrors.		
413	Luggage Net (2.8 Coupe)	160	180
435	Wood Trim (Roadster)	340	400
	NOT AVAILABLE with 396.		
481	Sport Seats (Roadster)	340	400
	REQUIRES 405. NOT AVAILABLE with Extended Leather.		
520	Fog Lights (2.3)	220	260
540	Cruise Control (2.3)	400	475
550	On Board Computer	260	300
658	BMW In-Dash CD	170	200
674	Harman Kardon Sound System (2.3)	570	675
982	Hard Top (Roadster)	1620	1900

TO PRICE YOUR TRADE-IN,
PURCHASE EDMUND'S® USED CAR PRICES AND RATINGS.

See page 6 for details.

Major Savings On An Extended Warranty

"YOU DESERVE THE BEST"
Call today for your free quote.
Pay up to 50% less than dealership prices!

http://www.edmunds.com/warranty 1-800-580-9889

CENTURY — BUICK

2000 CENTURY

2000 Buick Century

What's New?

Buick's midsize Century heads into the new millennium with a Special Edition model commemorating the turn of the century and more horsepower in all three models from a revised 3.1-liter 3100 V6.

Review

Back in 1997, a revamped Century hit the showrooms with a bigger, more ergonomic interior and roomier trunk, all wrapped in smooth, flowing sheetmetal that Buick stylists hoped would have a long shelf life. It appears they got their wish. Now four model-years old, today's Century has been growing in popularity each year, proving we shouldn't underestimate the market power of America's senior citizens, rental car companies or business-class road travelers.

While traditional Buick buyers might describe this car as clean or classic looking, younger buyers will likely find it as bland as baby food. The 2000 version does nothing to change any of that, so if you happen to like the look, you're in luck. Ditto for the interior design, which is certainly contemporary, thanks to large and legible gauges and controls facing a cabin roomy enough to carry six comfortably. Rear seating remains elevated theater-style, lending an overall airy feel inside.

The big news this year is the addition of a Special Edition to go along with the well-equipped Custom and the positively pampering Limited versions. According to Century brand manager Anthony Derhake, the Special Edition model was added after Buick figured that "the turn of the century is a great opportunity to celebrate Buick's Century."

Marketing aside, the Special Edition comes with blacked-out grille and trim, monochrome fascias and bodyside moldings and machined aluminum wheels. It also touts commemorative "2000" badging on its doors, taillamps and instrument panel and embroidered "Century 2000" lettering on its headrests and floor mats. The uplevel Special Edition adds leather-trimmed seats which come with a side airbag for the driver.

Other features packaged with this year's Special Edition model include body-color mirrors, cruise control, a six-way power driver's seat, trunk convenience net, AM/FM cassette player with steering wheel controls and a rear window antenna. Opt for the aforementioned uplevel package with leather and you'll also get electrochromic auto-dim rearview and illuminated visor

BUICK CENTURY

vanity mirrors, a six-way power front passenger seat and a split-fold pass-through rear seat. You also enjoy an AM/FM compact-disc player (or optional CD/cassette combination) with GM's Concert Sound III speaker system.

All 2000-model-year Centurys benefit from a revised 3100 V6 that makes 175 horsepower, up 15 horsepower from 1999, and 195 foot-pounds of torque, or 10 more than last year's engine. The 3.1's new intake and exhaust manifolds not only provide more power, but also increase projected highway fuel economy by one mile per gallon, to 30 mpg. Projected city mileage remains at 20 mpg. Century's four-speed automatic transmission has also been improved, featuring fully electronic controls and a larger torque converter for smoother shifting.

Other revisions for 2000 come inside, where newly designed and improved dual-zone climate controls are now standard on all models, allowing the driver and right-front passenger to select different temperatures. Electronic dual-zone climate control, which replaces slide-and-knob controls with push buttons and LED and digital indicators, is standard in the upper-level Special Edition and optional on the Limited.

All models come standard with such features as remote keyless entry, automatic power door locks, daytime running lamps with Twilight Sentinel (which automatically controls the headlamps based on lighting conditions), door courtesy lights, battery rundown protection, antilock brakes, traction control, a tire inflation monitor and GM's PASS-Key II theft-deterrent system.

Century also offers the new three-button OnStar driver assistance system as a dealer-installed option for the 2000 model year. OnStar provides a hands-free link to real-time, person-to-person in-vehicle safety, security and information services from GM's 24-hour, seven-day-a-week OnStar Center. The new three-button system eliminates the need for a customer to buy separate cellular telephone service to access OnStar.

Century stacks up well in the high-volume midsize sedan market, where it shows continued sales strength against its domestic rivals. But its GM stablemates seem to offer the strongest competition with similar vehicles that differ mainly in terms of styling and content. Oldsmobile's Euro-flavored Intrigue is arguably prettier, Chevrolet's Malibu is a strong value and Pontiac's sporty Grand Prix is one of our favorite sedans of any stripe.

Nonetheless, a good safety record and solid build quality makes the Buick Century an enduring favorite, while gaining "top buy" type acclaim from more than a few consumer publications and rating organizations along the way. With the highest customer loyalty rating in the segment, Century buyers seem prepared to stick with this Buick well into the next century.

Standard Equipment

CUSTOM (4A): 3.1L V6 OHV SMPI 12-valve engine; 4-speed electronic OD auto transmission with lock-up; battery with run down protection; front-wheel drive, traction control, 3.29 axle ratio; stainless steel exhaust; front independent strut suspension with anti-roll bar, front coil springs, rear independent strut suspension with anti-roll bar, rear coil springs; power rack-and-pinion steering; front disc/rear drum brakes with 4-wheel antilock braking system; 17.5 gal. capacity fuel tank; side impact bars; front and rear body-colored bumpers with chrome bumper insert; body-colored bodyside molding with chrome bodyside insert; monotone paint; aero-composite halogen fully auto headlamps with daytime running lights, delay-off feature; additional exterior lights include underhood light; driver's and passenger's power remote black folding outside mirrors; front and rear 15" x 6" steel wheels; P205/70SR15 A/S BSW front and rear tires; inside under cargo mounted compact steel spare wheel; dual zone front air conditioning, air filter, rear heat ducts; AM/FM stereo, clock, seek-scan, 6 performance speakers, and fixed antenna; power door locks, remote keyless entry, child safety rear door locks, power remote hatch/trunk release; 1 power accessory outlet, driver's foot rest, smokers' package; instrumentation display includes water temperature gauge, trip odometer; warning indicators include oil pressure, water temp, battery, low oil level, low coolant, lights on, key in ignition, low fuel, low washer fluid, door ajar, trunk ajar; driver's and passenger's front airbags; ignition disable, panic alarm; tinted windows, power front and rear windows with driver's 1-touch down; variable intermittent front windshield wipers, sun visor strip, rear window defroster; seating capacity of 6, 55-45 split-bench front seat, adjustable headrests, center armrest with storage, driver's seat includes 4-way direction control, passenger's seat includes 4-way direction control; rear bench seat with fixed headrests; front

CENTURY — BUICK

height adjustable seatbelts; cloth seats, cloth door trim insert, full cloth headliner, full carpet floor covering; interior lights include dome light with fade, front reading lights, illuminated entry; steering wheel with tilt adjustment; vanity mirrors, dual auxiliary visors; day/night rearview mirror; locking glove box with light, front cupholder, driver's and passenger's door bins, rear door bins; carpeted cargo floor, cargo light; chrome grille, chrome side window moldings, black front windshield molding, black rear window molding and body-colored door handles.

LIMITED (4A) (in addition to or instead of CUSTOM (4A) equipment): Power rack-and-pinion steering with vehicle speed-sensing assist; driver's and passenger's power remote body-colored heated folding outside mirrors; retained accessory power, seat mounted driver's side airbag; driver's seat includes 4-way power seat, 8-way direction control, rear center armrest; leather seats, leatherette door trim insert, carpeted floor mats; interior lights include front and rear reading lights; dual illuminated vanity mirrors, dual auxiliary visors and 2 seat back storage pockets.

Base Prices

Code	Description	Invoice	MSRP
S69	Custom (4A)	17936	19602
Y69	Limited (4A)	19889	21737
	Destination Charge:	560	560

Accessories

Code	Description	Invoice	MSRP
1SA	**Option Package 1SA (Custom)**	NC	NC
	Includes vehicle with standard equipment. NOT AVAILABLE with DH6, UK3, CF5, ULO, UPO, DD8, D85.		
1SB	**Option Package 1SB Popular (Custom)**	267	310
	Includes front carpet savers, rear carpet savers, electronic cruise control, trunk convenience net, AM/FM stereo with cassette, seek/scan and rear window antenna. NOT AVAILABLE with DH6, CF5, DD8, ULO, D85.		
1SC	**Option Package 1SC Premium (Custom)**	804	935
	Includes front carpet savers, rear carpet savers, electronic cruise control, trunk convenience net, AM/FM stereo with cassette, seek/scan, 6-way power's driver seat, rear window antenna and dual electric remote heated mirrors. NOT AVAILABLE with D85, UPO.		
1SD	**Option Package 1SD (Limited)**	NC	NC
	Includes vehicle with standard equipment. NOT AVAILABLE with CF5, DD8, ULO, AG2.		
1SE	**Option Package 1SE Luxury (Limited)**	396	460
	Includes electronic cruise control, AM/FM stereo with cassette, seek/scan and trunk convenience net. NOT AVAILABLE with CF5, UPO, AG2.		
1SF	**Option Package 1SF Prestige (Limited)**	1294	1505
	Includes electronic cruise control, trunk convenience net, air conditioning with dual temperature control, 6-way power passenger's seat, AM/FM stereo with cassette, seek/scan and Concert Sound III speakers. NOT AVAILABLE with UN6, UPO, U77, ULO.		
1SG	**Option Package 1SG Elite (Custom)**	933	1085
	Includes front carpet savers, rear carpet savers, electronic cruise control, trunk convenience net, 6-way power driver's seat, rear window antenna, dual electric		

BUICK — CENTURY

CODE	DESCRIPTION	INVOICE	MSRP
	remote heated mirrors, steering wheel mounted radio controls, AM/FM stereo with cassette and seek/scan. NOT AVAILABLE with UN6, UPO, ULO, 185.		
1SH	**Option Package 1SH Elite (Limited)**	727	845
	Includes electronic cruise control, trunk convenience net, air conditioning with dual temperature control and rear window antenna. MUST BE A RESIDENT OF California, Idaho, Oregon or Washington. NOT AVAILABLE with UN6, UPO, ULO.		
1SJ	**Option Package 1SJ Special Edition (Custom)**	1557	1810
	Manufacturer Discount	(430)	(500)
	Net Price	1127	1310
	Includes Century 2000 special appearance package, front carpet savers, rear carpet savers, electronic cruise control, trunk convenience net, 6-way power driver's seat, rear window antenna, dual electric remote heated mirrors, steering wheel mounted radio controls, AM/FM stereo with cassette, seek/scan and wheels: 15" aluminum. NOT AVAILABLE with QGZ, PH6, UN6, ULO, UPO.		
1SK	**Option Package 1SK Special Edition (Limited)**	2243	2608
	Manufacturer Discount	(430)	(500)
	Net Price	1813	2108
	Includes Century 2000 appearance package, electronic cruise control, trunk convenience net, air conditioning with dual temperature control, rear window antenna, 6-way power passenger's seat, AM/FM stereo with cassette, seek/scan and Concert Sound III speakers, wheels: 15" aluminum and split folding rear seat. NOT AVAILABLE with PH6, UN6, ULO, UPO.		
AG1	**6-Way Power Driver's Seat (Custom)**	284	330
	INCLUDED in 1SC, 1SG, 1SJ.		
AG2	**6-Way Power Passenger's Seat (Limited)**	284	330
	NOT AVAILABLE with 1SD, 1SE. INCLUDED in 1SF, 1SK.		
AM9	**Split Folding Rear Seat**	236	275
	Includes storage armrest and dual cup holders. INCLUDED in 1SK.		
AP9	**Trunk Convenience Net**	26	30
	INCLUDED in 1SD, 1SB, 1SE, 1SH, 1SC, 1SG, 1SF, 1SJ, 1SK.		
B34	**Front Carpet Savers (Custom)**	22	25
	REQUIRES B35. INCLUDED in 1SB, 1SC, 1SG, 1SJ.		
B35	**Rear Carpet Savers (Custom)**	17	20
	REQUIRES B34. INCLUDED in 1SB, 1SC, 1SG, 1SJ.		
CF5	**Electric Sliding and Tilting Sunroof**	598	695
	Includes power sunshade and reading lights. REQUIRES DD8 and DH6. NOT AVAILABLE with 1SA, 1SB, 1SD, 1SE.		
CJ2	**Air Conditioning with Dual Temp Control (Limited)**	168	195
	Includes auto ComforTemp climate control. INCLUDED in 1SH, 1SF, 1SK.		
D85	**Accent Stripes**	64	75
	NOT AVAILABLE with 1SA, 1SB, 1SC.		
DD8	**Electrochromic Interior Rearview Mirror**	103	120
	Includes auto dimming and heated outside rearview mirrors. REQUIRES DH6. NOT AVAILABLE with 1SA, 1SB, 1SD. INCLUDED in 1SF, 1SK.		
DE5	**Dual Electric Remote Heated Mirrors (Custom)**	52	60
	Body color. INCLUDED in 1SC, 1SG, 1SJ.		

CENTURY — BUICK

CODE	DESCRIPTION	INVOICE	MSRP
DH6	Dual Illuminated Visor Vanity Mirrors (Custom)	118	137
	Includes extendable sunshades, courtesy/reading lights and rear assist straps. NOT AVAILABLE with 1SA, 1SB.		
K05	Electric Engine Block Heater	15	18
K34	Cruise Control	202	235
	INCLUDED in 1SB, 1SC, 1SE, 1SF.		
PH6	Wheels: 15" Aluminum	322	375
	NOT AVAILABLE with 1SJ, 1SK.		
QGZ	Tires: P205/70R15 AS WSW SBR	129	150
	NOT AVAILABLE with 1SJ.		
U77	Rear Window Antenna	34	40
	NOT AVAILABLE with 1SF. INCLUDED in 1SA, 1SB, 1SH, 1SC, 1SG, 1SJ, 1SK.		
U85	Concert Sound III Speakers (Limited)	215	250
	Includes 8 speakers and diversity antenna. REQUIRES (1SD or 1SE) and (ULO or UPO). NOT AVAILABLE with UN6. INCLUDED in 1SF, 1SK.		
U85	Concert Sound III Speakers (Limited)	181	210
	Includes 8 speakers and diversity antenna. REQUIRES 1SH and (ULO or UPO). NOT AVAILABLE with UN6. INCLUDED in 1SF, 1SK.		
U85	Concert Sound III Speakers (Limited)	215	250
	Includes 8 speakers and diversity antenna. REQUIRES ULO or UPO. NOT AVAILABLE with UN6. INCLUDED with 1SF, 1SK.		
UK3	Steering Wheel Mounted Radio Controls	108	125
	REQUIRES ULO or UPO. NOT AVAILABLE with 1SA, UN6. INCLUDED in 1SH, 1SG, 1SF, 1SJ, 1SK.		
ULO	Radio: AM/FM Stereo with Cassette	189	220
	Includes power-loading cassette player, auto tone control, clock, digital display, preset of 12 FM/6 AM stations, backlit station-selector buttons and graphics, auto-preset station select, motorized volume control, separate bass/treble controls, fade/balance controls, auto CrO2 and Dolby B, preset scan, clean-tape-head indicator, radio monitor (allows radio to play while cassette player is fast forwarding/reversing), Theftlock and steering wheel controls; compatible with remote CD changer. NOT AVAILABLE with 1SA, UPO, UN6, 1SG, 1SE, 1SF, 1SK, 1SH. INCLUDED in 1SG, 1SJ.		
ULO	Radio: AM/FM Stereo with Cassette	22	25
	Includes power-loading cassette player, auto tone control, clock, digital display, preset of 12 FM/6 AM stations, backlit station-selector buttons and graphics, auto-preset station select, motorized volume control, separate bass/treble controls, fade/balance controls, auto CrO2 and Dolby B, preset scan, clean-tape-head indicator, radio monitor (allows radio to play while cassette player is fast forwarding/reversing), Theftlock and steering wheel controls; compatible with remote CD changer. REQUIRES 1SC. NOT AVAILABLE with 1SA, 1SB, 1SJ, UPO, UN6, 1SD, 1SF, 1SK, 1SH. INCLUDED in 1SG, 1SJ.		
UN6	Radio: AM/FM Stereo with Cassette	168	195
	Includes power-loading cassette player, clock, digital display, electronic tuning, preset scan, backlit station-selector buttons and graphics, auto CrO2 and Dolby B, separate bass/treble controls, fade/balance controls, clean-tape-head indicator and radio monitor (allows radio to play while cassette player is fast forwarding/reversing).		

BUICK — CENTURY / LESABRE

CODE	DESCRIPTION	INVOICE	MSRP
	NOT AVAILABLE with 1SF, 1SH, 1SK, U85, UK3, ULO, UPO. INCLUDED in 1SA, 1SB, 1SE, 1SC.		
UPO	Radio: AM/FM Stereo with CD and Cassette	172	200
	Includes power-loading CD and cassette players, auto tone control, seek/scan, clock, preset of 12 FM/6 AM stations, backlit station-selector buttons and graphics, preset scan, auto-preset station select, motorized volume control, separate bass/treble controls, fade/balance controls, auto CrO2 and Dolby B, clean-tape-head indicator, next/previous CD track selector, random play, radio monitor allows radio to play while cassette player is fast forwarding/reversing, Theftlock and steering wheel controls; compatible with remote CD changer. NOT AVAILABLE with 1SA, 1SB, 1SC, ULO, UN6, 1SD, 1SE. INCLUDED in 1SK.		
UPO	Radio: AM/FM Stereo with CD and Cassette	194	225
	Includes power-loading CD and cassette players, auto tone control, seek/scan, clock, preset of 12 FM/6 AM stations, backlit station-selector buttons and graphics, preset scan, auto-preset station select, motorized volume control, separate bass/treble controls, fade/balance controls, auto CrO2 and Dolby B, clean-tape-head indicator, next/previous CD track selector, random play, radio monitor, Theftlock and steering wheel controls; compatible with remote CD changer. NOT AVAILABLE with 1SA, 1SB, 1SJ, ULO, UN6, 1SD, 1SF, 1SE. INCLUDED in 1SK.		
UPO	Radio: AM/FM Stereo with CD and Cassette	361	420
	Includes power-loading CD and cassette players, auto tone control, seek/scan, clock, preset of 12 FM/6 AM stations, backlit station-selector buttons and graphics, preset scan, auto-preset station select, motorized volume control, separate bass/treble controls, fade/balance controls, auto CrO2 and Dolby B, clean-tape-head indicator, next/previous CD track selector, random play, radio monitor, Theftlock and steering wheel controls; compatible with remote CD changer. NOT AVAILABLE with 1SA, 1SC, 1SJ, ULO, UN6, 1SG, 1SF, 1SH. INCLUDED in 1SK.		

2000 LESABRE

What's New?

The best-selling U.S. full-size car for seven straight years, Buick's LeSabre has been totally redesigned for the 2000 model year. Though it looks a lot like a '99, this car has undergone a remarkable transformation, riding on a new platform with mildly tweaked sheetmetal and an entirely reworked cabin. Better ride, steering and seats, plus side airbags and integrated seatbelts, make it an even better value than before.

Review

Evolutionary in style outside, and revolutionary in style inside, the 2000 Buick LeSabre appears to have met its designers' goals — keep the good stuff and improve the rest. Give Buick credit for acting on customer input and coming up with a surprisingly competent overall package.

Though this big, front-drive sedan is about an inch narrower than its predecessor, much of its shape and many of its dimensions are little-changed from last year. Its new platform allows for moving the wheels farther out to the corners, making for an extra 1.4 inches of wheelbase to 112.2 inches, which is nearly as long as the so-called "cab-forward" designed Chrysler Concorde.

LESABRE

BUICK

| CODE | DESCRIPTION | INVOICE | MSRP |

Sure, Buick's traditional "waterfall" chrome grille is still there, but this new LeSabre also has fresher, cleaner-looking front and rear fascias, setting off clear-lens headlamps and bigger tail lamps. Flush, body-colored door handles replace the chrome pulls, and even the bodyside moldings have an integrated look.

The big news is inside, where that old, horizontal dashboard with small gauges has been replaced by a stylish, modern housing that delivers driving information in an easier-to-read format. Better still, the seats - long a sore spot with our testers - are comfy, yet supportive.

Interior storage and safety is also improved. In addition to incorporating side airbags, the front seats have built-in "self-aligning" head restraints, reducing the risk of whiplash. Front seatbelts are now integrated into the seat frames, and all five seating positions come equipped with shoulder and lap belts. The LeSabre's interior meets the government's new head-impact requirements ahead of the federal deadline.

Rear headroom is as good as in the Ford Crown Victoria or Mercury Grand Marquis, and though legroom back there has been slightly reduced, it is still comfortable. Larger rear-door glass lowers nearly all the way down into the doors for better ventilation. And trunk room has grown a full foot to 18 cubic feet, now bettering the 17 cubic feet found in the Concorde.

The new LeSabre platform makes for a stiffer, quieter body. While the front suspension remains MacPherson strut with coil springs, the rear's semi-trailing arm / coil-spring setup makes for a more-controlled ride. We'd opt for the LeSabre Limited with the Gran Touring Package, despite the fact that the top-of-the-line P255/60R-16 Firestones are not super handlers. Antilock brakes are standard, with the rear drums being upgraded to discs for better stopping power.

The only available powertrain in both the Custom and Limited models remains the trusty 3.8-liter Series II V6, mated to a smooth four-speed automatic transmission. While this motor still makes a healthy 205 horsepower at 5,200 rpm, its 230 foot-pounds of torque now peak at a more useable 3,700 rpm instead of up at 4,000. While the 4.6-liter V8 in the Grand Marquis boasts 275 foot-pounds of torque way down at 3,000 rpm, it has only 200 horses and its fuel economy is lower. What's more, GM's V6 meets federal 2001 low-emission vehicle (LEV) standards

LeSabres have consistently ranked better than average in owner trouble complaints over the years, and the 2000 model should even improve on that score. While the median age of most LeSabre buyers has long been in the 60s, this new-and-improved version is likely to draw younger, more family-oriented buyers into Buick showrooms. That will not only do much to help the brand shake some of its fuddy-duddy image, but also keep LeSabre among the best sellers.

2000 Buick LeSabre

EDMUND'S® NEW CARS www.edmunds.com

BUICK — LESABRE

| CODE | DESCRIPTION | INVOICE | MSRP |

Standard Equipment

CUSTOM (4A): 3.8L V6 OHV SMPI 12-valve engine; 4-speed electronic overdrive automatic transmission with lock-up; battery with run down protection; front wheel drive, 2.86 axle ratio; stainless steel exhaust; comfort ride suspension with auto-leveling, front independent strut suspension with anti-roll bar, front coil springs, rear independent suspension with anti-roll bar, rear coil springs; power rack-and-pinion steering; 4 wheel disc brakes with 4 wheel antilock braking system; 17.5 gal. capacity fuel tank; side impact bars; class I trailering; front and rear body-colored bumpers front with body-colored rub strip; body-colored bodyside molding; monotone paint; aero-composite halogen fully automatic headlamps with daytime running lights and delay-off feature; underhood light; driver's and passenger's power remote body-colored folding outside mirrors; front and rear 15" x 6" steel wheels; P215/70SR15 BSW AS front and rear tires; inside under cargo mounted compact steel spare wheel; air conditioning; AM/FM stereo with clock, seek-scan, 4 speakers and window grid diversity antenna; cruise control with steering wheel controls; power door locks with 2 stage unlock, remote keyless entry, child safety rear door locks, power remote hatch/trunk release; 2 power accessory outlets, driver's foot rest, retained accessory power, smoker's package; instrumentation display includes water temp gauge, trip odometer; warning indicators include water temp, battery, lights on, key in ignition; driver's and passenger's front airbags, driver's and front passenger's seat mounted side airbags; ignition disable, panic alarm; tinted windows, power front windows with driver's and passenger's 1-touch down, power rear windows; variable intermittent front windshield wipers, rear window defroster; seating capacity of 6, 55-45 split-bench front seat with adjustable headrests, center armrest with storage, driver's seat includes 2-way power seat with 4-way direction control and lumbar support, passenger's seat includes 2-way power seat with 4-way direction control; rear bench seat; cloth seats, vinyl door trim insert, full cloth headliner, full carpet floor covering with carpeted floor mats, simulated wood trim on instrument panel; interior lights include dome light with fade, front reading lights, illuminated entry; steering wheel with tilt adjustment; vanity mirrors, dual auxiliary visors; day-night rearview mirror; mini overhead console glove box with light, front cupholder, instrument panel covered bin, driver's and passenger's door bins; carpeted cargo floor, carpeted trunk lid, cargo light; chrome grille, chrome side window moldings, black front windshield molding, black rear window molding and body-colored door handles.

LIMITED (4A) (in addition to or instead of CUSTOM (4A) equipment): Front and rear body-colored bumpers with body-colored rub strip; monotone paint with bodyside accent stripe; additional exterior lights include cornering lights; dual zone front air conditioning with climate control, air filter; AM/FM stereo with clock, seek-scan, cassette, 6 performance speakers, automatic equalizer, theft deterrent, and window grid diversity antenna, radio steering wheel controls; instrumentation display includes tachometer, exterior temp; warning indicators include low oil level, low coolant, service interval; driver's seat includes 6-way power seat with lumbar support, passenger's seat includes 6-way power seat with lumbar support; rear bench seat with center pass-thru armrest; premium cloth seats; interior lights include front and rear reading lights, 4 door curb lights; dual illuminated vanity mirrors; auto-dimming day-night rearview mirror and cargo net.

Base Prices

Code	Description	Invoice	MSRP
4HP69	Custom (4A)	21260	23235
4HR69	Limited (4A)	25016	27340
Destination Charge:		615	615

Accessories

Code	Description	Invoice	MSRP
—	Leather Seat Trim (Limited)	632	735
—	Leather Trim (Custom)	598	695
	NOT AVAILABLE with 1SA.		

LESABRE / BUICK

CODE	DESCRIPTION	INVOICE	MSRP
1SA	**Custom Base Package 1SA (Custom)**	86	100
	Includes driver's and passenger's power recliners. NOT AVAILABLE with AG2, DH6, ULO, W02, Y56, UPO, CF5, NW9, U1S, UNO, (~~2) Leather Trim, N66.		
1SA	**Limited Package (Limited)**	NC	NC
	Includes vehicle with standard equipment. NOT AVAILABLE with A45, CF5, KA1, Y56.		
1SC	**Custom Premium Package 1SC (Custom)**	936	1088
	Includes driver's and passenger's power recliners, trunk convenience net, AM/FM stereo with cassette, radio steering wheel controls, 6-way power driver seat, bodyside stripe and wheels: 15" aluminum. NOT AVAILABLE with AG2, Y56, CF5, NW9, U1S, UPO, UNO.		
1SD	**Custom Luxury Package 1SD (Custom)**	1370	1593
	Includes driver's and passenger's power recliners, trunk convenience net, AM/FM stereo with cassette, 6 speaker concert sound system, radio steering wheel controls, 6-way power driver seat, bodyside stripe, wheels: 15" aluminum, gauge package, auto dimming rearview mirror and lighted visor vanity mirrors. NOT AVAILABLE with CF5, U1S, UPO, UNO, ULO.		
1SE	**Custom Prestige Package 1SE (Custom)**	2118	2463
	Includes driver's and passenger's power recliners, trunk convenience net, AM/FM stereo with cassette, 6 speaker concert sound system, radio steering wheel controls, 6-way power driver seat, bodyside stripe, wheels: 15" aluminum, gauge package, lighted visor vanity mirrors, air filtration system, electrochromic rearview mirror with compass, theft deterrent system, universal transmitter and moisture-sensing delay wipers. NOT AVAILABLE with UN6, UPO, ULO.		
1SE	**Limited Prestige Package 1SE (Limited)**	529	615
	Includes driver's and passenger power's recliners, electrochromic rearview mirror with compass, ETR AM/FM stereo with CD, cassette and automatic tone control, traction control system, universal transmitter and moisture-sensing delay wipers.		
A45	**Memory Driver's Seat (Limited)**	125	145
	Includes memory on outside mirrors and power lumbar. NOT AVAILABLE with 1SA.		
AG1	**6-Way Power Driver's Seat (Custom)**	364	423
	Includes passenger's side manual lumbar.		
AG2	**6-Way Power Passenger's Seat (Custom)**	284	330
	NOT AVAILABLE with 1SA, 1SC.		
AP9	**Trunk Convenience Net (Custom)**	26	30
CF5	**Astroroof (Custom)**	899	1045
	NOT AVAILABLE with 1SA, 1SC, 1SD.		
CF5	**Astroroof (Limited)**	856	995
	NOT AVAILABLE with 1SA.		
DD7	**Electrochromic Rearview Mirror (Limited)**	69	80
	Includes compass.		
DH6	**Driver's and Passenger's Lighted Visor Vanity Mirrors (Custom)**	79	92
	NOT AVAILABLE with 1SA.		
K05	**Engine Block Heater**	15	18
K12	**Air Filtration System (Custom)**	43	50
KA1	**Heated Front Seats (Limited)**	224	260
	Includes heated outside mirrors. NOT AVAILABLE with 1SA.		

BUICK — LESABRE

CODE	DESCRIPTION	INVOICE	MSRP
N66	Wheels: 16" Cross Lace Aluminum (Custom)	322	375
	NOT AVAILABLE with QPN, PH3, 1SC, 1SD, 1SE.		
N66	Wheels: 16" Cross Lace Aluminum	43	50
	REQUIRES 1SC, 1SD or 1SE (Custom). NOT AVAILABLE with QPN, PH3, 1SA.		
NW9	Traction Control System	150	175
	NOT AVAILABLE with 1SA, 1SC (Custom).		
PH3	Wheels: 15" Aluminum (Custom)	280	325
	NOT AVAILABLE with N66, QPN.		
QPN	Tires: P215/70R15 WW	60	70
	NOT AVAILABLE with PH3, N66, Y56.		
T1U	Driver Confidence Package	628	730
	Includes head-up display and StabiliTrak ICCS-3. REQUIRES 1SE, NW9 and Y56. NOT AVAILABLE with 1SA, 1SC, 1SD.		
T1U	Driver Confidence Package	757	880
	Includes head-up display, self sealing tires and StabiliTrak ICCS-3. REQUIRES 1SE, NW9 and N66. NOT AVAILABLE with 1SA, 1SC, 1SD.		
U1S	Trunk Mounted 12 Disc CD Changer	512	595
	Includes remote. NOT AVAILABLE with 1SA, 1SC, 1SD.		
UG1	Universal Transmitter (Limited)	86	100
	Includes 3 function remote. REQUIRES DD7.		
UL0	Radio: AM/FM Stereo with Cassette (Custom)	129	150
	Includes clock, seek-scan, auto tone control and steering wheel controls. REQUIES 1SC or 1SD. NOT AVAILABLE with 1SA, UN0, UN6, UP0, 1SE.		
UN0	Radio: AM/FM Stereo with CD (Custom)	215	250
	Includes clock, seek-scan, auto tone control and steering wheel controls. NOT AVAILABLE with 1SA, UL0, UP0, UN6, 1SE.		
UN0	Radio: AM/FM Stereo with CD (Custom)	86	100
	Includes clock, seek-scan, auto tone control and steering wheel controls. REQUIRES 1SE. NOT AVAILABLE with 1SA, 1SC, 1SD, UL0, UP0, UN6.		
UN6	Radio: AM/FM Stereo with Cassette (Custom)	142	165
	NOT AVAILABLE with 1SE, UN0, UP0, UL0.		
UP0	Radio: AM/FM Stereo with CD, Cassette, Automatic Tone Control (Custom)	301	350
	Includes power loading CD and cassette player with next/last CD track selector, seek/scan, clock and steering wheel radio controls. NOT AVAILABLE with 1SA, 1SE, UL0, UN0, UN6.		
UP0	Radio: AM/FM Stereo with CD, Cassette, Automatic Tone Control (Custom)	172	200
	Includes power loading CD and cassette player with next/last CD track selector, seek/scan, clock and steering wheel radio controls. REQUIRES 1SE. NOT AVAILABLE with 1SA, 1SC, 1SD, UL0, UN0, UN6.		
UP0	Radio: AM/FM Stereo with CD, Cassette, Automatic Tone Control (Limited)	172	200
	Includes power loading CD and cassette player with next/last CD track selector, seek/scan, clock and steering wheel radio controls.		
W02	5 Passenger Seating Package	60	70
	Includes convenience console with writing surface and cupholders, 45/45 bucket seats, two auxiliary 12V outlets, provisions for phone/fax and floor console. NOT AVAILABLE with 1SA.		

LESABRE / PARK AVENUE — BUICK

CODE	DESCRIPTION	INVOICE	MSRP
Y56	Gran Touring Package	159	185

Includes 3.05 axle ratio, gran touring suspension, wheels: 16" aluminum, tires: P225/60R16 Firestone touring, leather-wrapped steering wheel and magnetic variable assist steering. REQUIRES ULO or UNO or UPO (Custom). NOT AVAILABLE with 1SA or 1SC (Custom) or QPN.

2000 PARK AVENUE

2000 Buick Park Avenue

What's New?

Enjoying mild sales success since its 1997 redesign, Buick's full-size Park Avenue gets only minor refinements in the areas of safety, stability and comfort for 2000. The biggest news is the addition of StabiliTrak, GM's advanced vehicle stability control system.

Review

A mere two years after Buick engineers adopted chassis structures and styling cues from the trend-setting Riviera Coupe for a redesign of the Park Avenue Sedan, just look at how the fortunes of these sister cars have differed: The Park Avenue, a traditional favorite of the retirement-village set, racked up awards from several independent sources as it appealed to a wide audience. The Riv, as one of the dying breed of large personal-luxury sport coupe nameplates, struggled on the sales front until GM finally pulled the plug after only a couple of thousand units were produced for the 1999 model year.

While some auto analysts see a rebirth of the coupe segment on the horizon, nobody can argue with the viability of a well-executed, fully equipped large sedan in today's market. Clean design is the first thing you notice about the Park Avenue. It has a classy and dignified character without resorting to tacky chrome add-ons or exaggerated styling themes. Sure, a coupe this big would look downright silly (did somebody say Riviera?), but a sedan body looks right at home on this massive platform.

BUICK

PARK AVENUE

CODE	DESCRIPTION	INVOICE	MSRP

Ever think that redesigning a car to have larger exterior dimensions could cause some key interior dimensions to shrink? Well, such is the case with the Park Avenue. With that curvy body it gained in 1997 came the loss of a little front legroom and a whole cubic foot of cargo capacity. To compensate, Buick increased head-, rear leg- and hip room, while improving the lift-over into the trunk. The result is that many folks trading up to the newer Park Avenue think the car is more spacious than the old model.

Powertrains remain unchanged, and that's not a bad thing. GM's award-winning 3800 Series II engine provides V8-like power in a fuel-efficient, V6 package. The 240-horsepower supercharged edition of this engine is an absolute joy. Fortunately, it comes standard on the Ultra, which, when fully loaded, tips the scales at a hefty two tons.

There are two trim levels available, the well-equipped Park Avenue and upscale Ultra model. Ultras carry all the bells and whistles, including magnetic variable-assist steering that the dealership can reprogram for higher or lower steering effort. A variety of goodies are standard or optional on either, such as rain-sensing windshield wipers and a head-up display that projects speed, turn signals, high beams and idiot lights onto the lower portion of the windshield. There's also GM's "personal choice" and "convenience plus" option packages, as well as a "gran touring" package, which adds the programmable-effort steering, a beefier suspension, larger brake rotors, 16-inch alloy wheels riding on 225/60 blackwalls and a leather-wrapped steering wheel.

Topping the list of improvements for 2000 is StabiliTrak, an advanced integrated vehicle stability control system, which is standard on Ultra and optional on Park Avenue. StabiliTrak helps the driver maintain control by electronically comparing what the driver wants the car to do with information from sensors indicating how the car is actually responding. If the car is in danger of sliding or skidding, StabiliTrak slows and stabilizes the car to help the driver maintain control.

Safety is further enhanced this year with standard seat-mounted side airbags for the driver and right-front passenger, and rear child seat-tether anchors. Other interior improvements include a front-seat map pocket for expanded storage, optional separate heated seats, an optional trunk-mounted compact-disc player and additional sound-deadening measures.

Also available for the 2000 model year are new 16-inch wheels for both the Park Avenue and Ultra, as well as optional chrome wheels for both models. New exterior colors are Medium Red Pearl and Dark Blue Pearl. Bright White Diamond Tri-Coat also is available on Park Avenue. Inside, Medici Red is the new color option. Ultra models also will sport a new ebony instrument panel and door trim plates.

As on most premium GM models, buyers can opt for the dealer-installed, hands-free OnStar mobile communications system, which can not only be used for summoning all kinds of assistance, but also for automatic notification of airbag deployment, theft detection and stolen vehicle tracking.

Don't fix it if it ain't broke. Buick adhered to that wisdom for 1998-99 and again this year by making only minor modifications to the Park Avenue. Fact is, the Park Avenue is a quiet automobile, with solid build quality and interior ergonomics. It's no surprise to us that it garners high praise as a good value from auto reviewers, especially when compared to the sky-high price tag of some imported luxury sedans.

Standard Equipment

BASE (4A): 3.8L V6 OHV SMPI 12-valve engine; 4-speed electronic OD auto transmission with lock-up; HD battery with run down protection; front-wheel drive, 3.05 axle ratio; stainless steel exhaust; comfort ride suspension, auto-leveling suspension, front independent strut suspension with anti-roll bar, front coil springs, rear independent strut suspension with anti-roll bar, rear coil springs; power rack-and-pinion steering; 4-wheel disc brakes with 4-wheel antilock braking system; 18.5 gal. capacity fuel tank; side impact bars; front and rear body-colored bumpers with chrome bumper insert, body-colored rub strip; body-colored bodyside molding with chrome bodyside insert, rocker panel extensions; monotone paint with bodyside accent stripe; aero-composite halogen fully auto headlamps with daytime running lights, delay-off feature; additional exterior lights include cornering lights, underhood light; driver's and passenger's power remote body-colored folding outside mirrors; front and rear 16" x 6.5" silver alloy wheels; P225/60SR16 A/S BSW front and rear tires; inside under cargo mounted compact steel spare wheel; dual

PARK AVENUE — BUICK

CODE	DESCRIPTION	INVOICE	MSRP

zone front air conditioning with climate control, air filter, rear heat ducts; AM/FM stereo, clock, seek-scan, cassette, 6 performance speakers, theft deterrent, and window grid antenna; cruise control; power door locks, remote keyless entry, child safety rear door locks, power remote hatch/trunk release, power remote fuel release; 2 power accessory outlets, driver's foot rest, retained accessory power, smokers' package; instrumentation display includes tachometer, water temperature gauge, exterior temp, trip odometer; warning indicators include battery, lights on, key in ignition, low fuel; driver's and passenger's front airbags, driver's and front passenger's seat mounted side airbags; ignition disable, panic alarm, security system; tinted windows, power front and rear windows with driver's 1-touch down; variable intermittent front windshield wipers, sun visor strip, rear window defroster; seating capacity of 6, 55-45 split-bench front seat, power adjustable tilt headrests, center armrest with storage, driver's seat includes 6-way power seat, passenger's seat includes 6-way power seat; rear bench seat with fixed headrests, center pass-thru armrest; front height adjustable seatbelts; premium cloth seats, cloth door trim insert, full cloth headliner, full carpet floor covering with carpeted floor mats, simulated wood trim on instrument panel; interior lights include dome light with fade, front and rear reading lights, 4 door curb lights, illuminated entry; steering wheel with tilt adjustment; dual illuminated vanity mirrors, dual auxiliary visors; day/night rearview mirror; mini overhead console with storage, locking glove box with light, front and rear cupholders, 2 seat back storage pockets, driver's and passenger's door bins; carpeted cargo floor, cargo net, cargo light; chrome grille, chrome side window moldings, black front windshield molding, black rear window molding and body-colored door handles.

ULTRA (4A) (in addition to or instead of BASE (4A) equipment): 3.8L V6 OHV SMPI supercharger 12-valve engine, requires premium unleaded fuel; traction control, 2.93 axle ratio; electronic stability; power rack-and-pinion steering with vehicle speed-sensing assist; driver's and passenger's power remote body-colored heated electric folding outside mirrors; AM/FM stereo, clock, seek-scan, single CD, 9 performance speakers, amplifier, auto equalizer, theft deterrent, and window grid antenna, radio steering wheel controls; cell phone pre-wiring, garage door opener; instrumentation display includes compass, systems monitor, trip computer; warning indicators include low oil level, low coolant, low washer fluid, bulb failure, door ajar, trunk ajar, service interval; rain detecting wipers, heated-cushion 55-45 split-bench front seat; rear bench seat with tilt headrests, center pass-thru armrest with storage; leather seats, leatherette door trim insert; memory on driver's seat with 2 memory setting(s) includes settings for exterior mirrors, headrests; leather-wrapped steering wheel with tilt adjustment; auto-dimming day/night rearview mirror; rear illuminated vanity mirror and carpeted trunk lid.

Base Prices

Code	Description	Invoice	MSRP
W69	Base (4A)	28711	31725
U69	Ultra (4A)	33304	36800
	Destination Charge:	670	670

Accessories

Code	Description	Invoice	MSRP
—	Leather Seat Trim (Base)	645	750
	Includes leather-wrapped steering wheel. REQUIRES ULO or UNO or UPO. NOT AVAILABLE with Y56.		
1SA	Option Package 1SA (Base)	NC	NC
	Includes vehicle with standard equipment. NOT AVAILABLE with U99, UV6, Y56, CF5, NW9, UPO, UNO, KA1, U1S, U06, JL4.		
1SE	Option Package 1SE Prestige (Base)	968	1125
	Includes driver's information center, electrochromic heated rearview mirrors, electrochromic interior rearview mirror, integral digital compass, AM/FM stereo with		

BUICK — PARK AVENUE

CODE	DESCRIPTION	INVOICE	MSRP
	seek, scan and cassette, power driver's seat with memory, universal transmitter, driver's and passenger's power lumbars and rain-sensing windshield wiper system. NOT AVAILABLE with UPO.		
1SE	**Option Package 1SE Prestige (Ultra)**	NC	NC
	Includes vehicle with standard equipment.		
78U	**Bright White Diamond Paint**	387	450
CF5	**Electric Sliding and Tilting Sunroof**	942	1095
	Includes power sunshade and metaphoric switch design. NOT AVAILABLE with 1SA.		
DA1	**Rear Seat Storage Armrest (Base)**	43	50
	REQUIRES Leather Seat Trim.		
JL4	**StabiliTrak (Base)**	426	495
	Includes auto yaw rate correction system. REQUIRES NW9. NOT AVAILABLE with 1SA.		
K05	**Electric Engine Block Heater**	15	18
KA1	**Driver's and Front Passenger's Heated Seats (Base)**	194	225
	NOT AVAILABLE with 1SA.		
N98	**Wheels: 16" Chrome Plated Aluminum (Base)**	598	695
NW9	**Full Range Traction Control (Base)**	150	175
	NOT AVAILABLE with 1SA.		
P05	**Wheels: 16" Chrome Plated Aluminum (Ultra)**	598	695
QPY	**Tires: P225/60R16 AS WSW SBR**	129	150
	NOT AVAILABLE with Y56.		
U06	**Three Note Horn (Base)**	24	28
	NOT AVAILABLE with 1SA.		
U1S	**Trunk Mounted 12-Disc CD Changer**	512	595
	NOT AVAILABLE with 1SA.		
U99	**Concert Sound III Speakers (Base)**	241	280
	Includes 9-speaker equalized system with 154-Watt amplifier. NOT AVAILABLE with 1SA.		
UL0	**Radio: AM/FM Stereo with Cassette (Base)**	129	150
	Includes power-loading cassette, auto tone control, clock, digital display, preset of 12 FM/6 AM stations, backlit station-selector buttons and graphics, auto-preset station select, motorized volume control, separate bass/treble controls and fade/balance controls, auto CrO2 and Dolby B, preset scan, clean-tape-head indicator, radio monitor, Theftlock and steering wheel radio controls; compatible with remote CD changer. NOT AVAILABLE with UNO, UPO. INCLUDED in 1SE.		
UN0	**Radio: AM/FM Stereo with CD and Cassette (Base)**	215	250
	Includes power-loading CD and cassette players with auto tone control, clock, digital display, electronic tuning, preset of 12 FM/6 AM stations, backlit station-selector buttons and graphics, preset scan, auto preset station select, motorized volume control, fade/balance controls, auto CrO2 and Dolby B, clean-tape-head indicator, next/previous CD track selector, random play, radio monitor allows radio to play while cassette player is fast forwarding/reversing, Theftlock and steering-wheel controls; compatible with remote CD changer and OnStar three-button system. NOT AVAILABLE with UL0, UPO, 1SE.		

PARK AVENUE — BUICK

CODE	DESCRIPTION	INVOICE	MSRP
UN0	**Radio: AM/FM Stereo with CD and Cassette (Base)** .... Includes power-loading CD and cassette players with auto tone control, clock, digital display, electronic tuning, preset of 12 FM/6 AM stations, backlit station-selector buttons and graphics, preset scan, auto preset station select, motorized volume control, fade/balance controls, auto CrO2 and Dolby B, clean-tape-head indicator, next/previous CD track selector, radio monitor allows radio to play while cassette player is fast forwarding/reversing, Theftlock and steering-wheel controls; compatible with remote CD changer and OnStar three-button system. REQUIRES 1SE. NOT AVAILABLE with ULO, UP0, 1SA.	86	100
UP0	**Radio: AM/FM Stereo with CD and Cassette (Base)** .... Includes power-loading CD and cassette players with auto tone control, clock, preset of 12 FM/6 AM stations, backlit station-selector buttons and graphics, preset scan, auto-preset station select, motorized volume control, separate bass/treble controls, fade/balance controls, auto CrO2 and Dolby B, radio monitor allows radio to play while cassette player is fast forwarding/reversing, clean-tape-head indicator, next/previous CD track selector, random play, Theftlock and steering wheel controls; compatible with remote CD changer. NOT AVAILABLE with ULO, UNO, 1SE.	301	350
UP0	**Radio: AM/FM Stereo with CD and Cassette (Base)** .... Includes power-loading CD and cassette players with auto tone control, clock, preset of 12 FM/6 AM stations, backlit station-selector buttons and graphics, preset scan, auto-preset station select, motorized volume control, separate bass/treble controls, fade/balance controls, auto CrO2 and Dolby B, radio monitor allows radio to play while cassette player is fast forwarding/reversing, clean-tape-head indicator, next/previous CD track selector, random play, Theftlock and steering wheel controls; compatible with remote CD changer. REQUIRES 1SE. NOT AVAILABLE with ULO, UNO, 1SA.	172	200
UP0	**Radio: AM/FM Stereo with CD and Cassette (Ultra)** .... Includes power-loading CD and cassette players with auto tone control, clock, preset of 12 FM/6 AM stations, backlit station-selector buttons and graphics, preset scan, auto-preset station select, motorized volume control, separate bass/treble controls, fade/balance controls, auto CrO2 and Dolby B, radio monitor allows radio to play while cassette player is fast forwarding/reversing, clean-tape-head indicator, next/previous CD track selector, random play, Theftlock and steering wheel controls; compatible with remote CD changer.	86	100
UV6	**Eyecue Head-Up Windshield Display** .... Includes read-outs for speed, turn signals, high beam and check gauges telltale. NOT AVAILABLE with 1SA.	236	275
W02	**5-Passenger Seating (Ultra)** .... Includes 45/45 10-way power split-frame seats, convenience console with writing surface, dual cup holder, dual auxiliary power outlets, bi-level rear-seat Comfort Temp, convenience console package and dual auxiliary power outlets.	159	185
Y56	**Gran Touring Package (Base)** .... Includes dealer programmable magnetic variable effort steering, 16" aluminum wheels, Gran Touring suspension and tires: P225/60R16 TOURING BSW. REQUIRES NW9. NOT AVAILABLE with 1SA, QPY, Leather Seat Trim.	288	335

BUICK — PARK AVENUE / REGAL

CODE	DESCRIPTION	INVOICE	MSRP
Y56	**Gran Touring Package (Base)**	245	285
	Includes dealer programmable magnetic variable effort steering, 16" aluminum wheels, Gran Touring suspension, leather-wrapped steering wheel and tires: P225/60R16 TOURING BSW. REQUIRES NW9. NOT AVAILABLE with 1SA, QPY.		
Y56	**Gran Touring Package (Ultra)**	172	200
	Includes dealer programmable magnetic variable effort steering, 16" aluminum wheels, Gran Touring suspension and tires: P225/60R16 TOURING BSW. NOT AVAILABLE with QPY.		

2000 REGAL

2000 Buick Regal

What's New?

For the 2000 model year, the "Official Car of the Supercharged Family" gets new alloy wheels, a standard body-colored grille on the GS and two new colors, Gold Metallic and Sterling Silver. Inside, there's now a split-folding rear seat and an optional side airbag for the driver on leather-lined Regals.

Review

Back in 1997, Buick released a new Regal Sedan. The slow-selling coupe was dropped, leaving LS and GS versions of the four-door. This new Regal was larger in nearly every dimension, and was designed to reduce squeaks and rattles by increasing structural rigidity with one-piece side-panel stampings and cross bracing behind the instrument panel. A full load of standard equipment and reasonable prices have made this front-drive Regal competitive, and it continues to entice buyers who might normally limit themselves to Toyota or Nissan showrooms to at least visit a Buick store.

Think of the Regal as Park Avenue Light, or Century Deluxe. LS models are powered by GM's award-winning 3800 Series II V6, which boasts an even 200 horses. Move up to the GS, and you're getting an honest-to-goodness sport sedan equipped with a supercharged 3.8-liter V6

REGAL
BUICK

CODE	DESCRIPTION	INVOICE	MSRP

putting 240 horsepower through a heavy-duty version of Regal's four-speed automatic transmission. With a starting price of around $25,000, the suave, speedy Regal GS makes an excellent argument against purchasing any other sporty midsize V6 sedan.

Basic design is shared with the lower-rung Century. Regal has a unique front fascia, but barely different rear styling. LS versions are distinguished by a chrome-accented grille, while GS models have a body-colored grille this year, with P255/60 radials on restyled 16-inch alloy wheels (chrome is an option).

Inside, a comfortable interior beckons, and now features a split-folding rear seat to make hauling long items such as skis and fishing rods easier and more convenient. A 220-watt Monsoon audio system with eight speakers also is optional on GS models. Heated leather seats are again available, and with leather comes the option of a side airbag for the driver.

One thing this Buick offers that few in its class can is the availability of OnStar, an optional mobile communications system formerly available only on Cadillac models. OnStar provides a hands-free link to real-time, person-to-person in-vehicle safety, security and information services from GM's 24-hour, seven-day-a-week OnStar Center. A new three-button system eliminates the need for a customer to buy separate cellular phone service to access OnStar services.

The Regal GS comes equipped with full-range traction control, which uses the ABS and engine controls to reduce traction loss on slippery surfaces. Engine modulation provides traction-control assistance on LS versions. Four-wheel antilock disc brakes are standard on both models. An exceptional array of standard features and option packages make the LS a smart choice among premium midsize sedans. Yet pounding out 240 ponies to the pavement in the GS through its Gran Touring suspension leaves us wondering, where is Buick trying to go with this car?

Despite recent efforts at establishing strong GM brand identities for each division, sharing platforms between multiple divisions is likely to continue to be a problem. Pontiac's Grand Prix and Oldsmobile's Intrigue share Regal's underpinnings and basic structure. Grand Prix is obviously the driver's car with a youthful image and the "We Build Excitement" marketing theme. Intrigue is conservatively styled and import-oriented. So where does that leave the Buick Regal? Buick officials say the Regal is targeted at 40-49 year-olds with families who want a blend of performance, dependability and safety. Basically, Buick is going after the kinds of buyers who snap up thousands of Camrys every year.

The Camry is plainly styled, like the Regal. The Camry is a roomy, safe car, like the Regal. The Camry also has an outstanding reputation for reliability and resale value. Can the Regal compete in this arena as well? Given Buick's penchant for award-winning quality and continued refinement, we wouldn't be too surprised. For now, rest assured that the Regal is an excellent value, and with 240 supercharged horses under the hood, the GS model easily gets our nod.

Standard Equipment

LS (4A): 3.8L V6 OHV SMPI 12-valve engine; 4-speed electronic OD auto transmission with lock-up; battery with run down protection; front-wheel drive, traction control, 3.05 axle ratio; stainless steel exhaust; sport ride suspension, front independent strut suspension with anti-roll bar, front coil springs, rear independent strut suspension with anti-roll bar, rear coil springs; power rack-and-pinion steering with vehicle speed-sensing assist; 4-wheel disc brakes with 4-wheel antilock braking system; 17.5 gal. capacity fuel tank; side impact bars; front and rear body-colored bumpers with body-colored rub strip, chrome bumper insert; body-colored bodyside molding with chrome bodyside insert, body-colored bodyside cladding; monotone paint; aero-composite halogen fully auto headlamps with daytime running lights, delay-off feature; additional exterior lights include cornering lights, front fog/driving lights, underhood light; power remote body-colored folding driver's and passenger's heated outside mirror; front and rear 15" x 6" steel wheels; P215/70SR15 A/S BSW front and rear tires; inside under cargo mounted compact steel spare wheel; dual zone front air conditioning, air filter, rear heat ducts; AM/FM stereo, clock, seek-scan, cassette, 6 performance speakers, auto equalizer, theft deterrent, and window grid antenna; cruise control; power door locks with 2 stage unlock, remote keyless entry, child safety rear door locks, power remote hatch/trunk release; 2 power accessory outlets,

BUICK — REGAL

retained accessory power; instrumentation display includes tachometer, water temperature gauge, trip odometer; warning indicators include water temp, battery, low oil level, low coolant, lights on, key in ignition, low fuel, low washer fluid, door ajar, trunk ajar, service interval; driver's and passenger's front airbags; ignition disable, panic alarm; tinted windows, power front and rear windows with driver's 1-touch down; variable intermittent front windshield wipers, sun visor strip, rear window defroster; seating capacity of 5, front bucket seats adjustable, headrests, center armrest with storage, driver's seat includes 4-way direction control, passenger's seat includes 4-way direction control; 50-50 folding rear bench seat with fixed headrests, center armrest, with storage; front height adjustable seatbelts; cloth seats, vinyl door trim insert, full cloth headliner, full carpet floor covering, leather-wrapped gear shift knob; interior lights include dome light with fade, front reading lights, 2 door curb lights, illuminated entry; leather-wrapped steering wheel with tilt adjustment; vanity mirrors, dual auxiliary visors; day/night rearview mirror; full floor console, locking glove box with light, front and rear cupholders, 2 seat back storage pockets, driver's and passenger's door bins, rear door bins; carpeted cargo floor, cargo light; chrome grille, chrome side window moldings, black front windshield molding, black rear window molding and body-colored door handles.

GS (4A) (in addition to or instead of LS (4A) equipment): 3.8L V6 OHV SMPI supercharged 12-valve engine, requires premium unleaded fuel; driver's selectable multi-mode transmission; 2.93 axle ratio; stainless steel exhaust with chrome tip; touring ride suspension; black bumper insert; body-colored bodyside molding with black bodyside insert; lower accent two-tone paint; front and rear 16" x 6.5" silver alloy wheels; P225/60SR16 touring A/S BSW front and rear tires; instrumentation display includes trip computer; seat mounted driver's side airbag; driver's seat includes 4-way power seat, 8-way direction control; leather seats, leatherette door trim insert, full carpet floor covering with carpeted floor mats; interior lights include rear reading lights; dual illuminated vanity mirrors, cargo net; body-colored grille and black side window moldings.

Base Prices

Code	Description	Invoice	MSRP
4WB69	LS (4A)	20331	22220
4WF69	GS (4A)	22934	25065
	Destination Charge:	560	560

Accessories

Code	Description	Invoice	MSRP
—	Leather Trim (LS)	684	795
1SA	LS Base Package (LS)	NC	NC
	Includes vehicle with standard equipment. NOT AVAILABLE with CF5, DD8, KA1, PYO, U20, UK3, Y56, PW8, U85, AG2.		
1SB	LS Luxury Package (LS)	466	542
	Includes front carpet savers, rear carpet savers, 6-way power driver's seat, trunk convenience net, dual illuminated visor vanity mirrors, reading and courtesy lamps. NOT AVAILABLE with U20.		
1SC	LS Prestige Package (LS)	1017	1182
	Includes dual zone auto climate control, front carpet savers, rear carpet savers, electrochromic rearview mirror, electrochromic heated exterior mirrors, dual illuminated visor vanity mirrors, reading and courtesy lamps, AM/FM stereo, CD, cassette with seek and scan, steering wheel radio controls, 6-way power driver's seat and trunk convenience net.		
1SD	LS Touring Package (LS)	2070	2407
	Includes dual zone auto climate control, front carpet savers, rear carpet savers, Gran Touring package: wheels: 16" aluminum, tires: P225/60R16 TOURING A/S BSW;		

REGAL — BUICK

CODE	DESCRIPTION	INVOICE	MSRP
	electrochromic rearview mirror, electrochromic heated exterior mirrors, dual illuminated visor vanity mirrors, reading and courtesy lamps, AM/FM stereo, CD, cassette with seek and scan, monsoon 8-speaker system, steering wheel radio controls, diversity antenna, 6-way power driver's seat, 6-way power passenger's seat and trunk convenience net. NOT AVAILABLE with PW8.		
1SE	**GS Base Package (GS)**	NC	NC
	Includes vehicle with standard equipment. NOT AVAILABLE with KA1, CF5, UV7.		
1SF	**GS Luxury Package (GS)**	550	640
	Includes dual zone auto climate control, electrochromic rearview mirror, electrochromic heated exterior mirrors, AM/FM stereo, CD, cassette with seek and scan, steering wheel radio controls and 6-way power passenger's seat.		
AG1	**6-Way Power Driver's Seat (LS)**	284	330
	INCLUDED in 1SB, 1SC, 1SD.		
AG2	**6-Way Power Passenger's Seat (LS)**	284	330
	NOT AVAILABLE with 1SA. INCLUDED in 1SD.		
B34	**Front Carpet Savers**	22	25
	REQUIRES B35. INCLUDED in 1SB, 1SC, 1SD.		
B35	**Rear Carpet Savers**	17	20
	REQUIRES B34. INCLUDED in 1SB, 1SC, 1SD.		
CF5	**Electric Sliding Sunroof**	598	695
	REQUIRES DD8. NOT AVAILABLE with 1SA, 1SE.		
CJ2	**Dual Zone Automatic Climate Control**	168	195
	INCLUDED in 1SF, 1SC, 1SD.		
DD8	**Electrochromic Rearview Mirror**	103	120
	NOT AVAILABLE with 1SA. INCLUDED in 1SF, 1SC, 1SD.		
IP3	**Front Bucket Seats (LS)**	559	650
	Includes leather trim. NOT AVAILABLE with 1SA.		
K05	**Engine Block Heater**	15	18
KA1	**Driver's and Passenger's Heated Seats**	194	225
	NOT AVAILABLE with 1SA, 1SE.		
PW8	**Wheels: 15" Aluminum (LS)**	301	350
	NOT AVAILABLE with PY0, Y56, 1SA, 1SD.		
PY0	**Wheels: 16" Chrome Plated Aluminum**	559	650
	REQUIRES Y56. NOT AVAILABLE with PW8, 1SA, QD1.		
U20	**Driver's Information Center (LS)**	64	75
	Includes gauge cluster with speedometer, tachometer, temperature and fuel gauges. NOT AVAILABLE with 1SA, 1SB.		
U85	**Monsoon 8-Speaker System**	254	295
	Includes diversity antenna. NOT AVAILABLE with 1SA. INCLUDED in 1SD.		
UK3	**Steering Wheel Radio Controls**	108	125
	NOT AVAILABLE with 1SA. INCLUDED in 1SF, 1SC, 1SD.		
UP0	**Radio: AM/FM Stereo with CD and Cassette**	172	200
	Includes power-loading CD and cassette, auto tone control, clock, preset of 12 FM/6 AM stations, backlit station-selector buttons and graphics, preset scan, auto-preset station select, motorized volume control, separate bass/treble controls, fade/balance controls, auto CrO2 and Dolby B, clean-tape-head indicator, next/previous CD		

BUICK — REGAL

CODE	DESCRIPTION	INVOICE	MSRP
	track selector, random play, radio monitor (allows radio to play while cassette player is fast forwarding/rewinding) and Theftlock. Compatible with remote CD changer and steering wheel radio controls. INCLUDED in 1SF, 1SC, 1SD.		
Y56	Gran Touring Package (LS) .... Includes specific suspension tuning, magnetic variable effort steering, leather-wrapped steering wheel, rear stabilizer bar, 3.05 axle ratio, wheels: 16" aluminum and tires: P225/60R16 touring A/S BSW. NOT AVAILABLE with PW8, 1SA. INCLUDED in 1SD.	516	600

One 15-minute call could save you 15% or more on car insurance.

GEICO DIRECT

America's 6th Largest Automobile Insurance Company

1-800-555-2758

Save hundreds, even thousands, off the sticker price of the new car *you* want.

Call Autovantage® your FREE auto-buying service

1-800-201-7703

No purchase required. No fees.

CADILLAC
CATERA

1999 CATERA

1999 Cadillac Catera

What's New?

Catera's "black chrome" grille will be darkened this year, while new electronics and emissions systems make the '99 Catera the first Cadillac to meet the federal Low Emissions Vehicle (LEV) standards. There's also a redesigned fuel cap and tether with an instrument cluster telltale to indicate a loose fuel cap. Up to four remote entry key fobs can now be programmed for separate memory settings, all with enhanced automatic door lock/unlock functions.

Review

The entry-level luxury sedan market accounts for nearly half of all luxury car sales in the US, growing rapidly from 25% just a few years ago. Characteristically, Chrysler, Lincoln and Cadillac have been lethargically slow to react to shifting luxury car buyer tastes, while Lexus, Infiniti, Audi and BMW have been actively wooing these customers with fun-to-drive, lavishly appointed sedans and outstanding customer service. While companies from across either pond brought the ES300, 328i, and A4 to market, the Big Three produced the Eldorado, Continental and New Yorker during the same time period.

Cadillac was the first domestic luxury automaker to attack the entry-level market head-on with the introduction of the 1997 Catera. After its first full year on the market, Catera rolled up sales of 25,411 units, making it the most successful launch of an entry/luxury model in U.S. history. (The previous best was set by Acura, which sold 24,700 copies of its TL model in 1996.)

Based on the European-market Opel Omega MV6, the Catera features a 200-horsepower 3.0-liter DOHC V6 engine mated to a four-speed automatic transmission and rear-wheel drive. Built in Russelsheim, Germany, the Catera is touted by Cadillac as a blend of the best of German and American engineering. It features antilock brakes engineered for the German Autobahn, dual front airbags, traction control and an engine-disabling theft deterrent system.

With prices starting around $30,000, the Catera qualifies as a bona-fide bargain in this segment. Options are restricted to a power sunroof, power rear sunshade, heated front and rear seats, a Bose audio system, and chrome-plated aluminum wheels. Standard equipment includes power windows with express-down features for all four windows, remote keyless entry,

CADILLAC — CATERA

| CODE | DESCRIPTION | INVOICE | MSRP |

heated windshield washer nozzles, and an automatic dual-zone climate control system. Two models are available; a standard model and one appointed with leather.

The Catera also benefits from a roomy interior (it is classified a mid-size car by the EPA) with an outstanding dash layout featuring large, analog gauges and easy-to-use controls. Wood trimming is kept to a tasteful minimum, helping the Catera exude a level of interior luxury uncommon for the class.

But what about performance? With 0-60 mph arriving in about eight and a half seconds, the Catera holds its own. But we suspect there will be sales lost to the BMW 328i, Infiniti I30, Nissan Maxima and Audi A4 due to the Caddy's lack of a manual transmission. Cadillac also opted to limit the Catera's top speed to 125 mph so it could fit all-season rubber to the standard aluminum wheels. The result is a smoother, softer ride on America's often harsh pavement, and better wet-weather grip, but at the expense of dry-weather handling.

Still, the Catera is a fine effort from Cadillac, priced competitively and offering all the luxury and most of the performance a buyer could want from this segment. All it really needs is more low-end punch and an optional five-speed stick to stir up enthusiast interest.

Standard Equipment

CATERA (4A): 3.0L V6 DOHC SMPI 24-valve engine; 4-speed electronic overdrive automatic transmission with lock-up; 310-amp battery with run down protection; engine oil cooler; 120-amp alternator; driver selectable program transmission; rear wheel drive, traction control, 3.9 axle ratio; dual stainless steel exhaust with chrome tip; auto-leveling suspension, front independent strut suspension with anti-roll bar, front coil springs, rear independent multi-link suspension with anti-roll bar, rear coil springs; power re-circulating ball steering with vehicle speed-sensing assist; 4 wheel disc brakes with 4 wheel antilock braking system; 18 gal. capacity fuel tank; front and rear body-colored bumpers; body-colored bodyside molding; monotone paint; aero-composite halogen fully automatic headlamps with daytime running lights, delay-off feature; additional exterior lights include cornering lights, front fog/driving lights, center high mounted stop light; driver's and passenger's power remote body-colored heated folding outside mirrors; front and rear 16" x 7" silver alloy wheels; P225/55HR16 BSW AS front and rear tires; inside under cargo mounted full-size temporary steel spare wheel; dual zone front air conditioning with climate control, air filter, rear heat ducts; AM stereo/FM stereo with clock, seek-scan, cassette, CD changer pre-wiring, in-dash CD pre-wiring, 8 speakers, theft deterrent, and window grid diversity antenna; radio steering wheel controls; cruise control; power door locks with 2 stage unlock, remote keyless entry, child safety rear door locks, fuel filler door included with power doors, power remote hatch/trunk release, power remote fuel release; cell phone pre-wiring, 2 power accessory outlets, driver's foot rest, retained accessory power, garage door opener; instrumentation display includes tachometer, oil pressure gauge, water temp gauge, volt gauge, exterior temp, trip odometer; warning indicators include oil pressure, battery, low oil level, low coolant, lights on, key in ignition, low fuel, low washer fluid, door ajar, trunk ajar, service interval; dual airbags; ignition disable, security system; tinted windows, power front windows with front and rear 1-touch down, power rear windows; variable intermittent front windshield wipers with heated jets, rear window defroster; seating capacity of 5, front bucket seats with adjustable with tilt headrests, center armrest with storage, driver's seat includes 6-way power seat with lumbar support, passenger's seat includes 6-way power seat with lumbar support; 40-20-40 folding rear bench seat with tilting rear headrests, center pass-thru armrest; front and rear height adjustable seatbelts with front pretensioners; leather seats, leatherette door trim insert, full cloth headliner, full carpet floor covering with carpeted floor mats, wood trim; memory on driver's seat with 3 memory setting(s) includes settings for rearview mirror, exterior mirrors; interior lights include dome light, front and rear reading lights, 4 door curb lights, illuminated entry; leather-wrapped steering wheel with tilt adjustment; dual illuminated vanity mirrors; auto-dimming day-night rearview mirror; full floor console, locking glove box with light, front cupholder, 2 seat back storage pockets, driver's and passenger's door bins; carpeted cargo floor, carpeted trunk lid, cargo net, cargo light; chrome grille, black side window moldings, black front windshield molding, black rear window molding and body-colored door handles.

CADILLAC
CATERA / DEVILLE

CODE	DESCRIPTION	INVOICE	MSRP

Base Prices
6VR69	Catera (4A)	31772	34180
	Destination Charge:	640	640

Accessories
CF5	Sunroof with Express Open	846	995
DE1	Rear Power Sunshade	251	295
KA1	Heated Front and Rear Seats	340	400
P05	Chrome Wheels	507	795
UL6	Radio: Bose Sound System with CD and Cassette	827	973

Includes 8 speakers, AM stereo/FM stereo, signal seeking and scanner with digital display, single-slot CD player, weatherband, radio data system (RDS) and theftlock.

2000 DEVILLE

2000 Cadillac DeVille

What's New?

The 2000 DeVille is all-new inside and out and showcases new automotive technologies such as Night Vision, Ultrasonic Rear Parking Assist and the newest generation of GM's StabiliTrak traction-control system. It also boasts improvements to the Northstar V8 that not only improve fuel economy, but make this engine operate even smoother than before.

Review

Cadillac's DeVille brand celebrates its 50th anniversary in the marketplace with a completely revamped car and the introduction of groundbreaking high-tech features.

The new DeVille is evolutionary in design, yet is more than 2 inches shorter and narrower than last year's version, giving it a slightly trimmer, cleaner look. Its wheelbase is actually 1.5 inches

CADILLAC

DEVILLE

longer, while interior space is virtually as roomy as the 1999 car. It is available in three models: the base DeVille, a ritzy DeVille High Luxury Sedan (DHS) and a sporty, five-passenger DeVille Touring Sedan (DTS).

This year's car benefits from a stiffer body architecture that provides a notable increase in torsional rigidity. That not only allows for improvements in crashworthiness as well as noise, vibration and harshness (NVH) control, but also in handling dynamics. What's more, Cadillac's Northstar V8 has been redesigned from the inside out to achieve better mileage with regular fuel, smoother and quieter operation, and certification as a low-emission vehicle (LEV) for California and certain Northeast states.

Night Vision is the first automotive application of thermal-imaging technology that helps drivers avoid collisions by enhancing their ability to detect objects well beyond the normal range of their headlights. Another DeVille "first" is the use of Ultrasonic Rear Parking Assist, which uses an array of four sensors to help the driver in parking maneuvers. Then there's StabiliTrak 2.0, the latest version of GM's highly acclaimed stability-control system. It is enhanced for 2000 with the addition of active steering effort compensation, which slightly increases turning effort during sudden maneuvers, and side-slip-rate control, which responds to traction loss at all four wheels by gently applying both front brakes to help the driver regain control. In addition, the DeVille DTS will feature the second generation of Cadillac's continuously variable road-sensing suspension, called the CVRSS 2.0.

All DeVilles include leading-edge passive restraints, a CD-based navigation system and the OnStar communications system, as well as the industry's first light emitting diode (LED) taillight and center high-mounted stoplight combination. Building on its reputation for comfort and convenience, the 2000 DeVille also offers such luxury touches as three-zone climate control, adaptive seating, massaging lumbar seats and a new center seat/storage system. Rear-seat passengers enjoy a theater seating layout (for optimum forward visibility), heated seats and power lumbar adjustments.

As Cadillac's flagship sedan, the new DeVille is a sophisticated American luxury car that remains true to Cadillac's heritage, yet hints of the division's high-tech future. We think that mix will appeal to both the Town Car set and Cadillac purists alike.

Standard Equipment

BASE (4A): 4.6L V8 DOHC SMPI 32-valve engine; 4-speed electronic OD auto transmission with lock-up; battery with run down protection; 140-amp alternator; front-wheel drive, traction control, 3.11 axle ratio; stainless steel exhaust; comfort ride suspension, auto-leveling suspension, front independent strut suspension with anti-roll bar, front coil springs, rear independent multi-link suspension with anti-roll bar, rear coil springs; power rack-and-pinion steering with vehicle speed-sensing assist; 4-wheel disc brakes with 4-wheel antilock braking system; 18.5 gal. capacity fuel tank; front license plate bracket, side impact bars; front and rear body-colored bumpers; clearcoat monotone paint with bodyside accent stripe; aero-composite halogen fully auto headlamps with daytime running lights, delay-off feature; additional exterior lights include cornering lights, underhood light; driver's and passenger's power remote body-colored heated folding outside mirrors; front and rear 16" x 7" silver alloy wheels; P225/60SR16 A/S BSW front and rear tires; inside under cargo mounted compact steel spare wheel; dual zone front air conditioning with climate control, rear air conditioning with separate controls, air filter, rear heat ducts, auto air recirculation; AM stereo/FM stereo, clock, seek-scan, cassette, CD changer pre-wiring, in-dash CD pre-wiring, 8 speakers, theft deterrent, and window grid diversity antenna, radio steering wheel controls; cruise control with steering wheel controls; power door locks with 2 stage unlock, remote keyless entry, child safety rear door locks, power remote hatch/trunk release, power remote fuel release; cell phone pre-wiring, 3 power accessory outlets, trunk pulldown, retained accessory power; digital instrumentation display compass, exterior temp, systems monitor, trip computer, trip odometer; warning indicators include oil pressure, water temp, battery, lights on, key in ignition, low fuel, low washer fluid, door ajar, service interval; driver's and passenger's front airbags, driver's and front passenger's seat mounted side airbags; ignition disable, security system; tinted windows, power front and rear windows with front and rear 1-touch down; variable intermittent front windshield wipers, sun visor strip, rear

DEVILLE — CADILLAC

window defroster; seating capacity of 6, 40-20-40 split-bench front seat, adjustable tilt headrests, center armrest with storage, driver's seat includes 6-way power seat, passenger's seat includes 6-way power seat; rear bench seat with fixed headrests, center pass-thru armrest with storage; front height adjustable seatbelts with front pretensioners; cloth seats, cloth door trim insert, full cloth headliner, full color-keyed carpet floor covering with carpeted floor mats, simulated wood trim on instrument panel; interior lights include dome light with fade, front and rear reading lights, 4 door curb lights, illuminated entry; leather-wrapped steering wheel with tilt adjustment; dual illuminated vanity mirrors, dual auxiliary visors; auto-dimming day/night rearview mirror; mini overhead console with storage, locking glove box with light, front and rear cupholders, 2 seat back storage pockets, driver's and passenger's door bins; carpeted cargo floor, carpeted trunk lid, cargo net, cargo light; chrome grille, chrome side window moldings, black front windshield molding, black rear window molding and body-colored door handles.

DHS (4A) (in addition to or instead of BASE (4A) equipment): Ffront and rear 16" x 7" chrome alloy wheels; premium AM stereo/FM stereo, clock, seek-scan, cassette, single CD, 8 premium speakers, theft deterrent, and window grid diversity antenna; instrumentation display includes tachometer, water temperature gauge; sun blinds; rain detecting wipers, rear power blind; heated-cushion 40-20-40 split-bench front seat; heated rear bench seat with tilt headrests; leather seats, leatherette door trim insert, genuine wood trim on instrument panel, wood gear shift knob; memory on driver's seat with 2 memory setting(s) includes settings for exterior mirrors, steering wheel; steering wheel with power tilt and telescopic adjustment and rear illuminated vanity mirror.

DTS (4A) (in addition to or instead of DHS (4A) equipment): 3.71 axle ratio; auto ride control, adaptive auto-leveling suspension, electronic stability; additional exterior lights include cornering lights, front fog/driving lights, underhood light; front and rear 17" x 7.5" silver alloy wheels; P235/55HR17 performance A/S BSW front and rear tires; seating capacity of 5, heated-cushion front 40-40 bucket seats; heated rear bench seat with fixed headrests; leather-wrapped steering wheel with tilt adjustment and full floor console.

Base Prices

Code	Description	Invoice	MSRP
6KD69	Base (4A)	36298	39500
6KE69	DHS (4A)	41056	44700
6KF69	DTS (4A)	41056	44700
	Destination Charge:	670	670

Accessories

Code	Description	Invoice	MSRP
—	Trunk Storage System	225	265
86U	Crimson Pearl Paint	552	650
93U	White Diamond Paint	552	650
AC9	Front Adaptive Seats (DHS/DTS)	846	995
	REQUIRES WA7.		
AW9	Rear Seat Side Airbags	251	295
	NOT AVAILABLE with W20.		
CF5	Sunroof with Express Open	1318	1550
	Slightly reduces headroom.		
N30	Wood Trim Package (DTS)	506	595
	Includes wood steering wheel and wood shift knob.		
N94	Wheels: Chrome (DTS)	509	795
QC6	Wheels: Chrome (Base)	509	795

CADILLAC — DEVILLE / ELDORADO

CODE	DESCRIPTION	INVOICE	MSRP
U1R	Radio: AM Stereo/FM Stereo with Cassette (Base)	255	300
	Includes single slot CD, Theftlock and 8 speakers.		
U1Z	6-Disc CD Changer	506	595
	Located in glove box.		
UM9	Radio: AM Stereo/FM Stereo with Cassette and Mini-Disc (DHS/DTS)	255	300
	Includes weather band, Theftlock, Digital Signal Processing (DSP), Radio Data System (RDS) and 8-speaker Bose Acoustic System.		
UV2	Night Vision (DHS/DTS)	1696	1995
	REQUIRES WA8.		
UY4	On Board CD-ROM Based Navigation (DHS/DTS)	1696	1995
	Requires premium audio system and 6-disc CD changer.		
V92	3000 Lb Trailer Towing Provisions (DTS)	94	110
W20	Livery Package (Base)	136	160
	Includes on/off rocker switch, accent striping delete, engine oil cooler, full size spare tire, rear reading lamps, rear visor vanity dimmable mirrors and tires: whitewall. NOT AVAILABLE with AW9, V92.		
WA7	Comfort/Convenience Package (Base)	931	1095
	Includes 4-way power lumbar support, memory package, trunk mat, heated front and rear seats.		
WA7	Comfort/Convenience Package (DTS)	591	695
	Includes memory package, trunk mat, tilt and telescopic steering wheel column.		
WA8	Safety and Security Package (Base/DHS)	761	895
	Includes Stabilitrak, ultrasonic rear parking assist and 3-channel garage door opener.		
WA8	Safety and Security Package (DTS)	340	400
	Includes ultrasonic rear parking assist and 3-channel garage door opener.		
WJ7	Leather Seats (Base)	667	785

2000 ELDORADO

What's New?

The Northstar V8s have been improved, and the standard Eldorado gets a new logo, ESC (for Eldorado Sport Coupe). The racy Eldorado Touring Coupe (ETC) lands exterior enhancements such as body-color fascia moldings and side inserts (replacing chrome), new seven-spoke wheels with Cadillac logos in the center caps, and a new ETC decklid logo.

Review

One of the models that lured Cadillac back from the brink of becoming hopelessly behind the times was the current edition of the Eldorado. Introduced in 1992 to critical acclaim, and then substantially improved with the introduction of the Northstar V8 in 1993, the Eldorado (along with its sister car, the Seville) has helped bolster Cadillac's future.

While Eldorado lays claim to being the best-selling prestige luxury coupe in the United States, that's not saying a whole lot. In the wake of the deaths of the Lincoln Mark VIII and Buick Riviera, the Eldorado is currently the only luxury coupe built in North America. Consequently, some auto analysts have been crowing about the demise of the Eldo, but Cadillac insiders insist an all-new Eldorado with rear-drive and a smaller body will appear in the near future.

ELDORADO
CADILLAC

Meanwhile, traditional luxo-coupe buyers can contemplate the big, front-drive 2000 models, which gain revamped engines and minor exterior tweaks.

Both of Cadillac's 4.6-liter Northstar V8s (the 275-horsepower version in Eldorado and the 300-horse motor in the ETC) have been redesigned from the inside out to achieve better mileage with regular fuel, smoother and quieter operation, and certification as a low-emission vehicle (LEV) in some states. MagnaSteer variable-effort steering gear is standard. Optional on the base car and standard on the Touring Coupe is StabiliTrak, which includes stability enhancement and road texture detection. Stability enhancement is designed to correct skids automatically, allowing the Eldorado to better respond to driver inputs. Road texture detection reads the road surface, leading to better antilock brake performance.

The Eldorado's interior is rich with leather and wood. ETC models have memory systems that recall rearview mirror positions, climate-control settings, or even what CD and song the driver was listening to last. Standard is GM's new, three-button OnStar system that is now integrated into the Eldo's rearview mirror, eliminating the need for a separate cellular phone. With OnStar, a driver can alert emergency personnel to an exact location or simply get travel directions. The system can even track your Eldo if it's stolen, or locate the nearest ATM.

While today's Eldorado is on the bulky side and as gizmo-laden as they come, it still has a distinctive look and a wonderful engine, especially in ETC guise. Sure, the luxury SUV craze is killing off cars of this ilk, but we wouldn't be surprised to see an SUV backlash in the coming years, and comfy coupes like this Caddy may likely lead a truck-weary market charge back to cars.

2000 Cadillac Eldorado

Standard Equipment

ESC (4A): 4.6L V8 DOHC SMPI 32-valve engine, requires premium unleaded fuel; 4-speed electronic OD auto transmission with lock-up; 770-amp battery with run down protection; 140-amp alternator; front-wheel drive, traction control, 3.11 axle ratio; dual stainless steel exhaust with chrome tip; comfort ride suspension, auto-leveling suspension, front independent strut suspension with anti-roll bar, front coil springs, rear independent suspension with anti-roll bar, rear coil springs; power rack-and-pinion steering with vehicle speed-sensing assist; 4-wheel disc brakes with 4-wheel antilock braking system; 19 gal. capacity fuel tank; front license plate bracket, side impact bars; front and rear body-colored bumpers with chrome bumper insert; body-colored bodyside molding with chrome bodyside insert; monotone paint; aero-composite halogen fully auto headlamps with daytime running lights, delay-off feature; additional exterior lights include cornering lights, front fog/driving lights, underhood light; driver's and passenger's

CADILLAC — ELDORADO

power remote body-colored heated folding outside mirrors; front and rear 16" x 7" silver alloy wheels; P225/60SR16 A/S BSW front and rear tires; inside under cargo mounted compact steel spare wheel; dual zone front air conditioning with climate control, rear heat ducts, auto air recirculation; AM stereo/FM stereo, seek-scan, cassette, CD changer pre-wiring, in-dash CD pre-wiring, 6 speakers, theft deterrent, and power retractable antenna, radio steering wheel controls; cruise control; power door locks with 2 stage unlock, remote keyless entry, power remote hatch/trunk release, power remote fuel release; cell phone pre-wiring, 2 power accessory outlets, front & rear cigar lighter(s), trunk pulldown, retained accessory power, smokers' package; instrumentation display includes tachometer, water temperature gauge, in-dash clock, compass, exterior temp, systems monitor, trip computer, trip odometer; warning indicators include oil pressure, water temp, battery, lights on, key in ignition, low fuel, low washer fluid, door ajar, service interval; driver's and passenger's front airbags; ignition disable, security system; tinted windows, power windows with driver's 1-touch down; variable intermittent front windshield wipers, sun visor strip, rear window defroster; seating capacity of 5, front bucket seats, adjustable tilt headrests, center armrest with storage, driver's seat includes 6-way power seat, passenger's seat includes 6-way power seat; rear bench seat with fixed headrests, center armrest; seatbelts with front pretensioners; leather seats, leatherette door trim insert, full cloth headliner, full carpet floor covering with carpeted floor mats, genuine wood trim on instrument panel; interior lights include dome light, front and rear reading lights, 2 door curb lights, illuminated entry; leather-wrapped steering wheel with tilt adjustment; dual illuminated vanity mirrors, dual auxiliary visors; auto-dimming day/night rearview mirror; full floor console, mini overhead console with storage, locking glove box with light, front cupholder, 2 seat back storage pockets, driver's and passenger's door bins; carpeted cargo floor, carpeted trunk lid, cargo net, cargo light, cargo concealed storage; chrome grille, chrome side window moldings, black front windshield molding, black rear window molding and body-colored door handles.

ETC (4A) (in addition to or instead of ESC (4A) equipment): 3.71 axle ratio; electronic stability, touring ride suspension, auto ride control; P225/60HR16 A/S BSW front and rear tires; premium AM stereo/FM stereo, seek-scan, cassette, single CD, 4 premium speakers, theft deterrent, and power retractable antenna, radio steering wheel controls; rear center armrest with storage; leather-wrapped gear shift knob; memory on driver's seat with 2 memory setting(s) includes settings for exterior mirrors and body-colored grille.

Base Prices

Code	Description	Invoice	MSRP
6EL57	ESC (4A)	35950	39120
6ET57	ETC (4A)	39221	42695
	Destination Charge:	670	670

Accessories

Code	Description	Invoice	MSRP
—	Accent Stripe Color (ESC) *REQUIRES D98.*	NC	NC
86U	Crimson Pearl Paint (ESC)	552	650
93U	White Diamond Paint (ESC)	552	650
BNN	Trunk Storage System	225	265
CF5	Sunroof with Express Open *Deletes sunglass storage compartment and slightly reduces headroom.*	1318	1550
JL4	StabiliTrak (ESC)	421	495
N26	Wheels: Chrome (ETC)	509	795
N30	Wood Steering Wheel	336	395
QC8	Wheels: Chrome (ESC)	509	795
QDC	Tires: P235/60ZR16 Goodyear Eagle LS (ETC)	212	250

ELDORADO/SEVILLE — CADILLAC

CODE	DESCRIPTION	INVOICE	MSRP
U1S	12-Disc Trunk-Mounted Disc Changer	506	595
UG1	Programmable Garage Door Opener	91	107
UM5	Radio: BOSE Sound System with CD and Cassette (ESC)	1036	1219
	Includes AM stereo/FM stereo, cassette, single slot CD, weather band, digital signal processing (DSP), radio data system (RDS), Theftlock and Bose amplified speaker system.		
WA7	Comfort/Convenience Package (ESC)	737	867
	Includes 4-way power lumbar support, memory package and heated front seats.		

2000 SEVILLE

2000 Cadillac Seville

What's New?

The Northstar V8s have been improved, and all models get a new airbag suppression system and the revised version of GM's StabiliTrak. A new ultrasonic rear parking assist feature and an advanced navigation system is optional on STS and SLS. There are also two new exterior colors, Midnight Blue and Bronzemist.

Review

The world premiere of the 1998 Seville was held in September of '97 at the Frankfurt International Auto Show to exemplify the car's global focus. The first Cadillac ever to debut outside the United States, the Seville embodies not only the best America has to offer, but in many respects the best of what the world has to offer, too.

For 2000, Cadillac has redesigned its dual-overhead-cam 4.6-liter Northstar V8s from the inside out to achieve better mileage with regular fuel, smoother and quieter operation, and certification as a low-emission vehicle (LEV) in some states. A 275-horsepower version still powers the Seville SLS, while the STS again has an additional 25 ponies under the hood. But it's difficult to imagine these motors running smoother, as the Northstars are already among the most refined engines on the planet.

CADILLAC SEVILLE

| CODE | DESCRIPTION | INVOICE | MSRP |

Both the Seville STS and SLS come standard with a new version of StabiliTrak, which adds side slip-rate control and active steering effort compensation to an already impressive computer-controlled traction system. Also standard is the next generation of Cadillac's Continuously Variable Road-Sensing Suspension (CVRSS), which GM engineers say now includes inputs for transient roll control, lateral support and stability control interaction from StabiliTrak 2.0. The CVRSS system works like an electronic active suspension, reading the road surface and employing dampers at each corner to instantly adjust the Seville's ride and handling setup.

Inside, there's luxurious leather appointments (Zebrano wood trim is available) and an ergonomically functional control panel highlighted by electro-luminescent analog gauges as well as a driver information system. A heated seat is part of an adaptive seating package available on both models that uses a network of inflatable air cells installed in the seat cushion, seatback and side bolsters to adjust comfort and support. You can even opt for massaging lumbar seats on STS. Interior storage is outstanding, with a roomy glovebox, clamshell-design center armrest console, and a rear-seat pass-through. Standard on STS is the Bose 4.0 audio system, which provides superb sound reproduction through eight speakers and a trunk-mounted subwoofer.

Other notable features include a new airbag suppression system that uses sensors to determine if the front-passenger airbag should be disabled because the seat is either vacant or being occupied by a small child. Also new this year is an ultrasonic rear parking assist feature and GM's three-button OnStar communications service as standard equipment, and an optional advanced navigation system.

We could go on an on about other technology, such as the transmission's Performance Algorithm Shifting feature, or the Magnasteer variable-assist, speed-sensitive power rack-and-pinion unit, or the road-texture detection system, or the advanced radio data system stereo and any number of other Seville goodies, but space is limited. What we have here is an outstanding example of American design and engineering excellence. For our money, Seville is well worth every penny.

Standard Equipment

SLS (4A): 4.6L V8 DOHC SMPI 32-valve engine, requires premium unleaded fuel; 4-speed electronic OD auto transmission with lock-up; 770-amp battery with run down protection; 138-amp alternator; front-wheel drive, traction control, 3.71 axle ratio; stainless steel exhaust with chrome tip; comfort ride suspension, adaptive auto-leveling suspension, electronic stability, front independent strut suspension with anti-roll bar, front coil springs, rear independent multi-link suspension with anti-roll bar, rear coil springs; power rack-and-pinion steering with vehicle speed-sensing assist; 4-wheel disc brakes with 4-wheel antilock braking system; 18.5 gal. capacity fuel tank; front license plate bracket, rear lip spoiler, side impact bars; front and rear body-colored bumpers; body-colored bodyside molding; clearcoat monotone paint; projector beam halogen fully auto headlamps with daytime running lights, delay-off feature; additional exterior lights include cornering lights, underhood light; driver's and passenger's power remote body-colored heated folding outside mirrors; front and rear 16" x 7" silver alloy wheels; P235/60SR16 A/S BSW front and rear tires; inside under cargo mounted compact steel spare wheel; dual zone front air conditioning with climate control, air filter, rear heat ducts, auto air recirculation; AM stereo/FM stereo, clock, seek-scan, cassette, single CD, 8 speakers, amplifier, theft deterrent, and window grid diversity antenna, radio steering wheel controls; cruise control; power door locks with 2 stage unlock, remote keyless entry, child safety rear door locks, power remote hatch/trunk release, power remote fuel release; cell phone pre-wiring, 2 power accessory outlets, driver's foot rest, retained accessory power, smokers' package; instrumentation display includes tachometer, water temperature gauge, compass, exterior temp, systems monitor, trip computer, trip odometer; warning indicators include oil pressure, water temp, battery, lights on, key in ignition, low fuel, low washer fluid, door ajar, service interval; driver's and passenger's front airbags, driver's and front passenger's seat mounted side airbags; ignition disable, security system; tinted windows, power front and rear windows with front and rear 1-touch down; variable intermittent front windshield wipers, sun visor strip, rear window defroster; seating capacity of 5, front bucket seats, power adjustable tilt headrests, center armrest with

SEVILLE — CADILLAC

storage, driver's seat includes 6-way power seat, passenger's seat includes 6-way power seat; rear bench seat with tilt headrests, center pass-thru armrest with storage; front height adjustable seatbelts with front pretensioners; leather seats, leather door trim insert, full cloth headliner, full carpet floor covering with carpeted floor mats, genuine wood trim on instrument panel, leather-wrapped gear shift knob; interior lights include dome light, front and rear reading lights, 4 door curb lights, illuminated entry; leather-wrapped steering wheel with tilt adjustment; dual illuminated vanity mirrors, dual auxiliary visors; auto-dimming day/night rearview mirror; full floor console, mini overhead console with storage, locking glove box with light, front and rear cupholders, 2 seat back storage pockets, driver's and passenger's door bins; carpeted cargo floor, carpeted trunk lid, cargo net, cargo tie downs, cargo light, cargo concealed storage; chrome grille, chrome side window moldings, black front windshield molding, black rear window molding and body-colored door handles.

STS (4A) (in addition to or instead of SLS (4A) equipment): Additional exterior lights front fog/driving lights; premium AM stereo/FM stereo, clock, seek-scan, cassette, single CD, 8 premium speakers, premium amplifier, auto equalizer, theft deterrent, and window grid diversity antenna; rain detecting wipers, rear bench seat with power tilt headrests, center pass-thru armrest with storage; memory on driver's seat with 2 memory setting(s) includes settings for exterior mirrors, steering wheel, headrests and leather-wrapped steering wheel with power tilt and telescopic adjustment.

Base Prices

Code	Description	Invoice	MSRP
6KS69	SLS (4A)	40305	43880
6KY69	STS (4A)	44514	48480
	Destination Charge:	670	670

Accessories

Code	Description	Invoice	MSRP
1SB	SLS Convenience Package (SLS)	508	598
	Includes 4-way power lumbar support, RainSense windshield wiper system and garage door opener: 3-channel program.		
1SC	SLS Personalization Package (SLS)	1443	1698
	Includes 4-way power lumbar support, memory package, RainSense windshield wiper system, heated front and rear seats, power tilt and telescopic steering column and garage door opener: 3-channel program.		
1SD	STS Heated Seats Package (STS)	537	632
	Includes heated front and rear seats and garage door opener: 3-channel program.		
1SE	SLS Adaptive Seat Package (SLS)	2041	2401
	Includes driver's and front passenger's adaptive seats, memory package, RainSense windshield wiper system, heated front and rear seats, power tilt and telescopic steering column and garage door opener: 3-channel program.		
1SE	STS Adaptive Seat Package (STS)	1383	1627
	Includes driver's and front passenger's adaptive seats, heated front and rear seats and garage door opener: 3-channel program.		
86U	Crimson Pearl Paint	552	650
93U	White Diamond Paint	552	650
CF5	Sunroof with Express Open	1318	1550
	Slightly reduces headroom.		
D98	Accent Stripe Color (SLS)	64	75

CADILLAC — SEVILLE

CODE	DESCRIPTION	INVOICE	MSRP
FE9	Federal Emission Requirements	NC	NC
	NOT AVAILABLE with YF5.		
K05	Engine Block Heater	15	18
N30	Wood Trim Package	506	595
	Includes wood steering wheel and wood shift knob.		
P05	Wheels: Chrome (STS)	509	795
PX2	Wheels: Chrome (SLS)	509	795
QDC	Tires: P235/60ZR16 Goodyear Eagle LS (STS)	212	250
	Z-Rated Blackwall and extra capacity cooling system.		
U1Z	6-Disc CD Changer	506	595
	Located in center console. Also available as a dealer ordered and installed option.		
UD7	Ultrasonic Rear Parking Assist	251	295
UM5	Radio: AM Stereo/FM Stereo with CD Player (SLS)	808	950
	Includes cassette tape and single slot CD players, weatherband, digital signal processing, radio data system, auto volume control, Theftlock; Bose 4.0 music system (425-Watts) and 8 Bose speakers. NOT AVAILABLE with UM9.		
UM9	Radio: AM Stereo/FM Stereo with Mini-Disc (SLS)	1062	1250
	Includes cassette tape, weather band, digital signal processing, radio data system, auto volume control, Theftlock; Bose 4.0 music system (425-Watts) and 8 Bose speakers. NOT AVAILABLE with UM5.		
UM9	Radio: AM Stereo/FM Stereo with Mini-Disc (STS)	255	300
	Includes cassette tape, weather band, digital signal processing, radio data system, auto volume control, Theftlock; Bose 4.0 music system (425-Watts) and 8 Bose speakers.		
UY4	On Board CD-ROM Based Navigation (SLS)	2503	2945
	Includes premium audio system and 8 Bose speakers. REQUIRES U1Z.		
UY4	On Board CD-ROM Based Navigation (STS)	1696	1995
	Includes premium audio system and 8 Bose speakers. REQUIRES U1Z.		
YF5	California State Emission Requirements	NC	NC
	Required by state laws and regulations on new motor vehicles intended primarily for use or registration (sale, lease, rent, etc.) in the state of California. (Note: EPA Cross Border State Policy: FE9 of YF5 can be ordered in California contiguous states of Arizona, Nevada and Oregon.). NOT AVAILABLE with FE9.		

For a guaranteed low price on a new vehicle in your area, call

1-800-CAR-CLUB

CAMARO — CHEVROLET

2000 CAMARO

2000 Chevrolet Camaro

What's New?

New interior colors and fabrics, redundant steering-wheel radio controls, new alloy wheels, and a new exterior color spruce up the aging Camaro. V6 and V8 engines meet California's Low-Emission Vehicle (LEV) standards.

Review

"From the country that invented rock 'n' roll" claimed the advertisements for this Quebec, Canada-built sport coupe when it was redesigned in 1993. A small technicality, we suppose, but there are no technicalities when it comes to the Camaro's performance abilities, particularly in Z28 or SS guise. These Camaros are blazingly quick, hold the road tenaciously, cost less than the average price of a new car in this country and get decent gas mileage when they're not being hammered along a twisty, two-lane road.

Two trim levels are available for 2000, in either coupe or convertible bodystyles. Base Camaros are powered by a 3800 Series II V6 that makes 200 horsepower. Mated to a four-speed automatic or five-speed manual transmission, this sufficiently strong motor makes a strong argument for avoiding the higher insurance rates and prices of the Z28. An optional performance-handling package puts dual exhaust, tighter steering and a limited-slip differential on the V6 Camaro.

The Z28 is the go-faster Camaro. Equipped with a detuned Corvette 5.7-liter V8, the Z28 makes 305 horsepower, 45 more horses than the Mustang GT. Opt for the SS performance package and you get 320 horsepower (same as the Mustang Cobra), thanks to forced air induction through an aggressive-looking hood scoop. The SS gets to 60 mph from rest in a little over five seconds. SLP Engineering - known for working magic with GM's F-Bodies since the late '80s - supplies the parts to turn a Z28 into an SS. See your Chevy dealer for ordering details.

For 2000, revisions are few. New interior colors and fabrics, along with steering wheel-mounted stereo controls, freshen the passenger compartment. Engines meet LEV standards in California and other low-emission states, and one new exterior color is available. These changes are welcome. The new, more intricately laced alloy wheels that look like wheelcovers are not. They look difficult to clean, and these beautiful, fat, five-spokers on the SS have been sacrificed for the sake of change.

CHEVROLET — CAMARO

| CODE | DESCRIPTION | INVOICE | MSRP |

The interior of the Camaro is functional, but cheap in appearance. Visibility is nothing to brag about either. The Camaro holds a respectable amount of gear in the cargo hold (more than 33 cubic feet of space with the generally useless rear seats folded down), and airbags and antilock brakes are standard.

Rumors are flying that GM is set to kill the Camaro, and since no product is scheduled for the Canadian Camaro plant after 2002, those rumors are likely true. Steadily declining sales are to blame, and the company is eager to slice non-performing models from the lineup. If the Camaro dies, it would be a real shame because - from a bang-for-the-buck standpoint - the Z28 is unbeatable. More mature drivers can order traction control, but that option defeats some of the fun of Chevy's pony car: smoky, adolescent burnouts that leave the drivers behind choking on charred Goodyears.

Standard Equipment

BASE COUPE (5M): 3.8L V6 OHV SMPI 12-valve engine; 5-speed OD manual transmission; 690-amp battery with run down protection; 105-amp alternator; rear-wheel drive, 3.23 axle ratio; stainless steel exhaust; firm ride suspension, front independent suspension with anti-roll bar, front coil springs, gas-pressurized front shocks, rigid rear axle suspension with anti-roll bar, rear coil springs, gas-pressurized rear shocks; power rack-and-pinion steering; 4-wheel disc brakes with 4-wheel antilock braking system; 16.8 gal. capacity fuel tank; rear wing spoiler, side impact bars; front and rear body-colored bumpers; monotone paint; aero-composite halogen fully auto headlamps with daytime running lights; body-colored driver's manual remote outside mirror, passenger's body-colored manual outside mirror; front and rear 16" x 8" steel wheels; P215/60TR16 A/S BSW front and rear tires; inside mounted compact steel spare wheel; air conditioning; AM/FM stereo, clock, seek-scan, cassette, 4 speakers, and fixed antenna; 2 power accessory outlets, retained accessory power, smokers' package; instrumentation display includes tachometer, oil pressure gauge, water temperature gauge, volt gauge, trip odometer; warning indicators include low oil level, low coolant, lights on, key in ignition, low fuel, trunk ajar, service interval; driver's and passenger's front airbags; ignition disable; tinted windows; variable intermittent front windshield wipers, sun visor strip; seating capacity of 4, front bucket seats, fixed headrests, center armrest with storage, driver's seat includes 4-way direction control, passenger's seat includes 4-way direction control; full folding rear bench seat; cloth seats, cloth door trim insert, full cloth headliner, full carpet floor covering with floor mats, plastic/rubber gear shift knob; interior lights include dome light, front reading lights; steering wheel with tilt adjustment; vanity mirrors; day/night rearview mirror; full floor console, glove box with light, front cupholder, driver's and passenger's door bins; carpeted cargo floor, plastic trunk lid, cargo cover, cargo light; black side window moldings, black front windshield molding, black rear window molding and body-colored door handles.

Z28 COUPE (4A) (in addition to or instead of BASE COUPE (4A) equipment): 5.7L V8 OHV SMPI 16-valve engine; 4-speed electronic OD auto transmission with lock-up; 525-amp battery with run down protection; viscous limited slip differential, 2.73 axle ratio; stainless steel exhaust with chrome tip; sport ride suspension; black driver's manual remote outside mirror, passenger's black manual outside mirror; P235/55TR16 A/S BSW front and rear tires; premium AM/FM stereo, clock, seek-scan, cassette, 8 premium speakers, premium amplifier, auto equalizer, theft deterrent, and fixed antenna.

BASE CONVERTIBLE (5M) (in addition to or instead of BASE COUPE (5M) equipment): Power convertible roof with lining, glass rear window; additional exterior lights include front fog/driving lights; premium AM/FM stereo, clock, seek-scan, cassette, 8 premium speakers, premium amplifier, auto equalizer, theft deterrent, and fixed antenna, radio steering wheel controls; cruise control; power door locks, remote keyless entry, power remote hatch/trunk release; panic alarm, security system; power windows with driver's 1-touch down; rear window defroster and leather-wrapped steering wheel with tilt adjustment.

CAMARO CHEVROLET

| CODE | DESCRIPTION | INVOICE | MSRP |

Z28 CONVERTIBLE (4A) (in addition to or instead of Z28 COUPE (4A) equipment): Power convertible roof with lining, glass rear window; additional exterior lights include front fog/driving lights; radio steering wheel controls; cruise control; power remote hatch/trunk release; panic alarm, security system; power windows with driver's 1-touch down; driver's and passenger's power remote body-colored outside mirrors; driver's seat includes 4-way power seat, 8-way direction control and leather-wrapped gear shift knob.

Base Prices

Code	Description	Invoice	MSRP
1FP87	Base Coupe (5M)	15409	16840
1FP87-Z28	Z28 Coupe (4A)	19457	21265
1FP67	Base Convertible (5M)	22088	24140
1FP67-Z28	Z28 Convertible (4A)	25954	28365
	Destination Charge:	535	535

Accessories

Code	Description	Invoice	MSRP
—	Leather Seating Surfaces	445	500
	NOT AVAILABLE with 1SC.		
1LE	Performance Package (Z28 Coupe)	1136	1200
	Includes special handling suspension system, larger stabilizer bars, stiffer springs, dual adjustable shock absorbers, stiffer bushings and power steering cooler. Intended for serious perforance enthusiasts only. REQUIRES (QLC and MN6) or (QLC and GU5).		
1SA	Preferred Equipment Group 1SA (Base)	NC	NC
	Includes vehicle with standard equipment. REQUIRES C49 or R9W. NOT AVAILABLE with Y87, UK3.		
1SB	Preferred Equipment Group 1SB (Base Coupe)	1041	1170
	Includes electronic speed control with resume, remote keyless entry, illuminated entry, power door locks, fog lamps, power windows with driver's express down, dual sport electric remote mirrors, remote keyless entry, illuminated entry and theft deterrent alarm system. REQUIRES C49 or R9W.		
1SB	Preferred Equipment Group 1SB (Z28 Convertible)	NC	NC
	Includes vehicle with standard equipment.		
1SC	Preferred Equipment Group 1SC (Z28 Coupe)	NC	NC
	Includes vehicle with standard equipment. REQUIRES C49 or R9W. NOT AVAILABLE with NW9, Leather Seating Surfaces, B84, 1LE.		
1SD	Preferred Equipment Group 1SD (Z28 Coupe)	1526	1715
	Includes power door locks, remote keyless entry, illuminated entry, electronic speed control with resume, fog lamps, power windows with driver's express down, dual sport electric remote mirrors, leather-wrapped steering wheel, redundant radio controls, leather-wrapped shift knob, theft deterrent alarm system, 6-way power driver's seat, color-keyed body side moldings and carpeted rear floor mats. REQUIRES C49 or R9W.		
AG1	6-Way Power Driver's Seat (Base)	240	270
	INCLUDED in 1SB, 1SD.		
AU0	Remote Keyless Entry (Coupe)	214	240
	Includes illuminated entry. INCLUDED in 1SB, 1SD.		
B35	Carpeted Rear Floor Mats (Base Coupe)	13	15
B84	Color-Keyed Body Side Moldings (Base Coupe)	53	60

CHEVROLET — CAMARO

CODE	DESCRIPTION	INVOICE	MSRP
C49	Electric Rear Window Defogger (Coupe)	151	170
	NOT AVAILABLE with R9W.		
CC1	Transparent Removable Roof Panel (Coupe)	886	995
	Includes locks, lockable stowage provisions and sunshades. NOT AVAILABLE with 1LE.		
GU5	3.23 Performance Axle Ratio (Z28)	267	300
	REQUIRES QFZ or QLC. NOT AVAILABLE with MN6.		
MN6	Transmission: 6-Speed Manual (Z28)	NC	NC
	Includes 3.42 performance axle ratio. NOT AVAILABLE with GU5.		
MX0	Transmission: Electronic 4-Speed Automatic (Base)	725	815
	Includes 2nd gear start feature (when NW9 is not ordered) and 3.08 axle ratio.		
N96	Wheels: 16" Aluminum (Base)	245	275
	REQUIRES QCB. NOT AVAILABLE with PW7.		
NW9	Acceleration Slip Regulation (Base)	222	250
NW9	Acceleration Slip Regulation (Z28)	400	450
	QFZ tires recommended for optimum traction. NOT AVAILABLE with 1SC.		
PW7	Wheels: 16" Polished Aluminum (Base)	668	750
	REQUIRES QCB. NOT AVAILABLE with N96.		
PW7	Wheels: 16" Polished Aluminum (Z28)	445	500
	NOT AVAILABLE with WU8.		
QCB	Tires: P235/55R16 AS BSW (Base)	120	135
	REQUIRES N96 or PW7.		
QFZ	Tires: P245/50ZR16 AS Performance BW (Z28)	200	225
	NOT AVAILABLE with QLC.		
QLC	Tires: P245/50ZR16 Performance BW (Z28)	200	225
	NOT AVAILABLE with QFZ.		
R9W	Rear Window Defogger Not Desired (Coupe)	NC	NC
	NOT AVAILABLE with C49.		
U1S	Remote 12-Disc CD Changer	530	595
UK3	Leather-Wrapped Steering Wheel (Base Coupe)	151	170
	Includes leather-wrapped parking brake release handle, redundant radio controls and leather-wrapped shift knob. REQUIRES UL0 or UN0. NOT AVAILABLE with 1SA. INCLUDED in 1SD.		
UL0	Radio: AM/FM Stereo with Cassette and ATC (Base Coupe)	312	350
	Includes seek/scan, digital clock, auto tone control, theft lock, speed compensated volume, Monsoon 200-Watt sound system, 8 speakers and amplifier. NOT AVAILABLE with UN0.		
UN0	Radio: AM/FM Stereo with CD and ATC (Base Convertible/Z28)	89	100
	Includes seek/scan, digital clock, auto tone control, theft lock, speed compensated volume, Monsoon 200-Watt sound system, 8 speakers and amplifier. REQUIRES 1SC or 1SD.		
UN0	Radio: AM/FM Stereo with CD and Automatic Tone Control (Base Coupe)	400	450
	Includes seek/scan, digital clock, auto tone control, theft lock, speed compensated volume, Monsoon 200-Watt sound system, 8 speakers and amplifier. NOT AVAILABLE with UL0.		
V12	Power Steering Cooler (Z28)	89	100
	Intended for Gymkhana and Autocross-type applications.		

CAMARO / CAVALIER — CHEVROLET

CODE	DESCRIPTION	INVOICE	MSRP
WU8	SS Performance and Appearance Package (Z28)	3516	3950
	Includes 320 HP, forced air induction hood, specific SS spoiler, high-performance ride and handling package, low restriction dual exhaust, wheels: 17" aluminum, tires: 275/40ZR17 Goodyear Eagle F1, SS badging and power steering cooler. NOT AVAILABLE with Y3F, PW7.		
Y3F	Sport Appearance Package (Base)	1200	1348
	Includes spoiler extension, rocker and rear fascia moldings, wheels: 16" aluminum and tires: P235/55R16 A/S BSW.		
Y3F	Sport Appearance Package (Z28)	1562	1755
	Includes rocker and rear fascia moldings. NOT AVAILABLE with WU8.		
Y87	Performance Handling Package (Base)	245	275
	Includes dual outlet exhaust, sport steering ratio and Torsen limited slip differential. REQUIRES (1SB, QCB and (N96 or PW7)) or (1SB and Y3). NOT AVAILABLE with 1SA.		

2000 CAVALIER

2000 Chevrolet Cavalier

What's New?

Still available as a coupe, sedan or convertible, Chevy's best-selling car gets several subtle changes for 2000. Outside it has new body-colored front and rear facias, new headlamp/taillamp assemblies, new badging and restyled wheel covers/alloy rims. Inside, the instrument panel now features an electronic odometer and tripmeter, a revamped center console with three front cupholders and an improved storage area. Functionally, it gets a better-shifting five-speed manual transaxle, smoother operating ABS Passlock II security system and standard air-conditioning.

CHEVROLET — CAVALIER

| CODE | DESCRIPTION | INVOICE | MSRP |

Review

For nearly two decades the Cavalier has been a staple sales leader for Chevy dealers. Understandably so, because the Cavalier offers reasonable value and is priced low enough to compete favorably in the compact market, often undercutting smaller models from other manufacturers.

But small-car sales are suffering because of the strong economy and low fuel prices. Who needs a compact car when a roomy sedan or sport utility is within financial reach? Nonetheless, the Cavalier is good transportation, offering adequate room for four adults, decent performance and acceptable interior accommodations. Styling is attractive and contemporary, and there is a model to suit almost everyone's needs.

This year, Cavalier is offered in Base coupe and sedan, LS sedan and Z24 coupe and convertible. Fresh front and rear fascias debut on the 2000 Cavalier, but you'll need to be sharp-eyed to tell the difference. Here's a hint: the 2000 model has clear lens headlights. Z24 gets a more prominent spoiler, and two new five-spoke alloy wheel designs are available on upper trim levels. The Chevy bow tie returns to the decklid, after a one-year hiatus.

Inside, Cavalier is reasonably comfortable and well laid-out. A slightly revised instrument panel boasts new gauges, digital odometer and tripmeter, and stereo controls relocated above the climate controls for easier access. The center-console shift indicator is illuminated for 2000, and air-conditioning is standard on all Cavaliers. Stereos have been upgraded in terms of power output, while uplevel systems gain RDS technology and automatic theft protection. A dual-play cassette and compact-disc player is available.

GM's venerable 2.2-liter four-cylinder (whose droning exhaust note you are no doubt familiar with) is standard in the Cavalier. Equipped with this powerplant, Cavalier lags behind its primary domestic competition in power and acceleration. Optional in the LS sedan is a 2.4-liter, twin-cam engine hooked to a four-speed automatic transmission, a setup that features traction control. The Cavalier is a much more livable car with this engine, and we wish that Chevrolet offered this powertrain in base models as well. The twin-cam engine is standard in the sporty Z24 coupe and convertible. Manually shifted Z24 coupes are quick from rest to 60 mph. Antilock brakes are standard equipment, and are upgraded for 2000 to provide smoother operation and better response. A rear defogger is newly standard.

Cavalier is aging quickly, and there are no plans to replace this model until 2003 at the earliest. Still, it represents good value. The price is dead-on; low enough to make the Chevrolet Metro sedan an exercise in redundancy. We recommend that you check out the Cavalier if a compact car fits your needs.

Standard Equipment

BASE COUPE (5M): 2.2L I4 OHV SMPI 8-valve engine; 5-speed OD manual transmission; 525-amp battery with run down protection; 105-amp alternator; front-wheel drive, 3.94 axle ratio; stainless steel exhaust; touring ride suspension, front independent strut suspension with anti-roll bar, front coil springs, semi-independent rear suspension with coil springs; power rack-and-pinion steering; front disc/rear drum brakes with 4-wheel antilock braking system; 14.3 gal. capacity fuel tank; side impact bars; front and rear body-colored bumpers; monotone paint; aero-composite halogen headlamps with daytime running lights; black folding driver's manual remote outside mirror, passenger's manual outside mirror; front and rear 14" x 6" steel wheels; P195/70SR14 A/S BSW front and rear tires; inside under cargo mounted compact steel spare wheel; air conditioning, rear heat ducts; AM/FM stereo, clock, seek-scan, 4 speakers, and fixed antenna; 1 power accessory outlet, driver's foot rest; instrumentation display includes water temperature gauge; warning indicators include battery, low coolant, lights on, key in ignition; driver's and passenger's front airbags; ignition disable; tinted windows; fixed interval front windshield wipers, rear window defroster; seating capacity of 5, front bucket seats, adjustable headrests, center armrest with storage, driver's seat includes 4-way direction control, passenger's seat includes 4-way direction control; full folding rear bench seat; cloth seats, cloth door trim insert, full cloth headliner, full carpet floor covering, plastic/rubber gear shift knob; interior lights include dome light with fade; day/night rearview mirror; full floor console, glove box, front and

CAVALIER   CHEVROLET

CODE	DESCRIPTION	INVOICE	MSRP

rear cupholders, driver's and passenger's door bins; carpeted cargo floor, cargo light; black side window moldings, black front windshield molding, black rear window molding and black door handles.

Z24 COUPE (5M) (in addition to or instead of BASE COUPE (5M) equipment): 2.4L I4 DOHC SMPI 16-valve engine; sport ride suspension; rear lip spoiler; body-colored bodyside molding, rocker panel extensions; additional exterior lights include front fog/driving lights; driver's and passenger's power remote black folding outside mirrors; front and rear 16" x 6" silver alloy wheels; P205/55SR16 performance A/S RBL front and rear tires; AM/FM stereo, clock, seek-scan, single CD, 4 performance speakers, and fixed antenna; cruise control; power door locks with 2 stage unlock, remote keyless entry, power remote hatch/trunk release; instrumentation display includes tachometer, trip odometer; security system; power windows with driver's 1-touch down; variable intermittent front windshield wipers; passenger's seat includes, 4-way direction control, easy entry; premium cloth seats, carpeted floor mats; interior lights include front reading lights; steering wheel with tilt adjustment; vanity mirrors and cargo net.

Z24 CONVERTIBLE (5M) (in addition to or instead of Z24 COUPE (5M) equipment): 600-amp battery with run down protection; touring ride suspension; 15 gal. capacity fuel tank; power convertible roof with lining, glass rear window; front and rear 15" x 6" silver alloy wheels; P195/65SR15 touring BSW front and rear tires; warning indicators include low oil level and seating capacity of 4.

BASE SEDAN (5M) (in addition to or instead of BASE COUPE (5M) equipment): 3.58 axle ratio; child safety rear door locks; manual front and rear windows.

LS SEDAN (4A) (in addition to or instead of BASE SEDAN (4A) equipment): Four-speed electronic OD auto transmission with lock-up; traction control, 3.63 axle ratio; body-colored bodyside molding; front and rear 15" x 6" steel wheels; P195/65SR15 touring BSW front and rear tires; AM/FM stereo, clock, seek-scan, cassette, 4 speakers, and fixed antenna; cruise control; remote hatch/trunk release; instrumentation display includes tachometer, trip odometer; variable intermittent front windshield wipers, carpeted floor mats; interior lights include front reading lights, illuminated entry; steering wheel with tilt adjustment; vanity mirrors and cargo net.

Base Prices

Code	Description	Invoice	MSRP
1JC37	Base Coupe (5M)	12216	13065
1JF37	Z24 Coupe (5M)	15212	16270
1JF67	Z24 Convertible (5M)	18452	19735
1JC69	Base Sedan (5M)	12309	13165
1JF69	LS Sedan (4A)	13754	14710
	Destination Charge:	510	510

Accessories

Code	Description	Invoice	MSRP
—	Cloth Seat Trim (LS)	NC	NC
	Requires (92G/52G) Medium Gray or Neutral interior.		
—	Cloth Seat Trim (Z24)	NC	NC
	Requires (12H) Graphite interior.		
—	Vinyl Seat Trim (Z24 Convertible)	NC	NC
1SA	Preferred Equipment Group 1SA	NC	NC
	Includes vehicle with standard equipment. NOT AVAILABLE with CF5, V11, UPO, PF7, T43.		

CHEVROLET — CAVALIER

CODE	DESCRIPTION	INVOICE	MSRP
1SB	**Preferred Equipment Group 1SB (Base Coupe)**	387	430
	Includes body color side moldings, cargo area convenience net, front and rear carpeted floor mats, dual covered visor mirrors with map straps, front mud guards, passenger side easy entry seat, mechanical trunk opener, variable intermittent windshield wipers and AM/FM stereo with cassette.		
1SB	**Preferred Equipment Group 1SB (Base Sedan)**	372	413
	Includes body color side moldings, cargo area convenience net, front and rear carpeted floor mats, dual covered visor mirrors with map straps, front mud guards, mechanical trunk opener, variable intermittent windshield wipers and AM/FM stereo with cassette.		
1SB	**Preferred Equipment Group 1SB (LS)**	792	880
	Includes power mirrors, power windows with driver's express down, remote keyless entry, power door locks, content theft security system, AM/FM stereo with seek and scan and CD.		
1SC	**Preferred Equipment Group 1SC (Base Coupe)**	900	1000
	Includes 1SB: body color side moldings, cargo area convenience net, front and rear carpeted floor mats, dual covered visor mirrors with map straps, front mud guards, passenger side easy entry seat, mechanical trunk opener, variable intermittent windshield wipers; wheels: 15" with bolt-on covers, tires: P195/65R15 touring BSW, electronic speed control with resume speed, tilt steering wheel, AM/FM stereo with seek and scan and CD. NOT AVAILABLE with UM6.		
1SD	**Preferred Equipment Group 1SD (Base Coupe)**	1543	1714
	Includes 1SC: body color side moldings, cargo area convenience net, front and rear carpeted floor mats, dual covered visor mirrors with map straps, front mud guards, passenger side easy entry seat, mechanical trunk opener, variable intermittent windshield wipers; wheels: 15" with bolt-on covers, tires: P195/65R15 touring BSW, electronic speed control with resume speed, tilt steering wheel, AM/FM stereo with seek and scan and CD; power mirrors, power windows, remote keyless entry, power door locks and content theft security system. NOT AVAILABLE with UM6, MX1.		
40A	**White Stripe (Z24 Convertible)**	NC	NC
	REQUIRES WM1. NOT AVAILABLE with 75A, WM2.		
75A	**Red Stripe (Z24 Convertible)**	NC	NC
	REQUIRES WM1. NOT AVAILABLE with 40A, WM2.		
AS5	**Bucket Seats (Z24 Convertible)**	45	50
	Includes driver's side adjustable lumbar support.		
AU0	**Remote Keyless Entry (Base Coupe)**	333	370
	Includes power door locks and content theft security system. INCLUDED in 1SB, 1SC, 1SD.		
AU0	**Remote Keyless Entry (Sedan)**	369	410
	Includes power door locks and content theft security system. INCLUDED in 1SB.		
CF5	**Electric Sunroof (Coupe)**	536	595
	Includes mirror map light. NOT AVAILABLE with 1SA.		
K05	**Engine Block Heater**	27	30
KL6	**Natural Gas Provisions (Base Sedan)**	5342	5935
	Includes wheels: 15" and tires: 195/65R15. REQUIRES MX1.		

CAVALIER — CHEVROLET

CODE	DESCRIPTION	INVOICE	MSRP
LD9	Engine: 2.4L SFI L4 Twin Cam (LS)	405	450
	Includes 3.91 axle ratio.		
MX0	Transmission: 4-Speed Automatic (Z24)	702	780
	Includes traction control. NOT AVAILABLE with 1SA, 1SB, MX1.		
MX1	Transmission: 3-Speed Automatic (Base)	540	600
	Includes 3.18 axle ratio. NOT AVAILABLE with 1SD.		
NC7	Federal Emission Override (Sedan/Z24 Coupe)	NC	NC
PF7	Wheels: 15" Aluminum (Base Coupe/LS Sedan)	266	295
	NOT AVAILABLE with 1SA (Coupe).		
T43	Rear Spoiler (LS)	135	150
	NOT AVAILABLE with 1SA.		
U1C	Radio: AM/FM Stereo with CD (All Except Z24)	45	50
	Includes digital clock, speed compensated volume and premium front coaxial speakers. REQUIRES 1SB (Base). NOT AVAILABLE with UM6, UP0. INCLUDED in 1SB (LS), 1SC, 1SD.		
U1C	Radio: AM/FM Stereo with CD (Base)	194	215
	Includes digital clock, speed compensated volume and premium front coaxial speakers. REQUIRES 1SA. NOT AVAILABLE with UM6, UP0. INCLUDED in 1SB, 1SC, 1SD.		
UM6	Radio: AM/FM Stereo with Cassette (Base)	148	165
	Includes seek/scan and digital clock. NOT AVAILABLE with 1SC, 1SD, U1C, UP0, V11. INCLUDED in 1SB.		
UP0	Radio: AM/FM Stereo with CD and Cassette (Base Coupe)	207	230
	Includes seek/scan, digital clock, auto tone control, speed compensated volume, theft lock, radio data system controls and premium front coaxial speakers. REQUIRES 1SB. NOT AVAILABLE with UM6, U1C, V11, 1SA.		
UP0	Radio: AM/FM Stereo with CD and Cassette (Base Coupe)	162	180
	Includes seek/scan, digital clock, auto tone control, speed compensated volume, theft lock, radio data system controls and premium front coaxial speakers. REQUIRES V11, 1SC or 1SD. NOT AVAILABLE with UM6, U1C, 1SA.		
UP0	Radio: AM/FM Stereo with CD and Cassette (LS)	207	230
	Includes seek/scan, digital clock, auto tone control, speed compensated volume, theft lock, radio data system controls and premium front coaxial speakers. REQUIRES 1SA. NOT AVAILABLE with U1C.		
UP0	Radio: AM/FM Stereo with CD and Cassette (LS)	162	180
	Includes seek/scan, digital clock, auto tone control, speed compensated volume, theft lock, radio data system controls and premium front coaxial speakers. REQUIRES 1SB. NOT AVAILABLE with U1C.		
UP0	Radio: AM/FM Stereo with CD and Cassette (Z24)	162	180
	Includes seek/scan, digital clock, auto tone control, speed compensated volume, theft lock, radio data system controls and premium front coaxial speakers.		
V11	Sport Package (Base Coupe)	167	185
	Includes spoiler, AM/FM stereo with CD (U1C) and tachometer. REQUIRES 1SB. NOT AVAILABLE with 1SA, UP0, UM6.		
V11	Sport Package (Base Coupe)	122	135
	Includes spoiler, AM/FM stereo with CD (U1C) and tachometer. REQUIRES 1SC or 1SD. NOT AVAILABLE with 1SA, UP0, UM6.		

CHEVROLET — CAVALIER / CORVETTE

CODE	DESCRIPTION	INVOICE	MSRP
WM1	Heritage Stripe Package (Z24 Convertible) .... *NOT AVAILABLE with WM2.*	140	155
WM2	Winner's Circle Stripe Package (Z24 Convertible) .... *NOT AVAILABLE with WM1, 40A, 75A.*	252	280

2000 CORVETTE

2000 Chevrolet Corvette

What's New?

Minor refinements improve the Corvette for 2000. The Z51 performance-handling package has larger front and rear stabilizer bars for improved handling, while new, thin-spoke alloy wheels with optional high-polish finish subtly change the outward appearance. Two new colors are available on coupe and convertible: extra-cost Millennium Yellow and no-cost Dark Bowling Green Metallic. A garish Torch Red interior can be ordered, the stupendous LS1 5.7-liter V8 engine meets LEV regulations in California, the remote keyless-entry system has been upgraded, and the passenger door-lock cylinder has been deleted.

Review

   More than 40 years after the 1953 Corvette debuted, Chevrolet introduced the fifth-generation Corvette for 1997. The C5 almost didn't happen. Originally scheduled for release in 1993, the Corvette was killed for a short time before performance zealots within General Motors resuscitated the project and made the new car a reality. With the addition of a hardtop model to the lineup in 1999, three different Corvettes are available for 2000.

   Pushrod power - in the form of a reworked 5.7-liter V8 dubbed the LS1 that meets LEV standards for 2000 - motivates the Corvette. Horsepower is rated 345 at 5,600 rpm, while torque measures 350 foot-pounds at 4,400 rpm. The result? Equipped with the standard four-speed automatic transmission, the Corvette will hit 60 mph in a shade over five seconds. Opt for the six-speed manual transmission and you'll cut less than half a second off the trap time. To help reign the power in on slippery surfaces, acceleration slip regulation (a.k.a., traction control)

CORVETTE

is standard equipment. EPA mileage figures are phenomenal for this high-powered sports car; the Corvette will return 28 mpg on the highway with the manual tranny.

Four-wheel-disc antilock brakes keep stopping distances short, thanks to large rotors and pads. Front tires are 17 inches in diameter, and rears are a whopping 18 inches across - which contributes to prodigious amount of road grip. The rubber stays planted well, too, thanks to a fully independent four-wheel short/long-arm height-adjustable suspension. Optional on coupe and convertible is an Active Handling System (AHS), which keeps the Corvette in line even if the driver isn't.

Body panels are still composed of a material other than metal, though no longer fiberglass. Sheet-molded compound wraps around an ultra-stiff structure that features a full-length perimeter frame with tubular steel side rails. The windshield frame is aluminum, and the instrument panel is attached directly to a beefy crossmember designed to reduce noise and vibration. A sandwich composite floor with a lightweight balsa wood core damps noise and vibration while making the floor exceptionally stiff.

Inside, a dash with analog gauges and intuitive radio and climate controls greets passengers. A head-up display and a power tilt and telescoping steering wheel can be purchased for installation on the coupe and convertible. Also available on those two models is Twilight Sentinel, an automatic headlight system. Luggage space beneath the coupe's rear hatch glass is an incredible 25 cubic feet, made possible with the use of dual mid-ship-mounted fuel tanks that are snuggled within the Corvette's structure. Even the hardtop and convertible can tote more cargo than any Corvette in history. The car feels more airy inside, thanks to a narrower doorsill and taller height combined with a low cowl.

Improvements for 2000 are few but significant. To celebrate the turn of the century, buyers of the coupe and convertible can pay extra for Millennium Yellow premium tint coated bodywork. If spending extra money on paint isn't on the 'to do' list, you can set yourself apart from the crowd with Dark Bowling Green Metallic, named after the Kentucky city where the Corvette is assembled. A new interior color, Torch Red, debuts as well. New wheels with thinner spokes than before can be ordered with silver paint or a high polish finish - the optional magnesium wheels are still available. Other changes include a revised remote keyless-entry system, thicker stabilizer bars for the hardtop and models equipped with the Z51 performance and handling package, and the deletion of the passenger door-lock cylinder.

Yes, the Corvette is an outstanding effort and competes favorably with the best in the class. Unfortunately, it doesn't look like a million bucks, to our eyes. Long, low, and lean, the Corvette is certainly attractive. We take issue, however, with the thick truncated tail and the odd-looking air scoops for the front brakes. Other critics have complained of derivative styling cues and the lack of chrome-finished exhaust tips. Still, the Corvette's new shape will wear well into the next century, particularly in convertible format.

Don't let the fact that the C5 will swallow two golf bags sway you into thinking this a gentrified sporting coupe. The 2000 Corvette is among the best true sports cars your money can buy.

Standard Equipment

HARDTOP (6M): 5.7L V8 OHV SMPI 16-valve engine, requires premium unleaded fuel; 6-speed OD manual transmission; 600-amp battery with run down protection; engine block heater; 130-amp alternator; rear-wheel drive, limited slip differential, traction control, 3.42 axle ratio; dual stainless steel exhaust with chrome tip; sport ride suspension, front independent double wishbone suspension with anti-roll bar, front springs; rear independent double wishbone suspension with anti-roll bar, rear springs; power rack-and-pinion steering, power steering cooler; 4-wheel disc brakes with 4-wheel antilock braking system; 19.1 gal. capacity fuel tank; side impact bars; front and rear body-colored bumpers; clearcoat monotone paint; sealed beam halogen headlamps with daytime running lights; driver's and passenger's power remote body-colored heated folding outside mirrors; front 17" x 8.5" silver alloy wheels rear 18" x 9.5" silver alloy wheels; P245/45ZR17 performance A/S BSW front tires; 275/40R18 rear tires; air conditioning; premium AM/FM stereo, clock, seek-scan, cassette, 6 speakers, auto equalizer, theft deterrent, and fixed antenna; cruise control; power door locks, remote keyless entry, power remote hatch/trunk release, power remote fuel release; 1 power accessory outlet,

CHEVROLET CORVETTE

driver's foot rest, smokers' package; instrumentation display includes tachometer, oil pressure gauge, water temperature gauge, volt gauge, exterior temp, systems monitor, trip computer, trip odometer; warning indicators include oil pressure, water temp, battery, low oil level, low coolant, lights on, key in ignition, low fuel, low washer fluid, door ajar, trunk ajar, service interval, brake fluid; driver's and passenger's front airbags; ignition disable, panic alarm, security system; tinted windows with driver's and passenger's 1-touch down; variable intermittent front windshield wipers, sun visor strip, rear window defroster; seating capacity of 2, front bucket seats, fixed headrests, center armrest with storage, driver's seat includes 4-way direction control, passenger's seat includes 4-way direction control; front height adjustable seatbelts; leather seats, leatherette door trim insert, full cloth headliner, full carpet floor covering, deluxe sound insulation, leather-wrapped gear shift knob; interior lights include dome light, front reading lights, illuminated entry; leather-wrapped sport steering wheel with tilt adjustment; vanity mirrors; day/night rearview mirror; full floor console, locking glove box with light, front cupholder, interior concealed storage; carpeted cargo floor, plastic trunk lid, cargo concealed storage; black side window moldings, black front windshield molding, black rear window molding and body-colored door handles.

COUPE (4A) (in addition to or instead of HARDTOP (6M) equipment): Four-speed electronic OD auto transmission with lock-up; 2.73 axle ratio; power rack-and-pinion steering with vehicle speed-sensing assist; front manual targa steel removable roof; additional exterior lights include underhood light; Bose speakers, window grid antenna; driver's seat includes 4-way power seat, 8-way direction control; interior lights include 2 door curb lights; dual illuminated vanity mirrors and cargo light.

CONVERTIBLE (4A) (in addition to or instead of COUPE (4A) equipment): Manual convertible roof with lining, glass rear window; power retractable antenna and front cloth headliner.

Base Prices

Code	Description	Invoice	MSRP
1YY37	Hardtop (6M)	33530	38320
1YY07	Coupe (4A)	34033	38895
1YY67	Convertible (4A)	39655	45320
	Destination Charge:	580	580

Accessories

Code	Description	Invoice	MSRP
1SA	Preferred Equipment Group 1SA	NC	NC
	Includes vehicle with standard equipment.		
79U	Millennium Yellow (Convertible)	430	500
86U	Magnetic Red Metallic Paint (Coupe/Convertible)	430	500
AAB	Memory Package (Coupe/Convertible)	129	150
	Remembers settings for radio, HVAC controls, mirrors and driver's seat. REQUIRES CJ2.		
AG1	6-Way Power Driver's Seat (Hardtop)	262	305
AG2	6-Way Power Passenger's Seat (Coupe/Convertible)	262	305
AP9	Parcel Net (Hardtop)	13	15
AQ9	Adjustable Sport Buckets (Coupe/Convertible)	602	700
	REQUIRES AG2.		
B34	Front Floor Mats	22	25
B84	Body Side Moldings	64	75
C2L	Roof Package (Coupe)	817	950
	Includes standard solid panel and blue transparent roof panel.		
CC3	Blue Transparent Roof Panel (Coupe)	559	650

CORVETTE / IMPALA — CHEVROLET

CODE	DESCRIPTION	INVOICE	MSRP
CJ2	Dual Zone Electronic Air Conditioning (Coupe/Convertible)	314	365
CJ2	Dual Zone Electronic Air Conditioning (Hardtop)	314	365
D42	Luggage Shade and Parcel Net (Coupe)	43	50
F45	Selective Real Time Damping (Coupe/Convertible)	1458	1695
	The handling package for ultimate driver comfort and control through the use of a driver's adjustable ride control system. Includes standard suspension components and Delphi adjustable ride control system. NOT AVAILABLE with Z51.		
G92	3.15 Performance Axle Ratio (Coupe/Convertible)	86	100
JL4	Active Handling System	430	500
	The Active Handling System provides additional security in slippery conditions or in extreme handling maneuvers. The Active Handling System can automatically apply one of the vehicle's brakes to assist in correcting vehicle oversteer and understeer when the driver's intended direction differs from the vehicle's actual direction.		
MN6	Transmission: 6-Speed Manual (Coupe/Convertible)	701	815
	Includes 3.42 axle ratio. NOT AVAILABLE with G92.		
N37	Manual Tilt/Power Telescoping Steering (Coupe/Convertible)	301	350
	Includes memory steering wheel. REQUIRES AAB.		
N73	Wheels: Magnesium	1720	2000
	NOT AVAILABLE with QF5.		
QF5	Wheels: Polished Aluminum	770	895
	NOT AVAILABLE with N73.		
R8C	Corvette Museum Delivery	421	490
T82	Twilight Sentinel Lighting (Coupe/Convertible)	52	60
	Provides delay-off headlights.		
T96	Fog Lamps	59	69
TR9	Lighting (Hardtop)	82	95
	Includes cargo light, underhood light and illuminated vanity mirrors.		
U1S	Remote 12-Disc CD Changer	516	600
	REQUIRES UZ6 (Hardtop).		
UN0	Radio: Delco AM/FM Stereo with CD	86	100
	Includes seek/scan, auto tone control, digital clock, theft lock, speed compensated volume and Bose speaker system. REQUIRES UZ6 (Hardtop).		
UV6	Head-Up Display	322	375
UZ6	Bose Speaker System (Hardtop)	705	820
	Includes amplifier system.		
V49	Front License Plate Frame	13	15
Z51	Performance Handling Package (Coupe/Convertible)	301	350
	Performance oriented package for the Gymkhana/Autocross enthusiast, stiffer stabilizer bars and stiffer springs. REQUIRES G92. NOT AVAILABLE with F45.		

2000 IMPALA

What's New?

GM has resurrected the Impala nameplate (a staple in Chevy's lineup from 1959 to the early '80s and then briefly from 1994 to '96) and put it on an all-new, full-sized sedan body that rides

CHEVROLET

IMPALA

| CODE | DESCRIPTION | INVOICE | MSRP |

on the Lumina front-drive platform. Although the Lumina itself is back for the 2000-model year, Impala will eventually replace it as Chevy's large-car entry to battle the likes of Ford's Crown Victoria, Buick's LeSabre and Chrysler's LH cars.

Review

The Chevy Impala is back again, this time as a front-wheel-drive, V6-powered spin-off of the Lumina chassis. Designed to compete in the full-size market, the 2000 Impala is more aggressive-looking than its Lumina sister, with smoked headlight lenses, large circular tail lamps, and a shape that creates a "frown" both front and rear. Stylists looked to Impalas of the '60s for inspiration here, but its C-pillar badges mimic the surprisingly successful and often-mourned Impala SS of the '90s.

Available in base and LS trim levels, the 2000 Impala sedan holds six good-sized adults and 17.6 cubic feet of their luggage. Inside, a clean, straightforward layout features large, easy-to-find controls and gauges.

The standard 3.4-liter V6 engine was borrowed from the Venture minivan, making 180 horsepower at 5,200 rpm and 205 foot-pounds of torque at 4,000 rpm. Step up to LS trim and you get a 3.8-liter V6 making 200 horsepower at 5,200 rpm and 222 foot-pounds of torque at 4,000 rpm. Weighing just less than 3,400 pounds, Impala should move along with verve with either engine. A four-speed automatic is the only available transmission.

Structural enhancements make for a stiffer body, which allowed the engineers to reduce noise, vibration and harshness. It also allowed a more precisely tuned suspension to maximize both ride comfort and handling prowess. Standard 16-inch wheels and tires do much to help with both ride and grip, while Impala's standard four-wheel-disc brakes are rated for heavy-duty service in a new Impala police package. Antilock brakes, a tire inflation monitor and traction control are optional on base models and standard on LS.

Occupant safety will be a big selling point for the Impala. Head protection standards for 2003 have been met three years in advance, a side airbag is available, and rear-seat tethers will handle up to three child safety seats. Daytime running lights are standard.

Other standard equipment includes air conditioning with dual front temperature controls, rear defogger, rear-seat headrests, power windows and locks, and a Radio Data System (RDS) AM/FM stereo. Plus, the clock automatically adjusts when you drive across time zones, and Impala's remote keyless entry fobs can be programmed with the preferences of two different drivers.

Chevrolet has promised improved reliability, thanks to a simplified electrical system and fewer parts used in the assembly process. A coolant loss-protection system keeps the Impala moving even if all the coolant has been lost - just make sure to stop before you've traveled 50 miles. And, if you do get stranded, the available OnStar mobile communications system can help rescue you.

While not terribly exiting, middle-of-the-road buyers looking for a solid American sedan will likely be quite happy with this big new Impala.

Standard Equipment

BASE (4A): 3.4L V6 OHV SMPI 12-valve engine; 4-speed electronic overdrive automatic transmission with lock-up; battery with run down protection; front wheel drive, 3.05 axle ratio; stainless steel exhaust; comfort ride suspension, front independent strut suspension with anti-roll bar, front coil springs, rear independent strut suspension with anti-roll bar, rear coil springs; power rack-and-pinion steering; 4 wheel disc brakes; 17 gal. capacity fuel tank; front and rear body-colored bumpers with black rub strip; black bodyside molding, rocker panel extensions; monotone paint; aero-composite halogen fully automatic headlamps with daytime running lights; additional exterior lights include center high mounted stop light; driver's and passenger's power remote body-colored outside mirrors; front and rear 16" x 6.5" steel wheels; P225/60SR16 BSW AS front and rear tires; inside under cargo mounted compact steel spare wheel; air conditioning, rear heat ducts; AM/FM stereo with clock, seek-scan, 4 speakers, and fixed antenna; power door locks, child safety rear door locks, power remote hatch/trunk release; 1

IMPALA — CHEVROLET

| CODE | DESCRIPTION | INVOICE | MSRP |

power accessory outlet, driver's foot rest; instrumentation display includes tachometer, water temp gauge, trip odometer; warning indicators include oil pressure, water temp, battery, low oil level, low coolant, lights on, key in ignition, service interval; dual airbags; ignition disable; tinted windows, power front windows with driver's 1-touch down, power rear windows; variable intermittent front windshield wipers, rear window defroster; seating capacity of 6, 60-40 split-bench front seat with adjustable headrests, center armrest with storage, driver's seat includes 4-way direction control, passenger's seat includes 4-way direction control; rear bench seat with fixed headrests; front height adjustable seatbelts; cloth seats, cloth door trim insert, full cloth headliner, full carpet floor covering with carpeted floor mats; interior lights include dome light with fade, illuminated entry; steering wheel with tilt adjustment; vanity mirrors, dual auxiliary visors; day-night rearview mirror; mini overhead console, locking glove box with light, front cupholder, 2 seat back storage pockets, driver's and passenger's door bins; carpeted cargo floor, cargo light; chrome grille, black side window moldings, black front windshield molding, black rear window molding and body-colored door handles.

LS (4A) (in addition to or instead of BASE (4A) equipment): 3.8L V6 OHV SMPI 12-valve engine; front wheel drive, traction control; firm ride suspension; 4 wheel disc brakes with 4 wheel antilock braking system; rear wing spoiler; additional exterior lights include front fog/driving lights; driver's and passenger's power remote body-colored heated outside mirrors; dual zone front air conditioning, air filter; AM/FM stereo with clock, seek-scan, cassette, 6 performance speakers, automatic equalizer, theft deterrent, and fixed antenna; cruise control with steering wheel controls; remote keyless entry; seat mounted driver's side airbag; seating capacity of 5, front bucket seats with adjustable headrests, driver's seat includes 4-way power seat with 8-way direction control and lumbar support; 60-40 folding rear bench seat with fixed headrests; premium cloth seats; leather-wrapped steering wheel with tilt adjustment; dual illuminated vanity mirrors, driver's side auxiliary visor; full floor console; front and rear cupholders and cargo net.

2000 Chevrolet Impala

Base Prices

CODE	DESCRIPTION	INVOICE	MSRP
1WF19	Base (4A)	17115	18705
1WH19	LS (4A)	20464	22365
	Destination Charge:	560	560

CHEVROLET — IMPALA

CODE	DESCRIPTION	INVOICE	MSRP

Accessories

CODE	DESCRIPTION	INVOICE	MSRP
—	**Custom Cloth Seat Trim (Base)**	681	765
	Includes driver's and passenger's manual reclining seats, driver's side-impact air bag, driver's side lumbar and split folding rear seat. NOT AVAILABLE with 1SA, Leather Seat Trim, W01.		
—	**Leather Seat Trim (Base)**	1237	1390
	Includes driver's and passenger's manual reclining seats, driver's side-impact air bag, driver's side lumbar and split folding rear seat. REQUIRES (1SB and UK3) or 1SC. NOT AVAILABLE with 1SA, AR9, Custom Cloth Seat Trim, AG2.		
—	**Leather Trim (LS)**	556	625
1SB	**Preferred Equipment Group 1SB (Base)**	883	993
	Includes electronic speed control with resume speed, ETR AM/FM stereo with cassette and automatic tone control, remote keyless entry, dual illuminated visor mirrors, luggage area cargo net, overhead console with storage bins, three assist grips and electrochromic mirror. NOT AVAILABLE with 1SA, 1SC, UN0, UP0.		
1SB	**Preferred Equipment Group 1SB (LS)**	460	517
	Includes driver's information/convenience center: trip computer, outside temp and compass, universal garage door opener, anti-theft alarm system, electrochromic mirror with dual reading lamps and steering wheel radio controls. NOT AVAILABLE with 1SA.		
1SC	**Preferred Equipment Group 1SC (Base)**	1423	1599
	Includes electronic speed control with resume speed, ETR AM/FM stereo with cassette and automatic tone control, remote keyless entry, dual illuminated visor mirrors, luggage area cargo net, overhead console with storage bins, three assist grips, electrochromic mirror, driver's and passenger's temperature control, wheels: custom aluminum, power outside heated remote mirrors, steering wheel radio controls and leather-wrapped steering wheel. NOT AVAILABLE with 1SA, 1SB, UN0, UP0.		
AG2	**6-Way Power Passenger's Side Seat (Base)**	271	305
	NOT AVAILABLE with 1SA, AR9, Leather Seat Trim, W01.		
AM6	**60/40 Split Bench Seat (Base)**	681	765
	Includes custom cloth seat trim, 6-way power driver's seat, driver's side-impact inflatable air bag, driver's side lumbar and split folding rear seat. NOT AVAILABLE with AR9.		
AR9	**Bucket Seats (Base)**	725	815
	Includes custom cloth seat trim, power driver's seat, driver's side air bag, driver's side lumbar, split folding rear seat and center console. NOT AVAILABLE with AG2, Leather Seat Trim, 1SA, W01.		
CF5	**Electric Sliding Sunroof**	623	700
	NOT AVAILABLE with 1SA.		
D58	**Spoiler Delete (LS)**	(156)	(175)
JL9	**4-Wheel Disc Antilock Brakes (Base)**	534	600
	Includes tire inflation sensor.		
K05	**Engine Block Heater**	18	20
K34	**Electronic Speed Control with Resume Speed (Base)**	214	240

IMPALA / LUMINA — CHEVROLET

CODE	DESCRIPTION	INVOICE	MSRP
L36	Engine: 3.8L SFI V6 (Base)	878	986
	Includes 4-wheel disc antilock brakes, traction control, ride and handling suspension and tire inflation sensor. REQUIRES QD1 and QNX. NOT AVAILABLE with 1SA.		
QD1	Wheels: Custom Aluminum (Base)	267	300
	NOT AVAILABLE with 1SA.		
QNX	Tire: P225/60R16N Touring (Base)	40	45
	NOT AVAILABLE with 1SA.		
U68	Driver Information/Convenience Center (Base)	245	275
	Includes trip computer, outside temperature, compass, universal garage door opener and anti-theft alarm system. REQUIRES JL9. NOT AVAILABLE with 1SA.		
UK3	Steering Wheel Radio Controls (Base)	152	171
	Includes leather-wrapped steering wheel. NOT AVAILABLE with 1SA.		
UL0	Radio: AM/FM Stereo with Cassette and Automatic Tone Control (Base)	251	282
	Includes seek-scan, digital clock, theft lock, speed compensated volume and 6 speakers in stategic locations. NOT AVAILABLE with UN0, UP0.		
UN0	Radio: AM/FM Stereo with CD and Automatic Tone Control (Base)	360	405
	Includes seek-scan, digital clock, theft lock, speed compensated volume and performance 8 speaker system with auxiliary amplifier. NOT AVAILABLE with UL0, UP0, WX9, 1SB, 1SC.		
UN0	Radio: AM/FM Stereo with CD and Automatic Tone Control (LS)	109	123
	Includes seek-scan, digital clock, theft lock, speed compensated volume and performance 8 speaker system with auxiliary amplifier. NOT AVAILABLE with UP0, WX9.		
UP0	Radio: AM/FM Stereo with CD and Cassette (Base)	449	505
	Includes seek-scan, digital clock, automatic tone control, dual playback remote cassette, theft lock, speed compensated volume and performance 8 speaker system with auxiliary amplifier. NOT AVAILABLE with UL0, UN0, WX9, 1SB, 1SC.		
UP0	Radio: AM/FM Stereo with CD and Cassette (LS)	198	223
	Includes seek-scan, digital clock, automatic tone control, dual playback remote cassette, theft lock, speed compensated volume and performance 8 speaker system with auxiliary amplifier. NOT AVAILABLE with UN0, WX9.		
W01	Comfort Seating Package	378	425
	Includes heated front seats. REQUIRES Leather Seat Trim. NOT AVAILABLE with 1SA, AG2, AR9, Custom Cloth Seat Trim.		
WX9	Remote CD Wiring Harness	71	80
	Includes performance 8 speaker system with auxiliary amplifier. REQUIRES UL0. NOT AVAILABLE with UN0, UP0.		

2000 LUMINA

What's New?

Base models receive additional standard equipment, while the standard 3.1-liter V6 gets more power and torque. The sporty LTZ and upscale LS models are dropped. This is the final year for the Lumina.

CHEVROLET — LUMINA

Review

While in college, one of our staffers attended the 1989 North American International Auto Show in Detroit. The 1990 Chevrolet Lumina was displayed at the show in coupe and sedan form, and this young man thought the vehicle was some kind of funky, ill-conceived concept car, like those oddly shaped safetymobiles created during the 1970s. Few showgoers even seemed to notice the silly silver Luminas as he inspected the angular styling - all the while wondering if GM had missed the boat on Ford's success with the Taurus. When the Lumina hit the streets for the 1990 model year, he couldn't help but chuckle every time one passed him on the street. Amazingly, the Lumina went on to become a bestseller, due in part to strong fleet sales.

These days, a different Lumina occupies Chevy showrooms. Chevy engineers claim the current-generation Lumina is the result of intensive consumer clinics, and that the car was designed in accordance with the research findings. A vast improvement over the first-generation model, the current Lumina offers an ergonomically correct, straightforward dashboard. The exterior shape is modern, but somewhat dull. Styling was not a strong issue among sedan buyers, a point well proven by the popularity of the previous-generation Lumina. Fortunately, Chevy saw fit to give the Lumina a tidy, attractive look that is marred only by a somewhat characterless and protruding proboscis.

Inside, seats could use more support and firmer padding. Controls, however, are easy to see and use, and fabrics are treated with Scotchgard to repel the occasional Dairy Queen spill. Lumina can be equipped with GM's OnStar Mobile Communications system, which uses a cellular phone and global positioning satellite to pinpoint the car's location for emergency purposes. The system can also be used to get directions when the driver is lost, or book reservations with a restaurant or an airline.

This is the final year for the Lumina. For 2000, the model lineup is trimmed to a single entry. That base model receives added standard equipment like a rear window defroster, power windows, a cargo net, and an uplevel sound system. Options include a suspension package that provides for tauter, more responsive handling, and an appearance package that includes alloy wheels, CD player and nicer cloth upholstery. The 3.1-liter V6 gains power and torque, helping to fill the void left by the departure of the 200-horse, 3.8-liter V6 on the options list. Upscale LS and sporty LTZ trims have been discontinued.

With a competent car and a pricing structure that undercuts Ford and Chrysler, Chevy's 2000 Lumina offers a blend of function and value that many Americans might find appealing - at the rental counter.

2000 Chevrolet Lumina

LUMINA — CHEVROLET

CODE	DESCRIPTION	INVOICE	MSRP

Standard Equipment

LUMINA (4A): 3.1L V6 OHV SMPI 12-valve engine; 4-speed electronic OD auto transmission with lock-up; 600-amp battery; 100-amp alternator; front-wheel drive, 3.29 axle ratio; stainless steel exhaust; comfort ride suspension, front independent strut suspension with anti-roll bar, front coil springs, rear independent strut suspension with anti-roll bar, rear coil springs; power rack-and-pinion steering; front disc/rear drum brakes; 16.6 gal. capacity fuel tank; side impact bars; front and rear body-colored bumpers with chrome bumper insert; body-colored bodyside molding with chrome bodyside insert; monotone paint; aero-composite halogen fully auto headlamps with daytime running lights; additional exterior lights include underhood light; driver's and passenger's power remote black outside mirrors; front and rear 15" x 6" steel wheels; P205/70SR15 touring BSW front and rear tires; inside under cargo mounted compact steel spare wheel; air conditioning, rear heat ducts; AM/FM stereo, clock, seek-scan, cassette, 4 performance speakers, auto equalizer, theft deterrent, and fixed antenna; cruise control; power door locks, child safety rear door locks; 1 power accessory outlet, driver's foot rest, smokers' package; instrumentation display includes water temperature gauge, trip odometer; warning indicators include oil pressure, water temp, battery, low oil level, low coolant, lights on, key in ignition, service interval; driver's and passenger's front airbags; ignition disable; tinted windows, power front and rear windows with driver's 1-touch down; variable intermittent front windshield wipers, sun visor strip, rear window defroster; seating capacity of 6, 60-40 split-bench front seat, adjustable headrests, center armrest with storage, driver's seat includes 4-way direction control, passenger's seat includes 4-way direction control; rear bench seat; front height adjustable seatbelts; cloth seats, cloth door trim insert, full cloth headliner, full carpet floor covering; interior lights include dome light with fade, front reading lights; steering wheel with tilt adjustment; vanity mirrors; day/night rearview mirror; locking glove box with light, front cupholder, 2 seat back storage pockets, driver's and passenger's door bins; carpeted cargo floor, cargo light; body-colored grille, chrome side window moldings, black front windshield molding, black rear window molding and body-colored door handles.

Base Prices

Code	Description	Invoice	MSRP
1WL69	Lumina (4A)	15878	18790
	Destination Charge:	560	560

Accessories

Code	Description	Invoice	MSRP
—	Custom Cloth Seat Trim	134	150
1SA	Preferred Equipment Group 1SA	NC	NC
	Includes vehicle with standard equipment.		
1SB	Preferred Equipment Group 1SB	285	320
	Includes front carpeted color-keyed floor mats, rear carpeted color-keyed floor mats, power trunk opener and remote keyless entry.		
B34	Front Carpeted Color-Keyed Floor Mats	18	20
	INCLUDED in 1SB.		
B35	Rear Carpeted Color-Keyed Floor Mats	18	20
	INCLUDED in 1SB.		
JM4	4-Wheel Antilock Brakes	512	575
K05	Engine Block Heater	18	20
UN0	Radio: AM/FM Stereo with CD and Automatic Tone Control	83	93
	Includes seek/scan, digital clock, auto tone control, theft lock, speed compensated volume and premium front and rear coaxial speakers.		
WG1	Power Driver's Seat	271	305

EDMUND'S® NEW CARS

CHEVROLET — LUMINA / MALIBU

CODE	DESCRIPTION	INVOICE	MSRP
WS1	Appearance Package	639	718
	Includes wheels: 16" aluminum, tires: P225/60R16 TOURING BSW, 60/40 split bench seat, custom cloth seat trim, AM/FM stereo with CD and auto tone control.		

2000 MALIBU

2000 Chevrolet Malibu

What's New?

Revised front styling ties Malibu to Impala, while the 1999's perfectly good brushed-aluminum wheels have been redesigned to look like Prizm hubcaps. The 3.1-liter V6 engine is standard this year, and has been improved to offer more horsepower while meeting low-emission vehicle (LEV) standards. And hold on to your hats - a spoiler and a gold package are available. Yikes! Where are the landau roof and whitewall tires, Chevy?

Review

Chevrolet is producing good cars and trucks. Witness the excellent values to be found in the Blazer, Camaro, Cavalier and Impala. The Malibu is more of a good thing. In fact, this is one of the best family cars produced by any domestic automaker today.

Consumer clinics determined much of the Malibu's design. What consumers have demanded is a tight, solid, roomy, fun-to-drive midsized sedan. Guess what? Chevrolet delivers, and delivers big with this car. The Malibu is all of these things and more, wrapped in unobtrusive yet attractive sheetmetal and sold at a price that undercuts similarly equipped imports and domestics.

Two models are available. For 2000, the base Malibu features a substantially improved 3.1-liter V6 engine, now making 170 horsepower and 190 foot-pounds of torque. What's more, this venerable motor meets low-emission vehicle (LEV) standards. Gears are shifted automatically, and standard equipment includes four-wheel antilock brakes, four-wheel independent suspension, battery rundown protection, theft deterrent system, tachometer, air-conditioning, rear-seat heat ducts, tilt steering wheel and remote trunk release. Step up to LS trim and you leave the showroom in a fully loaded car. The LS includes aluminum wheels, fog lights, remote

MALIBU — CHEVROLET

keyless entry, power driver's seat, power windows and door locks, cruise control, uplevel stereo, and a trunk cargo net.

This Chevy goes, slows and turns corners well enough to be entertaining, particularly with this year's boost in power. Interior design elements include a handy, left-handed cupholder, backlighting for major controls and switches throughout the interior, and heating and air conditioning ducts located on the A-pillar to help direct air flow to rear-seat passengers. Also notable is the retro-style dash-mounted ignition switch, because the driver doesn't have to crane his neck around to find the key slot.

Malibu has safety concerns covered, too. Dual airbags, four-wheel antilock brakes and child-safe rear door locks are standard. According to Chevrolet, side-impact door beams exceed federal standards for protection, though federal side-impact crash tests indicate that occupants may actually be rather vulnerable in this car. Maintaining the Malibu has been made easy with platinum-tipped spark plugs that last up to 100,000 miles, engine coolant designed to last five years or 150,000 miles, and transmission fluid that never has to be changed or checked.

Our list of gripes is short. The fake wood in the LS, revised for 2000, is unnecessary. We also want to find an integrated child safety seat on the options list in the future. And why can buyers get traction control on the Cavalier but not the Malibu? The list of improvements for 2000 doesn't address our concerns. Assist handles have been added to the headliner, door lockout protection is standard, and seat fabric has been revised. Mudguards front and rear are now body-color, and base wheel covers are redesigned.

Still, the Malibu impresses us. It's one of the few domestic models that can go toe-to-toe with the imports on comfort and features, while beating them on price.

Standard Equipment

BASE (4A): 3.1L V6 OHV SMPI 12-valve engine; 4-speed electronic OD auto transmission with lock-up; 600-amp battery with run down protection; 105-amp alternator; front-wheel drive, 3.05 axle ratio; stainless steel exhaust; front independent strut suspension with anti-roll bar, front coil springs, independent rear suspension with anti-roll bar, rear coil springs; power rack-and-pinion steering; front disc/rear drum brakes with 4-wheel antilock braking system; 15 gal. capacity fuel tank; front license plate bracket, side impact bars; front and rear body-colored bumpers; body-colored bodyside molding, rocker panel extensions; clearcoat monotone paint; aero-composite halogen fully auto headlamps with daytime running lights; body-colored folding driver's manual remote outside mirror, passenger's manual outside mirror; front and rear 15" x 6" steel wheels; P215/60SR15 A/S BSW front and rear tires; inside under cargo mounted compact steel spare wheel; air conditioning, rear heat ducts; AM/FM stereo, clock, seek-scan, 4 speakers, and fixed antenna; child safety rear door locks, power remote hatch/trunk release; 2 power accessory outlets, smoker's package; instrumentation display includes tachometer, water temperature gauge, trip odometer; warning indicators include oil pressure, battery, low coolant, lights on, key in ignition, low fuel, low washer fluid, door ajar; driver's and passenger's front airbags; ignition disable; tinted windows, manual front and rear windows; variable intermittent front windshield wipers; seating capacity of 5, front bucket seats, adjustable headrests, center armrest with storage, driver's seat includes 4-way direction control, passenger's seat includes 4-way direction control; rear bench seat with fixed headrests; front height adjustable seatbelts; cloth seats, cloth door trim insert, full cloth headliner, full carpet floor covering; interior lights include dome light with fade; steering wheel with tilt adjustment; vanity mirrors; day/night rearview mirror; full floor console, locking glove box with light, front and rear cupholders, instrument panel bin, driver's and passenger's door bins; carpeted cargo floor, cargo light; chrome grille, black side window moldings, black front windshield molding, black rear window molding and body-colored door handles.

LS (4A) (in addition to or instead of BASE (4A) equipment): Front license plate bracket, body-colored front and rear mud flaps; additional exterior lights include front fog/driving lights; driver's and passenger's power remote body-colored folding outside mirrors; AM/FM stereo, clock, seek-scan, cassette, single CD, 4 speakers, auto equalizer, theft deterrent, and fixed antenna; cruise control with steering wheel controls; power door locks with 2 stage unlock, remote keyless

CHEVROLET — MALIBU

entry, power remote hatch/trunk release; warning indicators include low oil level; power front and rear windows with driver's 1-touch down; rear window defroster; driver's seat includes 4-way power seat, 8-way direction control; 60-40 folding rear bench seat with fixed headrests, center armrest; premium cloth seats, carpeted floor mats; interior lights include front reading lights, illuminated entry; passenger's side illuminated vanity mirror and cargo net.

Base Prices

CODE	DESCRIPTION	INVOICE	MSRP
1ND69	Base (4A)	15061	16460
1NE69	LS (4A)	17467	19090
	Destination Charge:	535	535

Accessories

CODE	DESCRIPTION	INVOICE	MSRP
—	LS Special Leather Seat Trim (LS)	536	595
	Includes split folding rear seat and luggage area cargo net. INCLUDED in 1SB.		
1SA	Preferred Equipment Group 1SA	NC	NC
	Includes vehicle with standard equipment. REQUIRES C49 or R9W. NOT AVAILABLE with PF7, AG1, AUO.		
1SB	Preferred Equipment Group 1SB (Base)	1242	1380
	Includes AM/FM stereo with seek, scan and cassette, front and rear carpeted floor mats, dual exterior power remote mirrors, electric rear window defogger, power door locks, power windows and electronic cruise control with resume speed. NOT AVAILABLE with R9W, UNO, UN8.		
1SB	Preferred Equipment Group 1SB (LS)	1188	1320
	Includes LS special leather seat trim, split folding rear seat, luggage area cargo net, rear spoiler and electric sliding sunroof.		
AG1	Driver's Side Power Seat Adjuster (Base)	279	310
	NOT AVAILABLE with 1SA.		
AM9	Split Folding Rear Seat (Base)	176	195
	Includes luggage area cargo net. NOT AVAILABLE with 1SA.		
AU0	Remote Keyless Entry (Base)	135	150
	Includes lock-out protection. NOT AVAILABLE with 1SA.		
AU3	Power Door Locks (Base)	234	260
	INCLUDED in 1SB.		
B37	Front and Rear Carpeted Floor Mats (Base)	36	40
	Color-keyed. INCLUDED in 1SB.		
C49	Electric Rear Window Defogger (Base)	162	180
	NOT AVAILABLE with R9W. INCLUDED in 1SB.		
CF5	Electric Sliding Sunroof (LS)	585	650
	INCLUDED in 1SB.		
K05	Engine Block Heater	27	30
K34	Electronic Cruise Control with Resume Speed (Base)	202	225
	INCLUDED in 1SB.		
PF7	Wheels: 15" Aluminum (Base)	279	310
	NOT AVAILABLE with 1SA.		
R9W	Rear Window Defogger Not Desired (Base)	NC	NC
	NOT AVAILABLE with C49, 1SB.		

MALIBU / METRO — CHEVROLET

CODE	DESCRIPTION	INVOICE	MSRP
T43	Rear Spoiler (LS)	158	175
	Includes center high-mounted stop light. INCLUDED in 1SB.		
UL0	Radio: AM/FM Stereo with Cassette (Base)	198	220
	Includes digital clock, theft lock, speed compensated volume and auto tone control. NOT AVAILABLE with UN0, UN8. INCLUDED in 1SB.		
UN0	Radio: AM/FM Stereo and CD (Base)	288	320
	Includes digital clock, theft lock, speed compensated volume and auto tone control. NOT AVAILABLE with UL0, UN8, 1SB.		
UN0	Radio: AM/FM Stereo and CD (Base)	90	100
	Includes digital clock, theft lock, speed compensated volume and auto tone control. REQUIRES 1SB. NOT AVAILABLE with UL0, UN8, 1SA.		
UN8	Radio: AM/FM Stereo with Cassette and CD (Base)	378	420
	Includes seek-scan, digital clock, theft lock, speed compensated volume and auto tone control. NOT AVAILABLE with UL0, UN0, 1SB.		
UN8	Radio: AM/FM Stereo with Cassette and CD (Base)	180	200
	Includes seek-scan, digital clock, theft lock, speed compensated volume and auto tone control. REQUIRES 1SB. NOT AVAILABLE with UL0, UN0, 1SA.		
VH4	Body Color Front and Rear Mud Guards (Base)	68	75
Y11	Gold Package (LS)	86	95
	Includes exterior front and rear and interior gold appearance emblems.		

2000 METRO

2000 Chevrolet Metro

What's New?

Two new colors help buyers differentiate between 1999 and 2000 Metros.

CHEVROLET — METRO

CODE	DESCRIPTION	INVOICE	MSRP

Review

General Motors calls the 2000 Metro "a low-cost vehicle that provides new-car peace of mind and excellent fuel economy to the buyer shopping for reliable transportation." Fair enough, being that most small cars are cheap and get good gas mileage. But what we have here is automotive transport in its most basic form competing with larger, more powerful Korean entries and certified used cars from big-brand Japanese automakers. This market climate does not spell success for Metro. As any good comparison shopper will tell you, a bargain is only a bargain in comparison to what else is available for the same price.

So what other new vehicles are even available in this class? Chevy lists only three direct competitors for the Metro, all of them imports: the Hyundai Accent, the Kia Sephia and Metro's twin, the Suzuki Swift. True, Hyundai's reliability record is unimpressive, but recent indicators point to improved build quality in the Accent, which has a longer list of standard equipment and a far better warranty than the little Chevy. Plus, it's been redesigned for 2000, and improved in every way. And for our money, Kia's Sephia feels more substantial than the Canadian-built Metro. In contrast, the Metro comes across as a tinny, bare bones econocar. Finally, the Swift is essentially identical to the Metro, but without the Chevy's roadside-assistance coverage or extensive dealership network. On the used-car market, a buyer could select a certified used Honda Civic or Toyota Corolla and get more passenger room, more powerful engines, and world-renowned reputations for reliability.

Metro does feature dual depowered airbags, but in the way of standard equipment the base hatchback comes with little else. LSi models add a few convenience items, but this trim level is the ticket to many much-desired accessories such as remote exterior mirrors, a rear wiper/washer and an automatic transmission. A tiny, 1.0-liter three-cylinder engine attempts to motivate the base Metro with its 55 horsepower, but we know of some personal watercraft with more oomph. The LSi gets a 79-horsepower four-cylinder. Still, the Metro LSi is no stoplight sprinter, and the base hatchback is pathetically sluggish.

We don't recommend the Metro, and new paint colors for 2000 aren't going to do much to change our opinion of the baby Chevy. Why not? Because a fully loaded LSi Sedan tops $14,000 with an automatic transmission and antilock brakes. That's Chevy Prizm and Ford Focus territory, folks, and they are both in a different - and, let's face it, a much better - league than the Metro. Our advice in this low-cost segment remains to try the Accent or Sephia. If a Korean-assembled car doesn't sit well with you, get a nice used Honda or Toyota. You will probably be happier with it.

Standard Equipment

BASE COUPE (5M): 1.0L I3 SOHC SPI 6-valve engine; 5-speed OD manual transmission; 390-amp battery; 55-amp alternator; front-wheel drive, 4.39 axle ratio; partial stainless steel exhaust; front independent strut suspension with anti-roll bar, front coil springs, rear independent strut suspension with anti-roll bar, rear coil springs; manual rack-and-pinion steering; front disc/rear drum brakes; 10.3 gal. capacity fuel tank; front and rear black bumpers; monotone paint; aero-composite halogen headlamps with daytime running lights; driver's and passenger's manual black outside mirrors; front and rear 13" x 4.5" steel wheels; P155/80SR13 A/S BSW front and rear tires; inside under cargo mounted compact steel spare wheel; radio prep, 4 speakers, and manual retractable antenna; 1 power accessory outlet, smokers' package; instrumentation display includes water temperature gauge; warning indicators include oil pressure, battery, lights on, key in ignition; driver's and passenger's front airbags; tinted windows, fixed rear windows; seating capacity of 4, front bucket seats, fixed headrests, driver's seat includes 4-way direction control, passenger's seat includes 4-way direction control; full folding rear bench seat; cloth seats, vinyl door trim insert, full cloth headliner, full carpet floor covering, plastic/rubber gear shift knob; interior lights include dome light; day/night rearview mirror; full floor console, glove box, front cupholder, instrument panel bin, driver's and passenger's door bins; carpeted cargo floor, plastic trunk lid; black side window moldings, black front windshield molding, black rear window molding and black door handles.

METRO — CHEVROLET

LSi COUPE (5M) (in addition to or instead of BASE COUPE (5M) equipment): 1.3L I4 SOHC MPI 16-valve engine; 3.79 axle ratio; front and rear body-colored bumpers; black bodyside molding; instrumentation display includes trip odometer; premium cloth seats and passenger's side vanity mirror.

LSi SEDAN (5M) (in addition to or instead of LSi COUPE (5M) equipment): Child safety rear door locks and manual front and rear windows.

Base Prices

Code	Description	Invoice	MSRP
1MR08	Base Coupe (5M)	8652	9185
1MR08-B4M	LSi Coupe (5M)	9353	10035
1MR69	LSi Sedan (5M)	9889	10610
	Destination Charge:	380	380

Accessories

Code	Description	Invoice	MSRP
1SA	Preferred Equipment Group 1SA (Base Coupe/Sedan) *Includes vehicle with standard equipment. REQUIRES (C60 or R6G) and (C49 or R9W). NOT AVAILABLE with 1SB.*	NC	NC
1SB	Preferred Equipment Group 1SB (Base Coupe) *Includes front and rear carpeted floor mats, body side moldings and easy entry passenger's seat. REQUIRES C60 and (C49 or R9W).*	102	115
1SB	Preferred Equipment Group 1SB (Sedan) *Includes air conditioning, AM/FM stereo with seek and clock, front and rear carpeted floor mats, convenience package: dual manual remote mirrors, remote trunk release, split folding rear seat, trunk light; power door locks and power steering. REQUIRES C49 or R9W. NOT AVAILABLE with 1SA, R6G, R9J.*	1593	1790
1SD	Preferred Equipment Group 1SD (LSi Coupe) *Includes vehicle with standard equipment. REQUIRES (C60 or R6G) and (C49 or R9W).*	NC	NC
B37	Front and Rear Carpeted Floor Mats (Base Coupe/LSi Sedan) *Color-Keyed. INCLUDED in 1SB.*	36	40
B84	Body Side Moldings (Base Coupe) *INCLUDED in 1SB.*	44	50
C25	Rear Window Wiper/Washer (LSi Coupe) *REQUIRES C49.*	111	125
C49	Rear Window Defogger *NOT AVAILABLE with R9W.*	142	160
C60	Air Conditioning *NOT AVAILABLE with R6G. INCLUDED in 1SB (Sedan).*	699	785
FE9	Federal Emission Requirements	NC	NC
JM4	4-Wheel Antilock Brakes	503	565
MX1	Transmission: 3-Speed Automatic (LSi) *Includes 3.61 axle ratio.*	530	595
N41	Power Steering (LSi Sedan) *INCLUDED in 1SB.*	258	290
NC7	Federal Emission Override (LSi Sedan) *REQUIRES YF5.*	NC	NC

CHEVROLET
METRO / MONTE CARLO

CODE	DESCRIPTION	INVOICE	MSRP
R6G	Air Conditioning	NC	NC
	NOT AVAILABLE with C60.		
R9J	Radio Provision	NC	NC
	NOT AVAILABLE with UM7, UM6, U1C, 1SB.		
R9W	Rear Window Defogger	NC	NC
	NOT AVAILABLE with C49.		
U16	Tachometer (LSi)	62	70
U16	Tachometer with Trip Odometer (Base Coupe)	62	70
U1C	Radio: AM/FM Stereo with CD (LSi Sedan)	236	265
	Includes seek, digital clock and theft lock. REQUIRES 1SB. NOT AVAILABLE with R9J, UM7, UM6.		
U1C	Radio: AM/FM Stereo with CD	530	595
	Includes seek/scan, digital clock, theft lock and 4 speakers. REQUIRES 1SA (Except LSi Coupe). NOT AVAILABLE with R9J, UM7, UM6.		
UM6	Radio: AM/FM Stereo with Cassette (LSi Sedan)	147	165
	Includes seek/scan, digital clock and 4 speakers. REQUIRES 1SB. NOT AVAILABLE with R9J, UM7, U1C.		
UM6	Radio: AM/FM Stereo with Cassette	441	495
	Includes seek/scan, digital clock and 4 speakers. REQUIRES 1SA (Except LSi Coupe). NOT AVAILABLE with R9J, UM7, U1C.		
UM7	Radio: AM/FM Stereo with Seek and Clock	294	330
	Includes 4 speakers. NOT AVAILABLE with R9J, UM6, U1C. INCLUDED in 1SB.		
YF5	California Emission Requirements	NC	NC
Z05	Convenience Package (LSi Coupe)	111	125
	Includes dual manual remote mirrors, cargo security cover and easy entry passenger seat. INCLUDED in 1SB.		

2000 MONTE CARLO

What's New?

Chevy's large personal-luxury coupe is all-new for 2000, based on the Impala platform and sporting distinctive, heritage styling cues.

Review

Heritage design is all the rage these days, and Chevrolet has employed this styling trend on the all-new 2000 Monte Carlo. From the traditional "Knight's Crest" badge, script lettering and distinctive headlight treatment to the sculpted fenders and vertical taillights, the new Monte Carlo strongly recalls the '70s and '80s models that made the nameplate a hit.

Under the skin, the Monte Carlo shares a platform with the Chevrolet Impala, which means this is a big coupe - a full Monte, if you will. Two models are available: LS comes equipped with a 3.4-liter V6 engine making 180 horsepower, while SS benefits from 20 additional ponies and more torque, thanks to the venerable 3.8-liter V6 under the hood. Either model comes well-equipped, but to emphasize performance, the SS gets fog lights, rocker-panel moldings, a rear spoiler, 16-inch alloy wheels, a full complement of gauges and twin exhaust outlets routed from dual mufflers.

A tower-to-tower structural brace under the hood, combined with a magnesium dashboard support beam, contributes to a rigid platform, improves handling and helps reduce squeaks

MONTE CARLO — CHEVROLET

| CODE | DESCRIPTION | INVOICE | MSRP |

and rattles. Large four-wheel antilock disc brakes with front cooling ducts provide confidence-inspiring stopping ability. A four-wheel independent MacPherson strut suspension is matched to front and rear stabilizer bars and meaty Goodyear Eagle RS-A performance tires to help make Monte Carlo fun in the curves. But you're going to have to settle for an automatic transmission in this Chevy; a manual is not available. Traction control is standard and available only on SS.

Inside, buyers looking for healthy doses of comfort will find it in Monte Carlo. Boasting plenty of interior room, the MC's innards were designed specifically to maximize harmony between the car and the driver. Special attention was paid to control placement and seat design, and engineers strove to provide top-notch brake pedal and steering feel. Good visibility, thanks to generous glass areas, a standard rear-window defogger, and large side-view mirrors, is a new Monte Carlo hallmark, though the wide C-pillars likely block vision in certain parking and lane change maneuvers.

All Monte Carlos come with air conditioning, power door locks, power windows, tilt steering wheel, a driver message center with oil life monitor, RDS radio technology, theatre-dimming interior lighting, daytime running lights, and a tire-pressure monitor. Step up to the SS model, and you get, in addition to traction control and performance/cosmetic enhancements, a cargo net, cruise control, leather-wrapped steering wheel with redundant audio controls, remote keyless entry, dual-zone temperature controls and a pollen filter. Options include leather seating, premium stereo with CD player, power front seats, heated exterior mirrors, and a power sunroof. If desired, the dealer can install GM's On Star communications system and a trap-resistant trunk kit designed to prevent a child from becoming locked in the luggage compartment.

By all indications, the 2000 Monte Carlo is a tremendous improvement over the bland Lumina-based coupe it replaces.

2000 Chevrolet Monte Carlo

Standard Equipment

LS (4A): 3.4L V6 OHV SMPI 12-valve engine; 4-speed electronic OD auto transmission with lock-up; 600-amp battery; 100-amp alternator; front-wheel drive, 2.86 axle ratio; stainless steel exhaust; touring ride suspension, front independent strut suspension with anti-roll bar, front coil springs, rear independent strut suspension with anti-roll bar, rear coil springs; power rack-and-pinion steering; 4-wheel disc brakes with 4-wheel antilock braking system; 17 gal. capacity fuel tank; side impact bars; front and rear body-colored bumpers with chrome bumper insert; body-colored bodyside molding rocker panel extensions; monotone paint; aero-composite halogen fully auto headlamps with daytime running lights; driver's and passenger's power remote body-

CHEVROLET — MONTE CARLO

colored outside mirrors; front and rear 16" x 6.5" steel wheels; P225/60SR16 touring A/S BSW front and rear tires; inside under cargo mounted compact steel spare wheel; air conditioning, rear heat ducts; AM/FM stereo, clock, seek-scan, cassette, 4 speakers, auto equalizer, theft deterrent, and window grid antenna; power door locks, power remote hatch/trunk release; 1 power accessory outlet, driver's foot rest, smokers' package; instrumentation display includes tachometer, water temperature gauge, trip odometer; warning indicators include battery, low oil level, low coolant, lights on, key in ignition, service interval; driver's and passenger's front airbags; ignition disable; tinted windows, power windows with driver's 1-touch down; variable intermittent front windshield wipers, sun visor strip, rear window defroster; seating capacity of 5, front bucket seats, adjustable headrests, center armrest with storage, driver's seat includes 4-way direction control, passenger's seat includes 4-way direction control; 60-40 folding rear bench seat with fixed headrests, center armrest; cloth seats, cloth door trim insert, full cloth headliner, full carpet floor covering with carpeted floor mats; interior lights include dome light with fade, front reading lights; steering wheel with tilt adjustment; vanity mirrors, dual auxiliary visors; day/night rearview mirror; full floor console, mini overhead console with storage, locking glove box with light, front and rear cupholders, 2 seat back storage pockets, driver's and passenger's door bins; carpeted cargo floor, cargo light; body-colored grille, black side window moldings, black front windshield molding, black rear window molding and body-colored door handles.

SS (4A) (in addition to or instead of LS (4A) equipment): 3.8L V6 OHV SMPI 12-valve engine; traction control, 3.29 axle ratio; sport ride suspension, rear wing spoiler; front and rear body-colored bumpers with black bumper insert; additional exterior lights include front fog/driving lights; P225/60SR16 performance A/S BSW front and rear tires; dual zone front air conditioning, air filter; radio steering wheel controls; power door locks with 2 stage unlock, remote keyless entry; instrumentation display includes oil pressure gauge, volt gauge; front sports seats, adjustable headrests, driver's seat includes 4-way direction control, lumbar support; interior lights include illuminated entry; leather-wrapped steering wheel with tilt adjustment; dual illuminated vanity mirrors and cargo net.

Base Prices

Code	Description	Invoice	MSRP
1WW27	LS (4A)	17650	19290
1WX27	SS (4A)	19888	21735
	Destination Charge:	560	560

Accessories

Code	Description	Invoice	MSRP
—	Leather Seat Trim *REQUIRES AG1.*	556	625
1SA	Preferred Equipment Group 1SA *Includes vehicle with standard equipment. NOT AVAILABLE with UK3, CF5, DK5, DD6.*	NC	NC
1SB	Preferred Equipment Group 1SB (LS) *Includes speed control with resume speed, driver's and passenger's temperature controls, remote keyless entry, dual illuminated visor vanity mirrors, cargo net and wheels: styled aluminum.*	817	918
1SB	Preferred Equipment Group 1SB (SS) *Includes driver's information convenience center, trip computer, outside temperature and compass display, programmable garage door opener, anti-theft alarm system, dual power exterior heated mirrors, 6-way power driver's seat and electrochromic rearview mirror.*	655	736
AG1	6-Way Power Driver's Seat *INCLUDED in 1SB (SS).*	271	305

MONTE CARLO / PRIZM — CHEVROLET

CODE	DESCRIPTION	INVOICE	MSRP
AG2	6-Way Power Passenger's Seat *REQUIRES AG1.*	271	305
AU0	Remote Keyless Entry (LS) *INCLUDED in 1SB.*	147	165
CF5	Electric Sliding Sunroof *NOT AVAILABLE with 1SA.*	623	700
CJ3	Driver's and Passenger's Temperature Controls (LS) *INCLUDED in 1SB.*	89	100
D58	Spoiler Delete (SS)	(156)	(175)
DD6	Electrochromic ISRV Mirror (LS) *Includes dual reading/map lamps. NOT AVAILABLE with 1SA.*	108	121
DK5	Dual Power Exterior Heated Mirrors (LS) *NOT AVAILABLE with 1SA.*	31	35
K05	Engine Block Heater	18	20
K34	Speed Control with Resume Speed (LS) *INCLUDED in 1SB.*	214	240
KA1	Driver's and Passenger's Heated Seats *REQUIRES AG1 and AG2 and Leather Seat Trim.*	107	120
QD1	Wheels: Styled Aluminum (LS) *INCLUDED in 1SB.*	267	300
U68	Driver's Information Convenience Center (LS) *Includes trip computer, outside temperature and compass display, programmable garage door opener and anti-theft alarm system. NOT AVAILABLE with 1SA.*	245	275
UK3	Steering Wheel Radio Controls (LS) *Includes leather-wrapped steering wheel. NOT AVAILABLE with 1SA.*	152	171
UN0	Radio: AM/FM Stereo with CD and Automatic Tone Control *Includes seek/scan, digital clock, auto tone control, theft lock, speed compensated volume, radio data system technology (RDS), antenna located in rear glass, premium 6 speaker system and auxiliary amplifier. NOT AVAILABLE with UP0, WX9.*	109	123
UP0	Radio: AM/FM Stereo with CD, Cassette and Automatic Tone Control *Includes seek/scan, digital clock, auto tone control, dual playback cassette, theft lock, speed compensated volume, radio data system technology (RDS), antenna located in rear glass, premium 6 speaker system and auxiliary amplifier. NOT AVAILABLE with UN0, WX9.*	198	223
VK3	Cosmetic Cover (SS) *Covers bumper molded license plate holder.*	NC	NC
WX9	Remote CD Wiring Harness *Includes premium 6 speaker system with auxiliary amplifier. NOT AVAILABLE with UN0, UP0.*	71	80

2000 PRIZM

What's New?

New standard features improve the Prizm's value quotient, and variable valve timing boosts power and torque. The tweaked engine now meets low-emission vehicle status in California, and three new colors freshen the exterior.

CHEVROLET — PRIZM

CODE	DESCRIPTION	INVOICE	MSRP

Review

In short, the Prizm is one of the best compact cars money can buy. It does everything well, and looks good too. Better yet, it is essentially a reskinned Toyota Corolla, which bodes well for reliability, but not necessarily resale value. To top things off, the Prizm has earned very high marks in past initial quality studies, scoring better than the Infiniti G20 and Honda Accord.

But there is a problem, and that problem is price. Slotted between the Cavalier and Malibu, the small Prizm is no bargain once options are added. A well-equipped Prizm can be more expensive than a similarly loaded Malibu. For 2000, Chevrolet is trying to boost Prizm's value by offering more standard equipment in the base price. Bottom-rung models get air conditioning, a four-speaker stereo, floor mats and wheel covers this year, while LSi buyers receive standard power windows, rear defogger, tachometer with outside temperature gauge, tilt steering column and larger tires.

Despite the price of entry, there are compelling reasons to choose the Prizm. Its excellent reliability record, coupled with tasteful styling and outstanding assembly quality, goes a long way toward selling consumers on the Prizm. The car feels substantial, conveying the impression that it will last quite a long time. In contrast, the Cavalier feels somewhat cheap, flimsy and unrefined. The solid Malibu doesn't appeal to buyers looking for a smaller package.

A 1.8-liter four-cylinder engine is standard on all Prizms, and for 2000, benefits from variable valve timing technology that certainly didn't come from GM. Toyota's VVTi system boosts power in Prizm to 125 horsepower and 125 foot-pounds of torque, both peaking at lower rpm than last year. Interestingly, side airbags are optional on this economy sedan. Front and rear stabilizer bars are standard to improve handling response from the four-wheel independent suspension. All interior fabrics feature Scotchgard stain protection and a power sunroof is available. As on last year's model - and in a break with GM tradition - antilock brakes are optional rather than standard.

Interior accommodations are rather sparse in base Prizms, but LSi's come with uplevel fittings and trim. Either model offers excellent ergonomics; all the switches and controls fall readily to hand and the gauges are clear and legible. The seats are firm but comfortable, and Chevrolet has deleted the optional integrated child safety seat for 2000. The clutch is a joy to work and the five-speed manual snicks fluidly from gear to gear.

Prizm is strictly econo-issue in base trim, but add aluminum wheels and a premium equipment package to an LSi and the Prizm transforms itself into a mini-Camry. Also available is a CD player and extended-range speakers that sound great. Truly, a fully loaded Prizm is a fine package. However, a Prizm LSi with every available option closes quickly on $20,000. For that kind of cash you can buy any number of larger and more substantial sedans. Keep a lid on the options, though and the Prizm makes much more sense.

Standard Equipment

BASE (5M): 1.8L I4 DOHC SMPI 16-valve engine; 5-speed OD manual transmission; 390-amp battery; 80-amp alternator; front-wheel drive, 3.72 axle ratio; stainless steel exhaust; front independent strut suspension with anti-roll bar, front coil springs, rear independent strut suspension with anti-roll bar, rear coil springs; power rack-and-pinion steering; front disc/rear drum brakes; 13.2 gal. capacity fuel tank; side impact bars; front and rear body-colored bumpers; black bodyside molding; monotone paint; aero-composite halogen fully auto headlamps with daytime running lights; driver's and passenger's manual remote black outside mirrors; front and rear 14" x 5.5" silver styled steel wheels; P175/65SR14 A/S BSW front and rear tires; inside under cargo mounted compact steel spare wheel; air conditioning, rear heat ducts; AM/FM stereo, clock, seek-scan, 4 speakers, and fixed antenna; child safety rear door locks, remote hatch/trunk release, remote fuel release; 1 power accessory outlet, driver's foot rest, smokers' package; instrumentation display includes water temperature gauge, trip odometer; warning indicators include oil pressure, water temp, battery, lights on, key in ignition, low fuel, door ajar, brake fluid; driver's and passenger's front airbags; tinted windows, manual front and rear windows; variable intermittent front windshield wipers, sun visor strip; seating capacity of 5, front bucket seats, adjustable headrests, driver's seat includes 4-way direction control, passenger's

PRIZM — CHEVROLET

seat includes 4-way direction control; rear bench seat with fixed headrests; front height adjustable seatbelts with front pretensioners; cloth seats, cloth door trim insert, full cloth headliner, full carpet floor covering with carpeted floor mats, plastic/rubber gear shift knob; interior lights include dome light with delay; vanity mirrors; day/night rearview mirror; full floor console, glove box with light, front and rear cupholders, instrument panel covered bin, driver's and passenger's door bins; carpeted cargo floor, cargo light; black grille, black side window moldings, black front windshield molding, black rear window molding and black door handles.

LSi (5M) (in addition to or instead of BASE (5M) equipment): Driver's and passenger's power remote black outside mirrors; P185/65SR14 A/S BSW front tires; AM/FM stereo, clock, seek-scan, cassette, 4 speakers, and fixed antenna; cruise control; power door locks, remote keyless entry; instrumentation display includes tachometer, exterior temp; power front and rear windows with driver's 1-touch down; rear window defroster; center armrest with storage; 60-40 folding rear bench seat with fixed headrests, center pass-thru armrest; premium cloth seats; interior lights include illuminated entry; steering wheel with tilt adjustment and 2 seat back storage pockets.

Base Prices

Code	Description	Invoice	MSRP
1SK19	Base (5M)	13153	13816
1SK19-B4M	LSi (5M)	14606	15842
	Destination Charge:	430	430

2000 Chevrolet Prizm

Accessories

Code	Description	Invoice	MSRP
—	Cloth Seat Trim (Base) *Dark charcoal.*	NC	NC
—	Cloth Seat Trim (Base) *Light neutral.*	NC	NC
1SA	Preferred Equipment Group 1 (Base) *Includes vehicle with standard equipment. REQUIRES R9W or C49.*	NC	NC

CHEVROLET — PRIZM

CODE	DESCRIPTION	INVOICE	MSRP
1SB	Preferred Equipment Group 2 (Base)	490	570
	Includes power door locks, AM/FM stereo with cassette and electronic cruise control with resume speed. REQUIRES C49 or R9W. NOT AVAILABLE with U1C.		
1SE	Preferred Equipment Group 1 (LSi)	NC	- NC
	Includes vehicle with standard equipment.		
9J6	Tilt Steering (Base)	69	80
A31	Power Windows (Base)	258	300
	REQUIRES AU3.		
AJ7	Driver's and Passenger's Side Airbags	254	295
AN2	Integrated Child Safety Seat (LSi)	108	125
	Located in right rear passenger's seat.		
AU3	Power Door Locks (Base)	189	220
	Includes driver's and passenger's side switch. INCLUDED in 1SB.		
C49	Rear Window Defogger (Base)	155	180
	NOT AVAILABLE with R9W.		
CF5	Electric Sunroof	580	675
	Includes map lights.		
JM4	4-Wheel Antilock Brakes	555	645
K34	Electronic Cruise Control with Resume Speed (Base)	159	185
	INCLUDED in 1SB.		
MS7	Transmission: 4-Speed Automatic	688	800
	Includes 2.65 axle ratio. NOT AVAILABLE with MX1.		
MX1	Transmission: 3-Speed Automatic	426	495
	Includes 3.23 axle ratio. NOT AVAILABLE with MS7.		
PG4	Wheels: 14" Alloy	243	283
R9W	Rear Window Defogger (Base)	NC	NC
	NOT AVAILABLE with C49.		
U16	Tachometer (Base)	60	70
	Includes outside temperature gauge.		
U1C	Radio: AM/FM Stereo with CD (Base)	185	215
	Includes digital clock, theft lock and 4 premium coaxial speakers. NOT AVAILABLE with UM6, 1SB.		
U1C	Radio: AM/FM Stereo with CD	43	50
	Includes digital clock, theft lock and 4 premium coaxial speakers. NOT AVAILABLE with UM6, 1SA.		
UM6	Radio: AM/FM Stereo with Cassette (Base)	142	165
	Includes seek/scan, digital clock and 4 premium coaxial speakers. NOT AVAILABLE with U1C. INCLUDED in 1SB.		

CHRYSLER

300M

| CODE | DESCRIPTION | INVOICE | MSRP |

2000 300M

2000 Chrysler 300M

What's New?

There are five new colors, interior upgrades such as rear-seat cupholders and color-keyed switches, and a four-disc in-dash CD player. The rear suspension has been improved for less noise, vibration and harshness. The 2000 has the brake-shift interlock safety feature, which won't allow the driver to shift out of "park" unless his foot is on the brake.

Review

The 300M is the year-old iteration of Chrysler's sport sedan. Its styling and letter-series designation pick up where the original '55-'65 muscle cars left off—take one look at its big center grille and fin-like taillights, and you'll be just a notch ahead of your flashback.

For this driver-oriented modernized muscle car, there's a 3.5-liter aluminum, high-output V6 (shared with the Chrysler LHS and the Plymouth Prowler), and it offers respectable power for its size: 253 horsepower at 6,400 rpm and 255 foot-pounds of torque at 3,950 rpm. That's more power than you'll find in such performance sedans as the BMW M3 (a 3.2-liter making 240 horses) and the Ford Taurus SHO (a 3.4-liter worth 235 horses). The next-generation 300M is scheduled for the '04 model year and will use Jeep Grand Cherokee-based V8 power (and maybe even rear-wheel drive), but until then, the V6 is a plenty potent engine.

The performance theme of the 300M continues underneath. The fully independent suspension has a soft-ride setting as standard, but there's an optional, more aggressive European-tuned performance choice should you want to let the car strut its stuff. We'd opt for the European suspension, just for the promise of enhanced driving experience. In either soft or taut setting, however, the steering remains first-rate.

The 300M is affectionately known as the 5-meter car (its length is 197.8 inches, or 5.02 meters)— Chrysler says that the length was an important consideration from the start, and claims that it can be parked in smaller European garages. The 300M's platform is shared between the Dodge Intrepid and the Chrysler Concorde and LHS, but the 300M is the best of the bunch in terms of sportiness and fun to drive.

We're disappointed that the 300M's only transmission is still just an automatic. Chrysler tried to make up for it with the AutoStick, which gives manual control of an auto transmission. But it's definitely not the same thing. In addition to the automatic, other standard features include a

CHRYSLER 300M

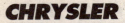

leather interior, air conditioning, four-wheel ABS, an Infinity 240-watt sound system, eight-way power seats (heated), and 17-inch wheels. New-for-2000 colors are Dark Garnet Red, Inferno Red Tinted Clear Coat, Shale Green Metallic, Steel Blue and Bright Silver Metallic.

Says Chrysler chief engineer Bob Rodger, "The 300 idea is the idea of a powerful, nimble, responsive automotive machine." Of course, Rodger made those comments more than 40 years ago. Amazing how history really does repeat itself.

Standard Equipment

300M (4A): 3.5L V6 SOHC SMPI 24-valve engine; 4-speed electronic OD auto transmission with lock-up; 600-amp battery with run down protection; HD radiator; 130-amp alternator; automanual transmission; front-wheel drive, traction control, 3.55 axle ratio; stainless steel exhaust; touring ride suspension, front independent strut suspension with anti-roll bar, front coil springs, rear independent multi-link suspension with anti-roll bar, rear coil springs; power rack-and-pinion steering; 4-wheel disc brakes with 4-wheel antilock braking system; 17 gal. capacity fuel tank; side impact bars; front and rear body-colored bumpers; body-colored bodyside molding, rocker panel extensions; monotone paint; aero-composite halogen fully auto headlamps, delay-off feature; additional exterior lights include front fog/driving lights; driver's and passenger's power remote black heated outside mirrors; front and rear 17" x 7" silver alloy wheels; P225/55SR17 touring A/S BSW front and rear tires; inside under cargo mounted compact steel spare wheel; air conditioning with climate control, rear heat ducts; AM stereo/FM stereo, seek-scan, cassette, single CD, 9 premium speakers, amplifier, graphic equalizer, and window grid antenna; cruise control with steering wheel controls; power door locks, remote keyless entry, child safety rear door locks, power remote hatch/trunk release; 1 power accessory outlet, driver's foot rest, garage door opener; instrumentation display includes tachometer, water temperature gauge, clock, compass, exterior temp, trip computer, trip odometer; warning indicators include oil pressure, water temp, battery, lights on, key in ignition, low fuel, low washer fluid, door ajar, trunk ajar; driver's and passenger's front airbags; ignition disable, panic alarm, security system; tinted windows, power front and rear windows with driver's 1-touch down; variable intermittent front windshield wipers, sun visor strip, rear window defroster; seating capacity of 5, heated-cushion front bucket seats, adjustable tilt headrests, center armrest with storage, driver's seat includes 6-way power seat, lumbar support, passenger's seat includes 6-way power seat; 60-40 folding rear bench seat with adjustable headrests, center armrest; front height adjustable seatbelts; leather seats, leatherette door trim insert, full cloth headliner, full carpet floor covering with carpeted floor mats, simulated wood trim on instrument panel, leather-wrapped gear shift knob; memory on driver's seat with 2 memory setting(s) includes settings for exterior mirrors; interior lights include dome light with fade, front and rear reading lights, 4 door curb lights, illuminated entry; leather-wrapped steering wheel with tilt adjustment; dual illuminated vanity mirrors, dual auxiliary visors; auto-dimming day/night rearview mirror; full floor console, mini overhead console locking glove box with light, front and rear cupholders, 2 seat back storage pockets, driver's and passenger's door bins; carpeted cargo floor, cargo net, cargo light; chrome grille, black side window moldings, black front windshield molding, black rear window molding and body-colored door handles.

Base Prices

Code	Description	Invoice	MSRP
LHYS41	300M (4A)	26661	29085
	Destination Charge:	605	605

Accessories

Code	Description	Invoice	MSRP
26M	Quick Order Package 26M	NC	NC
	Includes vehicle with standard equipment. REQUIRES EGG and DGB.		
ADE	Cold Weather Group	27	30
	Includes battery heater and engine block heater.		

300M / CIRRUS — CHRYSLER

CODE	DESCRIPTION	INVOICE	MSRP
ARF	Radio: AM/FM Cassette and CD Changer	458	515
	Includes 360-Watt amplifier, 4-disc in-dash CD changer with changer control and 11 Infinity speakers in 9 locations.		
AWS	Smokers' Group	18	20
	Includes front and rear ash receiver and cigar lighter.		
AWT	16" Performance Handling Group	445	500
	Includes performance 4-wheel antilock disc brakes, high speed engine controller, performance steering, performance suspension, tires: P225/60VR16 performance A/S BSW and wheels: 16" aluminum. NOT AVAILABLE with WFH.		
DGB	Transmission: 4-Speed Automatic	NC	NC
EGG	Engine: 3.5 L High Output V6 24V MPI	NC	NC
GWA	Power Sunroof	797	895
PEL	Inferno Red Tinted Pearl Coat	178	200
TBW	Tire: Full Size Spare	325	365
	Includes wheel: matching spare.		
TBW	Tire: Full Size Spare	191	215
	Includes wheel: matching spare. NOT AVAILABLE with WFH, WNE.		
WFH	Wheels: 17" Chrome Aluminum	668	750
	NOT AVAILABLE with AWT, WNE, TBW.		
WNE	Wheels: 16" Chrome Aluminum	668	750
	REQUIRES AWT. NOT AVAILABLE with WFH, TBW.		

2000 CIRRUS

What's New?

With a redesigned Cirrus modeled after the exceptionally attractive Concorde due in showrooms for 2001, the 2000 model is essentially a carryover model. Child-seat tethers have been added behind the back seat, and four new colors debut.

Review

We really like the Chrysler Cirrus. It offers more car for the money than nearly anything else in the compact class. With a standard-equipment list that includes everything from power goodies and a premium sound system to a 2.5-liter V6 engine and leather seats, Cirrus is actually competitive with many luxury sedans from the U.S. and Japan at a fraction of the price. All of these accouterments are perfect for turning the Cirrus into the ideal car for empty-nesters or young individuals who don't need or want a big car, but who like the luxurious touch.

But for that low price, you give up a certain degree of refinement. Cirrus is constructed using cheap materials, and can be loud on the highway. The standard Mitsubishi-sourced V6 thrashes when pushed. However, there is value here for people wanting amenities and interior space for a low price. Now, if that price isn't low enough for you, Chrysler has added a budget model to the lineup, the entry-level LX. It will have the same 2.4-liter four-cylinder engine as the Plymouth Breeze, and since pricing is barely a smidge higher than the Breeze, rumors are swirling about the possible demise of the Plymouth model following the intro of the LX.

If you can overlook the economy-car levels of refinement, the Cirrus is a pleasing driver. It handles well, and offers a high driving position with excellent forward visibility. Check your rearview mirror, however, and you'll be hard pressed to guess where the rear of the car is, much less whether traffic is following you. The rear deck on this car is quite tall.

CHRYSLER — CIRRUS

Trunk space, thanks to the bulging back end, is commodious, and there's plenty of room in back for the kids. But families may want to consider other models after checking crash-test scores for the Cirrus. Protection levels are not the best in the class.

We've seen the spy photos of the new Cirrus, due for 2001, and the car looks very similar to the current Concorde - in other words, delicious. Plus, the new car should be slightly larger and will certainly be more powerful. This means good deals can be made on the outgoing 2000 Cirrus, thanks to heavy incentives and rebates. With the average price of a new car creeping toward $25,000, it is uncommon to be able to purchase a heavily loaded sedan for this price. Cirrus represents value.

Standard Equipment

LX (5M): 2.0L I4 SOHC SMPI 16-valve engine; 5-speed OD manual transmission; 510-amp battery; 90-amp alternator; front-wheel drive, 3.94 axle ratio; stainless steel exhaust; touring ride suspension, front independent double wishbone suspension with anti-roll bar, front coil springs, rear independent multi-link suspension with anti-roll bar, rear coil springs; power rack-and-pinion steering; front disc/rear drum brakes; 16 gal. capacity fuel tank; front mud flaps, side impact bars; front and rear body-colored bumpers with chrome bumper insert; body-colored bodyside molding; monotone paint; aero-composite halogen headlamps with delay-off feature; driver's and passenger's manual remote black outside mirrors; front and rear 15" x 6" steel wheels; P195/65TR15 A/S BSW front and rear tires; inside under cargo mounted compact steel spare wheel; air conditioning, rear heat ducts; AM/FM stereo, clock, seek-scan, cassette, 6 speakers, and fixed antenna; child safety rear door locks, remote hatch/trunk release; 1 power accessory outlet, driver's foot rest; instrumentation display includes tachometer, water temperature gauge, trip odometer; warning indicators include oil pressure, water temp, battery, lights on, key in ignition, low fuel, door ajar; driver's and passenger's front airbags; tinted windows, manual front and rear windows; variable intermittent front windshield wipers, sun visor strip, rear window defroster; seating capacity of 5, front bucket seats, adjustable headrests, center armrest with storage, driver's seat includes 6-way direction control, lumbar support, passenger's seat includes 4-way direction control; full folding rear bench seat; front height adjustable seatbelts; premium cloth seats, cloth door trim insert, full cloth headliner, full carpet floor covering, simulated wood trim on instrument panel, plastic/rubber gear shift knob; interior lights include dome light; sport steering wheel with tilt adjustment; vanity mirrors; day/night rearview mirror; full floor console, locking glove box with light, front and rear cupholders, instrument panel bin, 1 seat back storage pocket, driver's and passenger's door bins; carpeted cargo floor, cargo light; black grille, black side window moldings, black front windshield molding, black rear window molding and body-colored door handles.

LXi (4A) (in addition to or instead of LX (5M) equipment): 2.5L V6 SOHC SMPI 24-valve engine; 4-speed electronic OD auto transmission with lock-up; 3.9 axle ratio; 4-wheel disc brakes with 4-wheel antilock braking system; additional exterior lights include front fog/driving lights; driver's and passenger's power remote black outside mirrors; cruise control with steering wheel controls; power door locks, remote keyless entry, power remote hatch/trunk release; garage door opener; panic alarm; power front and rear windows with driver's 1-touch down; carpeted floor mats, leather-wrapped gear shift knob; interior lights include front reading lights, illuminated entry; leather-wrapped steering wheel with tilt adjustment; dual illuminated vanity mirrors and cargo net.

Base Prices

CODE	DESCRIPTION	INVOICE	MSRP
JACH41	Cirrus LX (5M)	14791	16080
JACP41	Cirrus LXi (4A)	18222	19935
	Destination Charge:	545	545

CIRRUS
CHRYSLER

| CODE | DESCRIPTION | INVOICE | MSRP |

2000 Chrysler Cirrus

Accessories

Code	Description	Invoice	MSRP
21A	Quick Order Package 21A (LX)	NC	NC
	Includes vehicle with standard equipment. REQUIRES ECB and DD5. NOT AVAILABLE with BRJ, ARR, AR3, AR5, AJF, TBB, GWA, WJJ, DGB, EDZ.		
24B	Quick Order Package 24B (LX)	939	1055
	Manufacturer Discount	(939)	(1055)
	Net Price	NC	NC
	Includes front and rear floor mats, speed sensitive power locks, power mirrors, 8-way power driver's seat and power windows with driver's one-touch down. REQUIRES EDZ and DGB. NOT AVAILABLE with ECB, DD5.		
26K	Quick Order Package 26K (LXi)	1455	1635
	Manufacturer Discount	(1455)	(1635)
	Net Price	NC	NC
	Includes premium AM/FM stereo with cassette and CD ready, 8-way power driver's seat, leather low-back bucket seats and wheels: 15" aluminum. REQUIRES EEB and DGB.		
ADE	Engine Block and Battery Heater	27	30
AJF	Remote/Illuminated Entry Group (LX)	151	170
	NOT AVAILABLE with 21A.		
ALJ	Gold Package Edition (LXi)	315	500
	Includes silver accents, LXi badge, gold badging and wheels: 15" chrome with gold accents.		
AR3	Radio: Premium Cassette and CD Ready (LX)	303	340
	Includes 8 premium speakers in 6 locations, 100-Watt external amplifier, integral clock and CD changer control. NOT AVAILABLE with 21A, ARR, AR5. INCLUDED in 26K.		

EDMUND'S® NEW CARS

CHRYSLER — CIRRUS / CONCORDE

CODE	DESCRIPTION	INVOICE	MSRP
AR5	Radio: Premium Cassette with 6-Disc CD Changer (LX)	490	550
	Includes 6 speakers and CD changer control. NOT AVAILABLE with 21A, AR3, ARR.		
AR5	Radio: Premium Cassette with 6-Disc CD Changer (LXi)	187	210
	Includes 6 speakers and CD changer control.		
ARR	Radio: Premium with CD Player (LX)	178	200
	NOT AVAILABLE with 21A, AR3, AR5.		
AWS	Smokers' Group	18	20
	Includes front ash tray and cigar lighter.		
BRJ	Antilock Front Disc/Rear Drum Brakes (LX)	503	565
	NOT AVAILABLE with 21A.		
DD5	Transmission: 5-Speed Manual (LX)	NC	NC
	NOT AVAILABLE with 24B.		
DGB	Transmission: 4-Speed Automatic (LX)	935	1050
	NOT AVAILABLE with 21A.		
DGB	Transmission: 4-Speed Automatic (LXi)	NC	NC
ECB	Engine: 2.0L 4 Cyl. SOHC 16V SMPI (LX)	NC	NC
	NOT AVAILABLE with 24B.		
EDZ	Engine: 2.4L 4 Cyl. DOHC 16V SMPI (LX)	401	450
	Manufacturer Discount	(401)	(450)
	Net Price	NC	NC
	NOT AVAILABLE with 21A.		
EEB	Engine: 2.5L V6 SOHC 24V SMPI (LXi)	NC	NC
GWA	Power Sunroof (LX)	619	695
	NOT AVAILABLE with 21A.		
GWA	Power Sunroof (LXi)	516	580
LSA	Security Alarm (LXi)	156	175
	Includes Sentry Key theft deterrent system.		
PEL	Inferno Red Tinted Pearl Coat	178	200
TBB	Tire: Full Size Spare	111	125
	NOT AVAILABLE with 21A.		
WJJ	Wheels: 15" Aluminum (LX)	325	365
	NOT AVAILABLE with 21A.		
XL	Leather Low-Back Bucket Seats (LXi)	NC	NC
	INCLUDED in 26K.		

2000 CONCORDE

What's New?

All models are given a more refined touring suspension, and variable-assist, speed-proportional steering is standard on LXi. Five new colors come aboard, and the instrument panel has been freshened.

Review

The Concorde, along with its sibling Dodge Intrepid, went through a major redesign in 1998, and the folks at Chrysler got it right this time. The Concorde was actually designed and brought

CONCORDE   CHRYSLER

to life through the use of computers, and Chrysler ended up with a modern-day classic. With a front grille reminiscent of certain models from Ferrari, Chrysler brought class and style to full-size sedans.

But looks aren't everything, and sometimes it's what's on the inside that really counts. You can count on 225 horsepower and 225 foot-pounds of torque from the LXi's peppy 3.2-liter V6, which has strong midrange passing power and gets great mileage. The LX is outfitted with a 2.7-liter V6 worthy of 200 horsepower and 190 foot-pounds of torque. And you say you like 100,000-mile intervals between tune-ups? Your wish has been granted.

Only a four-speed automatic transmission is currently available, and don't look for an AutoStick anywhere in this lineup. Traction control is standard on the LXi and optional for LX seekers, and you can ditto that for ABS. Both the LX and LXi have a touring-tuned four-wheel independent suspension, which is quite compliant. The LXi has speed-sensitive power rack-and-pinion steering, and handling is precise — like a midsize sport sedan, not a car with a 113-inch wheelbase. The LX steers with a power rack-and-pinion system.

Besides V6 power differences between the LX and LXi, there are a few creature comforts made available only on the LXi, including a security system and automatic climate control. But many luxury items are either standard or available to the base model; cruise control, power windows, and front airbags head up the standard list, while a moon roof, a trip-computer/HomeLink package, and leather seats top the optionals. Packages are also available to the LX that earn the driver a leather-wrapped steering wheel, a 50/50 front bench seat, and eight-way power driver and passenger seats.

With the last redesign, Chrysler brought class and style to full-size sedans. If interior space is your No. 1 priority, the Concorde is hard to beat. This popular segment of the market is saturated with excellent cars, but Chrysler is making a strong case for itself. Want a sedan you can lust for? Take a good look at the Concorde. These looks will endure for years to come.

2000 Chrysler Concorde

Standard Equipment

LX (4A): 2.7L V6 DOHC SMPI 24-valve engine; 4-speed electronic OD auto transmission with lock-up; 500-amp battery with run down protection; 120-amp alternator; front-wheel drive, 3.55 axle ratio; stainless steel exhaust; touring ride suspension, front independent strut suspension with anti-roll bar, front coil springs, rear independent multi-link suspension with anti-roll bar, rear coil springs; power rack-and-pinion steering; 4-wheel disc brakes; 17 gal. capacity fuel tank; side impact bars; front and rear body-colored bumpers; body-colored bodyside molding, rocker panel extensions; monotone paint; aero-composite halogen headlamps, delay-off feature;

CHRYSLER CONCORDE

| CODE | DESCRIPTION | INVOICE | MSRP |

driver's and passenger's power remote black outside mirrors; front and rear 16" x 7" steel wheels; P225/60SR16 touring A/S BSW front and rear tires; inside under cargo mounted compact steel spare wheel; air conditioning, rear heat ducts; AM/FM stereo, clock, seek-scan, cassette, 4 speakers, and window grid antenna; cruise control with steering wheel controls; power door locks, remote keyless entry, child safety rear door locks, power remote hatch/trunk release; 1 power accessory outlet, driver's foot rest; instrumentation display includes tachometer, water temperature gauge, trip odometer; warning indicators include oil pressure, water temp, battery, lights on, key in ignition, low fuel, low washer fluid, door ajar, trunk ajar; driver's and passenger's front airbags; panic alarm; tinted windows, power front and rear windows with driver's 1-touch down; variable intermittent front windshield wipers, sun visor strip, rear window defroster; seating capacity of 5, front bucket seats, adjustable headrests, center armrest with storage, driver's seat includes 6-way power seat, lumbar support, passenger's seat includes 4-way direction control; rear bench seat with center pass-thru armrest and storage; front height adjustable seatbelts; premium cloth seats, cloth door trim insert, full cloth headliner, full carpet floor covering with carpeted floor mats, deluxe sound insulation, simulated wood trim on instrument panel, plastic/rubber gear shift knob; interior lights include dome light with fade, front and rear reading lights, 2 door curb lights, illuminated entry; steering wheel with tilt adjustment; dual illuminated vanity mirrors; day/night rearview mirror; full floor console, locking glove box with light, front and rear cupholders, 1 seat back storage pocket, driver's and passenger's door bins; carpeted cargo floor, cargo net, cargo light; chrome grille, black side window moldings, black front windshield molding, black rear window molding and body-colored door handles.

LXi (4A) (in addition to or instead of LX (4A) equipment): 3.2L V6 SOHC SMPI 24-valve engine; 600-amp battery with run down protection; traction control; power rack-and-pinion steering with vehicle speed-sensing assist; 4-wheel disc brakes with 4-wheel antilock braking system; front and rear 16" x 7" aluminum wheels; inside under cargo mounted full-size steel spare wheel; air conditioning with climate control; AM/FM stereo, clock, seek-scan, cassette, single CD, 8 speakers, amplifier, graphic equalizer, and window grid antenna; garage door opener; instrumentation display includes trip computer; ignition disable, security system; passenger's seat includes 6-way power seat; leather seats, leatherette door trim insert, leather-wrapped gear shift knob; leather-wrapped steering wheel with tilt adjustment; auto-dimming day/night rearview mirror and mini overhead console.

Base Prices

Code	Description	Invoice	MSRP
LHCH41	LX (4A)	20146	21990
LHCM41	LXi (4A)	23924	26235
	Destination Charge:	560	560

Accessories

Code	Description	Invoice	MSRP
22C	Quick Order Package 22C (LX)	NC	NC
	Includes vehicle with standard equipment. REQUIRES EER and DGB. NOT AVAILABLE with BNM, AJC, MP, ML, AR3.		
22D	Quick Order Package 22D (LX)	1001	1125
	Includes universal garage door opener, auto day/night mirror, 8-way power driver's and passenger's seats, 8 speakers in 6 locations, 120-Watt amplifier and trip computer. REQUIRES EER and DGB. NOT AVAILABLE with WNS.		
24F	Quick Order Package 24F (LXi)	(280)	(315)
	Includes vehicle with standard equipment. REQUIRES EGW and DGB.		
ADE	Cold Weather Group	27	30
	Includes battery heater and engine block heater.		

CONCORDE / LHS — CHRYSLER

CODE	DESCRIPTION	INVOICE	MSRP
AJC	Leather and Wheel Group (LX)	943	1060
	Manufacturer Discount	(267)	(300)
	Net Price	676	760
	Includes leather trimmed bucket seats, leather-wrapped shift knob, leather-wrapped steering wheel and wheels: 16" aluminum. NOT AVAILABLE with 22C, KF.		
AR3	Radio: Premium CD with Amplifier (LX)	200	225
	Includes 120-Watt amplifier, AM/FM stereo, cassette, equalizer and 8 speakers in 6 locations. NOT AVAILABLE with 22C.		
AR3	Radio: Premium CD with Amplifier (LX)	512	575
	Includes 120-Watt amplifier, AM/FM stereo, cassette, equalizer and 8 speakers in 6 locations. NOT AVAILABLE with 22D.		
ARE	Radio: AM/FM Stereo with Cassette and CD (LXi)	445	500
	Includes 240-Watt amplifier, 4-disc in-dash CD changer, CD changer control and 9 Infiniti speakers in 7 locations.		
AWS	Smokers' Group	18	20
	Includes front and rear ash receivers and cigar lighter.		
BNM	Traction Control (LX)	156	175
	NOT AVAILABLE with 22C.		
BR3	4-Wheel Disc Antilock Brakes (LX)	534	600
DGB	Transmission: 4-Speed Automatic	NC	NC
EER	Engine: 2.7L V6 DOHC 24V MPI (LX)	NC	NC
EGW	Engine: 3.2L V6 SOHC 24V MPI (LXi)	NC	NC
GWA	Power Sunroof	797	895
KF	Premium Cloth 50/50 Split Bench Seat (LX)	89	100
	NOT AVAILABLE with ML, MP, AJC.		
ML	Leather Trimmed Bucket Seats (LX)	NC	NC
	REQUIRES 22D and AJC. NOT AVAILABLE with 22C, MP, KF.		
MP	Leather Trimmed 50/50 Bench Seat	89	100
	Deletes floor console and shift knob. REQUIRES 22D and AJC (LX). NOT AVAILABLE with 22C, KF, ML.		
PEL	Inferno Red Tinted Pearl Coat	178	200
TBB	Tire: Full Size Spare (LX)	111	125
TBW	Full Size Spare with Matching Wheel (LXi)	214	240
	REQUIRES WNE.		
TBW	Full Size Spare with Matching Wheel (LXi)	80	90
WNE	Wheels: 16" Chrome Aluminum (LXi)	534	600
WNS	Wheels: 16" Aluminum (LX)	325	365
	NOT AVAILABLE with 22D.		

2000 LHS

What's New?

Nothing dramatically changes for 2000. There are interior upgrades, including a four-disc in-dash CD changer, and a modified rear suspension for less noise, vibration and harshness. An automatic transaxle brake-shift interlock is now standard, and there are four more color choices.

CHRYSLER LHS

| CODE | DESCRIPTION | INVOICE | MSRP |

Review

So you call yourself a luxury buyer? Then you've stopped at the right place. The Chrysler LHS is a fullsize sedan that is both affordable and easy on the eyes. It's built on the same platform as the Chrysler 300M, but the LHS is longer and has more interior and luggage space than its sibling.

If you're torn between the two, keep in mind that the LHS is more of a road pillow - its four-wheel independent suspension is tuned for leisurely driving, whereas the 300M's optional European-tuned suspension is all about performance.

Unfortunately the LHS's softer suspension results in some body roll while cornering, and although minor steering correction is required, we have to admit it still boasts agile handling. It's outfitted with a four-speed overdrive automatic transaxle, but we'd sure like to see Chrysler slide an AutoStick into the equation (it gives you manual control of your automatic tranny). While the AutoStick isn't a substitute for having a real manual transmission, Chrysler would sure score brownie points for making it an available option to consumers.

The LHS is powered by the same all-aluminum, 253-horsepower, 3.5-liter SOHC 24-valve V6 that gives life to both the 300M and the Plymouth Prowler. While it makes 39 more horsepower than the last-generation LHS, we'd love to see what a V8 could do to this car. Thankfully, that's predicted for the next generation. Still, 253 horsepower competes well against the output of luxury cars like the Oldsmobile Aurora and Lincoln Continental, both equipped with eight-cylinder engines.

The year 2000 didn't bring a heap of noteworthy changes, but there are more color options: Dark Garnet Red, Shale Green Metallic, Steel Blue and Bright Silver Metallic. Among the lavish standards are heated, leather-trimmed seats, eight-way power front seats, and glow-in-the-dark gauges. While the interior is virtually identical to the 300M's, the telltale sign that it's an LHS is the "Chrysler" wings on the steering wheel.

While the LHS may be a step down in performance from the 300M, it's tough to beat - a luxury sedan with handsome styling and an affordable price.

2000 Chrysler LHS

LHS — CHRYSLER

CODE	DESCRIPTION	INVOICE	MSRP

Standard Equipment

LHS (4A): 3.5L V6 SOHC SMPI 24-valve engine; 4-speed electronic OD auto transmission with lock-up; 600-amp battery with run down protection; HD radiator; 130-amp alternator; front-wheel drive, traction control, 3.55 axle ratio; stainless steel exhaust with chrome tip; touring ride suspension, front independent strut suspension with anti-roll bar, front coil springs, rear independent multi-link suspension with anti-roll bar, rear coil springs; power rack-and-pinion steering with vehicle speed-sensing assist; 4-wheel disc brakes with 4-wheel antilock braking system; 17 gal. capacity fuel tank; side impact bars; front and rear body-colored bumpers; body-colored bodyside molding, rocker panel extensions; monotone paint; aero-composite halogen fully auto headlamps, delay-off feature; additional exterior lights include front fog/driving lights; driver's and passenger's power remote black heated folding outside mirrors; front and rear 17" x 7" silver alloy wheels; P225/55SR17 touring A/S BSW front and rear tires; inside under cargo mounted compact steel spare wheel; air conditioning with climate control, rear heat ducts; AM/FM stereo, seek-scan, cassette, single CD, 9 premium speakers, amplifier, graphic equalizer, and window grid antenna; cruise control with steering wheel controls; power door locks, remote keyless entry, child safety rear door locks, power remote hatch/trunk release; 1 power accessory outlet, driver's foot rest, garage door opener; instrumentation display includes tachometer, water temperature gauge, clock, compass, exterior temp, trip computer, trip odometer; warning indicators include oil pressure, water temp, battery, lights on, key in ignition, low fuel, low washer fluid, door ajar, trunk ajar; driver's and passenger's front airbags; ignition disable, panic alarm, security system; tinted windows, power front and rear windows with driver's 1-touch down; variable intermittent front windshield wipers, sun visor strip, rear window defroster; seating capacity of 5, heated-cushion front bucket seats, adjustable tilt headrests, center armrest with storage, driver's seat includes 6-way power seat, lumbar support, passenger's seat includes 6-way power seat; rear bench seat with fixed headrests, center pass-thru armrest with storage; front height adjustable seatbelts; leather seats, leatherette door trim insert, full cloth headliner, full carpet floor covering with carpeted floor mats, deluxe sound insulation, simulated wood trim on instrument panel, leather-wrapped gear shift knob; memory on driver's seat with 2 memory setting(s) includes settings for exterior mirrors; interior lights include dome light with fade, front and rear reading lights, 4 door curb lights, illuminated entry; leather-wrapped steering wheel with tilt adjustment; dual illuminated vanity mirrors, dual auxiliary visors; auto-dimming day/night rearview mirror; full floor console, mini overhead console locking glove box with light, front and rear cupholders, 2 seat back storage pockets, driver's and passenger's door bins; carpeted cargo floor, cargo net, cargo light; chrome grille, black side window moldings, black front windshield molding, black rear window molding and body-colored door handles.

Base Prices

LHCP41	LHS (4A)		25775	28090
Destination Charge:			605	605

Accessories

26J	Quick Order Package 26J		NC	NC
	Includes vehicle with standard equipment. REQUIRES EGG and DGB.			
ADE	Cold Weather Group		27	30
	Includes battery heater and engine block heater.			
ARF	Radio: AM/FM Stereo with Cassette and CD Changer		458	515
	Includes 360-Watt amplifier, 4-disc in-dash CD changer with changer control, AM/FM stereo, cassette and 11 Infinity speakers in 9 locations.			
AWS	Smokers' Group		18	20
	Includes front and rear ash receiver and cigar lighter.			
DGB	Transmission: 4-Speed Automatic		NC	NC

CHRYSLER — LHS / SEBRING CONVERTIBLE

CODE	DESCRIPTION	INVOICE	MSRP
EGG	Engine: 3.5 L High Output V6 24V MPI	NC	NC
GWA	Power Sunroof	797	895
TBW	Full Size Spare Tire with Matching Wheel	191	215
	NOT AVAILABLE with WFH.		
TBW	Full Size Spare Tire with Matching Wheel	325	365
WFH	Wheels: 17" Chrome Aluminum	668	750

2000 SEBRING CONVERTIBLE

2000 Chrysler Sebring Convertible

What's New?

This year the rear suspension has been re-tuned for improved ride quality and reduced noise. Four colors have been added.

Review

Chrysler's Sebring Convertible gets people excited. "Finally, a convertible that doesn't make me feel like a college kid every time I put the top down." Basically, that's what Chrysler wants its Sebring buyers to proclaim. You see, there are plenty of fun convertibles, but most of them don't offer much practicality in day-to-day life. They're either stiff-riding hot rods, like the Camaro or Mustang, or too small to be practical for people who have kids.

Upon seeing this market opportunity, Chrysler went whole-hog when it debuted the Sebring in 1996. The car brought class, dignity and quite a bit of luxury to this otherwise whimsical segment, and became very successful with upscale buyers of all ages. There has been just minor retooling over the years, and 2000 is no exception, since the major redesign is scheduled for 2001.

The Sebring Convertible has little in common with the Sebring Coupe. The soft top is based on the Cirrus platform and shares its chassis and drivetrain components with that sedan. Its available engine is a 2.5-liter, SOHC V6, making 168 horsepower and 170 foot-pounds of torque, and it pulls quite well at slow speeds. The four-speed overdrive automatic transaxle is

SEBRING CONVERTIBLE — CHRYSLER

| CODE | DESCRIPTION | INVOICE | MSRP |

the only gearbox offered, but Limiteds have the AutoStick as part of the standard-feature package. Both the JX and JXi come with four-wheel ABS (front disc/rear drum braking), while the Limited has ABS, four-wheel discs and traction control, as well as chrome wheels and electro-luminescent instrument-panel lighting.

The rear suspension got tweaked this year to provide a better ride, but underneath remains the same four-wheel independent double-wishbone design. The JX has standard tuning, while the JXi and JXi Limited went the touring route. Firm-feel steering is provided for all three (as is minor understeer), and dual-outlet exhaust with a chrome-flashed tip passes gas.

The 2001 Sebring will have a brand-new platform and more potent power, but between now and then, the current Sebring Convertible is one of the few true four-seat drop tops on the market.

Standard Equipment

JX (4A): 2.5L V6 SOHC SMPI 24-valve engine; 4-speed electronic OD auto transmission with lock-up; 510-amp battery; 125-amp alternator; front-wheel drive, 3.9 axle ratio; stainless steel exhaust; front independent double wishbone suspension with anti-roll bar, front coil springs, rear independent multi-link suspension with anti-roll bar, rear coil springs; power rack-and-pinion steering with vehicle speed-sensing assist; front disc/rear drum brakes with 4-wheel antilock braking system; 16 gal. capacity fuel tank; side impact bars; power convertible roof with lining, glass rear window; front and rear body-colored bumpers; body-colored bodyside molding; monotone paint; aero-composite halogen headlamps with delay-off feature; driver's and passenger's power remote black heated folding outside mirrors; front and rear 15" x 6" steel wheels; P205/65SR15 A/S BSW front and rear tires; inside under cargo mounted compact steel spare wheel; air conditioning, rear heat ducts; AM/FM stereo, clock, seek-scan, cassette, CD changer pre-wiring, in-dash CD pre-wiring, 6 speakers, auto equalizer, and fixed antenna; cruise control with steering wheel controls; power door locks, remote keyless entry, power remote hatch/trunk release; 1 power accessory outlet, driver's foot rest; instrumentation display includes tachometer, water temperature gauge, trip odometer; warning indicators include oil pressure, water temp, battery, lights on, key in ignition, low fuel, low washer fluid, door ajar, trunk ajar; driver's and passenger's front airbags; panic alarm; tinted windows, power front and rear windows with driver's 1-touch down; variable intermittent front windshield wipers, sun visor strip, rear window defroster; seating capacity of 4, front bucket seats, adjustable headrests, center armrest with storage, driver's seat includes 4-way power seat, 8-way direction control, lumbar support, passenger's seat includes 4-way direction control, easy entry; rear bench seat; front height adjustable seatbelts; vinyl seats, vinyl door trim insert, full cloth headliner, full carpet floor covering with carpeted floor mats, plastic/rubber gear shift knob; interior lights include dome light with delay front reading lights, illuminated entry; steering wheel with tilt adjustment; dual illuminated vanity mirrors; day/night rearview mirror; full floor console, locking glove box with light, front cupholder, instrument panel bin, driver's and passenger's door bins; carpeted cargo floor, cargo light; black grille, black side window moldings, black front windshield molding, black rear window molding and black door handles.

JXi (4A) (in addition to or instead of JX (4A) equipment): Engine oil cooler; stainless steel exhaust with chrome tip; touring ride suspension; additional exterior lights include front fog/driving lights; front and rear 16" x 6.5" silver alloy wheels; P215/55SR16 touring A/S BSW front and rear tires; power retractable antenna; instrumentation display includes compass, exterior temp, trip computer; ignition disable, security system; leather seats, simulated wood trim on instrument panel, leather-wrapped gear shift knob; interior lights include 2 door curb lights, illuminated entry; leather-wrapped steering wheel with tilt adjustment; 1 seat back storage pocket and body-colored door handles.

CHRYSLER — SEBRING CONVERTIBLE

CODE	DESCRIPTION	INVOICE	MSRP

Base Prices

JXCH27	JX (4A)	22198	24245
JXCP27	JXi (4A)	24258	26560
Destination Charge:		545	545

Accessories

Code	Description	Invoice	MSRP
26B	Quick Order Package 26B (JX)	NC	NC
	Includes vehicle with standard equipment. REQUIRES EEB and DGB.		
26D	Quick Order Package 26D (JXi)	NC	NC
	Includes vehicle with standard equipment. REQUIRES EEB and DGB.		
26G	Quick Order Package 26G (JXi)	1682	1890
	Includes Autostick, 4-wheel antilock disc brakes, Limited Decor group, body color grille, leather low-back bucket seats, wheels: 16" x 6.5" chrome aluminum, luxury convenience group, universal garage door opener, auto day/night mirror, AM/FM stereo with cassette, CD and equalizer and traction control. REQUIRES EEB and DGB.		
6R2	Inferno Red Tinted PC with Black Vinyl Top	178	200
	NOT AVAILABLE with WNF, 26G.		
6R4	Inferno Red Tinted PC with Camel Vinyl Top	178	200
	NOT AVAILABLE with WNF, 26G.		
6R7	Inferno Red Tinted PC with Black Cloth Top (JXi)	178	200
6R8	Inferno Red Tint with Sandalwood Cloth Top (JXi)	178	200
ADE	Cold Weather Group	27	30
	Includes battery heater and engine block heater.		
AJB	Security Group (JX)	156	175
	Includes security alarm and power auto central locking locks.		
ALL	All Season Group (JXi)	659	740
	Manufacturer Discount	(303)	(340)
	Net Price	356	400
	Includes 4-wheel antilock disc brakes, luxury convenience group, universal garage door opener, auto day/night mirror, AM/FM stereo with cassette, CD and equalizer and traction control. NOT AVAILABLE with RDR, 26G.		
AR5	Radio: Premium AM/FM Cassette (JXi)	142	160
	Includes 6-disc CD changer in-dash and CD changer control. REQUIRES 26G.		
AWK	Luxury Convenience Group (JXi)	156	175
	Includes universal garage door opener and auto day/night mirror. INCLUDED in 26G.		
AY4	16" Aluminum Wheel Touring Group (JX)	441	495
	Includes firm feel power steering, white wheels when white paint is ordered, touring suspension, tires: P215/55R16 A/S BSW touring and wheels: 16" x 6.5" aluminum.		
D7	Premium Cloth Structural Bucket (JX)	85	95
DGB	Transmission: 4-Speed Automatic	NC	NC
EEB	Engine: 2.5L V6 SOHC 24V SMPI	NC	NC
RAZ	Radio: AM/FM Stereo with Cassette, CD and Equalizer (JX)	303	340
	INCLUDED in 26G.		

SEBRING CONVERTIBLE / COUPE — CHRYSLER

CODE	DESCRIPTION	INVOICE	MSRP
RDR	CD Changer 6-Disc In-Dash (JXi)	445	500
	NOT AVAILABLE with ALL.		
WNF	Wheels: 16" X 6.5" Aluminum (JX)	NC	NC
	REQUIRES AY4. NOT AVAILABLE with 6R2, 6R4.		
X7	Cloth Structural Bucket Seats (JXi)	(223)	(250)
	NOT AVAILABLE with 26G.		

2000 SEBRING COUPE

2000 Chrysler Sebring Coupe

What's New?

For 2000, the standard-equipment list has increased. Also, Ice Silver is the newest color, and the LX trim fabric has been updated.

Review

Chrysler has used the words "practicality" and "elegance" among the adjectives for the Sebring Coupe. It's hard to argue. This car can carry four occupants in comfort, possesses reasonable performance capability and struts around with suave good looks. Huge fog lights lend the sophisticated coupe an aggressive appearance, and the tastefully restrained rear styling exudes class. Buyers purchase nimble handling and up-market amenities for a down-market price.

Underneath the LXi's sheetmetal is a handling suspension that includes a rear stabilizer bar and four-wheel disc brakes. The LX has a more conservative touring-tuned independent double-wishbone setup coupled with four-wheel discs. ABS is optional for both models, but standard is a dual-outlet exhaust system accented by chrome tips. The LX and LXi also share a 163-horsepower, 2.5-liter SOHC V6 glued to a four-speed automatic transaxle. Power from this engine can be disappointing, but Chrysler plans to rectify the situation in 2001 by adding a 2.7-liter or 3.0-liter V6 to the lineup. The LXi sports larger tires and wheels than the LX, but,

CHRYSLER SEBRING COUPE

unfortunately, the cabin doesn't completely seal out the rubber-on-pavement noise. A speed-sensitive rack-and-pinion steering system completes the performance package.

You might be thinking that you can go either way on the tuned suspension, so what's the real difference between the LX and LXi? For a couple grand more, the LXi can boast among its standard features automatic night/day side mirrors, a compass, a CD player, leather seats and a leather-wrapped steering wheel, six-way power seating, remote entry, and the HomeLink home-security system. But the lower-level LX is nothing to spit at. Those features we just rattled off for the LXi are about the only ones not standard on the LX. It has power windows, air conditioning, and nearly everything else the LXi has, including access to a power sunroof, which is still only optional for the LXi.

There's one adjective Chrysler forgot to mention: affordable. Coming in at the lower end of the twenties for a well-equipped LXi, it pits the Sebring well against the Pontiac Grand Prix and various midsize coupes from Japan. Sure, the Grand Prix's 3.8-liter V6 offers more ponies for your money, but it's hard to overlook the Sebring's style, huge interior and trunk, and upscale standards.

Standard Equipment

LX (4A): 2.5L V6 SOHC SMPI 24-valve engine; 4-speed electronic OD auto transmission with lock-up; 525-amp battery; 90-amp alternator; front-wheel drive, 3.91 axle ratio; stainless steel exhaust; touring ride suspension, front independent double wishbone suspension with anti-roll bar, front coil springs, rear independent double wishbone suspension with rear coil springs; power rack-and-pinion steering with vehicle speed-sensing assist; 4-wheel disc brakes; 15.9 gal. capacity fuel tank; side impact bars; front and rear body-colored bumpers; body-colored bodyside cladding; monotone paint; aero-composite halogen headlamps; additional exterior lights include front fog/driving lights; driver's and passenger's power remote black outside mirrors; front and rear 16" x 6" steel wheels; P205/55HR16 performance A/S BSW front and rear tires; inside under cargo mounted compact steel spare wheel; air conditioning, rear heat ducts; AM/FM stereo, clock, seek-scan, cassette, 6 speakers, and fixed antenna; cruise control; power door locks, remote hatch/trunk release, remote fuel release; 1 power accessory outlet, driver's foot rest, smokers' package; instrumentation display includes tachometer, oil pressure gauge, water temperature gauge, trip odometer; warning indicators include oil pressure, water temp, battery, low coolant, lights on, key in ignition, low fuel, low washer fluid, door ajar, trunk ajar, brake fluid; driver's and passenger's front airbags; tinted windows, power windows with driver's 1-touch down; variable intermittent front windshield wipers, sun visor strip, rear window defroster; seating capacity of 5, front bucket seats, adjustable headrests, center armrest with storage, driver's seat includes 6-way direction control, passenger's seat includes 4-way direction control, easy entry; 60-40 folding rear bench seat; front height adjustable seatbelts; cloth seats, vinyl door trim insert, full cloth headliner, full carpet floor covering with carpeted floor mats, simulated wood trim on instrument panel, plastic/rubber gear shift knob; interior lights include dome light with fade, front reading lights; steering wheel with tilt adjustment; dual illuminated vanity mirrors; day/night rearview mirror; full floor console, locking glove box with light, front cupholder, driver's and passenger's door bins; carpeted cargo floor, cargo net, cargo light; black grille, black side window moldings, black front windshield molding, black rear window molding and body-colored door handles.

LXi (4A) (in addition to or instead of LX (4A) equipment): 110-amp alternator; stainless steel exhaust with chrome tip; sport ride suspension, rear independent double wishbone suspension with anti-roll bar; rear lip spoiler; driver's and passenger's power remote body-colored outside mirrors; front and rear 17" x 6.5" silver alloy wheels; P215/50HR17 performance A/S BSW front and rear tires; premium AM stereo/FM stereo, clock, seek-scan, cassette, single CD, 6 speakers, and fixed antenna; remote keyless entry, garage door opener; instrumentation display includes compass; panic alarm, security system; driver's seat includes 4-way power seat, 8-way direction control; leather seats; leather-wrapped steering wheel with tilt adjustment and auto-dimming day/night rearview mirror.

SEBRING COUPE — CHRYSLER

CODE	DESCRIPTION	INVOICE	MSRP

Base Prices

FJCS22	LX (4A)	18121	19765
FJCP22	LXi (4A)	20199	22100
Destination Charge:		545	545

Accessories

Code	Description	Invoice	MSRP
24H	Quick Order Package 24H (LX)	NC	NC
	Includes vehicle with standard equipment. REQUIRES EEB and DGB.		
24K	Quick Order Package 24K (LXi)	(561)	(630)
	Includes vehicle with standard equipment. REQUIRES EEB and DGB.		
BRF	4-Wheel Disc Antilock Brakes	534	600
DGB	Transmission: 4-Speed Automatic	NC	NC
EEB	Engine: 2.5L V6 SOHC 24V SMPI (LX)	(601)	(675)
EEB	Engine: 2.5L V6 SOHC 24V SMPI (LXi)	NC	NC
GWA	Power Sunroof	610	685
GXR	Remote Keyless Entry (LX)	271	305
	Includes 2 transmitters and panic alarm.		
JPS	6-Way Power Driver's Seat (LX)	182	205
RAZ	Radio: AM/FM Stereo with Cassette, CD and Equalizer (LX)	676	760
	Includes Infinity speaker system. NOT AVAILABLE with RBX.		
RAZ	Radio: AM/FM Stereo with Cassette, CD and Equalizer (LXi)	289	325
	Includes Infinity speaker system.		
RBX	Radio: AM/FM Stereo with Cassette and CD (LX)	387	435
	NOT AVAILABLE with RAZ.		

Major Savings On An Extended Warranty

"YOU DESERVE THE BEST"
Call today for your free quote.
Pay up to 50% less than dealership prices!

http://www.edmunds.com/warranty 1-800-580-9889

DAEWOO

LANOS

| CODE | DESCRIPTION | | INVOICE | MSRP |

1999 LANOS

1999 Daewoo Lanos

What's New? ───────

This entry into the subcompact class is Daewoo's attack on the Honda Civic.

Review ───────────

Daewoo, Korean for "Great Universe," has decided to take the U.S. market by storm with the Lanos. Trouble is, the U.S. market is already flooded with underpowered subcompact cars. Nevertheless, Daewoo is diving in, aiming sales squarely at loan-saddled college students. Interestingly, if you rearrange "Lanos" you get "Loans."

Available as a three-door hatchback or a four-door sedan, the Lanos is about the size of a Hyundai Accent. Because the Lanos is a small subcompact, anyone over six feet tall should not bother trying find a comfortable seating position. But the price matches the car's size.

The Lanos is available in three trim levels: S, SE and SX. Each comes with a 1.6-liter DOHC 16 valve engine that makes 105 horsepower at 5800 rpm and 107 foot-pounds of torque at 3400 rpm. A five-speed manual transmission is also standard, but buyers may choose a four-speed automatic, an $800 option.

While the S model is the base car, you have to go to the mid-level SE in order to purchase the optional ABS. SX trim buyers get a CD player, air conditioning, alloy wheels, fog lights and a tilt steering column. A moonroof is optional only on the SX.

Prices for this entry-level car range from about $9,000 for the bare bones model to just over $13,000 for a decently equipped SX. But with Daewoo's factory stores, modeled after Saturn's no-haggle price system, we have to wonder what the incentive is to drive away in an unproven Korean car of questionable reliability, when the Honda dealer down the street offers tried-and-true Civics and used Acura Integras for a similar price. And while you're at it, don't forget to shop the Dodge Neons, Saturn coupes and sedans, Nissan Sentras, Ford Escorts, Mercury Tracers, Mazda Proteges and Volkswagen Golfs. This segment is loaded with value.

Standard Equipment ──────

S HATCHBACK (5M): 1.6L I4 DOHC MPI 16-valve engine; 5-speed overdrive manual transmission; 55-amp battery; 85-amp alternator; front wheel drive; front independent strut suspension with anti-roll bar, front coil springs, rear independent multi-link suspension with anti-

---

148   www.edmunds.com   **EDMUND'S® NEW CARS**

LANOS — DAEWOO

roll bar, rear coil springs; power rack-and-pinion steering; front disc/rear drum brakes; 12.7 gal. capacity fuel tank; front and rear mud flaps, rear lip spoiler; front and rear body-colored bumpers; monotone paint; aero-composite halogen headlamps; additional exterior lights include center high mounted stop light; driver's and passenger's manual remote black folding outside mirrors; front and rear 14" x 5.5" steel wheels; P185/60SR14 BSW AS front and rear tires; inside under cargo mounted compact steel spare wheel; AM/FM stereo with seek-scan, cassette, 4 speakers, theft deterrent, and fixed antenna; 1 power accessory outlet, driver's foot rest; instrumentation display includes water temp gauge, in-dash clock, trip odometer; warning indicators include oil pressure, battery; dual airbags; tinted windows, vented rear windows; variable intermittent front windshield wipers, rear window defroster; seating capacity of 5, front bucket seats with adjustable headrests, driver's seat includes 6-way direction control, passenger's seat includes 4-way direction control with easy entry; 60-40 folding rear bench seat; front height adjustable seatbelts; cloth seats, vinyl door trim insert, full cloth headliner, full carpet floor covering; interior lights include dome light; day-night rearview mirror; partial floor console, glove box, front cupholder, driver's and passenger's door bins; carpeted cargo floor, cargo cover; chrome grille, black side window moldings, black front windshield molding, black rear window molding and black door handles.

SE HATCHBACK (5M) (in addition to or instead of S HATCHBACK (5M) equipment): Passenger's power remote outside mirror; power door locks, remote keyless entry; security system; power front windows with driver's 1-touch down and power rear windows.

SX HATCHBACK (5M) (in addition to or instead of SE HATCHBACK (5M) equipment): Additional exterior lights include front fog/driving lights; air conditioning; AM/FM stereo with seek-scan, cassette, single CD, 4 speakers, theft deterrent, and fixed antenna and steering wheel with tilt adjustment.

S SEDAN (5M) (in addition to or instead of S HATCHBACK (5M) equipment): Child safety rear door locks; manual rear windows; cloth door trim insert and full floor console.

SE SEDAN (5M) (in addition to or instead of SE HATCHBACK (5M) equipment): Child safety rear door locks; power rear windows; cloth door trim insert and full floor console.

SX SEDAN (5M) (in addition to or instead of SX Hatchback (5-speed) equipment): Child safety rear door locks; power rear windows; cloth door trim insert and full floor console.

Base Prices

Code	Description	Invoice	MSRP
D3LS5	S Hatchback (5M)	7649	8999
D3MS5	SE Hatchback (5M)	9010	10600
D3XS5	SX Hatchback (5M)	9944	11699
D4LS5	S Sedan (5M)	8244	9699
D4MS5	SE Sedan (5M)	9265	10900
D4XS5	SX Sedan (5M)	10174	11969
	Destination Charge:	250	250

Accessories

Code	Description	Invoice	MSRP
—	Air Conditioning (S/SE)	595	700
—	Antilock Braking System (SE/SX)	425	500
—	Floor Mats	76	90
—	Power Tilt/Slide Moon Roof (SX)	425	500
—	Transmission: 4-Speed Automatic	800	800

DAEWOO

LEGANZA

| CODE | DESCRIPTION | INVOICE | MSRP |

2000 LEGANZA

2000 Daewoo Leganza

What's New?

Content is pulled from the base SE model, but all Leganzas have new grilles, alloy wheels and seat fabrics.

Review

Leganza, whose name is derived from a combination of the Italian words "elegante" (elegant) and "forza" (power), is a midsize sedan from Korea marketed to would-be buyers of pedestrian Honda Accords and Toyota Camrys who want a full load of luxury amenities for a cut-rate bargain price.

While attractively styled and decently equipped, this unproven brand's most recent foray into the North American market was the joint venture that produced the Pontiac LeMans econo-car between 1988 and 1993. So notorious was that model for lousy quality that GM gave Daewoo the boot and halted production. Seven years later, Daewoo, trying to break into a fickle market saturated with established brands and excellent cars, was probably hoping you'd forgotten about the LeMans.

Yes, the Leganza is elegant, penned by ItalDesign whiz Giorgetto Giugiaro. But powerful? Hardly. Competing against vehicles commonly equipped with V6 engines, the Leganza is handicapped in the muscle department by its standard and only powerplant. A 2.2-liter, DOHC 16-valve engine making 131 horsepower at 5,200 rpm and 148 foot-pounds of torque at 2,800 rpm is charged with hauling around more than 3,000 pounds of sedan. Worse, a manual transmission, which can make the most of the meager power output, is available only on the bottom-feeder version.

Three trim levels are available on the Leganza: SE, SX and CDX. Standard equipment includes antilock front disc and rear drum brakes, a full-size spare tire, power windows and locks, air conditioning, remote keyless entry, and a tilt wheel. Step up to the SX, and you're rewarded with a CD player, leather seats, cruise control, and an automatic transmission. The luxurious CDX gets a power driver's seat, automatic temperature control, fake wood trim, power moonroof, and traction control.

British suspension expert Lotus tuned Leganza's four-wheel independent underpinnings, but Daewoo obviously wanted a cushy ride, and the Leganza delivers. Weak tires howl around turns, and we found the ABS to be substandard in refinement and effectiveness. Despite a

LEGANZA — DAEWOO

CODE	DESCRIPTION	INVOICE	MSRP

"Sport" mode for the automatic transmission, it's best to drive the Leganza less enthusiastically than you would, say, anything else on the market.

Inside, the interior feels smaller than many competitors. Ergonomics evidently doesn't translate into Korean, because the controls are haphazardly placed. One of our staffers said the leather in upmarket models was about as convincingly luxurious as a rubber football.

The biggest hurdle the Leganza faces is not Daewoo's no-haggle sales strategy or patchy dealer network, but the extremely fierce competition in the midsize sedan segment. Competing against such entities as the Chevrolet Malibu, Dodge Stratus, Ford Taurus, Honda Accord, Mazda 626, Mitsubishi Galant, Nissan Altima, Oldsmobile Alero, Saturn LS and Toyota Camry is no small order, especially when the American buying public already knows where to buy them.

Standard Equipment

SE (5M): 2.2L I4 DOHC MPI 16-valve engine; 5-speed OD manual transmission; 610-amp battery; 95-amp alternator; front-wheel drive, 3.72 axle ratio; partial stainless steel exhaust with chrome tip; front independent strut suspension with anti-roll bar, front coil springs, rear independent multi-link suspension with anti-roll bar, rear coil springs; power rack-and-pinion steering; 4-wheel disc brakes with 4-wheel antilock braking system; 17.2 gal. capacity fuel tank; side impact bars; front and rear body-colored bumpers; body-colored bodyside molding; monotone paint; projector beam halogen headlamps; additional exterior lights include front fog/driving lights; driver's and passenger's power remote body-colored heated folding outside mirrors; front and rear 15" x 6" steel wheels; P205/60SR15 A/S BSW front and rear tires; inside under cargo mounted full-size steel spare wheel; air conditioning, rear heat ducts; AM/FM stereo, seek-scan, cassette, 6 speakers, theft deterrent, and fixed antenna; power door locks, remote keyless entry, child safety rear door locks, remote fuel release; 1 power accessory outlet, driver's foot rest; instrumentation display includes tachometer, water temperature gauge, in-dash clock, trip odometer; warning indicators include oil pressure, battery, lights on, key in ignition, door ajar, trunk ajar; driver's and passenger's front airbags; security system; tinted windows, power front and rear windows with driver's 1-touch down; variable intermittent front windshield wipers, sun visor strip, rear window defroster; seating capacity of 5, front bucket seats, adjustable headrests, center armrest with storage, driver's seat includes 6-way direction control, passenger's seat includes 4-way direction control; 60-40 folding rear bench seat with fixed headrests; front height adjustable seatbelts; cloth seats, cloth door trim insert, full cloth headliner, full carpet floor covering, plastic/rubber gear shift knob; interior lights include dome light with fade, front reading lights, 2 door curb lights; steering wheel with tilt adjustment; dual illuminated vanity mirrors; day/night rearview mirror; full floor console, glove box, front cupholder, driver's and passenger's door bins; carpeted cargo floor, cargo light; chrome grille, black side window moldings, black front windshield molding, black rear window molding and body-colored door handles.

SX (4A) (in addition to or instead of SE (5M) equipment): Four-speed electronic auto transmission with lock-up; 2.65 axle ratio; power rack-and-pinion steering with vehicle speed-sensing assist; AM/FM stereo, seek-scan, cassette, single CD, 6 speakers, theft deterrent, and fixed antenna; leather seats, leatherette door trim insert and full carpet floor covering.

CDX (4A) (in addition to or instead of SX (4A) equipment): Traction control; front power sliding and tilting glass sunroof with sunshade; front and rear 15" x 6" alloy wheels; air conditioning with climate control; driver's seat includes 4-way power seat, 8-way direction control and simulated wood trim on instrument panel.

Base Prices

		Invoice	MSRP
F4MR5	Leganza SE (5M)	11630	13660
F4XR4	Leganza SX (4A)	14161	16660
F4CR4	Leganza CDX (4A)	15861	18660
Destination Charge:		330	330

DAEWOO
LEGANZA/NUBIRA

CODE	DESCRIPTION	INVOICE	MSRP

Accessories

—	6-Disc CD Changer (CDX)	383	450
—	Front and Rear Floor Mats	64	75
—	Power Glass Moon Roof (SX)	425	500
—	Transmission: 4-Speed Automatic (SE)	661	800
—	Wheels: Alloy (SX)	340	400

1999 NUBIRA

1999 Daewoo Nubira

What's New?

Want a car that looks just like a Nissan Maxima, yet costs thousands less? Daewoo's Nubira is it.

Review

Nubira. Sounds like a cloud formation, but it's actually the name of one of the three cars from Daewoo (pronounced DAY-woo) to debut in America this year.

The Nubira is available in two levels of trim: SX and CDX. The SX comes with power windows, locks and mirrors, as well as a height adjustable seat, air conditioning, tinted windows, alloy wheels and four-wheel disc brakes. The sole engine choice for the Nubira is a 2.0-liter with 128 horsepower at 5,400 rpm and 135 foot-pounds of torque at 2,800 rpm. All that for a mere $13,000. Floor mats are a $90 option. CDX trim buys cruise control, alloy wheels and antilock brakes, while leather seats and a moonroof are optional.

The compact Nubira is available as a four-door sedan, five-door hatchback, or wagon, and prices top out at around $16,000 for a fully-loaded wagon. The Nubira's size is about the same as a Ford Escort, though power is up with the base Ford Contour. That's a recipe for fun, since the Nubira comes with a five-speed manual transmission on both the SX and CDX trim (a four-speed automatic is optional). Add in the practicality of a hatchback or wagon, and the Nubira may be Daewoo's best shot at finding a niche in the crowded sub-$20,000 economy car market.

Now, if only buyers could haggle on the price a little?

NUBIRA   DAEWOO

CODE	DESCRIPTION	INVOICE	MSRP

Standard Equipment

SX SEDAN (5M): 2.0L I4 DOHC MPI 16-valve engine; 5-speed overdrive manual transmission; 55-amp battery; 85-amp alternator; front wheel drive, 3.55 axle ratio; steel exhaust; front independent strut suspension with anti-roll bar, front coil springs, rear independent multi-link suspension with anti-roll bar, rear coil springs; power rack-and-pinion steering; 4 wheel disc brakes; 13.7 gal. capacity fuel tank; front and rear mud flaps; front and rear body-colored bumpers; monotone paint; aero-composite halogen headlamps; additional exterior lights include front fog/driving lights, center high mounted stop light; driver's and passenger's power remote body-colored heated folding outside mirrors; front and rear 14" x 5.5" steel wheels; P185/65HR14 BSW AS front and rear tires; inside under cargo mounted compact steel spare wheel; air conditioning, rear heat ducts; AM/FM stereo with seek-scan, cassette, 6 speakers, theft deterrent, and fixed antenna; power door locks, remote keyless entry, child safety rear door locks, remote fuel release; 1 power accessory outlet; instrumentation display includes tachometer, water temp gauge, in-dash clock, trip odometer; warning indicators include oil pressure, battery; dual airbags; security system; tinted windows, power front windows with driver's 1-touch down, power rear windows; variable intermittent front windshield wipers, rear window defroster; seating capacity of 5, front bucket seats with adjustable headrests, center armrest with storage, driver's seat includes 6-way direction control, passenger's seat includes 4-way direction control; 60-40 folding rear bench seat with fixed headrests; front height adjustable seatbelts with front pretensioners; cloth seats, cloth door trim insert, full vinyl headliner, full carpet floor covering; interior lights include dome light; steering wheel with tilt adjustment; passenger's side vanity mirror; day-night rearview mirror; full floor console, glove box, front cupholder, driver's and passenger's door bins; carpeted cargo floor, cargo light; chrome grille, black side window moldings, black front windshield molding, black rear window molding and body-colored door handles.

SX 5-DOOR HATCHBACK/WAGON (5M) (in addition to or instead of SX SEDAN (5M) equipment): Front and rear mud flaps, rear lip spoiler; roof rack; AM/FM stereo seek-scan, cassette, 6 speakers, theft deterrent, and integrated roof antenna; variable intermittent front windshield wipers, rear window wiper; plastic trunk lid and cargo cover.

CDX SEDAN/5-DOOR HATCHBACK/WAGON (5M) (in addition to or instead SX SEDAN/5-DOOR HATCHBACK/WAGON (5M) equipment): Four wheel disc brakes with 4 wheel antilock braking system; alloy wheels, AM/FM stereo with seek-scan, cassette, single CD, 6 speakers, theft deterrent, and integrated roof antenna and cruise control.

Base Prices

Code	Description	Invoice	MSRP
E5XQ5	SX Hatchback (5M)	10630	12506
E5CQ5	CDX Hatchback (5M)	11739	13810
E4XQ5	SX Sedan (5M)	10630	12506
E4CQ5	CDX Sedan (5M)	11739	13810
EWXQ5	SX Wagon (5M)	11140	13106
EWCQ5	CDX Wagon (5M)	12249	14410
Destination Charge:		250	250

Accessories

Code	Description	Invoice	MSRP
—	Transmission: 4-Speed Automatic	800	800
ABS	Antilock Braking System (SX)	425	500
FM	Floor Mats	76	90
LSS	Leather Seating Surfaces (CDX)	425	500
SR	Power Tilt/Slide Moon Roof (CDX)	425	500

DODGE

AVENGER

CODE	DESCRIPTION	INVOICE	MSRP

2000 AVENGER

2000 Dodge Avenger

What's New?

Base Avengers get new standard equipment, including the 2.5-liter V6 and automatic transmission from the uplevel ES, new cloth fabric on the seats and standard 16-inch wheels with luxury wheelcovers. A sport package is newly optional. A power leather-trimmed driver's seat is included with ES trim for 2000. Two key fobs come with the remote keyless-entry system this year, and two new colors are available. The Avenger will be completely redesigned for 2001.

Review

Nobody misses the Dodge Daytona. You will recall that the Daytona was a front-wheel-drive sport coupe based on the K-Car chassis. After a decade on the market with minimal changes, Chrysler mercifully pulled the plug on the Daytona, replacing it with the Mitsubishi Galant-based Avenger in 1995.

Avenger competes with the Chevrolet Monte Carlo and Pontiac Grand Prix, whereas the Daytona was marketed as an alternative to the Ford Mustang and Chevrolet Camaro. Smaller, lighter and less powerful than the GP or the Monte, Dodge has managed to squeeze nearly as much interior space but not as much performance into the smoothly styled Avenger.

Base and ES flavors are available. For 2000, Dodge has dropped the four-cylinder engine and manual transmission, making a wheezy 163-horsepower, 2.5-liter Mitsubishi V6 hooked to a four-speed automatic the only powertrain choice. So equipped, the Avenger is woefully inadequate in terms of performance compared to the Grand Prix GT and Monte Carlo SS.

Refinement is not the Avenger's trump card, either. Both the Honda Accord Coupe and Toyota Camry Solara are better assembled and constructed of higher-quality materials. But, of course, you pay for perfection, and this sporty Dodge costs thousands less than competing models from Japan.

Other changes for 2000 include revised cloth seats and larger wheels and tires for the Base model. ES versions get a standard power driver's seat and leather upholstery. Ice Silver and Ruby Red paint colors debut. Next year, an all-new Avenger debuts and is expected to be larger, structurally stiffer, and powered by heartier four- and six-cylinder engines.

Overall, the 2000 Avenger is high on practicality and style but low on power and refinement. An accommodating coupe, the Avenger's only real shortcoming is its weak engine. If you're

AVENGER — DODGE

looking for performance, shop elsewhere. But with prices for the top-of-the-line Avenger ES on par with base editions of competing products, and substantial rebates sure to be a mainstay to move 2000 models off the lots, the Avenger is a tempting piece indeed.

Standard Equipment

BASE (4A): 2.5L V6 SOHC SMPI 24-valve engine; 4-speed electronic OD auto transmission with lock-up; 525-amp battery; 90-amp alternator; front-wheel drive, 3.2 axle ratio; stainless steel exhaust with chrome tip; touring ride suspension, front independent double wishbone suspension with anti-roll bar, front coil springs, rear independent double wishbone suspension with rear coil springs; power rack-and-pinion steering with vehicle speed-sensing assist; 4-wheel disc brakes; 15.9 gal. capacity fuel tank; rear lip spoiler, side impact bars; front and rear body-colored bumpers; body-colored bodyside molding; monotone paint; aero-composite halogen headlamps; driver's and passenger's manual remote black outside mirrors; front and rear 16" x 5.5" steel wheels; P205/55HR16 performance A/S BSW front and rear tires; inside under cargo mounted compact steel spare wheel; air conditioning, rear heat ducts; AM/FM stereo, clock, seek-scan, cassette, 6 speakers, and fixed antenna; cruise control; power door locks, remote hatch/trunk release, remote fuel release; 1 power accessory outlet, driver's foot rest, smokers' package; instrumentation display includes tachometer, water temperature gauge, trip odometer; warning indicators include oil pressure, battery, lights on, key in ignition, low fuel, door ajar, trunk ajar, brake fluid; driver's and passenger's front airbags; panic alarm; tinted windows, power windows with driver's 1-touch down; variable intermittent front windshield wipers, sun visor strip, rear window defroster; seating capacity of 5, front bucket seats, adjustable headrests, center armrest with storage, driver's seat includes 8-way direction control, passenger's seat includes 4-way direction control, easy entry; 60-40 folding rear bench seat with fixed headrests; front height adjustable seatbelts; cloth seats, vinyl door trim insert, full cloth headliner, full carpet floor covering with carpeted floor mats; interior lights include dome light, front reading lights; steering wheel with tilt adjustment; vanity mirrors; day/night rearview mirror; full floor console, locking glove box with light, front cupholder, driver's and passenger's door bins; carpeted cargo floor, cargo net, cargo light; black side window moldings, black front windshield molding, black rear window molding and body-colored door handles.

ES (4A) (in addition to or instead of BASE (4A) equipment): Sport ride suspension, rear independent double wishbone suspension with anti-roll bar; additional exterior lights include front fog/driving lights; front and rear 17" x 6.5" silver alloy wheels; P215/50HR17 performance A/S BSW front and rear tires; AM/FM stereo, clock, seek-scan, cassette, single CD, 6 speakers, and fixed antenna; garage door opener; remote keyless entry, panic alarm, security system; driver's seat includes 8-way direction control, lumbar support; leather seats, cloth door trim insert; leather-wrapped steering wheel with tilt adjustment and dual illuminated vanity mirrors.

Base Prices

Code	Description	Invoice	MSRP
FJDH22	Base (4A)	17338	18970
FJDS22	ES (4A)	19336	21215
Destination Charge:		545	545

Accessories

Code	Description	Invoice	MSRP
24E	Quick Order Package 24E (Base) *Includes vehicle with standard equipment. REQUIRES EEB and DGB.*	NC	NC
24F	Quick Order Package 24F (ES) *Includes vehicle with standard equipment. REQUIRES EEB and DGB.*	(561)	(630)
BRF	4-Wheel Antilock Disc Brakes (ES)	534	600
DGB	Transmission: 4-Speed Automatic	NC	NC

DODGE
AVENGER / INTREPID

CODE	DESCRIPTION	INVOICE	MSRP
EEB	Engine: 2.5L SOHC 24V V6 (Base)	(601)	(675)
EEB	Engine: 2.5L SOHC 24V V6 (ES)	NC	NC
GWA	Power Sunroof	610	685
GXR	Remote Keyless Entry (Base)	271	305
	Includes 2 transmitters and panic alarm.		
RAZ	Radio: AM/FM Stereo with Cassette, CD and Equalizer (ES)	289	325
RBX	Radio: AM/FM Stereo with Cassette and CD (Base)	387	435

2000 INTREPID

2000 Dodge Intrepid

What's New?

Dodge updates the Intrepid for 2000 by painting it in five new colors, replacing the seat fabric in base models, and adding horsepower and torque to ES models powered by the 2.7-liter V6. AutoStick is newly available with that engine, and ES buyers can order an in-dash CD changer. Tether-ready child seat anchors have been added behind the rear seat, and cars sold in California meet LEV standards.

Review

Family-sedan buyers typically want four things in a car: room, style, safety and reliability. Dodge delivers all of this and more in the modern-looking Intrepid. Equipped with a huge interior and gigantic trunk, cutting-edge cab-forward design, and proving itself dependable over the long haul (in our experience, anyway), the Dodge Intrepid represents an excellent argument to avoid cookie-cutter Accords and Camrys for a car with personality. Plus, it scores well in government crash tests.

Two trim levels are available: well-equipped base or sporty ES. Base models include four-wheel disc brakes, air conditioning, rear window defroster, power door locks and windows, cassette player, cruise control, power mirrors and a tilt steering wheel. ES adds antilock brakes, HomeLink integrated garage door opener, fog lights, premium sound, white-faced gauges,

156   www.edmunds.com

INTREPID — DODGE

CODE	DESCRIPTION	INVOICE	MSRP

alloy wheels, remote keyless entry, eight-way power driver's seat, leather-wrapped steering wheel and a full-size spare tire.

Base models, and bottom-rung ES versions, are powered by a twin-cam, 24-valve, 2.7-liter V6 based on an aluminum block. Making 200 horsepower at 5,800 rpm and 190 foot-pounds of torque at 4,850 rpm in base models, this engine moves the 3,400-pound Intrepid along adequately. More impressive is the SOHC, 24-valve, 3.2-liter V6 available in ES models. With 225 horsepower at 6,300 rpm and 225 foot-pounds of torque at 3,800 rpm, this engine's better low-end grunt gets the sportier ES off the line with verve.

Available only with an automatic transmission, Intrepid at least offers the enthusiast the option of AutoStick, which allows gears to be rowed manually for sporting driving. However, this feature, standard on ES models, is engineered for the lowest common denominator, and will shift automatically to avoid redlining the engine or fourth-gear starts from a light. Plus, it doesn't improve shift response or acceleration. So our question is, why bother? It's a gimmick, and fans of real manual transmissions will be turned off.

Intrepid is a sedan that has the graceful styling of a coupe, thanks to a continuation of Chrysler's cab-forward design. Dodge's trademark crosshair grille dominates the front end along with two large, sparkling headlights. A love-it-or-hate-it proposition, one thing about Intrepid's design is certain. It is almost impossible to discern the corners of this car when parking, and the hood protrudes further than one might think.

If interior space is your No. 1 priority in a sedan, the Intrepid is hard to beat. Rated a large car by the EPA, Intrepid competes with smaller models, both import and domestic, in price. Room is ample for five adults, and for a family of four, this Dodge seems downright cavernous. Rear-seat legroom, for example, measures a whopping 39.1 inches. In reality, it's almost limo-like.

Changes to the Intrepid are limited for 2000. Three tether-ready child seat anchorages have been added along the top edge of the rear seat, cars sold in California meet low-emission vehicle standards, and five new colors are available. A midline CD-cassette combination stereo is available, and Base models get new seat fabric. ES models have rear seat cupholders integrated with the armrest, and when equipped with the 2.7-liter V6, now come with AutoStick as well as a boost in power and torque, thanks to a new variable-intake system. ES also can be ordered with an in-dash four-disc CD changer.

The popular mid-priced sedan segment of the market is saturated with excellent cars, but Dodge is making a strong case for itself. The Intrepid, with its good looks and commodious cabin, has carved a niche on this crowded and scarred battleground.

Standard Equipment

BASE (4A): 2.7L V6 DOHC SMPI 24-valve engine; 4-speed electronic OD auto transmission with lock-up; 500-amp battery with run down protection; 120-amp alternator; transmission oil cooler; front-wheel drive, 3.55 axle ratio; stainless steel exhaust; touring ride suspension, front independent strut suspension with anti-roll bar, front coil springs, rear independent multi-link suspension with anti-roll bar, rear coil springs; power rack-and-pinion steering; 4-wheel disc brakes; 17 gal. capacity fuel tank; side impact bars; front and rear body-colored bumpers; body-colored bodyside molding, rocker panel extensions; monotone paint; aero-composite halogen headlamps, delay-off feature; driver's and passenger's power remote black outside mirrors; front and rear 16" x 7" steel wheels; P225/60SR16 A/S BSW front and rear tires; inside under cargo mounted compact steel spare wheel; air conditioning, rear heat ducts; AM/FM stereo, clock, seek-scan, cassette, 4 speakers, and fixed antenna; cruise control with steering wheel controls; power door locks, child safety rear door locks, power remote hatch/trunk release; 1 power accessory outlet, driver's foot rest; instrumentation display includes tachometer, water temperature gauge, trip odometer; warning indicators include oil pressure, water temp, battery, lights on, key in ignition, low fuel, low washer fluid, door ajar, trunk ajar; driver's and passenger's front airbags; tinted windows, power front and rear windows with driver's 1-touch down; variable intermittent front windshield wipers, sun visor strip, rear window defroster; seating capacity of 5, front bucket seats, adjustable headrests, center armrest with storage, driver's seat includes 4-way direction control, passenger's seat includes 4-way direction control; rear bench seat with fixed headrests; front height adjustable seatbelts; cloth seats, cloth door trim insert, full cloth

DODGE INTREPID

ES (4A) (in addition to or instead of BASE (4A) equipment): 2.7L V6 DOHC SMPI 24-valve engine with active intake, HD radiator, 125-amp alternator, automanual transmission; stainless steel exhaust with chrome tip; additional exterior lights include front fog/driving lights; front and rear 16" x 7" aluminum wheels; remote keyless entry; panic alarm; driver's seat includes 6-way power seat, lumbar support; 60-40 folding rear bench seat with fixed headrests, center armrest; premium cloth seats, leather-wrapped gear shift knob; interior lights include 2 door curb lights, illuminated entry and leather-wrapped steering wheel with tilt adjustment.

CODE	DESCRIPTION	INVOICE	MSRP

Base Prices

CODE	DESCRIPTION	INVOICE	MSRP
LHDH41	Base (4A)	18677	20390
LHDP41	ES (4A)	20186	22085
	Destination Charge:	560	560

Accessories

CODE	DESCRIPTION	INVOICE	MSRP
—	Inferno Red Tinted Pearl Coat	178	200
22C	Quick Order Package 22C (Base)	NC	NC
	Includes vehicle with standard equipment. REQUIRES EER and DGB.		
23L	Quick Order Package 23L (ES)	(102)	(115)
	Includes vehicle with standard equipment. REQUIRES EES and DGB. NOT AVAILABLE with EGW, CL, TBW.		
24L	Quick Order Package 24L (ES)	(102)	(115)
	Includes vehicle with standard equipment. REQUIRES EGW and DGB. NOT AVAILABLE with CL, EES, TBW.		
24M	Quick Order Package 24M (ES)	1041	1170
	Includes headliner module, universal garage door opener, auto day/night mirror, trip computer, comfort/security group; air conditioning with auto temperature control and security alarm; full size spare and traction control. REQUIRES EGW and DGB.		
ADE	Cold Weather Group	27	30
	Includes battery heater and engine block heater. NOT AVAILABLE with EER.		
AJF	Remote/Illuminated Entry Group (Base)	200	225
	Includes illuminated entry and keyless entry system.		
AJK	Comfort and Security Group (ES)	294	330
	Includes air conditioning with auto temperature control and security alarm. INCLUDED in 24M.		
AR3	Radio: Premium AM/FM Stereo with CD and Cassette	512	575
	Includes 120-W amplifier, equalizer and 8 speakers in 6 locations. REQUIRES 23L or 24L. NOT AVAILABLE with 24M.		
AWS	Smoker's Group	18	20
	Includes front/rear ash receiver and cigar lighter.		

INTREPID / NEON — DODGE

CODE	DESCRIPTION	INVOICE	MSRP
BF	Cloth 50/50 Bench Seat (ES)	89	100
	Includes floor console delete.		
BR3	Antilock Brakes (ES)	690	775
	Includes traction control. REQUIRES 24M. NOT AVAILABLE with 23L, 24L.		
BR3	Antilock Brakes	534	600
	NOT AVAILABLE with 24M.		
CL	Leather Trimmed Bucket Seats (ES)	890	1000
	Includes 8-way power driver/passenger seats. REQUIRES 24M. NOT AVAILABLE with 24L, 23L.		
DGB	Transmission: 4-Speed Automatic	NC	NC
EER	Engine: 2.7L V6 DOHC 24V MPI (Base)	NC	NC
EES	Engine: 2.7L V6 24V with Active Intake (ES)	NC	NC
	NOT AVAILABLE with 24L or 24M.		
EGW	Engine: 3.2L V6 SOHC 24V MPI (ES)	445	500
	NOT AVAILABLE with 23L.		
GWA	Power Sunroof	797	895
JPV	8-Way Power Driver's Seat (Base)	338	380
TBB	Tire: Full Size Spare	111	125
	NOT AVAILABLE with TBW. INCLUDED in 24M.		
TBW	Full Size Spare Tire with Matching Wheel (ES)	80	90
	REQUIRES 24M. NOT AVAILABLE with 24L, 23L, TBB.		

2000 NEON

What's New?

Everything's new inside and out, as the second-generation Neon grows up, not old. A totally redesigned suspension and steering system, low-speed traction control, and a complete exterior redesign head up the notable changes.

Review

The race to build the first 2000-model-year production car goes to DaimlerChrysler with the all-new Dodge and Plymouth Neons. However, the company's claim that "the 2000 Neon will be the first car of the new millennium" is not accurate; remember, historians, the new millennium technically starts in 2001. But "the first car of the last year of the old millennium" is probably too wordy for marketing purposes. Yet either way you look at it, the 2000 Neon is pretty futuristic when compared to its predecessor.

DaimlerChrysler is also billing the 2000 Neon as "quiet, sophisticated and still a lot of fun." Fun seems to be the catch word for the Neon. It's used repeatedly by the manufacturer including, "fun-to-drive handling and steering" and "fun-to-drive attributes." Its maker obviously wants people to know that while the Neon has grown up, it hasn't grown old. It's probably worthwhile for them to stress the fun factor, since the coupe version has been scrapped due to slow sales, meaning that a four-door sedan will have to suffice for all the entry-level economy car thrill-seekers.

Under the hood is the familiar 132-horsepower 2.0-liter inline four, but improvements to the air induction and intake manifold system provide torque over a broader rpm range. A new exhaust manifold, cylinder head and timing-belt cover also decrease overall engine noise, further boosting the new Neon's civilized character. Unfortunately, the 150-horsepower DOHC engine is no longer available.

DODGE

NEON

CODE	DESCRIPTION	INVOICE	MSRP

Thanks to increased wheel travel, the ride is smoother, and it's further enhanced with premium shock absorbers and rear sway bars. The power rack-and-pinion and revamped suspension also contribute to the cruising quality. Stopping power comes from a front disc/rear drum combo, but buyers may want to opt for four-wheel discs with ABS and traction control.

You won't have any problems distinguishing the 2000 model from previous Neons. Exterior changes include new, jewel-like headlamps, a smoother roofline and updated taillamps. By increasing the wheelbase and widening the track, the new Neon offers more interior room and a more stable ride than did its predecessor. And to quote Plymouth, the Neon has tons of interior "surprise and delight" features (hey, they're not fun?) that include a radio/cassette and four Big Gulp-sized cupholders.

For such a small increase in price from a year ago, the new Neon brings a lot to the table. It appears ready to capture the compact-car crown in terms of refinement and sophistication. Now, if only they'd make an optional engine, say, a 2.0-liter DOHC with 150 horsepower. That would be fun.

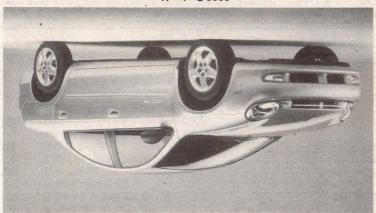

2000 Dodge Neon

Standard Equipment

HIGHLINE (5M): 2.0L I4 SOHC SMPI 16-valve engine; 5-speed overdrive manual transmission; 450-amp battery with run down protection; 83-amp alternator, front wheel drive, 3.54 axle ratio; stainless steel exhaust; touring ride suspension, front independent strut suspension with anti-roll bar, front coil springs, rear independent multi-link suspension with anti-roll bar, rear coil springs; power rack-and-pinion steering, power steering cooler; front disc/rear drum brakes; 12.5 gal. capacity fuel tank; front and rear body-colored bumpers; body-colored bodyside molding; monotone paint; aero-composite halogen headlamps; additional exterior lights include center high mounted stop light; black driver's manual remote outside mirror, passenger's manual outside mirror, front and rear 14" x 5.5" steel wheels; P185/65TR14 BSW AS front and rear tires; inside under cargo mounted compact steel spare wheel; AM/FM stereo, clock, seek-scan, cassette, CD changer pre-wiring, in-dash CD pre-wiring, 6 speakers, and fixed antenna; child safety rear door locks; 1 power accessory outlet; instrumentation display includes water temp gauge, trip odometer; warning indicators include oil pressure, battery, lights on, key in ignition, low fuel; dual airbags; tinted windows, manual rear windows; variable intermittent front windshield wipers, rear window defroster; seating capacity of 5; front bucket seats with adjustable headrests, center armrest with storage, driver's seat includes 4-way direction control, passenger's seat includes 4-way direction control; 60-40 folding rear bench seat with fixed rear headrest, cloth seats, cloth door trim insert, full cloth headliner, full carpet floor covering with carpeted floor

NEON — DODGE

mats, deluxe sound insulation; interior lights include dome light; driver's side vanity mirror; day-night rearview mirror; tilt steering column, full floor console, locking glove box, front and rear cupholders, instrument panel bin, driver's and passenger's door bins; carpeted cargo floor, carpeted trunk lid, cargo light; body-colored grille, black side window moldings, black front windshield molding, black rear window molding and body-colored door handles.

Base Prices

CODE	DESCRIPTION	INVOICE	MSRP
PLDH41	Highline (5M)	11499	12460
	Destination Charge:	510	510

Accessories

CODE	DESCRIPTION	INVOICE	MSRP
21D	Quick Order Package 21D	NC	NC
	Includes vehicle with standard equipment. REQUIRES DD5 and (HAA or 4XA).		
21G	ES Quick Order Package 21G	2234	2510
	Manufacturer Discount	(668)	(750)
	Net Price	1566	1760
	Includes ES badging, air conditioning, color-keyed instrument cluster bezel, keyless entry, power door locks with central locking, power heated exterior mirrors, security alarm, sentry key theft deterrent system, leather-wrapped steering wheel, leather-wrapped shift knob, power trucklid release, power windows, premium cloth low-back bucket seats, passenger assit handles, fog lamps, tachometer, P185/60R15 BSW touring tires and 15" wheel covers. REQUIRES DD5.		
22D	Quick Order Package 22D	NC	NC
	Includes vehicle with standard equipment. REQUIRES DGA and (HAA or 4XA).		
22G	ES Quick Order Package 22G	2234	2510
	Manufacturer Discount	(668)	(750)
	Net Price	1566	1760
	Includes ES badging, air conditioning, color-keyed instrument cluster bezel, keyless entry, power door locks with central locking, power heated exterior mirrors, security alarm, sentry key theft deterrent system, leather-wrapped steering wheel, leather-wrapped shift knob, power trucklid release, power windows, premium cloth low-back bucket seats, passenger assit handles, fog lamps, tachometer, P185/60R15 BSW touring tires and 15" wheel covers. REQUIRES DGA.		
4XA	Air Conditioning Bypass	NC	NC
	NOT AVAILABLE with 2*G, ADA, AJP, AJX, WJA.		
ADA	Light Group	116	130
	Includes console flood lamp, glove box lamp, underhood lamp, rearview mirror with reading lamps and illuminated visor vanity mirrors.		
ADR	Antilock Brake Group	748	840
	Manufacturer Discount	(218)	(245)
	Net Price	530	595
	Includes antilock 4-wheel-disc brakes, tachometer and traction control. REQUIRES 2*D.		
ADR	Antilock Brake Group	659	740
	Manufacturer Discount	(129)	(145)
	Net Price	530	595
	Includes antilock 4-wheel-disc brakes, tachometer and traction control. REQUIRES 2*G.		

DODGE
NEON / STRATUS

CODE	DESCRIPTION	INVOICE	MSRP
AJK	Deluxe Convenience Group	302	350
	Includes speed control and tilt steering column. REQUIRES HAA. NOT AVAILABLE with 2*G.		
AJP	Power Convenience Group	338	380
	Includes power heated fold-away mirrors and power front windows. REQUIRES AJX and HAA.		
AJX	Sentry Key Security Group	650	730
	Manufacturer Discount	(369)	(415)
	Net Price	281	315
	Includes keyless entry, power door locks with automatic central locking, security alarm, sentry key theft deterrent system, tachometer and power trunklid release. REQUIRES HAA.		
AWS	Smoker's Group	18	20
	Includes front ash tray and lighter.		
DD5	Transmission: 5-Speed Manual	NC	NC
DGA	Transmission: 3-Speed Automatic	534	600
	NOT AVAILABLE with 21D, 21G.		
HAA	Air Conditioning	890	1000
	NOT AVAILABLE with 4XA.		
NHK	Engine Block Heater	18	20
NHM	Speed Control	200	225
	REQUIRES 2*G.		
RBR	Radio: AM/FM Stereo with CD	111	125
WJA	Wheels: 15" Aluminum	316	355
	Includes tires: P185/60R15 BSW AS touring. REQUIRES 2*G.		

2000 STRATUS

What's New?

A new entry-level SE replaces last year's base model and comes with so much standard equipment and free optional equipment that you'll have a whole new kind of sticker shock! The upper-level ES steps up to a 2.5-liter V6, and new colors also debut.

Review

You want a car with room with five, oodles of cargo and interior space, and no-charge extras like air conditioning and eight-way power seats? Don't turn the page! With the Dodge Stratus you nab a midsize sedan with access to it all. Plus, the Stratus looks more stylish than its corporate cousin, the Chrysler Cirrus, thanks to its soft bulges and extreme cab-forward design that lend an air of character you can't always find in sedans.

Dodge's 5-year-old midsize returns with a new entry-level model, the SE. Now, you might be thinking entry level basically means a body, tires and a bunch of holes in the dash where the pricey options should go. Nope. The SE has standard A/C, a tilt steering column, tinted glass, a rear window defroster and a full-folding rear seat with a lockable seatback. And, for no additional money down, you can pump up the power parts, in the form of the windows, locks, mirrors and driver seat.

If all of that hasn't tantalized you enough, the Stratus also comes in a higher-end ES version. Optional (but free) upgrades are leather seats, an in-dash CD, remote entry and a security

STRATUS — DODGE

system. If you forego those, you still end up with the standard 2.5-liter V6, an AutoStick, lumbar support and fog lamps, among other features. If you want to impress your pals by spotting the difference between the ES and SE, here's your tip: The SE comes with steel wheels, while the ES has cast-aluminum. Not free but still available to both the SE and ES are such bonuses as a sunroof and a Cold Weather Group (engine-block and battery heaters).

Last year's 132-horsepower 2.0-liter inline four returns as the standard engine for the SE, but for no extra charge, there's an optional 150-horsepower 2.4-liter inline four. The 2.4-liter is hooked to a four-speed automatic transaxle, while the 2.0-liter buyers will be doing the work themselves with a five-speed manual transaxle. Available only to the ES is a 2.5-liter V6 putting out 168 horsepower, and it's mated to a four-speed automatic transaxle with the AutoStick. When you pop the hood, you'll appreciate that the vital fluids are well marked. Large block letters and yellow trim highlight the oil dipstick, coolant reservoir and windshield wiper fluid, among others.

Tucked underneath the Stratus is a modified double-wishbone independent suspension. The SE stops via power front disc and rear drum brakes, while the ES brings it to a halt with four-wheel ABS disc brakes; if you have the four-cylinder, it's a front-disc/rear-drum ABS combination. The steering system also varies between the models, with power rack-and-pinion standard for the SE, but speed-sensitive, variable-assist rack-and-pinion for the ES.

When the redesigned Stratus bows in 2001, it'll also be slightly larger, but the 2000 model is nothing to sneeze at. Pop the trunk and you'll find 15.7 cubic feet of storage. It's easy to load that space up with stuff too, because the lid opens up high and wide. No banged heads on protruding trunk latches here. Also watch for a 2.7-liter V6 to become available next year.

The Stratus is about ease of use and operation, as well as affordability. Perhaps it isn't as soul stirring as the Ford Contour V6, or as beautifully engineered as the Honda Civic, but it is a fantastic value, and we recommend that you consider the Stratus if a family sedan fits the bill.

2000 Dodge Stratus

Standard Equipment

SE (5M): 2.0L I4 SOHC SMPI 16-valve engine; 5-speed OD manual transmission; 510-amp battery; 90-amp alternator; front-wheel drive, 3.94 axle ratio; stainless steel exhaust; touring ride suspension, front independent double wishbone suspension with anti-roll bar, front coil springs, rear independent multi-link suspension with anti-roll bar, rear coil springs; power rack-and-pinion steering; front disc/rear drum brakes; 16 gal. capacity fuel tank; front mud flaps, rear lip spoiler, side impact bars; front and rear body-colored bumpers with body-colored bumper

DODGE STRATUS

CODE	DESCRIPTION	INVOICE	MSRP

insert; body-colored bodyside molding; monotone paint; aero-composite halogen headlamps; driver's and passenger's manual remote black outside mirrors; front and rear 14" x 6" steel wheels; P195/70SR14 A/S BSW front and rear tires; inside under cargo mounted compact steel spare wheel; air conditioning, rear heat ducts; AM/FM stereo, clock, seek-scan, cassette, 6 speakers, and fixed antenna; child safety rear door locks, remote hatch/trunk release; 1 power accessory outlet, driver's foot rest; instrumentation display includes tachometer, water temperature gauge, trip odometer; warning indicators include oil pressure, water temp, battery, lights on, key in ignition, low fuel, door ajar; driver's and passenger's front airbags; tinted windows, manual front and rear windows; variable intermittent front windshield wipers; sun visor strip, rear window defroster; seating capacity of 5; front bucket seats, adjustable headrests, center armrest with storage, driver's seat includes 4-way direction control, passenger's seat includes 4-way direction control; full folding rear bench seat; front height adjustable seatbelts; cloth seats, cloth door trim insert; full cloth headliner, full carpet floor covering with floor mats, plastic/rubber gear shift knob; interior lights include dome light; sport steering wheel with tilt adjustment, manual vanity mirrors, day/night rearview mirror; full floor console, locking glove box with light, front and rear cupholders; instrument panel bin, driver's and passenger's door bins; carpeted cargo floor, cargo light; body-colored grille, black side window moldings, black front windshield molding, black rear window molding and body-colored door handles.

ES (4A) (in addition to or instead of SE (4A) equipment): 2.5L V6 SOHC SMPI 24-valve engine; 4-speed electronic OD auto transmission with lock-up; automatic transmission; power rack-and-pinion steering with vehicle speed-sensing assist; 4-wheel disc brakes with 4-wheel antilock braking system; monotone paint with badging; additional exterior lights include front fog/driving lights; driver's and passenger's power remote black outside mirrors; front and rear 15" x 6" silver alloy wheels; P195/65HR15 A/S BSW front and rear tires; cruise control with steering wheel controls; power front and rear windows with driver's 1-touch down; driver's seat includes 4-way power driver's seat, lumbar support, premium cloth seats, carpeted floor mats; leather-wrapped gear shift knob; interior lights include front reading lights; leather-wrapped steering wheel with tilt adjustment, dual illuminated vanity mirrors and 1 seat back storage pocket.

Base Prices

JADH41	SE (5M)	14628	15930
JADP41	ES (4A)	18099	19830
	Destination Charge:	545	545

Accessories

21A	Quick Order Package 21A (SE)	NC	NC

Includes vehicle with standard equipment. REQUIRES ECB and DD5. NOT AVAILABLE with AJE, EDZ, DGB, GWA.

24B	Quick Order Package 24B (SE)	939	1055
	Manufacturer Discount	(939)	(1055)
	Net Price	NC	NC

Includes front and rear floor mats, speed sensitive power door locks, power mirrors, 8-way power driver's seat and power windows with driver's one-touch down. REQUIRES EDZ and DGB. NOT AVAILABLE with DD5, ECB.

26S	Quick Order Package 26S (ES)	1598	1795
	Manufacturer Discount	(1348)	(1515)
	Net Price	250	280

Includes cargo net, premium AM/FM stereo with cassette, 8-way power driver's seat, leather trimmed bucket seats, security alarm and sentry key theft deterrent system. REQUIRES FEB and DGB. NOT AVAILABLE with AR5.

STRATUS — DODGE

CODE	DESCRIPTION	INVOICE	MSRP
ADE	Engine Block and Battery Heater	27	30
AJF	Remote/Illuminated Entry Group	151	170
	Includes panic alarm, keyless entry system with 2 transmitters and illuminated entry. REQUIRES 24B. NOT AVAILABLE with 21A. INCLUDED in 26S.		
AR3	Radio: Premium AM/FM Stereo with Cassette	303	340
	Includes 8 speakers, 100-Watt external amplifier and CD changer control. NOT AVAILABLE with ARR, AR5. INCLUDED in 26S.		
AR5	Radio: Prem. AM/FM Cassette with 6-Disc CD Changer (ES)	187	210
	Includes CD changer control and 6 speakers. NOT AVAILABLE with AR3.		
AR5	Radio: Prem. AM/FM Cassette with 6-Disc CD Changer (SE)	490	550
	Includes CD changer control and 6 speakers. NOT AVAILABLE with AR3, ARR, 26S.		
ARR	Radio: Premium AM/FM Stereo with CD Player (SE)	178	200
	Includes 6 speakers. NOT AVAILABLE with AR3, AR5.		
AWS	Smokers' Group	18	20
	Includes front ash tray and cigar lighter.		
BRJ	Antilock Front Disc/Rear Drum Brakes (SE)	503	565
DD5	Transmission: 5-Speed Manual (SE)	NC	NC
	NOT AVAILABLE with DGB, EDZ, 24B.		
DGB	Transmission: 4-Speed Automatic (ES)	NC	NC
DGB	Transmission: 4-Speed Automatic (SE)	935	1050
	Includes electronic speed control. NOT AVAILABLE with DD5, ECB, 21A.		
ECB	Engine: 2.0L 4 Cyl. SOHC 16V SMPI (SE)	NC	NC
	NOT AVAILABLE with DGB, 24B.		
EDZ	Engine: 2.4L 4 Cyl. DOHC 16V SMPI (SE)	401	450
	Manufacturer Discount	(401)	(450)
	Net Price	NC	NC
	NOT AVAILABLE with DD5, 21A.		
EEB	Engine: 2.5L V6 SOHC 24V SMPI (ES)	NC	NC
GWA	Power Sunroof (ES)	516	580
	Includes passenger assist handles, front courtesy/reading lamps and illuminated visor vanity mirrors.		
GWA	Power Sunroof (SE)	619	695
	Includes passenger assist handles, front courtesy/reading lamps and illuminated visor vanity mirrors. REQUIRES 24B. NOT AVAILABLE with 21A.		
JPV	8-Way Power Driver's Seat (ES)	338	380
	INCLUDED in 26S.		
LL	Leather Trimmed Bucket Seats (ES)	NC	NC
	REQUIRES 26S.		
LSA	Security Alarm (ES)	156	175
	REQUIRES AJF. INCLUDED in 26S.		
PEL	Inferno Red Tinted Pearl Coat	178	200
TBB	Tire: Full Size Spare	111	125

FORD

CONTOUR

CODE	DESCRIPTION	INVOICE	MSRP

2000 CONTOUR

2000 Ford Contour

What's New?

Only one version of the Contour is available this year (not including the SVT). It is very similar to the 1999 Contour SE Sport series. New colors are offered and an emergency trunk-release handle is standard.

Review

There is nothing like a little sibling rivalry to shake things up. The arrival of the 2000 Ford Focus has affected both the Escort and the Contour. Effectively, the Focus will be slotted between the Escort and the Contour in terms of price. To avoid having the Focus steal sales away from the Contour, Ford has taken the Contour upscale, discontinuing the entry-level LX series from 1999.

The 2000 Contour is very similar to the '99 Contour SE Sport. The 2.5-liter Duratec V6, 15-inch, eight-spoke aluminum wheels, rear spoiler, remote keyless entry, body cladding and fog lamps are now standard. A 60/40 split-folding rear seat is also standard, though leather seats are no longer available.

Whether these upgrades will help alleviate the Contour's rental-fleet image, we're not quite sure. But we do know that when we've been behind the wheel of a V6-equipped Contour, we've generally had a good time. The V6 is just one part of an equation that makes this car such an excellent purchase for the shallow-pocketed enthusiast. The real excitement of the Contour's driving experience is the result of the car's excellent chassis, suspension and steering. Toss the Contour into a corner, and it's as easy to catch as softball thrown by a preschooler.

Since its introduction, the Contour has won plenty of awards and has received great press from automotive critics. In 1998, Ford gave the Contour an exterior freshening to make the car more distinctive in the crowded family-sedan marketplace. The interior still receives some gripes, however. It lacks some of the refinement found in competing cars and Ford has never been able to solve the lack of room for rear-seat passengers.

The SVT Contour continues into 2000. This vehicle is one of the best bang-for-the-buck performance sedans you can buy. It comes equipped with a 200-horsepower, 2.5-liter V6 and a sport-tuned suspension. The SVT Contour also benefits from larger brakes, 16-inch performance tires and wheels, leather seating, and unique front and rear styling.

166   www.edmunds.com   **EDMUND'S® NEW CARS**

CONTOUR — FORD

People less concerned about driving and more concerned about spaciousness may want to investigate the Dodge Stratus and Chevrolet Malibu. They aren't as exciting as the Contour, but they can hold people more comfortably. And if you're disappointed that the Contour LX is no longer available, you need not worry-a quick hop to your local Mercury dealership will net you a 2000 Mercury Mystique GS, which is effectively the same thing.

Standard Equipment

SE SPORT (5M): 2.5L V6 DOHC SMPI 24-valve engine; 5-speed OD manual transmission; 60-amp battery; 130-amp alternator; front-wheel drive, 4.06 axle ratio; partial stainless steel exhaust; front independent strut suspension with anti-roll bar, front strut springs, rear independent multi-link suspension with anti-roll bar, rear coil springs; power rack-and-pinion steering; front disc/rear drum brakes; 15 gal. capacity fuel tank; rear wing spoiler, side impact bars; front and rear body-colored bumpers; body-colored bodyside molding, rocker panel extensions; monotone paint; aero-composite halogen headlamps; additional exterior lights include front fog/driving lights; driver's and passenger's power remote body-colored folding outside mirrors; front and rear 15" x 5.5" silver alloy wheels; P205/60SR15 A/S BSW front and rear tires; inside under cargo mounted compact steel spare wheel; air conditioning, air filter, rear heat ducts; AM/FM stereo, seek-scan, cassette, 4 speakers, and fixed antenna; cruise control with steering wheel controls; power door locks with 2 stage unlock, child safety rear door locks, power remote hatch/trunk release; 1 power accessory outlet, driver's foot rest; instrumentation display includes tachometer, water temperature gauge, in-dash clock, trip odometer; warning indicators include oil pressure, battery, low oil level, lights on; driver's and passenger's front airbags; ignition disable; tinted windows, power front and rear windows with driver's 1-touch down; variable intermittent front windshield wipers, rear window defroster; seating capacity of 5, front bucket seats, adjustable headrests, driver's armrest, driver's seat includes 4-way direction control, passenger's seat includes 4-way direction control; 60-40 folding rear bench seat with center armrest; front height adjustable seatbelts; cloth seats, vinyl door trim insert, full cloth headliner, full carpet floor covering with carpeted floor mats, leather-wrapped gear shift knob; interior lights include dome light with fade, front reading lights, illuminated entry; leather-wrapped steering wheel with tilt adjustment; vanity mirrors; day/night rearview mirror; full floor console, glove box, front cupholder, driver's and passenger's door bins; carpeted cargo floor, cargo light; chrome grille, black side window moldings, black front windshield molding, black rear window molding and body-colored door handles.

Base Prices

Code	Description	Invoice	MSRP
P66	SE Sport (5M)	15332	16845
	Destination Charge:	560	560

Accessories

Code	Description	Invoice	MSRP
13B	Power Moonroof	530	595
21A	Power Driver's Seat	312	350
	Includes adjustment for seat forward/backward, seat up/down and seat front tilt/rear tilt.		
41H	Engine Block Heater	18	20
428	High Altitude Principal Use	NC	NC
429	Non-High Altitude Principal Use	NC	NC
44T	Transmission: 4-Speed Auto with OD	725	815
	Includes 3.77 axle ratio.		
552	Antilock Braking System	445	500
553	All-Speed Traction Control	156	175
	REQUIRES 552.		

FORD  CONTOUR / SVT CONTOUR

CODE	DESCRIPTION	INVOICE	MSRP
585	Radio: AM/FM Stereo with CD and Premium Sound	245	275
	Includes single CD player. Does not include cassette player. NOT AVAILABLE with 58P.		
58P	Radio: AM/FM Cassette with Premium Sound	120	135
	NOT AVAILABLE with 585.		
63B	Smoker's Package	13	15
	Includes ashtray and cigarette lighter.		

2000 SVT CONTOUR

2000 Ford SVT Contour

What's New?

The 2000 SVT Contour is unchanged from 1999.

Review

　　We've made no apologies for our unabashed appreciation of the Ford SVT Contour. A labor of love from the Ford Special Vehicle Team (the same folks who bring us the Mustang Cobra and F-150 Lightning), the SVT Contour is a must-drive for budget-minded sport-sedan shoppers. SVT's version of Ford's Contour comes fully loaded, packed with real enthusiast hardware, and is capable of zero-to-60 mph sprints in just seven-and-a-half seconds. It's no wonder the SVT Contour has been a frequent visitor on Edmunds.com's "Most Wanted" list.

　　Power comes from an SVT-modified 2.5-liter Duratec V6, which makes 200 horsepower at 6,600 rpm and 169 foot-pounds of torque at 5,500 rpm. The sweet-revving engine is all-too-willing to reach redline quickly, and the muted burble from the exhaust makes the $23,000 domestic sedan sound like an expensive, exotic sports machine.

　　The tires on the SVT Contour are considerably more performance oriented than those found on the regular Contour. For 2000, the SVT Contour is shod with 215/50ZR-16 BFGoodrich g-Force T/A KDW performance radials. The suspension is equally tweaked to increase handling ability. The sporty little front-driver is surefooted and nimble on curvy roads, and the performance brakes and standard ABS inspire confidence.

SVT CONTOUR — FORD

The SVT Contour looks good and performs a variety of functions well. It also does this without extracting a huge financial toll for your enthusiast yearnings. It's not perfect, mind you. The SVT version still inherits some of the Contour SE's faults, most of which concern the interior. The back seat is too small to comfortably fit three adults. There's also a difficult-to-operate stereo and too-small cupholders.

It is rumored that 2000 will be the final year for the SVT Contour. Oddly enough, the sport sedan is one of the few car segments that have held promise in the face of booming truck sales. In fact, most of Ford's major competitors now claim at least one strong-selling sport-sedan model in their 2000 lineups. If you want a sport sedan and there are no SVT Contours left, you might want to look at a Nissan Maxima SE, or an Audi A4.

Standard Equipment

SVT CONTOUR (5M): 2.5L V6 DOHC SMPI 24-valve engine, requires premium unleaded fuel; 5-speed OD manual transmission; 130-amp alternator; front-wheel drive, 4.06 axle ratio; stainless steel exhaust with chrome tip; sport ride suspension, front independent strut suspension with anti-roll bar, front coil springs, rear independent multi-link suspension with anti-roll bar, rear coil springs; power rack-and-pinion steering; 4-wheel disc brakes with 4-wheel antilock braking system; 14.5 gal. capacity fuel tank; side impact bars; front and rear body-colored bumpers; body-colored bodyside molding, rocker panel extensions; monotone paint; aero-composite halogen headlamps; additional exterior lights include front fog/driving lights; driver's and passenger's power remote body-colored folding outside mirrors; front and rear 16" x 6.5" silver alloy wheels; P215/50ZR16 A/S BSW front and rear tires; inside under cargo mounted compact steel spare wheel; air conditioning, air filter, rear heat ducts; AM/FM stereo, seek-scan, cassette, 4 performance speakers, amplifier, and power retractable antenna; cruise control with steering wheel controls; power door locks with 2 stage unlock, remote keyless entry, child safety rear door locks, remote hatch/trunk release; 1 power accessory outlet, driver's foot rest; instrumentation display includes tachometer, water temperature gauge, in-dash clock, trip odometer; warning indicators include oil pressure, battery, low coolant, lights on, key in ignition, low fuel; driver's and passenger's front airbags; ignition disable; tinted windows, power front and rear windows with driver's 1-touch down; variable intermittent front windshield wipers, sun visor strip, rear window defroster; seating capacity of 5, front sports seats, adjustable headrests, driver's seat includes 6-way power seat, power 2-way lumbar support, passenger's seat includes 4-way direction control; 60-40 folding rear bench seat with fixed headrests, center armrest; front height adjustable seatbelts; leather seats, vinyl door trim insert, full cloth headliner, full color-keyed carpet floor covering with carpeted floor mats, leather-wrapped gear shift knob; interior lights include dome light with delay front reading lights, illuminated entry; leather-wrapped steering wheel with tilt adjustment; dual illuminated vanity mirrors; day/night rearview mirror; full floor console, glove box, front cupholder, driver's and passenger's door bins; carpeted cargo floor, cargo light; chrome grille, black side window moldings, black front windshield molding, black rear window molding and body-colored door handles.

Base Prices

Code	Description	Invoice	MSRP
P68	SVT Contour (5M)	20556	22715
	Destination Charge:	560	560

Accessories

Code	Description	Invoice	MSRP
13B	Power Moonroof	NC	NC
13K	Raised Wing Spoiler	218	245
41H	Engine Block Immersion Heater (LPO)	18	20
428	High Altitude Principal Use	NC	NC

FORD
SVT CONTOUR / CROWN VICTORIA

CODE	DESCRIPTION	INVOICE	MSRP
429	Non-High Altitude Principal Use	NC	NC
585	Radio: Premium AM/FM Stereo with CD	NC	NC
	Includes amplifier. Does not include cassette player.		
63B	Smokers' Package	13	15
	Includes ashtray and cigarette lighter.		

2000 CROWN VICTORIA

2000 Ford Crown Victoria

_____ **What's New?** _____

New safety items have been added, including an emergency trunk release, child seat-anchor brackets, and the Belt Minder system. The rear-axle ratio for Crown Victorias with the handling package changes from 3.27 to 3.55. Two new shades of green are offered—Tropical Green and Dark Green Satin.

_____ **Review** _____

If you've been pinching your pennies to buy a new full-size, rear-drive American sedan, we hope you like Fords. The Blue Oval is the only manufacturer building such cars these days. Decades-old technology allows Ford to keep the prices low, and the car is a favorite among fleet buyers for taxi companies, police departments, or just those who need space and don't want a minivan or sport-ute.

The grand dame of the Ford lineup was redesigned in 1998, getting improved steering and handling, a formal roofline, a more prominent grille, a new hood and revised rear styling. Consequently, not much changes for 2000. The Crown Victoria does receive many of the safety changes that Ford has implemented across the line for 2000. The mobster—er, emergency trunk release allows people who are trapped in the trunk to release the hatch. The child seat anchor brackets in the back seat provide parents and caregivers an improved method to buckle in their child safety seats more securely. The system secures child safety seats using tethers that attach to the anchor brackets, in addition to traditional safety belts.

CROWN VICTORIA — FORD

| CODE | DESCRIPTION | INVOICE | MSRP |

These days the Ford Crown Victoria and its Mercury Grand Marquis stablemate offer much more value than most compact and midsize cars being peddled at your local auto mall. Think about this: the Crown Vic costs just over $26,000 fully loaded with electric everything and a leather interior. In contrast, a similarly equipped Toyota Avalon runs more than $30,000, and the much smaller Toyota Camry XLE costs $25,000; despite a wimpy (in comparison) V6, tight seating for five, and a comparatively small trunk.

In stock trim, the Crown Victoria drives and handles like you would expect a big American sedan to do. It's comfortable, but it's all too happy to float around over bumps. The handling and performance group adds a few horsepower and improves the car's stability in the twisties; we recommend it to anyone who enjoys backcountry highways more than mind-numbing interstates for their family vacations. The Watt's Linkage rear suspension gives this car's rear axle a 400 percent increase in rigidity, a real payoff in the handling department. Larger brake rotors with dual piston calipers were also added last year, and help pull the car down from high speeds without overheating. The Crown Victoria's traction control, also added in the 1998 redesign, operates at all speeds, using the antilock brakes and engine spark retardation to keep the rear wheels from slipping.

So, if you're one of the few people unwilling to pay for a sport utility's high insurance premiums and abysmal gas mileage and if you just can't stand the idea of a minivan, we hope that you like the Crown Victoria. It's your only choice for an American, full-size, rear-wheel-drive sedan.

Standard Equipment

BASE (4A): 4.6L V8 SOHC SMPI 16-valve engine; 4-speed electronic OD auto transmission with lock-up; battery with run down protection; 130-amp alternator; rear-wheel drive, 2.73 axle ratio; stainless steel exhaust; front independent suspension with anti-roll bar, front coil springs, rigid rear axle multi-link suspension with anti-roll bar, rear coil springs; power re-circulating ball steering with vehicle speed-sensing assist; 4-wheel disc brakes with 4-wheel antilock braking system; 19 gal. capacity fuel tank; side impact bars; front and rear body-colored bumpers with chrome bumper insert; body-colored bodyside molding; clearcoat monotone paint; aero-composite halogen fully auto headlamps with delay-off feature; additional exterior lights include cornering lights; driver's and passenger's power remote body-colored folding outside mirrors; front and rear 16" x 7" steel wheels; P225/60SR16 A/S BSW front and rear tires; inside mounted compact steel spare wheel; air conditioning, rear heat ducts; AM/FM stereo, seek-scan, cassette, 4 speakers, and window grid antenna; cruise control with steering wheel controls; power door locks, child safety rear door locks, power remote hatch/trunk release; 1 power accessory outlet, driver's foot rest, smokers' package; instrumentation display includes oil pressure gauge, water temperature gauge, volt gauge, in-dash clock, trip odometer; warning indicators include battery, lights on, key in ignition, low fuel, door ajar; driver's and passenger's front airbags; ignition disable; tinted windows, power front and rear windows with driver's 1-touch down; variable intermittent front windshield wipers, rear window defroster; seating capacity of 6, 50-50 split-bench front seat, adjustable headrests, center armrest, driver's seat includes 4-way direction control, passenger's seat includes 4-way direction control; rear bench seat; front height adjustable seatbelts; cloth seats, vinyl door trim insert, full cloth headliner, full color-keyed carpet floor covering, deluxe sound insulation, simulated wood trim on instrument panel; interior lights include dome light with delay, 4 door curb lights, illuminated entry; steering wheel with tilt adjustment; day/night rearview mirror; locking glove box with light, front cupholder, driver's and passenger's door bins; carpeted cargo floor, carpeted trunk lid, cargo light; chrome grille, chrome side window moldings, black front windshield molding, black rear window molding and chrome door handles.

LX (4A) (in addition to or instead of BASE (4A) equipment): Clearcoat monotone paint with bodyside accent stripe; remote keyless entry; ignition disable, panic alarm; driver's seat includes 6-way power seat, power 2-way lumbar support; rear bench seat with center armrest; premium cloth seats, carpeted lower door trim panel; interior lights include front reading lights; dual illuminated vanity mirrors and 2 seat back storage pockets.

FORD CROWN VICTORIA

CODE	DESCRIPTION	INVOICE	MSRP

Base Prices

P73	Base (4A)	20499	22005
P74	LX (4A)	22425	24120
	Destination Charge:	630	630

Accessories

12H	Front and Rear Floor Mats	49	55
144	Remote Keyless Entry (Base)	213	240
	NOT AVAILABLE with 999.		
175	Universal Garage Door Opener (LX)	102	115
	Can be programmed for 3 different transmitters.		
21A	Power Driver's Seat (Base)	321	360
41G	Handling and Performance Package (Base)	832	935
	Includes revised springs, shocks and stabilizer bar, tires: P225/60TR16 TOURING BSW, wheels: 16" cast aluminum, rear air suspension, dual exhaust, engine: 215 HP and 3.55 axle ratio. NOT AVAILABLE with T2A, 999, 72A.		
41G	Handling and Performance Package (LX)	658	740
	Includes revised springs, shocks and stabilizer bar, tires: P225/60TR16 TOURING BSW, wheels: 16" cast aluminum, rear air suspension, dual exhaust, engine: 215 HP and 3.55 axle ratio. NOT AVAILABLE with T2A, 65E, 65C, 999.		
41G	Handling and Performance Package (LX)	547	615
	Includes revised springs, shocks and stabilizer bar, tires: P225/60TR16 TOURING BSW, wheels: 16" cast aluminum, rear air suspension, dual exhaust, engine: 215 HP and 3.55 axle ratio. REQUIRES 65C or 65E. NOT AVAILABLE with T2A, 999.		
41H	Engine Block Immersion Heater (LPO)	23	25
428	High Altitude Principal Use	NC	NC
429	Non-High Altitude Principal Use	NC	NC
508	Conventional Spare Tire (LPO)	107	120
	Includes steel spare wheel at extra charge when ordered with 41G Handling Pkg. Replaces standard mini-spare. Includes full size steel wheel. NOT AVAILABLE with T2A, 999.		
508	Conventional Spare Tire (LPO)	93	105
	Replaces standard mini-spare. Includes full size steel wheel. NOT AVAILABLE with 41G.		
553	All-Speed Electronic Traction Control	156	175
	NOT AVAILABLE with 999.		
585	Radio: AM/FM Stereo with CD	124	140
	Replaces cassette. NOT AVAILABLE with 586, 65E.		
586	Radio: Premium AM/FM Stereo with Cassette (LX)	321	360
	Includes auto-set radio (selects 6 strongest listenable stations and stores them), seek and scan radio feature (seek also available with tape evaluation), distributed audio system, auto bass/loudness feature, self-diagnostic capability, 80-watt power, 4 speakers, Dolby sound and radio data system (RDS). REQUIRES 65C. NOT AVAILABLE with 999, 585.		

172 www.edmunds.com

CROWN VICTORIA / ESCORT — FORD

CODE	DESCRIPTION	INVOICE	MSRP
65C	LX Comfort Group (LX) .... *Includes air conditioning with auto temperature control, wheels: 12-spoke aluminum, power passenger's seat with lumbar, electronic auto dim rear view mirror, compass and leather-wrapped steering wheel. NOT AVAILABLE with 999.*	801	900
65E	LX Comfort Plus Group (LX) .... *Includes LX comfort group: air conditioning with auto temperature control, wheels: 12-spoke aluminum, power passenger's seat with lumbar, electronic auto dim rear view mirror, compass, leather-wrapped steering wheel, electronic instrumentation, tripminder computer, electronic digital instrumentation, leather seating surfaces and premium AM/FM stereo with cassette radio. NOT AVAILABLE with 999, 585.*	1914	2150
919	Trunk Mounted 6-Disc CD Changer (LX) .... *REQUIRES 586 and 65C. NOT AVAILABLE with 999.*	312	350
999	Engine: 4.6L Natural Gas .... *Includes engine compartment light and auto headlamp delete. NOT AVAILABLE with 41G, 553, T2A, 508, 144, L, 65C, 65E, 586, 919.*	5487	6165
L	Leather Seating Surfaces Split Bench (LX) .... *Includes driver's and passenger's power recliners, lumbar and vinyl headrests. REQUIRES 65C. NOT AVAILABLE with 999.*	654	735
T2A	Tires: P225/60SR16 WSW .... *NOT AVAILABLE with 41G, 999, 508.*	71	80

1999 ESCORT

What's New?

Ford's entry-level car gets new colors, new interior fabrics, and revised options. An AM/FM stereo with cassette is now standard on the Escort SE. An interior trunk release is now standard on all models. The sedans and wagon get all-door remote keyless entry added to their standard equipment lists. An integrated child seat is no longer available.

Review

The Escort has been Ford's bread-and-butter car for the last fifteen years. Think of it as the car that brings consumers into the Ford family. The Escort's low price, decent reliability and above average crash test scores have consistently offered recent college grads and young families an attractive set of American wheels. In 1997, Ford decided to redesign its entry-level vehicle.

Ford addressed three major areas when planning the current generation Escort: power, stiffness and build quality. Anyone familiar with the previous Escort's asthmatic engine knows that we are not exaggerating when we say that the new engine is an exponential improvement over the one powering the old model. The current motor is a 2.0-liter overhead cam engine that makes 110 horsepower and 125 foot-pounds of torque, enough to make the Escort sedan and wagon competitive with the Honda Civic, Hyundai Elantra and Mazda Protegé. The new engine is also quieter than the one it replaces, the overhead-cam design contributing to smoother delivery and more refined operation.

Ford also addressed body stiffness and vibration. Second-generation Escorts were notoriously wiggly over rough surfaces. The Escort's tendency to shake, which led to a lot of rattle-and-roll, could really punish passengers on long commutes. One-piece body construction, a cross-car

FORD
ESCORT

CODE	DESCRIPTION	INVOICE	MSRP

beam and stiffer stabilizer bars solved this problem by radically improving the current Escort's torsional stiffness.

Fit and finish, the Escort's third problem area, were also refined by the one-piece body construction. This makes the windows and doors fit better, meaning that they are less likely to let in the weather. The secondary control panel, a long-standing sore spot among Escort owners, was brought up to speed with the introduction of Ford's Integrated Control Panel, first seen on the 1996 Taurus. The ICP reduces dashboard clutter by combining the stereo and climate controls. The single-unit ICP is easier to use than the one found in Taurus, however, and allows eyes-on-the-road operation of its systems.

The major change for 1999 includes the addition of a new stereo with cassette to the standard equipment lists of the SE sedan and wagon. Other changes include adding a leather-wrapped steering wheel to the sedan sport group equipment and making all-door remote keyless entry standard on the SE models. Oddly, Ford dropped the integrated child seat from the wagon's optional equipment list. What happened to the safest car manufacturer in America image they've been pushing?

The Escort is a competent sedan in a crowded market. A competitive price, good lease deals, and ever-present incentives make it hard not to recommend the Escort.

1999 Ford Escort

Standard Equipment

LX SEDAN (5M): 2.0L I4 SOHC SMPI 8-valve engine; 5-speed overdrive manual transmission; 58-amp battery with run down protection; 48-amp HD alternator; front wheel drive, 3.85 axle ratio; stainless steel exhaust; front independent strut suspension with anti-roll bar, front coil springs, rear independent multi-link suspension with anti-roll bar, rear coil springs; power rack-and-pinion steering; front disc/rear drum brakes; 12.7 gal capacity fuel tank; front and rear body-colored bumpers; black bodyside molding; monotone paint; aero-composite halogen headlamps; additional exterior lights include center high mounted stop light; driver's and passenger's manual black folding outside mirrors; front and rear 14" x 5.5" steel wheels; P185/65SR14 BSW AS front and rear tires; inside under cargo mounted compact steel spare wheel; rear heat ducts; AM/FM stereo with seek-scan, 4 speakers, and manual retractable antenna; child safety rear door locks, remote hatch/trunk release; 1 power accessory outlet; instrumentation display includes water temp gauge, in-dash clock, trip odometer; warning indicators include oil pressure, battery, low coolant, lights on, key in ignition, low fuel, door ajar; dual airbags; tinted windows, manual rear windows; variable intermittent front windshield wipers; seating capacity of

174   www.edmunds.com   **EDMUND'S® NEW CARS**

ESCORT — FORD

CODE	DESCRIPTION	INVOICE	MSRP

5, front bucket seats with adjustable headrests, driver's seat includes 4-way direction control, passenger's seat includes 4-way direction control; 60-40 folding rear bench seat; front height adjustable seatbelts; cloth seats, vinyl door trim insert, full cloth headliner, full carpet floor covering; interior lights include dome light; vanity mirrors; day-night rearview mirror; full floor console, glove box, front and rear cupholders, instrument panel bin, driver's and passenger's door bins; carpeted cargo floor; black grille, body-colored side window moldings, black front windshield molding, black rear window molding and body-colored door handles.

SE SEDAN (5M) (in addition to or instead of LX SEDAN (5M) equipment): Air conditioning; AM/FM stereo with seek-scan, cassette, 4 speakers, and manual retractable antenna; power door locks, remote keyless entry, panic alarm, security system and rear window defroster.

SE WAGON (5M) (in addition to or instead of SE SEDAN (5M) equipment): Roof rack; power front windows with driver 1-touch down, power rear windows; rear window wiper, rear window defroster; carpeted cargo floor, plastic trunk lid and cargo cover.

Base Prices

CODE	DESCRIPTION	INVOICE	MSRP
P10	LX Sedan (5M)	10769	11505
P13	SE Sedan (5M)	12117	12985
P15	SE Wagon (5M)	13209	14185
	Destination Charge:	415	415

Accessories

CODE	DESCRIPTION	INVOICE	MSRP
12Y	Front and Rear Floor Mats	49	55
144	All-Door Remote Entry with Anti-Theft (LX Sedan)	147	165
	Includes 2 keyfobs.		
41H	Engine Block Heater	18	20
	REQUIRES 57Q.		
434	SE Sport Group (SE Sedan)	441	495
	Includes leather-wrapped steering wheel, rear spoiler, tachometer, bright-tip exhaust, unique sport bucket seats, 14" aluminum wheels and sport badging.		
44T	Transmission: 4-Speed Automatic	725	815
	Includes 3.74 axle ratio.		
50A	Comfort Group (SE)	307	345
	Includes tilt steering wheel, speed control and dual map lights.		
552	Antilock Braking System	356	400
572	Air Conditioning (LX Sedan)	708	795
57Q	Rear Window Defroster (LX Sedan)	169	190
58H	Radio: AM/FM Stereo with Cassette (LX Sedan)	165	185
	REQUIRES 572 or 57Q.		
60A	Power Group (SE Sedan)	307	345
	Includes power windows.		
63B	Smoker's Package	13	15
	Includes removable ashtray and cigarette lighter.		
64P	Wheels: 14" Aluminum (SE Sedan)	236	265
919	Radio: Premium AM/FM Stereo w/ Cass. and 6-Disc CD (SE Sedan)	263	295

FORD

ESCORT ZX2

CODE	DESCRIPTION	INVOICE	MSRP

2000 ESCORT ZX2

2000 Ford Escort ZX2

What's New?

The 2000 ZX2 has been simplified to a single series lineup, combining significant carryover features from the previous "Cool" and "Hot" series. The performance-oriented ZX2 S/R, a limited-production vehicle in 1999, is now an official "S/R" option package. The Power and Comfort option packages have been simplified.

Review

Based on the Escort platform, Ford's ZX2 Coupe competes in the entry-level performance-coupe market. We thought the ZX2 would be discontinued this year because of the arrival of the new Ford Focus, but Ford has decided to continue selling both cars. The Focus won't be offered in coupe format, so the ZX2 is Ford's only small coupe.

Buyers in this market are often looking for sporting fun. For horsepower, the ZX2 comes standard with a 2.0-liter, DOHC Zetec four-cylinder engine. It produces 130 horsepower at 5,750 rpm. The engine has plenty of torque, especially when compared to the Honda Civic's 1.6-liter engine. The torque comes in handy around town and when accelerating onto freeways. While it sounds uninspired, the engine is nevertheless quiet and fuel-efficient. The ZX2 powertrain is designed for low maintenance, with platinum-tipped spark plugs and a 100,000-mile tune-up interval under normal driving conditions.

Inside, the interior is functional, but suffers from styling attempts to make it hip. There are lots of angles and triangles used on the dash, which ultimately gives it a bizarre look. The interior also suffers from mushy seats and the manual-transmission shifter doesn't live up to the ZX2's performance-oriented aspirations. Rear-seat passenger room is only adequate for this class.

The 2000 ZX2 receives standardized key equipment, such as an AM/FM stereo cassette, power mirrors and a rear window defroster. The Power Group now includes power windows, power locks, and a remote entry with an anti-theft alarm. The Comfort Group now includes speed control, a tilt steering column, map lights and a leather-wrapped steering wheel. Like many other Fords for this year, the ZX2 also receives a new "belt-minder" safety feature (it beeps at you if you don't buckle your belt) and a rear seatback-release lever to prevent trunk entrapment.

ESCORT ZX2 — FORD

While handling is certainly acceptable on the ZX2, it can be improved considerably by ordering the S/R package. The S/R package adds stiffer suspension parts, additional horsepower (coming from a revised air intake, exhaust, and computer), rear disc brakes, a stronger clutch, a short-throw shifter, upgraded seats and a unique tire/wheel package. Even if the performance upgrades didn't work, the S/R package would still almost be worth it for the seats and shifter.

Even when the three-door Focus hatchback goes on sale, the ZX2 should still have enough positive attributes to attract attention. It's fun to drive and affordable, and the S/R package should attract enthusiasts who are looking for something more performance oriented.

Standard Equipment

ZX2 (5M): 2.0L I4 DOHC SMPI with variable valve timing 16-valve engine; 5-speed OD manual transmission; battery with run down protection; 48-amp HD alternator; front-wheel drive, 4.1 axle ratio; stainless steel exhaust; front independent strut suspension with anti-roll bar, front coil springs, rear independent multi-link suspension with anti-roll bar, rear coil springs; power rack-and-pinion steering; front disc/rear drum brakes; 12.7 gal. capacity fuel tank; front and rear mud flaps, rear wing spoiler; front and rear body-colored bumpers; body-colored bodyside molding; clearcoat monotone paint; aero-composite halogen headlamps; additional exterior lights include front fog/driving lights; driver's and passenger's power remote black folding outside mirrors; front and rear 15" x 5.5" silver alloy wheels; P185/60TR15 A/S BSW front and rear tires; inside under cargo mounted compact steel spare wheel; rear heat ducts; AM/FM stereo, seek-scan, 4 performance speakers, and manual retractable antenna; remote hatch/trunk release; 1 power accessory outlet, smokers' package; instrumentation display includes tachometer, water temperature gauge, in-dash clock, trip odometer; warning indicators include oil pressure, battery, low coolant, lights on, key in ignition, low fuel, door ajar; driver's and passenger's front airbags; tinted windows; variable intermittent front windshield wipers, rear window defroster; seating capacity of 4, front bucket seats adjustable headrests, driver's seat includes 4-way direction control, passenger's seat includes 4-way direction control, easy entry; 60-40 folding rear bench seat; front height adjustable seatbelts; cloth seats, cloth door trim insert, full cloth headliner, full carpet floor covering; interior lights include dome light; vanity mirrors; day/night rearview mirror; full floor console, glove box, front and rear cupholders, instrument panel bin, driver's and passenger's door bins; carpeted cargo floor, cargo light; black side window moldings, black front windshield molding, black rear window molding and body-colored door handles.

Base Prices

CODE	DESCRIPTION	INVOICE	MSRP
P11	ZX2 (5M)	10967	11760
	Destination Charge:	440	440

Accessories

CODE	DESCRIPTION	INVOICE	MSRP
12Y	Front and Rear Floor Mats	49	55
	NOT AVAILABLE with 67R.		
13B	Power Sliding Moonroof	530	595
	NOT AVAILABLE with 67R.		
41H	Engine Block Heater	18	20
428	High Altitude Principal Use	NC	NC
429	Non-High Altitude Principal Use	NC	NC
44T	Transmission: 4-Speed Auto with OD	725	815
	Includes 3.74 axle ratio.		
50A	Comfort Group	352	395
	Includes dual map lights, leather-wrapped steering wheel, speed control and tilt steering wheel. REQUIRES 572. NOT AVAILABLE with 67R.		

FORD
ESCORT ZX2 / FOCUS

CODE	DESCRIPTION	INVOICE	MSRP
552	Antilock Braking System	356	400
572	Air Conditioning	708	795
60A	Power Group	352	395
	Includes power windows, power door locks, all-door remote entry and anti theft		
	system.		
64A	Wheels: 14" Chrome 5-Spoke	530	595
	REQUIRES T71. NOT AVAILABLE with 67R.		
67R	S/R Package	1331	1495
	Includes performance clutch, exhaust, upgraded seats with ZX2 logo. floor mats,		
	performance rear disc brakes, performance suspension, performance shifter/boot/		
	knob, unique wheels, tires: P205/55ZR15 and rear spoiler delete. REQUIRES 572.		
	NOT AVAILABLE with 13B, 50A, T71, 64A, 12Y.		
919	Radio: Premium AM/FM Cassette with 6 Disc CD Changer	263	295
	Trunk mounted CD changer. Due to unique design of the ICP, aftermarket audio		
	upgrades are limited.		
A	Unique Leather Sport Buckets	352	395
T71	Tires: P185/65R14 BSW	NC	NC
	REQUIRES 64A. NOT AVAILABLE with 67R.		

2000 FOCUS

What's New?

This is Ford's all-new "world car" that will be sold concurrently with the Escort. Everything from interior room to performance has been addressed to make this European-engineered compact a winner in the small-car segment.

Review

"Smart design and spirited driving" were the guiding forces behind the development of the Focus. Targeted to be the new volume leader in Ford sales worldwide, the Focus is a highly evolved compact car with "New Edge" styling, a roomy interior, and excellent road manners.

Ford offers the Focus in three body styles: a three-door hatchback, a sedan and a wagon. The sedan can be ordered in one of three trim levels, starting with the base LX model and going up to the mid-level SE and highline ZTS trim. Wagons are available in SE trim only while the three-door coupe comes with a standard performance-oriented ZX3 package.

The base drivetrain for LX models is a 2.0-liter, 107-horsepower engine and five-speed manual transmission. This same drivetrain is standard in SE sedans, but ZTS sedans, along with SE wagons and the ZX3 coupe, get a more powerful 130-horsepower, 2.0-liter Zetec engine as standard equipment (wagons come with an automatic transmission only). The Zetec makes 130 foot-pounds of torque at an easily accessible 4,250 rpm. This is more peak torque than a Civic EX or Mazda Protege and more useable peak torque than anything else offered in the subcompact class.

The Focus rides on a four-wheel independent suspension with MacPherson struts up front and stabilizer bars both front and rear (except on the wagon). LX models come standard with 14-inch steel wheels while SE, ZTS and ZX3 models get 15-inch aluminum wheels with 60-series tires. Antilock brakes are standard on ZTS and ZX3 models and optional on LX and SE cars.

Besides its cutting-edge style and highly functional interior, the Focus boasts such innovative features as child-safety-seat anchors in the rear outboard seat locations and a glow-in-the-dark

FOCUS   FORD

rear seatback release to prevent trunk entrapment. All models come with rear defrost, manual seat-height adjustments, a center console and a 60/40 split-folding rear seat with flip-up rear seat cushion.

Ford is serious about retaining its share of the worldwide subcompact market. The Focus reflects not only the company's dedication to this goal, but also its ability to make solid, practical transportation for the 21st century.

2000 Ford Focus

Standard Equipment

ZX3 HATCHBACK (5M): 2.0L I4 DOHC SMPI with variable valve timing 16-valve engine; 5-speed OD manual transmission; battery with run down protection; 110-amp alternator; front-wheel drive, 3.82 axle ratio; stainless steel exhaust; front independent strut suspension with anti-roll bar, front coil springs, rear independent suspension with anti-roll bar, rear coil springs; power rack-and-pinion steering; front disc/rear drum brakes; 13.2 gal. capacity fuel tank; side impact bars; front and rear body-colored bumpers; black bodyside molding, rocker panel extensions; clearcoat monotone paint; aero-composite halogen headlamps; additional exterior lights include front fog/driving lights; driver's and passenger's manual remote black folding outside mirrors; front and rear 15" x 5.5" silver alloy wheels; P195/60SR15 A/S BSW front and rear tires; inside under cargo mounted compact steel spare wheel; rear heat ducts; AM/FM stereo, seek-scan, single CD, 4 speakers, and integrated roof antenna; remote hatch/trunk release; 1 power accessory outlet; instrumentation display includes tachometer, water temperature gauge, in-dash clock, trip odometer; warning indicators include oil pressure, battery, low coolant, lights on, key in ignition, low fuel, door ajar; driver's and passenger's front airbags; ignition disable; tinted windows; fixed interval front windshield wipers, rear window wiper, rear window defroster; seating capacity of 5, front sports seats, adjustable headrests, driver's seat includes 6-way direction control, easy entry, passenger's seat includes 6-way direction control, easy entry; 60-40 folding rear split-bench seat; front height adjustable seatbelts with front pretensioners; cloth seats, cloth door trim insert, full cloth headliner, full carpet floor covering, plastic/rubber gear shift knob; interior lights include dome light with fade; leather-wrapped steering wheel; vanity mirrors; day/night rearview mirror; full floor console, glove box, front and rear cupholders, driver's and passenger's door bins; carpeted cargo floor, cargo cover, cargo light; black side window moldings, black front windshield molding, black rear window molding and black door handles.

FORD

FOCUS

CODE	DESCRIPTION	INVOICE	MSRP

LX SEDAN (5M) (in addition to or instead of ZX3 HATCHBACK (5M) equipment): 2.0L I4 SOHC SMPI 8-valve engine; 3.61 axle ratio; rear independent suspension, rear coil springs, front and rear 14" x 5.5" steel wheels; P185/65SR14 A/S BSW front and rear tires; AM/FM stereo, seek-scan, cassette, 4 speakers, and integrated roof antenna; instrumentation display includes water temperature gauge, in-dash clock, trip odometer; child safety rear door locks, front bucket seats, adjustable headrests, driver's seat includes 6-way direction control, passenger's seat includes 6-way direction control; vinyl door trim insert and black grille.

SE SEDAN (5M) (in addition to or instead of LX SEDAN (5M) equipment): Body-colored bodyside molding; driver's and passenger's power remote black folding outside mirrors; front and rear 15" x 5.5" silver alloy wheels; P195/60SR15 A/S BSW front and rear tires; air conditioning, rear heat ducts; power door locks, remote keyless entry; ignition disable, panic alarm, security system; variable intermittent front windshield wipers and rear window defroster.

ZTS SEDAN (5M) (in addition to or instead of SE SEDAN (5M) equipment): 2.0L I4 DOHC SMPI with variable valve timing 16-valve engine; 3.82 axle ratio; front independent strut suspension with anti-roll bar, front coil springs, rear independent suspension with anti-roll bar, rear coil springs; front disc/rear drum brakes with 4-wheel antilock braking system; AM/FM stereo, seek-scan, single CD, 4 speakers, and integrated roof antenna; cruise control with steering wheel controls; instrumentation display includes tachometer; power front and rear windows with driver's 1-touch down; center armrest with storage, driver's seat includes 6-way direction control, lumbar support, cloth door trim insert; simulated wood trim on instrument panel; leather-wrapped steering wheel with tilt and telescopic adjustment; full floor console and 2 seat back storage pockets.

SE WAGON (4A) (in addition to or instead of SE SEDAN (4A) equipment): Four-speed electronic OD auto transmission with lock-up; 3.69 axle ratio; roof rack; warning indicators include trunk ajar; rear window wiper; plastic trunk lid, cargo cover and body-colored side window moldings.

Base Prices

Code	Description	Invoice	MSRP
P31	ZX3 Hatchback (5M)	11082	11865
P33	LX Sedan (5M)	11319	12125
P34	SE Sedan (5M)	12629	13565
P38	ZTS Sedan (5M)	14085	15165
P36	SE Wagon (4A)	14280	15380
	Destination Charge:	415	415

Accessories

Code	Description	Invoice	MSRP
12H	Front Floor Mats	27	30
12Q	Rear Floor Mats	23	25
144	All Door Remote Entry and Power Locks (ZX3/LX)	352	395
	Includes panic button and two keyfobs.		
41H	Engine Block Heater (LPO)	18	20
428	High Altitude Principle Use	NC	NC
	NOT AVAILABLE with 429, 93N.		
429	Non-High Altitude Principal Use	NC	NC
	NOT AVAILABLE with 428, 93N.		

FOCUS / MUSTANG — FORD

CODE	DESCRIPTION	INVOICE	MSRP
434	SE Sport Group (SE Sedan)	379	425
	Includes Securilock anti-theft system, engine: 2.0L DOHC 4-cylinder zetec, rear spoiler, integrated fog lamps and tachometer. REQUIRES 44A.		
43R	Power Windows (SE)	263	295
	Includes larger door trim map pockets.		
44A	Transmission: 4-Speed Automatic (All Except SE Wagon)	725	815
	REQUIRES 993 or 434.		
50A	SE Comfort Group (SE)	352	395
	Includes tilt/telescoping steering wheel, speed control, driver's armrest with storage and dual map lights.		
552	Antilock Braking System (ZX3/LX/SE)	356	400
572	Air Conditioning (ZX3/LX)	708	795
583	Radio: AM/FM Stereo with Single CD (LX/SE)	124	140
	Includes 4 speakers.		
59M	Side Impact Air Bags	312	350
63B	Smoker's Package	13	15
	Includes cigarette lighter and ash tray. Ash tray replaces storage area on instrument panel.		
64T	Wheels: 15" 5-Spoke Aluminum (LX)	321	360
8	Unique Leather Low Back Buckets (ZTS)	619	695
	Includes map pockets.		
993	Engine: 2.0L DOHC 4-Cylinder Zetec (SE)	178	200
	REQUIRES 44A.		

2000 MUSTANG

What's New?

The Mustang has three updated colors: Performance Red, Tropic Green and Sunburst Gold. A child-safety-seat anchoring system is standard on both the coupe and convertible. New 16-inch wheels and tires are offered as an option on appearance package-equipped V6 Mustangs. The 2000 Mustang also features a tri-color bar emblem on the sides of the front fenders.

Review

Now 36 years old, the Mustang is quickly approaching middle age. Fortunately, it received a facelift and a serious dose of testosterone in 1999. The facelift sharpened the Mustang's looks considerably (some people like it, some people don't). Changes in styling were applied to the doors, hood, decklid, quarter panels, taillights and headlights, rocker panel moldings, side scoops and C-pillar appliques. And even more importantly, both the V6 and V8 engines were modified to produce additional horsepower.

Ford's Mustang has outsold the Chevrolet Camaro and Pontiac Firebird for the last five years. This is in spite of the fact that the Mustang has suffered a performance disadvantage since its redesign in 1994. Nevertheless, Ford executives seem to have gotten sick of automotive journalists and gearheads moping about the Mustang's power deficit, so the Blue Oval gang massaged both the 3.8-liter V6 and the 4.6-liter V8, improving power output to more respectable levels. The V6 now makes 190 horsepower at 5,250 rpm and 220 ft-lbs. of torque at 3,000 rpm. The V8 that's found in the GT's engine bay makes 260 horsepower at 5,000 rpm and 302 ft-

FORD MUSTANG

CODE	DESCRIPTION	INVOICE	MSRP

lbs. of torque at 4,000 rpm. If that isn't enough for you, check out the Ford SVT Mustang Cobra. It generates 320 horsepower.

We think that part of the Mustang's sales success can be attributed to the car's comfortable interior. Since 1994, the 'Stang has offered drivers and passengers supportive, upright front chairs, well-placed controls, clear views out the front and side windows, and nice dashboard and seat materials. Ford improved the interior as part of the 1999 update. New interior colors and materials were added, and the driver and front-passenger seats were given an additional inch of aft adjustment. For 2000, the Mustang receives two permanent child-safety-seat tether anchors in the back seat. Unfortunately, in neither 1999 nor 2000 did Ford think it necessary to improve the stereo controls. We have always found them to be too small and hard to operate.

The Mustang driving experience is enhanced by steering improvements made in 1999. The steering has less kickback and gives the Mustang a tighter turning radius and increased road feel. The rear suspension has more travel than before, smoothing out the bumps that could easily upset the previous model. Ford has also made four-wheel antilock brakes standard on the GT.

The Mustang has always been crashworthy, offering drivers and front-seat passengers a high level of protection as rated by the National Highway Traffic Safety Administration. All-speed traction control (introduced last year) increases the Mustang's ability to stay out of a wreck, though Ford thoughtfully provides a traction-control defeat switch for the hooligan in all of us. Mustang is one of the most recognizable nameplates on the road. The improved horsepower, updated exterior and revised interior mean that it will likely maintain its spot in the hearts of American buyers. Heck, if the rumors at GM are true about the cancellation of the F-body Camaro and Firebird, this may be the only pony car left for the new millennium.

2000 Ford Mustang

Standard Equipment

BASE COUPE (5M): 3.8L V6 OHV SMPI 12-valve engine; 5-speed OD manual transmission; HD battery; 130-amp HD alternator; rear-wheel drive; 3.27 axle ratio; stainless steel exhaust; front independent strut suspension with anti-roll bar, front coil springs, gas-pressurized shocks, rigid rear axle multi-link suspension with anti-roll bar, rear coil springs, gas-pressurized rear shocks; power rack-and-pinion steering; 4-wheel disc brakes; 15.7 gal. capacity fuel tank; front license plate bracket, side impact bars; front and rear body-colored bumpers; rocker panel extensions; clearcoat monotone paint; aero-composite halogen headlamps; driver's and passenger's power remote black outside mirrors; front and rear 15" x 6.5" silver alloy wheels;

MUSTANG — FORD

CODE	DESCRIPTION	INVOICE	MSRP

P205/65TR15 A/S BSW front and rear tires; inside under cargo mounted compact steel spare wheel; air conditioning; premium AM/FM stereo, clock, seek-scan, cassette, single CD, 4 performance speakers, amplifier, and fixed antenna; power door locks, remote keyless entry, power remote hatch/trunk release; 2 power accessory outlets, driver's foot rest; instrumentation display includes tachometer, oil pressure gauge, water temperature gauge, volt gauge, trip odometer; warning indicators include battery, lights on, key in ignition; driver's and passenger's front airbags; ignition disable, panic alarm; tinted windows, power windows with driver's 1-touch down; variable intermittent front windshield wipers, sun visor strip; seating capacity of 4, front bucket seats, adjustable headrests, center armrest with storage, driver's seat includes 4-way direction control, passenger's seat includes 4-way direction control, easy entry; 50-50 folding rear bench seat; cloth seats, cloth door trim insert, full cloth headliner, full carpet floor covering; interior lights include dome light, front reading lights, illuminated entry; steering wheel with tilt adjustment; vanity mirrors; day/night rearview mirror; full floor console, locking glove box, front cupholder, instrument panel bin, driver's and passenger's door bins; carpeted cargo floor; black grille, black side window moldings, black front windshield molding, black rear window molding and body-colored door handles.

GT COUPE (5M) (in addition to or instead of BASE COUPE (5M) equipment): 4.6L V8 SOHC SMPI 16-valve engine; limited slip differential; dual stainless steel exhaust with chrome tip; sport ride suspension; 4-wheel disc brakes with 4-wheel antilock braking system; rear wing spoiler; additional exterior lights include front fog/driving lights; front and rear 16" x 7" silver alloy wheels; P225/55HR16 A/S BSW front and rear tires; warning indicators include low coolant; front sports seats, adjustable headrests; leather-wrapped steering wheel with tilt adjustment and cargo light.

CONVERTIBLE (5M) (in addition to or instead of COUPE (5M) equipment): Power convertible roof with lining, glass rear window and dual illuminated vanity mirrors.

Base Prices

Code	Description	Invoice	MSRP
P40	Base Coupe (5M)	15123	16520
P42	GT Coupe (5M)	19123	21015
P44	Base Convertible (5M)	19439	21370
P45	GT Convertible (5M)	22910	25270
	Destination Charge:	550	550

Accessories

Code	Description	Invoice	MSRP
-T	Free Leather Promotion (Base Convertible)	(445)	(500)
	Free leather promotion valid only on models ordered during October to December 1999 wholesale period. Check with salesperson for availability. REQUIRES T.		
13K	Single Wing Rear Spoiler (Base)	174	195
41H	Engine Block Immersion Heater	18	20
428	High Altitude Principal Use	NC	NC
429	Non-High Altitude Principal Use	NC	NC
44U	Transmission: 4-Speed Automatic with OD	725	815
54V	V6 Sport Appearance Group (Base)	276	310
	Includes wheels: 15" bright machined, rocker panel stripe, single wing rear spoiler and leather-wrapped steering wheel.		
552	Antilock Braking System (Base)	445	500
553	All Speed Traction Control	205	230
	REQUIRES 552 (Base).		

FORD MUSTANG / SVT MUSTANG COBRA

CODE	DESCRIPTION	INVOICE	MSRP
57O	Rear Window Defroster	169	190
58B	Radio: Mach 460 AM/FM Stereo	352	395
	Includes cassette, 230-watt RMS (460-watt peak) power, 60-watt parametrically equalized amplifier, (2) 85-watt subwoofer amplifiers, (4) 5.5 x 7.5 subwoofer speakers, (4) 2.5" midrange/tweeters, scan function (up/down), radio play during fast forward/rewind, soft touch tape controls, auto seek and station set, auto DNR, auto chromium oxide for tape, auto scan on tape and tape storage.		
60C	Convenience Group	490	550
	Includes front floor mats, speed control, rear window defroster and 6-way power driver's seat.		
63B	Smoker's Package	13	15
	Includes ashtray with cigarette lighter.		
64J	Wheels: 16" Bright Machined (Base)	169	190
	REQUIRES 54V.		
64X	Wheels: 17" Forged Aluminum (GT)	445	500
	Includes locking lug nuts and tires: P245/45ZR17 BSW performance.		
67T	Dual Illuminated Visor Mirrors (Coupe)	85	95
85A	Black Stripe (Base Convertible)	NC	NC
	REQUIRES 54V.		
85M	Parchment Stripe (Base Convertible)	NC	NC
	REQUIRES 54V.		
85W	White Stripe (Base Convertible)	NC	NC
	REQUIRES 54V.		
T	Leather Seating Surfaces (Base)	445	500
	Front buckets only.		
X	Leather Seating Surfaces (GT)	445	500
	Front buckets only.		

2000 SVT MUSTANG COBRA

What's New?

A child-safety-seat anchoring system is standard on both the coupe and convertible. Two new clearcoat-paint colors are offered: Silver Metallic and Atlantic Blue Metallic.

Review

The SVT Mustang Cobra is a high-performance Mustang that has been heavily modified by Ford's Special Vehicle Team (SVT). Available in either coupe or convertible, the SVT Cobra's main calling cards are a totally different engine, a revised suspension, and an improved interior. The Cobra's firepower comes from a 4.6-liter, 32-valve DOHC V8. While based on Ford's family of modular V8s, the Cobra's engine is considerably more advanced. The engine produces 320 horsepower at 6,000 rpm and 317 ft-lbs. of torque at 4,750 rpm. Intake-port geometry and the "tumble-port" combustion-chamber design provide engine efficiency and performance. Its coil-on-plug ignition system provides a high-energy spark in the combustion chamber for efficient burn characteristics. Precise control of potential detonation is made possible by use of an improved knock sensor. A stainless-steel dual-exhaust system is standard equipment.

SVT MUSTANG COBRA

| CODE | DESCRIPTION | INVOICE | MSRP |

Each 4.6-liter Cobra engine is hand-assembled at the Romeo Engine Plant in Romeo, Mich. After the two-person teams assemble the engine, located on a separate line from all other 4.6L engines, the team affixes a signature plate with their names on it onto the right cam cover.

Besides having generally more performance-oriented suspension pieces, the Cobra also has an independent rear suspension (IRS) that was just introduced last year. Compared to the GT's solid rear axle, the IRS reduces unsprung weight by 125 pounds and widens the rear track by 1.2 inches. The overall effect is better road feel and handling, especially on rough or bumpy pavement.

The Cobra sports leather seats as standard equipment. It also has a leather-trimmed steering wheel and shift knob. Other standard-equipment items of note include power-assisted four-wheel disc brakes with ABS, all-speed traction control, Ford's SecuriLock passive anti-theft system, remote keyless entry, and a Mach 460 electronic AM/FM/cassette and compact disc player system.

The DOHC V8 and improved suspension combine to give the Cobra a higher performance envelope than the regular Mustang GT. Though horsepower is similar, the Cobra is much more refined than a Camaro or Firebird. Ultimately, the question is whether the Cobra's price premium over the GT or Camaro/Firebird is worth it. We generally feel it is, though the gap has narrowed now that the GT produces 260 horsepower. But if all you're looking for is rear-drive muscle and not much else, a less-expensive Camaro/Firebird is a better choice.

2000 Ford SVT Mustang Cobra

Standard Equipment

COBRA COUPE (5M): 4.6L V8 DOHC SMPI 32-valve engine; 5-speed OD manual transmission; HD battery; engine oil cooler; 130-amp HD alternator; rear-wheel drive, limited slip differential, traction control, 3.27 axle ratio; dual stainless steel exhaust with chrome tip; sport ride suspension, front independent strut suspension with anti-roll bar, front coil springs, gas-pressurized front shocks, rear independent double wishbone suspension with anti-roll bar, rear coil springs, gas-pressurized rear shocks; power rack-and-pinion steering; 4-wheel disc brakes with 4-wheel antilock braking system; 15.7 gal. capacity fuel tank; front license plate bracket, side impact bars; front and rear body-colored bumpers; rocker panel extensions; clearcoat monotone paint; aero-composite halogen headlamps; additional exterior lights include front fog/driving lights; driver's and passenger's power remote black outside mirrors; front and rear 17" x 8" silver alloy wheels; P245/45ZR17 performance BSW front and rear tires; inside under cargo mounted compact alloy spare wheel; air conditioning; premium AM stereo/FM stereo, clock, seek-scan,

FORD
SVT MUSTANG COBRA / TAURUS

CODE	DESCRIPTION	INVOICE	MSRP

cassette, single CD, 8 performance speakers, premium amplifier, and fixed antenna; cruise control with steering wheel controls; power door locks, remote keyless entry, power remote hatch/trunk release; 2 power accessory outlets, driver's foot rest, smokers' package; instrumentation display includes tachometer, oil pressure gauge, water temperature gauge, volt gauge, trip odometer; warning indicators include battery, low oil level, low coolant, lights on, key in ignition; driver's and passenger's front airbags; ignition disable, panic alarm; tinted windows, power windows with driver's 1-touch down; variable intermittent front windshield wipers, sun visor strip, rear window defroster; seating capacity of 4, front sports seats, adjustable headrests, center armrest with storage, driver's seat includes 6-way power seat, power 2-way lumbar support, passenger's seat includes 4-way direction control, easy entry; 50-50 folding rear bench seat; leather seats, leatherette door trim insert, full cloth headliner, full color-keyed carpet floor covering with floor mats, leather-wrapped gear shift knob; interior lights include dome light, front reading lights, illuminated entry; leather-wrapped steering wheel with tilt adjustment; dual illuminated vanity mirrors; day/night rearview mirror; full floor console, locking glove box, front cupholder, instrument panel bin, driver's and passenger's door bins; carpeted cargo floor, cargo light; black grille, black side window moldings, black front windshield molding, black rear window molding and body-colored door handles.

COBRA CONVERTIBLE (5M) (in addition to or instead of COBRA COUPE (5M) equipment): Power convertible roof with lining and glass rear window.

Base Prices

		INVOICE	MSRP
P47	Cobra Coupe (5M)	24988	27605
P46	Cobra Convertible (5M)	28548	31605
Destination Charge:		550	550

Accessories

		INVOICE	MSRP
13K	Rear Spoiler	174	195
428	High Altitude Principal Use	NC	NC
429	Non-High Altitude Principal Use	NC	NC

2000 TAURUS

What's New?

Many changes are in store for the 2000 Taurus. Styling is the most obvious, with a new look for both the front and rear. Improved safety comes from a new airbag-deployment system, adjustable pedals, seatbelt pre-tensioners and child safety-seat anchors. The ride has been made more comfortable and the powertrain has been updated for more power and less noise. The V8-powered SHO has been dropped from the lineup.

Review

It's like the WWF, but for cars. Each year, Ford's Taurus jumps into the ring to duke it out with the Honda Accord and Toyota Camry. The goal? To earn the title of No. 1. You know that each company's marketing department can barely contain itself over the chance to call its respective car the "best-selling car in America!"

In hopes of putting the Taurus on top for 2000, Ford put its main contender through the automotive equivalent of a Tae-Bo class, endowing it with better safety, styling, power and suspension. Topping the safety list is Ford's Personal Safety System. It's a collection of

TAURUS — FORD

components that allows the car to more fully understand the nature of a crash and factors in whether or not the seatbelts are in use. With the system, the dual-stage airbags inflate at two different rates, depending on the situation. Additionally, safety belts are equipped with pre-tensioners that are designed to help reduce the risk of force-related injuries in a crash. Taurus also becomes the first car in North America to offer power-adjustable brake and accelerator pedals, allowing drivers of smaller stature to move the pedals toward their feet rather than moving the seat too close to the steering wheel.

The styling changes are a welcome improvement. All exterior panels on the 2000 Taurus are new with the exception of the doors. The grille opening is wider to give the car a larger, more substantial front-end appearance. Headlamps are larger and 20 percent brighter. These changes should add headroom and a bit of cargo room to an interior that already received high marks from us.

Ford says the chassis has been revised to give a smoother ride without adversely affecting handling. The company also says steering and alignment refinements give Taurus a better on-center feel and directional stability. Larger, 16-inch tires and wheels are standard.

The 2000 Taurus powertrains have been refined to increase power, improve midrange torque and reduce NVH. The Vulcan and Duratec V6s now generate 153 and 200 horsepower, respectively. Transmissions have been updated for smoother shifting. Both the Vulcan and Duratec engines meet low-emission vehicle (LEV) standards in California and the 13 Northeastern states.

The Taurus has always been a good value. Will the changes to styling, safety, horsepower and handling be enough to pin the Accord and Camry to the mat for a three-count? You, the consumer, will be the one to make that final decision.

2000 Ford Taurus

Standard Equipment

LX SEDAN (4A): 3.0L V6 OHV SMPI 12-valve engine; 4-speed electronic OD auto transmission with lock-up; battery with run down protection; 130-amp alternator; transmission oil cooler; front-wheel drive, 3.77 axle ratio; stainless steel exhaust; front independent strut suspension with anti-roll bar, front coil springs, rear independent strut suspension with anti-roll bar, rear coil springs; power rack-and-pinion steering with engine speed-sensing assist; front disc/rear drum brakes; 16 gal. capacity fuel tank; front and rear mud flaps, side impact bars; front and rear body-colored bumpers; body-colored bodyside molding, rocker panel extensions; clearcoat monotone paint; aero-composite halogen headlamps; driver's and passenger's power remote

FORD  TAURUS

| CODE | DESCRIPTION | INVOICE | MSRP |

black outside mirrors; front and rear 16" x 6" steel wheels; P215/65SR16 A/S BSW front and rear tires; inside under cargo mounted compact steel spare wheel; air conditioning, rear heat ducts; AM/FM stereo, seek-scan, 4 speakers, and fixed antenna; power door locks, child safety rear door locks, remote hatch/trunk release; 3 power accessory outlets, driver's foot rest, retained accessory power, smokers' package; instrumentation display includes tachometer, water temperature gauge, in-dash clock, trip odometer; warning indicators include oil pressure, battery, lights on, key in ignition, low fuel, door ajar, brake fluid; driver's and passenger's front airbags; ignition disable; tinted windows, power front and rear windows with driver's 1-touch down; variable intermittent front windshield wipers, sun visor strip, rear window defroster; seating capacity of 5, front bucket seats, adjustable headrests, center armrest with storage, driver's seat includes 4-way direction control, passenger's seat includes 4-way direction control; rear bench seat; front height adjustable seatbelts with front pretensioners; cloth seats, door trim full cloth headliner, full carpet floor covering; interior lights include dome light with delay, 2 door curb lights; steering wheel with tilt adjustment; vanity mirrors; day/night rearview mirror; partial floor console, locking glove box with light, front cupholder, 2 seat back storage pockets, driver's and passenger's door bins, rear door bins; carpeted cargo floor, cargo tie downs, cargo light; black grille, black side window moldings, black front windshield molding, black rear window molding and body-colored door handles.

SE-2V SEDAN (4A) (in addition to or instead of LX (4A) equipment): Driver's and passenger's power remote body-colored outside mirrors; air filter; AM/FM stereo, seek-scan, cassette, CD changer pre-wiring, in-dash CD pre-wiring, 4 speakers, and fixed antenna; cruise control with steering wheel controls; power door locks, remote keyless entry, power remote hatch/trunk release; ignition disable, panic alarm; rear bench seat with center armrest and interior lights include and illuminated entry.

SE-SVG SEDAN (4A) (in addition to or instead of SE-2V (4A) equipment): Front disc/rear drum brakes with 4-wheel antilock braking system; seating capacity of 6, front 40-20-40 bucket seats, adjustable headrests, driver's seat includes 4-way power seat, 8-way direction control, lumbar support; 60-40 folding rear bench seat with center armrest; interior lights include front reading lights, illuminated entry; dual illuminated vanity mirrors and dual auxiliary visors.

SE-COMFORT SEDAN (4A) (in addition to or instead of SE-SVG (4A) equipment): 3.0L V6 DOHC SMPI 24-valve engine; 3.98 axle ratio; aero-composite halogen fully auto headlamps; driver's and passenger's power remote body-colored heated outside mirrors; air conditioning with climate control and leather-wrapped steering wheel with tilt adjustment.

SE WAGON (4A) (in addition to or instead of SE-2V (4A) equipment): 4-wheel disc brakes; roof rack; front and rear body-colored bumpers with rear step; power retractable antenna; fixed 1/4 vent windows; flip-up rear window, rear window wiper; seating capacity of 6, front 40-20-40 bucket seats, adjustable headrests; plastic trunk lid, locking cargo concealed storage and chrome side window moldings.

Base Prices

Code	Description	Invoice	MSRP
P52	LX Sedan (4A)	16306	17695
P53	SE-2V Sedan (4A)	17063	18745
P55	SE-SVG Sedan (4A)	17842	19620
P56	SE-Comfort Sedan (4A)	18977	20895
P58	SE Wagon (4A)	18091	19900
Destination Charge:		550	550

188 www.edmunds.com **EDMUND'S® NEW CARS**

TAURUS — FORD

CODE	DESCRIPTION	INVOICE	MSRP
	Accessories		
12H	Front Floor Mats	27	30
12Q	Rear Floor Mats	23	25
13B	Power Moonroof (SE Except SE-2V)	747	840
	REQUIRES 85A (SE Wagon).		
184	6-Passenger Seating with Center Console	NC	NC
	Includes flip-fold center console. NOT AVAILABLE with 186.		
186	5-Passenger Seating with Floor Console (SE Sedan Except SE-2V)	93	105
	Includes floor shift.		
21A	Power Driver's Seat (SE-2V/SE Wagon)	NC	NC
	REQUIRES 642.		
21A	Power Driver's Seat (SE-2V/SE Wagon)	352	395
21J	Power Passenger's Seat (SE-Comfort)	312	350
	REQUIRES J and 61B.		
41H	Engine Block Heater (LPO)	31	35
428	High Altitude Principal Use	NC	NC
429	Non-High Altitude Principal Use	NC	NC
46S	Split-Fold Rear 60/40 Seat (SE-2V)	124	140
524	Leather-Wrapped Steering Wheel (SE-2V/SE Wagon)	NC	NC
	REQUIRES B3N and J.		
53A	Audio Group (SE Except SE-2V)	596	670
	Includes 6-disc CD changer and Mach stereo. REQUIRES 85A and 96W (Wagon).		
53C	LX Plus Goup (LX)	668	750
	Includes 5-spoke painted wheels, AM/FM stereo with cassette, power door locks, remote keyless entry system and speed control. REQUIRES B3C.		
54P	Heated Mirrors (SE-SVG/SE Wagon)	31	35
	REQUIRES 85A (Wagon).		
552	Antilock Braking System (LX/SE-2V/SE Wagon)	534	600
553	All-Speed Traction Control (All Except LX)	156	175
	REQUIRES 552 or 85A (Wagon). NOT AVAILABLE with 63D.		
59C	Adjustable Pedals (All Except LX)	107	120
	REQUIRES 21A (SE-2V/Wagon).		
61B	Side Impact Air Bags	347	390
	Upgrades LX trim to SE Cloth Buckets. REQUIRES 902 (LX).		
63D	Antilock Braking System Delete (LPO) (SE Except SE-2V)	(312)	(350)
	REQUIRES 85A (Wagon). NOT AVAILABLE with 553.		
642	Bolt-On Wheelcovers (SE-2V/Wagon)	NC	NC
	REQUIRES 21A. NOT AVAILABLE with 85A.		
85A	Special Value Group (Wagon)	801	900
	Includes antilock brakes, illuminated visor mirrors and power driver's seat. REQUIRES 96W. NOT AVAILABLE with 642.		
902	Power Door Locks (LX)	245	275
96W	Wagon Group (Wagon)	267	300
	Includes cargo cover and rear facing seat.		
992	Engine: 3.0L 2V V6 FFV (LX/SE-2V/SE-SVG)	NC	NC

FORD
TAURUS

CODE	DESCRIPTION	INVOICE	MSRP
99S	Engine: 3.0L 4V V6 (SE-SVG/SE Wagon)	619	695
	Includes 3.98 axle ratio. NOT AVAILABLE with 992.		
B3C	California/Orlando Regions Package (LX)	NC	NC
	REQUIRES 53C.		
B3N	No Charge Leather Seating Surfaces (SE - SVG/Comfort/Wagon)	(797)	(895)
	Available to residents of the Northeast Region only. REQUIRES 524 and J.		
J	Leather Seating Surfaces (SE - SVG/Comfort/Wagon)	797	895
	REQUIRES 524 or 85A or 96W (Wagon). NOT AVAILABLE with 63D.		

Major Savings On An Extended Warranty

"YOU DESERVE THE BEST"
Call today for your free quote.
Pay up to 50% less than dealership prices!

http://www.edmunds.com/warranty 1-800-580-9889

Save hundreds, even thousands, off the sticker price of the new car _you_ want.

Call Autovantage®
your FREE auto-buying service

1-800-201-7703

No purchase required. No fees.

ACCORD — HONDA

| CODE | DESCRIPTION | INVOICE | MSRP |

2000 ACCORD

2000 Honda Accord

What's New?

The four-cylinder engines now have a 100,000-mile no-tuneup service life. Side airbags are standard for all V6 models and EX four-cylinders with the leather interior. The feature-laden Accord SE sedan makes its debut this year. In the paint department, Nighthawk Black replaces Starlight Black, and Naples Gold Metallic replaces Heather Mist Metallic; Signet Silver Metallic, Raisin, and Currant have all been dropped.

Review

The benchmark. The best-selling car in America. The highest resale value in its class. These are all statements that have been made with regularity concerning the Honda Accord, a vehicle that is always on the short list of the most popular cars in this country. The Accord won a loyal base of customers by offering notable performance, room for four, frugal fuel economy and a virtual guarantee that, if cared for properly, it would not break. Totally redesigned two years ago, the Accord is considered by many to be a good value for a family sedan.

The sixth-generation Accord is available in coupe and sedan bodies, and LX and EX models come with a VTEC (Variable Valve Timing and Left Electronic Control) engine, be it a 2.3-liter four-cylinder (which gets 150 horsepower) or a 3.0-liter V6 (200 horsepower); the 3.0-liter is a model of refinement, revving smoothly and silently. The standard 2.3-liter four-banger in the DX Sedan was re-engineered last year and is worth 135 horses. It won't be until 2003 that the Accord sees even bigger and better power offerings.

Now that we've praised the living daylights out of this car, here's some bad news: The low price is accompanied by a low level of equipment. Also, the Accord is easy to drive, but it doesn't reward the driver much for the efforts. Despite minor body roll, braking and handling are good, the transmission shifts smoothly, and the steering is light and effortless.

As with the Toyota Camry, refinement and attention to detail are the Accord's strengths. Almost all interior materials are pleasing to the eye and touch, and are assembled with great care. Gap tolerances are about half what you'd find in American products. Storage room abounds; the Accord resembles a minivan with so many places to stash maps, drinks, change, and assorted detritus. Spacious, comfortable and quiet, the Accord will tote many happy

HONDA   ACCORD

| CODE | DESCRIPTION | INVOICE | MSRP |

campers for miles on end. The seats are comfortable, both front and rear. There is an immense amount of storage and passenger space inside the car, and ergonomics are nearly flawless.

While not exactly spicy, the Honda Accord is a quality, fine-tuned car exhibiting remarkable design because it is so functional and user-friendly. The bottom line is that Honda builds the ultimate midsize car. A low price, a high level of refinement, a cavernous interior, and a well-deserved reputation for reliability put the Accord at the top of the heap. Even a loaded top-of-the-line EX model with leather, alloy wheels, power moonroof, automatic climate control, CD player, premium sound, and steering-wheel radio controls stickers for about $25,000. The Accord is the definitive family sedan or coupe, and it's the benchmark by which all other midsize cars are measured.

Standard Equipment

2.3 DX SEDAN (5M): 2.3L I4 SOHC SMPI 16-valve engine; 5-speed OD manual transmission; 80-amp alternator; front-wheel drive, 4.06 axle ratio; steel exhaust; front independent double wishbone suspension with anti-roll bar, front coil springs, rear independent double wishbone suspension with rear coil springs; power rack-and-pinion steering with engine speed-sensing assist; front disc/rear drum brakes; 17.1 gal. capacity fuel tank; side impact bars; front and rear body-colored bumpers; black bodyside molding, rocker panel extensions; monotone paint; aero-composite halogen headlamps; driver's and passenger's manual remote black folding outside mirrors; front and rear 14" x 5.5" steel wheels; P195/70SR14 A/S BSW front and rear tires; inside under cargo mounted compact steel spare wheel; rear heat ducts; AM/FM stereo, seek-scan, cassette, 2 speakers, and window grid antenna; child safety rear door locks, remote hatch/trunk release, remote fuel release; 1 power accessory outlet, driver's foot rest; instrumentation display includes tachometer, water temperature gauge, in-dash clock, trip odometer; warning indicators include oil pressure, battery, lights on, key in ignition, low fuel, bulb failure, door ajar, trunk ajar, service interval; driver's and passenger's front airbags; ignition disable; tinted windows, manual front and rear windows; fixed interval front windshield wipers, sun visor strip, rear window defroster; seating capacity of 5, front bucket seats, adjustable headrests, center armrest with storage, driver's seat includes 4-way direction control, passenger's seat includes 4-way direction control; full folding rear bench seat with fixed headrests; front height adjustable seatbelts; cloth seats, cloth door trim insert, full vinyl headliner, full carpet floor covering, plastic/rubber gear shift knob; interior lights include dome light; steering wheel with tilt adjustment; vanity mirrors; day/night rearview mirror; full floor console, locking glove box with light, front cupholder, instrument panel bin, driver's and passenger's door bins, rear door bins; carpeted cargo floor, cargo light; body-colored grille, black side window moldings, black front windshield molding, black rear window molding and black door handles.

2.3 LX COUPE/SEDAN (5M) (in addition to or instead of 2.3 DX SEDAN (5M): 2.3L I4 SOHC SMPI with variable valve timing 16-valve engine; driver's and passenger's power remote body-colored folding outside mirrors; front and rear 15" x 6" steel wheels; P195/65HR15 A/S BSW front and rear tires; air conditioning, air filter; AM/FM stereo, seek-scan, cassette, CD changer pre-wiring, in-dash CD pre-wiring, 4 speakers, and window grid antenna; child safety rear door locks (Sedan), cruise control with steering wheel controls; power door locks with 2 stage unlock; power windows with driver's 1-touch down; variable intermittent front windshield wipers; driver's seat includes 6-way direction control, passenger's seat includes 4-way direction control, easy entry (Coupe); 60-40 folding rear bench seat with fixed headrests; interior lights front reading lights, 2 door curb lights; dual illuminated vanity mirrors; mini overhead console with storage, front and rear cupholders, rear door bins (Sedan); black grille, chrome side window moldings and body-colored door handles.

2.3 SE SEDAN (4A) (in addition to or instead of 2.3 LX COUPE/SEDAN (4A) equipment): 4-speed electronic OD auto transmission with lock-up; 4.46 axle ratio; front disc/rear drum brakes with 4-wheel antilock braking system; body-colored bodyside molding; front and rear 15" x 6" alloy wheels; remote keyless entry, power remote hatch/trunk release; security system and full carpet floor covering with carpeted floor mats.

192   www.edmunds.com   **EDMUND'S® NEW CARS**

ACCORD — HONDA

2.3 EX COUPE/SEDAN (5M) (in addition to or instead of 2.3 SE SEDAN (5M) equipment): 5-speed OD manual transmission; 4.06 axle ratio; 4-wheel disc brakes with 4-wheel antilock braking system; front power sliding and tilting glass sunroof with sunshade; aero-composite halogen auto off headlamps; AM/FM stereo, seek-scan, single CD, 6 speakers, theft deterrent, and window grid antenna; retained accessory power; ignition disable, panic alarm, security system; driver's seat includes 2-way power seat, 6-way direction control, lumbar support and cargo net.

3.0 LX COUPE/SEDAN (4A) (in addition to or instead of 2.3 LX COUPE/SEDAN (4A) equipment): 3.0L V6 SOHC SMPI with variable valve timing 24-valve engine; 4-speed electronic OD auto transmission with lock-up; 100-amp alternator; 4.2 axle ratio; front and rear 15" x 6.5" steel wheels; P205/65VR15 A/S BSW front and rear tires; driver's and front passenger's door mounted side airbags and driver's seat includes 6-way power seat.

3.0 EX COUPE/SEDAN (4A) (in addition to or instead of 3.0 LX COUPE/SEDAN (4A) equipment): Front power sliding and tilting glass sunroof with sunshade; aero-composite halogen auto off headlamps; front and rear 16" x 6.5" silver alloy wheels; P205/60VR16 A/S BSW front and rear tires; air conditioning with climate control; AM/FM stereo, seek-scan, single CD, 6 speakers, theft deterrent, and window grid antenna, radio steering wheel controls; remote keyless entry, power remote hatch/trunk release, retained accessory power, garage door opener; ignition disable, panic alarm, security system; driver's seat includes 6-way power seat, lumbar support; leather seats, leatherette door trim insert; leather-wrapped steering wheel with tilt adjustment and cargo net.

Base Prices

CODE	DESCRIPTION	INVOICE	MSRP
CG314YPBW	2.3 LX Coupe (5M)	16495	18540
CG315YJW	2.3 EX Coupe (5M)	18726	21050
CG224YPBW	3.0 LX Coupe (4A)	19526	21950
CG225YJNW	3.0 EX Coupe (4A)	21836	24550
CF854YPBW	2.3 DX Sedan (5M)	13661	15350
CG554YPBW	2.3 LX Sedan (5M)	16495	18540
CG567YEW	2.3 SE Sedan (4A)	18228	20490
CG565YJW	2.3 EX Sedan (5M)	18726	21050
CG164YPBW	3.0 LX Sedan (4A)	19526	21950
CG165YJNW	3.0 EX Sedan (4A)	21836	24550
Destination Charge:		415	415

Accessories

CODE	DESCRIPTION	INVOICE	MSRP
—	Antilock Braking System (2.3 LX)	533	600
	REQUIRES 4AT.		
—	Leather Seat Trim (2.3 EX)	1111	1250
	Includes driver's and passenger's side airbags, leather-wrapped steering wheel, 8-way power driver's seat and interior wood trim.		
4AT	Transmission: 4-Speed Automatic (2.3 Except SE)	711	800
	Includes 4.46 axle ratio.		
HC17	Engine: 2.3L ULEV (2.3 Except DX)	NC	NC

HONDA   CIVIC

CODE	DESCRIPTION	INVOICE	MSRP

2000 CIVIC

2000 Honda Civic

What's New?

No styling, content or trim changes for this year. The performance-oriented Si returns for 2000, and there have been paint comings and goings: Taffeta White has been added to the CX and DX Hatchback, and Dark Amethyst has been dropped; Titanium Metallic comes to the DX, LX and EX Sedan, and Vogue Silver is gone; and Vintage Plum is now available to the LX and EX Sedan, and Inza Red has been eliminated.

Review

More than two decades ago, Honda introduced the Civic. It was a small, anonymous, unassuming car, competing in a market saturated by mammoth sedans sporting ornate chrome, garish styling treatments, and acres of sheetmetal. The producers of these defunct dinosaurs didn't bat an eye at Honda's fuel-sipping entry, despite the fuel crisis of 1973. Big mistake.

Since then, Americans have seen six generations of the Civic come and go, each much improved over the previous model, and each becoming immensely popular with consumers. 1996 brought us a new generation; certainly improved but not so much so that we'd consider it revolutionary. Available in hatchback, sedan and coupe body styles, Honda has heeded customers who claimed the 1992-1995 Civic was too sporty looking. A grille was tacked on up front, sheetmetal contours provide a squarish profile, and larger rear taillamps give the Civic a more conservative look.

Dual airbags are part of the package, with antilock brakes standard on EX Sedan and Coupe models equipped with an automatic transmission. HX Coupes remain the only model to have available the continuously variable transmission, making it the most interesting Civic offered.

Three different versions of a 1.6-liter, SOHC four-cylinder aluminum engine are available on the Civic. The most common variety has an output of 106 horsepower at 6,200 rpm. EX models get 127 VTEC-inspired horsepower at 6,600 rpm, and the HX Coupe uses an economical VTEC-E engine with 115 horsepower at 6,300 rpm. The Si Coupe sports a DOHC four-cylinder that makes 160 horsepower at 7,000 rpm.

The Civic has few shortcomings, aside from its anonymous personality. Hondas tend to be on the expensive end of the scale when new, but over time, they are a far better value than most of their contemporaries. The Civic is no exception to the rule. It is a car for people who don't

194   www.edmunds.com   **EDMUND'S® NEW CARS**

CIVIC — HONDA

enjoy repair-shop waiting rooms. It is a car that holds its resale value better than most of the cars it competes with. It is a car that easily endears itself to its owner.

The Civic is a solid buy. For those who like a bit of fun in their commute, try the Si version of the coupe. Want a fuel miser? The HX Coupe is your car, getting up to 44 mpg. Strict budgets demand a look at the CX, while sedans are aimed more at the creature-comfort side of the scale. Style-conscious buyers will go for the svelte EX coupe, or the suave EX Sedan. Whatever your needs, Honda offers a Civic that will meet them—unless your needs include towing trailers or carrying a family of five.

Standard Equipment

CX HATCHBACK (5M): 1.6L I4 SOHC SMPI 16-valve engine; 5-speed OD manual transmission; 75-amp alternator; front-wheel drive, 3.72 axle ratio; steel exhaust; front independent double wishbone suspension front coil springs, rear independent double wishbone suspension with rear coil springs; manual rack-and-pinion steering; front disc/rear drum brakes; 11.9 gal. capacity fuel tank; rear lip spoiler, side impact bars; front and rear body-colored bumpers; black bodyside molding, rocker panel extensions; monotone paint; aero-composite halogen headlamps; driver's and passenger's manual remote black outside mirrors; front and rear 14" x 5" silver styled steel wheels; P185/65SR14 A/S BSW front and rear tires; inside under cargo mounted compact steel spare wheel; radio prep and manual retractable antenna; remote fuel release; 1 power accessory outlet, driver's foot rest; instrumentation display includes water temperature gauge, trip odometer; warning indicators include oil pressure, battery, lights on, key in ignition, trunk ajar, service interval; driver's and passenger's front airbags; tinted windows, fixed rear windows; fixed interval front windshield wipers, rear window defroster; seating capacity of 5, front bucket seats, adjustable headrests, driver's seat includes 4-way direction control, passenger's seat includes 4-way direction control; 50-50 folding rear bench seat; cloth seats, cloth door trim insert, full cloth headliner, full carpet floor covering, plastic/rubber gear shift knob; interior lights include dome light; steering wheel with tilt adjustment; vanity mirrors; day/night rearview mirror; partial floor console, glove box, front cupholder, instrument panel bin, driver's and passenger's door bins; carpeted cargo floor, plastic trunk lid; body-colored grille, black side window moldings, black front windshield molding, black rear window molding and black door handles.

DX HATCHBACK (5M) (in addition to or instead of CX HATCHBACK (5M) equipment): Power rack-and-pinion steering; AM/FM stereo, clock, seek-scan, CD changer pre-wiring, in-dash CD pre-wiring, 4 speakers, and manual retractable antenna; warning indicators include low fuel; rear window wiper; 1 seat back storage pocket and cargo cover.

DX COUPE (5M) (in addition to or instead of DX HATCHBACK (5M) equipment): 4.06 axle ratio; remote hatch/trunk release; 60-40 folding rear bench seat with fixed headrests and front and rear cupholders.

HX COUPE (5M) (in addition to or instead of DX COUPE (5M) equipment): 1.6L I4 SOHC SMPI with variable valve timing 16-valve engine; 3.72 axle ratio; driver's and passenger's power remote black outside mirrors; front and rear 14" x 5.5" silver alloy wheels; P185/65SR14 A/S BSW front and rear tires; instrumentation display includes tachometer; power windows with driver's 1-touch down; center armrest with storage, passenger's seat includes, 4-way direction control, easy entry; full floor console and cargo light.

EX COUPE (5M) (in addition to or instead of HX COUPE (5M) equipment): 4.25 axle ratio; front power sliding and tilting glass sunroof with sunshade; body-colored bodyside molding; driver's and passenger's power remote body-colored outside mirrors; front and rear 14" x 5.5" silver styled steel wheels; air conditioning; AM/FM stereo, clock, seek-scan, single CD, 6 speakers, and manual retractable antenna; cruise control with steering wheel controls; power door locks, remote keyless entry; panic alarm; driver's seat includes 6-way direction control; interior lights include front reading lights and body-colored door handles.

HONDA

CIVIC

| CODE | DESCRIPTION | INVOICE | MSRP |

Si COUPE (5M) (in addition to or instead of EX (5M) equipment): 1.6L I4 DOHC SMPI with variable valve timing 16-valve engine; 4.4 axle ratio; rear independent double wishbone suspension with anti-roll bar, rear coil springs; 4-wheel disc brakes; front and rear 15" x 6" silver alloy wheels; P195/55VR15 A/S BSW front and rear tires; unique cloth seats, leather-wrapped gear shift knob and leather-wrapped steering wheel with tilt adjustment.

DX SEDAN (5M) (in addition to or instead of DX COUPE (5M) equipment): Rear heat ducts; child safety rear door locks, smokers' package; manual front and rear windows; passenger's seat includes 4-way direction control and chrome grille.

LX SEDAN (5M) (in addition to or instead of DX SEDAN (5M) equipment): Driver's and passenger's power remote black outside mirrors; air conditioning; cruise control with steering wheel controls; instrumentation display includes tachometer; power front and rear windows with driver's 1-touch down; center armrest with storage; full floor console,1 seat back storage pocket; cargo light and chrome side window moldings.

EX SEDAN (5M) (in addition to or instead of LX SEDAN (5M) equipment): 1.6L I4 SOHC SMPI with variable valve timing 16-valve engine; 4.25 axle ratio; front disc/rear drum brakes with 4-wheel antilock braking system; front power sliding and tilting glass sunroof with sunshade; body-colored bodyside molding; driver's and passenger's power remote body-colored outside mirrors; AM/FM stereo, clock, seek-scan, single CD, 4 speakers, and window grid antenna; remote keyless entry; panic alarm; interior lights include front reading lights and body-colored door handles.

Base Prices

		INVOICE	MSRP
EJ632YBW	CX Hatchback (5M)	10157	10750
EJ634YPBW	DX Hatchback (5M)	11027	12200
EJ612YPBW	DX Coupe (5M)	11460	12680
EJ712YPBW	HX Coupe (5M)	12200	13500
EJ814YFW.	EX Coupe (5M)	14049	15550
EM115YFW	Si Coupe (5M)	15849	17545
EJ652YPBW	DX Sedan (5M)	11645	12885
EJ657YPBW	LX Sedan (5M)	13223	14930
EJ854YJW	EX Sedan (5M)	15204	16830
Destination Charge:		415	415

Accessories

		INVOICE	MSRP
—	4-Wheel Antilock Brakes (EX Coupe)	541	600
	REQUIRES 4AT.		
—	Value Package (DX Sedan)	943	1045
	Includes remote entry system, body-colored bodyside molding, air conditioning, AM/ FM stereo with CD, clock and 4 speakers, power door locks and front center armrest. REQUIRES 4AT.		
4AT	Transmission: 4-Speed Automatic (CX Hatchback)	943	1000
4AT	Transmission: 4-Speed Automatic (DX/LX/EX)	722	800
CVT	Transmission: Continuously Variable (HX Coupe)	902	1000

PRELUDE · HONDA

1999 PRELUDE

1999 Honda Prelude

What's New?

Prelude gets another five horsepower, bringing it up to 200 horsepower with the manual transmission and 195 horsepower with the automatic. A remote keyless entry system is added, as is an air filtration system, mesh-style grille and new interior color choices.

Review

The aptly-named Prelude has always been a symbol for great things to come; Honda has long used the Prelude to showcase their latest technological developments. Remember Honda's four-wheel steering system, designed to give drivers better control in tight corners? It first debuted on the 1988 Prelude. In 1993, the Prelude was also one of the first Hondas to receive a VTEC engine, first introduced in the 1991 Acura NSX. In 1997, Honda continued this tradition by showcasing their new Active Torque Transfer System (ATTS) on the Prelude Type SH.

ATTS is designed to give the Prelude rear-wheel drive cornering ability while retaining the wet-weather benefits of a traditional front-wheel drive car. The system works by monitoring the car's speed, steering angle, and yaw rate to determine if the car is following the driver's intended course. In a tight, fast corner the system works by increasing torque to the outboard front wheel, which in turn increases the vehicle's yaw rate, giving the driver better steering response. Basically, it neutralizes understeer for those times when the corners get a little too tight. What will they think of next.

The Prelude is powered by a VTEC engine that cranks out up to 200 horsepower at 7,000 rpm and 156 foot-pounds of torque at 5,250 rpm. Base models are available with a manual or automatic transmission, but if you want the high-tech Type SH, you better like rowing your own gears; it is available only with a five-speed manual gearbox. The five-speed manual is a carryover from the previous Prelude, but the new four-speed automatic features a Sequential SportShift that allows drivers the option of selecting their own gears, similar to a Porsche Tiptronic. Base and Type SH models get standard four-wheel antilock disc brakes that pull the car down quickly from the Prelude's estimated top-speed of 140 mph.

After receiving harsh criticism for the previous-generation Prelude's funky interior, Honda took a conservative approach to the dashboard layout of their revised sports coupe. It is disappointing

 **PRELUDE**

CODE	DESCRIPTION	INVOICE	MSRP

to note that they took an approach so conservative that when seated behind the Prelude's steering wheel, there is nothing to distinguish the car from a late-eighties Accord. Come on guys, you can do better than that.

Despite the interior shortcomings and the much-maligned headlamps, the Prelude is an outstanding sports coupe that offers the latest technology at a reasonably affordable price. If you are a gizmo hound, or you simply love to drive, this car must go on your shopping list.

Standard Equipment

BASE (5M): 2.2L I4 DOHC SMPI 16-valve engine with variable valve timing, requires premium unleaded fuel; 5-speed overdrive manual transmission; 55-amp battery; 100-amp alternator; front wheel drive, 4.27 axle ratio; steel exhaust with chrome tip; front independent double wishbone suspension with antiroll bar, front coil springs, rear independent double wishbone suspension with antiroll bar, rear coil springs; power rack-and-pinion steering with engine speed-sensing assist; 4 wheel disc brakes with 4 wheel antilock braking system; 15.9 gal. capacity fuel tank; front mud flaps; front power sliding and tilting glass sunroof; front and rear body-colored bumpers; rocker panel extensions; monotone paint; aero-composite halogen headlamps; additional exterior lights include center high mounted stop light; driver's and passenger's power remote body-colored folding outside mirrors; front and rear 16" x 6.5" silver alloy wheels; P205/50VR16 BSW AS front and rear tires; inside under cargo mounted compact steel spare wheel; air conditioning; air filter; AM/FM stereo seek-scan, single CD, 6 speakers, theft deterrent, and window grid antenna; cruise control with steering wheel controls; power door locks with 2 stage unlock, remote keyless entry, remote hatch/trunk release, remote fuel release; 1 power accessory outlet, driver's foot rest, retained accessory power; instrumentation display includes tachometer, water temp gauge, in-dash clock, trip odometer; warning indicators include oil pressure, water temp, battery, lights on, key in ignition, low fuel, bulb failure, door ajar, trunk ajar, service interval; dual airbags; ignition disable; tinted windows, power front windows with driver's 1-touch down, fixed rear windows; variable intermittent front windshield wipers, rear window defroster; seating capacity of 4, front bucket seats with fixed headrests, center armrest with storage, driver's seat includes 6-way direction control, passenger's seat includes 4-way direction control with easy entry; full folding rear bench seat; front height adjustable seatbelts; cloth seats, cloth door trim insert, full cloth headliner, full carpet floor covering; interior lights include dome light, front reading lights, 2 door curb lights; leather-wrapped steering wheel with tilt adjustment; vanity mirrors; day-night rearview mirror; partial floor console, locking glove box, front and rear cupholders, instrument panel bin, 1 seat back storage pocket, driver's and passenger's door bins; carpeted cargo floor, cargo light; black grille, black side window moldings, black front windshield molding, black rear window molding and body-colored door handles.

TYPE SH (5M) (in addition to or instead of BASE (5M) equipment): Active Torque Transfer System (ATTS); front mud flaps, rear wing spoiler and leather-wrapped gear shift knob.

Base Prices

BB614XJW	Base (5M)	20937	23450
BB615XJW	Type SH (5M)	23167	25950
Destination Charge:		415	415

Accessories

—	Transmission: 4-Speed Sequential Sport-Shift (Base)	892	1000
	Includes 4.79 axle ratio.		

S2000

| CODE | DESCRIPTION | INVOICE | MSRP |

2000 S2000

2000 Honda S2000

What's New?

The S2000 roadster is completely new for 2000.

Review

It's all about that little red button. Located on the left side of the driver's console and labeled "engine start," the button reflects the racing heritage found on the S2000 roadster.

Honda's new two-seat, open-topped roadster is based on the SSM concept car first shown at the 1995 Tokyo Motor Show. Designed to be fun to drive, the S2000 uses a front-engine, rear-wheel-drive configuration. As is often the case with Honda's newest performance vehicles, the S2000 contains many new technological advances that will surely trickle down to less-expensive models as time rolls by.

The centerpiece is an all-new, 2.0-liter, DOHC four-cylinder engine. It is equipped with an updated version of Honda's VTEC system, which can alter both valve timing and valve lift. The VTEC system allows the engine to produce maximum power while still being tractable enough for urban driving. If you need proof of Honda's technological prowess, look no further than the specifications: 240 horsepower at 8,300 rpm and 153 foot-pounds of torque at 7,500 rpm. Twist the key, hit the red start button, and the engine will give you the highest specific output (120 horsepower per liter) of any normally aspirated mass-production engine in the world. It will also spin to speeds that most other engines would choke on — redline is 8,900 rpm. If this still isn't impressive enough, Honda also says that the engine will meet low-emission vehicle status.

Power is routed though a six-speed, close-ratio transmission. The transmission is a compact design and features a direct shift linkage with excellent feel and short throws. A Torsen limited-slip differential is standard equipment.

Honda's expertise is also evident in the S2000's responsive handling. The exceptionally rigid chassis has an ideal 50/50 front-to-rear weight distribution. Both the suspension and power-steering systems feature new designs for Honda. The suspension is a four-wheel double-wishbone type with a racing-inspired "in-wheel" design. And in place of a conventional hydraulic power steering, the S2000 uses an electrically assisted system. This makes the steering feel much more responsive.

HONDA   S2000

| CODE | DESCRIPTION | INVOICE | MSRP |

Visually, the S2000 is compact and angular. The convertible top is power operated, but the rear window is plastic, not glass. There is only one version of the S2000, so all cars get 16-inch wheels and high-intensity discharge headlights as standard equipment. For occupant safety, Honda says it has designed the car to absorb as much crash energy as possible. It also has installed seatbelts with load limiters and pre-tensioners, driver and passenger airbags and roll bars. Inside, the S2000 comes with air conditioning, a digital instrument panel, a CD audio system, and leather seats.

Honda's new roadster should provide an excellent alternative to the BMW Z3, the Mercedes-Benz SLK, and the Porsche Boxster. Out of that group, the S2000 is the most performance-oriented. It's not as apt at city use, nor does it have the prestige that comes with owning a car with a BMW or Mercedes badge. But for a true (and less expensive) driving experience, the S2000 is the car to get.

Standard Equipment

BASE (6M): 2.0L I4 DOHC SMPI with variable valve timing 16-valve engine; 6-speed OD manual transmission; rear-wheel drive, limited slip differential, 4.1 axle ratio; stainless steel exhaust with chrome tip; front independent double wishbone suspension with anti-roll bar, front coil springs, rear independent double wishbone suspension with anti-roll bar, rear coil springs; power rack-and-pinion steering with vehicle speed-sensing assist; 4-wheel disc brakes with 4-wheel antilock braking system; 13.2 gal. capacity fuel tank; side impact bars; power convertible roof with lining, roll-over protection; front and rear body-colored bumpers; clearcoat monotone paint; projector beam high intensity headlamps ; driver's and passenger's power remote body-colored folding outside mirrors; front 16" x 6.5" silver alloy wheels rear 16" x 7.5" silver alloy wheels; P205/55WR16 A/S BSW front tires; 225/50WR16 A/S BSW rear tires; inside under cargo mounted compact steel spare wheel; air conditioning, air filter; AM/FM stereo, clock, seek-scan, single CD, 4 speakers, and fixed antenna; cruise control with steering wheel controls; power door locks, remote keyless entry, power remote hatch/trunk release, remote fuel release; 1 power accessory outlet, driver's foot rest; digital instrumentation display includes tachometer, water temperature gauge, trip odometer; warning indicators include oil pressure, battery, lights on, key in ignition, low fuel, trunk ajar, service interval; driver's and passenger's front airbags; ignition disable, panic alarm; tinted windows, power windows with driver's 1-touch down; variable intermittent front windshield wipers; seating capacity of 2, front bucket seats, fixed headrests, driver's seat includes 4-way direction control, passenger's seat includes 4-way direction control; seatbelts with front pretensioners; leather seats, leatherette door trim insert, full carpet floor covering, aluminum gear shift knob; interior lights include dome light, front reading lights; leather-wrapped steering wheel with tilt adjustment; day/night rearview mirror; full floor console, glove box, front cupholder; carpeted cargo floor; black side window moldings, black front windshield molding, black rear window molding and body-colored door handles.

Base Prices

AP114YENW S2000 Convertible (6M)	28456	32000
Destination Charge:	415	415

200   www.edmunds.com   **EDMUND'S® NEW CARS**

ACCENT　　　　　　　　　　　　　　　　　　HYUNDAI

| CODE | DESCRIPTION | INVOICE | MSRP |

1999 ACCENT

1999 Hyundai Accent

What's New?

The L model has power steering standard, the GS and GL models have standard alloy wheels and a couple of new paint options are available. Hyundai's new, industry leading buyer assurance program is also worth taking note of.

Review

This car is a pleasant surprise from Hyundai. The Accent is an in-your-face declaration from this Korean manufacturer that the days of selling shoddy, inept vehicles in the United States are over. The Accent is one of the better subcompacts in today's market.

However, you've got to pay for excellence, and the Accent is among the more expensive subcompacts. In contrast, a Chevrolet Metro sedan is a tad less pricey than the Accent. There is a reason for this: The Metro doesn't come standard with such niceties as power steering, rear window defogger, cargo area lighting, remote releases for the fuel door and trunk or digital clock. Additionally, the Accent benefits from single-piece side stampings, which contribute to stiffer body rigidity, and a 92-horsepower engine that far outranks the top-line 70-horse motor provided in the Chevy. Is the Hyundai worth the additional money over the Metro? Absolutely! The Metro feels a bit roomier, but the Accent offers more equipment and feels more solidly constructed than the tinny Chevrolet.

Unfortunately for Hyundai, another South Korean automaker has entered the U.S. market, expanding rapidly during the past couple of years. Kia builds the Sephia sedan, and it is larger and more powerful than the Hyundai.

Starting in 1999, Hyundai has a secret weapon: its new buyer assurance program, called "The Hyundai Advantage." With the purchase of any Hyundai vehicle, consumers will receive an awesome 10 year / 100,000-mile powertrain warranty. If the car is sold within those first 10 years, the new owner will still be entitled to a 5 year / 60,000-mile powertrain warranty. Also part of the program is 5 year / 100,000-mile corrosion coverage and a limited bumper-to-bumper warranty of 5 years or 60,000 miles. Additionally, the program offers free 24-hour roadside assistance for five years, which includes towing and lockout service.

Aside from the putrid seat fabrics, childish paint schemes and funky smell associated with all new Hyundais, we like the Accent. It's a great set of budget wheels, without the budget engineering or the budget-equipment levels.

HYUNDAI ACCENT

CODE	DESCRIPTION	INVOICE	MSRP

Standard Equipment

L HATCHBACK (5M): 1.5L I4 SOHC MPI 12-valve engine; 5-speed overdrive manual transmission; 55-amp battery; engine oil cooler; 75-amp alternator; front wheel drive; 3.84 axle ratio; partial stainless steel exhaust; front independent strut suspension with anti-roll bar, front coil springs, rear independent multi-link suspension with anti-roll bar, rear coil springs; power rack-and-pinion steering; front disc/rear drum brakes; 11.9 gal. capacity fuel tank; side impact bars; front and rear body-colored bumpers; black bodyside molding; monotone paint; aero-composite halogen headlamps; driver's and passenger's manual remote black folding outside mirrors; front and rear 13" x 5" silver steel wheels; P155/80SR13 BSW AS front and rear tires; inside under cargo mounted compact steel spare wheel; AM/FM stereo with seek-scan, cassette, 4 speakers, and fixed antenna; remote fuel release; 1 power accessory outlet, driver's foot rest, smoker's package; instrumentation display includes water temp gauge, trip odometer; warning indicators include oil pressure, battery, lights on, key in ignition, low fuel, door ajar, trunk ajar, brake fluid; dual airbags; tinted glass; vented rear windows; variable intermittent front windshield wipers; rear window defroster; seating capacity of 5; front bucket seats with adjustable headrests; driver's seat includes 4-way direction control; passenger's seat includes 4-way direction control with easy entry; full folding rear bench seat with fixed headrests; front height adjustable seatbelts; cloth seats; vinyl door trim insert; full cloth headliner; full carpet floor covering; interior lights include dome light; passenger's side vanity mirror; day-night rearview mirror; full floor console, glove box, front cupholder, driver's and passenger's door bins; carpeted cargo floor, cargo cover; body-colored grille; black side window moldings, black front windshield molding, black rear window molding and black door handles.

GS HATCHBACK (5M) (in addition to or instead of L HATCHBACK (5M) equipment): Body-colored bodyside molding; instrumentation display includes tachometer; rear window wiper; driver's seat includes 6-way direction control with lumbar support; 60-40 folding rear bench seat with rear headrest; cloth door trim insert and cargo light.

GL SEDAN (5M) (in addition to or instead of GS HATCHBACK (5M) equipment): Child safety rear door locks.

Base Prices

12303	L Hatchback (5M)	8371	8749
12373	GS Hatchback (5M)	8881	9499
12473	GL Sedan (5M)	8881	9499
	Destination Charge:	435	435

Accessories

—	4-Speed Automatic (GS/GL)	549	600
1AA	Package #1 (GS/GL)	NC	NC
	Includes vehicle with standard equipment.		
20AT	Package #2 (GS/GL)	651	750
	Includes air conditioning.		
21AU	Package #3 (GS)	1951	2200
	Includes AM/FM ETR stereo with CD, air conditioning, manual pop-up moonroof with sunshade, power front windows, power mirrors and Sporty Package upgrade; rear spoiler, front fog lamps, lower bodyside cladding, 14" alloy wheels and P175/65HR14 front and rear tires.		
CA	California Emissions	70	75
CF	Carpeted Floor Mats	38	60

ACCENT / ELANTRA — HYUNDAI

CODE	DESCRIPTION	INVOICE	MSRP
CN	Trunk Cargo Net	23	38
MG	Mud Guards	35	55
RC	Sports Rack	109	180
RS	Rear Spoiler	264	395
S1	Security System *Includes driver's door keyless entry.*	235	349
SS	Security System	160	249

2000 ELANTRA

2000 Hyundai Elantra

What's New?

The Elantra will receive a complete redesign in 2001, and the wagon model will be dropped. For 2000, the car is a carryover.

Review

In an effort to mold its image into that of a serious, first-rate automobile manufacturer, Hyundai has recently added standard equipment and enhanced the performance of several of its cars. The redesigned Accent and new Sonata are proving that this South Korean automaker has finally learned how to build a good car. The current Elantra provides even more proof, and the company offers an industry-leading warranty program to back it up.

Called the Hyundai Advantage, the new buyer-assurance program is a great incentive to buy a Hyundai over one of the many other compact choices on the market. With the purchase of any Hyundai vehicle, consumers will receive an awesome 10-year/100,000-mile powertrain warranty. If the car is sold within those first 10 years, the new owner will still be entitled to a 5-year/60,000-mile powertrain warranty. Also part of the program is 5-year/100,000-mile corrosion coverage and a limited bumper-to-bumper warranty for 5 years or 60,000 miles. Additionally, the program offers free 24-hour roadside assistance for five years, which includes towing and lockout service.

HYUNDAI  ELANTRA

CODE	DESCRIPTION	INVOICE	MSRP

Potential Elantra buyers can choose sedans or wagons in base or GLS trim levels. New under the hood of the Elantra is the 140-horsepower, 2.0-liter DOHC engine that powers the Tiburon. Riding on a four-wheel independent suspension, the Elantra features smooth, stable handling. A speed-sensitive rack-and-pinion steering system communicates improved road feel to the driver.

Designers fiddled around with the Elantra's exterior in 1999, restyling the front end with a bold new grille, sleek hood lines and a larger air-intake opening. Headlights feature a multi-focus reflector system and the Elantra gets revised turn-signal lamps.

Inside the Elantra, consumers will find rotary-type climate controls and a steering wheel that uses a low-weight magnesium core for greater strength and durability. To enhance ride comfort, front seatbacks have been slightly widened. Dual airbags are standard on the Elantra, housed in a two-piece dashboard designed to reduce squeaks and rattles. Adjustable headrests and seatbelt anchors are standard, and all models come with driver's side lumbar support and seat-height adjustments. Extensive use of sound-deadening materials helps quiet this compact car.

The five-speed sedan includes air conditioning, five-mph bumpers, rear window defroster, dual remote control mirrors, rear-seat heating ducts, intermittent windshield wipers, remote fuel and trunk releases, cassette stereo, tilt steering column, and speed-sensitive steering. Option packages can add automatic transmissions, power door locks, power outside mirrors, six-way adjustable driver's seat, 60/40 split folding rear seat, power windows, rear spoilers and antilock brakes.

The Hyundai Elantra is spunky, fun-to-drive and reliable, and has a buyer's program to prove it. If you're in the market for a compact sedan or wagon, Hyundai's Elantra is a serious contender.

Standard Equipment

GLS SEDAN (5M): 2.0L I4 DOHC MPI 16-valve engine; 5-speed OD manual transmission; engine oil cooler; 75-amp alternator; front-wheel drive, 3.65 axle ratio; steel exhaust with chrome tip; front independent strut suspension with anti-roll bar, front coil springs, rear independent multi-link suspension with anti-roll bar, rear coil springs; power rack-and-pinion steering with engine speed-sensing assist; 4-wheel disc brakes; 14.5 gal. capacity fuel tank; side impact bars; front and rear body-colored bumpers; body-colored bodyside molding with chrome bodyside insert; monotone paint; aero-composite halogen headlamps; driver's and passenger's power remote body-colored folding outside mirrors; front and rear 14" x 5.5" steel wheels; P195/60HR14 A/S BSW front and rear tires; inside under cargo mounted compact steel spare wheel; air conditioning, rear heat ducts; AM/FM stereo, seek-scan, cassette, 6 speakers, and fixed antenna; power door locks, child safety rear door locks, remote hatch/trunk release, remote fuel release; 1 power accessory outlet, smokers' package; instrumentation display includes tachometer, water temperature gauge, in-dash clock, trip odometer; warning indicators include oil pressure, battery, lights on, key in ignition, low fuel, door ajar, trunk ajar, brake fluid; driver's and passenger's front airbags; tinted windows, power front and rear windows with driver's 1-touch down; variable intermittent front windshield wipers, sun visor strip, rear window defroster; seating capacity of 5, front bucket seats, adjustable headrests, center armrest with storage, driver's seat includes 4-way direction control, lumbar support, passenger's seat includes 4-way direction control; 60-40 folding rear bench seat with fixed headrests; front height adjustable seatbelts with front pretensioners; premium cloth seats, cloth door trim insert, full cloth headliner, full carpet floor covering; interior lights include dome light, front reading lights; steering wheel with tilt adjustment; passenger's side vanity mirror; day/night rearview mirror; full floor console, locking glove box, front cupholder, instrument panel bin, driver's and passenger's door bins; carpeted cargo floor, cargo light; black grille, chrome side window moldings, chrome front windshield molding, chrome rear window molding and body-colored door handles.

GLS WAGON (5M) (in addition to or instead of GLS SEDAN (5M) equipment): Roof rack; rear window wiper, plastic trunk lid, cargo cover and black side window moldings.

204   www.edmunds.com   EDMUND'S® NEW CARS

ELANTRA / SONATA

CODE	DESCRIPTION	INVOICE	MSRP
	Base Prices		
41443	GLS Sedan (5M)	10860	11799
41543	GLS Wagon (5M)	11504	12499
Destination Charge:		435	435
	Accessories		
1AA	Package 1	NC	NC
	Includes vehicle with standard equipment.		
2AB	Package 2	166	200
	Includes cruise control.		
3AC	Package 3 (Sedan)	707	850
	Includes cruise control and power moonroof with sunshade.		
4AD	Package 4	767	925
	Includes cruise control, wheels: aluminum alloy and AM/FM stereo with CD.		
4AT	Transmission: 4-Speed Automatic	686	750
	Includes 3.66 axle ratio.		
5AE	Package 5	1251	1400
	Includes cruise control, AM/FM stereo with CD and antilock brakes.		
6AF	Package 6 (Sedan)	1475	1775
	Includes cruise control, power moonroof with sunshade, AM/FM stereo with CD, wheels: aluminum alloy, rear spoiler.		
AR	Console Armrest	79	125
	Includes center armrest with storage.		
CA	California Emissions	94	100
CF	Carpeted Floor Mats	40	70
CN	Trunk Cargo Net	23	38
MG	Mud Guards	38	60
RC	Sports Rack (Sedan)	109	180
RR	Roof Rack Cross Rails (Wagon)	85	140
RS	Rear Spoiler (Sedan)	264	395
S1	Security System with Drivers Door Keyless Entry	232	365
	NOT AVAILABLE with SS.		
SS	Security System	162	260
	NOT AVAILABLE with S1.		
WD	Sunroof Wind Deflector	35	62

2000 SONATA

What's New?

With new standard 15-inch alloy wheels, standard side airbags, and some option changes, Hyundai's 2000 Sonata maintains the same base MSRP as last year.

HYUNDAI

SONATA

CODE	DESCRIPTION	INVOICE	MSRP

Review

Hyundai got a fresh start with last year's well-received, redesigned midsize family sedan. The 1999 Sonata offered all-new and highly attractive sheetmetal, increased structural rigidity and reduced noise from outside the cabin. Using a supercomputer analysis, engineers were able to develop a rigid, stronger frame without adding extra weight to the car's body. Riding on a front double-wishbone suspension and a rear five-link setup, the Sonata's ride and handling is stable, smooth and responsive.

Under the hood of base models is a standard 2.4-liter DOHC engine making 149 horsepower and 156 foot-pounds of torque. Buyers can upgrade to a more powerful V6 or get it standard if they spring for the GLS trim. This V6 is an aluminum, 2.5-liter DOHC motor making 170 horsepower and 166 foot-pounds of torque that peaks at 4,000 rpm, which means power off the line can be a bit lacking. Sonata V6 sometimes has trouble climbing hills and getting up to speed quickly. Sonatas can be ordered with automatic or manual transmissions mated to either engine.

Inside the monochromatic cabin are plush seats, an adequate driving position and a nice-looking dashboard. Drivers will also find a leather shift knob, well-laid out radio and HVAC controls, and nifty pen holder. The trunk is spacious with an extremely low lift-in height for ease of use and rear seats on the GLS fold down conveniently in a 60/40 configuration to expand the cargo area.

2000-model-year Sonatas retain the same base MSRP as last year's models. For an inexpensive car, the Sonata is nicely equipped. The base model comes with air conditioning, rear window defroster, AM/FM stereo, rear child-safety door locks, power windows, power locks and power mirrors, seven-position tilt steering wheel, tinted glass, halogen headlamps, cruise control and seat-mounted side airbags. The step-up GLS brings with it a 100-watt, six-speaker stereo with CD player, air filtration system, center console with an armrest and storage space, heated side mirrors, cruise control, upgraded seat cloth, six-way adjustable driver's seat, split-folding rear seats and a V6 engine.

For the millennium, all Sonatas receive standard 15-inch alloy wheels, and the keyless remote feature is now offered as a $180 option (last year it was free). The MSRP of Sonata's leather package (which includes power driver's seat, power sunroof, ABS and traction control) has been lowered significantly, and the cassette/CD stereo is now available only as an option.

Hyundai has one big advantage over most other manufacturers peddling bread-and-butter sedans these days. Aptly called the Hyundai Advantage, the company's warranty program is a great incentive to buy a Hyundai over one of the many other choices on the market. With the purchase of any Hyundai vehicle, consumers will receive an awesome 10-year, 100,000-mile powertrain warranty, a five-year, 100,000-mile corrosion coverage and a limited bumper-to-bumper warranty for five years or 60,000 miles.

From powertrains to reliability to cutting-edge style, Hyundai has come a long way lately, and the Sonata is proof of it.

Standard Equipment

BASE (5M): 2.4L I4 DOHC MPI 16-valve engine; 5-speed OD manual transmission; 95-amp alternator; front-wheel drive, 3.88 axle ratio; partial stainless steel exhaust; front independent double wishbone suspension with anti-roll bar, front coil springs, rear independent multi-link suspension with anti-roll bar, rear coil springs; power rack-and-pinion steering with vehicle speed-sensing assist; front disc/rear drum brakes; 17.2 gal. capacity fuel tank; side impact bars; front and rear body-colored bumpers; body-colored bodyside molding; monotone paint; aero-composite halogen headlamps; driver's and passenger's power remote black folding outside mirrors; front and rear 15" x 6" silver alloy wheels; P205/60HR15 A/S BSW front and rear tires; inside under cargo mounted compact spare tire; air conditioning, rear heat ducts; AM/FM stereo, seek-scan, cassette, 4 speakers, and fixed antenna; cruise control with steering wheel controls; power door locks, child safety rear door locks, remote hatch/trunk release, remote fuel release; 2 power accessory outlets, driver's foot rest, retained accessory power, smokers' package; instrumentation display includes tachometer, water temperature gauge, in-

206   www.edmunds.com   **EDMUND'S® NEW CARS**

SONATA — HYUNDAI

dash clock, trip odometer; warning indicators include oil pressure, battery, lights on, key in ignition, low fuel, bulb failure, door ajar, trunk ajar, brake fluid; driver's and passenger's front airbags, driver's and front passenger's seat mounted side airbags; tinted windows, power front and rear windows with driver's 1-touch down; variable intermittent front windshield wipers, sun visor strip, rear window defroster; seating capacity of 5, front bucket seats, adjustable headrests, center armrest with storage, driver's seat includes 6-way direction control, passenger's seat includes 4-way direction control; rear bench seat with adjustable headrests; front height adjustable seatbelts with front pretensioners; cloth seats, cloth door trim insert, full cloth headliner, full carpet floor covering; interior lights include dome light with delay; steering wheel with tilt adjustment; passenger's side illuminated vanity mirror; day/night rearview mirror; full floor console, locking glove box with light, front cupholder, instrument panel bin, 2 seat back storage pockets, driver's and passenger's door bins; carpeted cargo floor, cargo light; body-colored grille, black side window moldings, black front windshield molding, black rear window molding and body-colored door handles.

GLS V6 (5M) (in addition to or instead of BASE (5M) equipment): 2.5L V6 DOHC MPI 24-valve engine; engine oil cooler; 4-wheel disc brakes; body-colored bodyside molding with chrome bodyside insert; driver's and passenger's power remote body-colored heated folding outside mirrors; cabin air filter; AM/FM stereo, seek-scan, single CD, 6 speakers, and power retractable antenna; adjustable tilt headrests, driver's seat includes 6-way direction control, lumbar support, 60-40 folding rear bench seat with adjustable headrests, center armrest with storage; premium cloth seats; interior lights include front reading lights, 2 door curb lights and dual illuminated vanity mirrors.

2000 Hyundai Sonata

Base Prices

CODE	DESCRIPTION	INVOICE	MSRP
23403	Base (5M)	13805	14999
23453	GLS V6 (5M)	15116	16999
	Destination Charge:	435	435

HYUNDAI SONATA / TIBURON

2000 TIBURON

What's New?

Hyundai's Tiburon is now offered in just one trim level. It receives new interior and exterior styling as well as alloy wheels, a power package, and four-wheel disc brakes standard.

Review

Several years ago, Hyundai displayed a mouth-watering concept car at national auto shows - the HCD-II. Showgoers could hardly swallow the fact that the same company that produced the Excel could, or would, dream up something like this futuristic sport coupe. Hyundai execs promised that a production version of the showcar was on the drawing board.

Accessories

CODE	DESCRIPTION	INVOICE	MSRP
—	Transmission: 4-Speed Automatic (Base)	499	500
	Includes 3.77 axle ratio.		
—	Transmission: 4-Speed Automatic (GLS)	499	500
	Includes 3.358 axle ratio.		
01AA	Package 1	NC	NC
	Includes vehicle with standard equipment.		
01AB	Package 2 (Base)	679	800
	Includes AM/FM stereo CD upgrade and power tilt/slide moonroof with sunshade.		
10AJ	Package 10 (GLS)	834	975
	Includes AM/FM stereo with CD and cassette upgrade and power tilt/slide moonroof with sunshade.		
11AK	Package 11 (GLS)	1171	1325
	Includes AM/FM stereo with CD and cassette upgrade, leather package with leather power driver's seat.		
12AL	Package 12 (GLS)	1629	1875
	Includes AM/FM stereo with CD and cassette upgrade, power tilt/slide moonroof with sunshade and leather package with leather power driver's seat.		
13AM	Package 13 (GLS)	2284	2575
	Includes AM/FM stereo with CD and cassette upgrade, power tilt/slide moonroof with sunshade, leather package with leather power driver's seat and antilock brakes with traction control.		
CA	California Emissions	100	100
CF	Carpeted Floor Mats	45	78
CN	Trunk Cargo Net	23	38
KR	Keyless Remote Entry System	107	180
MG	Mud Guards	43	75
RS	Rear Spoiler	295	440
SI	Security System Upgrade for Keyless Remote	132	205
WD	Sunroof Wind Deflector	35	62

TIBURON — HYUNDAI

The following year, HCD-III arrived and contained an innovative sidesaddle rear seat that a passenger could sit in sideways and stretch out. Excellent concept, Hyundai. Young consumers drooled in anticipation of the forthcoming HCD production car with the cool back seat.

Alas, it was not meant to be. The Tiburon arrived as a compromise between federal regulations and designer fantasy in base and FX trims. Still, its swoopy sheetmetal and sporty interior got it noticed. This year, both its sheetmetal and cockpit have been redesigned; it now sports large, bold quad projector-beam headlights, a revised rear fascia, and several hood creases that continue along the side panels.

For 2000, Hyundai has dropped the FX trim and is offering the car as one model, the Tiburon. New standard equipment includes 15-inch alloy wheels, power door locks and mirrors, and four-wheel disc brakes. Option packages three and four offer the features that were available only on last year's FX trim. And for 2000, consumers can get a Tiburon for the same $13,999 base price that was offered last year.

But that's not all. Hyundai customers also will be delighted with the company's buyer assurance program, called the "Hyundai Advantage." With the purchase of any Hyundai vehicle, consumers will receive an awesome 10 year / 100,000-mile powertrain warranty. If the car is sold within those first 10 years, the new owner will still be entitled to a 5 year / 60,000-mile powertrain warranty. Also part of the program is 5 year / 100,000-mile corrosion coverage and a limited bumper-to-bumper warranty of 5 years or 60,000 miles. Additionally, the program offers free 24-hour roadside assistance for five years, which includes towing and lockout service.

The Tiburon's target market is the same young, style-conscious, financially impaired bunch that buys the Ford Escort ZX2, Volkswagen GTI, Honda Civic Si and Pontiac Sunfire GT. The stylish Tiburon competes well and, with the Hyundai Advantage backing up the Tib's credentials, many young buyers may look at this coupe with newfound enthusiasm.

2000 Hyundai Tiburon

Standard Equipment

TIBURON (5M): 2.0L I4 DOHC MPI 16-valve engine; 5-speed OD manual transmission; 68-amp battery; 90-amp alternator; front-wheel drive, 3.84 axle ratio; partial stainless steel exhaust with chrome tip; sport ride suspension, front independent strut suspension with anti-roll bar, front coil springs, rear independent multi-link suspension with anti-roll bar, rear coil springs; power rack-and-pinion steering; 4-wheel disc brakes; 14.5 gal. capacity fuel tank; side impact bars; front and rear body-colored bumpers; monotone paint; aero-composite halogen headlamps; driver's and passenger's power remote body-colored folding outside mirrors; front and rear 15"

HYUNDAI
TIBURON

CODE	DESCRIPTION	INVOICE	MSRP

x 6" silver alloy wheels; P195/55HR15 A/S BSW front and rear tires; inside under cargo mounted compact steel spare wheel; air conditioning, rear heat ducts; AM/FM stereo, seek-scan, cassette, 4 speakers, and fixed antenna; cruise control with steering wheel controls; power door locks, remote hatch/trunk release, remote fuel release; 1 power accessory outlet, driver's foot rest; instrumentation display includes tachometer, water temperature gauge, in-dash clock, trip odometer; warning indicators include oil pressure, battery, lights on, key in ignition, low fuel, door ajar, trunk ajar, brake fluid; driver's and passenger's front airbags; tinted windows, power windows with driver's 1-touch down; variable intermittent front windshield wipers, rear window defröster; seating capacity of 4, front bucket seats, adjustable headrests, center armrest with storage, driver's seat includes 6-way direction control, passenger's seat includes 4-way direction control; 50-50 folding rear bench seat with fixed headrests; front height adjustable seatbelts; cloth seats, vinyl door trim insert, full vinyl headliner, full carpet floor covering; interior lights include dome light, front reading lights; steering wheel with tilt adjustment; passenger's side vanity mirror; day/night rearview mirror; full floor console, mini overhead console with storage, locking glove box, front cupholder, instrument panel bin, driver's and passenger's door bins; carpeted cargo floor, vinyl trunk lid, cargo cover, cargo light; black side window moldings, black front windshield molding, black rear window molding and body-colored door handles.

Base Prices

CODE	DESCRIPTION	INVOICE	MSRP
51323	Tiburon (5M)	12739	13999
	Destination Charge:	435	435

Accessories

CODE	DESCRIPTION	INVOICE	MSRP
—	**Transmission: 4-Speed Automatic**	686	750
	Includes 4.345 axle ratio.		
01AA	**Package 1**	NC	NC
	Includes vehicle with standard equipment.		
02AB	**Package 2**	1082	1300
	Includes AM/FM stereo with cassette and CD and power tilt/slide sunroof.		
03AC	**Package 3**	2143	2475
	Includes AM/FM stereo with cassette and CD, power tilt/slide sunroof, leather package: two-tone leather seat trim, black leather-wrapped steering wheel, black leather-wrapped shift knob and rear spoiler.		
04AD	**Package 4**	2868	3250
	Includes AM/FM stereo with cassette and CD, power tilt/slide sunroof, leather package: two-tone leather seat trim, black leather-wrapped steering wheel, black leather-wrapped shift knob; rear spoiler and antilock braking system.		
AR	**Console Armrest**	81	130
CA	**California Emissions**	117	125
CF	**Carpeted Floor Mats**	44	75
CN	**Trunk Cargo Net**	23	38
MG	**Mud Guards**	38	60
RS	**Rear Spoiler**	293	450
	INCLUDED in 03AC and 04AD.		
S1	**Security System**	242	385
	Includes keyless entry.		
SS	**Security System**	177	285

G20

INFINITI

2000 G20

2000 Infiniti G20

What's New?

The G20 entry-level compact receives numerous mechanical improvements, exterior and interior enhancements and safety additions for 2000, including more horsepower, revised transmissions, and a new muffler.

Review

Infiniti's original G20 departed the ranks in 1996, leaving a hole in Infiniti's entry-level slot, and was followed to pasture in 1997 by Infiniti's small-but-luxurious sedan, the J30. With the badge-engineered I30 and the slow-selling Q45 flagship as Infiniti's sole passenger-car offerings, the company needed a quick fix to bring people back into showrooms. Last year marked the return of an all-new G20 that was designed to breathe some life back into the Infiniti lineup.

Infiniti aims its G20 at the young, affluent 25- to 35-year-old demographic that snaps up hordes of Audi A4s, BMW 3 Series and Mercedes-Benz C-Class models every year. This small Infiniti promises buyers a stimulating and luxurious experience. Because prospective owners were concerned last year by the fact that this entry-luxury model had the lowest horsepower and torque ratings, the slowest acceleration times, and one of the stingiest standard-equipment lists in its class, Infiniti has made some changes to the car for 2000.

Gaining five extra horsepower, the G20's improved 2.0-liter, DOHC, 16-valve engine now makes 145 ponies. Two revamped transmissions are available: a new five-speed manual with revised first-, second- and fourth-gear ratios and a four-speed automatic with hydraulic control. Also new is a variable capacity muffler with dual tip outlets and a 100,000-mile tune-up interval.

Infiniti added anti-glare coating to the outside mirrors and an auto-off headlight function that turns the lights off 45 seconds after the key is removed from the ignition. For extra safety, Infiniti installed an engine immobilizer, revised remote keyless-entry transmitter with trunk release, and an optional In Vehicle Communication System (IVCS).

Inside, 2000 G20 buyers will find a power trunk release, one-touch up/down driver's window with safety reverse feature, retained accessory power for windows and sunroof, battery-saver feature, simulated wood trim, graphite-colored instrument panel, cruise-control activation switch moved to the steering wheel, and a newly shaped shift knob.

This year, options on the G20 include: an In Vehicle Communication System, power sunroof, leather/convenience package (for both base and touring models), and heated seats. The G20

INFINITI
G20

CODE	DESCRIPTION	INVOICE	MSRP

The G20 is an attractive set of wheels and, with its many improvements for 2000, it may compete better against the Audis and BMWs that young up-and-comers are interested in. We know that the Infiniti dealer body is respectful and courteous to consumers, and that the warranty coverage at Infiniti is more generous than at Nissan, but we aren't completely convinced that better deals can't be found elsewhere.

Standard Equipment

LUXURY (5M): 2.0L I4 DOHC SMPI 16-valve engine; 5-speed OD manual transmission; battery with run down protection; front-wheel drive, 4.18 axle ratio; steel exhaust; front independent suspension with anti-roll bar, front coil springs, rear non-independent multi-link suspension with anti-roll bar, rear coil springs; power rack-and-pinion steering with engine speed-sensing assist; 4-wheel disc brakes with 4-wheel antilock braking system; 15.9 gal. capacity fuel tank; side impact bars; front and rear body-colored bumpers; body-colored bodyside molding, rocker panel extensions; monotone paint; aero-composite halogen auto off headlamps; driver's and passenger's power remote body-colored folding outside mirrors; front and rear 15" x 6" silver alloy wheels; P195/65HR15 A/S BSW front and rear tires; inside under cargo mounted full-size alloy spare wheel; air conditioning, rear heat ducts; premium AM/FM stereo, clock, seek-scan, cassette, single CD, 6 premium speakers, and power retractable diversity antenna; cruise control with steering wheel controls; power door locks with 2 stage unlock, remote keyless entry, child safety rear door locks, power remote hatch/trunk release, remote fuel release; 1 power accessory outlet, driver's foot rest, retained accessory power; instrumentation display includes tachometer, water temperature gauge, trip computer, trip odometer; warning indicators include oil pressure, battery, lights on, key in ignition, low fuel, low washer fluid, door ajar, brake fluid; driver's and passenger's front airbags, driver's and front passenger's seat mounted side airbags; ignition disable, panic alarm, security system; tinted windows, power front and rear windows with driver's 1-touch down; variable intermittent front windshield wipers, sun visor strip, rear window defroster; seating capacity of 5, front bucket seats, adjustable headrests, center armrest with storage, driver's seat includes 8-way direction control, lumbar support, passenger's seat includes 4-way direction control; 60-40 folding rear bench seat with adjustable headrests, center armrest; front height adjustable seatbelts with front pretensioners; cloth seats, cloth door trim insert, full cloth headliner, full carpet floor covering with carpeted floor mats, simulated wood trim on instrument panel, plastic/rubber gear shift knob; interior lights include dome light with fade, front reading lights, illuminated entry; steering wheel with tilt adjustment; dual illuminated vanity mirrors; day/night rearview mirror; full floor console, locking glove box with light, front and rear cupholders, 2 seat back storage pockets, driver's and passenger's door bins; carpeted cargo floor, cargo net, cargo light; chrome grille, black side window moldings, black front windshield molding, black rear window molding and body-colored door handles.

TOURING (5M) (in addition to or instead of LUXURY (5M) equipment): Viscous limited slip differential; rear wing spoiler; additional exterior lights include front fog/driving lights; air conditioning with climate control, leather-wrapped gear shift knob and leather-wrapped steering wheel with tilt adjustment.

Base Prices

CODE	DESCRIPTION	INVOICE	MSRP
92050	Luxury (5M)	19422	21395
92850	Touring Model (5M)	20560	22895
Destination Charge:		525	525

Accessories

CODE	DESCRIPTION	INVOICE	MSRP
4AT	Transmission: 4-Speed Automatic (Luxury)	730	800
4AT	Transmission: 4-Speed Automatic (Touring)	722	800

212   www.edmunds.com   **EDMUND'S® NEW CARS**

G20 / I30 — INFINITI

CODE	DESCRIPTION	INVOICE	MSRP
H02	Infiniti Communicator	1378	1599
	Includes 4 years of Infiniti response center fees and cellular service fees. REQUIRES 4AT and V01.		
J01	Power Sliding Glass Sunroof with Sunshade (Touring)	819	950
	Includes rear tilt feature.		
K15	Painted Splash Guards	70	99
R12	6-Disc CD Changer	505	740
V01	Luxury Leather and Convenience Package (Luxury)	1132	1500
	Includes leather seating surfaces, leather-wrapped steering wheel, leather-wrapped shift knob, power sliding glass sunroof with sunshade, power driver's seat, auto temperature control, microfilter ventilation and Homelink universal transceiver. REQUIRES 4AT.		
V01	Touring Leather and Convenience Package (Touring)	904	1200
	Includes leather-appointed interior, leather door trim, leather seating surfaces, power sliding glass sunroof with sunshade, Homelink universal transceiver and microfilter ventilation.		
X03	Heated Seats Package	362	420
	Includes heated driver's and front passenger's seats and heated outside mirrors. REQUIRES 4AT and V01.		

2000 I30

What's New?

2000 marks the introduction of the all-new Infiniti I30.

Review

Our biggest complaint about the previous I30 was that it was too similar to Nissan Corporation's own affordable Maxima. This year, however, Infiniti's svelte sedan is completely new, inside and out, offering more power, extra features and updated styling-and making it more distinctive than ever.

Perhaps the biggest news is the 3.0-liter, 24-valve aluminum V6 engine that makes 227 horsepower-a 20 percent increase in power over last year's engine. Engine efficiency is increased as well. Molybdenum coated pistons help reduce friction while triple-forged crankshafts increase accuracy and weight balancing. The I30 gets computer-assisted, speed-sensitive power steering that automatically adjusts to driving conditions, providing more feel when needed for parallel parking, and more control at high speeds. The multi-link beam suspension has been enhanced with softer bushings for a smoother ride. Sixteen-inch aluminum alloy wheels now support P215/55R16 all season-tires that offer lightweight performance while directing cooling air over the brakes.

New styling elements include Xenon High-Intensity Discharge (HID) headlights (standard on Touring models only) which expands the area of illumination while minimizing glare to oncoming traffic. The driver's side windshield wiper is 4 inches longer this year, a streamlined rear-window design provides a more panoramic view, the front grille has been redesigned, and heat- and UV-resistant tinted glass keep occupants cool inside.

Available in two trim levels, Luxury and Touring, both Infiniti I30s come equipped with the new engine. Luxury models come with antilock brakes, power leather seats, express-open sliding and tilting glass sunroof with sunshade, air conditioning with climate control and rear heat ducts, 16-inch alloy wheels, AM/FM/cassette stereo with single CD player and seven speakers, cruise, cell phone pre-wiring, and tinted windows standard. Step up to the Touring model and

INFINITI

I30

| CODE | DESCRIPTION | INVOICE | MSRP |

Infiniti adds a viscous limited-slip differential, sport-ride suspension, aero-composite high-intensity fully automatic headlamps, 17-inch silver alloy wheels and P225/50VR17 A/S BSW tires.

Inside the I30, consumers will find seating for five adults, eight-way power-adjustable driver's seat with lumbar support, two-position memory and automatic entry/exit system, and a four-way power-adjustable passenger's seat. A height-adjustable center armrest, dual-level storage compartment, classy analog clock, one-touch open and close power windows, three front and two rear cupholders, and a power rear sunshade are also included.

Other innovations for 2000 include a Bose compact woofer, active front headrests, which automatically move up and forward during a rear-end collision to protect the head and neck, and a Homelink Universal Transceiver, which allows you to activate your house lights and garage door from inside the car.

Last year's Infiniti got you great service, extra convenience items, and one of the best warranties in the business. This year, the I30 will give you all that and much more.

2000 Infiniti I30

Standard Equipment

LUXURY (4A): 3.0L V6 DOHC SMPI 24-valve engine, requires premium unleaded fuel; 4-speed electronic OD auto transmission with lock-up; battery with run down protection; front-wheel drive, 3.8 axle ratio; stainless steel exhaust with chrome tip; comfort ride suspension, front independent strut suspension with anti-roll bar, front coil springs, rear non-independent multi-link suspension with anti-roll bar, rear coil springs; power rack-and-pinion steering with engine speed-sensing assist; 4-wheel disc brakes with 4-wheel antilock braking system; 18.5 gal. capacity fuel tank; side impact bars; front express open sliding and tilting glass sunroof with sunshade; front and rear body-colored bumpers with chrome bumper insert; body-colored bodyside molding; monotone paint; aero-composite halogen fully auto headlamps; additional exterior lights include cornering lights, front fog/driving lights; driver's and passenger's power remote body-colored folding outside mirrors; front and rear 16" x 6.5" silver alloy wheels; P215/55HR16 A/S BSW front and rear tires; inside under cargo mounted compact steel spare wheel; air conditioning with climate control, rear heat ducts; premium AM/FM stereo, seek-scan, cassette, single CD, 7 premium speakers, premium amplifier, auto equalizer, and window grid diversity antenna; cruise control with steering wheel controls; power door locks with 2 stage unlock, remote keyless entry, child safety rear door locks, power remote hatch/trunk release, power remote fuel release; cell phone pre-wiring, 2 power accessory outlets, driver's foot rest, retained accessory power, garage door opener; instrumentation display includes tachometer, water temperature gauge, clock, exterior temp, trip odometer; warning indicators include oil pressure, battery, lights on, key in ignition, low fuel, low washer fluid, bulb failure, door ajar;

214   www.edmunds.com   **EDMUND'S® NEW CARS**

I30 / Q45   INFINITI

driver's and passenger's front airbags, driver's and front passenger's seat mounted side airbags; ignition disable, panic alarm, security system; tinted windows, power front and rear windows with driver's and passenger's 1-touch down; variable intermittent front windshield wipers, sun visor strip, rear window defroster, rear power blind; seating capacity of 5, front bucket seats, adjustable headrests, center armrest with storage, driver's seat includes 6-way power seat, lumbar support, passenger's seat includes 4-way power seat; 60-40 folding rear bench seat with adjustable headrests, center armrest; front height adjustable seatbelts with front pretensioners; leather seats, leatherette door trim insert, full cloth headliner, full carpet floor covering with carpeted floor mats, leather-wrapped gear shift knob; memory on driver's seat with 2 memory setting(s); interior lights include dome light with fade, front reading lights, 2 door curb lights, illuminated entry; leather-wrapped steering wheel with tilt adjustment; dual illuminated vanity mirrors, dual auxiliary visors; auto-dimming day/night rearview mirror; full floor console, locking glove box with light, front and rear cupholders, instrument panel covered bin, 2 seat back storage pockets, driver's and passenger's door bins; carpeted cargo floor, carpeted trunk lid, cargo net, cargo light; chrome grille, chrome side window moldings, black front windshield molding, black rear window molding and chrome door handles.

TOURING (4A) (in addition to or instead of LUXURY (4A) equipment): Viscous limited slip differential; sport ride suspension; aero-composite high intensity fully auto headlamps; front and rear 17" x 7" silver alloy wheels and P225/50VR17 A/S BSW front and rear tires.

Base Prices

Code	Description	Invoice	MSRP
95010	Luxury (4A)	26835	29465
95710	Touring (4A)	27979	31540
	Destination Charge:	525	525

Accessories

Code	Description	Invoice	MSRP
H02	Infiniti Communicator	1378	1599
	Includes 4 years of Infiniti Response Center Service and 4 years cellular service fees. NOT AVAILABLE with J10.		
J10	Sunroof and Sunshade Delete (Luxury)	(868)	(1000)
	Deletes power rear sunshade. Deletes power sunroof with one-touch open feature. NOT AVAILABLE with H02, T01.		
K60	6-Disc CD Changer	511	740
	VPC installed accessory.		
S01	Touring Sport Package (Touring)	887	1000
	Includes rear spoiler and side sills.		
T01	Traction Control System	268	300
	REQUIRES X03. NOT AVAILABLE with J10.		
W11	Painted Splash Guards	97	130
X03	Heated Seats Package	374	420
	Includes front heated seats and heated sideview mirrors.		

1999 Q45

What's New?

Several small exterior and interior enhancements have been added to the Q for 1999, including a new sunroof, revised front styling and the return of the analog clock.

INFINITI

Q45

CODE	DESCRIPTION	INVOICE	MSRP

Review

As the second-generation Q45 enters its third year of production, Infiniti hopes that new exterior and interior appointments will help keep the vehicle flying high in the luxury performance sedan class. To that end, Infiniti continues its quest for enhanced comfort and convenience rather than building on the sporting nature of the original Q45. The sedan now offers a quiet, isolated ride worthy of dignified heads of state.

Just as one would expect inside a flagship sedan from a luxury marque, the Q overflows with sumptuous features such as power leather seats, wood accents, premium Bose sound system, driver's seat memory, automatic climate control, power sunroof and power tilt/telescoping steering wheel. This year, Infiniti also proves that it knows how to listen to its customers. The beautiful analog timepiece that adorned the dashboard of the first-generation Q45, and was replaced by a digital clock two years ago, is back. Additionally, the Q's full metal sunroof has been replaced with a power glass sunroof with tilt/slide, one-touch open and a sunshade.

Outside, Infiniti has touched up the styling of the vehicle by reducing the amount of chrome on the front grille, adding new high intensity discharge (HID) headlamps with Xenon gas bulbs and crystalline lenses, and introducing two round projector beam bulbs per side. The license plate finisher is now body-colored, the trunk has a power closure assist, and the outside mirrors have an anti-glare coating. New exterior colors for 1999 are Hunter Green, Aspen White Pearl and Titanium.

The 4.1-liter V8 engine is still in place, though some would be happy to see Infiniti bring back the 4.5-liter V8 that powered the sedan prior to 1997. Overall, though, the Q45 offers a nice ride that is perfect for cross-country cruising. If you are in the market for a large luxurious sedan, and are unwilling to fight the gremlins that habitually inhabit many competing luxo-cruisers, you owe it to yourself to test drive a Q45.

1999 Infiniti Q45

Standard Equipment

BASE (4A): 4.1L V8 DOHC SMPI with variable valve timing 32-valve engine, requires premium unleaded fuel; 4-speed electronic overdrive automatic transmission with lock-up; 110-amp alternator; rear wheel drive, viscous limited slip differential, traction control, 3.69 axle ratio; steel exhaust with chrome tip; front independent strut suspension with anti-roll bar, front coil springs, rear independent multi-link suspension with anti-roll bar, rear coil springs; power rack-and-pinion steering with vehicle speed-sensing assist; 4 wheel disc brakes with 4 wheel antilock braking

216   www.edmunds.com   **EDMUND'S® NEW CARS**

Q45

system; 21.4 gal capacity fuel tank; front power sliding and tilting sunroof with sunshade; front and rear body-colored bumpers with chrome bumper insert; chrome bodyside insert; monotone paint; aero-composite halogen fully automatic headlamps; additional exterior lights include front fog/driving lights, center high mounted stop light, underhood light; driver's and passenger's power remote body-colored heated folding outside mirrors; front and rear 16" x 7" silver alloy wheels; P215/60VR16 BSW AS front and rear tires; inside under cargo mounted compact alloy spare wheel; air conditioning with climate control, air filter, rear heat ducts; premium AM/FM stereo with seek-scan, cassette, single CD, 8 premium speakers, and power retractable diversity antenna; cruise control with steering wheel controls; power door locks with 2 stage unlock, remote keyless entry, child safety rear door locks, power remote hatch/trunk release, power remote fuel release; cell phone pre-wiring, 2 power accessory outlets, trunk pulldown, driver's foot rest, garage door opener; instrumentation display includes tachometer, water temp gauge, clock, exterior temp, trip odometer; warning indicators include oil pressure, battery, lights on, key in ignition, low fuel, low washer fluid, bulb failure, door ajar, trunk ajar, brake fluid; dual airbags, seat mounted side airbag; ignition disable, panic alarm, security system; tinted windows, power front windows with driver's 1-touch down, power rear windows; variable intermittent front windshield wipers, rear window defroster; seating capacity of 5, front bucket seats with adjustable tilt headrests, center armrest with storage, driver's seat includes 6-way power seat with power lumbar support and easy entry, passenger's seat includes 6-way power seat with power lumbar support; rear bench seat with fixed rear headrest, center armrest with storage; front height adjustable seatbelts with front pretensioners; leather seats, leatherette door trim insert, full cloth headliner, full carpet floor covering with carpeted floor mats, wood trim, leather-wrapped gear shift knob; memory on driver seat with 2 memory setting(s) includes settings for exterior mirrors, steering wheel; interior lights include dome light with fade, front and rear reading lights, 4 door curb lights, illuminated entry; leather-wrapped steering wheel with power tilt and telescopic adjustment; dual illuminated vanity mirrors, dual auxiliary visors; auto-dimming day-night rearview mirror; full floor console, locking glove box with light, front and rear cupholders, 2 seat back storage pockets, driver's and passenger's door bins, rear door bins; carpeted cargo floor, carpeted trunk lid, cargo net, cargo light; chrome grille, chrome side window moldings, chrome front windshield molding, chrome rear window molding and chrome door handles.

TOURING (4A) (in addition to or instead of BASE (4A) equipment): Electronically controlled suspension with driver selectable settings; front and rear 17" x 7" silver alloy wheels, P225/50VR 17 BSW AS front and rear tires; performance steering wheel and black chrome grille.

Base Prices

Code	Description	Invoice	MSRP
94319	Base (4A)	43255	48200
94819	Touring (4A)	44271	49900
	Destination Charge:	525	525

Accessories

Code	Description	Invoice	MSRP
E10	Two-Tone Paint	428	500
G50	Splash Guards	83	120
H02	Infiniti Communicator	1370	1599
	Includes 4 years of Infiniti Response Center Service.		
K55	Safe and Sound Package	650	940
	Includes 6-disc CD autochanger, splash guards, wheel locks and trunk mat.		
K60	6-Disc CD Autochanger	507	740
S92	Rear Spoiler (Touring)	352	510
X03	Heated Front Seats	376	420

JAGUAR

S-TYPE

CODE	DESCRIPTION	INVOICE	MSRP

2000 S-TYPE

2000 Jaguar S-Type

What's New?

From the ground up, this is a completely new sport sedan based on the Ford's midsize platform. Lincoln worked with Jaguar to develop this platform, which is also used for Lincoln's LS sedan.

Review

It makes sense that Lincoln and Jaguar worked together on the DEW98 platform because the midsize models that ride on this platform represent the same final goals for both companies. While Lincoln is hoping to add some spice to its stodgy image, Jaguar wants to give buyers an affordable luxury/performance model sporting a big cat on the hood. In the end, however, both automakers are hoping for the same result: increased sales from markets not normally associated with either car company.

The S-type's exterior is the first clue that this is no XJ/XK knock-off. The quad headlights and small front grille give the sedan a classic look not seen on Jaguars for 30 years. Small character lines run down the otherwise smooth body, ending at a taillight section that somewhat resembles a Chevy Lumina/Monte Carlo. Inside, the S-type is pure Jaguar with acres of wood and leather covering every surface. Despite its smaller exterior size, the S-type boasts a longer wheelbase than Jaguar's XJ models and interior dimensions on par with its larger sedans. A standard split-folding rear seat and optional roof rack further add to this Jag's utility.

Power for the S-type comes from either Jaguar's 4.0-liter V8 or Ford's 3.0-liter Duratec V6. While the V8 is a slightly less-powerful version of the V8 found in Jaguar's XK8, it still makes 281 horsepower and 287 foot-pounds of torque. The V6 uses a Ford block while Jaguar's variable-valve-timing heads, intake system and drive-by-wire throttle body top the Blue Oval low-end. These changes add 55 horsepower to the Duratec V6, giving it 240 horsepower and 212 foot-pounds of torque. A five-speed automatic is the only transmission available in the S-type.

As with the LS, suspension components in the S-type are primarily forged aluminum. Unlike the Lincoln, however, the Jaguar offers a sport package featuring a Computer Active Technology Suspension (CATS) system that constantly adjusts the car's Bilstein shocks. A yaw-control system is also on tap to keep the S-type from misbehaving even when the driver does.

S-TYPE — JAGUAR

| CODE | DESCRIPTION | INVOICE | MSRP |

Additional high-tech toys include an optional reverse-park control system, a GPS navigation system, and a voice-operated climate-control system.

Looks notwithstanding, the S-type is anything but a classic Jaguar, which, for the purposes of mass-market appeal, is not a bad thing.

Standard Equipment

3.0L V6 (5A): 3.0L V6 DOHC SMPI 24-valve engine, requires premium unleaded fuel; 5-speed electronic overdrive automatic transmission with lock-up; battery with run down protection; rear wheel drive, traction control, 3.31 axle ratio; dual stainless steel exhaust with chrome tip; front independent suspension with anti-roll bar, front coil springs, rear independent suspension with anti-roll bar, rear coil springs; power rack-and-pinion steering with vehicle speed-sensing assist; 4-wheel disc brakes with 4-wheel antilock braking system; 18.4 gal. capacity fuel tank; side impact bars; front and rear body-colored bumpers with chrome bumper insert; body-colored bodyside molding; monotone paint; aero-composite halogen fully automatic headlamps with washers and delay-off feature; additional exterior lights include front fog/driving lights; driver's and passenger's power remote body-colored heated folding outside mirrors; front and rear 16" x 7" silver alloy wheels; P225/55HR16 BSW AS front and rear tires; inside under cargo mounted full-size alloy spare wheel; dual zone front air conditioning with climate control, air filter, rear heat ducts; AM/FM stereo with clock, seek-scan, cassette, 4 speakers, and window grid diversity antenna; cruise control with steering wheel controls; power door locks, remote keyless entry, child safety rear door locks, power remote hatch/trunk release, power remote fuel release; cell phone pre-wiring, 2 power accessory outlets, driver's foot rest, retained accessory power, smoker's package; instrumentation display includes tachometer, water temp gauge, trip odometer; warning indicators include oil pressure, water temp, battery, low oil level, lights on, key in ignition, low fuel, low washer fluid, bulb failure, door ajar, trunk ajar; driver's and passenger's front airbags, driver's and front passenger's seat mounted side airbags; ignition disable, panic alarm, security system; tinted windows, power front windows with driver's 1-touch down, power rear windows; variable intermittent heated front windshield wipers, rear window defroster; seating capacity of 5, front bucket seats with adjustable tilt headrests, center armrest with storage, driver's seat includes 6-way power seat with lumbar support, passenger's seat includes 4-way power seat with 6-way direction control and lumbar support; 60-40 folding rear bench seat with fixed headrests, center armrest; front height adjustable seatbelts; leather seats, leather door trim insert, full cloth headliner, full carpet floor covering with carpeted floor mats, genuine wood trim on instrument panel, wood gear shift knob; interior lights include dome light with fade, front and rear reading lights, 2 door curb lights, illuminated entry; leather-wrapped with wood trim steering wheel with power tilt and telescopic adjustment; dual illuminated vanity mirrors; day-night rearview mirror; full floor console, locking glove box with light, front and rear cupholders, instrument panel covered bin, 2 seat back storage pockets, driver's and passenger's door bins; carpeted cargo floor, carpeted trunk lid, cargo light; chrome grille, chrome side window moldings, black front windshield molding, black rear window molding and body-colored door handles.

4.0L V8 (5A) (in addition to or instead of 3.0L V6 (5A) equipment): 4.0L V8 DOHC SMPI 32-valve engine, requires premium unleaded fuel; power glass moonroof, garage door opener; instrumentation display includes compass, exterior temp, systems monitor, trip computer; driver's seat includes 6-way power seat with power 2-way lumbar support, passenger's seat includes 4-way power seat with 6-way direction control and power 2-way lumbar support; 60-40 folding rear bench seat with adjustable headrests; memory on driver's seat with 2 memory setting(s) includes settings for exterior mirrors, steering wheel, headrests; auto-dimming day-night rearview mirror.

Base Prices

		Invoice	MSRP
JAG1	3.0L V6 (5A)	37128	42500
JAG2	4.0L V8 (5A)	41932	48000
Destination Charge:		580	580

JAGUAR   S-TYPE

CODE	DESCRIPTION	INVOICE	MSRP

Accessories

CODE	DESCRIPTION	INVOICE	MSRP
—	CA/CT/MA/NJ/NY/RI Emission Equipment	25	30
DC	Deluxe Communications Package	3644	4300
	Includes Jaguar assist, voice activated controls for sound system, climate control and cellular phone and GPS navigation system.		
NS	Navigation System	1680	2000
PM	Power/Memory Package (V6)	1596	1900
	Includes power glass moonroof, automatic day/night mirror with compass, garage door opener and memory on driver's seat with 2 memory settings including settings for exterior mirrors, steering wheel and headrest.		
PS	Premium Sound Radio Equipment	1260	1500
	Includes compact disc changer.		
PW	Weather Package (V6)	1008	1200
	Includes heated front seats, rain-sensing wipers and dynamic stability control. REQUIRES PM.		
RP	Reverse Park Control	336	400
SK	Sport Package	924	1100
	Includes wheels: sport, tires: P235/50ZR17 and Computer Active Technology Suspension (CATS).		
WT	Weather Package (V8)	1008	1200
	Includes heated front seats, rain-sensing wipers and dynamic stability control.		

Major Savings On An Extended Warranty

"YOU DESERVE THE BEST"
Call today for your free quote.
Pay up to 50% less than dealership prices!

http://www.edmunds.com/warranty 1-800-580-9889

SEPHIA

2000 SEPHIA

2000 Kia Sephia

What's New?

The Sephia has improved seat fabric, a new audio system and two new colors for 2000.

Review

The current Kia is bigger, stronger and more enticing than ever before. Two trim levels are offered and both come equipped with a Kia-built 1.8-liter that delivers 125 horsepower to the front wheels. The LS is the top-of-the-line model and includes power steering, bodyside molding, rear heat ducts, a remote hatch/trunk release, a tachometer, 60-40 split folding rear seat and a passenger-side vanity mirror.

The Sephia is a Korean product, but unfairly suffers the stigma attached to all autos from that country, depicting Korean cars as unreliable garbage. Thank Hyundai for that image, the first Korean automaker on U.S. soil. And Daewoo, who in 1988 unleashed a reliability nightmare, called the Pontiac LeMans, on the American public. The crummy Hyundais are history and the LeMans died at the end of 1993. Meanwhile, Kia was sending us small Fords, called the Festiva, which consistently ranked among the most reliable compact cars available.

We've determined that Kias are a step above other Korean cars; now the reasons you should consider one.

Base equipment levels are rather impressive; front and rear stabilizer bars, dual exterior mirrors, theft-deterrent system, rear defogger, remote fuel release, and fabric upholstery come standard. Dual airbags, a powerful engine, capable suspension and styling tweaks make it look more expensive than a car of this price has a right to look. Even build quality ranks high for a vehicle in this class. Slam any one of the four doors and you will be rewarded with an impressive "thunk" usually reserved for Hondas or Toyotas.

The Sephia is certainly not a performance car, despite its optional rear spoiler, but the 1.8-liter engine makes 108 ft-lbs. of torque. Combined with its 4.11 rear axle ratio, the little Kia scoots away from stoplights with authority, but doesn't generate much passing thrust at higher rpms where the engine makes more noise than horsepower. We'd like to see Kia replace the Sephia's factory Hankook tires with a more respected brand that offers superior all-around performance.

KIA

SEPHIA

| CODE | DESCRIPTION | INVOICE | MSRP |

Perhaps the Sephia's greatest strength lies in its roomy interior. With a truly useable rear seat, four adults can fit easily and five will manage as long as the rear-seat passengers are close friends. With base prices starting around $10,000, the Sephia offers better value than the Chevy Prizm, Honda Civic or Toyota Corolla, among others.

The company is slowly expanding, taking a lesson from the massive expansion that Hyundai embarked upon in the late '80s, only to see sales and quality suffer in the early '90s. Kia doesn't want to have a poor image to overcome, so they are taking their time. Take yours, too, and test drive a Sephia. We think you'll be pleasantly surprised.

Standard Equipment

BASE (5M): 1.8L I4 DOHC MPI 16-valve engine; 5-speed OD manual transmission; 48-amp battery; 70-amp alternator; front-wheel drive; partial stainless steel exhaust; front independent strut suspension with anti-roll bar, front coil springs, rear independent multi-link suspension with anti-roll bar, rear coil springs; manual rack-and-pinion steering; front disc/rear drum brakes; 13.2 gal. capacity fuel tank; side impact bars; front and rear body-colored bumpers; monotone paint; aero-composite halogen headlamps; driver's and passenger's manual remote body-colored folding outside mirrors; front and rear 14" x 5.5" silver styled steel wheels; P185/65SR14 A/S BSW front and rear tires; inside under cargo mounted compact steel spare wheel; child safety rear door locks, remote hatch/trunk release, remote fuel release; 1 power accessory outlet, driver's foot rest, smokers' package; instrumentation display includes water temperature gauge, trip odometer; warning indicators include battery, low fuel; driver's and passenger's front airbags; tinted windows, manual front and rear windows; fixed interval front windshield wipers, rear window defroster; seating capacity of 5, front bucket seats, adjustable headrests, center armrest with storage, driver's seat includes 4-way direction control, passenger's seat includes 4-way direction control; rear bench seat with fixed headrests; front height adjustable seatbelts; cloth seats, cloth door trim insert, full cloth headliner, full carpet floor covering, plastic/rubber gear shift knob; interior lights include dome light; day/night rearview mirror; full floor console, glove box, front cupholder, instrument panel bin, driver's and passenger's door bins; carpeted cargo floor; body-colored grille, black side window moldings, black front windshield molding, black rear window molding and body-colored door handles.

LS (5M) (in addition to or instead of BASE (5M) equipment): Power rack-and-pinion steering with engine speed-sensing assist; body-colored bodyside molding; rear heat ducts; driver's seat includes 6-way direction control; 60-40 folding rear bench seat with fixed headrests; premium cloth seats; steering wheel with tilt adjustment and passenger's side vanity mirror.

Base Prices

14201	Base (5M)	8996	9995
14221	LS (5M)	9791	10995
Destination Charge:		450	450

Accessories

AB	4-Wheel Antilock Brakes (LS)	745	800
AC	Air Conditioning	745	900
AP	Appearance Package (Base)	120	160
	Includes full wheel covers and body color bodyside molding.		
AT	Transmission: 4-Speed Automatic	860	975
	Includes 3.83 axle ratio.		
AW	Wheels: Alloy (LS)	274	340
BM	Body Color Bodyside Molding (Base)	60	85

222   www.edmunds.com   **EDMUND'S® NEW CARS**

SEPHIA — KIA

CODE	DESCRIPTION	INVOICE	MSRP
CD	Radio: AM/FM Stereo with CD	375	475
	NOT AVAILABLE with RM.		
CF	Carpeted Floor Mats	48	69
PP	Power Package (LS)	1950	2330
	Includes tachometer, air conditioning, AM/FM stereo with CD and 6 speakers, power windows, power door locks, power mirrors, cruise control and variable intermittent wipers.		
PS	Power Steering (Base)	224	260
RM	Radio: AM/FM with Mechanical Cassette Deck	250	320
	NOT AVAILABLE with CD.		
SP	Rear Spoiler	132	175
WG	Wood Grain Appearance Package	109	149

**TO PRICE YOUR TRADE-IN,
PURCHASE EDMUND'S® USED CAR
PRICES AND RATINGS.**

See page 6 for details.

Edmund's®
TOWN HALL

Get answers from our editors, discover smart shopping strategies and share your experiences in our new talk area. Just enter the following address into your web browser:

http://townhall.edmunds.com

Where smart shoppers talk about cars, trucks, and related consumer topics.

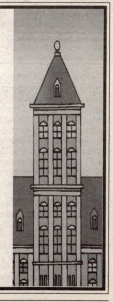

LEXUS

ES 300

CODE	DESCRIPTION	INVOICE	MSRP

2000 ES 300

2000 Lexus ES 300

What's New?

The Lexus ES 300 sports new front-end styling and taillights. The rearview and driver's side mirrors are now electrochromatic for improved nighttime performance. The interior gets new colors and additional wood trim on the audio/heater panel. The mirrors are added to the memory seat function. High-intensity discharge headlights are optional, as are 16-inch wheels. Brake Assist is included in the Vehicle Skid Control option. A particle-and-odor air filter is a new option. The ES 300 also receives child seat-anchor brackets and three new colors.

Review

More than just a fancy Toyota Camry, the ES 300 is an entry-level Lexus worthy of its nameplate. The most prominent feature of the ES 300 is its aggressive snout, which juts forward with a large lower air dam and prominent fog lamps. The ES 300's deep character lines along the hood and door panels work well, giving this car a distinguished appearance. This is backed up by a Lexus claim that 75 percent of its major components, including engine, transmission and interior components, are unique to the ES 300 or other Lexus models.

Last year, the ES 300 received a more-powerful 3.0-liter V6 engine. It produces 210 horsepower and 220 foot-pounds of torque. Even more impressive is the variable valve timing system (called VVT-i), capable of making 80 percent of peak torque available at 1,600 rpm. A four-speed automatic transmission uses computer control to adjust upshift and downshift patterns for improved responsiveness when climbing hills and enhanced engine braking when traveling down steep inclines.

2000-year changes, such as the electrochromatic mirrors and the high-intensity discharge headlights, only add to the ES 300's list of luxury convenience features. For example, a twist of the key fob will lower both front windows and open the power moonroof. A seven-speaker audio system with 195 watts of amplification is standard, and a 215-watt Nakamichi sound system is optional. Then there's the usual array of heated mirrors, automatic climate control, 10-way power-adjustable driver's seat, and California walnut wood throughout the interior. Front and side airbags, standard electronic traction control, daytime running lights, and three-point safety belts in all seating locations are the main safety features.   It's nice to see the people at Lexus taking their entry-level car seriously. Be aware, however, that many of the options on the ES 300

ES 300 — LEXUS

are standard on other vehicles, such as the Acura TL. Adding these features can quickly jack up the ES 300's price past its competitors.

Standard Equipment

ES 300 (4A): 3.0L V6 DOHC SMPI 24-valve engine, requires premium unleaded fuel; 4-speed electronic auto transmission with lock-up; 80-amp alternator; driver's selectable multi-mode transmission, transmission oil cooler; front-wheel drive, traction control, 2.64 axle ratio; stainless steel exhaust with chrome tip; front independent strut suspension with anti-roll bar, front coil springs, rear independent strut suspension with anti-roll bar, rear coil springs; power rack-and-pinion steering with engine speed-sensing assist; 4-wheel disc brakes with 4-wheel antilock braking system; 18.5 gal. capacity fuel tank; side impact bars; front and rear colored bumpers; colored bodyside cladding; monotone paint; aero-composite halogen fully auto headlamps with daytime running lights, delay-off feature; additional exterior lights include front fog/driving lights; driver's and passenger's power remote body-colored heated folding outside mirrors; front and rear 15" x 6" silver alloy wheels; P205/65VR15 performance BSW front and rear tires; inside under cargo mounted full-size steel spare wheel; air conditioning with climate control, rear heat ducts; premium AM/FM stereo, seek-scan, cassette, CD changer pre-wiring, in-dash CD pre-wiring, 7 performance speakers, amplifier, auto equalizer, theft deterrent, and window grid diversity antenna; cruise control; power door locks with 2 stage unlock, remote keyless entry, child safety rear door locks, power remote hatch/trunk release, power remote fuel release; cell phone pre-wiring, 3 power accessory outlets, driver's foot rest, retained accessory power, smokers' package; instrumentation display includes tachometer, water temperature gauge, in-dash clock, exterior temp, trip odometer; warning indicators include oil pressure, battery, low oil level, lights on, key in ignition, low fuel, low washer fluid, bulb failure, door ajar; driver's and passenger's front airbags, driver's and front passenger's seat mounted side airbags; ignition disable, panic alarm, security system; tinted windows, power front and rear windows with driver's and passenger's 1-touch down; variable intermittent front windshield wipers, sun visor strip, rear window defroster; seating capacity of 5, front bucket seats, adjustable tilt headrests, center armrest with storage, driver's seat includes 6-way power seat, power 2-way lumbar support, passenger's seat includes 6-way power seat; rear bench seat with adjustable headrests, center pass-thru armrest; front height adjustable seatbelts with front pretensioners; premium cloth seats, cloth door trim insert, full cloth headliner, full carpet floor covering with carpeted floor mats, leather-wrapped gear shift knob; interior lights include dome light, front reading lights, 4 door curb lights, illuminated entry; leather-wrapped steering wheel with tilt adjustment; dual illuminated vanity mirrors, dual auxiliary visors; auto-dimming day/night rearview mirror; full floor console, mini overhead console with storage, locking glove box with light, front and rear cupholders, instrument panel bin, 2 seat back storage pockets, driver's and passenger's door bins; carpeted cargo floor, carpeted trunk lid, cargo light; chrome grille, chrome side window moldings, black front windshield molding, black rear window molding and body-colored door handles.

Base Prices

Code	Description	Invoice	MSRP
9000	ES 300 (4A)	27278	31405
	Destination Charge:	495	495

Accessories

Code	Description	Invoice	MSRP
DC	6-Disc In-Dash CD Auto-Changer	864	1080
	NOT AVAILABLE with VK.		
EA	Adaptive Variable Suspension (AVS)	496	620
	REQUIRES LA or VP or VK.		
FT	Tires: All Season	NC	NC
	NOT AVAILABLE with TI, TU.		

LEXUS
ES 300 / GS-SERIES

CODE	DESCRIPTION	INVOICE	MSRP
HH	Heated Front Seats	352	440
	REQUIRES LA or VP or VK.		
HL	High Intensity Discharge (HID) Headlamps	412	515
LA	Leather Trim Package	1508	1885
	Includes interior air filter, leather seats, driver's seat with memory and programmable garage door opener.		
LM	Carpeted Trunk Mat	40	66
NK	Nakamichi Premium Audio System	1277	1630
	Includes 6-disc in-dash CD auto-changer. NOT AVAILABLE with VP.		
SR	Power Tilt/Slide Moonroof with Sunshade	800	1000
TI	Tires: 16" with Chrome Wheels	870	1740
	NOT AVAILABLE with TU, FT.		
TU	Tires: 16"	32	40
	Includes wheels. 16". NOT AVAILABLE with TI, FT.		
VK	Nakamichi Audio Package	2711	3015
	Includes Nakamichi premium audio system, 6-disc in-dash CD auto-changer, leather trim package: interior air filter, leather seats, driver's seat with memory, programmable garage door opener and power tilt/slide moonroof with sunshade. NOT AVAILABLE with VP, DC.		
VP	Lexus Value Package	2215	2465
	Includes leather trim package: interior air filter, leather seats, driver's seat with memory, programmable garage door opener, 6-disc in-dash CD auto-changer and power tilt/slide moonroof with sunshade. NOT AVAILABLE with VK, NK.		
VV	Vehicle Skid Control (VSC)	440	550
WL	Wheel Locks	30	44

2000 GS-SERIES

What's New?

Both the GS 300 and GS 400 get a new brake-assist system and child seat-anchor brackets. The GS 300 is certified as a low-emission vehicle. Crystal White and Millennium Silver Metallic replace Diamond White Pearl and Alpine Silver Metallic.

Review

Looking to create the ultimate sport sedan in both price and performance, Lexus redesigned its GS series in 1998 and came up with a truly exceptional car. Available in either GS 300 or GS 400 format, this is one model that can hang with the best Europe has to offer.

A distinctive quad-headlight design sweeps back into the hood and fenders in much the same manner as Mercedes' E-Class cars. Short front and rear overhangs give the GS a sporty look, and tidy hindquarters with creative rear taillights keep this car from blending in with the rest of today's high-line sport sedans.

The appearance of the car is supported by a powerful drivetrain. The GS 300 uses a 3.0-liter, inline six engine that develops 225 horsepower at 6,000 rpm and 200 foot-pounds of torque at 4,000 rpm. The GS 400 packs a 4.0-liter V8 that develops 300 horsepower at 6,000 rpm and 310 foot-pounds of torque at 4,000 rpm. Both of these engines use variable valve timing (called VVT-i) to promote additional power and fuel efficiency. A five-speed automatic is the only transmission available. To take advantage of the transmission's five forward gears, the GS 400

GS-SERIES — LEXUS

CODE	DESCRIPTION	INVOICE	MSRP

features manual upshift and downshift buttons on the steering wheel spokes, controlled by the thumb and forefinger of either hand.

The Lexus' roomy cabin provides the driver and front-seat occupant with excellent visibility and room to stretch out. An impressive 44 inches of legroom and 58 inches of shoulder room accommodates the long-limbed and broad-shouldered in the front seat. Rear-seat passengers don't fare as well, however, and get only 34.3 inches of legroom. Luxury touches include a standard dual-zone climate control, a power tilt and telescoping steering wheel, and all of the other power goodies typically found on luxury cars. Popular options include a Nakamichi premium sound system and a GPS-based navigation system that uses touch-screen controls.

Both models come standard with Vehicle Skid Control, which is a system that employs the sensors, actuators and computer electronics of the antilock braking and traction control systems to help reduce vehicle skids caused by understeer or oversteer conditions. ABS, front and side airbags, and traction control are all standard.

As with other vehicles in the Lexus line, road feel and absolute sportiness take a back seat to pure luxury and refinement. BMW's 5 Series offers a bit more fun, and the Mercedes E-Class has, well, the Mercedes emblem on the hood. But for all-around, everyday living with rock-solid reliability, you can't beat the GS series, especially if price is a consideration.

2000 Lexus GS 300

Standard Equipment

GS 300 (5A): 3.0L I6 DOHC SMPI with variable valve timing 24-valve engine, requires premium unleaded fuel; 5-speed electronic OD auto transmission with lock-up; HD battery; 100-amp alternator; driver's selectable multi-mode transmission; rear-wheel drive, traction control, 3.92 axle ratio; stainless steel exhaust with chrome tip; electronic stability, front independent double wishbone suspension with anti-roll bar, front coil springs, gas-pressurized front shocks, rear independent double wishbone suspension with anti-roll bar, rear coil springs, gas-pressurized rear shocks; power rack-and-pinion steering with vehicle speed-sensing assist; 4-wheel disc brakes with 4-wheel antilock braking system; 19.8 gal. capacity fuel tank; side impact bars; front and rear body-colored bumpers with chrome bumper insert; chrome bodyside insert, body-colored bodyside cladding; monotone paint; aero-composite halogen fully auto headlamps with daytime running lights, delay-off feature; additional exterior lights include front fog/driving lights; driver's and passenger's power remote body-colored heated folding outside mirrors; front and rear 16" x 7.5" silver alloy wheels; P215/60VR16 performance BSW front and rear tires; inside under cargo mounted full-size alloy spare wheel; dual zone front air conditioning with

LEXUS
GS-SERIES

CODE	DESCRIPTION	INVOICE	MSRP

climate control, air filter, rear heat ducts, auto air recirculation; premium AM/FM stereo, seek-scan, cassette, CD changer pre-wiring, in-dash CD pre-wiring, 7 performance speakers, amplifier, auto equalizer, theft deterrent, and window grid diversity antenna; cruise control; power door locks with 2 stage unlock, remote keyless entry, child safety rear door locks, power remote hatch/trunk release, power remote fuel release; cell phone pre-wiring, 2 power accessory outlets, driver's foot rest, retained accessory power, garage door opener, smokers' package; instrumentation display includes tachometer, water temperature gauge, in-dash clock, exterior temp, trip odometer; warning indicators include oil pressure, battery, lights on, key in ignition, low fuel, low washer fluid, door ajar; driver's and passenger's front airbags, driver's and front passenger's seat mounted side airbags; ignition disable, panic alarm, security system; tinted windows, power front and rear windows with front and rear 1-touch down; variable intermittent front windshield wipers, sun visor strip, rear window defroster; seating capacity of 5, front bucket seats, adjustable tilt headrests, center armrest with storage, driver's seat includes 6-way power seat, power 2-way lumbar support, passenger's seat includes 6-way power seat, power 2-way lumbar support; rear bench seat with adjustable headrests, center armrest; front height adjustable seatbelts with front pretensioners; cloth seats, cloth door trim insert, full cloth headliner, full color-keyed carpet floor covering with carpeted floor mats, leather-wrapped gear shift knob; interior lights include dome light, front and rear reading lights, 4 door curb lights, illuminated entry; leather-wrapped sport steering wheel with power tilt and telescopic adjustment; dual illuminated vanity mirrors, dual auxiliary visors; auto-dimming day/night rearview mirror; full floor console, locking glove box with light, front and rear cupholders, 2 seat back storage pockets, driver's and passenger's door bins; carpeted cargo floor, carpeted trunk lid, cargo light; chrome grille, chrome side window moldings, black front windshield molding, black rear window molding and body-colored door handles.

GS 400 (5A) (in addition to or instead of GS300 (5A) equipment): 4.0L V8 DOHC SMPI with variable valve timing 32-valve engine, requires premium unleaded fuel; driver's selectable multi-mode automanual transmission; 3.27 axle ratio; P225/55VR16 performance BSW front and rear tires; leather seats, leather door trim insert and memory on driver's seat with 2 memory setting(s) includes settings for exterior mirrors and steering wheel.

Base Prices

CODE	DESCRIPTION	INVOICE	MSRP
9300	GS 300 (5A)	32663	37605
9320	GS 400 (5A)	39495	46005
	Destination Charge:	495	495

Accessories

CODE	DESCRIPTION	INVOICE	MSRP
CW	Wheels: Chrome	850	1700
	NOT AVAILABLE with TI, TU.		
DC	6-Disc In-Dash CD Auto-Changer	864	1080
FK	Chrome Wheels with All-Season Tires	850	1700
	NOT AVAILABLE with TI, TU.		
FT	Tires: 215/60VR16 AS SBR (GS300)	NC	NC
FT	Tires: All Season (GS400)	NC	NC
	NOT AVAILABLE with TI, TU.		
HH	Heated Front Seats (GS300)	352	440
	REQUIRES PM.		
LA	Leather Trim Package with Memory System (GS300)	1408	1760
	Includes leather seating surfaces and driver's seat 2-position memory.		
LM	Carpeted Trunk Mat	40	66

GS-SERIES — LEXUS

CODE	DESCRIPTION	INVOICE	MSRP
ND	**Navigation Package (GS300)**	5765	7065
	Includes navigation system, leather trim package with memory system: leather seating surfaces, driver's seat 2 position memory; 6-disc in-dash CD auto-changer, power tilt/slide moonroof with sunshade, heated front seats, electrochromic outside mirrors and high intensity discharge headlights. NOT AVAILABLE with NI, PM.		
ND	**Navigation System Package (GS400)**	4357	5305
	Includes navigation system, 6-disc in-dash CD auto-changer, power tilt/slide moonroof with sunshade, heated front seats and high intensity discharge headlights. NOT AVAILABLE with NI, PM.		
NI	**Nakamichi Audio System Package (GS300)**	4752	6015
	Includes Nakamichi premium audio system, 6-disc in-dash CD auto-changer, leather trim package with memory system: leather seating surfaces, driver's seat 2 position memory; power tilt/slide moonroof with sunshade, heated front seats, electrochromic outside mirrors and high intensity discharge headlights. NOT AVAILABLE with ND, PM.		
NI	**Nakamichi Audio System Package (GS400)**	3344	4255
	Includes Nakamichi premium audio system, 6-disc in-dash CD auto-changer, power tilt/slide moonroof with sunshade, heated front seats and high intensity discharge headlights. NOT AVAILABLE with ND, PM.		
PM	**Premium Package (GS300)**	3088	3860
	Includes leather trim package with memory system: leather seating surfaces, driver's seat 2 position memory; 6-disc in-dash CD auto-changer, electrochromic outside mirrors and power tilt/slide moonroof with sunshade. NOT AVAILABLE with ND, NI.		
PM	**Premium Package (GS400)**	2444	3055
	Includes 6-disc in-dash CD auto-changer, power tilt/slide moonroof with sunshade, heated front seats and high intensity discharge headlights. NOT AVAILABLE with ND, NI.		
RF	**Rear Spoiler (GS400)**	352	440
	REQUIRES PM or NI or ND.		
SR	**Power Tilt/Slide Moonroof with Sunshade**	816	1020
TI	**Upgraded Tire Package with Chrome Wheels (GS400)**	958	1915
	Includes wheels: 17" chrome. NOT AVAILABLE with CW, FT, FK, TU.		
TU	**Upgraded Tire Package (GS400)**	172	215
	Includes wheels: 17" cast aluminum. NOT AVAILABLE with CW, FT, FK, TI.		
WL	**16" Wheel Locks (GS400)**	28	42
	NOT AVAILABLE with TU, TI.		
WL	**17" Wheel Locks (GS400)**	25	37
	NOT AVAILABLE with FK, FT, CW.		
WL	**Wheel Locks (GS300)**	30	44

LEXUS

LS 400

| CODE | DESCRIPTION | INVOICE | MSRP |

2000 LS 400

2000 Lexus LS 400

What's New?

Only minor changes are scheduled for 2000 LS 400s. Brake assist has been added to the Vehicle Skid Control system. A new onboard refueling vapor recovery system allows the LS 400 to meet transitional low-emission vehicle status. Child seat anchor-brackets are standard.

Review

The Lexus LS 400 was first introduced in 1989 as an alternative to European sedans. It offered superior build quality and refinement at a lower price. Eleven years later, the LS continues to be one of the top luxury sedans available. However, its European competition has improved considerably on the value equation, and now the LS 400's price is quite similar to that of the BMW 540i and the Mercedes Benz E430.

A 4.0-liter V8 engine powers the LS 400. Equipped with a variable valve timing system (Lexus calls it VVT-i), this engine generates 290 horsepower at 6,000 rpm and 300 foot-pounds of torque at 4,000 rpm. Power delivery is exceptionally smooth and quiet. A five-speed electronically controlled automatic transmission transfers power to the rear wheels. Lexus says the LS 400 can sprint from zero-to-60 in 6.6 seconds.

A Vehicle Skid Control system, which helps maintain traction under demanding conditions by detecting and correcting wheel spin, is standard. For 2000, Lexus has integrated a brake-assist system to VSC. The brake-assist system interprets a quick, hard push of the brake pedal as emergency braking and, if the driver has not stepped hard enough on the brake pedal to activate the antilock braking system, supplements the applied braking pressure.

Inside you'll find a high level of comfort and features. Impressive amounts of leather and walnut wood trim are used throughout. Four different colors of leather are available. The automatic climate control features an activated charcoal filter to trap dust and pollen. A smog sensor automatically switches the system into recirculation mode when it detects certain levels of pollution outside. Both the driver and passenger get 10-way power-adjustable seats, and heated seats are optional. The electroluminescent gauge cluster is easy to read and, when combined with the optional navigation screen, gives the Lexus a very high-tech aura.

The navigation system's screen is touch-operated and incorporates the audio- and climate-control systems. The navigation system provides turn-by-turn guidance by voice and on-screen

230   www.edmunds.com   EDMUND'S® NEW CARS

LS 400 — LEXUS

prompts. Instead of CDs, the LS 400's system uses a 2.0-gigabyte hard drive to store all major highways and about 90 U.S. metropolitan cities.

The LS 400 is a car that does everything for its driver. It is quick, exceptionally quiet, and comfortable. It is also exceptionally safe, with front and side airbags, a rigid chassis and optional high-intensity discharge xenon headlights. Lexus has crafted a near-perfect luxury car to get from point A to point B. However, some people feel that the Lexus isolates the driver too much from the driving experience.

Standard Equipment

LS 400 (5A): 4.0L V8 DOHC SMPI with variable valve timing 32-valve engine, requires premium unleaded fuel; 5-speed electronic OD auto transmission with lock-up; 750-amp battery; 100-amp alternator; driver's selectable multi-mode transmission; rear-wheel drive, traction control, electronic stability, 3.27 axle ratio; dual stainless steel exhaust with chrome tip; adaptive front independent double wishbone suspension with anti-roll bar, front coil springs, rear independent double wishbone suspension with anti-roll bar, rear coil springs; power rack-and-pinion steering with vehicle speed-sensing assist; 4-wheel disc brakes with 4-wheel antilock braking system; 22.5 gal. capacity fuel tank; side impact bars; front and rear colored bumpers with chrome bumper insert; chrome bodyside insert, colored bodyside cladding; monotone paint; aero-composite halogen fully auto headlamps with daytime running lights, delay-off feature; additional exterior lights include cornering lights, front fog/driving lights; driver's and passenger's power remote body-colored heated folding outside mirrors; front and rear 16" x 7" silver alloy wheels; P225/60VR16 performance BSW front and rear tires; inside under cargo mounted full-size alloy spare wheel; dual zone front air conditioning with climate control, air filter, rear heat ducts; premium AM/FM stereo, seek-scan, cassette, CD changer pre-wiring, in-dash CD pre-wiring, 7 premium speakers, amplifier, auto equalizer, theft deterrent, and window grid diversity antenna; cruise control; power door locks with 2 stage unlock, remote keyless entry, child safety rear door locks, power remote hatch/trunk release, power remote fuel release; cell phone pre-wiring, 3 power accessory outlets, driver's foot rest, retained accessory power, garage door opener; instrumentation display includes tachometer, water temperature gauge, in-dash clock, exterior temp, trip computer, trip odometer; warning indicators include oil pressure, battery, low coolant, key in ignition, low fuel, low washer fluid, bulb failure, door ajar; driver's and passenger's front airbags, driver's and front passenger's seat mounted side airbags; ignition disable, panic alarm, security system; tinted windows, power front and rear windows with front and rear 1-touch down; variable intermittent front windshield wipers, electrically heated windshield, rear window defroster; seating capacity of 5, front bucket seats, power adjustable tilt headrests, center armrest with storage, driver's seat includes 6-way power seat, power 2-way lumbar support, passenger's seat includes 6-way power seat, power 2-way lumbar support; rear bench seat with tilt headrests, center armrest with storage; front height adjustable seatbelts with front pretensioners; leather seats, leather door trim insert, full cloth headliner, full carpet floor covering with carpeted floor mats, genuine wood trim on instrument panel, leather-wrapped gear shift knob; memory on driver's seat with 2 memory setting(s) includes settings for exterior mirrors, steering wheel; interior lights include dome light, front and rear reading lights, 4 door curb lights, illuminated entry; steering wheel with power tilt and telescopic adjustment; dual illuminated vanity mirrors, dual auxiliary visors; auto-dimming day/night rearview mirror; full floor console, locking glove box with light, front and rear cupholders, instrument panel covered bin, 2 seat back storage pockets, driver's and passenger's door bins, rear door bins; carpeted cargo floor, carpeted trunk lid, cargo light; chrome grille, chrome side window moldings, black front windshield molding, chrome rear window molding and body-colored door handles.

Base Prices

CODE	DESCRIPTION	INVOICE	MSRP
9100	LS 400 (5A)	45648	53805
	Destination Charge:	495	495

LEXUS LS 400 / SC-SERIES

CODE	DESCRIPTION	INVOICE	MSRP
	Accessories		
CW	Wheels: Chrome	850	1700
DC	Lexus In-Dash 6 CD Auto-Changer	864	1080
FK	Chrome Wheels with All-Season Tires	850	1700
FT	Tires: All Season	NC	NC
HH	Heated Front Seats	352	440
	REQUIRES PM.		
LM	Trunk Mat	40	66
ND	Navigation System Package	4437	5405
	Includes navigation system, heated front seats, Premium package; Lexus in-dash 6 CD auto-changer, power tilt/slide moonroof with sunshade and high intensity discharge headlamps. NOT AVAILABLE with NI.		
NI	Nakamichi Audio System Package	3424	4355
	Includes Nakamichi premium audio, heated front seats, Premium package; Lexus in-dash 6 CD auto-changer, power tilt/slide moonroof with sunshade and high intensity discharge headlamps. NOT AVAILABLE with ND.		
PM	Premium Package	2172	2715
	Includes Lexus in-dash 6 CD auto-changer, power tilt/slide moonroof with sunshade and high intensity discharge headlamps.		
SA	Electronic Air Suspension Package	1524	1905
	Includes Lexus ride control. REQUIRES NI or ND.		
SR	Power Tilt/Slide Moonroof with Sunshade	896	1120
WL	Wheel Locks	30	44

2000 SC-SERIES

What's New?

The 2000 Lexus SC 300 and SC 400 are unchanged mechanically. For paint selection, Cinnabar Pearl replaces Baroque Red Metallic.

Review

Way back in the day (early '90s, actually), the then-new Lexus SC 300 and SC 400 were a huge hit with both the public and the automotive press. They offered features and pricing that no other car could match. But like an aging rock band, the SC Coupes still have the same moves and songs as they did when they were new. This has opened opportunities for younger stars (like the Mercedes Benz CLK430) to steal their fan base.

When Lexus came out with the SC Coupes, it did things a bit differently. First, a stylish, sexy body was penned that didn't look much like the mini chrome-barges that usually populate the personal-luxury segment. Aggressive and lacking a traditional grille, the SC looked like nothing else. But that basic shape remains today, and it has grown a bit tired. The SC 300 is powered by a 3.0-liter inline six that generates 225 horsepower at 6,000 rpm and 220 foot-pounds of torque at 4,000 rpm. The SC 400 uses the same V8 that is found in the Lexus LS 400. It puts out 290 horsepower at 6,000 rpm and 300 foot-pounds of peak torque at 4,000 rpm. Both engines are super-smooth and feature a variable valve timing system (Toyota calls its system VVT-i). This system optimizes valve overlap throughout the engine's speed range and in operating conditions, eliminating the traditional compromise between low-end torque and high-rpm horsepower. Both

SC-SERIES — LEXUS

SC engines use an electronic throttle control system (ETCS). The inline six features a four-speed automatic transmission and the V8 has a five-speed automatic.

Both interiors are exceptionally quiet. Special materials are used to filter out noise, vibration and harshness (NVH) to give the SC Coupes a serenely quiet ride. Heat and UV-reducing light-green tinted glass helps keep the interior cool on bright days and also helps reduce premature aging of interior materials. Those luxurious interior materials include sumptuous perforated leather seat inserts and trim (optional on the SC 300), wood and leather shift knob, plus elegant wood trim around the center console, doors and instrument panel. There's also amenities such as automatic climate control, 10-way power front seats, and a Lexus/Pioneer audio system. A premium 280-watt Lexus/Nakamichi unit is optional.

While the SC 300 and 400 are both good cars, the truth is that the SC Coupe platform is a 9-year-old design that simply can't compete in today's market. For the money, you'll find better personal-luxury coupes elsewhere.

2000 Lexus SC 400

Standard Equipment

SC 300 (4A): 3.0L I6 DOHC SMPI with variable valve timing 24-valve engine, requires premium unleaded fuel; 4-speed electronic OD auto transmission with lock-up; 600-amp battery; 80-amp alternator; driver's selectable multi-mode transmission, transmission oil cooler; rear-wheel drive, 4.27 axle ratio; dual stainless steel exhaust with chrome tip; front independent double wishbone suspension with anti-roll bar, front coil springs, rear independent double wishbone suspension with anti-roll bar, rear coil springs; power rack-and-pinion steering with vehicle speed-sensing assist; 4-wheel disc brakes with 4-wheel antilock braking system; 20.6 gal. capacity fuel tank; side impact bars; front and rear body-colored bumpers; rocker panel extensions; monotone paint; projector beam halogen fully auto headlamps with daytime running lights, delay-off feature; additional exterior lights include front fog/driving lights; driver's and passenger's power remote body-colored heated folding outside mirrors; front and rear 16" x 6.5" silver alloy wheels; P225/55VR16 performance BSW front and rear tires; inside under cargo mounted full-size steel spare wheel; air conditioning with climate control; premium AM/FM stereo, seek-scan, cassette, trunk-mounted 6-disc CD changer, 7 premium speakers, amplifier, auto equalizer, theft deterrent, and power retractable diversity antenna; cruise control; power door locks with 2 stage unlock, remote keyless entry, power remote hatch/trunk release, power remote fuel release; cell phone pre-wiring, 1 power accessory outlet, driver's foot rest, retained accessory power, smokers' package; instrumentation display includes tachometer, water temperature gauge, in-dash clock, exterior temp, trip computer, trip odometer; warning indicators include oil

LEXUS SC-SERIES

CODE	DESCRIPTION	INVOICE	MSRP

pressure, battery, low oil level, low coolant, lights on, key in ignition, low fuel, bulb failure, door ajar, driver's and passenger's front airbags; ignition disable, panic alarm, security system; tinted windows, power front windows with driver's 1-touch down; variable intermittent front windshield wipers, sun visor strip, rear window defroster; seating capacity of 4, front bucket seats, adjustable tilt headrests, center armrest with storage, driver's seat includes 6-way power seat, power 2-way lumbar support, passenger's seat includes 6-way power seat, power 2-way lumbar support, rear bench seat with fixed headrests; front height adjustable seatbelts with front pretensioners; premium cloth seats, cloth door trim insert, full cloth headliner, full carpet floor covering with carpeted floor mats, genuine wood trim on instrument panel, leather/wood gear shift knob; interior lights include dome light, front reading lights, 2 door curb lights, illuminated entry; leather-wrapped steering wheel with tilt and telescopic adjustment; dual illuminated vanity mirrors, driver's side auxiliary visor, auto-dimming day/night rearview mirror; full floor console, locking glove box with light, front cupholder, 2 seat back storage pockets, driver's and passenger's door bins; carpeted cargo floor, carpeted trunk lid, cargo light; chrome grille, chrome side window moldings, black front windshield molding, black rear window molding and body-colored door handles.

SC 400 (5A) (in addition to or instead of SC300 (5A) equipment): 4.0L V8 DOHC SMPI with variable valve timing 32-valve engine, requires premium unleaded fuel; 5-speed electronic OD auto transmission with lock-up; 750-amp battery, 3.27 axle ratio; warning indicators low washer fluid, electrically heated windshield, sun visor strip, rear window defroster; leather seats, leather door trim insert, memory on driver's seat with 2 memory setting(s) includes settings for exterior mirrors, steering wheel and leather-wrapped steering wheel with power tilt and telescopic adjustment.

Base Prices

9200	SC 300 (4A)	37701	43405
9220	SC 400 (5A)	47994	55905
	Destination Charge:	495	495

Accessories

CW	Wheels: Chrome	850	1700
FK	Chrome Wheels with All-Season Tires	850	1700
FT	Tires: All Season	NC	NC
LA	Leather Trim Package with Memory System (SC300)	1688	2110
	Includes electrochromic outside mirrors, Lexus memory system and leather seating surfaces.		
ML	Carpeted Trunk Mat with CD Changer	40	66
NK	Lexus/Nakamichi Premium Audio System	900	1200
RF	Color-Keyed Rear Spoiler	352	440
	Includes LED high mount stop lamp.		
SR	Power Tilt/Slide Moonroof with Sunshade	904	1130
TN	Traction Control System	992	1240
	REQUIRES LA (SC300) and (FT or FK).		
WL	Wheel Locks (SC400)	28	42
WL	Wheel Locks	30	44
	NOT AVAILABLE with TN.		

LINCOLN
CONTINENTAL

CODE	DESCRIPTION	INVOICE	MSRP

2000 CONTINENTAL

2000 Lincoln Continental

What's New?

The Continental receives additional safety features, including side airbags, an emergency trunk release, child seat-anchor brackets, and Lincoln's Belt Minder system.

Review

It's not easy to find a rear-drive, luxury car built in America, and Lincoln's Continental is no exception. Making the jump to front-wheel drive in 1988, the Continental has been with Lincoln since 1940 but is fully modernized and features a potent 275 horsepower, 4.6-liter V8. This engine also makes 275 foot-pounds of torque at 4,750 rpm. Gas mileage remains in the acceptable range with a 17/24 mpg rating for city/highway driving.

A fully independent suspension and gas pressurized shocks come standard on all Continentals, but a check on the driver's control package option adds three-way adjustable, semi-active suspension for plush, normal or firm ride control. There's also an Alpine audio system option group for audiophiles, a luxury package with upgraded interior and exterior trim pieces, and a personal security package with a low tire-pressure warning system and a programmable garage door opener. For the ultimate in secure travel, a RESCU package is available with Lincoln's Remote Emergency Satellite Cellular Unit to call for assistance and transmit the vehicle's location within 100 feet via a global positioning satellite (GPS) network.

In addition to the new standard side airbags for 2000, the Continental receives many of the same safety changes that Ford has implemented across most of its model line. The emergency trunk release allows people who are trapped in the trunk to release the hatch. The child seat-anchor brackets in the back seat provide parents and caregivers an improved method to buckle in their child safety seats more securely. The system secures child safety seats using tethers that attach to the anchor brackets, in addition to traditional safety belts. The Belt Minder system consists of a chime and an indicator light to remind drivers and passengers to buckle up.

The Continental's exterior remains unchanged for the 2000 model year. The wide front grille is retained, as are the dual exhaust outlets and the swoopy hood line. This gives the Lincoln a .32 coefficient of drag which, as luxury sedans go, is fairly slippery. If you really want to set yourself apart from other Continentals, the optional six-spoke chrome wheels can add to the car's classic look.

LINCOLN

CONTINENTAL

CODE	DESCRIPTION	INVOICE	MSRP

The Lincoln Continental is a roomy, competent, attractive sedan. It faces tough competition from Acura, BMW, Cadillac, Lexus and Mercedes Benz. The new 2000 Lincoln LS will be another vehicle to consider. Many of the vehicles from these manufacturers offer high levels of ride and handling refinement without resorting to gee-whiz gadgetry like the Driver's Select System.

─────────────── **Standard Equipment** ───────────────

CONTINENTAL (4A): 4.6L V8 DOHC SMPI 32-valve engine, requires premium unleaded fuel; 4-speed electronic OD auto transmission with lock-up; HD battery with run down protection; 125-amp alternator; front-wheel drive, traction control, 3.56 axle ratio; stainless steel exhaust with chrome tip; adaptive auto-leveling suspension, front independent strut suspension with anti-roll bar, front coil springs, rear independent suspension with anti-roll bar, rear air springs; power rack-and-pinion steering with vehicle speed-sensing assist; 4-wheel disc brakes with 4-wheel antilock braking system; 20 gal. capacity fuel tank; side impact bars; front and rear body-colored bumpers with chrome bumper insert; body-colored bodyside molding with chrome bodyside insert; monotone paint; aero-composite halogen fully auto headlamps with delay-off feature; additional exterior lights include cornering lights; driver's and passenger's power remote body-colored heated outside mirrors; front and rear 16" x 7" silver alloy wheels; P225/60HR16 A/S BSW front and rear tires; inside under cargo mounted compact steel spare wheel; air conditioning with climate control, air filter, rear heat ducts; premium AM/FM stereo, seek-scan, cassette, 4 speakers, amplifier, and window grid antenna; cruise control with steering wheel controls; power door locks, remote keyless entry, child safety rear door locks, power remote hatch/trunk release, power remote fuel release; 2 power accessory outlets, trunk pulldown, driver's foot rest, retained accessory power; instrumentation display includes tachometer, water temperature gauge, clock, compass, exterior temp, systems monitor, trip computer, trip odometer; warning indicators include oil pressure, water temp, battery, low oil level, low coolant, lights on, key in ignition, low fuel, low washer fluid, bulb failure, door ajar, trunk ajar, service interval; driver's and passenger's front airbags, driver's and front passenger's seat mounted side airbags; ignition disable, panic alarm, security system; tinted windows, power front and rear windows with driver's 1-touch down; variable intermittent front windshield wipers, sun visor strip, rear window defroster; seating capacity of 5, front bucket seats, adjustable headrests, center armrest with storage, driver's seat includes 6-way power seat, power 2-way lumbar support, easy entry, passenger's seat includes 6-way power seat, power 2-way lumbar support; rear bench seat, center armrest with storage; front height adjustable seatbelts; leather seats, leatherette door trim insert, full cloth headliner, full carpet floor covering with carpeted floor mats, genuine wood trim on instrument panel, leather-wrapped gear shift knob; memory on driver's seat with 2 memory setting(s) includes settings for exterior mirrors; interior lights include dome light with fade, front reading lights, 2 door curb lights, illuminated entry; leather-wrapped steering wheel with tilt adjustment; dual illuminated vanity mirrors, dual auxiliary visors; auto-dimming day/night rearview mirror; full floor console, mini overhead console with storage, locking glove box with light, front and rear cupholders, 2 seat back storage pockets, driver's and passenger's door bins; carpeted cargo floor, carpeted trunk lid, cargo light; chrome grille, chrome side window moldings, black front windshield molding, black rear window molding and chrome door handles.

─────────────── **Base Prices** ───────────────

CODE	DESCRIPTION	INVOICE	MSRP
M97	Continental (4A)	35408	38880
Destination Charge:		695	695

236   www.edmunds.com   **EDMUND'S® NEW CARS**

CONTINENTAL — LINCOLN

Accessories

CODE	DESCRIPTION	INVOICE	MSRP
—	Tri Coat Paint Charge	314	365
	NOT AVAILABLE with 933.		
13B	Power Moonroof	1302	1515
	Includes color-keyed sunshade. REQUIRES 175.		
175	Programmable Garage Door Opener	104	120
	REQUIRES 13B.		
41H	Engine Block Immersion Heater (LPO)	52	60
428	High Altitude Principal Use	NC	NC
429	Non-High Altitude Principal Use	NC	NC
467	Heated Seats	250	290
	Includes distinct settings for back and bottom heating and 5 temperature settings.		
516	Portable/Convertible Cellular Telephone	680	790
	Cellular services may not be available in all areas. Includes voice activated, hands free operations and in-car charger. Phone numbers, signal strength and time length of call displayed in message center. Located in console on 5-passenger and in passenger-side armrest on 6-passenger. REQUIRES 916.		
54A	Luxury Appearance Package	942	1095
	Includes tu-tone leather seating surfaces, chrome/argent grille, wheels: 6-spoke chrome, real wood trim steering wheel and unique front floor mats. REQUIRES 667. NOT AVAILABLE with 675.		
64F	Wheels: 16" Highly Polished Aluminum	302	350
	NOT AVAILABLE with 64G.		
64G	Wheels: 6-Spoke Chrome	726	845
	NOT AVAILABLE with 675, 64F, T23.		
667	Driver's Select System	512	595
	Includes driver's adjustable ride control (firm, normal and plush), memory profile system that allows 2 drivers to personalize settings for 11 features, auto-dimming outside driver's side view mirror, semi-active suspension and steering wheel mounted radio controls. REQUIRES 916.		
675	Personal Security Package	646	750
	Includes tires: run-flat, programmable garage door opener and pressure alert warning system. REQUIRES 64F. NOT AVAILABLE with 64G, 54A.		
67F	RESCU Package	2016	2345
	Includes Lincoln RESCU, portable/convertible cellular telephone, Alpine audio system radio and programmable garage door opener. Automatic activation with air bag deployment.		
67F	RESCU Package	1914	2225
	Includes Lincoln RESCU, portable/convertible cellular telephone, Alpine audio system radio and programmable garage door opener. Automatic activation with air bag deployment. REQUIRES 675.		
7	Twin Comfort Seats (6-Passenger)	NC	NC
	Includes leather seating surfaces, storage armrests, cupholders, column shift and mini console with ashtray.		

LINCOLN
CONTINENTAL / LS

CODE	DESCRIPTION	INVOICE	MSRP
916	Radio: Alpine Audio System	486	565
	Includes digital signal processing (DSP), separate subwoofer amplifier, 5-1/2" x 7-1/2" door speakers in rear doors, 5-1/4" round coaxial speakers in front doors and 2 6x9 sub-woofers added to rear package tray.		
919	Alpine 6-Disc CD/DJ Changer	512	595
	Located in console for 5-passenger seating and mini-console for 6-passenger. *REQUIRES 916.*		
B3E	No Charge Moonroof Package	(1406)	(1635)
	Customers whose residence or place of business is located within the New York Region or the State of New York and serviced by the Pittsburgh Region are eligible. Commercial, repurchase, LMCRS and Government sales (including price concessions) are not eligible. REQUIRES 13B and 175.		
T23	Tires: P225/60VR16 BSW	NC	NC
	REQUIRES 64F. NOT AVAILABLE with 64G.		

2000 LS

2000 Lincoln LS

What's New?

From the ground up, this is a completely new sport sedan based on the Ford's mid-size platform. Lincoln worked with Jaguar to develop this platform, which is also used for Jaguar's S-type sedan. It is the first Lincoln in over two decades not classified as a full-size vehicle, and should appeal to buyers looking for something sportier and smaller than the Town Car or Continental.

Review

Lincoln is on a mission to redefine its image, and the LS model will lead the charge when it goes on sale in the spring of 1999 as the company's first 2000 model. With a sticker price, overall size and base horsepower nearly identical to Cadillac's Catera, Lincoln hopes to offer more in

LS   LINCOLN

the areas of performance and passion than GM's Opel-based Caddy.

The first clue to this Lincoln's sporting nature is its optional Getrag five-speed manual transmission, which can be mated to the standard 3.0-liter V6 engine. This base engine makes 210 peak horsepower and 205 foot-pounds of torque. If more go-power is required, an optional 3.9-liter V8, making 252 horsepower and 267 foot-pounds of torque, can be ordered, but not with a manual transmission.

For those who like the idea of shifting, but not necessarily using a clutch, an optional SelectShift 5-speed automatic is available with either engine. The SelectShift automatic is part of the LS Sport Package, which includes 17-inch aluminum wheels, European suspension, body-colored bumpers and a leather-wrapped steering wheel.

Suspension is another area where Lincoln took the high road when creating the LS. An all-aluminum, four-wheel independent setup means the days of the Lincoln Land Yacht may finally be over. With a 52/48 percent weight distribution (V8) between the front and rear axles, this may be the first "European-inspired" luxury sedan that will truly feel European when attacking twisty roads. There's even an optional Advance-Trac yaw control system available for when your driving enthusiasm exceeds your driving ability.

Despite its sporting nature, the LS is still a Lincoln at heart, and standard features like dual automatic temperature control, leather seating, rear armrests with cupholders and an air filtration system speak to those who won't compromise luxury for the sake of performance. A Convenience Package adds further to the LS' posh nature with a memory driver's seat/steering wheel/exterior mirror position, power lumbar support for driver and passenger, a universal garage door opener and moisture-sensitive wipers.

Standard Equipment

V6 AUTOMATIC (5A): 3.0L V6 DOHC SMPI 24-valve engine; 5-speed electronic overdrive automatic transmission with lock-up; 72-amp battery with run down protection; 110-amp alternator; rear wheel drive, traction control, 3.58 axle ratio; dual stainless steel exhaust; front independent suspension with anti-roll bar, front coil springs, rear independent suspension with anti-roll bar, rear coil springs; power rack-and-pinion steering with vehicle speed-sensing assist; 4 wheel disc brakes with 4 wheel antilock braking system; 18.3 gal. capacity fuel tank; front and rear body-colored bumpers with chrome bumper insert; body-colored bodyside molding; monotone paint; aero-composite halogen fully automatic headlamps with delay-off feature; additional exterior lights include front fog/driving lights, center high mounted stop light; driver's and passenger's power remote body-colored heated outside mirrors; front and rear 16" x 7" silver alloy wheels; P215/60HR16 BSW AS front and rear tires; inside under cargo mounted compact steel spare wheel; dual zone front air conditioning with climate control, air filter, rear heat ducts; premium AM/FM stereo with clock, seek-scan, cassette, 6 speakers, automatic equalizer, and window grid diversity antenna; cruise control with steering wheel controls; power door locks, remote keyless entry, child safety rear door locks, power remote hatch/trunk release, power remote fuel release; cell phone pre-wiring, 2 power accessory outlets, driver's foot rest, retained accessory power; instrumentation display includes tachometer, water temp gauge, trip odometer; warning indicators include oil pressure, water temp, battery, low oil level, lights on, key in ignition, low fuel, low washer fluid, bulb failure, door ajar, trunk ajar; dual airbags, seat mounted side airbags; ignition disable, panic alarm, security system; tinted windows, power front windows with driver's 1-touch down, power rear windows; variable intermittent heated front windshield wipers, rear window defroster; seating capacity of 5, front bucket seats with adjustable headrests, center armrest with storage, driver's seat includes 6-way power seat with lumbar support, passenger's seat includes 4-way power seat with 8-way direction control and lumbar support; 60-40 folding rear bench seat with fixed headrests, center armrest; front height adjustable seatbelts; leather seats, leather door trim, full cloth headliner, full carpet floor covering with carpeted floor mats, wood trim; interior lights include dome light with fade, front and rear reading lights, 2 door curb lights, illuminated entry; steering wheel with power tilt and telescopic adjustment; dual illuminated vanity mirrors; day-night rearview mirror; full floor console, locking glove box with light, front and rear cupholders, instrument panel covered bin, 2 seat back storage pockets, driver's and passenger's door bins; carpeted cargo floor, carpeted trunk lid, cargo light; chrome grille,

LINCOLN

LS

CODE	DESCRIPTION	INVOICE	MSRP

chrome side window moldings, black front windshield molding, black rear window molding and body-colored door handles.

V6 MANUAL (5M) (in addition to or instead of V6 AUTOMATIC (5A) equipment): 5-speed overdrive manual transmission; engine oil cooler; 3.31 axle ratio; sport ride suspension; front and rear body-colored bumpers with body-colored bumper insert; front and rear 17" x 7" silver alloy wheels; inside under cargo mounted full-size conventional alloy spare wheel; leather-wrapped steering wheel with power tilt and telescopic adjustment.

V8 AUTO (5A) (in addition to or instead of V6 MANUAL (5M) equipment): 3.9L V8 DOHC SMPI 32-valve engine; 5-speed electronic overdrive automatic transmission with lock-up; 3.58 axle ratio; front and rear body-colored bumpers with chrome bumper insert; front and rear 16" x 7" silver alloy wheels; inside under cargo mounted compact steel spare wheel; instrumentation display includes exterior temp, systems monitor, trip computer; rain detecting wiper; 60-40 folding rear bench seat with adjustable rear headrests; memory on driver's seat with 2 memory setting(s) includes settings for exterior mirrors, steering wheel and auto-dimming day-night rearview mirror.

Base Prices

Code	Description	Invoice	MSRP
M86	V6 Auto (5A)	28264	30915
GMI	V6 Manual (5M)	28976	31715
M87	V8 Auto (5A)	31624	34690
	Destination Charge:	560	560

Accessories

Code	Description	Invoice	MSRP
13B	Power Moonroof	856	995
	Includes keyfob sunroof control.		
41H	Engine Block Immersion Heater	52	60
518	Portable Hands Free Cellular Telephone	598	695
	Analog frequency. NOT AVAILABLE with 67B.		
556	Advance Trac (Automatic)	624	725
60L	Convenience Package (V6)	732	850
	Includes electrochromic rearview mirror, universal garage door opener, moisture sensitive wipers, memory settings, power driver's and passenger's lumbar. STANDARD on V8.		
60N	Sport Package (Automatic)	860	1000
	Includes wheels: 17" super silver aluminum, tires: P235/50VR17 BSW, full size spare tire with matching wheel, European sport suspension tuning, selectshift automatic transmission, body colored bumpers, engine oil cooler, leather-wrapped steering wheel and leather-wrapped shift knob. NOT AVAILABLE with 64X.		
632	Heated Front Seats	250	290
	Includes heated cushions and seatbacks.		
64X	Wheels: 16" 5-Spoke High-Polished Aluminum (Automatic)	340	395
	NOT AVAILABLE with 60N.		
67B	RESCU System (V8)	826	960
	Includes portable hands free cellular telephone. NOT AVAILABLE with 518.		
916	Alpine Audiophile System	486	565
	Includes 260-watt amplifier and 12 speaker system with subwoofer.		

LS / TOWN CAR — LINCOLN

CODE	DESCRIPTION	INVOICE	MSRP
919	6-Disc CD Changer	512	595
	Glovebox mounted.		
LCC	Tri Coat Paint	314	365

2000 TOWN CAR

2000 Lincoln Town Car

What's New?

The Town Car receives additional safety features, including an emergency trunk release, child seat-anchor brackets, and Lincoln's Belt Minder system. A new storage armrest has been placed on the front-passenger door-trim panel. One new exterior color has been added: Autumn Red Clearcoat Metallic.

Review

Lincolns have always been big, comfortable cruisers designed to coddle drivers and passengers in silent, swift comfort. In 1998, the Town Car was updated with new exterior styling, a new interior, traction control, and an improved rear suspension. Overall, the new style is clean, with a profile that is chiseled and strong. The only discordant element is the strange headlamp design that appears as though penned by an action comic-book artist.

Three trim levels of the Town Car are available: the base Executive, midline Signature, and top-of-the-heap Cartier. The Executive comes loaded with luxury: leather seating, power-adjusted front seats with power recliners and automatic climate control are all included in the entry-level Town Car (why Lincoln spoiled this classic name with that "Executive" tag is beyond us). Safety features abound as well, with antilock brakes, traction control and front side-impact airbags among the standard fare. Stepping up to the Signature adds a few perks such as power lumbar supports in front, a powerful Alpine stereo system, and steering wheel-mounted controls for the stereo and climate-control systems. The Cartier gilds the lily with higher-grade leather, heated seats, chrome wheels and, of course, a Cartier clock.

The 2000 Town Car continues this tradition with a 4.6-liter V8 that makes 205 horsepower and 280 foot-pounds of torque. The Cartier and Signature Touring Sedan Town Car models are

LINCOLN
TOWN CAR

CODE	DESCRIPTION	INVOICE	MSRP

equipped with a dual exhaust system and deliver 220 horsepower and 290 foot-pounds of torque at 3,500 rpm. While not exactly a performance car, the Town Car will get you up to speed with little effort and even less drama.

The changes for 2000 consist of the same safety changes that Ford has implemented across most of its model line. The emergency trunk release allows people who are trapped in the trunk to release the hatch. The child seat-anchor brackets in the back seat provide parents and caregivers an improved method to buckle in their child safety seats more securely. The system secures child safety seats using tethers that attach to the anchor brackets, in addition to traditional safety belts. The Belt Minder system consists of a chime and an indicator light to remind drivers and passengers to buckle up.

The Town Car hasn't had any domestic competition since the rear-drive Fleetwood and Buick Roadmaster were canceled in 1996. Strangely enough, the 2000 Town Car might find competition from within the Ford camp. While it's smaller, the new Lincoln LS offers a considerably more refined and sporting character.

Standard Equipment

EXECUTIVE (4A): 4.6L V8 SOHC SMPI 16-valve engine; 4-speed electronic OD auto transmission with lock-up; HD battery with run down protection; 130-amp alternator; rear-wheel drive, traction control, 3.08 axle ratio; stainless steel exhaust; auto-leveling suspension, front independent suspension with anti-roll bar, front coil springs, gas-pressurized front shocks, rigid rear axle multi-link suspension with anti-roll bar, rear air springs, gas-pressurized rear shocks; power re-circulating ball steering with vehicle speed-sensing assist, power steering cooler; 4-wheel disc brakes with 4-wheel antilock braking system; 19 gal. capacity fuel tank; side impact bars; front and rear body-colored bumpers with chrome bumper insert; chrome bodyside insert, body-colored bodyside cladding; monotone paint; aero-composite halogen fully auto headlamps with delay-off feature; additional exterior lights include cornering lights; driver's and passenger's power remote body-colored heated folding outside mirrors; front and rear 16" x 7" silver alloy wheels; P225/60SR16 A/S BSW front and rear tires; trunk mounted compact steel spare wheel; air conditioning with climate control, rear heat ducts; premium AM/FM stereo, clock, seek-scan, cassette, 4 speakers, and window grid diversity antenna; cruise control with steering wheel controls; power door locks, remote keyless entry, child safety rear door locks, power remote hatch/trunk release, power remote fuel release; 2 power accessory outlets, driver's foot rest, retained accessory power; instrumentation display includes water temperature gauge, exterior temp, systems monitor, trip computer, trip odometer; warning indicators include oil pressure, water temp, battery, low oil level, lights on, key in ignition, low fuel, low washer fluid, bulb failure, door ajar, trunk ajar; driver's and passenger's front airbags, driver's and front passenger's door mounted side airbags; ignition disable, panic alarm; tinted windows, power front and rear windows with driver's 1-touch down; variable intermittent front windshield wipers, sun visor strip, rear window defroster; seating capacity of 6, 40-20-40 split-bench front seat, adjustable headrests, center armrest with storage, driver's seat includes 6-way power seat, passenger's seat includes 6-way power seat; rear bench seat with fixed headrests, center armrest with storage; front height adjustable seatbelts; leather seats, leatherette door trim insert, full cloth headliner, full carpet floor covering with carpeted floor mats; interior lights include dome light with fade, front and rear reading lights, 4 door curb lights, illuminated entry; leather-wrapped steering wheel with tilt adjustment; dual illuminated vanity mirrors; day/night rearview mirror; locking glove box with light, front and rear cupholders, interior concealed storage, 2 seat back storage pockets, driver's door bin; carpeted cargo floor, carpeted trunk lid, cargo light; chrome grille, chrome side window moldings, black front windshield molding, black rear window molding and chrome door handles.

SIGNATURE (4A) (in addition to or instead of EXECUTIVE (4A) equipment): Premium AM/FM stereo, clock, seek-scan, cassette, 5 premium speakers, amplifier, and window grid diversity antenna, radio steering wheel controls; garage door opener; instrumentation display includes compass; driver's seat includes 6-way power seat, power 2-way lumbar support, passenger's seat includes 6-way power seat, power 2-way lumbar support; genuine wood trim on instrument

242   www.edmunds.com   **EDMUND'S® NEW CARS**

TOWN CAR — LINCOLN

panel; memory on driver's seat with 2 memory setting(s) includes settings for exterior mirrors and auto-dimming day/night rearview mirror.

CARTIER (4A) (in addition to or instead of SIGNATURE (4A) equipment): Dual stainless steel exhaust; monotone paint with bodyside accent gold trim package; instrumentation display includes clock; heated-cushion 40-20-40 split-bench front seat and rear vanity mirror.

Base Prices

CODE	DESCRIPTION	INVOICE	MSRP
M81	Executive (4A)	35186	38630
M82	Signature (4A)	36966	40630
M83	Cartier (4A)	39191	43130
	Destination Charge:	695	695

Accessories

CODE	DESCRIPTION	INVOICE	MSRP
13B	Power Moonroof (Signature/Cartier)	1302	1515
41H	Heater: Engine Block Immersion	52	60
428	High Altitude Principal Use	NC	NC
429	Non-High Altitude Principal Use	NC	NC
467	Driver's and Passenger's Heated Seats (Signature)	250	290
503	Conventional Spare Tire	104	120
	Includes matching steel wheel.		
518	Cellular Telephone (Signature/Cartier)	680	790
	Integrated voice activated, portable, convertable and rechargeable features. Cellular services may not be available in all areas.		
535	Livery Package (LPO) (Executive)	216	250
	Includes single exhaust, heavy duty steering gear, upgraded front and rear stabilizer bar, 3.08 axle ratio, wider opening rear door hinges, rear seat armrest with cupholders, center front seat fold-down storage armrest, mini spare tire loose in trunk, 78-amp HD battery, HD front springs, tires: P225/60SR16 A/S BSW and AM/FM stereo cassette radio.		
60P	Premium Package (Signature/Cartier)	1814	2110
	Includes power moonroof and trunk-mounted CD changer.		
615	Electrochromic Mirrors and Compass Group (Executive)	210	245
	Includes electrochromic driver's mirror, electrochromic interior rearview mirror and compass. Automatically dims to precise level to eliminate headlight glare from following vehicles, returns to clear state when glare subsides. Mirrors return to clear state when vehicle is in reverse mode.		
663	Signature Touring Sedan Package (Signature)	602	700
	Includes argent painted grille with chrome surround, Birdseye woodgrain (black) trim on instrument panel and door trim, revised springs and shocks, 30mm front stabilizer bar, 18mm rear stabilizer bar, unique badge, unique torque converter, leather perforated seating surfaces, monotone lower bodyside cladding/fascia, 3.55 axle ratio, tires: P235/60TR16 BSW, wheels: 16" chrome tech aluminum, dual exhaust and engine: 4.6l EFI V8 with dual exhaust. Available in 6 exterior colors and 3 interior colors. NOT AVAILABLE with 954, T2A.		
919	Trunk Mounted Compact Disc Changer (Signature/Cartier)	512	595

LINCOLN
TOWN CAR

CODE	DESCRIPTION	INVOICE	MSRP
954	Two-Tone Paint (Signature)	216	250
	NOT AVAILABLE with 663.		
T2A	Tires: P225/60SR16 WSW AS	82	95
	NOT AVAILABLE with 663.		
UTO	Premium Package Discount (Signature/Cartier)	(442)	(515)
	REQUIRES 60P.		
WF	White Pearlescent Clearcoat Metalic (Executive/Signature)	314	365
X	Leather Perforated Seating Surfaces (Signature)	NC	NC
	Includes individual comfort 40-20-40 lounge.		

**One 15-minute call
could save you 15% or more
on car insurance.**

**GEICO
DIRECT**

America's 6th Largest Automobile Insurance Company

1-800-555-2758

***Save hundreds, even thousands,
off the sticker price
of the new car you want.***

**Call Autovantage®
your FREE auto-buying service**

1-800-201-7703

No purchase required. No fees.

626 MAZDA

2000 626

2000 Mazda 626

What's New?

Improvements in styling, handling, steering, interior content, and options are the highlights of the 2000 626.

Review

The Mazda 626 has been somewhat of a wallflower these past few years, watching the Honda Accord and the Toyota Camry receive the most attention from people looking to buy a four-door sedan. That's a bit unfortunate, as the 626 harnesses some solid attributes, especially in 2000. All models this year receive updated styling, revised interiors, and added content.

The Mazda comes in four trim levels: LX, LX-V6, ES, and ES-V6. The exterior has been altered this year by adding a new five-point grille with a large Mazda symbol, new headlights and taillights, and revised front-end styling. LX and ES models now have 15-inch wheels as standard, and the ES-V6 gets 16-inch wheels. It looks better, but the 626 still doesn't stand out very much.

Mazda prides itself on building cars that are fun to drive. For 2000, the 626 receives changes to further this characteristic. The body structure is stiffer than before, with strengthened front and rear suspension towers. The actual suspension design is still MacPherson struts up front and Mazda's Twin-Trapezoidal Link (TTL) at the rear, but there are now thicker front and rear antiroll bars. Mazda says these changes improve handling, and NVH has been reduced to improve comfort.

The steering, braking, and overall road feel of the 626 are better and more responsive than last year. The steering system has been altered to more closely feel like the Mazda Miata's, and the brake system benefits from revised components.

For power, the LX and ES feature a more powerful 2.0-liter four-cylinder engine producing 130 horsepower and 130 foot-pounds of torque. LX and ES cars fitted with the 2.0-liter engine now qualify as ultra-low-emission vehicles. The V6 puts out 170 horsepower and 163 foot-pounds of torque. While both engines are competent, they do lack power when compared to the engines found in the Accord, Camry or Galant. Both 626 engines are available with either a five-speed manual or a four-speed automatic transmission.

MAZDA   626

CODE	DESCRIPTION	INVOICE	MSRP

The interior is still the same as it was when this 626 generation debuted in 1998, but 2000 brings minor updates. The big news is optional side airbags. But there's also a new center console, cloth or leather covers for the center armrest, chrome-plated door handles, different cloth and leather seat patterns, and illumination for more buttons and switches. Additional interior changes include a new rear-seat armrest, rear-seat heater ducts, and new gauge graphics.

The 626 (built in Flat Rock, Mich.) was the first Japanese-branded sedan to be called a true domestic by government agencies. With an upscale image and nimble handling manners, our favorite model is the ES V6 with a five-speed manual transmission. Though the 2000-year changes probably won't push the 626's sales past the Accord or Camry, they certainly make Mazda's mid-priced four-door sedan a much more attractive purchase for people looking for something a bit different.

Standard Equipment

LX (5M): 2.0L I4 DOHC SMPI 16-valve engine; 5-speed OD manual transmission; 582-amp battery; 80-amp alternator; front-wheel drive, 4.11 axle ratio; partial stainless steel exhaust; front independent strut suspension with anti-roll bar, front coil springs, rear independent multi-link suspension with anti-roll bar, rear coil springs; power rack-and-pinion steering with engine speed-sensing assist; front disc/rear drum brakes; 16.9 gal. capacity fuel tank; side impact bars; front and rear body-colored bumpers; body-colored bodyside molding; monotone paint; aero-composite halogen auto off headlamps; driver's and passenger's power remote body-colored outside mirrors; front and rear 15" x 6" steel wheels; P205/60SR15 A/S BSW front and rear tires; inside under cargo mounted compact steel spare wheel; air conditioning, rear heat ducts; AM/FM stereo, clock, seek-scan, single CD, 4 speakers, amplifier, and window grid antenna; cruise control with steering wheel controls; power door locks with 2 stage unlock, remote keyless entry, child safety rear door locks, power remote hatch/trunk release, remote fuel release; 2 power accessory outlets, driver's foot rest; instrumentation display includes tachometer, water temperature gauge, trip odometer; warning indicators include oil pressure, battery, low oil level, lights on, key in ignition, low fuel, low washer fluid, bulb failure, door ajar, brake fluid; driver's and passenger's front airbags; tinted windows, power front and rear windows with driver's 1-touch down; variable intermittent front windshield wipers, sun visor strip, rear window defroster; seating capacity of 5, front bucket seats, adjustable headrests, center armrest with storage, driver's seat includes 6-way direction control, passenger's seat includes 4-way direction control; 40-60 folding rear bench seat with fixed headrests, center armrest with storage; front height adjustable seatbelts; premium cloth seats, cloth door trim insert, full cloth headliner, full carpet floor covering, plastic/rubber gear shift knob; interior lights include dome light with fade, front reading lights, 2 door curb lights; steering wheel with tilt adjustment; dual illuminated vanity mirrors; day/night rearview mirror; full floor console, locking glove box with light, front and rear cupholders, instrument panel covered bin, 2 seat back storage pockets, driver's and passenger's door bins; carpeted cargo floor, cargo light; chrome grille, chrome side window moldings, black front windshield molding, black rear window molding and body-colored door handles.

LX V6 (5M) (in addition to or instead of LX (5M) equipment): 2.5L V6 DOHC SMPI 24-valve engine, requires premium unleaded fuel; 90-amp alternator; 4-wheel disc brakes; front and rear 15" x 6" alloy wheels and interior lights include illuminated entry.

ES (4A) (in addition to or instead of LX (5M) equipment): 4-speed electronic OD auto transmission with lock-up; leather seats, vinyl door trim insert, carpeted floor mats and leather-wrapped steering wheel with tilt adjustment.

ES V6 (5M) (in addition to or instead of ES (5M) equipment): 2.5L V6 DOHC SMPI 24-valve engine, requires premium unleaded fuel; 5-speed OD manual transmission; 90-amp alternator; 4-wheel disc brakes; front power sliding and tilting glass sunroof with sunshade; driver's and passenger's power remote body-colored heated outside mirrors; front and rear 16" x 6" silver alloy wheels; P205/55HR16 A/S BSW front and rear tires; AM/FM stereo, clock, seek-scan,

246   www.edmunds.com   **EDMUND'S® NEW CARS**

626 MAZDA

cassette, single CD, 4 premium speakers, amplifier, and window grid antenna; ignition disable, security system; driver's seat includes 4-way power seat, 8-way direction control; leather-wrapped gear shift knob; interior lights include illuminated entry; mini overhead console with storage and carpeted trunk lid.

Base Prices

CODE	DESCRIPTION	INVOICE	MSRP
626LX4P	LX (5M)	16642	18245
626LX6P	LX V6 (5M)	17735	19445
626ES4A	ES (4A)	18645	20445
626ES6P	ES V6 (5M)	20465	22445
Destination Charge:		450	450

Accessories

CODE	DESCRIPTION	INVOICE	MSRP
1AB	ABS Brakes (V6)	760	950
	Includes traction control system and side airbags.		
1ES	ES Luxury Package (ES)	1040	1300
	Includes power moonroof, mini overhead console, anti-theft alarm, 6-way power driver's seat and heated mirrors.		
1LX	LX Luxury Package (LX)	1440	1800
	Includes wheels: 15" alloy with locks, power moonroof, mini overhead console, anti-theft alarm, 6-way power driver's seat, floor mats and heated mirrors. NOT AVAILABLE with FLM.		
1WP	Wheels: 16" Alloy with Locks (LX V6)	506	595
	Includes tires: P205/55R16.		
2LX	LX-V6 Premium Package (LX V6)	1480	1850
	Includes wheels: 16" alloy with locks, tires: P205/55R16, power moonroof, mini overhead console, 6-way power driver's seat, floor mats, heated mirrors and anti-theft alarm. NOT AVAILABLE with FLM.		
2WP	Wheels: 15" Alloy with Locks (LX)	383	450
3LX	LX-V6 Audio Package (LX V6)	480	600
	Includes Bose AM/FM stereo with CD and cassette.		
AB3	ABS with Side Airbags (LX/ES)	640	800
	Includes side airbags.		
AT1	Transmission: 4-Speed Automatic (All Except ES)	696	800
CAS	Cassette Deck (All Except ES V6)	170	200
CD2	6-Disc CD Changer (ES V6)	180	225
CE1	Transitional Low Emissions Vehicles TLEV (V6)	126	150
CE1	UltraLow Emissions Vehicles ULEV (LX/ES)	126	150
FLM	Floor Mats (LX/LX V6)	56	80
	NOT AVAILABLE with 1LX, 2LX.		
RSP	Rear Spoiler	295	395

MAZDA

MIATA

| CODE | DESCRIPTION | INVOICE | MSRP |

2000 MIATA

2000 Mazda Miata

What's New?

The Miata's option packages have been simplified. There are now two models—Miata and Miata L—and three option packages. Power steering, a power antenna, a leather-wrapped Nardi steering wheel, power windows, and power mirrors are standard on all models. Fourteen-inch alloy wheels are standard on base Miatas, and 15-inch alloy wheels are standard on the Miata L. A new Revolution Orange Mica exterior color has been added. Logically, last year's limited-edition 10th Anniversary Miata is no longer available.

Review

Financially, it certainly pays to buy in bulk. To own a big and bad 2000 Ford Excursion, you'll have to pay only about $5 per pound (based on MSRP for a base model). To own a lithe 2000 Mazda Miata, you'll have to pay close to $9 per pound. But hey, sometimes you just have to pay more to get the good stuff.

While it seems strange to pay over $20,000 for a Miata, the price is still considerably less than those asked for newcomers like the BMW Z3, Mercedes Benz SLK, Porsche Boxster, and Honda S2000. And while the Miata might not be able to match these cars' absolute performance numbers, it certainly equals or exceeds them in the intangibles.

The Miata is about simplicity in design and operation. It's about having fun behind the wheel. It's about feeling free and young on warm summer nights. Not a serious car, the Miata, but that's part of its charm. Redesigned from the ground up in 1999, the 2000 Miata is faster, more rigid, and more functional than the previous generation. But it doesn't stray too far from the original Miata's heritage of offering reliable and fun transportation. The updated styling is more aggressive, but it's still instantly recognizable as a Miata. In some ways, the new car is better looking than the first-generation model, thanks to its wider tail and more sculpted bodywork. Some people still miss the pop-up headlights, however.

Though the Miata's trunk is miniscule when compared to what can be crammed into the latest SUVs, the Miata can handle daily commuting or weekend getaways. The shifter moves with quick and short precision. All of the switchgear is easy to reach and use. The option packages have been altered for 2000, but the same basic equipment is still available.

MIATA

MAZDA

Droning trips on American interstates are not the Miata's forte. But with a lowered top and an open road, the Miata has few equals. The 140-horsepower, 1.8-liter engine is perfectly matched to the suspension and steering. The Miata is simply a joy to pilot on curving roads. When equipped with the 15-inch wheels and the suspension package (which includes items like a Torsen limited-slip differential and upgraded shock absorbers), the Miata's performance envelope is higher, but some fun is lost in not being able to adjust the tail easily via the throttle.

In our opinion, you can utilize 90 percent of the Miata's abilities under normal driving conditions, while a BMW Z3 2.8 driver is lucky to experience 60 percent of that car's potential most of the time. From this perspective, the Miata is a better value and the reason why it continues to be on Edmunds.com's Most Wanted list.

Standard Equipment

BASE (5M): 1.8L I4 DOHC SMPI 16-valve engine; 5-speed OD manual transmission; 70-amp alternator; rear-wheel drive, 4.3 axle ratio; partial stainless steel exhaust with chrome tip; front independent double wishbone suspension with anti-roll bar, front coil springs, gas-pressurized front shocks, rear independent double wishbone suspension with anti-roll bar, rear coil springs, gas-pressurized rear shocks; power rack-and-pinion steering with engine speed-sensing assist; 4-wheel disc brakes; 12.7 gal. capacity fuel tank; side impact bars; manual convertible roof with glass rear window; front and rear body-colored bumpers; monotone paint; aero-composite halogen headlamps; driver's and passenger's power remote body-colored folding outside mirrors; front and rear 14" x 5.5" silver alloy wheels; P185/60HR14 A/S BSW front and rear tires; inside under cargo mounted compact steel spare wheel; AM/FM stereo, clock, seek-scan, single CD, 2 speakers, theft deterrent, and power retractable antenna; remote hatch/trunk release, remote fuel release; 1 power accessory outlet, front cigar lighter(s), driver's foot rest, smokers' package; instrumentation display includes tachometer, oil pressure gauge, water temperature gauge, trip odometer; warning indicators include oil pressure, battery, lights on, key in ignition; driver's front airbag, passenger's cancelable front airbag; tinted windows; fixed interval front windshield wipers, rear window defroster; seating capacity of 2, front bucket seats, fixed headrests, center armrest with storage, driver's seat includes 4-way direction control, passenger's seat includes 4-way direction control; cloth seats, full carpet floor covering; interior lights include dome light; leather-wrapped steering wheel; passenger's side vanity mirror; day/night rearview mirror; full floor console, locking glove box, front cupholder, instrument panel bin, 1 seat back storage pocket, driver's and passenger's door bins; carpeted cargo floor, cargo light; black side window moldings, black front windshield molding, black rear window molding and body-colored door handles.

LS (5M) (in addition to or instead of BASE (5M) equipment): Limited slip differential, front and rear 15" x 6" silver alloy wheels; P195/50VR15 performance A/S BSW front and rear tires; premium AM/FM stereo, clock, seek-scan, cassette, single CD, 4 premium speakers, theft deterrent, and power retractable antenna; cruise control; leather seats and full carpet floor covering with floor mats.

Base Prices

CODE	DESCRIPTION	INVOICE	MSRP
MIACP	Base (5M)	19499	21245
MIALP	LS (5M)	22018	23995
	Destination Charge:	450	450

Accessories

CODE	DESCRIPTION	INVOICE	MSRP
1AP	Appearance Package	476	595
	Includes front air dam, side sills and rear mudguards.		
AB1	Antilock Brake System (LS)	468	550
ACA	Air Conditioning	720	900

MAZDA
MIATA / MILLENIA

CODE	DESCRIPTION	INVOICE	MSRP
AT1	Transmission: Electronic 4-Speed Auto	782	900
	Includes 4.10 rear axle ratio.		
CAS	Cassette Player (Base)	213	250
CE1	LEV Emissions	126	150
	Low Emissions Vehicle as required.		
CV1	Convenience Package (Base)	668	795
	Includes power door locks, cruise control, windblocker and tweeter speakers. NOT AVAILABLE with SP1.		
FLM	Floor Mats (Base)	56	80
FOG	Fog Lights	200	250
HT1	Detachable Hardtop	1215	1500
MGB	Front and Rear Mud Guards	100	125
RSP	Rear Spoiler	236	295
SD1	Torsen Limited Slip Differential (Base)	332	395
SP1	Suspension Package (Base)	836	995
	Includes strut tower brace, sport suspension, Bilstein shock absorbers, Torsen limited slip differential, wheels: 15" alloy with locks and tires: 195/50VR15 Michelin. NOT AVAILABLE with CV1.		
SP2	Suspension Package (LS)	416	495
	Includes strut tower brace, sport suspension and Bilstein shock absorbers.		
WNB	Windblocker (Base)	120	150
	Includes anti-draft panel with integral storage pouch.		

2000 MILLENIA

What's New?

Millenia models receive considerable price reductions to make them more competitive in the market. Mazda is also offering a special 2000 Millenium edition of the Millenia. This version comes with 17-inch chrome wheels, an in-dash six-disc CD changer, suede seat and door trim, and a choice of either Highlight Silver Mica or Millennium Red Mica paint.

Review

The Mazda Millenia leads a dual-purpose life. It comes in two versions: the base Millenia and the Millenia S. The base Millenia competes against cars like the Honda Accord V6 and the Toyota Camry V6. The Millenia S goes up against entry-luxury cars like the Audi A4, Acura TL and Toyota Avalon.

Base Millenias come with standard features like a wood-trimmed center console, a power-operated driver's seat, and antilock brakes. To get a power-adjustable passenger seat, leather, a moonroof, and remote keyless entry, you'll need to order the premium package. Traction control and heated front seats are part of the 4-Seasons package.

The Millenia S comes standard with all of the features included in the premium package, as well as a Bose audio system and 17-inch wheels. The main difference lies in the engine. The base Millenia is powered by a 2.5-liter V6 that makes 170 horsepower. The S version gets a supercharged 2.3-liter V6 that generates 210 horsepower.

For 2000, Mazda is also offering a mouthful: the Mazda Millenia Millennium Edition. Commemorating the new millennium (shh—don't tell Mazda it doesn't mathematically start until 2001), this version will be limited to a total production of 3,000. Although ultimately a Millenia S

MILLENIA   MAZDA

| CODE | DESCRIPTION | INVOICE | MSRP |

with special badging, the Millennium Edition does come with a six-disc CD changer and standard 17-inch chrome wheels.

The Millenia's interior is better than those found in the Accord or Camry, but it lacks quality and amenities when compared to higher-end cars. With the Millenia S, acceleration is strong. The supercharger does a good job of providing low-end power for easy passing. On the road, the Millenia's suspension does a good job of soaking up broken pavement. The over-boosted steering detracts from overall driving pleasure, however.

Mazda considers the Nissan Maxima, the Infiniti I30, the Toyota Avalon, and the Acura TL to be the Millenia's primary competitors. We would say that this is the case for the Millenia S, not the base version. Considering that the Maxima, I30 and Avalon have all been updated for 2000, the Millenia S has its work cut out for it. And if you're looking to buy an entry-level luxury sedan, the extra money you'll pay for an Audi A4 or a BMW 3 Series is most likely worth it.

2000 Mazda Millenia

Standard Equipment

BASE (4A): 2.5L V6 DOHC SMPI 24-valve engine, requires premium unleaded fuel; 4-speed electronic OD auto transmission with lock-up; 90-amp alternator; front-wheel drive, 4.38 axle ratio; partial stainless steel exhaust with chrome tip; front independent suspension with anti-roll bar, front coil springs, rear independent multi-link suspension with rear coil springs; power rack-and-pinion steering with engine speed-sensing assist; 4-wheel disc brakes with 4-wheel antilock braking system; 18 gal. capacity fuel tank; side impact bars; front and rear body-colored bumpers; body-colored bodyside cladding, rocker panel extensions; monotone paint; aero-composite halogen auto off headlamps; additional exterior lights include front fog/driving lights; driver's and passenger's power remote body-colored heated folding outside mirrors; front and rear 16" x 6.5" silver alloy wheels; P215/55VR16 A/S BSW front and rear tires; inside under cargo mounted compact steel spare wheel; air conditioning with climate control, rear heat ducts; AM/FM stereo, seek-scan, cassette, single CD, 4 speakers, and window grid diversity antenna; cruise control with steering wheel controls; power door locks with 2 stage unlock, remote keyless entry, child safety rear door locks, power remote hatch/trunk release, power remote fuel release; 1 power accessory outlet, front cigar lighter(s), driver's foot rest, smokers' package; instrumentation display includes tachometer, water temperature gauge, in-dash clock, exterior temp, trip odometer; warning indicators include oil pressure, battery, low oil level, lights on, key in ignition, low fuel, door ajar; driver's and passenger's front airbags; panic alarm, security system; tinted windows, power front and rear windows with driver's 1-touch down; variable intermittent front windshield wipers, rear window defroster; seating capacity of 5, front

MAZDA
MILLENIA

CODE	DESCRIPTION	INVOICE	MSRP

bucket seats, adjustable headrests, center armrest with storage, driver's seat includes 6-way power seat, passenger's seat includes 4-way power seat; rear bench seat with fixed headrests, center pass-thru armrest; front height adjustable seatbelts; cloth seats, cloth door trim insert, full cloth headliner, full carpet floor covering with carpeted floor mats, plastic/rubber gear shift knob; interior lights include dome light with fade, front and rear reading lights, illuminated entry; leather-wrapped steering wheel with power tilt adjustment; dual illuminated vanity mirrors, driver's side auxiliary visor; day/night rearview mirror; full floor console, locking glove box with light, front cupholder, 2 seat back storage pockets, driver's and passenger's door bins; carpeted cargo floor, carpeted trunk lid, cargo light; chrome grille, chrome side window moldings, black front windshield molding, black rear window molding and body-colored door handles.

S (4A) (in addition to or instead of BASE (4A) equipment): 2.3L V6 DOHC SMPI intercooled supercharged 24-valve engine, requires premium unleaded fuel; 110-amp alternator; traction control, 3.8 axle ratio; front power sliding and tilting glass sunroof with sunshade; front and rear 17" x 6.5" silver alloy wheels; P215/50VR17 A/S BSW front and rear tires; AM/FM stereo, seek-scan, cassette, single CD, 5 premium speakers, premium amplifier, and window grid diversity antenna; passenger's seat includes 6-way power seat; leather seats and leatherette door trim insert.

MILLENNIUM EDITION (4A) (in addition to or instead of S (4A) equipment: Front and rear 17" x 6.5" chrome alloy wheels; AM/FM stereo, seek-scan, cassette 6-disc CD changer, 5 premium speakers, premium amplifier, auto equalizer, and window grid diversity antenna; premium suede seats, suede door trim insert, unique wood pattern trim, leather-wrapped brake handle, leather-wrapped gear shift knob and unique interior and exterior badging.

Base Prices

CODE	DESCRIPTION	INVOICE	MSRP
MILCA	Base (4A)	22840	24995
MILSA	S (4A)	27400	29995
MILMA	Millennium Edition (4A)	28312	30995
	Destination Charge:	450	450

Accessories

CODE	DESCRIPTION	INVOICE	MSRP
1PR	Premium Package (Base)	1720	2000

Includes power moonroof, leather trimmed interior and 8-way power passenger's seat.

1RA	Bose Speaker System (Base)	588	700

Includes Double-DIN AM/FM stereo with full logic auto-reverse cassette, 1-disc CD player, backlit green LCD readout illumination, 100W power amplifier, 2 front door Bose speaker enclosures, (2) 6 x 9" Bose rear full range speakers, 2.0" Bose centerfill tweeter with 12.5 W amplifier, rear-window mount twin-diversity antenna and faceplate control for accessory CD changer. REQUIRES 1PR.

2CO	4-Seasons Package (Base)	504	600

Includes heavy-duty windshield wiper motor, large capacity windshield washer tank, heavy duty heated mirrors, two position windshield wipers, electronic traction control, heated front seats, rear compartment heater ducts, heavy duty battery and windshield washer fluid indicator light. REQUIRES 1PR.

3CO	4-Seasons Package (S/Millennium Edition)	252	300

Includes heavy-duty windshield wiper motor, large capacity windshield wiper tank, heavy duty heated mirrors, two position windshield wipers, heated front seats, rear compartment heater ducts, heavy duty battery and windshield washer fluid indicator light.

MILLENIA / PROTEGÉ — MAZDA

CODE	DESCRIPTION	INVOICE	MSRP
JCP	Two-Tone Paint (Base/S) .... *REQUIRES 1PR (Base).*	319	380
JCR	White Pearl MC Paint (Base/S) .... *REQUIRES 1PR (Base).*	319	380
PA5	Wheels: 17" Chrome Alloy (S)	420	500

2000 PROTEGÉ

2000 Mazda Protegé

What's New?

Front-seat side airbags and an improved ABS system are new to the LX premium and ES premium packages. The LX and ES also get illuminated power window switches. Chrome plating has been added to the inner door handles, the Mazda symbol on the steering wheel, the parking brake button, and the automatic transmission shift-lever button. The Twilight Blue Mica exterior color has been discontinued and replaced with Midnight Blue Mica.

Review

Now in its second model year, Mazda's current Protegé is a snappy car that competes against vehicles like the Honda Civic, the Toyota Corolla, and the Ford Focus. Sold only as a four-door sedan, the Protegé is available in three trim levels: DX, LX and ES. The base-model DX comes with standard features like power steering, tilt steering wheel and a split folding seatback. For options like a driver's height-adjustable seat, power windows and locks, a tachometer, and cruise control, you'll have to step up to either the LX or the ES. The ES also comes with features like standard air conditioning, 15-inch alloy wheels, and optional ABS.

Both the DX and the LX use a 1.6-liter four-cylinder engine that makes 105 horsepower and 107 foot-pounds of torque. Power from the 1.6-liter is tolerable, but buyers looking for more acceleration should go for the ES. This version gets a 1.8-liter engine that puts out 122 horsepower and 120 foot-pounds of torque.

The Protegé is one of the best-looking economy sedans on the market. The creased and folded sheetmetal lends the car a more elegant and sophisticated look than you find on a Ford

MAZDA

PROTEGÉ

CODE	DESCRIPTION	INVOICE	MSRP

Escort or Nissan Sentra. The attractive brushed-aluminum wheels go a long way toward achieving this upscale appearance. Jewel-like headlight reflectors, angular taillights and chrome accents give the impression of a more expensive car.

The firm seats are comfortable, and the seat-height and cushion-angle adjustments (on the LX and ES) are greatly appreciated. The driving position is excellent, with a thick steering wheel rim to grip and a properly placed dead pedal for the left foot. There's also a proper Germanic front-passenger door grip, nicely padded upper door panels where elbows often rest, lots of storage nooks and crannies, a large rear seat, a commodious 12.9 cubic foot trunk, and a great stereo. Too bad Mazda decided to go with standard-issue econobox interior plastics, however. While not an unpleasant place to spend time, the Protegé's interior is simply an example of form following function. For safety, there's standard dual front airbags and load-limiting front seatbelts with height adjustment.

On the road, the Protegé is a bit louder than expected, but it does provide a good drive. The suspension is equal in both performance and ride quality when compared to the other top cars found in this class. Both engines come with either a five-speed manual or four-speed automatic transmission.

The Mazda Protegé is a long time favorite of ours. And although the new Ford Focus will be getting a lot of hype this year, the Protegé deserves the attention of commuters looking for a comfortably quick commuter with spicy style and a good reliability record.

Standard Equipment

DX (5M): 1.6L I4 DOHC SMPI 16-valve engine; 5-speed OD manual transmission; 70-amp alternator; front-wheel drive, 3.85 axle ratio; steel exhaust with chrome tip; front independent strut suspension with anti-roll bar, front coil springs, rear independent strut suspension with anti-roll bar, rear coil springs; power rack-and-pinion steering with engine speed-sensing assist; front disc/rear drum brakes; 13.2 gal. capacity fuel tank; side impact bars; front and rear body-colored bumpers; black bodyside molding; clearcoat monotone paint; aero-composite halogen headlamps; driver's and passenger's manual remote black folding outside mirrors; front and rear 14" x 5.5" styled steel wheels; P185/65SR14 A/S BSW front and rear tires; inside under cargo mounted compact steel spare wheel; rear heat ducts; radio prep, 4 speakers, and manual retractable antenna; child safety rear door locks, remote hatch/trunk release, remote fuel release; 1 power accessory outlet, driver's foot rest, smokers' package; instrumentation display includes water temperature gauge, trip odometer; warning indicators include oil pressure, battery, lights on, low fuel, door ajar; driver's and passenger's front airbags; tinted windows, manual front and rear windows; fixed interval front windshield wipers, rear window defroster; seating capacity of 5, front bucket seats, adjustable headrests, driver's seat includes 4-way direction control, passenger's seat includes 4-way direction control; 60-40 folding rear bench seat; front height adjustable seatbelts; cloth seats, cloth door trim insert, full cloth headliner, full carpet floor covering, plastic/rubber gear shift knob; interior lights include dome light; steering wheel with tilt adjustment; vanity mirrors; day/night rearview mirror; full floor console, glove box, front cupholder, instrument panel covered bin, interior concealed storage, driver's and passenger's door bins; carpeted cargo floor, cargo light; chrome grille, black side window moldings, black front windshield molding, black rear window molding and black door handles.

LX (5M) (in addition to or instead of DX (5M) equipment): Body-colored bodyside molding; driver's and passenger's power remote black folding outside mirrors; AM/FM stereo, clock, seek-scan, single CD, 4 speakers, and manual retractable antenna; cruise control; instrumentation display includes tachometer; power front and rear windows with driver's 1-touch down; center armrest with storage, driver's seat includes 6-way direction control; 60-40 folding rear bench seat with fixed headrests and body-colored door handles.

ES (5M) (in addition to or instead of LX (5M) equipment): 1.8L I4 DOHC SMPI 16-valve engine; 80-amp alternator; 4.11 axle ratio; front and rear 15" x 6" silver alloy wheels; P195/55VR15 A/S BSW front and rear tires; air conditioning, rear heat ducts; power door locks with 2 stage unlock, remote keyless entry; premium cloth seats and interior lights include illuminated entry.

254　　www.edmunds.com　　**EDMUND'S® NEW CARS**

PROTEGÉ — MAZDA

CODE	DESCRIPTION	INVOICE	MSRP

Base Prices

CODE	DESCRIPTION	INVOICE	MSRP
PRODXP	DX (5M)	11445	11970
PROLXP	LX (5M)	12389	13245
PROESP	ES (5M)	13909	15040
	Destination Charge:	450	450

Accessories

CODE	DESCRIPTION	INVOICE	MSRP
1ES	ES Premium Package (ES)	1296	1580
	Includes side airbags, antilock braking system, power moonroof and carpeted floor mats.		
1LX	LX Premium Package (LX)	1312	1600
	Includes side airbags, antilock braking system, power moonroof, dual front seat map lights, keyless entry and illuminated entry. REQUIRES LXC.		
AT1	Transmission: Electronic 4-Speed Auto with OD	720	800
	Includes 3.90 axle ratio.		
CAS	Cassette Player	213	250
	REQUIRES DXC.		
CE1	NLEV Emissions	84	100
DXC	DX Convenience Package (DX)	1292	1575
	Includes air conditioning, AM/FM stereo with CD and carpeted floor mats.		
FLM	Carpeted Floor Mats	64	80
KE1	Keyless Entry (LX)	80	100
	Includes illuminated entry.		
LXC	LX Comfort Package (LX)	939	1145
	Includes air conditioning and carpeted floor mats.		
MR1	Power Moonroof (LX/ES)	560	700
	Includes dual front seat map lights. REQUIRES KE1.		
RSP	Rear Spoiler	246	330

**TO PRICE YOUR TRADE-IN,
PURCHASE EDMUND'S® USED CAR
PRICES AND RATINGS.**

See page 6 for details.

MERCEDES-BENZ   C-CLASS

| CODE | DESCRIPTION | INVOICE | MSRP |

2000 C-CLASS

2000 Mercedes-Benz C-Class

What's New?

TeleAid, which can assist in summoning help if you're ill or involved in a crash, is a brilliant new standard feature. A Touch Shift automanual transmission is added to all C-Class models, and stability control is standard this year. C-Class now comes with free scheduled service for the duration of the warranty period.

Review

Many aspire to own a car with the three-pointed star on the hood, but few have the means. For those on the fence, the entry-level C-Class is the way to get a foot in the door. But don't let the term "entry level" fool you. Even the most basic C230 is well equipped with luxury amenities and infused with the solid engineering that is a Mercedes-Benz hallmark. Despite its age, this 7-year-old sedan still entices with ample room for four, rich wood and leather, sprightly performance and that world-renowned ornament above the grille.

Three C-Class models are available for the final year of this design cycle. The C230 Kompressor is powered by the same supercharged 2.3-liter four cylinder found in the SLK roadster. Making 185 horsepower and 200 ft-lbs. of torque, the C230 runs from zero to 60 mph in about 8 seconds. A five-speed adaptive logic automatic transmission transfers power to the rear wheels, and features Touch Shift gear selection for 2000 to appeal to fans of manual gearboxes.

Standard equipment on the C230 includes front and side airbags, traction control, stability control, ABS with Brake Assist, and a BabySmart child-seat recognition system. Leather and burled walnut wood trim are included in the base price, as are an automatic climate-control system, integrated garage door opener, power driver's seat with 10-way adjustment and heated exterior mirrors. The optional $900 sport package is worth considering, and includes sport seats, larger wheels and tires, a firmer suspension, telescoping steering wheel, and special trim.

Stepping up to the C280 nets additional goodies like a Bose audio system and power passenger's seat, but the premium paid for this pricey C primarily covers the silky-smooth 2.8-liter aluminum V6 under the hood. It doesn't make a C280 get up and go any quicker than the blown four on the C230. The benefit of C280 ownership is refinement. For those needing

256   www.edmunds.com   **EDMUND'S® NEW CARS**

C-CLASS — MERCEDES-BENZ

CODE	DESCRIPTION	INVOICE	MSRP

maximum performance and guaranteed exclusivity, Mercedes offers the AMG-massaged C43, which is discussed separately from the C230 and C280.

Handling is sure-footed with either the C230 or the C280, and braking ability is astounding in panic situations, although the C230, at 100 fewer pounds than the C280, feels somewhat more agile. Frankly, we fail to see how Mercedes justifies the premium commanded by the C280. In fact, the only complaint we can voice about the C230 is that the grumbling exhaust note doesn't impart much of a sense of luxury or prestige. But if you can get beyond that and the fact that the nomenclature on the decklid indicates to others that you bought the cheap car, a C230 Sport is the way to go.

But you've really gotta want a Benz to buy the aging C-Class. It's not a bargain, and there are less expensive ways to obtain a small luxury-brand sedan. A BMW 323i is a better deal, for example, or an Acura 3.2TL. For some, however, the lure of that three-pointed star outweighs a kidney-shaped grille topped with a blue and white roundel. You could do worse than to select the nicely appointed and eminently capable C-Class.

Standard Equipment

C230 KOMPRESSOR (5A): 2.3L I4 DOHC SMPI intercooled supercharger with variable valve timing 16-valve engine, requires premium unleaded fuel; 5-speed electronic OD auto transmission with lock-up; HD battery; 90-amp alternator; driver's selectable multi-mode automanual transmission; rear-wheel drive, traction control, 3.27 axle ratio; stainless steel exhaust; electronic stability, front independent double wishbone suspension with anti-roll bar, front coil springs, gas-pressurized front shocks, rear independent multi-link suspension with anti-roll bar, rear coil springs, gas-pressurized rear shocks; power re-circulating ball steering; 4-wheel disc brakes with 4-wheel antilock braking system; 16.4 gal. capacity fuel tank; side impact bars; front and rear body-colored bumpers with body-colored rub strip, chrome bumper insert; body-colored bodyside molding with chrome bodyside insert; monotone paint; aero-composite halogen headlamps with delay-off feature; additional exterior lights include front fog/driving lights; driver's and passenger's power remote body-colored heated folding outside mirrors; front and rear 15" x 7" silver alloy wheels; P205/60HR15 A/S BSW front and rear tires; inside under cargo mounted full-size alloy spare wheel; dual zone front air conditioning, air filter; AM/FM stereo, seek-scan, cassette, CD changer pre-wiring, in-dash CD pre-wiring, 8 speakers, auto equalizer, theft deterrent, and window grid antenna; cruise control; power door locks with 2 stage unlock, remote keyless entry, child safety rear door locks, power remote hatch/trunk release, power remote fuel release; cell phone pre-wiring, 1 power accessory outlet, front cigar lighter(s), driver's foot rest, garage door opener, smokers' package, emergency "S.O.S"; instrumentation display includes tachometer, water temperature gauge, in-dash clock, exterior temp, systems monitor, trip odometer; warning indicators include water temp, battery, low oil level, low coolant, lights on, key in ignition, low fuel, low washer fluid, bulb failure, service interval, brake fluid; driver's and passenger's front airbags, driver's and front passenger's door mounted side airbags; ignition disable, panic alarm, security system; tinted windows, power front and rear windows with front and rear 1-touch down; heated jet variable intermittent front windshield wipers, sun visor strip, rear window defroster; seating capacity of 5, front bucket seats, adjustable tilt headrests, center armrest with storage, driver's seat includes 6-way power seat, passenger's seat includes 8-way direction control; rear bench seat with power adjustable headrests, center armrest; front height adjustable seatbelts; leather seating inserts, leatherette door trim insert, full cloth headliner, full carpet floor covering with carpeted floor mats, genuine wood trim on instrument panel, leather-wrapped gear shift knob; interior lights include dome light with fade, front reading lights, illuminated entry; leather-wrapped steering wheel with telescopic adjustment; dual illuminated vanity mirrors; auto-dimming day/night rearview mirror; full floor console, locking glove box with light, front and rear cupholders, instrument panel bin, 2 seat back storage pockets, driver's and passenger's door bins; carpeted cargo floor, carpeted trunk lid, cargo light; chrome grille, black side window moldings, black front windshield molding, black rear window molding and chrome door handles.

MERCEDES-BENZ

C-CLASS

CODE	DESCRIPTION	INVOICE	MSRP

C280 (5A) (in addition to or instead of C230 KOMPRESSOR (5A) equipment): 2.8L V6 SOHC SMPI 18-valve engine, requires premium unleaded fuel; 115-amp alternator; 3.07 axle ratio; air conditioning with climate control; premium AM/FM stereo, seek-scan, cassette, CD changer pre-wiring, in-dash CD pre-wiring, 8 premium speakers, auto equalizer, theft deterrent, and window grid antenna and passenger's seat includes 6-way power seat.

Base Prices

CODE	DESCRIPTION	INVOICE	MSRP
C230 Komp	C230 Kompressor (5A)	29528	31750
C280 W	C280 (5A)	33434	35950
Destination Charge:		595	595

Accessories

CODE	DESCRIPTION	INVOICE	MSRP
—	Leather Interior	1251	1345
—	Metallic Paint	567	610
—	Special Order Personalization Charge	930	1000
143	Option Package C1	419	450
	Includes rain sensor wipers and headlamp washer system.		
165	Option Package C2 (C280)	1181	1270
	Includes electronic glass sunroof with pop up feature, sunroof extra fob controls and split folding rear seat.		
166	Option Package C2 (C230)	1581	1700
	Includes electronic glass sunroof with pop up feature, sunroof extra fob controls, split folding rear seat and power passenger's seat.		
177	Option Package K2	1454	1795
	Includes CDMA integrated portable telephone and integrated 6-disc CD changer. NOT AVAILABLE with 178.		
178	Option Package K2	1454	1795
	Includes TDMA integrated portable telephone and integrated 6-disc CD changer. NOT AVAILABLE with 177.		
282	Ski Sack	186	200
	REQUIRES Special Order Personalization Charge.		
406	Multi-Contour Driver's and Passenger's Seats	660	710
	REQUIRES Special Order Personalization Charge.		
414	Glass Sunroof with Pop Up Feature	1051	1130
	Includes sunroof extra fob controls.		
612	Xenon Headlights	884	950
	REQUIRES Special Order Personalization Charge.		
772	Option Package C6	837	900
	Includes sport interior trim, ivory-colored instrument gauges, wheels: 7" x 16" 6-spoke alloy, tires: 205/55R16-91H performance, sport tuned suspension, sport B-pillar trim, color keyed bodyside/bumper moldings, sport emblems, front sport-contoured seats and sport steering wheel with telescopic column.		
810	Bose Premium Sound System (C230)	539	580
873	Electrically Heated Front Seats	563	605

258   www.edmunds.com   **EDMUND'S® NEW CARS**

C43 MERCEDES-BENZ

| CODE | DESCRIPTION | INVOICE | MSRP |

2000 C43

2000 Mercedes-Benz C43

What's New?

TeleAid, which can assist in summoning help if you're ill or involved in a crash, is a new standard feature. A Touch Shift automanual transmission is added to simulate the thrill of shifting gears manually. Free scheduled service for the duration of the warranty period has been added to the lengthy standard equipment list.

Review

Two years ago, high-performance tuner AMG, long associated with Mercedes-Benz products, dropped a 302-horsepower 4.3-liter V8 engine into the engine bay of the tidy little C-Class sedan. The result was nothing short of sensational, so Mercedes, long considered BMW's sullen stepsister, decided to create a limited-production run of the muscular model to generate interest in the aging C-Class lineup.

The C43, now entering its third and final year in current guise, accelerates from zero to 60 in less than six seconds. Other go-fast goodies include a special two-stage resonance intake manifold, a Touch Shift automanual transmission pilfered from the SL500 roadster for its higher torque capacity, and performance-tuned gear ratios for maximum acceleration capability.

Underneath the sedate bodywork, the four-wheel independent suspension gets higher-rate springs, solid 27mm stabilizer bars and degressive-action Bilstein shocks front and rear. Full-range traction control uses the braking system and throttle to keep power to the ground, while Brake Assist and upgraded vented discs front and rear haul the C43 down from triple-digit speeds swiftly and surely.

Electronic Stability Programming (ESP), otherwise known as stability control, keeps the C43 in line if the driver manages to exceed the lofty adhesion limits of the wide 17-inch tires mounted to five-spoke AMG rims. Quicker-ratio power recirculating ball steering gear and a high-performance exhaust system complete the hardware changes that make a C43 a C43.

Don't expect a smooth ride from this bad boy. It rides stiffly, but the trade-off is astounding grip and minimal body roll in smoothly paved corners. The steering feels a little lifeless, but responds well off center. The brakes are ridiculously competent, and ESP works as advertised. We haven't tried the Touch Shift tranny yet, but in a sport sedan, pseudo-gearchanging is better than automatic gearchanging any day of the week. Still, a manual would be ideal.

MERCEDES-BENZ   C43

CODE	DESCRIPTION	INVOICE	MSRP

Inside, the C43 gets multi-adjustable sport seats with pneumatic bolstering, exclusive two-tone leather appointments, and special ivory-colored gauges. Additionally, the C43's steep $53,000 price tag includes a power sunroof, Bose audio system, automatic climate control and a manually telescoping steering column. TeleAid is newly standard for 2000, and it automatically summons assistance if your airbags have deployed in an accident. TeleAid also helps in medical emergencies with an SOS feature, and allows the C43 owner to query live operators about specific features of the car or call upon Mercedes-Benz roadside assistance. Because TeleAid contains a GPS unit, the car can also be tracked easily if it is stolen.

But, is this limited-production car worth the premium? Can a monster engine, tight suspension, superb performance and exclusivity be valued so highly? Enough people think so to keep the C43 in the lineup for 2000.

Standard Equipment

C43 (5A): 4.3L V8 SOHC SMPI 24-valve engine, requires premium unleaded fuel; 5-speed electronic OD auto transmission with lock-up; HD battery; 115-amp alternator; driver's selectable multi-mode automanual transmission, transmission oil cooler; rear-wheel drive, traction control, 3.07 axle ratio; stainless steel exhaust with chrome tip; sport ride suspension, electronic stability, front independent double wishbone suspension with anti-roll bar, front coil springs, premium front shocks, rear independent multi-link suspension with anti-roll bar, rear coil springs, premium rear shocks; power re-circulating ball steering; 4-wheel disc brakes with 4-wheel antilock braking system; 16.4 gal. capacity fuel tank; side impact bars; front power sliding and tilting glass sunroof with sunshade; front and rear body-colored bumpers with body-colored rub strip; body-colored bodyside molding with body-colored bodyside insert, rocker panel extensions; monotone paint; aero-composite halogen headlamps with delay-off feature; additional exterior lights include front fog/driving lights; driver's and passenger's power remote body-colored heated folding outside mirrors; front 17" x 7.5" silver alloy wheels rear 17" x 8.5" silver alloy wheels; P225/45ZR17 performance BSW front tires; 245/40ZR17 performance BSW rear tires; inside under cargo mounted full-size alloy spare wheel; air conditioning with climate control, air filter; AM/FM stereo, seek-scan, cassette, CD changer pre-wiring, in-dash CD pre-wiring, 8 premium speakers, auto equalizer, theft deterrent, and window grid antenna; cruise control; power door locks with 2 stage unlock, remote keyless entry, child safety rear door locks, power remote hatch/trunk release, power remote fuel release; cell phone pre-wiring, 1 power accessory outlet, front cigar lighter(s), driver's foot rest, garage door opener, smokers' package, emergency "S.O.S"; instrumentation display includes tachometer, water temperature gauge, in-dash clock, exterior temp, systems monitor, trip odometer; warning indicators include water temp, battery, low oil level, low coolant, lights on, key in ignition, low fuel, low washer fluid, bulb failure, service interval, brake fluid; driver's and passenger's front airbags, driver's and front passenger's door mounted side airbags; ignition disable, panic alarm, security system; tinted windows, power front and rear windows with front and rear 1-touch down; heated washer bottle, variable intermittent front windshield wipers, sun visor strip, rear window defroster; seating capacity of 5, heated-cushion front premium bucket seats, power adjustable tilt headrests, center armrest with storage, driver's seat includes 10-way power seat, power 2-way lumbar support, passenger's seat includes 10-way power seat, power 2-way lumbar support; 60-40 folding rear bench seat with power adjustable headrests, center pass-thru armrest with skibag; front height adjustable seatbelts; leather seats, leather door trim insert, full cloth headliner, full carpet floor covering with carpeted floor mats, genuine wood trim on instrument panel, leather-wrapped gear shift knob; interior lights include dome light with fade, front reading lights, illuminated entry; leather-wrapped sport steering wheel with telescopic adjustment; dual illuminated vanity mirrors; auto-dimming day/night rearview mirror; full floor console, locking glove box with light, front and rear cupholders, instrument panel bin, 2 seat back storage pockets, driver's and passenger's door bins; carpeted cargo floor, carpeted trunk lid, cargo light; chrome grille, black side window moldings, black front windshield molding, black rear window molding and black door handles.

C43 / CLK — MERCEDES-BENZ

CODE	DESCRIPTION	INVOICE	MSRP

Base Prices

C43 AMG	C43 (5A)	49290	53000
Destination Charge:		595	595

Accessories

CODE	DESCRIPTION	INVOICE	MSRP
—	Metallic Paint	567	610
—	Special Order Personalization Charge	930	1000
143	Option Package C1	419	450
	Includes rain sensor wipers and headlamp washer system.		
177	Option Package K2	1454	1795
	Includes CDMA integrated portable telephone and integrated 6-disc CD changer. NOT AVAILABLE with 178.		
178	Option Package K2	1454	1795
	Includes TDMA integrated portable telephone and integrated 6-disc CD changer. NOT AVAILABLE with 177.		
282	Ski Sack	186	200
	REQUIRES Special Order Personalization Charge.		
406	Multi-Contour Driver's and Passenger's Seats	660	710
	REQUIRES Special Order Personalization Charge.		
612	Xenon Headlights	884	950
	REQUIRES Special Order Personalization Charge.		

2000 CLK-CLASS

What's New?

The CLK430 Convertible debuts, reminding us, for a premium price, what a drop-top muscle car from the '70s was like. Turn-signal indicators have been added to exterior mirrors, stability control is standard on all models, automatics get Touch Shift manual gear selection, and TeleAid emergency cellular service is standard. A new instrument cluster and multi-function steering wheel are added, and buyers can opt for the confusing COMAND navigation/phone/trip computer/sound system. CLK320s benefit from exterior cosmetic changes including new wheels, while 430s are enhanced inside with new black birdseye maple wood trim. Free maintenance for the duration of the warranty is now included.

Review

Don't ever call the gang at the three-pointed star lazy; they've been rolling out new cars faster than Hot Wheels. One of their latest efforts is the CLK, the latest in a string of Mercedes-Benz victories that will undoubtedly stretch into the next century.

Luxury is synonymous with Mercedes, and the CLK lives up to that name. Standard equipment is generous, and the interior is swathed in wood and leather. Based on C-Class sedan running gear and available with either a V6 or V8 in coupe or convertible format, the CLK appeals to people who place sports car performance and the availability of manual transmissions secondary to comfort and convenience. But this Benz is no slouch in the driving satisfaction department.

CLK320 models are powered by a 3.2-liter V6 engine making 215 horsepower and 229 foot-pounds of torque. Mercedes asserts that the 320 Coupe goes from zero to 60 mph in 6.9 seconds. CLK430 models receive a 275-horsepower, 4.3-liter V8 engine, which cranks out 295

MERCEDES-BENZ

CLK

CODE	DESCRIPTION	INVOICE	MSRP

ft-lbs. of twist. This shaves nearly a second off the 320's zero-to-sixty time. Power is transmitted to the rear wheels through an adaptive logic five-speed automatic transmission that features Touch Shift manual control for 2000. Either car feels well balanced in turns, but a little heavy. The 320 drives more like a sedan than a sports car: surefooted and steady rather than agile and quick. The speedy 430, on the other hand, is tuned for a firm ride and taut handling. In either case, the CLK is an attractive car that turns heads.

Safety is addressed by the CLK as well as beauty. Antilock brakes with Brake Assist and full-range Automatic Slip Control (ASR) traction control come standard. Other standard features include front and side airbags and BabySmart child-detection protection for the front passenger seat. For 2000, Electronic Stability Programming (ESP), which reduces understeer and oversteer by applying braking force to the wheel that needs it, is standard as well. TeleAid service is also standard, and will notify emergency personnel if your airbags deploy or will put you in touch with a live operator to summon medical or police assistance.

One option on the list for 2000 is the Cockpit Management and Data (COMAND) system that debuted on the redesigned S-Class. Integrating radio, navigation, telephone and trip-computer functions into one unit that displays data on a small dash-mounted screen, COMAND is fussy and distracting to operate. Unless you absolutely must have a navigation system on board, skip this option.

The CLK impresses, from the classic and elegant styling, to the smooth and powerful engines, to the comfortable and well-appointed cabin. If you're in the market for a satisfying luxury coupe, it's hard to go wrong with this beautiful Benz.

2000 Mercedes-Benz CLK

Standard Equipment

CLK320 COUPE (5A): 3.2L V6 SOHC SMPI 18-valve engine, requires premium unleaded fuel; 5-speed electronic OD auto transmission with lock-up; HD battery; 115-amp alternator; driver's selectable multi-mode transmission; rear-wheel drive, traction control, 3.07 axle ratio; stainless steel exhaust; electronic stability, front independent double wishbone suspension with anti-roll bar, front coil springs, gas-pressurized front shocks, rear independent multi-link suspension with anti-roll bar, rear coil springs, gas-pressurized rear shocks; power re-circulating ball steering; 4-wheel disc brakes with 4-wheel antilock braking system; 16.4 gal. capacity fuel tank; side impact bars; front and rear body-colored bumpers with body-colored rub strip; body-colored bodyside molding, rocker panel extensions; clearcoat monotone paint; aero-composite halogen headlamps with delay-off feature; additional exterior lights include front fog/driving

262   www.edmunds.com   **EDMUND'S® NEW CARS**

CLK — MERCEDES-BENZ

lights; driver's and passenger's power remote body-colored heated folding outside mirrors; front and rear 16" x 7" silver alloy wheels; P205/55HR16 A/S BSW front and rear tires; inside under cargo mounted full-size alloy spare wheel; dual zone front air conditioning with climate control, air filter; premium AM/FM stereo, seek-scan, cassette, CD changer pre-wiring, in-dash CD pre-wiring, 8 premium speakers, auto equalizer, theft deterrent, and window grid antenna; cruise control; power door locks with 2 stage unlock, remote keyless entry, power remote hatch/trunk release, power remote fuel release; cell phone pre-wiring, 1 power accessory outlet, driver's foot rest, garage door opener; instrumentation display includes tachometer, water temperature gauge, in-dash clock, exterior temp, systems monitor, trip odometer; warning indicators include water temp, battery, low oil level, low coolant, lights on, key in ignition, low fuel, low washer fluid, bulb failure, service interval, brake fluid; driver's and passenger's front airbags, driver's and front passenger's door mounted side airbags; ignition disable, panic alarm, security system; tinted windows with driver's and passenger's 1-touch down; variable intermittent front windshield wipers, heated jets, sun visor strip, rear window defroster; seating capacity of 4, front bucket seats, power adjustable tilt headrests, center armrest with storage, driver's seat includes 6-way power seat, easy entry, passenger's seat includes 6-way power seat, easy entry; 60-40 folding rear split-bench seat with power adjustable headrests, center armrest; front and rear height adjustable seatbelts with front pretensioners; leather seats, leather door trim insert, full cloth headliner, full carpet floor covering with carpeted floor mats, genuine wood trim on instrument panel, leather-wrapped gear shift knob; memory on driver's and passenger's seats with 3 memory setting(s) includes settings for exterior mirrors, headrests; interior lights include dome light with fade, front reading lights, illuminated entry; leather-wrapped steering wheel with telescopic adjustment; dual illuminated vanity mirrors; auto-dimming day/night rearview mirror; full floor console, rear console with storage, locking glove box with light, front and rear cupholders, instrument panel bin, 2 seat back storage pockets, driver's and passenger's door bins; carpeted cargo floor, carpeted trunk lid, cargo light; chrome grille, chrome side window moldings, black front windshield molding, black rear window molding and body-colored door handles.

CLK430 COUPE (5A) (in addition to or instead of CLK320 COUPE (5A) equipment): 4.3L V8 SOHC SMPI 24-valve engine, requires premium unleaded fuel; 2.87 axle ratio; sport ride suspension; front 17" x 7.5" body-colored superior alloy wheels, rear 17" x 8.5" body-colored superior alloy wheels; P225/45ZR17 performance BSW front tires; 245/40ZR17 performance BSW rear tires and black side window moldings.

CONVERTIBLE (5A) (in addition to or instead of COUPE (5A) equipment): Power convertible roof with lining, glass rear window, roll-over protection; premium AM/FM stereo, seek-scan, cassette, CD changer pre-wiring, in-dash CD pre-wiring, 7 premium speakers, auto equalizer, theft deterrent, and window grid antenna and power front and rear windows with front and rear 1-touch down.

Base Prices

Code	Description	Invoice	MSRP
CLK320 C	CLK320 Coupe (5A)	38688	41600
CLK430 C	CLK430 Coupe (5A)	45663	49100
CLK320 A	CLK320 Convertible (5A)	44733	48100
CLK430 A	CLK430 Convertible (5A)	51708	55600
	Destination Charge:	595	595

Accessories

Code	Description	Invoice	MSRP
—	Metallic Paint	567	610
—	Special Order Personalization Charge	930	1000
149	Option Package K3 (Coupe)	1218	1310
	Includes power glass sunroof, rain sensor and electric rear window sunshade.		

MERCEDES-BENZ   CLK / E-CLASS

CODE	DESCRIPTION	INVOICE	MSRP
150	Option Package K4 (Coupe)	1409	1515
	Includes Xenon headlights, headlight washer and wiper system.		
159	Option Package K4 (Convertible)	1502	1615
	Includes heated seats, Xenon headlights, headlight washer and wiper system and rain sensor.		
177	Option Package K2	1454	1795
	Includes CDMA integrated portable cellular telephone and integrated 6-disc CD changer. NOT AVAILABLE with 178, 179, 180.		
178	Option Package K2	1454	1795
	Includes TDMA integrated portable cellular telephone and integrated 6-disc CD changer. NOT AVAILABLE with 177, 179, 180.		
179	Option Package K2a	1774	2190
	Includes CDMA integrated portable cellular telephone with voice recognition and integrated 6-disc CD changer. NOT AVAILABLE with 177, 178, 180.		
180	Option Package K2a	1774	2190
	Includes TDMA integrated portable cellular telephone with voice recognition and integrated 6-disc CD changer. NOT AVAILABLE with 177, 178, 179.		
192	Designo Package-Espresso Edition	5487	5900
	REQUIRES 873 or 740.		
193	Designo Package Slate Blue Edition	6231	6700
	REQUIRES 873 or 740.		
282	Ski Sack (Coupe)	186	200
352	COMAND System	1855	1995
	Includes navigation or CD music capability and provides a connection for a portable audio player in the glove box.		
406	Multi-Contour Driver's and Passenger's Seats	660	710
873	Heated Seats	563	605

2000 E-CLASS

What's New?

Though it might not look different, the E-Class receives a substantial freshening for 2000, with an entirely new front end and a revised interior. Stability control, a Touch Shift automanual transmission, and side airbags for all outboard seating positions are now standard. A multi-function steering wheel debuts, and E430 models can be equipped with 4matic all-wheel drive. TeleAid, a cellular emergency service, is standard and the confounding COMAND system is optional. For 2000, free maintenance is provided for the duration of the warranty period. The E300 turbodiesel model has been dropped. Other changes are limited to minor cosmetic and functional upgrades.

Review

Thanks to a booming economy and strong stock market, sales of luxury sedans have never been stronger. The very popular E-Class has proven to be a solid home run since its last redesign four years ago, but Mercedes is no longer content to rest on its laurels between design cycles. The days of yore when a Benz had a shelf life of a decade or more are over. As

E-CLASS — MERCEDES-BENZ

| CODE | DESCRIPTION | INVOICE | MSRP |

such, the engineers in Stuttgart have given the 2000 E-Class a substantial freshening to keep it competitive in a hot market.

Four different models are available this year. The E320 Sedan and Wagon come equipped with a strong 3.2-liter V6 engine making 221 horsepower and capable of propelling these models from a standstill to 60 mph in 7 to 8 seconds, depending on equipment. The E430 Sedan, available with 4matic all-wheel drive for the first time this year, has a 4.3-liter V8 good for 275 horsepower and runs to 60 mph in the low- to mid-sixes. The ground-tromping E55, discussed on our Web site, comes with a massive 349-horsepower 5.5-liter V8. All models have a Touch Shift automanual transmission for 2000, which lets the driver select his own gears or leave the slushbox to do the dirty work. Last year's turbodiesel E300 has been dropped for 2000, because its inline cylinder configuration couldn't be stuffed under the E's revised front bodywork.

Outside, the E gets a new, but familiar, face. The CLK-inspired front end is more tapered than before, with a lower hoodline, raked-back headlamps and seamlessly integrated bumpers. In back, a new bumper and revised taillights update traditional Benz styling. Along the sides exterior mirrors have integrated turn signals and trim is body-colored.

Inside, enhancements to the quality of the wood and leather aren't so obvious. The new-for-2000 multi-function steering wheel, revised instrument cluster and display screen for the optional (but not recommended) Cockpit Management and Data (COMAND) are more apparent. Side airbags are available in each of the four doors, and E320 Wagons come with inflatable side curtains for the first time. TeleAid is a standard service, and it can put you in touch with emergency personnel if your airbags deploy or if you suffer a sudden medical problem.

In addition to TeleAid, E-Class comes with a full roster of standard safety equipment. Antilock brakes with Brake Assist, traction control and stability control keep the E-Class going safely and securely in the direction it's been pointed. A BabySmart system automatically deactivates the front passenger airbag when a special dealer-installed child seat is present, but in an E-Class, there's plenty of room in back for the kiddies.

Thanks to a long list of improvements for 2000, the E-Class continues to represent the epitome of luxury, giving its owners a technologically magnificent vehicle in a striking package. The Mercedes E-Class cars make a statement. They say, "I'm rich." Then they add, "But I'm also an intelligent buyer who wants a comfortable and safe car, and that's what I'm paying for." Quite talkative, these cars. But they're correct.

2000 Mercedes-Benz E430

MERCEDES-BENZ
E-CLASS

CODE	DESCRIPTION	INVOICE	MSRP

Standard Equipment

E320 RWD SEDAN (5A): 3.2L V6 SOHC SMPI 18-valve engine, requires premium unleaded fuel; 5-speed electronic OD auto transmission with lock-up; 100-amp alternator; driver's selectable multi-mode transmission; rear-wheel drive, traction control, 3.07 axle ratio; stainless steel exhaust; electronic stability, front independent double wishbone suspension with anti-roll bar, front coil springs, rear independent multi-link suspension with anti-roll bar, rear coil springs; power rack-and-pinion steering with vehicle speed-sensing assist; 4-wheel disc brakes with 4-wheel antilock braking system; 21.1 gal. capacity fuel tank; side impact bars; front and rear body-colored bumpers with body-colored rub strip, chrome bumper insert; body-colored bodyside molding with chrome bodyside insert; monotone paint; aero-composite halogen headlamps with delay-off feature; additional exterior lights include front fog/driving lights; driver's and passenger's power remote body-colored heated folding outside mirrors; front and rear 15" x 7" silver alloy wheels; P205/65HR15 A/S BSW front and rear tires; inside under cargo mounted full-size alloy spare wheel; dual zone front air conditioning with climate control, air filter, rear heat ducts, auto air recirculation; premium AM/FM stereo, seek-scan, cassette, CD changer pre-wiring, in-dash CD pre-wiring, 8 speakers, auto equalizer, theft deterrent, and window grid antenna; cruise control; power door locks with 2 stage unlock, remote keyless entry, child safety rear door locks, power remote hatch/trunk release, power remote fuel release; cell phone pre-wiring, 1 power accessory outlet, driver's foot rest, retained accessory power, garage door opener, emergency "S.O.S"; instrumentation display includes tachometer, water temperature gauge, in-dash clock, exterior temp, systems monitor, trip odometer; warning indicators include water temp, battery, low oil level, low coolant, lights on, key in ignition, low fuel, low washer fluid, bulb failure, service interval, brake fluid; driver's and passenger's front airbags, driver's and front passenger's door mounted side airbags, overhead airbag; ignition disable, panic alarm, security system; tinted windows, power front and rear windows with front and rear 1-touch down; heated jet variable intermittent front windshield wipers, sun visor strip, rear window defroster; seating capacity of 5, front bucket seats, power adjustable tilt headrests, center armrest with storage, driver's seat includes 6-way power seat, passenger's seat includes 6-way power seat; rear bench seat with adjustable headrests, center armrest with storage; front and rear height adjustable seatbelts with front pretensioners; leather seats, leather door trim insert, full cloth headliner, full carpet floor covering with carpeted floor mats, genuine wood trim on instrument panel, leather-wrapped gear shift knob; memory on driver's and passenger's seats with 3 memory setting(s) includes settings for exterior mirrors, steering wheel, headrests; interior lights include dome light with fade, front reading lights, 4 door curb lights, illuminated entry; leather-wrapped steering wheel with power tilt and telescopic adjustment; dual illuminated vanity mirrors, dual auxiliary visors; auto-dimming day/night rearview mirror; full floor console, locking glove box with light, front and rear cupholders, instrument panel covered bin, 2 seat back storage pockets, refrigerated box, driver's and passenger's door bins, rear door bins; carpeted cargo floor, carpeted trunk lid, cargo light; chrome grille, black side window moldings, black front windshield molding, black rear window molding and body-colored door handles.

E430 RWD SEDAN (5A) (in addition to or instead of E320 RWD SEDAN (5A) equipment): 4.3L V8 SOHC SMPI 24-valve engine, 2.82 axle ratio; adjustable shocks; front and rear 16" x 7.5" silver alloy wheels; P215/55HR16 A/S BSW front and rear tires and premium AM/FM stereo, seek-scan, cassette, CD changer pre-wiring, in-dash CD pre-wiring, 8 premium speakers, auto equalizer, theft deterrent, and window grid antenna.

E320 RWD WAGON (5A) (in addition to or instead of E320 RWD SEDAN (5A) equipment): Auto-leveling suspension; 18.5 gal. capacity fuel tank; 2 power accessory outlets, trunk pulldown; fixed 1/4 vent windows; fixed interval rear wiper with heated jets; seating capacity of 7; full folding rear bench 2nd row seat with adjustable headrests, center armrest with storage; full folding 3rd row rear facing bench seat; leatherette door trim insert, genuine wood trim on instrument panel, leather-wrapped gear shift knob; cargo cover, cargo net and cargo tie downs.

4MATIC AWD (5A) (in addition to or instead of RWD (5A) equipment): Full-time 4-wheel drive.

E-CLASS MERCEDES-BENZ

CODE	DESCRIPTION	INVOICE	MSRP
Base Prices			
E320 W	E320 RWD Sedan (5A)	43803	47100
E320 W/4	E320 4MATIC AWD Sedan (5A)	46407	49900
E430 W	E430 RWD Sedan (5A)	48779	52450
E430 W/4	E430 4MATIC AWD Sedan (5A)	51383	55250
E320 S	E320 RWD Wagon (5A)	44594	47950
E320 S/4	E320 4MATIC AWD Wagon (5A)	47198	50750
Destination Charge:		595	595
Accessories			
—	Leather Interior (E320 Wagon)	1251	1345
—	Metallic Paint (E320)	567	610
—	Metallic Paint (E430)	NC	NC
—	Nappa Leather (Sedan)	651	700
	REQUIRES Special Order Personalization Charge. NOT AVAILABLE with 185,186.		
—	Special Order Personalization Charge	930	1000
147	Option Package E1	1465	1575
	Includes Xenon headlights, headlamp washer system and electrically heated front seats.		
148	Option Package E2 (E320)	1465	1575
	Includes Bose premium sound system, electronic glass sunroof with pop up feature and rain sensor wipers.		
148	Option Package E2 (E430)	1116	1200
	Includes electronic glass sunroof with pop up feature and rain sensor wipers.		
177	Option Package K2	1454	1795
	Includes CDMA integrated portable cellular telephone and integrated 6-disc CD changer. NOT AVAILABLE with 179, 178, 180.		
178	Option Package K2	1454	1795
	Includes TDMA integrated portable cellular telephone and integrated 6-disc CD changer. NOT AVAILABLE with 177, 179, 180.		
179	Option Package K2a	1774	2190
	Includes CDMA integrated portable cellular telephone and integrated 6-disc CD changer. NOT AVAILABLE with 177, 178, 180.		
180	Option Package K2a	1774	2190
	Includes TDMA integrated portable cellular telephone and integrated 6-disc CD changer. NOT AVAILABLE with 177, 178, 179.		
185	Designo Package-Espresso Edition (E320 RWD Wagon)	6045	6500
	Includes Designo light brown leather, center console, wood/leather-wrapped steering wheel, wood and leather trimmed knobs and floor mats. REQUIRES 873. NOT AVAILABLE with 186.		
185	Designo Package-Espresso Edition (RWD Sedan)	5487	5900
	Includes Designo light brown leather, center console, wood/leather-wrapped steering wheel, wood and leather trimmed knobs and floor mats. REQUIRES 873. NOT AVAILABLE with 186.		

MERCEDES-BENZ

E-CLASS / SLK

CODE	DESCRIPTION	INVOICE	MSRP
186	**Designo Package-Silver Edition (E320 RWD Wagon)**	6045	6500
	Includes Designo dark green/charcoal leather, center console, wood/leather-wrapped steering wheel, wood and leather trimmed knobs and floor mats. REQUIRES 873. NOT AVAILABLE with 185.		
186	**Designo Package-Silver Edition (RWD Sedan)**	5487	5900
	Includes Designo dark green/charcoal leather, center console, wood/leather-wrapped steering wheel, wood and leather trimmed knobs and floor mats. REQUIRES 873. NOT AVAILABLE with 185.		
220	**Parktronic System**	907	975
352	**COMAND System**	1855	1995
	Includes color 5" liquid crystal display with auto day/night modes, integrated navigation system (GPS), AM/FM weatherband radio with single CD, steering wheel controls for all functions (radio/navigation system/CD/telephone), telephone keypad (for 10 radio presets/optional digital StarTAC dialing) and separate COMAND mode display in instrument panel. Comand stands for Cockpit Management and Data System.		
406	**Multi-Contour Driver's and Passenger's Seats**	660	710
414	**Glass Sunrooof with Pop Up Feature**	1051	1130
540	**Electric Rear Window Sunshade (Sedan)**	381	410
722	**Integrated Luggage Rack (Wagon)**	419	450
772	**Option Package E3 (E430 RWD)**	3729	4010
	Includes sculpted front air dam with internal projector beam front fog lights, sport shift knob, wheels: 17" x 8" 5-spoke alloy, tires: 235/45ZR 17, side skirts and sport emblems.		
873	**Electrically Heated Front Seats**	563	605

2000 SLK230

What's New?

Designo editions debut and include special paint and trim in either Copper or Electric Green hues.

Review

A few years ago, the gang at the three-pointed star decided that it was time to ditch their dowdy image and begin attracting younger buyers. The result of that decision is the SLK roadster, introduced in 1997 to instant critical acclaim. The SLK's big selling point is its exclusive retractable steel roof that, when raised, makes the car seem as tight and insulated as a Benz sedan. In less than 30 seconds, you can convert the SLK from a closed coupe to a cool convertible without leaving the driver's seat.

Mercedes got the recipe almost right the first time. The original was available only with an automatic transmission, which sent sports car purists packing. Last year, Mercedes equipped the car with a manual transmission as standard equipment, making the slushbox optional. While not appreciably quicker, the manual at least offers buyers the option of selecting their own gears, which is fun when combined with the SLK's precise steering, willing supercharged powerplant, and wonderfully damped suspension.

The 185-horsepower SLK's 2.3-liter four-cylinder engine provides 200 foot-pounds of torque,

268   www.edmunds.com   **EDMUND'S® NEW CARS**

MERCEDES-BENZ
SLK

available between 2,500 and 4,800 rpm, making it a choice convertible for carving through traffic or up a spiraling mountain road. The SLK races to 60 mph in about seven seconds, but some think the exhaust note sounds more flatulent than fiery.

An optional sport package doesn't cure the exhaust blat, but does include a muscular-looking body kit and thick 17-inch treads mounted to AMG Monoblock wheels. Designo editions with special paint and trim are also available this year. The Copper and Electric Green models include plenty of interior and exterior trim in those colors. Yikes.

Front and side airbags are standard, along with ABS and automatic slip control. The SLK also has a super-reinforced A-pillar, integrated roll bars behind each seat and emergency tensioning seatbelt retractors for enhanced rollover protection. Brake Assist applies full braking force before you can. A BabySmart system allows owners to use a special car seat sold by Benz dealers that keeps the passenger airbag from deploying in an accident. Here's our question: Why no cutoff switch like Mazda and other makers offer?

Inside, the SLK charms with retro gauges and polished aluminum bezels. Stainless steel, chrome and carbon fiber accents, along with available two-tone leather, complete the look. Bose audio and automatic dual-zone climate controls are standard. Metallic paint and heated seats are not.

Roadsters are plentiful these days. Many makers are introducing them, and others are infusing existing models with more power and equipment. The SLK is aging rapidly in this quickly changing segment, but is still the only one to offer the convenience of a hardtop and the benefits of top-down cruising in a single, easy-to-use package. That might be all it needs to ensure continued success. But we'd like more power to make the price palatable.

2000 Mercedes-Benz SLK230

Standard Equipment

SLK230 KOMPRESSOR (5M): 2.3L I4 DOHC SMPI intercooled supercharged with variable valve timing 16-valve engine, requires premium unleaded fuel; 5-speed OD manual transmission; HD battery; engine block heater; 90-amp alternator; rear-wheel drive, traction control, 3.46 axle ratio; stainless steel exhaust; front independent double wishbone suspension with anti-roll bar, front coil springs, rear independent multi-link suspension with anti-roll bar, rear coil springs; power re-circulating ball steering; 4-wheel disc brakes with 4-wheel antilock braking system; 14 gal. capacity fuel tank; side impact bars; power convertible hardtop roof with lining, glass rear window, roll-over protection; front and rear body-colored bumpers with body-colored rub strip; rocker panel extensions; monotone paint; aero-composite halogen headlamps with washer,

MERCEDES-BENZ
SLK

CODE	DESCRIPTION	INVOICE	MSRP

delay-off feature; additional exterior lights include front fog/driving lights; driver's and passenger's power remote body-colored heated folding outside mirrors; front 16" x 7" silver alloy wheels, rear 16" x 8" silver alloy wheels; P205/55VR16 performance BSW front tires; 225/50VR 16 performance BSW rear tires; inside under cargo mounted compact steel spare wheel; dual zone front air conditioning, air filter, auto air recirculation; premium AM/FM stereo, seek-scan, cassette, CD changer pre-wiring, in-dash CD pre-wiring, 6 premium speakers, auto equalizer, theft deterrent, and fixed antenna; cruise control; power door locks with 2 stage unlock, remote keyless entry, power remote hatch/trunk release, power remote fuel release; cell phone pre-wiring, 1 power accessory outlet, driver's foot rest, garage door opener, smokers' package; instrumentation display includes tachometer, water temperature gauge, in-dash clock, exterior temp, systems monitor, trip odometer; warning indicators include water temp, battery, low oil level, low coolant, lights on, key in ignition, low fuel, low washer fluid, bulb failure, door ajar, service interval; driver's and passenger's front airbags, driver's and front passenger's door mounted side airbags; ignition disable, panic alarm, security system; tinted windows, power windows with driver's and passenger's 1-touch down; heated washer bottle variable intermittent front windshield wipers, sun visor strip, rear window defroster; seating capacity of 2, front bucket seats, adjustable headrests, center armrest with storage, driver's seat includes 8-way direction control, passenger's seat includes 8-way direction control; leather seats, leather door trim insert, full cloth headliner, full carpet floor covering, carbon fiber gear shift knob; interior lights include dome light with fade, illuminated entry; leather-wrapped steering wheel with telescopic adjustment; vanity mirrors; auto-dimming day/night rearview mirror; full floor console, locking glove box with light, front cupholder, instrument panel bin, interior concealed storage, driver's and passenger's door bins; carpeted cargo floor, cargo light; black grille, black side window moldings, black front windshield molding, black rear window molding and black door handles.

Base Prices

SLK230 Komp SLK230 Kompressor (5M)		38130	41000
Destination Charge:		595	595

Accessories

CODE	DESCRIPTION	INVOICE	MSRP
—	Metallic Paint	567	610
177	K2 Package	1454	1795
	Includes integrated CD changer and integrated portable cellular telephone.		
194	Designo Package Copper Edition	4371	4700
	Includes designo copper/charcoal leather interior. REQUIRES 873. NOT AVAILABLE with 195.		
195	Designo Package Electric Green Edition	3953	4250
	Includes designo charcoal leather interior. REQUIRES 873. NOT AVAILABLE with 194.		
5AT	Transmission: 5-Speed Automatic	837	900
	Includes driver selectable program and 3.27 axle ratio.		
772	Sport Package	3767	4050
	Includes sculpted front apron with integrated projector beam fog lights, sculpted rear apron, wheels: 17" x 7.5" Monoblock alloy, tires: 225/45ZR17 front and 245/40ZR17 rear, sculpted side skirts and sport emblems.		
873	Electrically Heated Front Seats	563	605

COUGAR — MERCURY

| CODE | DESCRIPTION | INVOICE | MSRP |

2000 COUGAR

2000 Mercury Cougar

What's New?

The Cougar receives an emergency trunk release as standard equipment. The floor console has been redesigned. Citrus Gold, Light Blue, and Light Sapphire are the three new clearcoat metallic paints available.

Review

One of the most distinctly styled vehicles on the road today, the Mercury Cougar enters its second year of production in 2000. Don't expect Cougar customers to be cross-shopping for the 2000 Grand Marquis; this kitty cat is aimed at a much younger crowd.

The Cougar is the first production vehicle to receive a full New Edge facelift. Ford's New Edge styling theme was concocted in its European design studios to put an end to the egg-shaped styling that the company went overboard on, most notably with the 1996 Taurus redesign. It combines sleek, rounded main forms with creased straight-edge detail. The most interesting parts of the Cougar's appearance are the cat-eye headlamps with smoked lenses, large triangular taillights, sculpted doors and hood, and the character line that runs along the lower portion of the greenhouse and sweeps downward at the rear quarter panel.

Underneath this eye-catching skin are components that are much more familiar. The Cougar is built on the same platform as the Ford Contour and Mercury Mystique. It also shares roughly 70 percent of its parts with these two entry-level sedans. This is important to Ford, because it keeps the cost of the Cougar down. It is important to you, because it virtually guarantees that the Cougar will be one of the best driving coupes on the market.

The Cougar is blessed with an excellent suspension, neutral handling characteristics, and powerful brakes. This translates to plenty of fun on curvy roads. The only thing slowing the Cougar down is an overly heavy steering feel and a set of engines that don't quite measure up to the car's exciting looks. Ford offers either a 125-horsepower, four-cylinder engine or a 2.5-liter V6 that produces 170 horsepower. These are the same engines found in the Contour/Mystique and, while they might be fine for a sedan, they don't measure up to the powerful offerings in the Mitsubishi Eclipse or the Volkswagen GTI.

Inside, you'll find a conventional control layout but a decidedly unconventional appearance. Still, form followed function for the most part, and while we might complain about minor

MERCURY
COUGAR

CODE	DESCRIPTION	INVOICE	MSRP

ergonomic problems found within the Cougar, the car is reasonably satisfying. Accessing the back seat is a breeze, thanks to a front passenger seat that slides forward when the backrest is folded and then returns to its preset position once riders are secured in back. The rear seats are firm and place the rider high in the car, but taller adults will find that their heads are squashed into the headliner.

Despite the relative lack of power, the Cougar has a lot to offer. It's affordable, functional, fun to drive, and neat to look at.

Standard Equipment

I4 (5M): 2.0L I4 DOHC SMPI with variable valve timing 16-valve engine; 5-speed OD manual transmission; 105-amp alternator; front-wheel drive, 3.82 axle ratio; stainless steel exhaust; front independent strut suspension with anti-roll bar, front coil springs, rear independent multi-link suspension with anti-roll bar, rear coil springs; power rack-and-pinion steering; front disc/rear drum brakes; 16 gal. capacity fuel tank; side impact bars; front and rear body-colored bumpers; monotone paint; projector beam halogen headlamps; driver's and passenger's power remote body-colored heated folding outside mirrors; front and rear 15" x 6" silver alloy wheels; P205/60SR15 A/S BSW front and rear tires; inside under cargo mounted compact steel spare wheel; air conditioning, air filter, rear heat ducts; premium AM/FM stereo, seek-scan, cassette, 4 speakers, and integrated roof antenna; power door locks, power remote hatch/trunk release; 2 power accessory outlets, driver's foot rest; instrumentation display includes tachometer; water temperature gauge, in-dash clock, exterior temp, trip computer, trip odometer; warning indicators include oil pressure, battery, lights on, key in ignition, low fuel; driver's and passenger's front airbags; ignition disable; tinted windows, power windows with driver's 1-touch down; variable intermittent front windshield wipers, rear window defroster; seating capacity of 4, front bucket seats, fixed headrests, driver's seat includes 2-way power seat, 6-way direction control, passenger's seat includes 4-way direction control, easy entry; 50-50 folding rear bucket seats with fixed headrests; front and rear height adjustable seatbelts; cloth seats, cloth door trim insert, full cloth headliner, full carpet floor covering with floor mats, plastic/rubber gear shift knob; interior lights include dome light with delay; steering wheel with tilt adjustment; driver's side vanity mirror; day/night rearview mirror; full floor console, glove box, front cupholder, instrument panel bin, driver's and passenger's door bins; carpeted cargo floor, plastic trunk lid, cargo cover, cargo light; black grille, black side window moldings, black front windshield molding, black rear window molding and body-colored door handles.

V6 (5M) (in addition to or instead of I4 (5M) equipment): 2.5L V6 DOHC SMPI 24-valve engine; 130-amp alternator; 4.06 axle ratio; stainless steel exhaust with chrome tip and sport ride suspension.

Base Prices

CODE	DESCRIPTION	INVOICE	MSRP
T60	Cougar 4-Cyl. (5M)	15021	16445
T61	Cougar V6 (5M)	15466	16945
	Destination Charge:	425	425

Accessories

CODE	DESCRIPTION	INVOICE	MSRP
—	Smokers' Package	13	15
13E	Power Tilt/Slide Sunroof	547	615
13K	Spoiler (4-Cyl.)	209	235
21A	6-Way Power Driver's Seat (V6)	209	235
	Includes power fore/aft adjustment, power lumbar and recline. REQUIRES 97S.		
41H	Engine Block Immersion Heater	18	20
428	High Altitude Principal Use	NC	NC

COUGAR / GRAND MARQUIS — MERCURY

CODE	DESCRIPTION	INVOICE	MSRP
429	Non-High Altitude Principal Use	NC	NC
433	Rear Spoiler Delete (V6)	(209)	(235)
	REQUIRES 97S.		
44T	Transmission: 4-Speed Automatic with Overdirve (V6)	725	815
	Includes 3.77 axle ratio.		
552	Antilock Braking System	445	500
553	Traction Control (V6)	209	235
	REQUIRES 552.		
583	Radio: AM/FM Stereo with CD	124	140
	Includes premium sound. NOT AVAILABLE with 58K.		
58K	Radio: AM/FM Stereo with CD and Cassette (V6)	71	80
	Includes premium sound. NOT AVAILABLE with 583, 919.		
58K	Radio: AM/FM Stereo with CD and Cassette	196	220
	Includes premium sound. NOT AVAILABLE with 583, 919, 60L.		
59M	Side Air Bags	347	390
60L	V6 Convenience Group (V6)	641	720
	Includes speed control, remote keyless entry, remote trunk release with keyfob, panic alarm, illuminated entry, rear window wiper/washer and AM/FM stereo with CD.		
646	Wheels: 16" Machined Aluminum (V6)	223	250
	REQUIRES 97S.		
8	Leather Bucket Seats (V6)	797	895
	REQUIRES 21A and 97S.		
919	Trunk Mounted Compact Disc Changer	312	350
	NOT AVAILABLE with 58K.		
94A	4-Cyl. Convenience Group (4-Cyl.)	547	615
	Includes speed control, remote keyless entry, remote trunk release with keyfob, panic alarm, illuminated entry and rear window wiper/washer.		
96G	Bodyside Moldings	45	50
97S	V6 Sport Group (V6)	725	815
	Includes bright door sill plate, leather-wrapped steering wheel, leather-wrapped shift knob, light group: auxiliary warning system, glove box light, driver's side illuminated visor mirror; fog lamps, spoiler, 4-wheel disc brakes, wheels: 16" aluminum, upgraded sport seats and tires: P215/50X16 BSW.		

2000 GRAND MARQUIS

What's New?

The Marquis receives additional safety features, including an emergency trunk release, child seat-anchor brackets, and Mercury's Belt Minder system. The interior gets a new trim color, Dark Charcoal. One new exterior color will be offered, Tropic Green. The handling package's rear-axle ratio changes from 3.27 to 3.55. The Grand Marquis Limited will be offered later in the 2000 model year.

MERCURY — GRAND MARQUIS

CODE	DESCRIPTION	INVOICE	MSRP

Review

It is so cool that a car like this still exists. While just about every other American manufacturer has run screaming from its past, the Grand Marquis embraces it with a big V8 under the hood and two rear wheels doing the pushing.

Despite this all-but-extinct layout, the Grand Marquis offers some high-tech options like ABS and traction control. It also comes standard with dual front airbags, rear-door child safety locks, and dynamic side-impact protection. For 2000, the Grand Marquis receives many of the safety changes that Ford has implemented across most of its model line. The emergency trunk release allows people who are trapped in the trunk to release the hatch. The child seat-anchor brackets in the back seat provide parents and caregivers an improved method to buckle in their child safety seats more securely. The system secures child safety seats using tethers that attach to the anchor brackets, in addition to traditional safety belts. The Belt Minder system consists of a chime and an indicator light to remind drivers and passengers to buckle up.

Power comes from a 4.6-liter V8 with 200 horsepower and 275 foot-pounds of torque. These numbers can be upped to 215 and 285, respectively, by ordering the handling package that includes dual exhaust, 16-inch aluminum wheels, a higher rear-axle ratio, larger-diameter front and rear stabilizer bars, and rear air springs. Automatic load leveling is a side benefit with this option. If you're after luxury and not performance, options like automatic temperature control, auto-dimming rearview mirror, and premium AM/FM stereo with trunk-mounted CD changer can be ordered separately or as part of a luxury package.

The shape of this car contributes to its rather brick-like coefficient of drag (.37) and at 17 mpg in the city it's certainly no econobox. With Mercury constantly improving this traditional model, the company has managed to bring together something old and something new. A V8, rear-drive sedan with traction control and ABS is something most American automakers abandoned long ago. If nothing else, Mercury gets credit for going its own route and not playing follow-the-leader.

2000 Mercury Grand Marquis

Standard Equipment

GS (4A): 4.6L V8 SOHC SMPI 16-valve engine; 4-speed electronic OD auto transmission with lock-up; battery with run down protection; 130-amp alternator; rear-wheel drive, 2.73 axle ratio; stainless steel exhaust; front independent suspension with anti-roll bar, front coil springs, rigid rear axle multi-link suspension with anti-roll bar, rear coil springs; power re-circulating ball

274   www.edmunds.com   **EDMUND'S® NEW CARS**

GRAND MARQUIS — MERCURY

CODE	DESCRIPTION	INVOICE	MSRP

steering with vehicle speed-sensing assist; 4-wheel disc brakes; 19 gal. capacity fuel tank; side impact bars; front and rear body-colored bumpers with body-colored rub strip, chrome bumper insert; body-colored bodyside molding with chrome bodyside insert; monotone paint; aero-composite halogen fully auto headlamps with delay-off feature; additional exterior lights include cornering lights; driver's and passenger's power remote body-colored folding outside mirrors; front and rear 16" x 7" steel wheels; P225/60SR16 A/S WSW front and rear tires; inside mounted compact steel spare wheel; air conditioning, rear heat ducts; AM/FM stereo, seek-scan, cassette, 4 speakers, and window grid antenna; cruise control with steering wheel controls; power door locks, child safety rear door locks, power remote hatch/trunk release; 1 power accessory outlet, driver's foot rest, smokers' package; instrumentation display includes oil pressure gauge, water temperature gauge, volt gauge, in-dash clock, trip odometer; warning indicators include battery, lights on, key in ignition, low fuel; driver's and passenger's front airbags; tinted windows, power front and rear windows with driver's 1-touch down; variable intermittent front windshield wipers, sun visor strip, rear window defroster; seating capacity of 6, 50-50 split-bench front seat, adjustable headrests, center armrest, driver's seat includes 6-way power seat, passenger's seat includes 4-way direction control; rear bench seat with fixed headrests; front height adjustable seatbelts; cloth seats, vinyl door trim insert, full cloth headliner, full carpet floor covering with carpeted floor mats, deluxe sound insulation, simulated wood trim on instrument panel; interior lights include dome light with fade, illuminated entry; steering wheel with tilt adjustment; passenger's side vanity mirror; day/night rearview mirror; locking glove box with light, front cupholder, 2 seat back storage pockets, driver's and passenger's door bins; carpeted cargo floor, cargo light; chrome grille, chrome side window moldings, black front windshield molding, black rear window molding and chrome door handles.

LS (4A) (in addition to or instead of GS (4A) equipment): Rocker panel extensions; monotone paint with bodyside accent stripe; remote keyless entry; driver's seat includes 6-way power seat, power 2-way lumbar support, rear center armrest; premium cloth seats; interior lights include front and rear reading lights and dual illuminated vanity mirrors.

Base Prices

Code	Description	Invoice	MSRP
M74	GS (4A)	20897	22415
M75	LS (4A)	22626	24315
	Destination Charge:	630	630

Accessories

Code	Description	Invoice	MSRP
144	Remote Keyless Entry System (GS) *Includes keypad and 2 remotes.*	213	240
155	Electronic Instrumentation (LS) *REQUIRES 573.*	379	425
175	Homelink Universal Garage Door Opener (LS)	102	115
41G	Handling Package (LS) *Includes larger diameter rear stabilizer bar, unique tuned suspension (shocks, spring rates), 3.55 axle ratio, tires: P225/60R16 handling BSW, rear air suspension with unique springs, wheels: 16" lacy-spoke aluminum, dual exhaust and larger rear stabilizer bar. REQUIRES 64R. NOT AVAILABLE with 66B.*	476	535
41G	Handling Package *Includes larger diameter rear stabilizer bar, unique tuned suspension (shocks, spring rates), 3.55 axle ratio, tires: P225/60R16 handling BSW, rear air suspension with unique springs, wheels: 16" lacy-spoke aluminum, dual exhaust and larger rear stabilizer bar. NOT AVAILABLE with 66B, 64R.*	761	855

MERCURY
GRAND MARQUIS

CODE	DESCRIPTION	INVOICE	MSRP
41H	Engine Block Heater (LPO)	23	25
428	High Altitude Principal Use	NC	*NC
	NOT AVAILABLE with 429, 93N.		
429	Non-High Altitude Principal Use	NC	NC
	NOT AVAILABLE with 428, 93N.		
508	Tires: Conventional Spare (LPO)	93	105
	Replaces standard mini-spare with full-size steel wheel and ground position tire.		
508	Tires: Conventional Spare (LPO)	107	120
	Replaces standard mini-spare with full-size steel wheel and ground position tire.		
	REQUIRES 41G.		
552	Antilock Braking System	534	600
553	Traction Control	690	775
	Includes antilock braking system.		
573	Electronic Automatic Temperature Control (LS)	156	175
	Includes outside temperature display.		
585	Single Disc CD Player (GS)	124	140
	Replaces cassette.		
586	Radio: Premium AM/FM Stereo with Cassette (LS)	321	360
	Includes the following upgrades from 58H cassette radio: radio/tape scan, AM stereo, auto memory set, unique 4-channel premium amplifier with 80 total Watts RMS, Auto Dynamic Noise Reduction (DNR) on FM, CrO2 capability on tape, radio play with tape rewind/fast forward, premium dual cone rear speakers, premium front door speakers, CD changer compatible and radio data system (RDS).		
60C	GS Standard Equipment Group (GS)	NC	NC
	Includes remote keyless entry system, body side paint stripe and luxury light group: dual illuminated visor mirrors and dual beam dome/map lamp. Available only to residents of California and Hawaii. NOT AVAILABLE with 943.		
60L	LS Standard Equipment Groups (LS)	NC	NC
	Includes GS Standard Equipment Group: remote keyless entry system, body side paint stripe and luxury light group: dual illuminated visor mirrors and dual beam dome/map lamp; electronic instrumentation, electronic automatic temperature control, auto dimming rear view mirror, radio: premium AM stereo/FM stereo with cassette, amplifier, dynamic noise reduction, RDS, 4 premium speakers and CD changer controls, wheels: 16" Teardrop aluminum, leather twin conmfort seats, power 8-way passenger's seat, Homelink garage door opener and leather-wrapped steering wheel. Available only to residents of California and Hawaii. NOT AVAILABLE with 943.		
64R	Wheels: 16" Teardrop Aluminum (LS)	285	320
	NOT AVAILABLE with 41G, 68E, 68F.		
66B	Rear Air Suspension (LS)	240	270
	Tuned for softer ride. NOT AVAILABLE with 41G.		
68E	Premium Package (LS)	890	1000
	Includes leather-wrapped steering wheel, electronic auto temperature control, outside temperature display, 8-way power passenger's seat, auto dimming rearview mirror and compass. REQUIRES 99W. NOT AVAILABLE with 64R.		

GRAND MARQUIS / MYSTIQUE — MERCURY

CODE	DESCRIPTION	INVOICE	MSRP
68F	Ultimate Package (LS)	2136	2400
	Includes Premium Package: leather-wrapped steering wheel, electronic auto temperature control, outside temperature display, 8-way power passenger's seat, auto dimming rearview mirror and compass; traction control, antilock braking system, electronic instrumentation and premium AM/FM stereo with cassette. NOT AVAILABLE with 64R.		
919	6-Disc CD Changer (LS)	312	350
	Trunk mounted. REQUIRES 586.		
943	Luxury Light Group (GS)	169	190
	Includes dual illuminated visor mirrors and dual beam dome/map lamp.		
972	Bodyside Paint Stripe (GS)	54	60
99W	Engine: 4.6L SEFI V8	NC	NC
	Horsepower on engine increases from 200 to 215 with dual exhaust (41G).		
J	Leather Twin Comfort Seats (LS)	654	735
	REQUIRES 68E or 68F.		

2000 MYSTIQUE

2000 Mercury Mystique

What's New?

The Mystique comes standard with an emergency glow-in-the-dark trunk release, designed to allow a child or adult trapped in the trunk to open it from the inside. The Mystique also receives two new exterior colors.

Review

Since its introduction in 1995, the Mystique has been Mercury's counterpart to the Ford Contour. Based on the same platform, the Mercury has differentiated itself by having different

MERCURY

MYSTIQUE

CODE	DESCRIPTION	INVOICE	MSRP

styling and trim packages. But for all intensive purposes, the Contour and Mystique were the same car.

The Contour and Mystique are still the same car for 2000, but there is an added difference: the Mystique is the only one to offer a four-cylinder engine. To avoid having the new Ford Focus steal sales away from the Contour, Ford has taken the Contour upscale, discontinuing the entry-level LX series. The remaining 2000 Contour comes only with a V6 engine.

Customers looking to purchase a more fuel-efficient (and less expensive) four-cylinder should check out the Mystique GS. The Zetec DOHC 16-valve four produces 125 horsepower at 5,500 rpm and 130 foot-pounds of torque at 4,000 rpm. The GS also comes with a rear spoiler, a leather-wrapped steering wheel, fog lamps and special floor mats. While we still aren't sold on the exterior look, the Mystique GS has plenty to offer the small-sedan shopper. The body structure is stiff, and the ergonomically correct instrument panel features legible dials and controls. The interior still receives some gripes, however. It lacks some of the refinement found in competing cars and Mercury has never been able to solve the lack of room for rear-seat passengers.

The more upscale Mystique LS comes standard with the 24-valve Duratec V6 engine, which develops 170 horsepower at 6,250 rpm and 165 foot-pounds of torque at 4,250 rpm. Improvements over the LS include leather bucket seats, 15-inch alloy wheels, larger tires, a performance-tuned suspension, a 60/40 split-folding rear seat and four-wheel disc brakes on manual transmission-equipped cars.

When we've been behind the wheel of V6-powered Mystiques, we've generally had a good time. The V6 is just one part of an equation that makes this car such an excellent purchase for the shallow-pocketed enthusiast. The real excitement of the Mystique's driving experience is the result of the car's excellent chassis, suspension and steering.

Since its introduction, the Contour/Mystique platform has won plenty of awards and has received great press from automotive critics. In 1998, Mercury gave the Mystique an exterior freshening to make the car more distinctive in the crowded family-sedan marketplace.

The Dodge Stratus and Chevrolet Malibu may offer greater interior volume, but for pure road-going thrills in a well thought-out package, the Mystique makes for a fun car at a great price.

Standard Equipment

GS (5M): 2.0L I4 DOHC SMPI 16-valve engine; 5-speed OD manual transmission; HD battery; 130-amp alternator; front-wheel drive, 3.84 axle ratio; stainless steel exhaust; front independent strut suspension with anti-roll bar, front coil springs, rear independent multi-link suspension with anti-roll bar, rear coil springs; power rack-and-pinion steering; front disc/rear drum brakes; 15 gal. capacity fuel tank; side impact bars; front and rear body-colored bumpers; body-colored bodyside molding; monotone paint; aero-composite halogen headlamps; driver's and passenger's power remote body-colored outside mirrors; front and rear 14" x 5.5" steel wheels; P185/70SR14 A/S BSW front and rear tires; inside under cargo mounted compact steel spare wheel; air conditioning, air filter, rear heat ducts; AM/FM stereo, clock, seek-scan, cassette, 4 speakers, and fixed antenna; cruise control with steering wheel controls; power door locks, child safety rear door locks, remote hatch/trunk release; 1 power accessory outlet, driver's foot rest; instrumentation display includes tachometer, water temperature gauge, trip odometer; warning indicators include oil pressure, lights on, key in ignition, low fuel; driver's and passenger's front airbags; tinted windows, power front and rear windows with driver's 1-touch down; fixed interval front windshield wipers, rear window defroster; seating capacity of 5, front bucket seats, adjustable tilt headrests, center armrest, driver's seat includes 4-way direction control, passenger's seat includes 4-way direction control; rear bench seat; front height adjustable seatbelts; cloth seats, cloth door trim insert, full cloth headliner, full carpet floor covering, simulated wood trim on instrument panel, plastic/rubber gear shift knob; interior lights include dome light with fade, front and rear reading lights, 4 door curb lights; steering wheel with tilt adjustment; vanity mirrors; day/night rearview mirror; full floor console, glove box, front cupholder, instrument panel bin, 2 seat back storage pockets, driver's and passenger's door bins; carpeted cargo floor, cargo light; chrome grille, black side window moldings, black front windshield molding, black rear window molding and body-colored door handles.

278   www.edmunds.com   **EDMUND'S® NEW CARS**

MYSTIQUE   MERCURY

CODE	DESCRIPTION	INVOICE	MSRP

LS (5M) (in addition to or instead of GS (5M) equipment): 2.5L V6 DOHC SMPI 24-valve engine; 4.06 axle ratio; sport ride suspension; 4-wheel disc brakes; additional exterior lights include front fog/driving lights; front and rear 15" x 6" silver alloy wheels; P205/60SR15 A/S BSW front and rear tires; remote keyless entry; ignition disable, panic alarm; variable intermittent front windshield wipers; driver's seat includes 6-way power seat, power 2-way lumbar support; 60-40 folding rear bench seat with center armrest; leather seats, carpeted floor mats, simulated wood trim on instrument panel; leather-wrapped steering wheel with tilt adjustment and passenger's side illuminated vanity mirror.

Base Prices

Code	Description	Invoice	MSRP
M65	GS (5M)	14714	16145
M66	LS (5M)	15871	17445
	Destination Charge:	560	560

Accessories

Code	Description	Invoice	MSRP
12Y	Front and Rear Carpeted Floor Mats (GS)	49	55
13B	Power Moonroof (LS)	NC	NC
	REQUIRES B3M. NOT AVAILABLE with B3E.		
13B	Power Moonroof	530	595
13K	Rear Spoiler (LS)	218	245
143	Remote Keyless Entry (GS)	169	190
	Includes illuminated entry and panic alarm.		
219	60/40 Split Folding Rear Seat (GS)	182	205
21A	6-Way Power Driver's Seat (LS)	312	350
	Includes adjustments for seat forward/seat backward, seat up/seat down and front seat tilt/rear seat tilt.		
41H	Engine Block Immersion Heater (LPO)	18	20
428	High Altitude Principal Use	NC	NC
429	Non-High Altitude Principal Use	NC	NC
	NOT AVAILABLE with 428, 93N.		
44T	Transmission: 4-Speed Automatic with OD	725	815
53G	GS Sport Group (GS)	174	195
	Includes rear spoiler, leather-wrapped shift knob, leather-wrapped steering wheel, fog lamps, floor mats and sport badging.		
552	Antilock Braking System	445	500
553	Traction Control (LS)	156	175
	REQUIRES 552.		
585	Radio: AM/FM Stereo with CD and Premium Sound	245	275
	Includes amplifier. Does not include cassette player. NOT AVAILABLE with 58P.		
58P	Radio: AM/FM Cassette and Premium Sound	120	135
	Includes amplifier. NOT AVAILABLE with 585.		
63B	Smoker's Package	13	15
	Includes drop-in ashtray and cigarette lighter.		
64M	Wheels: 15" 6-Spoke Polished Mach Alloy (GS)	423	475
	Includes tires: P205/60R15 BSW. NOT AVAILABLE with 64Y.		
64Y	Wheels: 15" Mach Alloy (GS)	423	475
	Includes tires: P205/60R15 BSW. NOT AVAILABLE with 64M.		

MERCURY
MYSTIQUE / SABLE

CODE	DESCRIPTION	INVOICE	MSRP
91H	Power Antenna (LS)	85	95
B3E	Regional Discount (LS)	(445)	(500)
	Includes Chicago, Orlando, Southwest, Atlanta, Twin Cities and Detroit (South Bend and Fort Wayne LMDA's only) Regions. NOT AVAILABLE with B3M, 13B.		
B3M	Regional Discount (LS)	NC	NC
	Includes Boston, New York, Philadelphia, Washington D.C, Pittsburgh (the state of New York and Pittsburgh LMDA), Cincinnati and Kansas City Regions. NOT AVAILABLE with B3E.		

2000 SABLE

2000 Mercury Sable

What's New?

The 2000 Mercury Sable gains new sheetmetal and additional refinements. The freshened styling includes a raised hood and decklid, a larger grille, improved headlamps and taillights, and new mirrors. The instrument panel has been updated, and the new integrated control panel provides better functionality. The Sable also gains significant improvements to its safety and powertrain components.

Review

Like its near twin, the Ford Taurus, the Mercury Sable receives some welcome changes in 2000. Mercury hopes these changes will improve the Sable's chances against the competition. Compared to the 1999 Sable, the most obvious change is styling. Both the public and the media generally disliked the older car's looks. And while the exterior enhancements are evolutionary in nature, they certainly are an improvement. The car now has a larger, higher, wider and more substantial appearance. All exterior body panels, except the doors and greenhouse, are new. The headlights are now larger and 20 percent more powerful. All Sables receive new 16-inch wheels and 215/60R16 tires as standard equipment.

SABLE — MERCURY

| CODE | DESCRIPTION | INVOICE | MSRP |

The Sable has earned a good reputation for safety, thanks to its solid performances in U.S. government crash testing. Mercury builds on that rep with the Sable's new Advanced Restraints System. This system adapts airbag deployment depending upon impact severity, safety-belt usage and driver-seat position. The ARS includes safety-belt pre-tensioners and retractors. Head-and-chest side airbags are optional for front occupants. Additional safety changes include a new emergency trunk release (for those times when you accidentally lock yourself in your own trunk), child-safety-seat anchors and locking front-seat head restraints.

Inside, the Sable now has power-adjustable accelerator and brake pedals. With the touch of a button, the brake and accelerator pedals can, together, be horizontally adjusted up to 3 inches toward the driver from the standard location to provide added driving comfort for a wider range of drivers. Audio and climate controls are grouped in a new soft-cornered rectilinear shape. Controls are operated by square buttons, which are arranged in a conventional linear grid fashion for more intuitive use. The flip/fold console in the six-passenger Sable now folds down flat to the floor, allowing better access to the lower part of the integrated control panel.

Powertrain choices have been refined for 2000. Both the standard Vulcan 3.0-liter V6 and the optional Duratec 3.0-liter V6 gain horsepower and torque. Improvements have been made in the reduction of noise, vibration and harshness. Both the Vulcan and Duratec engines meet Low-Emissions Vehicle (LEV) standards in California and 13 Northeastern states. Mercury also says that the transmissions for both engines shift smoother, and suspension and steering refinements help to improve ride smoothness without taking away from overall handling.

We've always liked the Sable and Taurus, but thought they were edged out when compared to the Accord or Camry. The changes introduced for 2000 should help narrow the gap.

Standard Equipment

GS SEDAN (4A): 3.0L V6 OHV SMPI 12-valve engine; 4-speed electronic OD auto transmission with lock-up; battery with run down protection; 130-amp alternator; transmission oil cooler; front-wheel drive, 3.77 axle ratio; stainless steel exhaust; front independent strut suspension with anti-roll bar, front coil springs, gas-pressurized front shocks, rear independent multi-link suspension with rear coil springs, gas-pressurized rear shocks; power rack-and-pinion steering with vehicle speed-sensing assist; front disc/rear drum brakes; 16 gal. capacity fuel tank; side impact bars; front and rear body-colored bumpers; body-colored bodyside molding with chrome bodyside insert, rocker panel extensions; clearcoat monotone paint; aero-composite halogen headlamps; driver's and passenger's power remote body-colored outside mirrors; front and rear 15" x 6" steel wheels; P205/65TR15 A/S BSW front and rear tires; inside under cargo mounted compact steel spare wheel; air conditioning, rear heat ducts; AM/FM stereo, clock, seek-scan, cassette, 4 speakers, and fixed antenna; cruise control with steering wheel controls; power door locks, remote keyless entry, child safety rear door locks, power remote hatch/trunk release; 2 power accessory outlets, driver's foot rest, retained accessory power, smokers' package; instrumentation display includes tachometer, water temperature gauge, trip odometer; warning indicators include oil pressure, battery, lights on, key in ignition, low fuel, door ajar, brake fluid; driver's and passenger's front airbags; ignition disable, panic alarm; tinted windows, power front and rear windows with driver's 1-touch down; variable intermittent front windshield wipers, sun visor strip, rear window defroster; seating capacity of 6, front 40-20-40 bucket seats, adjustable headrests, center armrest with storage, driver's seat includes 4-way direction control, lumbar support, passenger's seat includes 4-way direction control; rear bench seat; front height adjustable seatbelts with front pretensioners; cloth seats, full cloth headliner, full carpet floor covering with carpeted floor mats, deluxe sound insulation, simulated wood trim on instrument panel, plastic/rubber gear shift knob; interior lights include dome light with delay, front reading lights; steering wheel with tilt adjustment; vanity mirrors; day/night rearview mirror; partial floor console, locking glove box with light, front cupholder, 2 seat back storage pockets, driver's and passenger's door bins; carpeted cargo floor, cargo light; chrome grille, black side window moldings, black front windshield molding, black rear window molding and body-colored door handles.

MERCURY
SABLE

CODE	DESCRIPTION	INVOICE	MSRP

LS SEDAN (4A) (in addition to or instead of GS SEDAN (4A) equipment): Driver's and passenger's power remote body-colored heated outside mirrors; front and rear 15" x 6" alloy wheels, seating capacity of 5, front bucket seats, adjustable headrests, center armrest with storage, driver's seat includes 4-way power seat, 8-way direction control, power 2-way lumbar support; 60-40 folding rear bench seat; leather-wrapped steering wheel with tilt adjustment, adjustable gas and brake pedals and full floor console.

LS PREMIUM SEDAN (4A) (in addition to or instead of LS SEDAN (4A) equipment): 3.0L V6 DOHC SMPI 24-valve engine; 3.98 axle ratio; aero-composite halogen fully auto headlamps; additional exterior lights include front fog/driving lights; air conditioning with climate control; security system; 60-40 folding rear bench seat with center armrest; leather seats, dual illuminated vanity mirrors and dual auxiliary visors.

GS WAGON/LS PREMIUM WAGON (4A) (in addition to or instead of GS SEDAN/LS PREMIUM SEDAN (4A) equipment): 4-wheel disc brakes; roof rack; rear step; power retractable antenna; mechanical rear window remote release; flip-up rear window, rear window wiper; seating capacity of 8 (7 - LS); full folding rear facing 3rd row bench seat; plastic trunk lid, cargo cover, cargo tie downs, cargo concealed storage and chrome side window moldings.

Base Prices

CODE	DESCRIPTION	INVOICE	MSRP
M50	GS Sedan (4A)	17177	18845
M53	LS Sedan (4A)	18156	19945
M55	LS Premium Sedan (4A)	19313	21245
M58	GS Wagon (4A)	18779	20645
M59	LS Premium Wagon (4A)	20292	22345
	Destination Charge:	550	550

Accessories

CODE	DESCRIPTION	INVOICE	MSRP
13B	Power Moonroof (LS)	747	840
13B	Power Moonroof with California/Hawaii (LS Premium Sedan)	NC	NC
13B	Power Moonroof with Northeast (LS Premium Sedan)	NC	NC
186	5-Passenger Seating (GS Sedan)	93	105
	Includes floor shift.		
21A	Power Driver's Seat (GS)	352	395
21J	Power Passenger's Seat (LS Premium)	312	350
	REQUIRES 61B.		
428	High Altitude Principal Use	NC	NC
429	Non-High Altitude Principal Use	NC	NC
53A	Audio Group (LS)	597	670
	Includes MACH AM/FM stereo with cassette, 6 premium speakers, vehicle-specific equalization, 80-watt external amplifier and 6-disc CD changer.		
552	Antilock Braking System	534	600
552	Antilock Braking System with Northeast (LS Premium)	NC	NC
553	All-Speed Traction Control (LS)	156	175
	REQUIRES 552.		
59C	Adjustable Pedals (GS)	107	120
	REQUIRES 21A.		

SABLE — MERCURY

CODE	DESCRIPTION	INVOICE	MSRP
61B	Side Impact Air Bags	347	390
64N	Wheels: 7-Spoke Machined Alloy (GS Sedan)	352	395
64W	Wheels: Chrometec (LS)	263	295
99S	Engine: 3.0L Duratec 4V V6 (LS Sedan)	619	695
	Includes 3.98 axle ratio.		

TO PRICE YOUR TRADE-IN,
PURCHASE EDMUND'S® USED CAR PRICES AND RATINGS.

See page 6 for details.

Edmund's® TOWN HALL

Get answers from our editors, discover smart shopping strategies and share your experiences in our new talk area. Just enter the following address into your web browser:

http://townhall.edmunds.com

Where smart shoppers talk about cars, trucks, and related consumer topics.

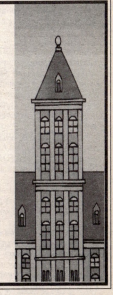

MITSUBISHI

DIAMANTE

CODE	DESCRIPTION	INVOICE	MSRP

1999 DIAMANTE

1999 Mitsubishi Diamante

What's New?

Only one Diamante model is available for 1999, replacing the ES and LS models. Mitsubishi also adds some new standard features, options and exterior colors to this top-level model.

Review

To achieve success in the near-luxury market, an automaker must possess a strong brand image that consumers associate with prestige. Mitsubishi does not, and this partly explains the dismal failure that the first Diamante luxury sedan suffered in the United States. It wasn't a bad car, just a little dull looking and loaded with so much techno-wizardry that it cost far more than its perceived worth. That changed last year, when the Diamante appeared worth more than its price. For 1999, Mitsubishi builds upon last year's success, offering more standard equipment than before.

The same 3.5-liter V6 drives the front wheels, making 210 horsepower and upholding the Diamante's standing as one of the most powerful sedans in its class. The Diamante will go from zero to 60 in about 8.5 seconds, and, if you make this Mitsu perform this way often, the four-speed automatic transmission is supposed to learn that you're a lead foot, and adjust itself accordingly.

Exterior styling features a chiseled, BMW-like appearance that is bolder than the smooth silhouette of the previous car. Chrome appears in the window moldings, surrounding the license plate, grille trim and alloy wheels. For 1999, the Diamante displays a centered Mitsubishi Motors decklid badge. The Diamante's interior is tastefully trimmed, though the stereo is fitted with a ridiculous number of buttons. Gauges emit a Lexus-like glow at night, and the automatic climate controls feature innovative pictograms to convey fan mode.

Standard features now include driver and front passenger illuminated visor mirrors, front and rear map lights and power trunk and fuel door releases. Our biggest complaint about the Diamante last year, the lack of traction control, has been addressed and is now offered as an option. Both traction control and heated front seats are available for 1999 with the new Platinum Package. To top it off, Mitsubishi has added a new tan color seat fabric selection and three new exterior paint colors: Richmond Red Pearl, Lexington Green Metallic and Platinum White Pearl.

284   www.edmunds.com   **EDMUND'S® NEW CARS**

DIAMANTE — MITSUBISHI

For 1999, the Diamante's MSRP is less than $28,000 including destination charge- that's $5,000 less than the 1998 Diamante LS and about $8,000 less than the 194-horsepower Mercedes-Benz C280, though the Benz provides standard traction control. This year's Diamante is priced about the same as the Acura 3.2 TL, but the Acura gets you 15 more horsepower and heated seats standard. Both the 'Benz and the Honda have superior transmissions and are better cars overall.

Standard Equipment

DIAMANTE (4A): 3.5L V6 SOHC MPI 24-valve engine; 4-speed electronic overdrive automatic transmission with lock-up; 110-amp alternator; front wheel drive, 2.95 axle ratio; stainless steel exhaust with chrome tip; front independent strut suspension with anti-roll bar, front coil springs, rear independent multi-link suspension with anti-roll bar, rear coil springs; power rack-and-pinion steering with engine speed-sensing assist; 4 wheel disc brakes with 4 wheel antilock braking system; 19 gal. capacity fuel tank; front and rear body-colored bumpers; black bodyside molding; monotone paint; aero-composite halogen auto off headlamps; additional exterior lights include center high mounted stop light; driver's and passenger's power remote body-colored folding outside mirrors; front and rear 15" x 6" steel wheels; P205/65HR15 BSW AS front and rear tires; inside under cargo mounted full-size conventional steel spare wheel; air conditioning with climate control, rear heat ducts; AM/FM stereo with seek-scan, cassette, 6 speakers, theft deterrent, and power retractable diversity antenna; cruise control; power door locks with 2 stage unlock, remote keyless entry, child safety rear door locks, power remote hatch/trunk release, power remote fuel release; 1 power accessory outlet, driver's foot rest, retained accessory power; instrumentation display includes tachometer, water temp gauge, in-dash clock, trip odometer; warning indicators include oil pressure, battery, key in ignition, low fuel, door ajar, trunk ajar; dual airbags; panic alarm, security system; tinted windows, power front windows with driver's 1-touch down, power rear windows; variable intermittent front windshield wipers, rear window defroster; seating capacity of 5, front bucket seats with adjustable headrests, center armrest with storage, driver's seat includes 8-way direction control, passenger's seat includes 8-way direction control; rear bench seat with adjustable headrests, center armrest; front height adjustable seatbelts with front pretensioners; cloth seats, cloth door trim insert, full cloth headliner, full carpet floor covering with carpeted floor mats; interior lights include dome light with fade, front reading lights, 2 door curb lights, illuminated entry; steering wheel with tilt adjustment; dual illuminated vanity mirrors; day-night rearview mirror; full floor console, locking glove box with light, front and rear cupholders, 2 seat back storage pockets, driver's and passenger's door bins; carpeted cargo floor, cargo net, cargo light; chrome grille, chrome side window moldings, black front windshield molding, black rear window molding and chrome door handles.

Base Prices

Code	Description	Invoice	MSRP
DM42B	Diamante	24749	27199
	Destination Charge:	470	470

Accessories

Code	Description	Invoice	MSRP
—	Alaska Destination Surcharge	120	120
—	California/NLEV Emissions	70	70
C3	CD Player	307	399
	NOT AVAILABLE with P2, P3.		
C4	10-Disc CD Changer	411	599
MG	Mudguards	90	125

MITSUBISHI

DIAMANTE / ECLIPSE

CODE	DESCRIPTION	INVOICE	MSRP
P1	Luxury Package	1925	2291
	Includes alloy wheels, 215/60R16 tires, leather seats, power driver's seat, driver's seat memory system, fog lights, power sunroof, leather-wrapped steering wheel, heated door mirrors, HomeLink system, woodgrain accent, color keyed bodyside molding and wheel locks. NOT AVAILABLE with W1, P2, P3.		
P2	Premium Package	2605	3101
	Includes alloy wheels, 215/60R16 tires, power leather seats, fog lights, power sunroof, wheel locks, premium Infinity AM/FM stereo with cassette and CD, leather-wrapped steering wheel, heated door mirrors, HomeLink system, woodgrain accent and color keyed bodyside molding. NOT AVAILABLE with P1, P3.		
P3	Platinum Package	3151	3751
	Includes alloy wheels, 215/60R16 tires, power heated leather seats, power sunroof, fog lights, premium Infinity AM/FM stereo with cassette and CD, traction control, leather-wrapped steering wheel, heated door mirrors, HomeLink system, wood grain accent, color keyed bodyside molding and wheel locks. NOT AVAILABLE with P1, P2.		
W1	Wheels: Chrome Alloy Upgrade	706	840
	REQUIRES P2 or P3. NOT AVAILABLE with P1.		

2000 ECLIPSE

2000 Mitsubishi Eclipse

_____ **What's New?** _____

Mitsubishi's 2000 Eclipse is redesigned inside and out and based on the Galant sedan platform, embodying a youthful image and providing a sporty drive. But the turbocharged engine is gone and all-wheel drive is no longer on the menu.

ECLIPSE MITSUBISHI

| CODE | DESCRIPTION | INVOICE | MSRP |

Review

Since 1990, the Eclipse has been giving budget-minded enthusiasts edgy style and quick performance at bargain prices. The 1995 redesign improved on this idea and for 2000, the Eclipse once again gets a makeover complete with enhanced four-cylinder engine performance, sophisticated technology and a whole new image.

Mitsubishi calls the new Eclipse's styling geo-mechanical, and what that means is the car has an unbroken roof arch, a swell in the hood that rolls across the upper fenders, a crease that runs along the car's sides and ribbed contours in its doors and front fascia. In layman's terms, geo-mechanical is a hard-edged, industrial look.

Inside, styling is one part futuristic and two parts sporty with a dash of luxury sprinkled in. With a twin-cockpit design, the interior is symmetrical and functional, with some components appearing melded into the dash while others, like the fuel and temperature gauge, protrude aggressively. Materials include soft-touch appointments with crude titanium-finish details, but on the lesser trim levels, they look a bit low-grade.

The two-plus-two Eclipse is now offered in three trim levels RS, GS and GT. The base four-cylinder engine found in the RS and GS models has grown from 2.0 liters to 2.4 liters and gone from 140 horsepower to 155 horsepower. This 15-horsepower gain feels even more substantial because the power peak is 500 rpm lower in the rev range. The high-end GT model comes equipped with a 3.0-liter V6 engine making 205 horsepower that offers split-second responsiveness and high-rpm refinement. The turbo engine has been dropped in favor of the more refined V6. Regardless of which engine is selected, a five-speed manual transmission is standard on the Eclipse. For those who desire an automatic tranny, Mitsubishi offers a four-speed automatic with "learned control" that tailors its shifting characteristics to an individual driver's style, or a new Sportronic automanual transmission that allows drivers to change their own gears without using a clutch.

The 2000 Eclipse also incorporates a new suspension system under its sheetmetal, using large-diameter MacPherson front struts for straight-line stability and a multi-link rear suspension with stronger tubular steel arms. A more rigid sub-frame and a longer wheelbase also debut. Structurally, the Eclipse is now 40 percent stronger in terms of bending rigidity, and 26 percent better at resisting twist. Safety improvements include front-seat force-limiter seatbelts, which gradually ease pressure on the passenger's shoulder and front seat-mounted side airbags that are optional on the GT model. Traction control is offered only on Eclipse GT with an automatic transmission, which leaves us wondering why it isn't available with the manual. And why can't buyers of the RS and GS models get antilock brakes, either?

Mitsubishi claims that with all these improvements, the value of Eclipse hasn't been lost. Standard equipment on every 2000 model includes power windows and door locks, an engine immobilizer and anti-theft system, microfiltered air conditioning, height-adjustable driver's seat, CD player, auto-off headlights with three-minute time delay, and alloy wheels. The mid-level GS also gets standard 16-inch wheels, cruise control, power sunroof, remote keyless entry, fog lamps, lumbar support and a split-folding rear seat. Step up to the GT and consumers will receive the larger engine, 17-inch wheels, improved brakes, upgraded seat fabric and wider tires. The power sunroof is optional on the GT even though it comes standard on the GS. Also optional on the GT is an audio package and a premium package.

Hardcore Eclipse fans are disturbed that Mitsubishi has decided to drop the turbo motor and the all-weather GSX model this year, and instead seems to be focusing on attracting middle-market buyers. And, accusations about whether Mitsubishi has turned the Eclipse into a me-too kind of car have been bandied about. There's certainly no denying the huge leap that Mitsubishi has taken with the 2000 Eclipse. From its styling to its drivetrain, the car is totally different from anything that's previously worn an "Eclipse" badge. Take a drive and see if the changes suit you.

Standard Equipment

RS (5M): 2.4L I4 SOHC SMPI 16-valve engine; 5-speed OD manual transmission; front-wheel drive, 4.85 axle ratio; stainless steel exhaust; front independent strut suspension with anti-roll

MITSUBISHI ECLIPSE

CODE	DESCRIPTION	INVOICE	MSRP

bar, front coil springs, rear independent multi-link suspension with rear coil springs; power rack-and-pinion steering with engine speed-sensing assist; front disc/rear drum brakes; 15.9 gal. capacity fuel tank; side impact bars; front and rear body-colored bumpers; monotone paint; aero-composite halogen headlamps; driver's and passenger's manual black outside mirrors; front and rear 15" x 6" silver alloy wheels; P195/65HR15 A/S BSW front and rear tires; inside under cargo mounted compact steel spare wheel; air conditioning; air filter; AM/FM stereo, seek-scan, single CD, 4 speakers, theft deterrent, and fixed antenna; power door locks; remote hatch/trunk release, remote fuel release; 2 power accessory outlets, driver's foot rest; instrumentation display includes tachometer, water temperature gauge, in-dash clock, trip odometer; warning indicators include oil pressure, battery, lights on, low fuel, door ajar, trunk ajar, brake fluid, driver's and passenger's airbags, ignition disable; tinted windows, power windows with driver's 1-touch down; variable intermittent front windshield wipers; rear window defroster; seating capacity of 4, front sports seats, adjustable headrests, driver's seat includes 6-way direction control, passenger's seat includes 4-way direction control; full folding rear bench seat; front height adjustable seatbelts; cloth seats, front cloth headliner, full carpet floor covering, aluminum gear shift knob; interior lights include dome light with delay, front reading lights; steering wheel with tilt adjustment; passenger's side vanity mirror; day/night rearview mirror; full floor console, glove box, front cupholder, driver's and passenger's door bins; carpeted cargo floor, plastic trunk lid; black side window moldings, black front windshield molding, black rear window molding and body-colored door handles.

GS (5M) (in addition to or instead of RS (5M) equipment): Rear independent multi-link suspension with anti-roll bar, rear coil springs; 4-wheel disc brakes; rocker panel extensions; additional exterior lights include front fog/driving lights; driver's and passenger's power remote body-colored outside mirrors; power tilt and retract sunroof; front and rear 16" x 6" silver steel wheels; P205/55HR16 A/S BSW front and rear tires; AM/FM stereo, seek-scan, single CD, 6 speakers, theft deterrent, and window grid diversity antenna; cruise control; remote keyless entry, garage door opener; sun visor strip; center armrest with storage, driver's seat includes 6-way direction control, lumbar support; 50-50 folding rear bench seat; cloth door trim insert; leather-wrapped steering wheel with tilt adjustment; cargo cover, cargo net and cargo light.

GT (5M) (in addition to or instead of GS (5M) equipment): 3.0L V6 SOHC SMPI 24-valve engine; engine oil cooler; stainless steel exhaust with chrome tip; premium front shocks, premium rear shocks; front and rear 17" x 6.5" silver alloy wheels; P215/50VR17 A/S BSW front and rear tires; AM/FM stereo, seek-scan, single CD, 6 speakers, amplifier, theft deterrent, and window grid diversity antenna; instrumentation display includes oil pressure gauge and premium cloth seats. (Note: Power sunroof is optional on GT, standard on GS.)

Base Prices

EC24-G	RS (5M)	16193	17697
EC24-K	GS (5M)	17428	19047
EC24-P	GT (5M)	18470	20187
	Destination Charge:	435	435

Accessories

—	Destination Surcharge: Alaska	125	125
4AT	Transmission: 4-Speed Auto with OD (RS)	650	730
	Includes oil temperature warning light.		
4AT	Transmission: Sportronic 4-Speed Automatic with OD (GS)	649	720
	Includes adaptive transmission control management; ECM/TCM and oil temperature warning light.		

ECLIPSE / GALANT — MITSUBISHI

CODE	DESCRIPTION	INVOICE	MSRP
4AT	Transmission: Sportronic 4-Speed Automatic with OD (GT)	785	880
	Includes adaptive transmission control management, ECM/TCM and oil temperature warning light.		
CX	4-Disc In-Dash CD Changer (GS)	299	399
P1	GS Sport and Sound Package (GS)	609	700
	Includes security system, Infinity AM/FM cassette with CD and rear spoiler.		
P2	GT Sun and Sound Package (GT)	1175	1350
	Includes security system, Infinity AM/FM cassette with CD and power glass sunroof.		
P4	GT Sun and Sound Package (GT)	1436	1670
	Includes security system, Infinity AM/FM cassette with CD, power glass sunroof and rear spoiler.		
P5	GT Premium Package (GT)	2262	2600
	Includes Infinity AM/FM stereo with cassette, 4-disc CD changer, leather front seats, power driver's seat, antilock brakes, front side impact air bags, rear wiper and power glass sunroof. NOT AVAILABLE with P2.		
P6	GT Premium Package (GT)	2523	2920
	Includes Infinity AM/FM stereo with cassette, 4-disc CD changer, leather front seats, power driver's seat, antilock brakes, front side impact air bags, rear wiper, power glass sunroof and rear spoiler. NOT AVAILABLE with P2 or P4.		
P7	GT Premium Package (GT)	2512	2890
	Includes Infinity AM/FM stereo with cassette, 4-disc CD changer, leather front seats, power driver's seat, antilock brakes, front side impact air bags, security system with panic alarm, power glass sunroof, rear wiper and traction control. REQUIRES 4AT. NOT AVAILABLE with P2.		
P8	GT Premium Package (GT)	2773	3210
	Includes Infinity AM/FM stereo with cassette, 4-disc CD changer, leather front seats, power driver's seat, antilock brakes, front side impact air bags, security system with panic alarm, power glass sunroof, rear wiper, traction control and rear spoiler. REQUIRES 4AT. NOT AVAILABLE with P2 or P4.		

2000 GALANT

What's New?

Mitsubishi's fourth-generation Galant features some new standard and optional equipment, like cruise-control memory function, an in-dash CD player, larger tires and four new colors.

Review

Mitsubishi has done a lot of work lately to bring its bread-and-butter vehicle up to snuff with the hot-selling competitors that had been beating it in the sales game during the past few years. The all-new Galant debuted last year, and featured V6 power, BMW knock-off styling, and lots of standard equipment to combat its opponents. It was tailored to appease power-hungry Americans by offering a choice of two engines: a high-torque four-cylinder or a 195-horsepower V6.

Going fast is second nature to the Galant. The vehicle exhibits a smooth powertrain with a Saab-like thrust of forward movement the second your foot hits the gas. Its torquey, 2.4-liter, 16-valve, SOHC four-cylinder engine produces 145 horsepower and 155 foot-pounds of torque,

MITSUBISHI   GALANT

CODE	DESCRIPTION	INVOICE	MSRP

and quells noise and vibration nicely. The 3.0-liter, 24-valve, SOHC V6 makes 205 foot-pounds of torque at 4,500 rpm, placing it on par power-wise with the Toyota Camry, Honda Accord and Mazda 626.

The Galant is offered in four trim levels: DE, ES, LS and GTZ. The economical DE is built with the four-cylinder engine, the ES can be purchased with either a four-banger or a V6, and the luxury LS and sport-tuned GTZ both come with V6 power standard. All Galants come with a standard automatic transmission (stick shifts are available on four-cylinder models), A/C, power package, variable intermittent wipers, AM/FM/CD stereo, auxiliary power outlet, tinted glass and dual trip odometers. Safety features include available front seat-mounted side airbags, automatic headlight shut-off and a collapsible steering column.

The ES model comes with a cruise-control memory function, an optional sunroof, and an optional premium package with adjustable driver's lumbar support and an Infinity sound system. If you opt for the LS, you'll automatically receive the premium package, standard V6 engine and traction control. The GTZ model also comes with a V6 engine, color-keyed grille, rear spoiler, leather trim and black-on-white instrument gauges. These refinements, coupled with the sport-tuned suspension, make GTZ the high-end Galant for those seeking crisp handling and the most fun-to-drive ride in the line.

Inside, styling is clean and simple, with appealing interior wood appointments, a thick, leather-wrapped steering wheel, and functional interior controls. The stereo unit is positioned above the automatic climate controls for easier driver access and the console-mounted cupholders don't block any part of the dashboard and hold a variety of drinks, including an extremely fat water bottle. The front center armrest also folds rearward to serve as a cupholder for those in the back seat. Seating in the Galant is comfortable with a good driving position and excellent visibility. This year's lumbar support option should make things even better.

Additions to all 2000 Galants include a new anti-theft engine immobilizer, continuous seatbelt warning lamp, rear center three-point safety belt, larger 195/65R15 tires, front cupholder spacers, four new exterior color choices, and an optional in-dash, six-disc CD changer.

With its balance of styling, performance and standard content, the Galant is an impressive vehicle and one we would recommend to those in the market for a fun family sedan.

2000 Mitsubishi Galant

Standard Equipment

DE (4A): 2.4L I4 SOHC SMPI 16-valve engine; 4-speed electronic OD auto transmission with lock-up; 90-amp alternator; front-wheel drive, 4.04 axle ratio; stainless steel exhaust; front independent strut suspension with anti-roll bar, front coil springs, rear independent multi-link

290   www.edmunds.com   EDMUND'S® NEW CARS

GALANT — MITSUBISHI

suspension with rear coil springs; power rack-and-pinion steering; front disc/rear drum brakes; 16.3 gal. capacity fuel tank; side impact bars; front and rear body-colored bumpers; black bodyside molding; monotone paint; aero-composite halogen auto off headlamps; driver's and passenger's manual remote black outside mirrors; front and rear 15" x 6" steel wheels; P195/65HR15 A/S BSW front and rear tires; inside under cargo mounted compact steel spare wheel; air filter; AM/FM stereo, clock, seek-scan, single CD, 4 speakers, and fixed antenna; power door locks with 2 stage unlock, child safety rear door locks, remote hatch/trunk release, remote fuel release; 2 power accessory outlets, driver's foot rest, retained accessory power; instrumentation display includes tachometer, water temperature gauge, trip odometer; warning indicators include oil pressure, battery, lights on, key in ignition; driver's and passenger's front airbags; ignition disable; tinted windows, power front and rear windows with driver's 1-touch down; fixed interval front windshield wipers, sun visor strip, rear window defroster; seating capacity of 5, front bucket seats, adjustable headrests, center armrest with storage, driver's seat includes 8-way direction control, passenger's seat includes 4-way direction control; rear bench seat; front height adjustable seatbelts; cloth seats, vinyl door trim insert, full cloth headliner, full carpet floor covering with carpeted floor mats, plastic/rubber gear shift knob; interior lights include dome light with fade, front reading lights; steering wheel with tilt adjustment; driver's side vanity mirror; day/night rearview mirror; full floor console, locking glove box, front and rear cupholders, instrument panel bin, driver's and passenger's door bins; carpeted cargo floor, cargo light; black grille, black side window moldings, black front windshield molding, black rear window molding and body-colored door handles.

ES (4A) (in addition to or instead of DE (4A) equipment): Rear independent multi-link suspension with anti-roll bar; body-colored bodyside molding; additional exterior lights include front fog/driving lights; driver's and passenger's power remote body-colored outside mirrors; air conditioning; AM/FM stereo, clock, seek-scan, single CD, 4 speakers, and window grid antenna; cruise control; remote keyless entry; panic alarm; variable intermittent front windshield wipers; folding rear split-bench seat with fixed headrests; premium cloth seats, cloth door trim insert; simulated wood trim on instrument panel; leather-wrapped steering wheel with tilt adjustment; dual illuminated vanity mirrors; locking glove box with light; chrome grille and chrome side window moldings.

ES V6 (4A) (in addition to or instead of ES (4A) equipment): 3.0L V6 SOHC SMPI 24-valve engine; 3.5 axle ratio; 4-wheel disc brakes with 4-wheel antilock braking system; driver's and passenger's power remote body-colored heated outside mirrors; front and rear 16" x 6" steel wheels and P205/55HR16 A/S BSW front and rear tires.

LS V6 (4A) (in addition to or instead of ES V6 (4A) equipment): Traction control; rear wing spoiler; front power sliding and tilting glass sunroof with sunshade; body-colored bodyside cladding; front and rear 16" x 6" alloy wheels; premium AM/FM stereo, clock, seek-scan, single CD, 7 premium speakers, amplifier, theft deterrent, and window grid diversity antenna; driver's and front passenger's seat mounted side airbags; driver's seat includes 6-way power seat, lumbar support; leather seats, leatherette door trim insert; leather-wrapped gear shift knob; 2 seat back storage pockets and body-colored grille.

GTZ-V6 (4A) (in addition to or instead of LS V6 (4A) equipment): Sport ride suspension and garage door opener.

Base Prices

CODE	DESCRIPTION	INVOICE	MSRP
GA41-B	DE (4A)	15963	17357
GA41-G	ES (4A)	16615	18257
GA41-K	ES V6 (4A)	18338	20157
GA41-X	LS V6 (4A)	21524	23657
GA41-P	GTZ-V6 (4A)	21617	23757
Destination Charge:		435	435

MITSUBISHI   GALANT / MIRAGE

CODE	DESCRIPTION	INVOICE	MSRP

Accessories

—	Destination Charge (Alaska)	125	125
P1	ES Premium Package (ES 4-Cyl)	2257	2600
	Includes antilock brakes, side air bag system, security system, wheels: 15" alloy, rear seat heater ducts, heated door mirrors, power glass sunroof, driver's adjustable lumbar support and Infinity AM/FM stereo with CD. NOT AVAILABLE with SR.		
P2	ES-V6 Premium Package (ES V6)	2087	2400
	Includes side air bag system, security system, wheels: 16" alloy, power glass sunroof, driver's adjustable lumbar support and Infinity AM/FM stereo with CD. NOT AVAILABLE with SR.		
SR	Power Glass Sunroof (ES)	697	850
	NOT AVAILABLE with P1, P2.		

2000 MIRAGE

2000 Mitsubishi Mirage

What's New?

The DE Sedan now comes with the more powerful 1.8-liter engine in place of last year's base 1.5-liter powerplant. All DE models (sedans and coupes) get a host of luxury items and larger brakes as standard equipment. The LS Sedan also gets a few more standard goodies for 2000.

Review

Available as a coupe or sedan in DE and LS trim levels, the Mirage is now better-equipped to battle with sales favorites like the Honda Civic and Toyota Corolla as well as Korean upstarts like the Kia Sephia and Hyundai Accent.

The entry-level DE Coupe has a 92-horsepower, 1.5-liter engine mated to either a five-speed manual transmission or four-speed automatic transmission. The DE Sedan now comes with the larger 1.8-liter, 113-horsepower engine that was formerly reserved for LS trim models. This same

MIRAGE MITSUBISHI

sedan also has a front stabilizer bar that helps the car move nimbly between potholes and slow-moving traffic, and both the DE Coupe and Sedan have a four-wheel independent suspension. Several standard features have been added to the DE trim level this year, including tilt steering, remote outside mirrors and intermittent wipers.

All LS models, which are meant to appeal to the features-conscious crowd, have the larger 1.8-liter engine, front bucket seats, a six-way adjustable driver's seat, rear window defroster, a body-colored grille and body-colored door handles. Other upgrades include alloy wheels, a chrome-tipped exhaust, tilt steering, a stereo with integrated CD controls and, new for the 2000 LS Sedan, a standard sunroof.

If you want your Mirage with some "sport" thrown in, the LS Coupe can be ordered with an optional sport package that includes a rear spoiler, chrome tailpipe extension, a sunroof and side air dams. All LS Coupes come with air conditioning, an AM/FM stereo with CD player, a tachometer and a split folding rear bench seat for increased cargo capacity.

Regardless of the specific body style and trim level you order, you can be sure your Mirage won't blend in with the other small cars in the parking lot. Its shape offers more personality than the Toyota Corolla or Honda Civic, giving the Mirage "coolest-looking kid on the block" status in the subcompact class. Too bad it's not the most refined, best-handling or lowest-priced car in its class and too bad the Mirage's crash-test scores are less than impressive.

Generally we like the Mirage. It's got a good look, a quiet interior, stable road characteristics and comfy seats. But the Kia Sephia is still a better value and the redesigned 2000 Accent looks to be a strong contender in terms of refinement, interior space and overall design. And while the Civic and Corolla may not be as sexy, they do come with legendary reliability at a comparable price. Competition in the small-car segment continues to heat up, and we fear the Mirage may be fading.

Standard Equipment

DE COUPE (5M): 1.5L I4 SOHC MPI 12-valve engine; 5-speed OD manual transmission; 420-amp battery; 80-amp alternator; front-wheel drive, 3.72 axle ratio; stainless steel exhaust; front independent strut suspension front coil springs, rear independent multi-link suspension with rear coil springs; power rack-and-pinion steering; front disc/rear drum brakes; 12.4 gal. capacity fuel tank; side impact bars; front and rear body-colored bumpers; monotone paint; aero-composite halogen headlamps; driver's and passenger's manual remote black folding outside mirrors; front and rear 14" x 5.5" steel wheels; P175/65SR14 A/S BSW front tires; inside under cargo mounted compact steel spare wheel; radio prep, manual retractable antenna; remote hatch/trunk release, remote fuel release; 1 power accessory outlet, driver's foot rest, smokers' package; instrumentation display includes water temperature gauge, in-dash clock, trip odometer; warning indicators include oil pressure, battery, lights on, key in ignition, low fuel, door ajar; driver's and passenger's front airbags; tinted windows, fixed rear windows; fixed interval front windshield wipers, rear window defroster; seating capacity of 5, front bucket seats, fixed headrests, driver's seat includes 6-way direction control, passenger's seat includes 4-way direction control; rear bench seat with fixed headrests; front height adjustable seatbelts; cloth seats, cloth door trim insert, full cloth headliner, full carpet floor covering; interior lights include dome light; steering wheel with tilt adjustment; vanity mirrors; day/night rearview mirror; full floor console, glove box, front cupholder, instrument panel bin, driver's and passenger's door bins; carpeted cargo floor, cargo light; black side window moldings, black front windshield molding, black rear window molding and black door handles.

LS COUPE (5M) (in addition to or instead of DE COUPE (5M) equipment): 1.8L I4 SOHC MPI 16-valve engine; 433-amp battery; rear independent multi-link suspension with rear coil springs; rocker panel extensions; driver's and passenger's power remote body-colored folding outside mirrors; P185/65HR14 A/S BSW front and rear tires; air conditioning; AM/FM stereo, seek-scan, single CD, 4 speakers, and manual retractable antenna; cruise control; instrumentation display includes tachometer; variable intermittent front windshield wipers; front sports seats, adjustable headrests, center armrest with storage; 60-40 folding rear bench seat with fixed headrests;

MITSUBISHI MIRAGE

interior lights include front reading lights; mini overhead console with storage and body-colored door handles.

DE SEDAN (5M) (in addition to or instead of DE COUPE (5M) equipment): 13.2 gal. capacity fuel tank; passenger's manual outside mirror; power door locks, child safety rear door locks, power front and rear windows and body-colored grille.

LS SEDAN (4A) (in addition to or instead of LS COUPE (5M) equipment): 4-speed electronic OD auto transmission with lock-up; stainless steel exhaust with chrome tip; front power sliding and tilting glass sunroof with sunshade; passenger's manual remote outside mirror and front and rear 14" x 5.5" alloy wheels.

Base Prices

CODE	DESCRIPTION	INVOICE	MSRP
M621-B	DE Coupe (5M)	10815	11757
M621-G	LS Coupe (5M)	13433	14607
M641-B	DE Sedan (5M)	12870	13987
M641-G	LS Sedan (4A)	15587	16947
	Destination Charge:	425	425

Accessories

CODE	DESCRIPTION	INVOICE	MSRP
4AT	Transmission: 4-Speed Automatic with ELC (DE Coupe)	735	800
4AT	Transmission: 4-Speed Automatic with ELC (DE Sedan)	729	800
4AT	Transmission: 4-Speed Automatic with ELC (LS Coupe)	739	800
AC	Air Conditioning (DE Coupe)	720	880
C3	Single Disc CD Player (LS Sedan)	299	399
CN	Cargo Net	23	36
FM	Floor Mats (Coupe)	43	65
KE	Keyless Entry System (All Except DE Coupe)	161	248
MG	Mudguards	53	81
P1	Convenience Package (DE Coupe). Includes air conditioning, full cloth seat, power door locks, power windows, 60/40 split fold rear seat and AM/FM stereo with CD. NOT AVAILABLE with R9, R3.	1491	1820
P1	Premium Package (DE Sedan). Includes dual power color-keyed mirrors, color-keyed door handles, cruise control, variable intermittent wipers, tachometer and map lamps.	336	410
P2	Sport Package (LS Coupe). Includes side air dam, white face guages, wheels: 14" alloy, chrome exhaust tip, fog lights and rear spoiler.	844	1030
R3	Radio: AM/FM Stereo Without CD Controls (DE Coupe). Includes cassette and clock. NOT AVAILABLE with P1.	247	352
R9	Radio: AM/FM Stereo with CD (DE Coupe). NOT AVAILABLE with P1.	333	473
WL	Wheel Locks (LS)	26	37

ALTIMA — NISSAN

| CODE | DESCRIPTION | INVOICE | MSRP |

2000 ALTIMA

2000 Nissan Altima

What's New?

2000 Altimas receive fresh sheetmetal, comfort and convenience enhancements, engine refinements, and a revised suspension.

Review

When Nissan introduced the Infiniti J30-like Altima in 1993, it was an instant hit. The term "affordable luxury" became synonymous with Altima, and those who wouldn't have been caught dead in the Altima's predecessor, the unloved Stanza, rushed out in droves to buy this car. Five years later, the Altima was redesigned with the goal of improving on its original style and appeal. Unfortunately, the second-generation Altima didn't have the attractive looks and luxurious feel that the original car possessed and sales suffered.

So for 2000, Nissan has made substantial refinements to the Altima. Styling has been upgraded, thanks to an aggressive front fascia, new grille and integrated clear-lens headlights with turn signals and cornering lamps in a one-piece, wraparound design. They've also lowered the front of the car, giving the vehicle a more pronounced rake. Altima's rear fascia has been redesigned as well, with bright red taillights, a new rear decklid finisher, and 2 inches of increased length.

Inside, new seats improve driving comfort and a new instrument cluster exhibits an LCD odometer with dual trip meters. Also provided is a revamped center console for cars equipped with automatic transmissions, a vehicle immobilizer system, redesigned sunvisors and new audio units. Side airbags are now standard on the GLE model and optional on the GXE and SE trims.

Altima's 2.4-liter inline four-cylinder engine has been refined, resulting in quicker acceleration, performance enhancements, increased horsepower and more torque down low in the rev range. All trims have a standard five-speed manual transmission except the GLE, which receives a four-speed automatic standard. Noise, vibration and harshness levels have also been reduced, thanks to new outside mirrors, use of expandable foam in windshield pillars, roof rails, front doors and sills, a new driveshaft design, and thicker glass.

Increased stiffness in the four-wheel independent-strut suspension helps, too. This responsive setup, with coil springs and rear Super Toe Control, features a new acceleration-sensitive strut

NISSAN

ALTIMA

CODE	DESCRIPTION	INVOICE	MSRP

design (available with 16-inch wheels and tires only) that automatically adjusts dampening firmness to improve handling.

With these improvements, the Altima should prove to be fun to drive, offering plenty of entertainment for enthusiasts. Its crisp steering and peppy engine will provide drivers with the tools to go fast and have a good time. And if you didn't like the car's styling before, take a gander at this new and improved Altima before crossing it off your shopping list.

Standard Equipment

XE (5M): 2.4L I4 DOHC SMPI 16-valve engine; 5-speed OD manual transmission; 100-amp alternator; front-wheel drive, 3.62 axle ratio; steel exhaust; front independent strut suspension with anti-roll bar, front coil springs, rear independent strut suspension with anti-roll bar, rear coil springs; power rack-and-pinion steering; front disc/rear drum brakes; 15.9 gal. capacity fuel tank; side impact bars; front and rear body-colored bumpers; body-colored bodyside molding; monotone paint; aero-composite halogen headlamps; driver's and passenger's power remote black outside mirrors; front and rear 15" x 6" steel wheels; P195/65SR15 A/S BSW front and rear tires; inside under cargo mounted compact steel spare wheel; rear heat ducts; fixed antenna; child safety rear door locks, remote hatch/trunk release, remote fuel release; 1 power accessory outlet, driver's foot rest, smokers' package; instrumentation display includes tachometer, water temperature gauge, trip odometer; warning indicators include oil pressure, battery, lights on, key in ignition, low fuel, door ajar; driver's and passenger's front airbags; ignition disable; tinted windows, power front and rear windows with driver's 1-touch down; fixed interval front windshield wipers, sun visor strip, rear window defroster; seating capacity of 5, front bucket seats, adjustable headrests, center armrest with storage, driver's seat includes 4-way direction control, passenger's seat includes 4-way direction control; rear bench seat with fixed headrests; front height adjustable seatbelts with front pretensioners; cloth seats, full cloth headliner, full carpet floor covering, plastic/rubber gear shift knob; interior lights include dome light; steering wheel with tilt adjustment; dual auxiliary visors, passenger's side vanity mirror; day/night rearview mirror; full floor console, glove box, front cupholder, instrument panel bin, driver's and passenger's door bins; carpeted cargo floor, carpeted trunk lid, cargo light; chrome grille, chrome side window moldings, black front windshield molding, black rear window molding and body-colored door handles.

GXE (5M) (in addition to or instead of XE (5M) equipment): Driver's and passenger's power remote body-colored outside mirrors; AM/FM stereo, clock, seek-scan, single CD, 4 speakers, and fixed antenna; driver's seat includes 8-way direction control; 60-40 folding rear bench seat with fixed headrests, center armrest; premium cloth seats, cloth door trim insert, simulated wood trim on instrument panel, instrument panel covered bin and 1 seat back storage pocket.

SE (5M) (in addition to or instead of GXE (5M) equipment): Battery with run down protection; steel exhaust with chrome tip; sport ride suspension; 4-wheel disc brakes; rear wing spoiler, additional exterior lights include front fog/driving lights; front and rear 16" x 6" silver alloy wheels; P205/55HR16 A/S BSW front and rear tires; air conditioning; AM/FM stereo, clock, seek-scan, cassette, single CD, 6 speakers, amplifier, and fixed antenna; cruise control with steering wheel controls; power door locks with 2 stage unlock, remote keyless entry, power remote hatch/trunk release, garage door opener; ignition disable, panic alarm; variable intermittent front windshield wipers; driver's seat includes 8-way direction control, lumbar support; leather-wrapped gear shift knob; interior lights include dome light with fade, front reading lights, illuminated entry; leather-wrapped steering wheel with tilt adjustment; dual illuminated vanity mirrors; mini overhead console with storage, locking glove box with light, cargo net and body-colored grille.

GLE (4A) (in addition to or instead of SE (4A) equipment): 4-speed electronic OD auto transmission with lock-up; comfort ride suspension; front disc/rear drum brakes; P205/55TR16 A/S BSW front and rear tires; 2 power accessory outlets, driver's and front passenger's door mounted side airbags; driver's seat includes 6-way power seat, lumbar support; leather seats, leatherette door trim insert and chrome grille.

ALTIMA / MAXIMA — NISSAN

CODE	DESCRIPTION	INVOICE	MSRP

Base Prices

Code	Description	Invoice	MSRP
05650	XE (5M)	14547	15140
05750	GXE (5M)	15016	16340
05950	SE (5M)	16935	18640
05810	GLE (4A)	18525	20390
	Destination Charge:	520	520

Accessories

Code	Description	Invoice	MSRP
—	Transmission: 4-Speed Automatic (GXE)	735	800
—	Transmission: 4-Speed Automatic (SE) *Includes rear cupholders and power outlet.*	727	800
—	Transmission: 4-Speed Automatic (XE)	768	800
B07	Antilock Braking System (GXE/SE/GLE) REQUIRES S01.	454	499
F02	XE Option Package (XE) *Includes CFC-Free air conditioning, cruise control and AM/FM stereo with CD.*	1734	1999
G03	Appearance and Convenience Package (GXE) *Includes strut tower brace, AM/FM stereo with CD and cassette, tires: 16", wheels: 16" alloy, luxury tuned suspension and cargo net. REQUIRES V01.*	519	599
H01	Immobilizer Enhancement System (SE/GLE)	172	199
J01	Power Sliding Glass Sunroof (GXE/SE/GLE) *REQUIRES G03 and V01 (GXE).*	737	849
K02	Color-Keyed Rear Spoiler (GXE/GLE)	289	409
L92	Floor Mats	58	79
M02	Splash Guards (GXE/SE/GLE)	63	89
P94	Fog Lights (XE/GXE)	234	299
S01	Front Side Airbags (GXE/SE)	227	249
V01	GXE VOP Package (GXE) *Includes slant cut tailpipe, CFC-Free air conditioning, AM/FM stereo with CD, cruise control, power door locks, remote keyless entry system, variable intermittent wipers, dual illuminated visor vanity mirrors, locking and lighted glove box, dual overhead map lamps, battery saver system, sunglass holder and exit fade out system.*	918	999
X03	Leather Seat Trim/Power Driver's Seat (SE) *REQUIRES S01.*	1126	1299

2000 MAXIMA

What's New?

The Maxima has been (controversially) redesigned, providing more power, more room and more amenities to the luxury/performance sedan buyer. Key among the improvements is 222 horsepower from the standard V6, a boost in rear-seat legroom and an available 200-watt Bose audio system.

NISSAN   MAXIMA

CODE	DESCRIPTION	INVOICE	MSRP

2000 Nissan Maxima

Review

Sometimes, a car doesn't have to be visually appealing to instill desire. Since 1995, the Nissan Maxima has been such a car. This self-proclaimed "four-door sports car" went from beauty to beast that year, but the mechanics underneath the bodywork created a symphony no enthusiast could resist. A 1997 reskin helped in the styling department, but the real draw continued to be the stunningly smooth 3.0-liter dual-overhead-cam V6 engine, which Ward's Auto World dubbed "the best V6 engine available in America."

For 2000, a struggling Nissan releases a redesigned Maxima with more of what's good about the car (luxury and performance) and more of what's controversial (odd styling cues ladled over a dull shape). Let's start with the controversial. Wheel arches ripped off from Audi. A gaping, slat-toothed grille that would look right at home on a Buick Regal. Teardrop taillights with smoked lens surrounds (SE only) that appear out of place in a sea of body-color plastic and metal. Love it or hate it, at least it's more distinctive than the car it replaces.

Besides, from behind the steering wheel you won't care one whit what the outside looks like. This car is a sheer joy to drive. The V6 benefits from a horsepower and torque boost, from 190 horses to 222 at 6,400 rpm and from 205 to 217 foot-pounds of twisting force at 4,000 rpm. New intake and exhaust manifolds, a Nissan Variable Induction System (NVIS), equal-length exhaust pipes, and a variable-capacity muffler (that reduces exhaust-system back pressure when the engine is revved above 2,400 rpm) are responsible for the added go-power.

And rev it above 2,400 rpm you will, regardless of whether you select the standard five-speed manual transmission or the available four-speed automatic. Handling is enhanced thanks to suspension refinements. Thicker stabilizer bars have been added front and back, while the multi-link beam rear suspension gets larger, softer trailing-link bushings and a relocated lateral link that provides more stability at the limit. Four-wheel disc antilock brakes are standard, and traction control is available with the automatic gearbox.

Inside, the sport-oriented theme continues from the previous car, with the usual luxury enhancements. Midlevel SE models get titanium-faced gauges, replacing the white dials of 1999, while all models have a new 60/40 split-bench seat. A longer wheelbase creates a larger interior; rear-seat riders get 1.9 more inches of legroom, and the trunk has grown from 14.5 to 15.1 cubic feet. An adjustable center armrest is available, which, along with increased headroom and redesigned seats, improves passenger comfort.

298   www.edmunds.com   **EDMUND'S® NEW CARS**

MAXIMA

NISSAN

CODE	DESCRIPTION	INVOICE	MSRP

Maxima is available in three flavors: basic GXE, sporty SE and luxurious GLE. Standard equipment on all Maximas includes air conditioning, remote keyless entry, and various power accoutrements. SE adds racy alloy wheels, special gauges, a sport suspension, fog lights and a rear decklid spoiler. GLE models have fake-wood accents, leather seats, a 200-watt Bose audio system, and automatic climate control. A power sunroof, heated seats and side airbags can be added to any model.

A treat to drive, the new Maxima is an enthusiast's alternative to staid models from Honda and Toyota. But consider the artful Volkswagen Passat before making any final decisions on Nissan's performance/luxury offering.

Standard Equipment

GXE (5M): 3.0L V6 DOHC SMPI 24-valve engine, requires premium unleaded fuel; 5-speed overdrive manual transmission; battery with run down protection; 110-amp alternator; front-wheel drive, 3.62 axle ratio; stainless steel exhaust; front independent strut suspension with anti-roll bar, front coil springs, non-independent multi-link suspension with rear coil springs; power rack-and-pinion steering with engine speed-sensing assist; 4-wheel disc brakes with 4-wheel antilock braking system; 18.5 gal. capacity fuel tank; side impact bars; front and rear body-colored bumpers; body-colored bodyside molding; monotone paint; aero-composite halogen fully automatic headlamps; driver's and passenger's power remote body-colored folding outside mirrors; front and rear 15" x 6" steel wheels; P205/65SR15 A/S BSW front and rear tires; inside under cargo mounted compact steel spare wheel; air conditioning, rear heat ducts; AM/FM stereo, seek-scan, cassette, 4 speakers, and window grid antenna; cruise control with steering wheel controls; power door locks with 2 stage unlock, remote keyless entry, child safety rear door locks, remote hatch/trunk release, remote fuel release; cell phone pre-wiring, 1 power accessory outlet, driver's foot rest, retained accessory power; instrumentation display includes tachometer, water temp gauge, in-dash clock, trip odometer; warning indicators include oil pressure, battery, lights on, key in ignition, low fuel, door ajar; driver's and passenger's front airbags; ignition disable, panic alarm; tinted windows, power front windows with driver's 1-touch down, power rear windows; fixed interval front windshield wipers, sun visor strip, rear window defroster; seating capacity of 5, front bucket seats, adjustable headrests, center armrest with storage, driver's seat includes 8-way direction control, lumbar support, passenger's seat includes 4-way direction control; 60-40 folding rear bench seat with fixed headrests, center armrest; front height adjustable seatbelts; premium cloth seats, cloth door trim insert, full cloth headliner, full carpet floor covering, plastic/rubber gear shift knob; interior lights include dome light with fade, front reading lights, illuminated entry; steering wheel with tilt adjustment; dual illuminated vanity mirrors, dual auxiliary visors; day/night rearview mirror; full floor console, locking glove box with light, front and rear cupholders, driver's and passenger's door bins; carpeted cargo floor, carpeted trunk lid, cargo light; chrome grille, chrome side window moldings, black front windshield molding, black rear window molding and chrome door handles.

SE (5M) (in addition to or instead of GXE (5M) equipment): Viscous limited slip differential, 3.62 axle ratio; stainless steel exhaust with chrome tip; sport ride suspension, front independent strut suspension with HD anti-roll bar, front coil springs, non-independent multi-link suspension with HD rear coil springs, premium rear shocks; rear wing spoiler; additional exterior lights include front fog/driving lights; front and rear 16" x 6.5" silver alloy wheels; P215/55HR16 A/S BSW front and rear tires; AM/FM stereo, seek-scan, cassette, single CD, 6 speakers, amplifier, and power window grid diversity antenna; leather-wrapped gear shift knob; leather-wrapped steering wheel with tilt adjustment; body-colored grille, black side window moldings and body-colored door handles.

GLE (4A) (in addition to or instead of SE (4A) equipment): 4-speed electronic overdrive automatic transmission with lock-up; front independent strut suspension with anti-roll bar, front coil springs, non-independent multi-link suspension with rear coil springs; P215/55SR16 A/S BSW front and rear tires; air conditioning with climate control; premium AM/FM stereo, seek-scan, cassette, single CD, 7 premium speakers, premium amplifier, and power window grid

NISSAN MAXIMA

CODE	DESCRIPTION	INVOICE	MSRP

diversity antenna; power remote hatch/trunk release; garage door opener; instrumentation display includes exterior temp; security system; variable intermittent front windshield wipers, driver's seat includes 6-way power seat, lumbar support, passenger's seat includes 4-way power seat; leather seats, leatherette door trim insert, simulated wood trim on instrument panel; interior lights include 2 door curb lights; 1 seat back storage pocket, cargo net; chrome grille; chrome side window moldings and chrome door handles.

Base Prices

08450	GXE (5M)	19247	21049
08250	SE (5M)	21253	23649
08910	GLE (4A)	23590	26249
Destination Charge:		520	520

Accessories

4AT	Transmission: 4-Speed Automatic (GXE)	1316	1700
	Includes 3.62 axle ratio.		
4AT	Transmission: 4-Speed Automatic (SE)	450	500
	Includes 3.62 axle ratio.		
F93	Gold Badging (GXE/GLE)	123	389
H07	Radio: Bose Audio System (SE)	798	898
	REQUIRES V02.		
J01	Power Sliding Glass Sunroof (GXE/GLE)	779	899
	REQUIRES V01 and 4AT.		
K93	Sunroof Wind Deflector	42	59
	REQUIRES (4AT) Transmission: 4-Speed Automatic and V01 and J01 or V02.		
L97	Floor Mats	58	79
M92	Splash Guards	74	99
S92	Rear Spoiler (GXE/GLE)	361	479
T01	Traction Control System (SE/GLE)	259	299
	REQUIRES 4AT.		
V01	Comfort and Convenience Package (GXE)	950	1069
	Includes wheels: 16" alloy, 8-way power driver's seat, premium ETR AM/FM stereo with cassette and CD, variable intermittent windshield wipers, cargo net and integrated Homelink transceiver. REQUIRES 4AT.		
V02	Comfort and Convenience Package (SE)	1420	1599
	Includes power sliding glass sunroof, wheels: 17" alloy, 8-way power driver's seat, integrated Homelink transceiver, variable intermittent windshield wipers and cargo net.		
W08	Deluxe Seating Package	467	539
	Includes heated front seats, heated outside mirrors, low window washer fluid light, front seat side airbags and trunklid trim. REQUIRES 4AT and V01 or V02.		
X03	SE Leather Trim Package (SE)	1171	1349
	Includes leather seating surfaces, automatic temperature control, 4-way power passenger's seat, simulated leather door trim, passenger's seatback pocket and outside temperature display. REQUIRES V02 and H07.		

1999 SENTRA

1999 Nissan Sentra

What's New?

Fresh front-end styling, a Limited Edition Option Package for GXE models, and some new paint colors constitute the changes for 1999. Nissan also renamed the SE trim level the SE-Limited (SE-L) and added more features.

Review

Though it is refined, roomy and reliable, Nissan's smallest sedan has not been the success Nissan hoped for during the past three years. Offered in three trim levels (XE, GXE and SE-L), the current generation Sentra debuted in 1995 and has failed to become a hot seller because of the car's frumpy looks. In defense of its styling elements, Nissan attributes its low 0.33 coefficient of drag to the car's high rear decklid, steeply raked windshield and low hood line. The design also provides enhanced visibility and a spacious trunk. This year, at least Nissan gave the car's front-end a once-over, adding a new headlight treatment, grille and front fascia.

Unlike its exterior, the Sentra's guts have never been a problem. An impressive 1.6-liter DOHC four-cylinder engine that cranks out 115 horsepower and 115 foot-pounds of torque powers the XE and GXE Sentras. The top-of-the-line SE-Limited model is equipped with the 2.0-liter DOHC 140-horsepower engine that first appeared on the now defunct 200SX SE-R sport coupe. Smart customers looking for a fast set of wheels will pick this engine over the offerings from Honda and Toyota; the Civic and Corolla can't touch the Sentra SE-L in the fun-to-drive department.

The GXE trim level has been tinkered with this year as well and is now available with a Limited Edition Option Package that includes an AM/FM/CD audio system, remote keyless entry with selective unlocking, 14-inch alloy wheels, sport seats, tachometer, door ajar warning light, front stabilizer bar, floor mats, body-color mirrors, door handles and side moldings, and a Limited Edition badge.

Other pluses in the Sentra's credit column include standard air conditioning, power door locks and power windows on all but the XE. All models include a tilt steering wheel, two-speed intermittent wipers, side-window demisters and rear window defoggers. In 1999, Nissan adds three new exterior paint color options for Sentra buyers: Charcoal Mist, Vivid Teal and Ruby Pearl.

NISSAN
SENTRA

CODE	DESCRIPTION	INVOICE	MSRP

To our eyes, the Sentra's styling is still plain vanilla, but beneath its countenance, consumers will find a willing, reliable vehicle that is surprisingly well assembled and quite affordable. And if your taste in driving runs toward the quick and curvy, you won't be able to find a better pocket rocket than the Sentra SE-L.

Standard Equipment

XE (5M): 1.6L I4 DOHC SMPI with variable valve timing 16-valve engine; 5-speed overdrive manual transmission; 80-amp alternator; front wheel drive, 3.83 axle ratio; stainless steel exhaust; front independent strut suspension front coil springs, rear non-independent multi-link suspension with anti-roll bar, rear coil springs; power rack-and-pinion steering; front disc/rear drum brakes; 13.2 gal capacity fuel tank; front and rear body-colored bumpers; monotone paint; aero-composite halogen headlamps; additional exterior lights include center high mounted stop light; driver's and passenger's manual black outside mirrors; front and rear 13" x 5" steel wheels; P175/70SR13 BSW AS front and rear tires; inside under cargo mounted compact steel spare wheel; rear heat ducts; AM/FM stereo with clock, seek-scan, cassette, 4 speakers, and fixed antenna; child safety rear door locks, remote hatch/trunk release, remote fuel release; 1 power accessory outlet, driver's foot rest; instrumentation display includes water temp gauge, trip odometer; warning indicators include oil pressure, battery, lights on, key in ignition, low washer fluid; dual airbags; tinted windows, manual rear windows; fixed interval front windshield wipers, rear window defroster; seating capacity of 5, front bucket seats with adjustable headrests, driver's seat includes 4-way direction control, passenger's seat includes 4-way direction control; rear bench seat with fixed headrests; front height adjustable seatbelts; cloth seats, vinyl door trim insert, full cloth headliner, full carpet floor covering; interior lights include dome light; steering wheel with tilt adjustment; day-night rearview mirror; full floor console, glove box, front cupholder, instrument panel bin, driver's and passenger's door bins; carpeted cargo floor; body-colored grille, black side window moldings, black front windshield molding, black rear window molding and black door handles.

GXE (5M) (in addition to or instead of XE (5M) equipment): Black bodyside molding; driver's and passenger's power remote black outside mirrors; front and rear 14" x 5.5" steel wheels; air conditioning; cruise control with steering wheel controls; warning indicators low fuel; tinted windows, power front windows with driver's 1-touch down, power rear windows; 60-40 folding rear bench seat with fixed rear headrest; cloth door trim insert; passenger side vanity mirror and cargo light.

SE LIMITED (5M) (in addition to or instead of GXE (5M) equipment): 2.0L I-4 DOHC SMPI 16-valve engine; stainless steel exhaust with chrome tip; sport ride suspension, front independent strut suspension with anti-roll bar, front coil springs; 4 wheel disc brakes; rear wing spoiler; body-colored bodyside molding, rocker panel extensions; additional exterior lights include front fog/driving lights; driver's and passenger's power remote body-colored outside mirrors; front and rear 15" x 5.5" titanium tinted alloy wheels; instrumentation display includes titanium-tinted gauges, tachometer; warning indicators include door ajar; front sports seats with adjustable headrests; SE Limited floor mats, leather-wrapped gear shift knob; leather-wrapped steering wheel with tilt adjustment; body-colored grille and body-colored door handles.

Base Prices

Code	Description	Invoice	MSRP
42159	XE (5M)	11097	11799
42259	GXE (5M)	12880	14199
42459	SE Limited (5M)	13787	15199
Destination Charge:		520	520

302   www.edmunds.com   **EDMUND'S® NEW CARS**

SENTRA   NISSAN

CODE	DESCRIPTION	INVOICE	MSRP
	Accessories		
—	Transmission: 4-Speed Automatic (XE)	752	800
B07	4-Wheel Antilock Brakes (GXE/SE-L)	454	499
F05	XE Option Package (XE)	867	1000
	Includes AM/FM stereo with cassette and in-dash clock and air conditioning.		
G92	Wood Trim with Armrest	252	359
H04	Radio: AM/FM Stereo with CD (SE-L)	86	100
	NOT AVAILABLE with V02.		
H96	CD Player (GXE)	310	469
	NOT AVAILABLE with V10.		
K92	Rear Spoiler (GXE/SE-L)	248	339
L92	Floor Mats	53	79
	NOT AVAILABLE with V10.		
M94	Wheels: Alloy (GXE)	419	599
	NOT AVAILABLE with V10.		
N05	Remote Keyless Entry (SE-L)	131	150
	Includes select unlock.		
P94	Fog Lights (GXE)	185	249
R92	Splash Guards (XE/GXE)	63	89
V02	SE-L Option Package (SE-L)	NC	NC
	Includes 100-watt AM/FM stereo with cassette and CD, power sliding glass sunroof and vehicle security system. NOT AVAILABLE with H04.		
V10	LE Option Package (GXE)	179	190
	Includes AM/FM stereo with CD, 14" alloy wheels, body-colored mirrors, body-colored door handles, body-colored mirrors, sport seats, tachometer, front stabilizer bar, chrome tailpipe finisher, floor mats and Limited Edition badge.		

**One 15-minute call
could save you 15% or more
on car insurance.**

America's 6th Largest Automobile Insurance Company

1-800-555-2758

OLDSMOBILE

ALERO

CODE	DESCRIPTION	INVOICE	MSRP

2000 ALERO

2000 Oldsmobile Alero

What's New?

A five-speed manual transmission is now available on the Alero GX and GL, with the latter gaining a performance suspension option. The four-cylinder gets a composite intake manifold, while all models benefit from the addition of three rear-shelf anchors for child safety-seat restraints. If glitz is your thing, you can now opt for a new gold package on GL and GLS versions.

Review

Introduced to the public at the 1998 North American International Auto Show, the Oldsmobile Alero was an instant hit with the automotive press and consumers alike. Both a sedan and a coupe are available, with your choice of three trim levels and two engines. While the Alero is technically a replacement for the Achieva, this stylish compact is light years ahead of previous attempts by the division to build and market a small car.

Like big-brother Intrigue, the Alero is entertaining to drive. GX and GL models come with a 2.4-liter dual-overhead-cam four-cylinder engine that makes 150 horsepower. Standard on the GX and optional on the GL is a new Getrag five-speed manual transaxle. A four-speed automatic is also available. Optional on GL and standard on GLS is a 3.4-liter V6 that makes 170 horsepower mated only to the automatic. Both engines now meet low-emission vehicle (LEV) standards.

While neither engine is particularly quiet during operation, they both deliver spirited performance. Alero employs what Olds engineers call an Active Response System (ARS) to increase driver enjoyment. ARS is simply a combination of 16 desirable attributes, such as a stiff body structure, four-wheel independent suspension, all-speed traction control and four-wheel disc brakes with ABS. New this year is a performance suspension that previously was offered only on the GLS Coupe. As part of an optional sport package for the GL or GLS Sedan, the firmer-riding suspension rolls on upsized, V-rated 16-inch performance rubber.

Inside, the Alero is a four-fifths version of the Intrigue. Well laid-out with seating for five, this car has features such as air conditioning, power locks, rear window defogger and split/folding rear seats all standard. But side airbags, offered by some under-$20,000 competitors from Toyota

304   www.edmunds.com   **EDMUND'S® NEW CARS**

ALERO — OLDSMOBILE

and Chevrolet, aren't available or planned. On the minus side, the cloth upholstery isn't very attractive, and the leather looks and feels too much like vinyl for our tastes.

Overall, the Alero is a stylish, powerful, sporting car that is willing to play if you are. It can serve family duty when necessary, won't embarrass the owner when pulling up to a swanky restaurant, zooms confidently along when the road turns twisty, and won't break the bank when the payment book arrives in the mail. However appealing, it will need continuous refinement and a reputation for durability to avoid the destiny met by previous small Oldsmobiles.

Standard Equipment

GX COUPE (5M): 2.4L I4 DOHC SMPI 16-valve engine; 5-speed OD manual transmission; 600-amp battery with run down protection; 105-amp alternator; front-wheel drive, traction control, 3.92 axle ratio; stainless steel exhaust; front independent strut suspension with anti-roll bar, front coil springs, rear independent multi-link suspension with anti-roll bar, rear coil springs; power rack-and-pinion steering; 4-wheel disc brakes with 4-wheel antilock braking system; 15 gal. capacity fuel tank; front license plate bracket, side impact bars; front and rear body-colored bumpers; body-colored bodyside molding; monotone paint; aero-composite halogen fully auto headlamps with daytime running lights, delay-off feature; additional exterior lights include underhood light; black folding driver's manual remote outside mirror, passenger's manual outside mirror; front and rear 15" x 6" steel wheels; P215/60SR15 touring A/S BSW front and rear tires; inside under cargo mounted compact steel spare wheel; air conditioning, rear heat ducts; AM/FM stereo, clock, seek-scan, 4 speakers, auto equalizer, theft deterrent, and window grid antenna; power door locks with 2 stage unlock, power remote hatch/trunk release, remote fuel release; 2 power accessory outlets, smokers' package; instrumentation display includes tachometer, water temperature gauge, trip odometer; warning indicators include oil pressure, battery, low coolant, lights on, key in ignition, low fuel, low washer fluid; driver's and passenger's front airbags; ignition disable; tinted windows, fixed rear windows; variable intermittent front windshield wipers, sun visor strip, rear window defroster; seating capacity of 5, front bucket seats, adjustable headrests, center armrest with storage, driver's seat includes 4-way direction control, passenger's seat includes 4-way direction control, easy entry; 60-40 folding rear bench seat; cloth seats, vinyl door trim insert, full cloth headliner, full carpet floor covering with carpeted floor mats, plastic/rubber gear shift knob; interior lights include dome light with fade, front reading lights, 2 door curb lights, illuminated entry; steering wheel with tilt adjustment; vanity mirrors; day/night rearview mirror; full floor console, mini overhead console with storage, locking glove box with light, front and rear cupholders, instrument panel bin, 2 seat back storage pockets; carpeted cargo floor, cargo light; chrome side window moldings, black front windshield molding, black rear window molding and body-colored door handles.

GL1 COUPE (5M) (in addition to or instead of GX COUPE (5M) equipment): Power rack-and-pinion steering with vehicle speed-sensing assist; driver's and passenger's power remote body-colored folding outside mirrors; P215/60SR15 touring A/S BSW front and rear tires; AM/FM stereo, clock, seek-scan, cassette, 6 performance speakers, amplifier, auto equalizer, theft deterrent, and window grid antenna; cruise control with steering wheel controls; power windows with driver's 1-touch down; driver's seat includes 2-way power seat, 6-way direction control, lumbar support; dual auxiliary visors; driver's and passenger's door bins and cargo net.

GL2 COUPE (4A) (in addition to or instead of GL1 COUPE (4A) equipment): 4-speed electronic OD auto transmission with lock-up and 3.42 axle ratio.

GL3 COUPE (4A) (in addition to or instead of GL2 COUPE (4A) equipment): 3.4L V6 OHV SMPI 12-valve engine and 3.05 axle ratio.

GLS COUPE (4A) (in addition to or instead of GL3 COUPE (4A) equipment): Additional exterior lights include front fog/driving lights; front and rear 16" x 6.5" polished alloy wheels; P225/50SR16 touring A/S BSW front and rear tires; AM/FM stereo, clock, seek-scan, cassette, single CD, 6 performance speakers, amplifier, auto equalizer, theft deterrent, and window grid antenna;

OLDSMOBILE

ALERO

CODE	DESCRIPTION	INVOICE	MSRP

remote keyless entry; warning indicators include low oil level; ignition disable, panic alarm; driver's seat includes 4-way power seat, 8-way direction control, lumbar support; leather seats, leatherette door trim insert, leather-wrapped gear shift knob and leather-wrapped steering wheel with tilt adjustment.

SEDAN (in addition to or instead of COUPE equipment): Child safety rear door locks.

Base Prices

CODE	DESCRIPTION	INVOICE	MSRP
3NK37	GX Coupe (5M)	14656	15675
3NL37	GL1 Coupe (5M)	16150	17650
3NL37	GL2 Coupe (4A)	16717	18270
3NL37	GL3 Coupe (4A)	17271	18875
3NF37	GLS Coupe (4A)	19335	21365
3NK69	GX Sedan (5M)	14656	15675
3NL69	GL1 Sedan (5M)	16150	17650
3NL69	GL2 Sedan (4A)	16717	18270
3NL69	GL3 Sedan (4A)	17271	18875
3NF69	GLS Sedan (4A)	19335	21365
Destination Charge:		535	535

Accessories

CODE	DESCRIPTION	INVOICE	MSRP
1SA	GL1 Package (GL1)	NC	NC
	Includes vehicle with standard equipment.		
1SA	GLS Package (GLS)	NC	NC
	Includes vehicle with standard equipment		
1SA	GX Package (GX)	NC	NC
	Includes vehicle with standard equipment.		
1SB	GL2 Package (GL2)	NC	NC
	Includes vehicle with standard equipment.		
1SC	GL3 Package (GL3)	NC	NC
	Includes vehicle with standard equipment. NOT AVAILABLE with R7Y.		
AG1	6-Way Power Driver's Seat (GL)	271	305
CF5	Power Sunroof	578	650
	Includes electric sliding glass panel in gray tint with tilt feature. Reduces headroom. REQUIRES R7T.		
K05	Engine Block Heater	18	20
K34	Cruise Control (GX)	200	225
	Includes steering wheel controls and resume and acceleration features.		
MX0	Transmission: Electric 4-Speed Automatic with Overdrive (GX)	699	785
	Includes 3.42 axle ratio.		
R7T	Feature Package (GL)	699	785
	Manufacturer Discount	(178)	(200)
	Net Price	521	585
	Includes wheels: 15" aluminum, remote keyless entry, fog lamps, leather-wrapped steering wheel and leather-wrapped shift knob.		

306   www.edmunds.com   **EDMUND'S® NEW CARS**

ALERO / AURORA — OLDSMOBILE

CODE	DESCRIPTION	INVOICE	MSRP
R7X	Sport Package (GL)	823	925
	Manufacturer Discount	(423)	(475)
	Net Price	400	450
	Includes wheels: 16" aluminum, performance suspension package, tires: P225/50R16 performance and rear decklid spoiler. REQUIRES R7T.		
R7Y	Leather Package (GL1/GL2)	1295	1455
	Manufacturer Discount	(383)	(430)
	Net Price	912	1025
	Includes leather seating surfaces, 6-way power driver's seat, Delco AM/FM stereo with CD and cassette, feature package: wheels: 15" aluminum, remote keyless entry, fog lamps, leather-wrapped steering wheel and leather-wrapped shift knob. REQUIRES R7T. NOT AVAILABLE with 1SC.		
R9P	Performance Suspension Package (GLS)	222	250
	Includes tires: P225/50R16 performance.		
T43	Rear Decklid Spoiler (GL/GLS)	200	225
UL0	Radio: Delco AM/FM Stereo with Cassette (GX)	196	220
	Includes auto-reverse cassette, auto tone control, digital display clock and 4-speaker extended range sound system.		
UP0	Radio: Delco AM/FM Stereo with CD and Cassette (GL)	178	200
	Includes auto-reverse cassette, auto tone control, digital display clock and 6-speaker Dimensional Sound system.		
UP0	Radio: Delco AM/FM Stereo with CD and Cassette (GX)	427	480
	Includes auto-reverse cassette, auto tone control, digital display clock and 6-speaker Dimensional Sound system.		
UQ3	Audio System: 100-Watt Dynamic Bass (GL/GLS)	134	150
	REQUIRES R7T.		
Y11	Gold Package (GL/GLS)	134	150
	Includes gold-tinted front and rear emblems, "Alero" and "Oldsmobile" lettering on rear panel.		

1999 AURORA

What's New?

It's the status quo again in Auroraville, except this year Olds has added two more hydraulic engine mounts (for a total of three to better isolate engine vibrations. Other than that, a few new colors have been added (Galaxy Silver, Copper Nightmist and Dark Bronzemist).

Review

We want to like the Aurora. On paper, it seems to have everything in place to whip the competition. Strong performance, a Northstar-derived V8 engine, standard antilock brakes and traction control, svelte sheetmetal and prices that top out just over $40,000 fully loaded. Sounds great, doesn't it?

While it is a slick overall package, the Aurora could be confused with an overgrown 1995 Saturn SL that underwent minor reconstructive surgery. It weighs two tons. Its wheels still look like Aunt Polly's holiday condiment dishes. And it barely avoids the dreaded gas-guzzler tax.

OLDSMOBILE

AURORA

CODE	DESCRIPTION	INVOICE	MSRP

Yes, the Aurora has done its job setting a new image for Oldsmobile as the division's flagship model. And yes, the Aurora has been selling to expectations. (Thanks to minor improvements with each model year, it is actually on a rising sales curve.) But neither the luxury sedan market nor the enthusiast world has embraced the Aurora the way Oldsmobile had hoped. Oh, from a design and engineering standpoint, the Aurora certainly moved the needle at Olds. In fact, steering, braking and suspension tweaks over the last few years have made the car better. But from a sales standpoint, it is becoming obvious that luxury car buyers are not looking to Oldsmobile in great numbers to meet their needs.

The Aurora has lots of little luxury goodies. The right exterior mirror dips down while reversing to help the driver see the curb or other obstructions to the rear of the car. The rearview mirror has an integrated compass. A three-channel garage door opener is standard, and the Bose sound system provides an in-dash CD player. Every one that comes off the assembly line is fully loaded; there are few options.

So, what is the Aurora's competition? Olds sees the Mercedes-Benz E320, Lexus ES300 and the Lincoln Continental at its primary targets. General Motors itself positions the Buick Park Avenue Ultra and Pontiac Bonneville SSE in this segment, but those cars don't carry Aurora's cool sophistication and, hence, aren't worthy alternatives. Chrysler's LHS is nice, but lacks the oomph of a V8. The Audi A6 could be worth consideration, given its new range of powerful engines. Cars like the BMW 528i are substantially more expensive than the Aurora when comparably equipped.

Yes, while the Aurora blends enough luxury and performance into a stylish, competitively priced near-luxury sedan that can go toe-to-toe with the likes of Lincoln, we just can't shake the feeling that this package doesn't have the kind of absolutely stellar credentials needed to battle the higher-priced imports.

1999 Oldsmobile Aurora

Standard Equipment

AURORA (4A): 4.0L V8 DOHC SMPI 32-valve engine, requires premium unleaded fuel; 4-speed electronic overdrive automatic transmission with lock-up; 970-amp battery with run down protection; 140-amp alternator; driver selectable program transmission; front wheel drive, traction control, 3.48 axle ratio; dual stainless steel exhaust; touring ride suspension with auto-leveling, front independent strut suspension with anti-roll bar, front coil springs, rear independent multi-link suspension with anti-roll bar, rear coil springs; power rack-and-pinion steering with vehicle speed-sensing assist; 4 wheel disc brakes with 4 wheel antilock braking system; 18.5 gal

AURORA

OLDSMOBILE

CODE	DESCRIPTION	INVOICE	MSRP

capacity fuel tank; front and rear body-colored bumpers; body-colored bodyside molding, rocker panel extensions; monotone paint; aero-composite halogen fully automatic headlamps with daytime running lights, delay-off feature; additional exterior lights include cornering lights, front fog/driving lights, center high mounted stop light; driver's and passenger's power remote body-colored heated outside mirrors; front and rear 16" x 7" silver alloy wheels; P235/60SR16 BSW AS front and rear tires; inside under cargo mounted compact steel spare wheel; dual zone front air conditioning with climate control, rear heat ducts; AM/FM stereo with clock, seek-scan, cassette, single CD, 6 speakers, automatic equalizer, and power retractable antenna, radio steering wheel controls; cruise control; power door locks with 2 stage unlock, remote keyless entry, child safety rear door locks; power remote hatch/trunk release, power remote fuel release; cell phone pre-wiring, 2 power accessory outlets, retained accessory power, garage door opener; instrumentation display includes tachometer, water temp gauge, compass, exterior temp, systems monitor, trip computer, trip odometer; dual airbags; ignition disable, panic alarm, security system; tinted windows, power front windows with driver's 1-touch down, power rear windows; variable intermittent front windshield wipers, rear window defroster; seating capacity of 5, front bucket seats with adjustable tilt headrests, center armrest with storage, driver's seat includes 6-way power seat with power lumbar support, passenger's seat includes 6-way power seat with power lumbar support; rear bench seat with fixed rear headrest, center pass-thru armrest with storage; leather seats, leatherette door trim insert, full cloth headliner, full carpet floor covering with carpeted floor mats, wood trim, leather-wrapped gear shift knob; memory on driver's seat with 2 memory setting(s) includes settings for exterior mirrors; interior lights include dome light with fade, front and rear reading lights, 4 door curb lights, illuminated entry; leather-wrapped steering wheel with tilt adjustment; dual illuminated vanity mirrors, dual auxiliary visors; auto-dimming day-night rearview mirror; full floor console, mini overhead console with storage, locking glove box with light, front and rear cupholders, 2 seat back storage pockets, driver's and passenger's door bins, rear door bins; carpeted cargo floor, carpeted trunk lid, cargo net, cargo light.

Base Prices

Code	Description	Invoice	MSRP
3GR29	Aurora	32787	36229
	Destination Charge:	670	670

Accessories

Code	Description	Invoice	MSRP
1SA	Option Package 1SA	NC	NC
	Includes vehicle with standard equipment.		
78U	White Diamond Paint	352	395
BA5	Gold Package	156	175
	Includes gold finish on hood emblem and rear panel script.		
CF5	Power Astroroof	975	1095
	Includes electric sliding glass panel in gray tint with sunshade.		
K05	Engine Block Heater	18	20
KA1	Heated Front Seats	307	345
N98	Wheels: 16" Chrome	712	800
	6-spoke.		
QQX	Autobahn Package	352	395
	Includes 3.71 axle ratio and P235/60VR16 BSW AS tires.		
U1F	Radio: Bose Acoustimass System	775	871
	Includes ETR AM/FM stereo with seek-scan, auto-reverse cassette, CD player, speaker system with rear package shelf module incorporating one woofer, plus 6 additional speakers and rear quarter power antenna.		
U1S	Disc Changer: 12-Disc Trunk Mounted	409	460

OLDSMOBILE

INTRIGUE

CODE	DESCRIPTION	INVOICE	MSRP

2000 INTRIGUE

2000 Oldsmobile Intrigue

What's New?

All Intrigues get restyled six-spoke 16-inch alloy wheels in either silver argent paint or chrome, and the option of adding Oldsmobile's Precision Control System (PCS). The full-function traction-control unit that's standard on the GL and GLS is now available on the GX. Retained accessory power becomes standard, and GL buyers can opt for the revised heated seats on the GLS.

Review

Since being introduced in the 1998 model year, the Intrigue has played a key role in helping Oldsmobile redefine its struggling brand identity. Aimed squarely at the imports, Intrigue features a functional sedan design inside and out that delivers a minimum of glitz and a maximum of ergonomic operation. Providing space for five adults, the Intrigue offers appreciably more interior room than its major competitors, yet without the bulky exterior size or hefty curb weight.

Built off a rigid structural backbone, Olds gave its midsize front-driver four-wheel independent suspension, disc brakes and ABS. The GX is a fully equipped base model, while moving up to the GL nets extras such as a dual-zone air conditioner, fog lamps, keyless entry and upgraded mirrors, seats and sound system. The GLS pops for top-of-the-line items such as leather, fake wood trim, CD player and the like. Need more pizzazz? The gold exterior badge package and special Sterling (as in silver) Edition model offered in mid-'99 remain available for 2000.

All Intrigues are now powered by GM's new, 24-valve 3.5-liter V6 (based on the Aurora V8) that sends a torquey 215 horsepower through a smooth-shifting four-speed electronically controlled transaxle. New this year is the optional PCS driver control system that uses sensors to measure the speed of each wheel as well as steering and yaw angles. If a panic stop, quick swerve or slick pavement forces the car into a skid, the system hydraulically adjusts the individual ABS unit(s) needed to bring the car back under control.

Driving the Intrigue feels much more like driving an import than an Olds. Speed-sensitive steering offers good feedback, and the brake pedal is easy to modulate. Seats are comfy and supportive. While the car is fairly big, it doesn't feel like it from the driver's seat, thanks to responsive handling and good visibility. Understated styling provides strong family ties to the flagship Aurora in the headlights, front fascia and rear quarters. And Intrigue's twin-cam V6 not

310   www.edmunds.com   **EDMUND'S® NEW CARS**

INTRIGUE   OLDSMOBILE

only provides stout acceleration and good fuel economy, but it does so without the need for premium fuel, unlike many other performance-oriented V6 powerplants in this class.

Pricing is in line with the Toyota Camry LE and XLE V6, the Nissan Maxima SE and GLE, and the Mercury Sable LS. Offering style, room and power, the Oldsmobile Intrigue is one sedan priced in the mid-20s that shoppers should have on their must-drive list.

Standard Equipment

GX (4A): 3.5L V6 DOHC SMPI 24-valve engine; 4-speed electronic OD auto transmission with lock-up; 690-amp battery with run down protection; 105-amp alternator; front-wheel drive, 3.05 axle ratio; stainless steel exhaust; touring ride suspension, front independent strut suspension with anti-roll bar, front coil springs, rear independent strut suspension with anti-roll bar, rear coil springs; power rack-and-pinion steering with vehicle speed-sensing assist; 4-wheel disc brakes with 4-wheel antilock braking system; 18 gal. capacity fuel tank; front and rear body-colored bumpers; body-colored bodyside molding; monotone paint; aero-composite halogen fully auto headlamps with daytime running lights; additional exterior lights include cornering lights; driver's and passenger's power remote black folding outside mirrors; front and rear 16" x 6.5" silver alloy wheels; P225/60SR16 touring A/S BSW front and rear tires; inside under cargo mounted compact steel spare wheel; air conditioning, rear heat ducts; AM/FM stereo, clock, seek-scan, cassette, 4 speakers, auto equalizer, theft deterrent, and window grid antenna; cruise control with steering wheel controls; power door locks, child safety rear door locks, power remote hatch/trunk release, power remote fuel release; 2 power accessory outlets, driver's foot rest, retained accessory power; instrumentation display includes tachometer, water temperature gauge, systems monitor, trip odometer; warning indicators include oil pressure, battery, low oil level, low coolant, lights on, key in ignition, low fuel, low washer fluid, service interval; driver's and passenger's front airbags; ignition disable; tinted windows, power front and rear windows with driver's 1-touch down; variable intermittent front windshield wipers, sun visor strip, rear window defroster; seating capacity of 5, front bucket seats, adjustable headrests, center armrest with storage, driver's seat includes 4-way direction control, passenger's seat includes 4-way direction control; rear bench seat with fixed headrests, center armrest; front height adjustable seatbelts; cloth seats, cloth door trim insert, full cloth headliner, full carpet floor covering with carpeted floor mats; interior lights include dome light with fade, front and rear reading lights, illuminated entry; steering wheel with tilt adjustment; vanity mirrors; day/night rearview mirror; full floor console, locking glove box with light, front and rear cupholders, instrument panel covered bin, 2 seat back storage pockets, driver's and passenger's door bins, rear door bins; carpeted cargo floor, cargo light; chrome side window moldings, black front windshield molding, black rear window molding and body-colored door handles.

GL (4A) (in addition to or instead of GX (4A) equipment): Traction control; additional exterior lights include front fog/driving lights; driver's and passenger's power remote body-colored heated folding outside mirrors; dual zone front air conditioning with climate control; AM/FM stereo, clock, seek-scan, cassette, 6 performance speakers, auto equalizer, theft deterrent, and window grid antenna; remote keyless entry; instrumentation display includes exterior temp; panic alarm; driver's seat includes 4-way power seat, 8-way direction control, lumbar support; 60-40 folding rear bench seat with fixed headrests; premium cloth seats, leather-wrapped gear shift knob; leather-wrapped steering wheel with tilt adjustment; dual illuminated vanity mirrors and cargo net.

GLS (4A) (in addition to or instead of GL (4A) equipment): AM/FM stereo, clock, seek-scan, cassette, single CD, 6 performance speakers, auto equalizer, theft deterrent, and window grid antenna, radio steering wheel controls; instrumentation display includes compass; heated-cushion front bucket seats, passenger's seat includes 4-way power seat, 8-way direction control; leather seats, leatherette door trim insert, faux woodgrain interior accents on console and door trim switch plates and auto-dimming day/night rearview mirror.

OLDSMOBILE

INTRIGUE

CODE	DESCRIPTION	INVOICE	MSRP

Base Prices

Code	Description	Invoice	MSRP
3WH69	GX (4A)	20212	22090
3WS69	GL (4A)	21704	23720
3WX69	GLS (4A)	23534	25720
Destination Charge:		560	560

Accessories

Code	Description	Invoice	MSRP
—	Leather Trim (GL)	886	995
	Includes contour front bucket seats with reclining seat backs plus driver's side seat adjuster. INCLUDED in 1SC.		
1SA	Option Package 1SA (GX)	NC	NC
	Includes vehicle with standard equipment.		
1SB	Option Package 1SB (GL)	NC	NC
	Includes vehicle with standard equipment.		
1SC	Option Package 1SC (GLS)	NC	NC
	Includes vehicle with standard equipment.		
AG1	6-Way Power Driver's Seat Adjuster (GX)	271	305
AG2	6-Way Passenger's Side Power Seat Adjuster (GL)	271	305
	REQUIRES KA1. INCLUDED in 1SC.		
AM9	60/40 Split Folding Rear Seats (GX)	134	150
AU0	Keyless Remote Lock Control (GX)	134	150
	Includes illuminated entry feature, two key-chain transmitters and panic alarm. INCLUDED in 1SB, 1SC.		
CF5	Power Sliding Glass Sunroof	668	750
	Includes panel in gray tint with tilt feature (reduces headroom).		
D81	Rear Decklid Spoiler	200	225
JL4	Precision Control System	530	595
	Includes Precision Control System componentry, Magnasteer II, 3.29 axle ratio and tires: P225/60R16 H BSW. REQUIRES NW9 (GX).		
K05	Engine Block Heater	18	20
K11	Air Filtration System	22	25
	Includes replaceable filter.		
KA1	Heated Front Seats (GL)	263	295
	REQUIRES AG2. INCLUDED in 1SC.		
NP5	Leather-Wrapped Steering Wheel (GX)	107	120
	Includes leather-wrapped armrest and leather-wrapped shift knob. INCLUDED in 1SB, 1SC.		
NW9	Traction Control System (GX)	129	145
	INCLUDED in 1SB, 1SC.		
PY1	Wheels: 16" Chrome Plated Aluminum (GL/GLS)	619	695
U1F	Radio: Bose AM/FM Stereo with CD and Cassette (GL/GLS)	445	500
	Includes seek-scan, digital display clock and 8-speaker sound system powered by a rear shelf amplifier. NOT AVAILABLE with UP0, U1S.		
U1S	12-Disc CD Changer Trunk-Mounted (GL/GLS)	409	460
	NOT AVAILABLE with UP0, U1F.		

INTRIGUE — OLDSMOBILE

CODE	DESCRIPTION	INVOICE	MSRP
UK3	Steering Wheel Mounted Radio Controls (GL)	111	125
UP0	Radio: AM/FM Stereo with CD and Cassette (GL)	178	200
	Includes auto tone control and digital display clock. INCLUDED in 1SC.		
UP0	Radio: AM/FM Stereo with CD and Cassette (GX)	240	270
	Includes auto tone control, digital display clock and 6 speaker dimensional sound system. INCLUDED in 1SC.		
UQ3	6-Speaker Dimensional Sound System (GX)	62	70
	INCLUDED in 1SB, 1SC.		
Y11	Gold Package	134	150
	Includes exterior gold emblems and lettering.		

**One 15-minute call
could save you 15% or more
on car insurance.**

America's 6th Largest Automobile Insurance Company

1-800-555-2758

***Save hundreds, even thousands,
off the sticker price
of the new car you want.***

Call Autovantage®
your FREE auto-buying service

1-800-201-7703

No purchase required. No fees.

PLYMOUTH

BREEZE

CODE	DESCRIPTION	INVOICE	MSRP

2000 BREEZE

2000 Plymouth Breeze

What's New?

New colors and child-seat tether anchorages update the Breeze for 2000.

Review

Despite predictions that the Plymouth brand is doomed (Chrysler killed Plymouth in Canada and has not earmarked any new product beyond the 2000 Neon for the division in the States), the Breeze is still gusting along. The Breeze, a sibling of the Dodge Stratus and Chrysler Cirrus, was originally poised to lead Plymouth's revival as Chrysler's value brand by offering a stylish, roomy four-door sedan with a decent level of standard equipment for a low price. But that marketing plan, and Breeze sales, are faltering.

The Breeze comes standard with air conditioning, tilt steering, six-speaker stereo, rear-window defroster, remote trunk release and a folding rear seat. The short options list includes antilock brakes, power door locks and windows, power sunroof, and a choice of stereos. A five-speed manual transmission is standard and a four-speed automatic is optional.

Power comes from a 132-horsepower, 2.0-liter four-cylinder engine lifted from the smaller Neon. Also available is a 2.4-liter engine, which brings 150 horsepower and 167 foot-pounds of torque, and that's just what the Breeze needs to try to live up to its name. Sadly, a manual transmission is not available with this larger powerplant. Both engines meet California's low-emission vehicle regulations.

Driving the Breeze proves it to be a strictly point A to point B kind of conveyance. Equipped with an automatic transmission, as most are, the car is dreadfully slow to accelerate with the base 2.0-liter engine, and only marginally quicker to speed with the optional 2.4-liter motor. Handling is surprisingly good, with responsive steering and a flat cornering stance, thanks to a four-wheel independent suspension with front and rear stabilizer bars.

Interior trim is low-rent in feel and appearance, but ergonomics are generally good. Forward visibility is excellent, but the high rear deck and narrow backlight mean reversing can become a guessing game. The raucous engines make lots of racket, and road rumble is plainly evident on the highway. This is not a quiet car.

Breeze differs from the Stratus and Cirrus primarily in front and rear appearances and available equipment. When it premiered in 1996, the Breeze was a real value, giving buyers a

314   www.edmunds.com   **EDMUND'S® NEW CARS**

BREEZE PLYMOUTH

midsize-car package on a small-car budget. While it is still a relatively inexpensive car, it's no longer an exceptional value when equipped with options. Plus, buyers looking for more variety or a V6 engine will want to choose the Chrysler or Dodge models. No wonder Plymouth is living on borrowed time.

Standard Equipment

BREEZE (5M): 2.0L I4 SOHC SMPI 16-valve engine; 5-speed OD manual transmission; 510-amp battery; 90-amp alternator; front-wheel drive, 3.93 axle ratio; stainless steel exhaust; touring ride suspension, front independent double wishbone suspension with anti-roll bar, front coil springs, rear independent multi-link suspension with anti-roll bar, rear coil springs; power rack-and-pinion steering; front disc/rear drum brakes; 16 gal. capacity fuel tank; front mud flaps, side impact bars; front and rear body-colored bumpers with body-colored bumper insert; body-colored bodyside molding; monotone paint; aero-composite halogen headlamps; driver's and passenger's manual remote black outside mirrors; front and rear 14" x 6" steel wheels; P195/70SR14 A/S BSW front and rear tires; inside under cargo mounted compact steel spare wheel; air conditioning, rear heat ducts; AM/FM stereo, clock, seek-scan, cassette, 6 speakers, and fixed antenna; child safety rear door locks, remote hatch/trunk release; 1 power accessory outlet, driver's foot rest; instrumentation display includes tachometer, water temperature gauge, trip odometer; warning indicators include oil pressure, water temp, battery, lights on, key in ignition, low fuel, door ajar; driver's and passenger's front airbags; tinted windows, manual front and rear windows; variable intermittent front windshield wipers, sun visor strip, rear window defroster; seating capacity of 5, front bucket seats, adjustable headrests, center armrest with storage, driver's seat includes 4-way direction control, passenger's seat includes 4-way direction control; full folding rear bench seat; front height adjustable seatbelts; cloth seats, cloth door trim insert, full cloth headliner, full carpet floor covering, plastic/rubber gear shift knob; interior lights include dome light; sport steering wheel with tilt adjustment; vanity mirrors; day/night rearview mirror; full floor console, locking glove box with light, front and rear cupholders, instrument panel bin, driver's and passenger's door bins; carpeted cargo floor, cargo light; body-colored grille, black side window moldings, black front windshield molding, black rear window molding and black door handles.

Base Prices

CODE	DESCRIPTION	INVOICE	MSRP
JAPH41	Breeze (5M)	14603	15930
	Destination Charge:	545	545

Accessories

CODE	DESCRIPTION	INVOICE	MSRP
21A	Quick Order Package 21A	NC	NC
	Includes vehicle with standard equipment. REQUIRES ECB and DD5. NOT AVAILABLE with AJF, GWA, AR3.		
24B	Quick Order Package 24B	939	1055
	Manufacturer Discount	(939)	(1055)
	Net Price	NC	NC
	Includes front and rear floor mats, speed sensitive power door locks, power mirrors, 8-way power driver's seat and power windows with driver's 1-touch down. REQUIRES EDZ and DGB.		
ADE	Engine Block and Battery Heater	27	30
AJF	Remote/Illuminated Entry Group	151	170
	Includes illuminated entry, remote keyless entry and panic alarm. NOT AVAILABLE with 21A.		

PLYMOUTH BREEZE / NEON

CODE	DESCRIPTION	INVOICE	MSRP
AR3	Radio: AM/FM Premium Cassette	303	340
	Includes CD changer control, 8 speakers and 100-watt amplifier. NOT AVAILABLE with 21A.		
AR5	Radio: Premium AM/FM with CD and Cassette	490	550
	Includes 6-disc in-dash CD changer with control and 6 speakers. NOT AVAILABLE with ARR.		
ARR	Radio: Premium AM/FM with CD	178	200
	Includes 6 speakers. NOT AVAILABLE with AR5.		
AWS	Smokers' Group	18	20
	Includes front ash tray and cigar lighter.		
BRJ	Antilock Front Disc/Rear Drum Brakes	503	565
DD5	Transmission: 5-Speed Manual	NC	NC
DGB	Transmission: 4-Speed Automatic	935	1050
	Includes electronic speed control.		
ECB	Engine: 2.0L 4 Cyl. SOHC 16V SMPI	NC	NC
EDZ	Engine: 2.4L 4 Cyl. DOHC 16V SMPI	401	450
	Manufacturer Discount	(401)	(450)
	Net Price	NC	NC
GWA	Power Sunroof	619	695
	Includes passenger's assist handles, front courtesy/reading lamps and illuminated visor vanity mirrors. NOT AVAILABLE with 21A.		
PFL	Inferno Red Tinted Pearl Coat	178	200
TBB	Tire: Full Size Spare	111	125

2000 NEON

What's New?

Everything's new inside and out, as the second-generation Neon grows up, not old. A totally redesigned suspension and steering system, low-speed traction control, and a complete exterior redesign head up the notable changes.

Review

The race to build the first 2000-model-year production car goes to DaimlerChrysler with the all-new Dodge and Plymouth Neons. However, the company's claim that "the 2000 Neon will be the first car of the new millennium" is not accurate; remember, the new millennium technically starts in 2001. But "the first car of the last year of the old millennium" is probably too wordy for marketing purposes. Yet either way you look at it, the 2000 Neon is pretty futuristic when compared to its predecessor.

DaimlerChrysler is also billing the 2000 Neon as "quiet, sophisticated and still a lot of fun." Fun seems to be the catch word for the Neon. It's used repeatedly by the manufacturer including, "fun-to-drive handling and steering" and "fun-to-drive attributes." Its maker obviously wants people to know that while the Neon has grown up, it hasn't grown old. It's probably worthwhile for them to stress the fun factor, since the coupe version has been scrapped due to slow sales, meaning that a four-door sedan will have to suffice for all the entry-level economy car thrill-seekers.

Under the hood is the familiar 2.0-liter inline four, but improvements to the air induction and intake manifold system provide torque over a broader rpm range. A new exhaust

NEON PLYMOUTH

manifold, cylinder head and timing-belt cover also decrease overall engine noise, further boosting the new Neon's civilized character. Unfortunately, the 150-horsepower DOHC engine is no longer available.

Thanks to increased wheel travel, the ride is smoother, and it's further enhanced with premium shock absorbers and rear sway bars. The power rack-and-pinion and revamped suspension also contribute to the cruising quality. Stopping power comes from a front disc/rear drum combo, but buyers may want to opt for four-wheel discs with ABS and traction control.

You won't have any problems distinguishing the 2000 model from previous Neons. Exterior changes include new, jewel-like headlamps, a smoother roofline and updated taillamps. By increasing the wheelbase and widening the track, the new Neon offers more interior room and a more stable ride than did its predecessor. And to quote Plymouth, the Neon has tons of interior "surprise and delight" features (hey, they're not fun?) that include a radio/cassette and four Big Gulp-sized cupholders.

For such a small increase in price from a year ago, the new Neon brings a lot to the table. It appears ready to capture the compact-car crown in terms of refinement and sophistication. Now, if only they'd make an optional engine, say, a 2.0-liter DOHC with 150 horsepower. That would be fun.

2000 Plymouth Neon

Standard Equipment

HIGHLINE (5M): 2.0L I4 SOHC SMPI 16-valve engine; 5-speed overdrive manual transmission; 450-amp battery with run down protection; 83-amp alternator; front wheel drive, 3.54 axle ratio; stainless steel exhaust; touring ride suspension, front independent strut suspension with anti-roll bar, front coil springs, rear independent multi-link suspension with anti-roll bar, rear coil springs; power rack-and-pinion steering, power steering cooler; front disc/rear drum brakes; 12.5 gal. capacity fuel tank; front and rear body-colored bumpers; body-colored bodyside molding; monotone paint; aero-composite halogen headlamps; additional exterior lights include center high mounted stop light; black driver's manual remote outside mirror, passenger's manual outside mirror; front and rear 14" x 5.5" steel wheels; P185/65TR14 BSW AS front and rear tires; inside under cargo mounted compact steel spare wheel;AM/FM stereo, clock, seek-scan, cassette, CD changer pre-wiring, in-dash CD pre-wiring, 6 speakers, and fixed antenna; child safety rear door locks; 1 power accessory outlet; instrumentation display includes water temp gauge, trip odometer; warning indicators include oil pressure, battery, lights on, key in ignition, low fuel; dual airbags; tinted windows, manual rear windows; variable intermittent front

PLYMOUTH   NEON

CODE	DESCRIPTION	INVOICE	MSRP

windshield wipers, rear window defroster; seating capacity of 5, front bucket seats with adjustable headrests, center armrest with storage, driver's seat includes 4-way direction control, passenger's seat includes 4-way direction control; 60-40 folding rear bench seat with fixed rear headrest; cloth seats, cloth door trim insert, full cloth headliner, full carpet floor covering with carpeted floor mats, deluxe sound insulation; interior lights include dome light; driver's side vanity mirror; day-night rearview mirror; tilt steering column, full floor console, locking glove box, front and rear cupholders, instrument panel bin, driver's and passenger's door bins; carpeted cargo floor, carpeted trunk lid, cargo light; body-colored grille, black side window moldings, black front windshield molding, black rear window molding and body-colored door handles.

LX (5M) (in addition to or instead of HIGHLINE (5M) equipment): (REQUIRES 2*G Option Package) Air conditioning, passenger's assist handles, LX badge, color keyed instrument cluster bezel, fog lamps, keyless entry, illuminated entry, power automatic central locks, power heated fold-away mirrors, premium cloth low back bucket seats, security alarm, sentry key theft deterrent system, leather-wrapped shift knob, leather-wrapped steering wheel, tachometer, front and rear P185/60R15 BSW AS touring tires, 15" wheel covers, power trunklid release and power front windows.

Base Prices

CODE	DESCRIPTION	INVOICE	MSRP
PLPH41	Highline (5M)	11499	12460
Destination Charge:		510	510

Accessories

CODE	DESCRIPTION	INVOICE	MSRP
21D	Quick Order Package 21D	NC	NC
	Includes vehicle with standard equipment. REQUIRES HAA or 4XA and ECB and DD5. NOT AVAILABLE with DGA.		
21G	LX Quick Order Package 21G	2234	2510
	Manufacturer Discount	(668)	(750)
	Net Price	1566	1760
	Includes LX badging, air conditioning, color-keyed instrument cluster bezel, keyless entry, power door locks with central locking, power heated exterior mirrors, security alarm, sentry key theft deterrent system, leather-wrapped steering wheel, leather-wrapped shift knob, power trucklid release, power windows, premium cloth low-back bucket seats, passenger assit handles, fog lamps, tachometer, P185/60R15 BSW touring tires and 15" wheel covers. REQUIRES ECB and DD5. NOT AVAILABLE with DGA.		
22D	Quick Order Package 22D	NC	NC
	Includes vehicle with standard equipment. REQUIRES HAA or 4XA and ECB and DGA. NOT AVAILABLE with DD5.		
22G	LX Quick Order Package 22G	2234	2510
	Manufacturer Discount	(668)	(750)
	Net Price	1566	1760
	Includes LX badging, air conditioning, color-keyed instrument cluster bezel, keyless entry, power door locks with central locking, power heated exterior mirrors, security alarm, sentry key theft deterrent system, leather-wrapped steering wheel, leather-wrapped shift knob, power trucklid release, power windows, premium cloth low-back bucket seats, passenger assit handles, fog lamps, tachometer, P185/60R15 BSW touring tires and 15" wheel covers. REQUIRES ECB and DGA. NOT AVAILABLE with DD5.		

318   www.edmunds.com   **EDMUND'S® NEW CARS**

NEON PLYMOUTH

CODE	DESCRIPTION	INVOICE	MSRP
4XA	Air Conditioning Bypass	NC	NC
ADA	Light Group	116	130
	Includes console flood lamp, glove box lamp, underhood lamp, rearview mirror with reading lamps and dual illuminated visor vanity mirrors.		
ADR	Antilock Brake Group	748	840
	Manufacturer Discount	(218)	(245)
	Net Price	530	595
	Includes antilock 4-wheel-disc brakes, tachometer and traction control. REQUIRES 2*D.		
ADR	Antilock Brake Group	659	740
	Manufacturer Discount	(129)	(145)
	Net Price	530	595
	Includes antilock 4-wheel-disc brakes, tachometer and traction control. REQUIRES 2*G.		
AJK	Deluxe Convenience Group	312	350
	Includes speed control and tilt steering column. REQUIRES 2*D.		
AJP	Power Convenience Group	338	380
	Includes power heated fold-away mirrors and power front windows. REQUIRES HAA and AJX.		
AJX	Sentry Key Theft Group	650	730
	Manufacturer Discount	(369)	(415)
	Net Price	281	315
	Includes keyless entry, power door locks with automatic central locking, security alarm, sentry key theft deterrent system, tachometer and power trunklid release. REQUIRES HAA.		
AWS	Smoker's Group	18	20
	Includes front ashtray and lighter.		
DD5	Transmission: 5-Speed Manual	NC	NC
	NOT AVAILABLE with 22D, 22G, DGA.		
DGA	Transmission: 3-Speed Automatic	534	600
	NOT AVAILABLE with 21D, 21G, DD5.		
ECB	Engine: 2.0L 4 Cyl. SOHC 16V SMPI	NC	NC
HAA	Air Conditioning	890	1000
	NOT AVAILABLE with 4XA.		
NHK	Engine Block Heater	18	20
NHM	Speed Control	200	225
	REQUIRES 2*G.		
RBR	Radio: AM/FM Stereo with CD	111	125
WJA	Wheels: 15" Aluminum	365	410
	Includes tires: P185/60R15 BSW AS touring. REQUIRES 2*D and HAA.		
WJA	Wheels: 15" Aluminum	316	355
	Includes tires: P185/60R15 BSW AS touring. REQUIRES 2*G.		

EDMUND'S® NEW CARS

PLYMOUTH

PROWLER

| CODE | DESCRIPTION | INVOICE | MSRP |

2000 PROWLER

2000 Plymouth Prowler

What's New?

Prowler Purple is discontinued, replaced by Prowler Silver for 2000. Chrome wheels are standard, as is a new leather shift boot and speed-sensitive volume for the stereo.

Review

Chrysler has taken the drawing board directly into the manufacturing plant. The Prowler is simply a concept car that has magically seen the light of day, and though it's not the most impressive car performance-wise, it is a most impressive display of Chrysler's commitment to fun.

Modeled after traditional hot rods of the 1950's, the Prowler certainly looks the part, despite the federally mandated but truly dopey-looking gray front bumpers. Painted red, black, yellow or silver for 2000, Prowler is equipped with massive 20-inch wheels in back (fronts are 17s). New this year is standard chrome plating on the attractive alloys. With its extremely high sill, you'll feel like you're treading water in a pool, and with the top up, visibility is a joke. Trunk space is even more amusing — there isn't any to speak of.

The retro aluminum bodywork is wrapped around an all-aluminum frame supported by an aluminum four-wheel independent suspension, but you can't wrap leftovers with the Prowler. You can't get a smooth ride either, as this roadster rides harshly. Lousy leather-wrapped seats don't promote comfort over the long-haul, but you won't care much because the interior, aside from some bargain-basement Chrysler parts-bin bits, is delicious. And if the styling isn't attracting enough attention, you can crank up the 320-watt Infinity sound system (with speed-compensated volume control for 2000) to garner even more attention.

Prowler's powertrain somewhat disappoints. A stout 3.5-liter SOHC V6 engine, capable of producing 253 horsepower and 255 foot-pounds of torque, powers this Plymouth from rest to 60 mph quickly, but without fanfare. It's mated to Chrysler's lame AutoStick automanual transmission, which is certainly no substitute for a real manual gearbox. So, no V8 and no stick: if this constitutes the hardware of the modern hot rod, we'll take a pass. The Prowler is just for show.

But what a show. This car is guaranteed to turn heads in traffic. If you're not a celebrity but you want to feel like one, here's the recipe: buy a Plymouth Prowler. Drop the top. Cruise up

PROWLER — PLYMOUTH

and down your local strip. Wave at the gawking crowd. Just don't try to drag race any real muscle cars.

Standard Equipment

PROWLER: 3.5L V6 SOHC SMPI 24-valve engine, requires premium unleaded fuel; 4-speed electronic overdrive automatic transmission with lock-up; 525-amp battery; 90-amp alternator; tip-auto; rear wheel drive, 3.89 axle ratio; dual stainless steel exhaust with chrome tip; front independent suspension with anti-roll bar, front coil springs, brand name front shocks, rear independent suspension with anti-roll bar, rear coil springs, brand name rear shocks; power rack-and-pinion steering; 4 wheel disc brakes; 12.0 gal capacity fuel tank; manual convertible roof with glass rear window, roll-over protection; front and rear colored bumpers; rocker panel extensions; monotone paint; projector beam halogen headlamps; additional exterior lights include center high mounted stop light; front 17" x 7.5" silver alloy wheels, rear 20" x 10" silver alloy wheels; 225/45R17 front tires; 295/40R20 rear tires; inside under cargo mounted full-size temporary alloy spare wheel; air conditioning; premium AM/FM stereo with cassette, seek-scan, 7 performance speakers, premium amplifier, graphic equalizer, window grid antenna, radio steering wheel controls; cruise control with steering wheel controls; power door locks, remote keyless entry, remote hatch/trunk release; 1 power accessory outlet, driver foot rest; analog instrumentation display includes tachometer, oil pressure gauge, water temp gauge, volt gauge, in-dash clock, trip odometer; warning indicators include oil pressure, water temp warning, battery, lights on, key in ignition, low fuel, low washer fluid, door ajar, trunk ajar; driver side airbag, passenger side cancellable airbag; ignition disable, panic alarm, security system; tinted windows, power front windows with driver 1-touch down; variable intermittent front windshield wipers, rear window defroster; seating capacity of 2, front bucket seats with fixed headrests, center armrest with storage, driver seat includes 6-way direction control, passenger seat includes 4-way direction control; leather seats, leatherette door trim insert, full carpet floor covering with carpeted floor mats, leather gear shift knob; interior lights include dome light, front reading lights, illuminated entry; leather-wrapped steering wheel with tilt adjustment; vanity mirrors; day-night rearview mirror; full floor console, glove box with light, front cupholder, 2 seat back storage pockets; carpeted cargo floor; body-colored grille, black front windshield molding, body-colored door handles.

Base Prices

CODE	DESCRIPTION	INVOICE	MSRP
PRPS27	Prowler (4A)	36773	39300
	Destination Charge:	700	700

Accessories

CODE	DESCRIPTION	INVOICE	MSRP
2*A	Quick Order Package 2*A	NC	NC
	Includes vehicle with standard equipment.		
MDA	Front License Plate Bracket	NC	NC

PONTIAC

BONNEVILLE

| CODE | DESCRIPTION | INVOICE | MSRP |

2000 BONNEVILLE

2000 Pontiac Bonneville

What's New?

Brand-new from the ground up, Pontiac's flagship sedan moves onto the Cadillac Seville's platform with rakish styling and high-tech goodies such as an integrated chassis control system.

Review

Billed as "Luxury With Attitude," the 2000 Pontiac Bonneville has been completely redesigned on a bigger and better platform with an all-new look. This new architecture results in a 62 percent improvement in torsional stiffness over the old car, which provides a rigid body shell for a solid, quiet ride. Rolling on a 112-inch wheelbase, the new Bonny backs up Pontiac's "Wide Track" marketing pitch with a class-leading 62.6-inch front and 62.1-inch rear footprint.

Styling combines a steeper hood and windshield rake with an aggressive roofline to impart a decidedly wedge-like profile. But the new Bonneville still retains such traditional Pontiac design cues as cat's-eye headlamps with large, round fog lamps, a V-shaped hood, and sculpted bodyside with muscular haunches. As before, three models are available, SE, SLE and SSEi.

While the look is fresh, you'll recognize the powertrains. Standard on the SE and SLE is GM's 3800 Series II V6 that not only pumps out 205 horsepower though a four-speed automatic transmission, but also can get an amazing 30 miles per gallon on the highway. Move to the SSEi and you get a healthy, 240-horsepower supercharged variant of the 3.8-liter V6 that makes you almost forget that this full-size luxury sport sedan is not available with V8 power.

The base SE is fully equipped, with new standard features such as seat-mounted safety belts, driver and front-passenger side-impact airbags, and four-wheel antilock brakes. Other optional items have been made standard, including 16-inch wheels and tires, power mirrors and illuminated entry. The midlevel SLE adds dual climate controls, a programmable driver information center, four-wheel disc brakes with ABS, and an upgrade to 17-inch wheels.

Of course, the SSEi not only packs supercharged punch, but ups the equipment ante with dual exhaust, high-performance 17-inch wheels and tires, GM's StabiliTrak suspension system, and a Bose eight-speaker premium audio unit. You also get other high-tech goodies, such as EyeCue head-up display, variable-effort steering, and 12-way power leather front buckets with memory.

322 www.edmunds.com **EDMUND'S® NEW CARS**

BONNEVILLE

PONTIAC

Speaking of the interior, many features have been borrowed from Seville. But in the Bonneville, all controls are canted toward the driver in true Pontiac tradition, with full instrumentation backlit in the brand-signature red lighting. If your needs call for six-passenger capability, a 55/45 bench seat with center storage armrest is available on the SE (in cloth only). An all-new lineup of Delco radios is offered, as is GM's new three-button OnStar communications system.

Overall, the new Bonneville is a stylish and speedy full-size sedan built off a true, world-class platform that has won critical acclaim beneath Cadillac's Seville. If the Bonneville's racy new looks suit you, the only way to improve the breed would be to borrow the Caddy's Northstar V8.

Standard Equipment

SE (4A): 3.8L V6 OHV SMPI 12-valve engine; 4-speed electronic OD auto transmission with lock-up; 690-amp battery with run down protection; 140-amp alternator; transmission oil cooler; front-wheel drive, 3.06 axle ratio; stainless steel exhaust; comfort ride suspension, front independent strut suspension with anti-roll bar, front coil springs, rear independent suspension with anti-roll bar, rear coil springs; power rack-and-pinion steering; 4-wheel disc brakes with 4-wheel antilock braking system; 17.5 gal. capacity fuel tank; side impact bars; front and rear body-colored bumpers with chrome bumper insert; body-colored bodyside molding with chrome bodyside insert; monotone paint; aero-composite halogen fully auto headlamps with daytime running lights, delay-off feature; additional exterior lights include front fog/driving lights, underhood light; body-colored driver's manual remote outside mirror, passenger's manual outside mirror; front and rear 16" x 7" steel wheels; P225/60SR16 A/S BSW front and rear tires; inside under cargo mounted compact steel spare wheel; air conditioning, rear heat ducts; AM/FM stereo, clock, seek-scan, 4 speakers, and window grid antenna; cruise control; power door locks with 2 stage unlock, child safety rear door locks; 2 power accessory outlets, driver's foot rest; instrumentation display includes tachometer, oil pressure gauge, water temperature gauge, volt gauge, systems monitor, trip odometer; warning indicators include oil pressure, water temp, battery, low oil level, lights on, key in ignition, service interval; driver's and passenger's front airbags, driver's and front passenger's seat mounted side airbags; ignition disable; tinted windows, power front and rear windows with driver's 1-touch down; variable intermittent front windshield wipers, sun visor strip, rear window defroster; seating capacity of 5, front 45-45 bucket seats, adjustable headrests, center armrest with storage, driver's seat includes 4-way direction control, passenger's seat includes 4-way direction control; rear bench seat with fixed headrests, center pass-thru armrest; front height adjustable seatbelts; cloth seats, cloth door trim insert, full cloth headliner, full carpet floor covering with carpeted floor mats, plastic/rubber gear shift knob; interior lights include dome light with fade, front and rear reading lights, 4 door curb lights; steering wheel with tilt adjustment; vanity mirrors; day/night rearview mirror; full floor console, mini overhead console locking glove box with light, front and rear cupholders, driver's and passenger's door bins; carpeted cargo floor, cargo light; body-colored grille, black side window moldings, black front windshield molding, black rear window molding and body-colored door handles.

SLE (4A) (in addition to or instead of SE (4A) equipment): 3.05 axle ratio; stainless steel exhaust with chrome tip; rear lip spoiler; driver's and passenger's power remote body-colored outside mirrors; front and rear 17" x 7.5" silver alloy wheels; P235/55HR17 A/S BSW front and rear tires; dual zone front air conditioning with climate control, air filter; AM/FM stereo, clock, seek-scan, cassette, 6 speakers, graphic equalizer, and window grid antenna, radio steering wheel controls; remote keyless entry, power remote hatch/trunk release; retained accessory power; warning indicators include low coolant, low washer fluid, bulb failure, trunk ajar; panic alarm, security system; driver's seat includes 4-way power seat, 8-way direction control, center pass-thru armrest with storage; interior lights include illuminated entry; leather-wrapped steering wheel with tilt adjustment; dual illuminated vanity mirrors and cargo net.

SSEi (4A) (in addition to or instead of SLE (4A) equipment): 3.8L V6 OHV SMPI supercharger 12-valve engine, requires premium unleaded fuel; traction control, 2.93 axle ratio; electronic stability, power rack-and-pinion steering with vehicle speed-sensing assist; 18.5 gal. capacity

PONTIAC

BONNEVILLE

CODE	DESCRIPTION	INVOICE	MSRP

fuel tank; body-colored bodyside cladding; AM/FM stereo, clock, seek-scan, cassette, single CD, 8 premium speakers, auto equalizer, and window grid antenna, radio steering wheel controls; garage door opener, emergency "S.O.S"; instrumentation display includes head-up display, exterior temp; driver's seat includes 6-way power seat, passenger's seat includes 6-way power seat; leather seats, leatherette door trim insert, leather-wrapped gear shift knob; memory on driver's seat with 2 memory setting(s) includes settings for exterior mirrors and auto-dimming day/night rearview mirror.

Base Prices

CODE	DESCRIPTION	INVOICE	MSRP
2HX69	SE (4A)	21667	23680
2HY69	SLE (4A)	25053	27380
2HZ69	SSEi (4A)	28946	31635
Destination Charge:	....	615	615

Accessories

CODE	DESCRIPTION	INVOICE	MSRP
—	**Prado Leather Seat Trim (SE)**	756	850
	Includes leather-wrapped steering wheel, steering wheel mounted radio controls and rear armrest with storage. REQUIRES 1SB. NOT AVAILABLE with 1SA, AM6. INCLUDED in 1SC.		
—	**Prado Leather Seat Trim (SLE)**	756	850
	Includes leather-wrapped steering wheel with radio controls and rear armrest with storage.		
1SA	**Option Package 1SA (SE/SLE)**	NC	NC
	Includes vehicle with standard equipment. NOT AVAILABLE with Prado Leather Seat Trim (SE), AG2, U1P, U1Q, U1S, UW6, D58, CF5, UG1.		
1SB	**Option Package 1SB (SE)**	743	835
	Includes trunk storage net, 6-way power driver's seat, remote keyless entry: panic mode, activation verification, retained accessory power, remote trunk release and personalization; dual illuminated visor vanity mirrors and theft deterrent system. NOT AVAILABLE with U1S, D58, UG1.		
1SB	**Option Package 1SB (SSEi)**	NC	NC
	Includes vehicle with standard equipment.		
1SC	**Option Package 1SC (SE)**	2363	2655
	Includes trunk storage net, 6-way power driver's seat, remote keyless entry: panic mode, activation verification, retained accessory power, remote trunk release and personalization; dual illuminated visor vanity mirrors and theft deterrent system, leather-wrapped steering wheel, steering wheel mounted radio controls, rear Deck spoiler, wheels: 16" 5-spoke aluminum, 6-speaker sound system, dual zone auto air conditioning, 3.05 performance axle ratio, 45/45 bucket seats, Prado leather seat trim and rear armrest with storage. NOT AVAILABLE with AM6.		
AG1	**6-Way Power Driver's Seat (SE)**	271	305
	INCLUDED in 1SB, 1SC.		
AG2	**6-Way Power Passenger Seat (SE/SLE)**	271	305
	REQUIRES 1SB or 1SC (SE). NOT AVAILABLE with 1SA (SE).		
AM6	**45-55 Split Bench Seat (SE)**	134	150
	Includes floor console delete and rear air vent delete. REQUIRES 1SA or 1SB. NOT AVAILABLE with 1SC.		

324   www.edmunds.com   **EDMUND'S® NEW CARS**

BONNEVILLE / FIREBIRD — PONTIAC

CODE	DESCRIPTION	INVOICE	MSRP
CF5	Power Glass Sunroof	872	980
	REQUIRES 1SB or 1SC on SE. NOT AVAILABLE with 1SA (SE).		
D58	Rear Deck Spoiler Delete	(98)	(110)
	REQUIRES 1SC (SE). NOT AVAILABLE with 1SA or 1SB on SE.		
F83	Performance Axle Ratio 3.05 (SE)	18	20
	NOT AVAILABLE with 1SA. INCLUDED in 1SC.		
K05	Engine Block Heater	31	35
KA1	Driver's and Passenger's Heated Seats (SSEi)	174	195
N94	Wheels: 17" Chrome Plated Aluminum (SLE/SSEi)	530	595
	3 Blade.		
NP5	Leather-Wrapped Steering Wheel (SE)	156	175
	Includes steering wheel mounted radio controls. REQUIRES 1SB. NOT AVAILABLE with 1SA. INCLUDED in 1SC.		
NW9	Traction Control (SE/SLE)	156	175
	REQUIRES 1SB or 1SC on SE. NOT AVAILABLE with 1SA (SE).		
PF5	Wheels: 16" 5-Spoke Aluminum (SE)	254	285
	INCLUDED in 1SC.		
T43	Rear Deck Spoiler (SE)	98	110
	INCLUDED in 1SC.		
U1P	Radio: AM/FM Stereo with CD (SE/SLE)	89	100
	Includes programmable EQ and RDS. REQUIRES 1SB or 1SC on SE. NOT AVAILABLE with 1SA, U1Q.		
U1Q	Radio: AM/FM Stereo with CD and Cassette (SE)	178	200
	Includes programmable EQ and RDS. REQUIRES 1SB or 1SC. NOT AVAILABLE with 1SA, U1P.		
U1Q	Radio: AM/FM Stereo with CD and Cassette (SLE)	178	200
	Includes programmable EQ and RDS. NOT AVAILABLE with U1P.		
U1S	12-Disc Trunk-Mounted CD Changer	530	595
	REQUIRES 1SC (SE).		
UG1	Universal Garage Door Opener (SE/SLE)	89	100
	REQUIRES 1SC (SE).		
UW6	6-Speaker Sound System (SE)	89	100
	NOT AVAILABLE with 1SA. INCLUDED in 1SC.		
VK4	Front Licence Plate Depression Cover	9	10

2000 FIREBIRD

What's New?

New wheels, exterior and interior colors, and engine revisions for improved emissions and better throttle response on manual-transmission-equipped cars top the list of Firebird changes for 2000.

Review

The Pontiac Firebird is a car meant to convey sex appeal. Its blend of angular greenhouse lines and softly bulging sheetmetal creates the automotive equivalent of a supermodel in a silk

PONTIAC
FIREBIRD

CODE	DESCRIPTION	INVOICE	MSRP

nightgown. Unfortunately, the bespoilered Trans Am (with its aero skirting, decklid "batwing" and louvered side scoops) ruins the effect. Not to worry; the midlevel Formula provides all of the T/A's hardware and go-fast goodies in a more restrained-looking, lighter, less-costly package.

The Firebird's cockpit is a futuristic blend of style and function, and is better executed than that of its corporate twin, the Chevrolet Camaro. Dual airbags and antilock brakes are standard, and the optional traction-control system can be ordered on all models. Additionally, convertible versions of Firebird and Trans Am are available (but not as a Formula), for a corresponding boost in price.

Performance from the Corvette-derived LS1 V8 is nothing short of astounding, providing enough grunt to get the Firebird to 60 mph faster than your 10-year-old can get to 40 yards. The pushrod 5.7-liter that comes standard on Formula and Trans Am makes 305 horsepower, and a more-important 335 foot-pounds of tire-blistering torque. Want even more? A Ram Air WS6 performance and handling package for the Formula Coupes and T/A is available, featuring twin hood scoops that force cool air into the engine, resulting in 15 extra ponies. WS6 suspension tuning and 275/40ZR-17 rubber keep the Ram Air Firebird planted to the ground, while a dual-outlet exhaust system is the last thing most poor souls trying to catch you will see.

All V8 models come standard with a four-speed automatic transmission; a six-speed manual is a no-cost option. Base Firebirds are powered by a 3800 Series II V6 that makes a peppy 200 horsepower, and can be optioned with a performance package of their own. This "insurance special" includes bigger tires, a limited-slip differential, dual exhaust and uplevel steering. A slick-shifting five-speed manual transmission is standard on the V6.

With world-class powertrains and hot-looking sheetmetal at a low base price, the Firebird fries Ford's Mustang, not only at the stoplight but also at the racetrack. Problem is, Ford's beloved pony car, freshened last year, is pummeling Pontiac's performance flagship in dealer showrooms, outselling this GM F-body at better than a 3-to-1 clip. While Mustang's packaging and refinement may have earned it a wider audience, Firebird wears its modern-day muscle-car crown well.

If this powerful pony car legend has been on your wish list for a while, the time to act is now. The current F-body's days are numbered. If the Camaro/Firebird nameplates live on into the new millennium, look for them to be reborn in a vastly different form on an all-new platform.

2000 Pontiac Firebird

Standard Equipment

BASE COUPE (5M): 3.8L V6 OHV SMPI 12-valve engine; 5-speed OD manual transmission; 690-amp battery; 105-amp alternator; rear-wheel drive, 3.23 axle ratio; stainless steel exhaust; firm ride suspension, front independent suspension with anti-roll bar, front coil springs, rigid rear

FIREBIRD — PONTIAC

axle suspension with anti-roll bar, rear coil springs; power rack-and-pinion steering; 4-wheel disc brakes with 4-wheel antilock braking system; 16.8 gal. capacity fuel tank; front license plate bracket, rear wing spoiler, side impact bars; front and rear body-colored bumpers; body-colored bodyside molding; monotone paint; sealed beam halogen fully auto headlamps with daytime running lights; additional exterior lights include front fog/driving lights; body-colored driver's and passenger's manual remote outside mirrors; front and rear 16" x 8" silver alloy wheels; P215/60SR16 touring A/S BSW front and rear tires; inside mounted compact steel spare wheel; air conditioning; AM/FM stereo, clock, seek-scan, single CD, 4 speakers, graphic equalizer, theft deterrent, and fixed antenna; cruise control; power remote hatch/trunk release; 2 power accessory outlets, driver's foot rest, smokers' package; instrumentation display includes tachometer, oil pressure gauge, water temperature gauge, volt gauge, trip odometer; warning indicators include battery, low oil level, lights on, key in ignition, service interval; driver's and passenger's front airbags; ignition disable; tinted windows; variable intermittent front windshield wipers, sun visor strip, rear window defroster; seating capacity of 4, front bucket seats, adjustable headrests, center armrest with storage, driver's seat includes 6-way direction control, passenger's seat includes 4-way direction control; full folding rear bench seat; cloth seats, vinyl door trim insert, full cloth headliner, full carpet floor covering with carpeted floor mats; interior lights include dome light, front reading lights; steering wheel with tilt adjustment; vanity mirrors; day/night rearview mirror; full floor console, glove box with light, front and rear cupholders, 2 seat back storage pockets, driver's and passenger's door bins; carpeted cargo floor, plastic trunk lid, cargo light; black side window moldings, black front windshield molding, black rear window molding and body-colored door handles.

FORMULA COUPE (4A) (in addition to or instead of BASE COUPE (4A) equipment): 5.7L V8 OHV SMPI 16-valve engine; 4-speed electronic OD auto transmission with lock-up; 525-amp battery; transmission oil cooler; limited slip differential, 2.73 axle ratio; stainless steel exhaust with chrome tip; sport ride suspension; driver's and passenger's power remote body-colored outside mirrors; P245/50ZR16 performance A/S BSW front and rear tires; premium AM/FM stereo, clock, seek-scan, single CD, 10 performance speakers, premium amplifier, graphic equalizer, theft deterrent, and power retractable antenna, radio steering wheel controls; retained accessory power; warning indicators include low coolant; power windows with driver's 1-touch down; leather-wrapped gear shift knob and leather-wrapped steering wheel with tilt adjustment.

TRANS AM COUPE (4A) (in addition to or instead of FORMULA COUPE (4A) equipment): Front manual t-bar glass sunroof with sunshade; rocker panel extensions; leather seats; interior lights include illuminated entry.

BASE CONVERTIBLE (5M) (in addition to or instead of BASE COUPE (5M) equipment): Power convertible roof with lining, glass rear window; premium AM/FM stereo, clock, seek-scan, single CD, 8 performance speakers, premium amplifier, graphic equalizer, theft deterrent, and power retractable antenna, radio steering wheel controls; power door locks with 2 stage unlock, remote keyless entry; ignition disable, panic alarm, security system and driver's seat includes 4-way power seat, 8-way direction control.

TRANS AM CONVERTIBLE (4A) (in addition to or instead of TRANS AM COUPE (4A) equipment): Power convertible roof with lining and glass rear window.

Base Prices

CODE	DESCRIPTION	INVOICE	MSRP
2FS87	Base Coupe (5M)	16918	18490
2FV87-W66	Formula Coupe (4A)	21521	23520
2FS67	Base Convertible (5M)	22976	25110
2FV87	Trans Am Coupe (4A)	24366	26630
2FV67	Trans Am Convertible (4A)	28090	30700
Destination Charge:		535	535

PONTIAC FIREBIRD

CODE	DESCRIPTION	INVOICE	MSRP

Accessories

—	Custom Fitted Car Cover with Tote Bag (Firebird/Trans Am) .... Premium grade, breathable, water-resistant fabric. Includes cable, lock and silk-screened Firehawk graphics. REQUIRES WU6.	140	159
—	High Performance Lubricants Package (Firebird/Trans Am) .... Includes Castrol "Syntec" full synthetic engine oil. REQUIRES WU6.	69	79
—	High Torque Performance Differential (Formula/Trans Am) .... Auburn with aluminum cooling cover. Combination of leading edge Auburn Gear and American Axle Manufacturing technology enhances traction and helps reduce differential operating temperatures under certain driving conditions. System detects variance in the gripping force of each rear and redistributes the engine load as road conditions change, thereby enhancing vehicle performance and stability. REQUIRES WU6.	800	899
—	Prado Leather Seat Trim (Base/Formula) .... NOT AVAILABLE with 1SA, 1SB (Firebird).	512	575
—	Prado Leather Seat Trim (Trans Am) .... REQUIRES AQ9.	NC	NC
—	Premium Front Floor Mats (Firebird/Trans Am) .... Includes Firehawk logo and heavy duty custom-fitted carpeting with aggressive nubs to hold mats firmly in place. REQUIRES WU6.	87	99
—	Wheels: 17" x 9" Chrome Plated Aluminum (Formula/Trans Am) .... 5-spoke design. REQUIRES WU6.	703	799
1SA	Option Group 1SA .... Includes vehicle with standard equipment. NOT AVAILABLE with W68, W54, W55, R7X, P05, QCB.	NC	NC
1SB	Option Group 1SB (Base Coupe) .... Includes power package: power door locks, power windows with driver's express down, dual power sport mirrors, power antenna and transmission: 4-speed automatic.	1344	1510
1SB	Option Group 1SB (Formula) .... Includes 6-way power driver's seat, security package: theft deterrent system, remote keyless entry and removable T-top roof. REQUIRES QCB.	1339	1505
1SC	Option Group 1SC (Base Coupe) .... Includes power package: power door locks, power windows with driver's express down, dual power sport mirrors, power antenna, transmission: 4-speed automatic, leather-wrapped steering wheel, 6-way power driver's seat and security package: theft deterrent system and remote keyless entry. REQUIRES QCB.	2180	2450
A61	6-Way Power Driver's Seat (Coupe - Base/Formula) .... NOT AVAILABLE with 1SA. INCLUDED in 1SB (Formula), 1SC.	240	270
AQ9	Custom Bucket Seats (Trans Am) .... Includes adjustable lumbar supports. REQUIRES Prado Leather Seats.	165	185
B85	Hurst Shifter (Formula/Trans Am) .... REQUIRES MN6.	289	325
CC1	Removable Hatch Roof (Coupe - Base/Formula) .... Includes locks, sun shades and stowage. INCLUDED in 1SB (Formula).	886	995
GU5	3.23 Axle Ratio (Formula/Trans Am) .... NOT AVAILABLE with MN6.	267	300

FIREBIRD — PONTIAC

CODE	DESCRIPTION	INVOICE	MSRP
MN6	Transmission: 6-Speed Manual (Formula/Trans Am)	NC	NC
	Includes 3.42 axle ratio. NOT AVAILABLE with GU5.		
MX0	Transmission: 4-Speed Automatic (Base)	725	815
	INCLUDED in 1SB, 1SC.		
NW9	Traction Control (Base)	222	250
NW9	Traction Control (Formula/Trans Am)	400	450
P05	Wheels: 16" Chromed Aluminum	530	595
	NOT AVAILABLE with WS6, 1SA (Base/Formula).		
QCB	Tires: P235/55R16 BSW Touring (Base)	120	135
	REQUIRES 1SB or 1SC. NOT AVAILABLE with 1SA.		
QFK	Tires: P275/40ZR17 Speed Rated (Formula/Trans Am)	NC	NC
	NOT AVAILABLE with QLC.		
QLC	Tires: P245/50ZR16 BSW STL (Formula/Trans Am)	NC	NC
	High performance. NOT AVAILABLE with WS6.		
R7X	Security Package (Coupe - Base/Formula)	214	240
	Includes theft deterrent system and remote keyless entry. NOT AVAILABLE with 1SA (Base). INCLUDED in 1SB (Formula), 1SC (Base).		
U1S	12-Disc Trunk-Mounted Disc Changer	530	595
V12	Power Steering Cooler (Trans Am Convertible)	89	100
V12	Power Steering Cooling System (Coupe - Formula/Trans Am)	89	100
W54	Radio: AM/FM Stereo with Cassette and Equalizer (Base Coupe)	294	330
	Includes graphic equalizer, auto reverse cassette, clock, seek up/down, remote CD pre-wiring, Monsoon 500-Watt peak power amplifier, 10-speaker premium sound system and leather-wrapped steering wheel with radio controls. REQUIRES 1SB. NOT AVAILABLE with 1SA, W55.		
W54	Radio: AM/FM Stereo with Cassette and Equalizer (Coupe)	(89)	(100)
	Includes graphic equalizer, auto reverse cassette, clock, seek up/down, remote CD pre-wiring, Monsoon 500-Watt peak power amplifier, 10-speaker premium sound system and leather-wrapped steering wheel with radio controls. REQUIRES 1SC (Base Coupe). NOT AVAILABLE with W55.		
W55	Radio: AM/FM Stereo with CD and Equalizer (Base Coupe)	383	430
	Includes graphic equalizer, clock, seek up/down, remote CD pre-wiring, Monsoon 500-Watt peak power amplifier, 10-speaker premium sound system and leather-wrapped steering wheel with radio controls. NOT AVAILABLE with 1SA, W54. INCLUDED in 1SB, 1SC.		
W68	Sport Appearance Package (Base)	926	1040
	Includes specific aero appearance and dual outlet exhaust. REQUIRES QCB and (1SB or 1SC). NOT AVAILABLE with Y87, 1SA.		
WS6	Ram Air Performance/Handling Package (Formula/Trans Am)	2804	3150
	Includes ram air induction system, functional air scoops, specific tuned suspension, wheels: 17" high polish aluminum, tires: P275/40ZR17 and low restriction dual exhaust system. REQUIRES MX0. NOT AVAILABLE with P05, QLC.		
WU6	Firehawk Package (Firebird/Trans Am)	3559	3999
	Includes Firehawk exclusive composite hood with 2 functional scoops, 2 hood mounted heat extractors, Firehawk front fascia badge, underhood forced air induction system, cat-back stainless steel exhaust system with twin dual tips, upgraded		

PONTIAC
FIREBIRD / GRAND AM

CODE	DESCRIPTION	INVOICE	MSRP
	suspension components, interior dash plaque, exterior Frehawk graphics, two key fobs, tires: 275/40ZR17 SZ50 and wheels: 17" x 9" painted aluminum. REQUIRES V12. NOT AVAILABLE with QLC, QFK, P05, WS6.		
X10	Radio: AM/FM Stereo with Cassette and Equalizer (Convertible)	(89)	(100)
	Includes graphic equalizer, auto reverse cassette, clock, seek up/down, remote CD pre-wiring, Monsoon 500-Watt peak power amplifier, 10-speaker premium sound system and leather-wrapped steering wheel with radio controls.		
Y87	3800 Performance Package (Base)	436	490
	Includes uplevel steering, Torsen limited slip rear differential, dual outlet exhaust and tires: P235/55R16 BSW touring. NOT AVAILABLE with W68.		

2000 GRAND AM

2000 Pontiac Grand Am

What's New?

In the wake of its 1999 redesign, Grand Am gets engine improvements, interior upgrades (including a revamped center console), new exterior appearance packages and paint choices. A five-speed manual transmission has been added for four-cylinder-equipped models.

Review

Pontiac revised its volume-leading model for 1999 with an all-new car, inside and out. Boasting a bold new style and a wider stance, the sporty Grand Am bears a strong family resemblance to its big brother, the Grand Prix. One noteworthy design quirk is the use of large, round cornering lamps at the lower edges of the rear fascia, looking much like the fog/driving lamps in the front.

Overall, the new design is pleasing to the eye because the car's proportions are more balanced than the previous model. The Grand Am can be had as a coupe or sedan, in two distinct models (SE and GT) plus three option packages (SE1, SE2 and GT1). Base SE Sedans and Coupes are powered by a 150-horse, twin cam 2.4-liter four-cylinder that has been fitted with a redesigned composite intake manifold for better fuel economy and lower emissions. The

GRAND AM — PONTIAC

base cars also feature air conditioning, antilock brakes, 15-inch wheels and an AM/FM stereo cassette.

SE and SE1 models are equipped with an all-new Getrag five-speed manual transmission, a feature we'd wished for last year. (Sorry, sports fans, but the stick shift is not available with the V6.) An electronically controlled four-speed automatic is optional on four-cylinder SE1s, and standard on all V6-powered models (SE2, GT and GT1). The SE1 includes cruise, power seats, windows and mirrors, and can be optioned with 16-inch alloys, a CD player and decklid spoiler.

Once you get to the SE2, you gain a 170-horsepower 3.4-liter V6 that has been reworked for better durability and lower emissions. You also get all the SE1 options as well as traction control and remote keyless entry. Go for the sporty GT, and you'll benefit from a stiffer suspension, four-wheel disc brakes, a set of 16-inch five-spoke wheels and a unique look, including special front and rear fascias and bodyside cladding. GT1 adds a six-way power driver's seat, high-power audio system and power sunroof. Leather seating and chrome wheels are also available.

Grand Am's interior is driver-oriented, with all center panel controls angled toward the cockpit, centered around a contemporary circular cluster panel housing red backlit gauges. Surfaces are soft-touch and low-gloss while control knobs are easy to see and use. By putting money into driver-oriented hardware instead of flashy doodads, Pontiac has bolstered Grand Am's market position. This car packs lots of equipment into a well-screwed-together package. But don't look for real enthusiasts to embrace the Grand Am until a five-speed is available in the V6 GT model.

Standard Equipment

SE COUPE (5M): 2.4L I4 DOHC SMPI 16-valve engine; 5-speed OD manual transmission; 600-amp battery with run down protection; 105-amp alternator; front-wheel drive, traction control, 3.29 axle ratio; stainless steel exhaust; touring ride suspension, front independent strut suspension with anti-roll bar, front coil springs, rear independent multi-link suspension with anti-roll bar, rear coil springs; power rack-and-pinion steering; front disc/rear drum brakes with 4-wheel antilock braking system; 15.2 gal. capacity fuel tank; front license plate bracket, side impact bars; front and rear body-colored bumpers; body-colored bodyside molding; monotone paint; aero-composite halogen fully auto headlamps with daytime running lights, delay-off feature; additional exterior lights include cornering lights, front fog/driving lights, underhood light; black driver's manual remote outside mirror, passenger's manual outside mirror; front and rear 15" x 6" steel wheels; P215/60SR15 touring BSW front and rear tires; inside under cargo mounted compact steel spare wheel; air conditioning, rear heat ducts; AM/FM stereo, clock, seek-scan, cassette, 4 speakers, and fixed antenna; power door locks with 2 stage unlock, power remote hatch/trunk release, remote fuel release; 1 power accessory outlet, driver's foot rest, smokers' package; instrumentation display includes tachometer, water temperature gauge, trip odometer; warning indicators include oil pressure, battery, lights on, key in ignition, low washer fluid, bulb failure, door ajar, service interval; driver's and passenger's front airbags; ignition disable; tinted windows; variable intermittent front windshield wipers, sun visor strip, rear window defroster; seating capacity of 5, front bucket seats, adjustable headrests, center armrest with storage, driver's seat includes 4-way direction control, passenger's seat includes 4-way direction control, easy entry; rear bench seat with fixed headrests; front height adjustable seatbelts; cloth seats, cloth door trim insert, full cloth headliner, full carpet floor covering with carpeted floor mats, plastic/rubber gear shift knob; interior lights include dome light with fade, illuminated entry; sport steering wheel with tilt adjustment; vanity mirrors; day/night rearview mirror; full floor console, glove box with light, front cupholder, instrument panel bin, driver's and passenger's door bins; carpeted cargo floor, cargo light; chrome grille, chrome side window moldings, black front windshield molding, black rear window molding and body-colored door handles.

SE1 COUPE (5M) (in addition to or instead of SE COUPE (5M) equipment): Driver's and passenger's power remote black outside mirrors; cruise control with steering wheel controls; power windows with driver's 1-touch down; driver's seat includes 2-way power seat, 6-way direction control and 60-40 folding rear bench seat with fixed headrests.

PONTIAC
GRAND AM

CODE	DESCRIPTION	INVOICE	MSRP

SE2 COUPE (4A) (in addition to or instead of SE1 COUPE (4A) equipment): 3.4L V6 OHV SMPI 12-valve engine; 4-speed electronic OD auto transmission with lock-up; power rack-and-pinion steering with vehicle speed-sensing assist; front and rear 16" x 6" silver alloy wheels; P225/50SR16 touring BSW front and rear tires; AM/FM stereo, clock, seek-scan, single CD, 6 performance speakers, graphic equalizer, and fixed antenna, radio steering wheel controls; power door locks with 2 stage unlock, remote keyless entry; front sports seats, adjustable headrests, center armrest with storage, driver's seat includes 2-way power seat, 6-way direction control, lumbar support; leather-wrapped gear shift knob; interior lights include front reading lights; leather-wrapped sport steering wheel with tilt adjustment; dual auxiliary visors; 2 seat back storage pockets and cargo net.

GT COUPE (4A) (in addition to or instead of SE2 COUPE (4A) equipment): Stainless steel exhaust with chrome tip; 4-wheel disc brakes with 4-wheel antilock braking system; front license plate bracket, rear wing spoiler; driver's and passenger's power remote body-colored outside mirrors; P225/50VR16 performance BSW front and rear tires; AM/FM stereo, clock, seek-scan, cassette, 4 speakers, and fixed antenna; power door locks with 2 stage unlock.

GT1 COUPE (4A) (in addition to or instead of GT COUPE (4A) equipment): Front power sliding and tilting glass sunroof with sunshade; AM/FM stereo, clock, seek-scan, single CD, 6 performance speakers, graphic equalizer, and fixed antenna, radio steering wheel controls; power door locks with 2 stage unlock, remote keyless entry; driver's seat includes 4-way power seat, 8-way direction control and lumbar support.

SEDAN (in addition to or instead of COUPE equipment): Child safety rear door locks.

Base Prices

CODE	DESCRIPTION	INVOICE	MSRP
2NE37	SE Coupe (5M)	14567	15920
2NF37	SE1 Coupe (5M)	15674	17130
2NG37	SE2 Coupe (4A)	17806	19460
2NW37	GT Coupe (4A)	17888	19550
2NV37	GT1 Coupe (4A)	19261	21050
2NE69	SE Sedan (5M)	14841	16220
2NF69	SE1 Sedan (5M)	15948	17430
2NG69	SE2 Sedan (4A)	18080	19760
2NW69	GT Sedan (4A)	18163	19850
2NV69	GT1 Sedan (4A)	19535	21350
Destination Charge:		535	535

Accessories

CODE	DESCRIPTION	INVOICE	MSRP
—	Prado Leather Seat Trim (SE2/GT/GT1)	423	475
	Includes reading and courtesy lamps, up-level seat design, manual driver's lumbar adjustment, seat back pockets, trunk storage net, leather-wrapped steering wheel, leather-wrapped shift knob and leather-wrapped park brake handle.		
1SA	Option Package 1SA	NC	NC
	Includes vehicle with standard equipment.		
AG1	6-Way Power Driver's Seat (SE2/GT Sedan)	236	265
AU0	Remote Keyless Entry (SE1/GT)	134	150
CF5	Power Glass Sunroof (SE1/SE2 Sedan/GT)	578	650
K05	Engine Block Heater	18	20

GRAND AM / GRAND PRIX — PONTIAC

CODE	DESCRIPTION	INVOICE	MSRP
K34	Cruise Control with Resume Speed (SE)	209	235
LA1	Engine: 3.4L V6 SFI OHV (SE1)	583	655
	Includes variable effort power steering. NOT AVAILABLE with R6B.		
MX0	Transmission: 4-Speed Automatic (SE/SE1)	699	785
PY0	Wheels: 16" Aluminum Multi Spoke (SE1)	436	490
	Includes tires: P225/50R16 BSW STL touring.		
PY1	Wheels: 16" Chrome Tech Aluminum (GT/GT1)	574	645
R6B	Solid Style Appearance Package (SE1)	1509	1695
	Manufacturer Discount	(556)	(625)
	Net Price	953	1070
	Includes wheels: 16" aluminum multi-spoke, tires: P225/50R16 BSW STL TOURING, AM/FM stereo with CD and rear deck spoiler. NOT AVAILABLE with LA1, UN1.		
R6B	Solid Sun Appearance Package (GT)	1704	1915
	Manufacturer Discount	(556)	(625)
	Net Price	1148	1290
	Includes power glass sunroof and wheels: 16" chrome tech aluminum.		
R6D	Solid Sound Appearance Package (GT1)	1170	1315
	Manufacturer Discount	(285)	(320)
	Net Price	885	995
	Includes AM/FM stereo with CD and cassette, wheels: 16" chrome tech aluminum and Prado leather seat trim.		
T43	Rear Deck Spoiler (SE/SE1/SE2)	174	195
UN1	Radio: AM/FM Stereo with CD and Cassette (SE/SE1/GT)	418	470
	Includes 7-band equalizer. NOT AVAILABLE with R6B, UP3.		
UN1	Radio: AM/FM Stereo with CD and Cassette (SE2/GT1)	174	195
	Includes 7-band equalizer.		
UP3	Radio: AM/FM Stereo with CD (SE/SE1/GT)	245	275
	Includes 7-band equalizer. NOT AVAILABLE with UN1.		
UP3	Radio: AM/FM Stereo with CD (SE/SE1/GT)	187	210
	Includes 7-band equalizer. REQUIRES UQ2. NOT AVAILABLE with UN1.		
UQ2	6-Speaker Sound System (SE/SE1/GT)	NC	NC
	REQUIRES UP3.		
UQ3	High Performance Sound System (SE/SE1/GT)	NC	NC
	REQUIRES UN1 or UP3. NOT AVAILABLE with UQ2.		
VK4	Front Licence Plate Depression Cover	NC	NC

2000 GRAND PRIX

What's New?

Improvements to the base 3.1-liter V6 net a gain of 15 horsepower, as well as improved durability, reduced noise and lower emissions. A limited run (2000 coupes) of Daytona Pace Car replicas will be built, featuring unique exterior and interior details. Also new are a revised antitheft system, five-spoke silver-painted wheels, three new exterior colors and Cyclone cloth upholstery.

PONTIAC
GRAND PRIX

CODE	DESCRIPTION	INVOICE	MSRP

Review

Loaded with standard features and available in a potent, supercharged 240-horsepower edition, Pontiac's Grand Prix successfully blends form, function and performance into one appealing and affordable package. Buyers can select from one of three models: SE (in sedan form only), GT (coupe or sedan) and GTP, the latter a stand-alone model as either a coupe or sedan.

The SE is powered by a revised 3.1-liter V6 that now makes 175 horsepower (up from 160 last year). Cylinder head, camshaft and intake manifold changes provide 10 more foot-pounds of torque, and the addition of an Air Injection Reaction (AIR) system means the 3.1 now meets Low Emissions Vehicle (LEV) standards. (The supercharged 3.8 does so without the AIR system, and the naturally aspirated 3.8 with AIR now meets Ultra-Low Emissions Vehicle (ULEV) standards.) Despite the improved 3.1, we recommend the 200-horsepower 3800 Series II V6 (optional on SE Sedan and standard on GT). The award-winning 3.8 offers more power yet still delivers about 19 mpg in the city and 30 mpg on the highway, figures that nearly match the base motor.

GTP models come equipped with a supercharged version of the 3800 V6 that makes a whopping 240 horsepower. Traction control works in conjunction with four-wheel antilock disc brakes, which include beefy rotors and state-of-the-art calipers for better stopping ability. Power is put through the front wheels via a standard four-speed, electronically controlled automatic transmission. The GTP gets a heavy-duty version that allows drivers to pick "normal" or "performance" shift modes.

All Grand Prix models benefit from new hydraulic engine mounts to isolate noise and vibration normally transmitted into the cabin. And all powertrains feature long-life fluids and parts, such as coolant designed to last five years or 50,000 miles, and platinum-tipped spark plugs that last 100,000 miles under optimal conditions. Interiors feature analog instrumentation and large, easy-to-use controls. In the Pontiac tradition, the dashboard is a cockpit-style arrangement with gauges designed to look like those in a jet fighter, all backlit in a soothing red glow at night.

This year, Pontiac has dropped the split-bench front seat in SE Sedans, putting the Grand Prix out of contention when considering a six-place four-door. But dual airbags, air conditioning, power windows, door locks and mirrors are all standard fare. And if you like high-tech, you can opt for the EyeCue head-up display, which projects driver data onto the windshield for easy viewing. Should sporty performance be part of your car-buying equation, Grand Prix delivers in the grand American tradition. This Pontiac packs plenty of power and a wide array of safety and convenience features in a package that's as easy to drive as it is on the pocketbook.

Standard Equipment

SE SEDAN (4A): 3.1L V6 OHV SMPI 12-valve engine; 4-speed electronic OD auto transmission with lock-up; 600-amp battery with run down protection; 105-amp alternator; transmission oil cooler; front-wheel drive, traction control, 2.93 axle ratio; stainless steel exhaust; touring ride suspension, front independent strut suspension with anti-roll bar, front coil springs, rear independent multi-link suspension with anti-roll bar, rear coil springs; power rack-and-pinion steering; 4-wheel disc brakes with 4-wheel antilock braking system; 18 gal. capacity fuel tank; side impact bars; front and rear body-colored bumpers; body-colored bodyside molding; monotone paint; aero-composite halogen headlamps with daytime running lights, delay-off feature; additional exterior lights include front fog/driving lights; driver's and passenger's power remote body-colored outside mirrors; front and rear 15" x 6" steel wheels; P205/70SR15 A/S BSW front and rear tires; inside under cargo mounted compact steel spare wheel; air conditioning; AM/FM stereo, clock, seek-scan, cassette, 6 speakers, theft deterrent, and fixed antenna; power door locks, child safety rear door locks; 2 power accessory outlets, driver's foot rest, retained accessory power; instrumentation display includes tachometer, water temperature gauge, trip odometer; warning indicators include oil pressure, battery, low oil level, low coolant, lights on, key in ignition, low fuel, low washer fluid, door ajar, trunk ajar, service interval; driver's and passenger's front airbags; tinted windows, power front and rear windows with driver's 1-touch down; variable intermittent front windshield wipers, sun visor strip, rear window defroster;

334   www.edmunds.com   **EDMUND'S® NEW CARS**

GRAND PRIX — PONTIAC

seating capacity of 5, front bucket seats, adjustable headrests, center armrest with storage, driver's seat includes 4-way direction control, lumbar support, passenger's seat includes 4-way direction control; rear bench seat with fixed headrests; front height adjustable seatbelts; cloth seats, cloth door trim insert, full cloth headliner, full carpet floor covering with carpeted floor mats, plastic/rubber gear shift knob; interior lights include dome light with fade, front reading lights; sport steering wheel with tilt adjustment; vanity mirrors; day/night rearview mirror; full floor console, locking glove box with light, front cupholder, 2 seat back storage pockets, driver's and passenger's door bins; carpeted cargo floor, cargo light; body-colored grille, black side window moldings, black front windshield molding, black rear window molding and body-colored door handles.

GT SEDAN/COUPE (4A) (in addition to or instead of SE SEDAN (4A) equipment): 3.8L V6 OHV SMPI 12-valve engine; 690-amp battery with run down protection; stainless steel exhaust with chrome tip; power rack-and-pinion steering with vehicle speed-sensing assist; rear lip spoiler, body-colored bodyside cladding; front and rear 16" x 6.5" silver alloy wheels; P225/60SR16 touring BSW front and rear tires; cruise control; power remote hatch/trunk release and passenger's seat includes 4-way direction control and easy entry (Coupe).

GTP (in addition to or instead of GT equipment): 3.8L V6 OHV SMPI supercharger 12-valve engine, requires premium unleaded fuel; 770-amp battery with run down protection; driver's selectable multi-mode transmission; traction control, 2.93 axle ratio; P225/60SR16 performance A/S BSW front and rear tires; dual zone front air conditioning with climate control; AM/FM stereo, clock, seek-scan, single CD, 6 speakers, graphic equalizer, theft deterrent, and window grid antenna, radio steering wheel controls; power door locks with 2 stage unlock, remote keyless entry; instrumentation display includes exterior temp, trip computer; panic alarm, security system; driver's seat includes 4-way power seat, 8-way direction control, lumbar support, rear center pass-thru armrest with storage; leather-wrapped gear shift knob; leather-wrapped sport steering wheel with tilt adjustment; full overhead console with storage, front and rear cupholders and cargo net.

2000 Pontiac Grand Prix

Base Prices

Code	Description	Invoice	MSRP
2WJ69	SE Sedan (4A)	18131	19815
2WP37	GT Coupe (4A)	19576	21395

PONTIAC GRAND PRIX

CODE	DESCRIPTION	INVOICE	MSRP
2WP69	GT Sedan (4A)	19714	21545
2WR37	GTP Coupe (4A)	22106	24160
2WR69	GTP Sedan (4A)	22244	24310
	Destination Charge:	560	560

Accessories

1SA	Option Package 1SA	NC	NC

Includes vehicle with standard equipment. NOT AVAILABLE with CF5, V2C, U85, A66, Leather, UTC, KA1, L36, QNX, R7X, QD1, PY0.

| 1SB | Option Package 1SB (GT) | 725 | 815 |

Includes AM/FM stereo with cassette and 6 speakers, overhead console, rear seat pass through, leather-wrapped steering wheel with radio controls, 6-way power driver's seat, trunk cargo net and security package: remote keyless entry and theft deterrent system.

| 1SB | Option Package 1SB (GTP Coupe) | 467 | 525 |

Includes AM/FM stereo with CD, graphic equilizer and 6 speakers, rear window antenna, 6-way power driver's seat with 4-way power lumbar, premium lighting package: illuminated visor mirrors, assist handles, electrochromic rearview mirror and EyeCue head-up display.

| 1SB | Option Package 1SB (GTP Sedan) | 494 | 555 |

Includes remote Decklid release, cruise control with resume speed, variable effort power steering, rear Decklid spoiler, AM/FM stereo with CD radio, rear window antenna, 6-way power driver seat, 4-way power lumbar driver's seat, premium lighting package, illuminated visor mirrors, assist handles, electrochromic rearview mirror and EyeCue head-up display.

| 1SB | Option Package 1SB (SE) | 307 | 345 |

Includes remote decklid release, cruise control with resume speed, AM/FM stereo with cassette and rear seat pass through. NOT AVAILABLE with L36, A66, Leather, KA1.

| 1SC | Option Package 1SC (GT Coupe) | 1210 | 1360 |

Includes AM/FM stereo with cassette and 6 speakers, overhead console, rear seat pass through, leather-wrapped steering wheel with radio controls, 6-way power driver's seat, trunk cargo net, security package: remote keyless entry and theft deterrent system, trip computer, auto dual zone air conditioning, premium lighting package: illuminated visor mirrors, assist handles and electrochromic rearview mirror.

| 1SC | Option Package 1SC (GT Sedan) | 1237 | 1390 |

Includes AM/FM stereo with cassette and 6 speakers, overhead console, rear seat pass through, leather-wrapped steering wheel with radio controls, 6-way power driver's seat, trunk cargo net, security package: remote keyless entry and theft deterrent system, trip computer, auto dual zone air conditioning, premium lighting package: illuminated visor mirrors, assist handles and electrochromic rearview mirror.

| 1SC | Option Package 1SC (GTP Coupe) | 1442 | 1620 |

Includes remote Decklid release, cruise control with resume speed, variable effort power steering, rear Decklid spoiler, AM/FM stereo with CD radio, rear window antenna, 6-way power driver seat, 4-way power lumbar driver's seat, premium lighting package, illuminated visor mirrors, assist handles, electrochromic rearview

GRAND PRIX — PONTIAC

CODE	DESCRIPTION	INVOICE	MSRP
	mirror and EyeCue head-up display; Prado leather seat trim and power spoiler type glass sunroof.		
1SC	Option Package 1SC (GTP Sedan)	1468	1650
	Includes remote Decklid release, cruise control with resume speed, variable effort power steering, rear Decklid spoiler, AM/FM stereo with CD radio, rear window antenna, 6-way power driver seat, 4-way power lumbar driver's seat, premium lighting package, illuminated visor mirrors, assist handles, electrochromic rearview mirror and EyeCue head-up display; Prado leather seat trim and power spoiler type glass sunroof.		
1SC	Option Package 1SC (SE Sedan)	1144	1285
	Includes remote decklid release, cruise control with resume speed, rear decklid spoiler, AM/FM stereo with cassette and 6 speakers, overhead console, rear seat pass through, leather-wrapped steering wheel with radio controls, 6-way power driver's seat, trunk cargo net, security package: remote keyless entry and theft deterrent system. REQUIRES L36 and QNX.		
1SD	Option Package 1SD (GT Coupe)	2519	2830
	Includes AM/FM stereo with cassette and 6 speakers, overhead console, rear seat pass through, leather-wrapped steering wheel with radio controls, 6-way power driver's seat, trunk cargo net, security package: remote keyless entry and theft deterrent system; trip computer, auto dual zone air conditioning, premium lighting package: illuminated visor mirrors, assist handles and electrochromic rearview mirror; EyeCue head-up display, Prado leather seat trim, power spoiler type glass sunroof and heated driver's seat. NOT AVAILABLE with CF5.		
1SD	Option Package 1SD (GT Sedan)	2545	2860
	Includes AM/FM stereo with cassette and 6 speakers, overhead console, rear seat pass through, leather-wrapped steering wheel with radio controls, 6-way power driver's seat, trunk cargo net, security package: remote keyless entry and theft deterrent system; trip computer, auto dual zone air conditioning, premium lighting package: illuminated visor mirrors, assist handles and electrochromic rearview mirror; EyeCue head-up display, Prado leather seat trim, power spoiler type glass sunroof and heated driver's seat. NOT AVAILABLE with CF5.		
AG1	6-Way Power Driver's Seat (SE/GT)	240	270
	NOT AVAILABLE with 1SA. INCLUDED in 1SB, 1SC, 1SD.		
AG6	4-Way Power Lumbar Driver's Seat (SE/GT)	89	100
	NOT AVAILABLE with 1SA, 1SB. INCLUDED in 1SB, 1SC, 1SD.		
CF5	Power Spoiler Type Glass Sunroof	507	570
	Includes overhead console delete. NOT AVAILABLE with 1SA. INCLUDED in 1SC (GTP), 1SD (GT).		
D81	Rear Decklid Spoiler (SE)	156	175
	REQUIRES 1SB. NOT AVAILABLE with 1SA. INCLUDED in 1SC.		
K05	Engine Block Heater	18	20
K34	Cruise Control with Resume Speed (SE)	209	235
	INCLUDED in 1SB, 1SC.		
KA1	Heated Driver's Seat	44	50
	REQUIRES AG6 and Leather. INCLUDED in 1SC (GTP), 1SD (GT).		
L36	Engine: 3800 V6 SFI Series II (SE)	369	415
	REQUIRES 1SC. NOT AVAILABLE with 1SA, 1SB.		

PONTIAC — GRAND PRIX

CODE	DESCRIPTION	INVOICE	MSRP
Leather	Prado Leather Seat Trim (All Except GTP Sedan)	423	475
	NOT AVAILABLE with 1SA, 1SB, INCLUDED in 1SC, 1SD.		
Leather	Prado Leather Seat Trim (GTP Sedan)	423	475
	NOT AVAILABLE with 1SA, 1SB, INCLUDED in 1SC, 1SD.		
PY0	Wheels: 16" Aluminum Silver Crosslace (SE)	263	295
	NOT AVAILABLE with 1SA, INCLUDED in 1SC, 1SD.		
QD1	Wheels: 16" 5-Spoke Aluminum (SE)	263	295
	REQUIRES (1SB or 1SC) and QNX. NOT AVAILABLE with 1SA, QD1.		
QNX	Tires: P225/60R16 Touring BSW (SE)	142	160
	Silver painted. REQUIRES (1SB or 1SC) and QNX. NOT AVAILABLE with 1SA, PY0.		
R7X	Security Package (SE)	187	210
	Includes remote keyless entry and theft deterrent system. REQUIRES 1SB. NOT AVAILABLE with 1SA, INCLUDED 1SC.		
U1C	AM/FM Stereo with CD (GT)	476	535
	Includes 6-speaker system and rear window antenna. REQUIRES U85. NOT AVAILABLE with 1SA.		
U1C	AM/FM Stereo with CD (GTP)	NC	NC
	Includes 6-speaker system and rear window antenna. NOT AVAILABLE with 1SA.		
U1C	AM/FM Stereo with CD (SE/GT)	125	140
	Includes 6-speaker system and rear window antenna. NOT AVAILABLE with U85, 1SA.		
U85	Bose Premium Sound System (GT)	NC	NC
	REQUIRES 1SB or 1SC or 1SD. NOT AVAILABLE with 1SA.		
U85	Bose Premium Sound System (GTP)	329	370
	REQUIRES U1C. NOT AVAILABLE with 1SA.		
U85	Bose Premium Sound System (GTP)	240	270
	REQUIRES UN6. NOT AVAILABLE with 1SA.		
UN6	AM/FM Stereo with Cassette (GT)	387	435
	Includes Bose premium sound system and rear window antenna. REQUIRES U85. NOT AVAILABLE with U1C, 1SA.		
UP3	Radio: AM/FM Stereo with CD (SE/GT)	147	165
	Includes graphic equalizer, 6-speaker system and rear window antenna. REQUIRES 1SC (SE) or 1SD (GT). NOT AVAILABLE with 1SA, U1C, U85.		
UV6	EYECUE Head-Up Display (GT)	245	275
	REQUIRES 1SC or 1SD. NOT AVAILABLE with 1SA, 1SB.		
V2C	Wheels: High Polished Aluminum (GT/GTP)	289	325
	5-Spoke torque star silver painted. NOT AVAILABLE with 1SA, PY0.		
VK4	Front Licence Plate Depression Cover (GT/GTP)	NC	NC
	Included at no charge for states with out a front plate requirement.		

SUNFIRE — PONTIAC

| CODE | DESCRIPTION | INVOICE | MSRP |

2000 SUNFIRE

2000 Pontiac Sunfire

What's New?

Redesigned front and rear fascias for a sportier appearance, a new five-speed manual transmission and the availability of the premium Monsoon audio system lead Sunfire's upgrade list for 2000. There are also restyled rocker-panel moldings, new wheels and exterior colors, as well as a revised instrument panel cluster, floor console and upholstery.

Review

Pontiac's Sunfire is poised to take on the Cavalier, Escort ZX2, Neon and assorted import compacts by offering value, sporty styling and good performance in a well-rounded package. Wearing revised front and rear fascias with integrated lamps, Sunfire is available as a coupe, sedan or convertible in SE (base) trim, and as a coupe or convertible in the GT (uplevel) series.

Dual airbags, ABS and an anti-theft system are standard equipment. Base models come with a 2.2-liter four-cylinder engine. Power is rated at 115 horsepower, and can be fed through the standard five-speed manual or optional three- and four-speed automatics. GT models get a slightly larger 16-valve four-cylinder, good for 150 horsepower. The GT's 2.4-liter, twin-cam motor is optional on the SE, and we highly recommend it, particularly mated to this year's new, smoother-shifting Getrag five-speed manual transmission.

Equipped with the bigger engine and a stick shift, a Sunfire is downright speedy when compared to other four-banger compacts. The automatic raises acceleration times by about a second in the dash to 60 mph. Options on the Sunfire include sharp new alloy wheels, a power sunroof and a variety of uplevel sound systems, including the 200-watt Monsoon unit. Equip an SE Coupe to the gills, watch the price soar to the mid-18s, and suddenly Sunfire isn't such a hot deal. But fiddling with the options sheet should land you a sporty, well-equipped coupe priced at around $16,000.

The move to more aggressive-looking fascias and rocker-panel moldings was intended to boost Sunfire's image with young buyers. That goal also fueled the move to better sound systems, as well as improvements in interior functionality, features and storage space for things like compact discs or cassettes. And Pontiac even adds a racy decklid spoiler (optional on sedans).

PONTIAC   SUNFIRE

| CODE | DESCRIPTION | INVOICE | MSRP |

Our only complaint about driving the Sunfire is that when it is pushed to its limits, it tends to exhibit an excessive amount of body roll, especially the heavier convertible version. We think the ragtop and GT models should offer a more sporting suspension to back up the car's sporty looks. On the plus side, all the well-equipped models we've tested so far carried an affordable price tag.

We think the Sunfire has what it takes to succeed in the crowded compact marketplace. Feature for feature, Sunfire makes a strong argument against purchasing its slightly larger stablemate, the Grand Am, or its more pedestrian twin at Chevy dealers, the Cavalier. If you're interested in a Sunfire Convertible, this'll likely be you last chance, as it is rumored to be dropped later this year. But even if you're left to choose from only the coupe or sedan, the Sunfire deserves a look.

Standard Equipment

SE COUPE (5M): 2.2L I4 OHV SMPI 8-valve engine; 5-speed OD manual transmission; 525-amp battery with run down protection; 105-amp alternator; front-wheel drive, 3.94 axle ratio; stainless steel exhaust; touring ride suspension, front independent strut suspension with anti-roll bar, front coil springs, rear semi-independent suspension with rear coil springs; power rack-and-pinion steering; front disc/rear drum brakes with 4-wheel antilock braking system; 15 gal. capacity fuel tank; rear wing spoiler, side impact bars; front and rear body-colored bumpers; body-colored bodyside molding rocker panel extensions; monotone paint; aero-composite halogen headlamps with daytime running lights; black folding driver's manual remote outside mirror, passenger's manual outside mirror; front and rear 14" x 6" steel wheels; P195/70SR14 A/S BSW front and rear tires; inside under cargo mounted compact steel spare wheel; air conditioning, rear heat ducts; AM/FM stereo, clock, seek-scan, 4 speakers, and fixed antenna; 1 power accessory outlet, driver's foot rest, smokers' package; instrumentation display includes tachometer, water temperature gauge, trip odometer; warning indicators include battery, low coolant, lights on, key in ignition; driver's and passenger's front airbags; ignition disable; tinted windows; fixed interval front windshield wipers, rear window defroster; seating capacity of 5, front bucket seats, adjustable headrests, center armrest with storage, driver's seat includes 4-way direction control, passenger's seat includes 4-way direction control, easy entry; full folding rear bench seat with fixed headrests; cloth seats, cloth door trim insert, full cloth headliner, full carpet floor covering with carpeted floor mats; interior lights include dome light with fade; sport steering wheel; vanity mirrors; day/night rearview mirror; full floor console, locking glove box with light, front and rear cupholders, driver's and passenger's door bins; carpeted cargo floor, cargo light; black grille, black side window moldings, black front windshield molding, black rear window molding and black door handles.

GT COUPE (5M) (in addition to or instead of SE COUPE (5M) equipment): 2.4L I4 DOHC SMPI 16-valve engine; stainless steel exhaust with chrome tip; sport ride suspension, rear semi-independent suspension with anti-roll bar; body-colored bodyside cladding, rocker panel extensions; front and rear 16" x 6" silver alloy wheels; P205/55SR16 performance A/S BSW front and rear tires; AM/FM stereo, clock, seek-scan, single CD, 6 performance speakers, graphic equalizer, and fixed antenna; front sports seats, adjustable headrests, center armrest with storage, driver's seat includes 4-way direction control, lumbar support, passenger's seat includes 4-way direction control, lumbar support, easy entry; leather-wrapped gear shift knob; leather-wrapped sport steering wheel with tilt adjustment; full floor console, 1 seat back storage pocket and body-colored grille.

GT CONVERTIBLE (4A) (in addition to or instead of GT COUPE (4A) equipment): Four-speed electronic OD auto transmission with lock-up; traction control, 3.91 axle ratio; touring ride suspension, rear semi-independent suspension with rear coil springs; power convertible roof with lining, glass rear window; driver's and passenger's power remote black folding outside mirrors; front and rear 15" x 6" silver alloy wheels; P195/65SR15 touring A/S BSW front and rear tires; cruise control; power door locks, remote keyless entry; security system; power front and

340   www.edmunds.com   **EDMUND'S® NEW CARS**

SUNFIRE — PONTIAC

| CODE | DESCRIPTION | INVOICE | MSRP |

rear windows; variable intermittent front windshield wipers; seating capacity of 4; interior lights include front reading lights and cargo net.

SE SEDAN (5M) (in addition to or instead of SE COUPE (5M) equipment): 3.58 axle ratio; child safety rear door locks; manual front and rear windows; passenger's seat includes 4-way direction control and front height adjustable seatbelts.

Base Prices

Code	Description	Invoice	MSRP
2JB37	SE Coupe (5M)	12867	13910
2JD37	GT Coupe (5M)	14994	16210
2JB67	GT Convertible (4A)	19989	21610
2JB69	SE Sedan (5M)	12959	14010
	Destination Charge:	510	510

Accessories

Code	Description	Invoice	MSRP
1SA	Option Package 1SA	NC	NC
	Includes vehicle with standard equipment. NOT AVAILABLE with MX0, PB1, PG1, R6B, R7X, R9P, U1Q, U85, K34, MM5, CF5, R6D.		
1SB	Option Package 1SB (GT Coupe)	1317	1480
	Includes transmission: 4-speed automatic, variable intermitant wipers, security package: remote keyless entry, power door locks, content theft alarm and cruise control with resume speed.		
1SB	Option Package 1SB (SE Coupe)	952	1070
	Includes transmission: 3-speed automatic, rear deck spoiler, AM/FM stereo with CD, RDS, equalizer, 6 speakers and tilt steering wheel. NOT AVAILABLE with R9P, UM6.		
1SB	Option Package 1SB (SE Sedan)	1086	1220
	Includes transmission: 3-speed automatic, rear deck spoiler, AM/FM stereo with CD, RDS, equalizer, 6 speakers and tilt steering wheel. NOT AVAILABLE with R7X, UM6.		
1SC	Option Package 1SC (GT Coupe)	1900	2135
	Includes transmission: 4-speed automatic, variable intermitant wipers, security package: remote keyless entry, power door locks, content theft alarm, cruise control with resume speed, power package: dual power mirrors and power windows; Monsoon premium audio system and convenience package: trunk net, reading lamps and overhead storage.		
1SC	Option Package 1SC (SE Coupe)	1620	1820
	Includes transmission: 3-speed automatic, rear deck spoiler, AM/FM stereo with CD, RDS, equalizer, 6 speakers, tilt steering wheel, cruise control with resume speed, variable intermitant wipers, convenience package: trunk net, reading lamps, overhead storage and assist handles and security package: remote keyless entry, power door locks, content theft alarm. NOT AVAILABLE with UM6, R6B.		
1SC	Option Package 1SC (SE Sedan)	1789	2010
	Includes transmission: 3-speed automatic, rear deck spoiler, AM/FM stereo with CD, RDS, equalizer, 6 speakers, tilt steering wheel, cruise control with resume speed, variable intermitant wipers, convenience package: trunk net, reading lamps, overhead storage and assist handles and security package: remote keyless entry, power door locks, content theft alarm. NOT AVAILABLE with UM6, R6D.		

PONTIAC

SUNFIRE

CODE	DESCRIPTION	INVOICE	MSRP
CF5	Power Sliding Glass Sunroof (GT Coupe)	494	555
	Includes overhead console delete. REQUIRES 1SC. NOT AVAILABLE with 1SA.		
CF5	Power Sliding Glass Sunroof (GT Coupe)	530	595
	REQUIRES 1SB. NOT AVAILABLE with 1SA.		
K05	Engine Block Heater	18	20
K34	Cruise Control with Resume Speed (SE)	209	235
	NOT AVAILABLE with 1SA. INCLUDED in 1SB, 1SC.		
LD9	Engine: 2.4L SFI L4 Twin Cam (SE)	400	450
	REQUIRES 1SC and (MM5 or MX0). NOT AVAILABLE with MX1, 1SA, 1SB.		
MM5	Transmission: 5-Speed Manual (GT)	(721)	(810)
	REQUIRES 1SB or 1SC. NOT AVAILABLE with 1SA.		
MM5	Transmission: 5-Speed Manual (SE)	(534)	(600)
	REQUIRES 1SB or 1SC. NOT AVAILABLE with 1SA.		
MX0	Transmission: 4-Speed Automatic (GT Coupe)	721	810
	INCLUDED in 1SB, 1SC.		
MX0	Transmission: 4-Speed Automatic (SE)	187	210
	NOT AVAILABLE with 1SA.		
MX1	Transmission: 3-Speed Automatic (SE)	534	600
	INCLUDED in 1SB, 1SC.		
PB1	15" Bolt On Chrome Full Wheels Covers (SE)	49	55
	NOT AVAILABLE with PG1, 1SA.		
PF7	Wheels: 15" Aluminum (SE)	263	295
	NOT AVAILABLE with PB1, PG1, 1SA.		
PG1	Wheels: 15" Bolt-On Covers (SE)	NC	NC
	NOT AVAILABLE with PB1, 1SA.		
QPD	Tires: P195/65R15 BSW STL Touring (SE)	120	135
	NOT AVAILABLE with 1SA.		
R6B	Sun and Sound Package (SE Coupe)	2234	2510
	Manufacturer Discount	(378)	(425)
	Net Price	1856	2085
	Includes tires: P195/65R15 BSW STL touring, AM/FM with CD, equalizer, 6 speakers, RDS and power sliding glass sunroof. NOT AVAILABLE with 1SA.		
R6B	Sun and Sound Package (SE Coupe)	1602	1800
	Manufacturer Discount	(378)	(425)
	Net Price	1224	1375
	Includes tires: P195/65R15 BSW STL touring, AM/FM with CD, equalizer, 6 speakers, RDS and power sliding glass sunroof. REQUIRES 1SB. NOT AVAILABLE with 1SA, 1SC.		
R6D	Special Edition Package (SE Sedan)	1967	2210
	Manufacturer Discount	(516)	(580)
	Net Price	1451	1630
	Includes security package: remote keyless entry, power door locks, content theft alarm; power package: dual power mirrors and power windows; and tires: P195/65R15 BSW STL touring. REQUIRES 1SB. NOT AVAILABLE with 1SA, 1SC.		

SUNFIRE PONTIAC

CODE	DESCRIPTION	INVOICE	MSRP
R6D	Special Edition Package (SE Sedan)	2305	2590
	Manufacturer Discount	(516)	(580)
	Net Price	1789	2010
	Includes security package: remote keyless entry, power door locks, content theft alarm; power package: dual power mirrors and power windows; and tires: P195/65R15 BSW STL touring. REQUIRES 1SC. NOT AVAILABLE with 1SA, 1SB.		
R7X	Security Package (SE Coupe)	329	370
	Includes remote keyless entry, power door locks and content theft alarm. NOT AVAILABLE with 1SA. INCLUDED in 1SB, 1SC.		
R9P	Power Package (Coupe)	338	380
	Includes dual power mirrors and power windows. REQUIRES R7X. NOT AVAILABLE with 1SA, 1SB. INCLUDED in 1SC.		
T43	Rear Deck Spoiler (SE Sedan)	134	150
	INCLUDED in 1SB, 1SC.		
U1P	Radio: AM/FM with CD (SE)	285	320
	Includes equalizer, RDS, and 6 speakers. NOT AVAILABLE with U1Q, UM6. INCLUDED in 1SB, 1SC.		
U1Q	Radio: AM/FM with CD and Cassette	89	100
	Includes equalizer, RDS, and 6 speakers. NOT AVAILABLE with 1SA, U1P, UM6.		
U85	MONSOON Premium Audio System (Coupe)	174	195
	REQUIRES (1SB and R7X) or 1SC (SE). NOT AVAILABLE with 1SA. INCLUDED in 1SC (GT).		
UM6	Radio: AM/FM Stereo with Cassette (SE)	147	165
	REQUIRES 1SA. NOT AVAILABLE with 1SC, 1SB, U1P, U1Q.		
UM6	Radio: AM/FM Stereo with Cassette (SE)	(138)	(155)
	REQUIRES 1SB. NOT AVAILABLE with 1SC, 1SA, U1P, U1Q.		
VK4	Front Licence Plate Depression Cover (GT)	9	10
	Included at no charge for states without a front plate requirment.		

One 15-minute call could save you 15% or more on car insurance.

GEICO DIRECT

America's 6th Largest Automobile Insurance Company

1-800-555-2758

PORSCHE

BOXSTER

CODE	DESCRIPTION	INVOICE	MSRP

1999 BOXSTER

1999 Porsche Boxster

What's New?

The Boxster is slowly adding features and options. This year, a Classic Package includes metallic paint and all-leather seats, and adds special highlights to the interior. The gas tank is increased from a 12.5- to a 14.1- gallon capacity, and gas-discharge Litronic headlights are optional. All the features in the Sport Package are individually optional this year, and 18-inch wheels are now available.

Review

Car buff magazines have been proclaiming the rebirth of the sports car market since the introduction of the BMW Z3 in the winter of 1996. One year later, their prediction was validated with the introduction of the Mercedes SLK and Porsche Boxster. The most anticipated of these wonderfully impractical cars, however, has to be the Boxster. Porsche is slow to change, and even slower to introduce new products. (The previous 911 design had been around for an astounding 30 years before it was completely revised.) When Porsche does introduce a new product, it is guaranteed to cause a stir.

The Boxster was a clean-sheet design that was built around an all-new horizontally opposed (boxer type) engine. The engine is mounted mid-ship for ideal weight distribution and displaces a relatively thrifty 2.5 liters. This is Porsche's first use of water-cooling and four-valve technology on a six-cylinder engine. The engine produces 201 horsepower and 181 foot-pounds of torque, which is plenty of grunt for an open-air roadster.

The Boxster is available with a five-speed manual or a five-speed Tiptronic transmission. The Tiptronic transmission features five forward speeds and has manual mode gear selector switches mounted exclusively on the steering wheel.

Aside from the mechanical innovations, the Boxster also features a few practical features that buyers will appreciate. First, the Boxster offers more cargo area than any of its competitors due to the inclusion of front and rear trunks. This front/rear trunk design produces an impressive 9.1 cubic feet of cargo space, and is made possible by the mid-engine design. Second, the Boxster's livable cockpit has a good deal of space for two occupants and features wonderful, cradling seats. For safety, side airbags are standard and roll bars are built in behind the seats.

344   www.edmunds.com

EDMUND'S® NEW CARS

BOXSTER — PORSCHE

Finally, the Boxster has the fastest closing automatic top in the business, going from completely open to completely closed in a scant twelve seconds — perfect for those unexpected rain showers.

This year, the Boxster has added a new option package called "Classic". The Classic Package features metallic exterior paint and all-leather seats, as well as granite and amber paintwork on the interior. Sport Package options are individually optional (including features like sport seats or a sports suspension with short springs and hard dampeners).

The real reason that people will buy this car, however, rests with the fact that it is a Porsche that many people can afford. With prices starting at $24,000 under the 911 Carrera Coupe, the Boxster's price tag leaves enough money in the bank to park a practical sedan or sport utility next to it in the garage. If you're looking for the most prestigious set of wheels under $45,000, you've found it.

Standard Equipment

BOXSTER (5M): 2.5L H6 DOHC SMPI with variable valve timing 24-valve engine, requires premium unleaded fuel; 5-speed overdrive manual transmission; 70-amp battery; engine oil cooler; 120-amp alternator; transmission oil cooler; rear wheel drive, 3.89 axle ratio; dual stainless steel exhaust with chrome tip; front independent strut suspension with anti-roll bar, front coil springs, rear independent strut suspension with anti-roll bar, rear coil springs; power rack-and-pinion steering with engine speed-sensing assist; 4 wheel disc brakes with 4 wheel antilock braking system; 17 gal. capacity fuel tank; rear lip spoiler; power convertible roof with lining, roll-over protection; front and rear body-colored bumpers; monotone paint; aero-composite halogen headlamps; additional exterior lights include front fog/driving lights, center high mounted stop light; driver's and passenger's power remote body-colored heated folding outside mirrors; front 16" x 6" silver alloy wheels rear 16" x 7" silver alloy wheels; 205/55 front tires; 225/50 rear tires; inside mounted full-size temporary alloy spare wheel; air conditioning with climate control, air filter; AM/FM stereo with seek-scan, cassette, 4 speakers, theft deterrent, and window grid diversity antenna; power door locks; 1 power accessory outlet, driver's foot rest; instrumentation display includes tachometer, water temp gauge, clock, trip odometer; warning indicators include water temp, battery, low oil level, lights on, key in ignition, low fuel; dual airbags, door mounted side airbags; ignition disable; tinted windows, power front windows with driver's 1-touch down; windshield wipers with heated jets; seating capacity of 2, front sports seats with fixed headrests, center armrest with storage, driver's seat includes 2-way power seat with 6-way direction control, passenger's seat includes 2-way power seat with 4-way direction control; leather seats, leather door trim insert, full cloth headliner, full carpet floor covering, leather-wrapped gear shift knob; interior lights include dome light with fade, 2 door curb lights; leather-wrapped steering wheel with telescopic adjustment; vanity mirrors; day-night rearview mirror; full floor console, locking glove box with light, driver's and passenger's door bins; carpeted cargo floor, cargo net; black side window moldings, black front windshield molding and body-colored door handles.

Base Prices

Code	Description	Invoice	MSRP
986310	Boxster (5M)	35895	41000
	Destination Charge:	765	765

Accessories

Code	Description	Invoice	MSRP
—	Metallic Paint	607	805
	Environmentally compatible water based metallic paint.		
274	Dual Illuminated Visor Vanity Mirrors	123	145
288	Headlamp Washers	193	225
396	Wheels: 17" Boxster Design	1257	1479
	Includes wheel locks and 205/50ZR17 front tires and 255/40ZR17 rear tires. NOT AVAILABLE with P84, XRA, XRB, P85, XRH.		

PORSCHE | BOXSTER

CODE	DESCRIPTION	INVOICE	MSRP
421	Cassette Shelf (Center Console)	34	40
	NOT AVAILABLE with 688, 424, P63, P84, 662.		
424	CD Storage Shelf In Center Front Console	34	40
	NOT AVAILABLE with 421.		
446	Wheel Caps with Colored Crest	146	170
454	Speed Control	477	561
490	Hi-Fi Sound Package	512	602
	Includes 8 speakers and amplifier.		
498	Delete Model Designation	NC	NC
513	Passenger's Lumbar Support Adjuster	320	375
	REQUIRES P15.		
535	Remote Control Alarm System	481	612
540	Passenger's Height Seat Adjuster	125	145
	NOT AVAILABLE with P15.		
550	Hard Top	1960	2295
	Includes rear window defroster.		
551	Wind Deflector	312	367
571	Active Carbon Filter	393	460
580	Non-Smoker Package	NC	NC
	Includes storage compartment in place of ash tray and removable plug over cigarette lighter.		
586	Driver's Adjustable Lumbar Support	320	375
	REQUIRES P15.		
635	Park Assist System	444	520
	System is activated whenever the reverse gear is engaged, an acoustical signal will be heard in intervals whenever the vehicle backs up and approaches an object that is closer than 5 feet and at a distance of 1 foot the tone is continuous.		
659	On-Board Computer	381	449
662	Navigation System	2986	3540
	Includes climate control indicator and on-board computer. NOT AVAILABLE with 421.		
688	Radio: AM/FM Stereo with CD and Cassette	273	315
	NOT AVAILABLE with 421.		
692	Remote 6-Disc CD Changer	707	831
	Replaces CD in dash. NOT AVAILABLE with P64.		
982	Soft Look Leather Seats	303	355
	In interior color. REQUIRES ALTHR. NOT AVAILABLE with P69, SLTHR.		
ALTHR	All Leather Seat/Interior Trim	1699	1990
	Includes seat trim and dashboard top and bottom. NOT AVAILABLE with SLTHR.		
M6*	Floor Mats	78	92
P14	Heated Front Seats	341	400
P15	Dual Power Seats	1298	1520
	Includes driver's seat memory system. NOT AVAILABLE with P69, 540.		
P37	Traction Control	737	870
	Includes on/off switch and active brake differential.		
P38	Technic Sport Package	1655	1940
	Includes stiffer springs, shock absorbers and stabilizer bars, traction control and upgraded suspension. NOT AVAILABLE with P84, P64, XRA, XRB, XRH, P63, P85.		

346 www.edmunds.com EDMUND'S® NEW CARS

BOXSTER — PORSCHE

CODE	DESCRIPTION	INVOICE	MSRP
P49	Digital Sound Processing	1003	1175

Includes hi-fi sound package. NOT AVAILABLE with P63, P64, P84, P85.

P63	Sport Package	2817	3295

Includes hi-fi sound package, speed control, remote control alarm system, wind deflector, AM/FM stereo with CD, 17" Boxster design alloy wheels and 205/50ZR17 front tires and 255/40ZR17 rear tires. NOT AVAILABLE with P84, P69, P85, P38, XRA, XRB, XRH, P49, 421.

P64	Sport Touring Package	5795	6791

Includes sport package: hi-fi sound package, speed control, remote control alarm system, wind deflector, AM/FM stereo with CD, 17" Boxster design alloy wheels, 205/50ZR17 front tires and 255/40ZR17 rear tires, remote 6-disc CD changer, on board computer, aluminum instrument dials, roll bar painted silver, stainless steel door sills with insignia, aluminum/leather brake/shifter and chrome oval center exhaust pipe. NOT AVAILABLE with P84, P38, XRA, XRB, 692, P69, P85, XRH, P49, Y03, XMT, XMU, X69.

P69	Sport Design Package	1383	1620

Requires interior color AS. Includes leather sport bucket seats, leather air bag cover, roll bar trim, center console cover and upper part of instrument cover, leatherette center console sides and front, dashboard and door trim panels and painted grey roll bar and interior trim. NOT AVAILABLE with P63, P84, P64, P85, 982, P15, Y06, XMY.

P84	Sport Package	3905	4570

Includes hi-fi sound package, speed control, remote control alarm system, wind deflector, AM/FM stereo with CD, 17" Sport Classic design alloy wheels and 205/50ZR17 front tires and 255/40ZR17 rear tires. NOT AVAILABLE with P64, P38, 396, XRB, P63, P69, XRH, P49, Y03, 421.

P85	Sport Touring Package	6884	8066

Includes sport package: hi-fi sound package, speed control, remote control alarm system, wind deflector, AM/FM stereo with CD, 17" Sport Classic design alloy wheels, 205/50ZR17 front tires and 255/40ZR17 rear tires, remote 6 disc CD changer, on board computer, aluminum instrument dials, roll bar painted silver, aluminum/leather brake/shifter, stainless steel door sills with insignia and chrome oval center exhaust pipe. NOT AVAILABLE with P63, P69, P64, P38, 396, XRB, XRH, P49, Y03, XMU, XMT, X69.

SLTHR	Special Leather Seat and Interior Trim	2023	2370

Includes seat trim, console cover, dashboard top and bottom and door trim panels, top of instrument cluster, storage shelf and roll bar cover and carpeting in color to match special leather. NOT AVAILABLE with ALTHR, 982.

TT3	Transmission: 5-Speed Tiptronic with Overdrive	2657	3210

Includes floor shift. NOT AVAILABLE with P64.

X26	Leather Steering Wheel	1091	1278

In matching interior color. NOT AVAILABLE with XNE, X77, XNT.

X68	Tonneau Cover In Matching Top Color	1077	1262
X69	Carbon Door Sills with Insignia	723	847

NOT AVAILABLE with P64, P85, X70.

PORSCHE — BOXSTER

CODE	DESCRIPTION	INVOICE	MSRP
X70	Stainless Steel Door Sills with Insignia	354	415
	NOT AVAILABLE with X69.		
X71	Aluminum Instrument Dials	567	664
X77	Carbon/Leather Steering Wheel	1403	1643
	In matching interior color. NOT AVAILABLE with XNE, X26, XNT.		
X89	Rim Caps with Porsche Crest	245	292
XAA	Aero Kit Front and Rear Spoilers	5314	6225
	Includes left and right rocker panel covers.		
XAB	Rear Speedster in Matching Exterior Color	1247	1461
XD9	Rims Painted in Exterior Color	1141	1336
	REQUIRES X89.		
XE3	Automatic Day/Night Mirror	482	564
XIA	Chrome Oval Center Exhaust Pipe	347	407
XMK	Roll Bar Painted in Exterior Color	439	515
	NOT AVAILABLE with XMY.		
XMT	Leather/Wood Brake/Shifter	709	830
	NOT AVAILABLE with Y03, XMU, Y06, P64, P85.		
XMU	Leather/Wood/Aluminum Brake/Shifter	709	830
	NOT AVAILABLE with Y03, XMT, Y06, P64, P85.		
XMY	Roll Bar Painted Silver	439	515
	NOT AVAILABLE with P69, XMK.		
XNE	Aluminum/Leather/Wood Steering Wheel	1403	1643
	NOT AVAILABLE with X77, X26, XNT.		
XNG	Instrument Housing/Upper Panel Leather Trim	248	291
XNJ	Speaker Covers with Leather Trim	376	440
	In matching interior color.		
XNN	Mid Air Vents/Heat Controls Leather Trim	354	415
XNT	Wood/Leather Steering Wheel	1403	1643
	In matching interior color. NOT AVAILABLE with XNE, X77, X26.		
XRA	Wheels: 17" Sport Classic	2126	2490
	Includes wheel locks and 205/50ZR17 front tires and 255/40ZR17 rear tires.		
	NOT AVAILABLE with P38, P64, 396, XRB, P63, XRH.		
XRB	Wheels: 18" Sport Classic	3486	4084
	Includes wheel locks and 255/40ZR18 front tires and 265/35ZR18 rear tires.		
	NOT AVAILABLE with XRA, 396, P64, P84, P38, P63, P85, XRH.		
XRH	Wheels: 17" Dyno-Design	1960	2334
	Includes wheel locks and 205/50ZR17 front tires and 255/40ZR17 rear tires.		
	NOT AVAILABLE with P38, P63, P64, P84, P85, XRA, XRB, 396.		
XXZ	Footwell Lights	623	730
Y03	Carbon/Leather Brake/Shifter	709	830
	NOT AVAILABLE with XMT, XMU, Y06, P64, P85, P84.		
Y06	Aluminum/Leather Brake/Shifter	709	830
	NOT AVAILABLE with Y03, XMT, XMU, P69.		

9-3

2000 9-3

2000 Saab 9-3

What's New?

The base model gets restyled 15-inch alloy wheels, while the SE version gains performance enhancements and increased horsepower. The sporty 9-3 Viggen offers even more power, and is available as a five-door or convertible in addition to the coupe. All engines are now LEV compliant and GM's OnStar "Telematics" System becomes optional across the model lineup.

Review

Despite some obvious shortcomings, we're fond of Saab. Last year, the old 900 model was replaced with the 9-3, which is actually just an updated 900. The base 9-3 comes in three-door coupe, five-door hatchback and two-door convertible models. All come equipped with a powerful 185-horsepower four-cylinder engine. This turbocharged 2.0-liter produces stunning acceleration that can char the front tires into bits if the driver so chooses.

Move up to the even more feature-laden SE five-door or convertible, and you're opting for even more performance. All SEs are powered by a high-output version of the turbo four that spins an amazing 205 horses (that's better than 100 horsepower per liter of displacement!) through either a four-speed automatic or five-speed manual gearbox. Perhaps even more impressive is that in stick-shift models, this motor makes its 209 foot-pounds of torque at an amazingly low 2,200 rpm, and then maintains peak torque all the way up to 4,500 rpm. Talk about a useable power band!

In addition to getting bigger wheels and tires, the uplevel SE also boasts a sportier look with a front chin spoiler, flared rocker panels, a new rear valence, body-colored mirrors, chrome exhaust tip and a sports steering wheel. The SE Convertible models add a rear spoiler, while five-door versions come equipped with a specially tuned sport suspension for more responsive handling. For pure enthusiasts, Saab offers the high-performance 9-3 Viggen. Now with 230 horsepower and a healthy 258 foot-pounds of torque from its high-output turbo 2.3-liter, the Viggen can be had as a coupe, hatch or rag top, and either in black, silver or the original Lightning Blue. Less than 3,000 Viggens will be produced in model year 2000, with 1,000 of them coming to the U.S.

SAAB
9-3

CODE	DESCRIPTION	INVOICE	MSRP

All 9-3 models feature Saab's patented pendulum-design B-pillar, which deflects side impacts away from head and chest areas; the world's first head restraint system to reduce the risk of whiplash-type injuries; and seat-mounted, two-stage inflating head and chest side airbags.

The Saab 9-3 is a fun-to-drive, equipment-laden near-luxury car that competes against entries from Volvo, BMW and Mercedes. While the 9-3 is a good car in its own right, the problem is that there are plenty of good cars in the 9-3's price class. If your tastes run a bit on the eccentric side, however, this car's personality and quirkiness may be a better choice for you than a BMW 323is or Mercedes C280. You'll certainly stand out more in the crowd, and have fun doing it.

―――――――――――― **Standard Equipment** ――――――――――――

BASE 2-DOOR HATCHBACK (5M): 2.0L I4 DOHC MPI intercooled turbo 16-valve engine; 5-speed manual transmission; 65-amp alternator; front-wheel drive, 3.82 axle ratio; steel exhaust with chrome tip; front independent strut suspension with anti-roll bar, front coil springs, gas-pressurized front shocks, rear non-independent suspension with anti-roll bar, rear coil springs, gas-pressurized rear shocks; power rack-and-pinion steering; 4-wheel disc brakes with 4-wheel antilock braking system; 16.9 gal. capacity fuel tank; front mud flaps, rear wing spoiler, side impact bars; front and rear body-colored bumpers with black rub strip; black bodyside molding; monotone paint; aero-composite halogen auto off headlamps with washer and wiper, daytime running lights, delay-off feature; additional exterior lights include cornering lights, front fog/driving lights; driver's and passenger's power remote black heated folding outside mirrors; front and rear 15" x 6.5" silver alloy wheels; P195/60VR15 A/S BSW front and rear tires; inside under cargo mounted compact steel spare wheel; air conditioning, air filter, rear heat ducts; AM/FM stereo, seek-scan, cassette, CD changer pre-wiring, in-dash CD pre-wiring, 4 speakers, amplifier, theft deterrent, and power retractable antenna, radio steering wheel controls; cruise control; power door locks with 2 stage unlock, remote keyless entry, power remote hatch/trunk release; 1 power accessory outlet, driver's foot rest; instrumentation display includes tachometer, water temperature gauge, in-dash clock, exterior temp, systems monitor, trip odometer; warning indicators include oil pressure, battery, low oil level, lights on, key in ignition, low fuel, low washer fluid, bulb failure, door ajar, service interval, brake fluid; driver's and passenger's front airbags, driver's and front passenger's seat mounted side airbags; ignition disable, security system; tinted windows, power windows with driver's and passenger's 1-touch down; variable intermittent front windshield wipers, rear window wiper, rear window defroster; seating capacity of 5, front bucket seats, adjustable headrests, center armrest with storage, driver's seat includes 6-way direction control, lumbar support, easy entry, passenger's seat includes 4-way direction control, easy entry; 60-40 folding rear bench seat with adjustable headrests, center pass-thru armrest; front height adjustable seatbelts with front pretensioners; premium cloth seats, cloth door trim insert, full cloth headliner, full carpet floor covering with carpeted floor mats, plastic/rubber gear shift knob; interior lights include dome light with fade, front and rear reading lights, illuminated entry; steering wheel with telescopic adjustment; dual illuminated vanity mirrors; day/night rearview mirror; full floor console, locking glove box with light, front cupholder, instrument panel bin, 2 seat back storage pockets, driver's and passenger's door bins; carpeted cargo floor, vinyl trunk lid, cargo cover, cargo tie downs, cargo light; chrome grille, black side window moldings, black front windshield molding, black rear window molding and black door handles.

BASE 4-DOOR HATCHBACK (5M) (in addition to or instead of BASE 2-DOOR HATCHBACK (5M) equipment): Child safety rear door locks and power front and rear windows with driver's and passenger's 1-touch down.

SE HOT 4-DOOR HATCHBACK (5M) (in addition to or instead of BASE 4-DOOR HATCHBACK (5M) equipment): 2.0L I4 DOHC MPI intercooled high-output turbo 16-valve engine; 130-amp alternator; sport ride suspension; front power sliding and tilting glass sunroof with sunshade; rocker panel extensions; driver's and passenger's power remote body-colored heated folding outside mirrors; front and rear 16" x 6.5" silver alloy wheels; P205/50ZR16 A/S BSW front and rear tires; air conditioning with climate control; AM/FM stereo, seek-scan, cassette, CD changer

350   www.edmunds.com   **EDMUND'S® NEW CARS**

SAAB 9-3

pre-wiring, in-dash CD pre-wiring, 6 speakers, amplifier, theft deterrent, and power retractable antenna; cell phone pre-wiring; instrumentation display includes trip computer; driver's seat includes 6-way power seat, lumbar support, passenger's seat includes 6-way power seat; leather seats; genuine wood trim on instrument panel, leather-wrapped gear shift knob; memory on driver's seat with 3 memory setting(s); leather-wrapped sport steering wheel with telescopic adjustment.

VIGGEN 2-DOOR HATCHBACK (5M) (in addition to or instead of SE HOT HATCHBACK (5M) equipment): 2.3L I4 DOHC MPI intercooled turbo 16-valve engine; 4.05 axle ratio; front and rear body-colored bumpers with black bumper insert; front and rear 17" x 7.5" silver alloy wheels; P215/45VR17 A/S BSW front and rear tires; integrated roof antenna; driver's seat includes 6-way power seat, lumbar support, easy entry and passenger's seat includes 6-way power seat and easy entry.

VIGGEN 4-DOOR HATCHBACK (5M) (in addition to or instead of VIGGEN 2-DOOR HATCHBACK (5M) equipment): Child safety rear door locks and power front and rear windows with driver's and passenger's 1-touch down.

BASE CONVERTIBLE (5M) (in addition to or instead of BASE 2-DOOR HATCHBACK (5M) equipment): Power convertible roof with lining, glass rear window; power front and rear windows with front and rear 1-touch down; seating capacity of 4 and full folding rear bench seat with adjustable headrests.

SE HOT CONVERTIBLE (5M) (in addition to or instead of SE HOT 2-DOOR HATCHBACK (5M) equipment): Front mud flaps, rear wing spoiler; power convertible roof with lining, glass rear window; power front and rear windows with front and rear 1-touch down; seating capacity of 4 and full folding rear bench seat with adjustable headrests.

VIGGEN CONVERTIBLE (5M) (in addition to or instead of VIGGEN 2-DOOR HATCHBACK (5M) equipment): Front mud flaps, rear wing spoiler; power convertible roof with lining, glass rear window; power front and rear windows with front and rear 1-touch down; seating capacity of 4 and full folding rear bench seat with adjustable headrests.

Base Prices

CODE	DESCRIPTION	INVOICE	MSRP
323M	Base 2-Door Hatchback (5M)	24346	25900
325M	Base 4-Door Hatchback (5M)	24578	26400
355MSR	SE HOT 4-Door Hatchback (5M)	29758	31895
383MSR	Viggen 2-Door Hatchback (5M)	34353	37750
385MSR	Viggen 4-Door Hatchback (5M)	34353	37750
322MT1	Base Convertible (5M)	36491	39450
352MT1	SE HOT Convertible (5M)	39770	42995
382MT1	Viggen Convertible (5M)	40945	44995
	Destination Charge:	575	575

Accessories

CODE	DESCRIPTION	INVOICE	MSRP
—	Front Heated Seats	318	370
—	Front and Rear Heated Seats (SE 4-Door)	447	520
—	Leather Package (All Except Convertible)	1161	1350
	Includes classic leather seat trim.		
—	Mica/Metallic Paint	301	350

EDMUND'S® NEW CARS

SAAB
9-3 / 9-5

CODE	DESCRIPTION	INVOICE	MSRP
—	OnStar Telematics System	740	895
—	Prep. and Handling	95	NC
4AT	Transmission: 4-Speed Automatic (All Except Viggen)	1032	1200
AS2/AS3	In Dash CD Player	NC	NC
SR	Power Glass Sunroof (Base Hatchback)	989	1150
SR	Sunroof Delete (Hatchback - SE/Viggen)	NC	NC
T2	Blue Convertible Top (Convertible - Base/SE)	NC	NC

2000 9-5

2000 Saab 9-5

What's New?

Intended to do for the 9-5 line what the Viggen does for the 9-3, Saab debuts a high-performance 9-5 Aero Sedan with 230 horsepower. Entry-level sedans and wagons sport new 16-inch 10-spoke alloy wheels, and all SE versions now offer a V6 and auto-dimming rearview mirror. A sunroof and traction-control system (TCS) have been added to the standard equipment list.

Review

Saab's premium 9-5 Sedan is designed to compete with everything from near-luxury models such as the Lexus ES 300 and Cadillac Catera, to full-blown sport sedans such as the Mercedes-Benz E430 and BMW 540i. But because the 9-5 is a Saab, this car looks and feels a bit different.

The sedan lineup consists of a fully equipped base 9-5 model or an SE version with all the bells and whistles. The 9-5 comes standard with a 2.3-liter turbo four-cylinder that produces 170 horsepower, mated to a five-speed manual or optional four-speed auto gearbox. All SEs are powered by a 3.0-liter turbo V6 that requires a driver-selectable four-speed automatic. The V6 makes 200 ponies and 229 foot-pounds of torque from 2,500 rpm through the 4,000-rpm mark.

The 9-5's standard equipment list is long, offering upmarket items such as antilock brakes, automatic climate controls, premium stereo, side-impact airbags, an active head-restraint system,

352   www.edmunds.com

EDMUND'S® NEW CARS

9-5 SAAB

even traction control and a sunroof. Heated front and rear seats are optional, but Saab's cool ventilated front seats and a 200-watt stereo/CD/cassette come standard on the SE. If you want some of the SE's luxury but can't bear doing without a stick shift, Saab makes the base 9-5 available with a new premium package that adds leather and upgraded seats and audio system.

Saab purists who bemoan the fact that the 9-5 is not available as a hatchback need only to drive the wagon. Offered in both turbo four and V6 versions, the 9-5 Wagon boasts almost 73 cubic feet of cargo space with the rear seat folded. What's more, the same kind of fresh thinking that went into the 9-5's safety technology is evident in the kind of convenience features found in the wagon. Unique ideas such as a refrigerated glove box, an aircraft-inspired "CargoTracks" load-securing system, a removable rigid cargo shelf, and even a sliding load floor to ease loading and unloading, all help to make the 9-5 Wagon handle just about any hauling task with ease.

But perhaps the nicest thing about the big Saab is its sporting character, with precise steering and powerful brakes that enhance the driving experience. Enthusiasts can even opt for the new 9-5 Aero Sedan, complete with a 230-horse, 2.3-liter turbo four, upgraded suspension and brakes with 17-inch tires, and sporty exterior and interior upgrades. Even in base form, the 9-5's high level of standard equipment and a sticker price of around $30K make it a bargain for most people shopping the near-luxury class. If you look at the 9-5 before traipsing off the lot with an Acura TL or Lexus ES 300, you'll be rewarded with a unique car that is both comfortable and fun to drive.

Standard Equipment

2.3t SEDAN (5M): 2.3L I4 DOHC MPI intercooled turbo 16-valve engine; 5-speed OD manual transmission; battery with run down protection; 130-amp alternator; front-wheel drive, traction control, 4.05 axle ratio; steel exhaust; touring ride suspension, front independent strut suspension with anti-roll bar, front coil springs, gas-pressurized front shocks, rear independent multi-link suspension with anti-roll bar, rear coil springs, gas-pressurized rear shocks; power rack-and-pinion steering; 4-wheel disc brakes with 4-wheel antilock braking system; 18.5 gal. capacity fuel tank; front license plate bracket, side impact bars; front power sliding and tilting glass sunroof with sunshade; front and rear body-colored bumpers with black rub strip; black bodyside molding, rocker panel extensions; monotone paint; aero-composite halogen auto off headlamps with washer and wiper, daytime running lights, delay-off feature; additional exterior lights include cornering lights, front fog/driving lights; driver's and passenger's power remote body-colored heated folding outside mirrors; front and rear 16" x 6.5" silver alloy wheels; P215/55VR16 A/S BSW front and rear tires; inside under cargo mounted compact steel spare wheel; dual zone front air conditioning with climate control, air filter, rear heat ducts; premium AM/FM stereo, seek-scan, cassette, single CD, 7 performance speakers, amplifier, theft deterrent, and window grid diversity antenna, radio steering wheel controls; cruise control; power door locks with 2 stage unlock, remote keyless entry, child safety rear door locks, power remote hatch/trunk release, power remote fuel release; cell phone pre-wiring, 2 power accessory outlets, driver's foot rest; instrumentation display includes tachometer, water temperature gauge, in-dash clock, exterior temp, systems monitor, trip computer, trip odometer; warning indicators include oil pressure, battery, low oil level, low coolant, lights on, key in ignition, low fuel, low washer fluid, bulb failure, door ajar, trunk ajar, brake fluid; driver's and passenger's front airbags, driver's and front passenger's seat mounted side airbags; ignition disable, panic alarm, security system; tinted windows, power front and rear windows with driver's and passenger's 1-touch down; variable intermittent front windshield wipers, rear window defroster; seating capacity of 5, front bucket seats, adjustable headrests, center armrest with storage, driver's seat includes 6-way power seat, lumbar support, passenger's seat includes 6-way power seat, lumbar support; 60-40 folding rear bench seat with adjustable headrests, center pass-thru armrest with skibag and storage; front and rear height adjustable seatbelts with front pretensioners; premium cloth seats, cloth door trim insert, full cloth headliner, full carpet floor covering with carpeted floor mats, genuine wood trim on instrument panel, leather-wrapped gear shift knob; interior lights include dome light with fade, front and rear reading lights, 4 door curb lights, illuminated entry; leather-wrapped steering wheel with tilt and telescopic adjustment; dual illuminated vanity

SAAB
9-5

| CODE | DESCRIPTION | INVOICE | MSRP |

mirrors, dual auxiliary visors; day/night rearview mirror; full floor console, mini overhead console, locking glove box with light, front and rear cupholders, 2 seat back storage pockets, driver's and passenger's door bins, rear door bins; carpeted cargo floor, carpeted trunk lid, cargo net, cargo tie downs, cargo light; chrome grille, black side window moldings, black front windshield molding, black rear window molding and black door handles.

SE V6t SEDAN (4A) (in addition to or instead of 2.3t SEDAN (5M) equipment): 3.0L V6 DOHC MPI intercooled turbo 24-valve engine; 4-speed electronic OD auto transmission with lock-up; driver's selectable multi-mode transmission; 2.56 axle ration; premium AM/FM stereo, seek-scan, cassette, single CD, 9 premium speakers, premium amplifier, theft deterrent, and window grid diversity antenna, radio steering wheel controls; leather seats, leatherette door trim insert and memory on driver's seat with 3 memory setting(s) includes settings for exterior mirrors; auto-dimming day/night rearview mirror.

AERO SEDAN (5M) (in addition to or instead of SE V6T SEDAN (4A) equipment): 2.3L I4 DOHC MPI intercooled turbo 16-valve engine; 5-speed OD manual transmission; 4.05 axle ratio; front and rear 17" x 6.5" silver alloy wheels and P225/45YR17 A/S BSW front and rear tires.

WAGON (in addition to or instead of SEDAN equipment): Roof rack; fixed 1/4 vent windows; rear window wiper and rear center armrest with storage.

Base Prices

CODE	DESCRIPTION	INVOICE	MSRP
504MSR	2.3t Sedan (5M)	30295	32575
575ASR	SE V6t Sedan (4A)	34919	37750
584MSR	Aero Sedan (5M)	36792	39775
505MSR	2.3t Wagon (5M)	30295	32575
575ASR	SE V6t Wagon (4A)	34919	37750
Destination Charge:		575	575

Accessories

CODE	DESCRIPTION	INVOICE	MSRP
—	BBS 17" 1-Piece Wheel/Tire Pkg (All Except Aero)	1615	1950
—	BBS 17" 2-Piece Wheel Upgrade (Aero)	1370	1650
—	Front and Rear Heated Seats	447	520
—	Leather Ventilated Seats (2.3t/Aero)	817	950
	REQUIRES PREM.		
—	Leather Ventilated Seats (SE)	817	950
—	Mica/Metallic Paint	301	350
—	OnStar Telematics System	740	895
—	Prep. and Handling	95	NC
—	Sunroof Delete	NC	NC
08	Vented Seats with Perforated Leather	NC	NC
10	Classic Leather Seat Trim	NC	NC
4AT	Transmission: 4-Speed Automatic (2.3t)	1032	1200
4AT	Transmission: 4-Speed Automatic (Aero)	1032	1200
PREM	Premium Package (All Except SE Wagon)	1716	1995
	Includes Harman/Kardon audio system and leather seat trim.		

L-SERIES

2000 L-SERIES

2000 Saturn LS

What's New?

The L-Series is a new midsize line of sedans and wagons that was developed for Saturn customers moving up from the smaller cars. Offered in three trim levels, with two engines and manual or automatic transmissions (depending on model), the L-Series is based on the European-market Opel Vectra platform, and consequently carries a distinct import feel.

Review

While Saturn enjoys strong customer loyalty with its line of small cars (almost 50 percent return to buy another Saturn), GM researchers found that when owners move on, they most often move up to a midsize vehicle. So a medium-sized entry makes perfect sense for both Saturn and its loyal customer base. Enter the 2000 Saturn L-Series, American-built Opel-based sedans and wagons designed and priced to compete with top imports such as Toyota's Camry and Honda's Accord.

With an overall length of just over 190 inches, the L-Series slots nicely in-between the segment-leading Camry Sedan and the redesigned 2000 Ford Taurus. Available as base LS, midlevel LS1 or top-line LS2 Sedans as well as fully equipped LW1 or upmarket LW2 Wagons, all models include air conditioning, four-wheel independent suspension, theft-deterrent system, and front disc/rear drum brakes (disc/disc standard on LS2 and LW2; ABS with traction control is optional).

Inside, the L-Series features a spacious interior with logical, easy-to-use controls. Seats have been designed for all-day comfort. Sedans offer 18 cubic feet of trunk space, which is a full 4 cubic feet more than you'll find in either Camry or Accord. And with rear seats folded, cargo capacity in the wagon is a generous 59 cubic feet. Unlike other Saturns, the L-Series has steel quarter panels (remember, this is built off an Opel platform); nevertheless, engineers were able to fit Saturn's signature dent-resistant polymer panels on the doors and fenders.

A pair of DOHC four-valve engines are offered: an all-new, Saturn-exclusive 2.2-liter, 137-horsepower four-cylinder with twin balance shafts, and a 3.0-liter, 182-horse V6. The four is standard on LS, LS1 and LW1 and comes with a five-speed manual transmission. An electronically controlled four-speed automatic is optional. The V6 is available only in the LS2 and LW2 and must be mated to an auto box. (Sorry, no V6 stick for sport sedan or wagon wannabes!)

SATURN

L-SERIES

| CODE | DESCRIPTION | INVOICE | MSRP |

The L-Series will be built in Saturn's new assembly plant in Wilmington, Del. How many are built and sold depends on consumer demand, of course, but offering a midsize model opens Saturn up to 41 percent of the total U.S. vehicle market, which isn't a bad thing. Competitively priced, the only question marks hanging over the debut of the L-Series are build quality and just how well this Euro-designed platform holds up to the rigors of American roads and consumers.

Standard Equipment

LS SEDAN(5M): 2.2L I4 DOHC SMPI 16-valve engine; 5-speed OD manual transmission; 525-amp battery; 96-amp alternator; front-wheel drive, 4.5 axle ratio; stainless steel exhaust; front independent strut suspension with anti-roll bar, front coil springs, gas-pressurized front shocks, rear independent strut suspension with rear coil springs, gas-pressurized rear shocks; power rack-and-pinion steering; front disc/rear drum brakes; 13.1 gal. capacity fuel tank; front license plate bracket, side impact bars; front and rear body-colored bumpers; monotone paint; aero-composite halogen headlamps with daytime running lights; driver's and passenger's manual remote body-colored outside mirrors; front and rear 15" x 6" steel wheels; P195/65TR15 touring BSW front and rear tires; inside under cargo mounted compact steel spare wheel; air conditioning, air filter, rear heat ducts; AM/FM stereo, clock, seek-scan, 8 speakers, and fixed antenna; child safety rear door locks, power remote hatch/trunk release; 2 power accessory outlets, driver's foot rest, smokers' package; instrumentation display includes tachometer, water temperature gauge, trip odometer; warning indicators include battery, low coolant, lights on, key in ignition, low fuel, low washer fluid, service interval, brake fluid; driver's and passenger's front airbags; ignition disable; tinted windows, manual front and rear windows; variable intermittent front windshield wipers, rear window defroster; seating capacity of 5, front bucket seats, adjustable headrests, driver's seat includes 4-way direction control, passenger's seat includes 4-way direction control; 60-40 folding rear bench seat; front height adjustable seatbelts; cloth seats, cloth door trim insert, full cloth headliner, full carpet floor covering, plastic/rubber gear shift knob; interior lights include dome light; steering wheel with tilt adjustment; vanity mirrors; day/night rearview mirror; full floor console, glove box, front cupholder, instrument panel bin, dashboard storage, driver's and passenger's door bins; carpeted cargo floor, cargo light; black side window moldings, black front windshield molding, black rear window molding and body-colored door handles.

LS1 SEDAN (5M) (in addition to or instead of LS SEDAN(5M) equipment): 525-amp battery with run down protection; driver's and passenger's power remote body-colored heated outside mirrors; AM/FM stereo, clock, seek-scan, single CD, 8 speakers, and fixed antenna; cruise control with steering wheel controls; power door locks with 2 stage unlock, remote keyless entry; panic alarm, security system; power front and rear windows with driver's 1-touch down; center armrest with storage, driver's seat includes 6-way direction control; simulated wood trim on instrument panel; interior lights include front reading lights and vanity mirrors with driver's side illuminated.

LS2 SEDAN (4A) (in addition to or instead of LS1 SEDAN (5M) equipment): 3.0L V6 DOHC SMPI 24-valve engine, requires premium unleaded fuel; 4-speed electronic OD auto transmission with lock-up; 3.29 axle ratio; stainless steel exhaust with chrome tip; sport ride suspension; 4-wheel disc brakes; additional exterior lights include front fog/driving lights; front and rear 15" x 7" alloy wheels; P205/65HR15 performance BSW front and rear tires; AM/FM stereo, clock, seek-scan, cassette, single CD, 8 speakers, auto equalizer, and fixed antenna; driver's seat includes 6-way direction control, lumbar support; 60-40 folding rear bench seat with fixed headrests; premium cloth seats, carpeted floor mats; interior lights include rear reading lights; leather-wrapped steering wheel with tilt adjustment and dual illuminated vanity mirrors.

LW1 WAGON (4A) (in addition to or instead of LS1 SEDAN (5M) equipment): 4-speed electronic OD auto transmission with lock-up; front-wheel drive, 3.29 axle ratio; roof rack; front and rear body-colored bumpers with rear step; warning indicators include oil pressure, trunk ajar; fixed 1/4 vent windows; rear window wiper; carpeted trunk lid, cargo cover and cargo net.

356   www.edmunds.com   **EDMUND'S® NEW CARS**

L-SERIES SATURN

CODE	DESCRIPTION	INVOICE	MSRP

LW2 WAGON (4A) (in addition to or instead of LS2 SEDAN (4A) equipment): Roof rack; front and rear body-colored bumpers with rear step; warning indicators include oil pressure, trunk ajar; fixed 1/4 vent windows; rear window wiper; carpeted trunk lid, cargo cover and cargo net.

Base Prices

Code	Description	Invoice	MSRP
ZJR19	LS Sedan (5M)	13359	15010
ZJT19	LS1 Sedan (5M)	14908	16750
ZJW19	LS2 Sedan (4A)	17920	20135
ZJU35	LW1 Wagon (4A)	16763	18835
ZJW35	LW2 Wagon (4A)	19010	21360
	Destination Charge:	440	440

Accessories

Code	Description	Invoice	MSRP
—	Leather Seating Surface (All Except LS)	975	1095
	Includes leather-wrapped parking brake grip, heated front seats, leather door trim panels and leather-wrapped auto shifter. REQUIRES AG1.		
—	Transmission: 4-Speed Automatic (LS/LS1)	765	860
AG1	6-Way Power Driver's Seat (All Except LS)	289	325
B58	Front and Rear Carpeted Floor Mats (LS/LS1/LW1)	62	70
CF5	Power Sunroof (LS1/LS2)	645	725
D80	Rear Spoiler (LS1/LS2)	200	225
JL9	Antilock Braking System (LS2/LW2)	619	695
	Includes traction control.		
JM4	Antilock Braking System (LS/LS1/LW1)	619	695
	Includes traction control.		
QE9	Wheels: 15" Alloy (LS1/LW1)	312	350
T96	Fog Lamps (LS1/LW1)	151	170
U67	Saturn Advanced Audio System (All Except LS)	196	220
	Includes amplifier, sub-woofer and premium speakers. REQUIRES ULO or UPO.		
UIC	Radio: AM/FM Stereo with CD and Clock (LS)	258	290
	Includes eight speakers. NOT AVAILABLE with ULO, UPO.		
ULO	Radio: AM/FM Stereo with Cassette and Clock (LS)	347	390
	Includes auto tone control, theft protection and eight speakers. NOT AVAILABLE with UIC, UPO.		
ULO	Radio: AM/FM Stereo with Cassette and Clock (LS1/LW1)	89	100
	Includes auto tone control, theft protection and eight speakers. NOT AVAILABLE with UPO.		
UPO	Radio: AM/FM Stereo with Clock, Cassette and CD (LS)	454	510
	Includes auto tone control, theft protection and eight speakers. NOT AVAILABLE with UIC, ULO.		
UPO	Radio: AM/FM Stereo with Clock, Cassette and CD (LS1/LW1)	196	220
	Includes auto tone control, theft protection and eight speakers. NOT AVAILABLE with ULO.		

SATURN

S-SERIES

| CODE | DESCRIPTION | INVOICE | MSRP |

2000 S-SERIES

2000 Saturn SL2

What's New?

Saturn has redesigned the body panels and cockpit of its S-Series SL Sedan and SW Wagon this year, leaving changes for the SC Coupe for January of 2000 as a 2001 model. GM's OnStar communications system will now be available as a dealer-installed option across the Saturn line.

Review

Saturn's small cars have enjoyed quite a following over the years, proving both fun to drive and reliable. And Saturn dealers have almost single-handedly sparked a retail revolution that emphasizes the ownership experience over sales commissions. Unfortunately, we want more from Saturn, such as more comfortable seats and better quality switchgear and interior trim.

For 2000, Saturn is freshening the looks of its SL Sedan and SW Wagon, and holding off on changes to the SC Coupe. The ding-, dent- and rust-resistant polymer exterior panels have been restyled from the beltline down, giving SL and SW models a contour line that runs the length of the vehicle for a more angular appearance. The SC Coupes, which are scheduled for a facelift early in 2000, still come with the driver's-side third door, providing better access to the back seat.

Inside, the small sedans and wagons get a new, one-piece instrument panel cover, eliminating miscolored plastic pieces and ill-fitting seams, as well as a redesigned console for improved ergonomics. Other changes aren't as noticeable, such as the adoption of some componentry from the new L-Series cars to reduce costs through parts commonality. Unfortunately, the seating position remains low to the floor, while the seats themselves feel too flimsy for long-haul comfort.

Two engine choices are on the S-Series roster, a 100-horsepower, 1.9-liter four-cylinder or a twin-cam version of the same that generates 124 ponies, with either a five-speed manual or four-speed auto box. Long accused of having buzzy engines, Saturn redesigned the reciprocating internals in '99 to bring some refinement to these otherwise acceptable powerplants. We find the twin-cam engine makes for a less-pedestrian sedan or wagon, and is a must if you plan spirited driving in your SC2 Coupe. Sadly, Saturn last year moved to rear drum brakes on all models, replacing the rear discs that had been available on upmarket versions with the optional ABS.

S-SERIES   SATURN

| CODE | DESCRIPTION | INVOICE | MSRP |

Sedans can be had as a base SL, midrange SL1 or uplevel SL2; wagons are available as the standard SW1 or high-end SW2. Coupes come as the basic SC1 or sportier SC2. Be aware that the standard equipment list is short on all base versions and that features are not packaged well enough to sell you on the midrange models. That means you may be forced into pricey, high-end versions to get the kind of equipment you really want, which puts the price near some imports. Packaging aside, Saturn's excellent dealer network, money-back guarantee, customer-first philosophy and reputation for reliability make it hard to go wrong with the S-Series cars.

Standard Equipment

SL SEDAN (5M): 1.9L I4 SOHC SMPI 8-valve engine; 5-speed OD manual transmission; 525-amp battery; 90-amp alternator; front-wheel drive, 4.06 axle ratio; stainless steel exhaust; front independent strut suspension with anti-roll bar, front coil springs, rear independent strut suspension with rear coil springs; manual rack-and-pinion steering; front disc/rear drum brakes; 12.1 gal. capacity fuel tank; side impact bars; front and rear black bumpers; clearcoat monotone paint; aero-composite halogen headlamps with daytime running lights; driver's manual remote black outside mirror; front and rear 14" x 5.5" steel wheels; P185/65SR14 A/S BSW front and rear tires; inside under cargo mounted compact steel spare wheel; rear heat ducts; AM/FM stereo, clock, seek-scan, 2 speakers, and fixed antenna; child safety rear door locks, remote hatch/trunk release, remote fuel release; 1 power accessory outlet, driver's foot rest, smokers' package; instrumentation display includes tachometer, water temperature gauge, trip odometer; warning indicators include oil pressure, battery, lights on, key in ignition, low fuel, low washer fluid, trunk ajar, brake fluid; driver's and passenger's front airbags; tinted windows, manual front and rear windows; variable intermittent front windshield wipers, rear window defroster; seating capacity of 5, front bucket seats, fixed headrests, driver's seat includes 4-way direction control, passenger's seat includes 4-way direction control; 60-40 folding rear bench seat; front height adjustable seatbelts; cloth seats, cloth door trim insert, full cloth headliner, full carpet floor covering, plastic/rubber gear shift knob; interior lights include dome light with delay; steering wheel with tilt adjustment; passenger's side vanity mirror; day/night rearview mirror; full floor console, glove box, front cupholder, dashboard storage, driver's and passenger's door bins; carpeted cargo floor, cargo light; black side window moldings, black front windshield molding, black rear window molding and black door handles.

SL1 SEDAN (5M) (in addition to or instead of SL SEDAN (5M) equipment): Power rack-and-pinion steering; passenger's manual outside mirror; AM/FM stereo, clock, seek-scan, 4 speakers, and fixed antenna and warning indicators service interval.

SL2 SEDAN (5M) (in addition to or instead of SL1 SEDAN (5M) equipment): 1.9L I4 DOHC SMPI 16-valve engine; sport ride suspension, rear independent strut suspension with anti-roll bar; power rack-and-pinion steering with vehicle speed-sensing assist; front and rear body-colored bumpers; front and rear 15" x 6" steel wheels; P185/65TR15 touring A/S BSW front and rear tires; air conditioning, rear heat ducts; center armrest with storage, driver's seat includes 6-way direction control, lumbar support; 1 seat back storage pocket and body-colored door handles.

SC1 COUPE (5M) (in addition to or instead of SL1 SEDAN (5M) equipment): Front and rear body-colored bumpers; fixed rear windows; seating capacity of 4, passenger's seat includes 4-way direction control, easy entry; rear console with storage and front and rear cupholders.

SC2 COUPE (5M) (in addition to or instead of SC1 COUPE (5M) equipment): 1.9L I4 DOHC SMPI 16-valve engine; sport ride suspension, rear independent strut suspension with anti-roll bar; power rack-and-pinion steering with vehicle speed-sensing assist; rear wing spoiler; additional exterior lights include front fog/driving lights; body-colored driver's manual remote outside mirror, body-colored passenger's manual outside mirror; front and rear 15" x 6" steel wheels; P195/60HR15 performance A/S BSW front and rear tires; air conditioning; center armrest with

SATURN S-SERIES

CODE	DESCRIPTION	INVOICE	MSRP

storage, driver's seat includes 6-way direction control, lumbar support; leather-wrapped steering wheel with tilt adjustment; 1 seat back storage pocket and body-colored door handles.

SW2 WAGON (5M) (in addition to or instead of SL2 SEDAN (5M) equipment): Front and rear body-colored bumpers with rear step; warning indicators include low coolant; fixed 1/4 vent windows; rear window wiper; interior lights include dome light with fade; plastic trunk lid, cargo cover and cargo net.

Base Prices

CODE	DESCRIPTION	INVOICE	MSRP
ZZN27	SC1 Coupe (5M)	10905	12535
ZZR77	SC2 Coupe (5M)	13176	15145
ZZF69	SL Sedan (5M)	9276	10685
ZZZ69	SL1 Sedan (5M)	9992	11485
ZZJ69	SL2 Sedan (5M)	11219	12895
ZZI35	SW2 Wagon (5M)	12432	14290
	Destination Charge:	440	440

Accessories

CODE	DESCRIPTION	INVOICE	MSRP
—	Leather Appointments (SL2/SC2/SW2) *Includes leather-wrapped parking brake grip. REQUIRES HK1 or HP1 or HN1.*	609	700
—	Transmission: Electric 4-Speed Auto with OD (SL1/SL2/SC1/SC2/SW2)	748	860
AU0	Saturn Security System (SL1/SL2/SW2) *Includes antilockout feature, door alarm, panic/alert mode and power trunklid/liftgate release and power door locks.*	322	370
B58	Carpeted Front and Rear Floor Mats	61	70
C60	Air Conditioning (SL/SL1/SC1)	835	960
CF5	Power Sunroof (SL1/SL2/SC1/SC2)	631	725
D35	Manual Right Side Mirror (SL)	35	40
D80	Rear Spoiler (SC1)	213	245
D80	Rear Spoiler (SL2)	196	225
HK1	Option Package 1 (SW2) *Includes cruise control, Saturn security system, power door locks, power windows and power remote control side mirrors.*	983	1130
HL1	Option Package 1 (SC1) *Includes air conditioning, cruise control, Saturn security system, power door locks, power windows and power remote control side mirrors.*	1710	1965
HM1	Option Package (SL1) *Includes air conditioning, cruise control, power remote control side mirrors, power windows, Saturn security system and power door locks.*	1818	2090
HN1	Option Package 2 (SL2) *Includes cruise control, Saturn security system, power door locks, power windows, power remote control side mirrors and wheels; 15" alloy.*	1288	1480
HP1	Option Package 1 (SC2) *Includes cruise control, Saturn security system, power door locks, power windows, power remote control side mirrors and wheels; 15" alloy.*	1179	1355

S-SERIES — SATURN

CODE	DESCRIPTION	INVOICE	MSRP
JM4	Antilock Braking System *Includes traction control.*	605	695
PG5	Wheels: 15" Alloy (SC2)	304	350
PH6	Wheels: 15" Alloy (SC1) *Includes tires: P185/65R15 touring A/S SBR BW.*	392	450
PH6	Wheels: 15" Alloy (SL2/SW2)	304	350
T96	Fog Lamps (SL2/SW2)	148	170
U1C	Radio: AM/FM Stereo with CD (SL) *Includes four coaxial speakers. NOT AVAILABLE with ULO, UPO.*	278	320
U1C	Radio: AM/FM Stereo with CD (SL1/SL2/SC1SC2/SW2) *Includes four coaxial speakers. NOT AVAILABLE with ULO, UPO.*	252	290
ULO	Radio: AM/FM Stereo with Cassette (SL) *Includes auto tone control, theft protection and four coaxial speakers. NOT AVAILABLE with U1C, UPO.*	365	420
ULO	Radio: AM/FM Stereo with Cassette (SL1/SL2/SC1SC2/SW2) *Includes auto tone control, theft protection and four coaxial speakers. NOT AVAILABLE with U1C, UPO.*	339	390
UPO	Radio: AM/FM Stereo with CD and Cassette (SC2) *Includes auto tone control, theft protection and four coaxial speakers. NOT AVAILABLE with U1C, ULO.*	351	390
UPO	Radio: AM/FM Stereo with CD and Cassette (SL) *Includes auto tone control, theft protection and four coaxial speakers. NOT AVAILABLE with U1C, ULO.*	470	540
UPO	Radio: AM/FM Stereo with CD and Cassette (SL1/SW2) *Includes auto tone control, theft protection and four coaxial speakers. NOT AVAILABLE with U1C, ULO.*	444	510
UPO	Radio: AM/FM Stereo with CD and Cassette (SL2/SC1) *Includes auto tone control, theft protection and four coaxial speakers. NOT AVAILABLE with U1C, ULO.*	444	510

One 15-minute call could save you 15% or more on car insurance.

America's 6th Largest Automobile Insurance Company

1-800-555-2758

SUBARU

IMPREZA

CODE	DESCRIPTION	INVOICE	MSRP

2000 IMPREZA

2000 Subaru Impreza

What's New?

For 2000, Subaru introduces the new Impreza 2.5 RS Sedan, a cross between aggressive driver's car and a sedan. More standard equipment comes on the 2.5 Coupe and Sedan while the L model remains unchanged. All Impreza models now come with 24-hour roadside assistance.

Review

The Impreza was originally built to battle the Ford Escorts, Toyota Corollas and Chevy Cavaliers that sold so well to young adults, but a zippy advertising campaign touting the underpowered Impreza as "What to Drive" alienated traditional Sube buyers and turned off the young adults it was supposed to attract. Sales of the Impreza were less than successful, and Subaru scrambled to find a solution.

Wonder of wonders, the company decided to reacquaint itself with its legendary all-wheel-drive system. Subaru emphasizes AWD in every ad, article and brochure you can lay your hands on. Ah yes, "The Beauty Of All-Wheel Drive." This AWD model is available in coupe, sedan, and wagon format. Traditional front-wheel-drive editions have been banished from the roster.

For 2000, Subaru introduces the Impreza 2.5 RS Sedan, a vehicle that combines the performance and handling of the race rally-inspired 2.5 RS Coupe with the comfort and convenience of a four-door sedan. For a $100 base price increase, the 2.5 RS Coupe and Sedan receive more standard fare, including cruise control and viscous limited-slip rear differential.

Overall, we find much to like about the Impreza. We've driven 2.5 RS and L Coupe models, and thoroughly enjoyed them. All Imprezas behave like street-legal rally cars, and they're a hoot to toss around. Fling one into a corner, and it clings to the pavement. Imprezas are a blast to drive hard and fast, and the all-wheel-drive system performs brilliantly on a variety of road surfaces. Each Impreza model is available with an $800 automatic transmission. Interiors are comfortable—though the side glass feels a bit too close—and steering and braking are communicative.

There is one thing that bothers us about the Impreza lineup, and that's the lack of an antilock brake option on the L model. To get ABS, you must order the 2.5 RS. This doesn't make much sense coming from a company touting safety in its advertising. We'd also like Subaru to offer

362   www.edmunds.com   **EDMUND'S® NEW CARS**

IMPREZA — SUBARU

one of their turbocharged engines in the 2.5 RS. The company makes an amazing Japan-only performance car, based on the 2.5 RS, called the 22B. Alas, this twin-turbocharged monster is not available in the United States.

Though prices haven't changed much for the millennium, we've always thought they were a bit on the high side to begin with. Despite the benefits of all-wheel drive, the budget-minded compact shopper must ask whether the price commanded by this Subaru is worth it. As much as we like the Impreza, we're skeptical.

Standard Equipment

L AWD COUPE (5M): 2.2L H4 SOHC SMPI 16-valve engine; 5-speed OD manual transmission; 75-amp alternator; full-time all-wheel drive, 3.9 axle ratio; stainless steel exhaust; front independent strut suspension with anti-roll bar, front coil springs, rear independent strut suspension with anti-roll bar, rear coil springs; power rack-and-pinion steering with engine speed-sensing assist; front disc/rear drum brakes; 15.9 gal. capacity fuel tank; rear wing spoiler, side impact bars; front and rear body-colored bumpers; black bodyside molding; monotone paint; aero-composite halogen auto off headlamps; driver's and passenger's power remote black folding outside mirrors; front and rear 15" x 6" steel wheels; P195/60HR15 A/S BSW front and rear tires; inside under cargo mounted compact steel spare wheel; air conditioning, rear heat ducts; AM/FM stereo, clock, seek-scan, cassette, 4 speakers, and manual retractable antenna; power door locks with 2 stage unlock, remote hatch/trunk release, remote fuel release; 1 power accessory outlet, driver's foot rest, smokers' package; instrumentation display includes tachometer, water temperature gauge, trip odometer; warning indicators include oil pressure, battery, key in ignition, low fuel, door ajar; driver's and passenger's front airbags; tinted windows, power windows with driver's 1-touch down; variable intermittent front windshield wipers, rear window defroster; seating capacity of 5, front bucket seats, adjustable headrests, center armrest with storage, driver's seat includes 4-way direction control, passenger's seat includes 4-way direction control, easy entry; rear bench seat with fixed headrests; cloth seats, cloth door trim insert, full cloth headliner, full color-keyed carpet floor covering, plastic/rubber gear shift knob; interior lights include dome light; steering wheel with tilt adjustment; passenger's side vanity mirror; day/night rearview mirror; full floor console, locking glove box, front cupholder, instrument panel bin, driver's and passenger's door bins; carpeted cargo floor; black grille, black side window moldings, black front windshield molding, black rear window molding and black door handles.

2.5 RS AWD COUPE (5M) (in addition to or instead of L AWD COUPE (5M) equipment): 2.5L H4 SOHC SMPI 16-valve engine; viscous limited slip differential, 4.11 axle ratio; stainless steel exhaust with chrome tip; sport ride suspension; 4-wheel disc brakes with 4-wheel antilock braking system; front power sliding and tilting steel sunroof; body-colored bodyside molding, rocker panel extensions; additional exterior lights include front fog/driving lights; driver's and passenger's power remote body-colored folding outside mirrors; front and rear 16" x 7" silver alloy wheels; P205/55VR16 A/S BSW front and rear tires; cruise control; front sports seats, adjustable headrests; leather-wrapped gear shift knob; interior lights include front reading lights; leather-wrapped steering wheel with tilt adjustment body-colored door handles.

SEDAN (in addition to or instead of COUPE equipment): Child safety rear door locks.

WAGON (in addition to or instead of SEDAN equipment): Front and rear body-colored bumpers with rear step; fixed 1/4 windows; rear window wiper; 60-40 folding rear bench seat; plastic trunk lid and cargo cover.

Base Prices

CODE	DESCRIPTION	INVOICE	MSRP
YMA	L AWD Coupe (5M)	14604	15895
YMC	2.5 RS AWD Coupe (5M)	17686	19295
YJA	L AWD Sedan (5M)	14604	15895

SUBARU IMPREZA

CODE	DESCRIPTION	INVOICE	MSRP
YJC	2.5 RS AWD Sedan (5M)	17686	19295
YLA	L AWD Wagon (5M)	14967	16295
	Destination Charge:	495	495

Accessories

4AT	Transmission: 4-Speed Automatic (2.5 RS)	725	800
4AT	Transmission: 4-Speed Automatic (L)	725	800
BWH	Beige Carpet Floor Covers (L)	48	74
BWI	Gray Carpet Floor Covers (L)	48	74
BWK	Gray Carpet Floor Covers (2.5 RS)	48	74
DWB	Subwoofer/Amplifier	169	260
DWD	Upgraded Speakers (Coupe/Sedan)	65	100
DWE	Upgraded Speakers (Wagon)	127	195
DXA	Tweeter Kit (Pair)	65	100
EWB	CD Player	264	350
F06	Security Package 1	237	365
	Manufacturer Discount	(12)	NC
	Net Price	225	365
	Includes keyless entry system and security system upgrade kit.		
FPD	Roof Rack (Wagon)	157	241
HWB	Wheels: 15" Alloy (L)	413	550
	Includes attachment set.		
106	Premium Sound Package 1 (Wagon)	625	905
	Manufacturer Discount	(100)	(210)
	Net Price	525	695
	Includes CD player, upgraded speakers, subwoofer/amplifier and tweeter kit (pair).		
107	Premium Sound Package 1 (Coupe/Sedan)	563	810
	Manufacturer Discount	(93)	(185)
	Net Price	470	625
	Includes CD player, upgraded speakers, subwoofer/amplifier and tweeter kit (pair).		
13A	Popular Equipment Group 1 (Wagon)	280	430
	Manufacturer Discount	(15)	NC
	Net Price	265	430
	Includes custom tail pipe cover, roof rack, splash guards and beige carpet floor covers.		
13B	Popular Equipment Group 1 (Wagon)	280	430
	Manufacturer Discount	(15)	NC
	Net Price	265	430
	Includes custom tail pipe cover, roof rack, splash guards and gray carpet floor covers.		
14A	Popular Equipment Group II (L)	123	189
	Manufacturer Discount	(7)	NC
	Net Price	116	189
	Includes custom tail pipe cover, splash guards and beige carpet floor covers.		
14B	Popular Equipment Group II (L)	123	189
	Manufacturer Discount	(7)	NC
	Net Price	116	189
	Includes custom tail pipe cover, splash guards and gray carpet floor covers.		

IMPREZA / IMPREZA OUTBACK SPORT — SUBARU

CODE	DESCRIPTION	INVOICE	MSRP
JVA	Fog Lamps (L)	160	245
KWA	Air Filter *Includes air filter cover.*	56	85
KWD	Gray Armrest Extender (L)	62	94
KWE	Beige Armrest Extender (L)	62	94
KWF	Gray Armrest Extender (2.5 RS)	62	94
LPA	Splash Guards (L)	55	84
LSE	Custom Tail Pipe Cover (L)	20	31
LTB	Rear Bumper Cover	39	57
LWI	Moon Roof Air Deflector (2.5 RS)	39	60
MSP	Roof Visor (L)	69	134
MSS	Trunk Net (Coupe/Sedan)	25	39
MSV	Wheel Locks	22	34
MVF	Cargo Net (Wagon)	25	39
MVG	Cargo Tray (Wagon)	47	73
NWF	Gauge Pack (L)	296	395
NWG	Gauge Pack	296	395
PXB	Rear Differential Protector	57	88
RWA	Keyless Entry System	146	225
RWB	Security System Upgrade Kit	91	140

2000 IMPREZA OUTBACK

What's New?

For 2000, Subaru's Impreza Outback Sport receives some exterior design changes and 24-hour roadside assistance.

Review

All-wheel drive wagons are making a comeback, and Subaru is leading the charge. While European automakers build a variety of AWD family haulers, none can be had for less than 30 grand. This leaves quite a hole in the low-priced, all-weather wagon market, and Subaru is happy to fill it with the company's expanding Outback line.

The first Subaru to wear an Outback badge was the Impreza Outback Sport wagon in 1994. The success of this model led to the Legacy-based Outback Wagon in 1995 and the mini-SUV-challenging Forester in 1998.

Features unique to this version of the Impreza include a heavy-duty four-wheel independent suspension with 6.5 inches of ground clearance, 205/60 R15 M+S tires, splash guards, a two-tone paint scheme, and a rear bumper step pad. The wagon has a small cargo area when the rear seat is raised, partially due to the steeply raked rear window. Drop the seat, though, and you've got 62 cubic feet to mess around with. Quibbles about the Outback Sport include a cramped rear seat and ugly plastic wheelcovers.

Like most Subarus, the Impreza Outback Sport comes with a long list of standard features. Air conditioning, antilock brakes, power windows, a 12-volt power outlet in the cargo area, power side-view mirrors, a tilt steering column and a roof rack are all included in the base price. Those looking to spend more can opt for one of the all-weather packages and get items like a CD player, heated outside mirrors, heated seats, a viscous limited-slip rear differential, side-impact airbags, dual power moonroofs, leather upholstery and a front windshield wiper de-icer.

SUBARU
IMPREZA OUTBACK

CODE	DESCRIPTION	INVOICE	MSRP

For 2000, Subaru's Outback Sport model receives a more aggressive look with the addition of bi-level spoilers and body-colored side mirrors, door handles and side molding. Cruise control is now standard along with 24-hour roadside assistance.

We've driven the Outback Sport and thoroughly enjoyed it. All Imprezas behave like street-legal rally cars, and they're a hoot to toss around. Fling one into a corner, and it clings to the pavement. They are a blast to drive hard and fast, and the all-wheel-drive system performs brilliantly on a variety of road surfaces. Each model is available with an automatic transmission, but to take full advantage of the 2.2-liter, 142-horsepower boxer engine, we prefer the five-speed manual transmission. Interiors are comfortable—though the side glass feels a bit too close—and steering and braking are communicative.

The Impreza Outback Sport offers a unique combination of utility and fun. If you need a serious people mover or a fully capable off-road vehicle, it likely won't meet your demands. If, however, you want to avoid the mob mentality of buying a mini-SUV while still being able to occasionally take the road less traveled, the Outback Sport could be the ride you've been waiting for.

2000 Subaru Impreza Outback

Standard Equipment

OUTBACK SPORT (5M): 2.2L H4 SOHC SMPI 16-valve engine; 5-speed OD manual transmission; 75-amp alternator; full-time 4-wheel drive, 4.11 axle ratio; stainless steel exhaust; HD ride suspension, front independent strut suspension with anti-roll bar, front coil springs, rear independent strut suspension with anti-roll bar, rear coil springs; power rack-and-pinion steering with engine speed-sensing assist; front disc/rear drum brakes with 4-wheel antilock braking system; 13.2 gal. capacity fuel tank; front and rear mud flaps, side impact bars; roof rack; front and rear body-colored bumpers with rear step; black bodyside molding; lower accent two-tone paint with badging; aero-composite halogen auto off headlamps; driver's and passenger's power remote black folding outside mirrors; front and rear 15" x 6" steel wheels; P205/60SR15 A/S RWL front and rear tires; inside under cargo mounted compact steel spare wheel; air conditioning, rear heat ducts; AM/FM stereo, clock, seek-scan, cassette, 4 speakers, and manual retractable antenna; power door locks with 2 stage unlock, child safety rear door locks, remote fuel release; 2 power accessory outlets, driver's foot rest; instrumentation display includes tachometer, water temperature gauge, trip odometer; warning indicators include oil pressure, battery, key in ignition, low fuel, door ajar; driver's and passenger's front airbags; tinted windows,

366   www.edmunds.com   **EDMUND'S® NEW CARS**

IMPREZA OUTBACK SPORT — SUBARU

power front and rear windows with driver's 1-touch down, fixed 1/4 vent windows; fixed interval front windshield wipers, rear window wiper, rear window defroster; seating capacity of 5, front bucket seats, adjustable headrests, center armrest with storage, driver's seat includes 4-way direction control, passenger's seat includes 4-way direction control; 60-40 folding rear bench seat; front height adjustable seatbelts; cloth seats, cloth door trim insert, full vinyl headliner, full carpet floor covering; interior lights include dome light; steering wheel with tilt adjustment; passenger's side vanity mirror; day/night rearview mirror; full floor console, locking glove box, front cupholder, instrument panel bin, driver's and passenger's door bins; carpeted cargo floor, plastic trunk lid, cargo cover, cargo tie downs, cargo light; black grille, black side window moldings, black front windshield molding, black rear window molding and black door handles.

Base Prices

Code	Description	Invoice	MSRP
YLC	Impreza Outback Sport Wagon (5M)	16592	18095
	Destination Charge:	495	495

Accessories

Code	Description	Invoice	MSRP
4EAT	Transmission: Electric 4-Speed Auto with OD	725	800
BWI	Gray Carpet Floor Covers	48	74
DWB	Subwoofer/Amplifier	169	260
DWE	Upgraded Speakers	127	195
DXA	Tweeter Kit (Pair)	65	100
EWB	CD Player	264	350
F06	Security Package 1	237	365
	Manufacturer Discount	(12)	NC
	Net Price	225	365
	Includes keyless entry system and security system upgrade kit.		
HWB	Wheels: 15" Alloy	413	550
I06	Premium Sound Package I	625	905
	Manufacturer Discount	(100)	(210)
	Net Price	525	695
	Includes CD player, upgraded speakers, subwoofer/amplifier and tweeter kit (pair).		
JVA	Fog Lamps	160	245
KWA	Air Filter	56	85
KWD	Gray Armrest Extender	62	94
LSE	Custom Tail Pipe Cover	20	31
MSP	Roof Visor	69	134
MSV	Wheel Locks	22	34
MVF	Cargo Net	25	39
NWG	Gauge Pack	296	395
	Includes gray gauge pack housing.		
PXB	Rear Differential Protector	57	88
RWA	Keyless Entry System	146	225
RWB	Security System Upgrade Kit	91	140

SUBARU

LEGACY

| CODE | DESCRIPTION | | INVOICE | MSRP |

2000 LEGACY

2000 Subaru Legacy

What's New?

Subaru's hot-selling Legacy is completely redesigned for the millennium.

Review

All-wheel drive is Subaru's mantra, and every vehicle they sell in America comes equipped with it. This includes the entire Legacy lineup of sedans and wagons that offer passenger-car styling with sport utility-like grip in inclement weather. The 2000 Legacy has been improved in several key areas while maintaining its unique position in the automotive pantheon.

While not a clean-sheet redesign, enough has changed to call it new. The sedan lineup now consists of the base L model, the GT and the luxurious GT Limited, while wagons come in value-packed Brighton trim, midlevel L trim, or top-of-the-line GT trim. All Legacys will be powered by a Phase II 2.5-liter, 16-valve, 165-horsepower boxer engine under the hood and the lineup switches from a dual-overhead-cam engine to a single, making the car's performance livelier, thanks to 166 foot-pounds of torque @ 4,000 rpm. All models come with either a five-speed manual or four-speed automatic transmission.

Additionally, Legacys receive a new body shape and front grille that improves aerodynamics with a low 0.31 coefficient of drag (Cd) for the sedan and 0.32 Cd for the wagon. A hidden tailpipe, standard breakaway mirrors, and improved front and rear cupholders contribute to the new Legacy's appeal. All-weather packages now include a limited-slip rear differential, the GT gets multi-reflection headlights, and the GT wagon receives a dual moonroof. New safety features include daytime running lights, front seatbelt pre-tensioners and load limiters, and a three-point seatbelt for the rear-seat center position. Side-impact airbags are now standard on the GT Limited, Brighton Wagons get ABS with rear drum brakes, and all models except Brighton add rear-seat outboard and center headrests.

Structural refinement was also addressed in the latest redesign with an innovative "Ring-Shaped Reinforcement" body structure. This design provides greater protection in a wide variety of collisions, including frontal, offset, side and rear. The new body also comes with two safety beams in each front door and one beam in each of the rear doors to further isolate passengers from side-impact collisions.

LEGACY SUBARU

CODE	DESCRIPTION	INVOICE	MSRP

The interior has been revamped as well. Subaru ditched the tiny stereo buttons that made changing radio stations in the previous model an exercise in microsurgery. They've also enlarged the instrument panel and relocated the power door lock and window switches to a more user-friendly location on the door panel. The dashboard, center stack and instrument panel now has an organic flow that moves nicely across the interior, and the quality of the interior materials has been improved.

Subaru has a good thing going with its Legacy, which offers a little something for everyone. Roomy, comfortable, safe and loaded with utility, the model's standard all-wheel drive, along with its many new technical and stylistic innovations, and its reputation for stalwart reliability, should entice you to take a close look.

Standard Equipment

BRIGHTON AWD WAGON (5M): 2.5L H4 SOHC SMPI 16-valve engine; 5-speed OD manual transmission; 430-amp battery; 90-amp alternator; full-time 4-wheel drive, 3.9 axle ratio; steel exhaust; front independent strut suspension with anti-roll bar, front coil springs, rear independent multi-link suspension with anti-roll bar, rear coil springs; power rack-and-pinion steering with engine speed-sensing assist; front disc/rear drum brakes with 4-wheel antilock braking system; 16.9 gal. capacity fuel tank; side impact bars; front and rear body-colored bumpers with rear step; black bodyside molding; monotone paint; aero-composite halogen auto off headlamps with daytime running lights; driver's and passenger's manual black outside mirrors; front and rear 15" x 6" steel wheels; P195/60HR15 A/S BSW front and rear tires; inside under cargo mounted compact steel spare wheel; air conditioning, rear heat ducts; AM/FM stereo, clock, seek-scan, cassette, 2 speakers, and manual retractable antenna; power door locks, child safety rear door locks, remote fuel release; 1 power accessory outlet, driver's foot rest, smokers' package; instrumentation display includes water temperature gauge, trip odometer; warning indicators include oil pressure, battery, key in ignition, low fuel, door ajar, trunk ajar; driver's and passenger's front airbags; tinted windows, power front and rear windows with driver's 1-touch down, fixed 1/4 vent windows; fixed interval front windshield wipers, sun visor strip, fixed interval rear wiper, rear window defroster; seating capacity of 5, front bucket seats, adjustable headrests, center armrest with storage, driver's seat includes 4-way direction control, passenger's seat includes 4-way direction control; 60-40 folding rear bench seat; front height adjustable seatbelts; cloth seats, cloth door trim insert, full cloth headliner, full carpet floor covering, plastic/rubber gear shift knob; interior lights include dome light; steering wheel with tilt adjustment; day/night rearview mirror; full floor console, locking glove box with light, front and rear cupholders, instrument panel bin, driver's and passenger's door bins; carpeted cargo floor, plastic trunk lid, cargo light; chrome grille, black side window moldings, black front windshield molding, black rear window molding and black door handles.

L AWD SEDAN/WAGON (5M) (in addition to or instead of BRIGHTON AWD WAGON (5M) equipment): Four-wheel disc brakes with 4-wheel antilock braking system; P205/60HR15 A/S BSW front and rear tires; AM/FM stereo, clock, seek-scan, cassette, 4 speakers, and manual retractable antenna; cruise control; remote hatch/trunk release; instrumentation display includes tachometer; rear bench seat with adjustable headrests, center pass-thru armrest; interior lights include front reading lights; passenger's side vanity mirror and cargo concealed storage.

GT AWD SEDAN/WAGON (5M) (in addition to or instead of L AWD SEDAN (5M) equipment): Full-time viscous limited slip differential, 4.11 axle ratio; sport ride suspension; rear wing spoiler; front power sliding and tilting glass sunroof with sunshade; body-colored bodyside molding, rocker panel extensions; additional exterior lights include front fog/driving lights; driver's and passenger's power remote body-colored outside mirrors; front and rear 16" x 6.5" silver alloy wheels; P205/55HR16 A/S BSW front and rear tires; AM/FM stereo, clock, seek-scan, cassette, 4 speakers, and window grid antenna; power door locks with 2 stage unlock, remote keyless entry; variable intermittent front windshield wipers; driver's seat includes 4-way power seat, 6-way direction control, lumbar support; premium cloth seats, deluxe sound insulation, leather-wrapped gear shift knob; interior lights include 2 door curb lights; leather-wrapped steering wheel with tilt adjustment; dual illuminated vanity mirrors and body-colored door handles.

SUBARU LEGACY

CODE	DESCRIPTION	INVOICE	MSRP

GT LIMITED AWD SEDAN (5M) (in addition to or instead of GT AWD SEDAN (5M) equipment): AM/FM stereo, clock, seek-scan, cassette, single CD, 6 speakers, and window grid antenna; driver's and front passenger's seat mounted side airbags; leather seats and leatherette door trim insert.

Base Prices

CODE	DESCRIPTION	INVOICE	MSRP
YAA	L AWD Sedan (5M)	17470	19195
YAC	GT AWD Sedan (5M)	20681	22795
YAE	GT Limited AWD Sedan (5M)	22019	24295
YBA	Brighton AWD Wagon (5M)	17353	18395
YBC	L AWD Wagon (5M)	18097	19895
YBE	GT AWD Wagon (5M)	21487	23695
	Destination Charge:	495	495

Accessories

CODE	DESCRIPTION	INVOICE	MSRP
—	6 Pair Ski Attachment (Cross Bars) (Wagon - L/GT)	81	125
	Dealer installed accessory. Includes ski mounting clamps.		
—	6 Pair Ski Attachment (Round Cross Bars) (Wagon - L/GT)	81	125
	Dealer installed accessory. Includes ski, kayak and roof basket mounting clamps.		
—	6-Disc In-Dash CD Changer (GT/Limited)	371	495
	Dealer installed accessory.		
—	Air Filtration System	26	40
	Dealer installed accessory.		
—	Anti-Skip Mat	13	20
	Dealer installed accessory.		
—	Battery Warmer	19	30
	Dealer installed accessory.		
—	Bike Attachment Set (Cross Bars) (Wagon - L/GT)	84	130
	Dealer installed accessory. Includes bike, kayak and roof basket mounting clamps.		
—	Bike Attachment Set (Cross Bars) (Wagon - L/GT)	149	230
	Dealer installed accessory. Includes bike, kayak and roof basket mounting clamps.		
—	Bike Attachment Set (Round Cross Bars) (Wagon - L/GT)	149	230
	Dealer installed accessory. Includes bike mounting clamps.		
—	Bike Attachment Set (Round Cross Bars) (Wagon - L/GT)	84	130
	Dealer installed accessory. Includes ski, kayak and roof basket mounting clamps.		
—	CD Player (All Except Limited)	251	335
	Dealer installed accessory.		
—	Car Cover	65	100
	Dealer installed accessory.		
—	Car Cover Bag	6	10
	Dealer installed accessory.		
—	Cargo Bin (Wagon)	84	130
	Dealer installed accessory.		
—	Cargo Net (Wagon)	23	35
	Dealer installed accessory.		

LEGACY — SUBARU

CODE	DESCRIPTION	INVOICE	MSRP
—	Cargo Tray/Mat (Wagon)	45	70
	Dealer installed accessory.		
—	Compartment Sep/Dog Guard (Wagon)	91	140
	Dealer installed accessory.		
—	Cross Bar Set Round (Wagon - L/GT)	104	160
	Dealer installed accessory.		
—	Cross Bars (Wagon - L/GT)	104	160
	Dealer installed accessory. NOT AVAILABLE with Cross Bar Set Round, Kayak Carrier Set, 6 Pair Ski Attachment, Bike Attachment Set, Bike Attachment Set.		
—	Engine Block Heater	19	30
	Dealer installed accessory.		
—	Full Front End Cover (Sedan)	78	120
	Dealer installed accessory.		
—	Full Front End Cover (Wagon)	78	120
	Dealer installed accessory.		
—	Gray Carpet Floor Covers	45	70
	Dealer installed accessory.		
—	Gray Illuminated Vanity Visor (L/Brighton)	63	97
	Dealer installed accessory.		
—	Gray Luggage Compartment Cover (Brighton)	81	125
	Dealer installed accessory.		
—	Hood Front End Cover (Sedan)	32	50
	Dealer installed accessory.		
—	Hood Front End Cover (Wagon)	32	50
	Dealer installed accessory.		
—	Kayak Carrier Set (Cross Bars) (Wagon - L/GT)	83	127
	Dealer installed accessory. Includes bike, kayak and roof basket mounting clamps.		
—	Kayak Carrier Set (Round Cross Bars) (Wagon - L/GT)	83	127
	Dealer installed accessory. Includes bike, kayak and roof basket mounting clamps.		
—	Keyless Entry System (L)	102	157
	Dealer installed accessory.		
—	Leather Shift Knob - A/T (GT Wagon)	38	59
	Dealer installed accessory. REQUIRES 4AT.		
—	Leather Shift Knob - A/T (L/Brighton)	38	59
	Dealer installed accessory. REQUIRES 4AT.		
—	Leather Shift Knob - M/T (Sedan L/Wagon)	32	49
	Dealer installed accessory.		
—	Moon Roof Air Deflector (Sedan - GT/Limited)	29	45
	Dealer installed accessory.		
—	Multi-Reflector Fog Lights (L/Brighton)	149	230
	Dealer installed accessory.		
—	Power Outlet (GT/Limited)	32	50
	Dealer installed accessory. REQUIRES 4AT.		
—	Power Outlet (L/Brighton)	32	50
	Dealer installed accessory. REQUIRES 4AT.		
—	Rear Bumper Corner Molding (2 Pair)	38	58
	Dealer installed accessory.		

SUBARU

LEGACY

CODE	DESCRIPTION	INVOICE	MSRP
—	Rear Bumper Cover (Wagon)	26	40
	Dealer installed accessory.		
—	Rear Differential Protector	45	70
	Dealer installed accessory.		
—	Rear Gate Bar (Wagon)	29	45
	Dealer installed accessory.		
—	Rear Window Dust Deflector (Wagon)	46	71
	Dealer installed accessory.		
—	Roof Cargo Carrier (Wagon - L/GT)	296	395
	Dealer installed accessory.		
—	Rubber Floor Mats	32	50
	Dealer installed accessory.		
—	SD Black Granite Spoiler (Sedan - GT/Limited)	185	285
	Dealer installed accessory.		
—	SD Deep Sapphire Pearl Spoiler (L Sedan)	185	285
	Dealer installed accessory.		
—	SD Primed Spoiler (Sedan)	162	250
	Dealer installed accessory.		
—	SD Rio Red Spoiler (Sedan - GT/Limited)	185	285
	Dealer installed accessory.		
—	SD Timberline Green Pearl Spoiler (Sedan)	185	285
	Dealer installed accessory.		
—	SD Titanium Pearl Spoiler (Sedan - GT/Limited)	185	285
	Dealer installed accessory.		
—	SD White Birch Spoiler (Sedan)	185	285
	Dealer installed accessory.		
—	SD Winestone Pearl Spoiler (L Sedan)	185	285
	Dealer installed accessory.		
—	SD Wintergreen Metallic Spoiler (L Sedan)	185	285
	Dealer installed accessory.		
—	Security System Upgrade (All Except Brighton)	104	160
	Dealer installed accessory.		
—	Splash Guards (L/Brighton)	45	70
	Dealer installed accessory.		
—	Stabilizing Brackets (4) (Wagon - L/GT)	26	40
	Dealer installed accessory.		
—	Subwoofer/Amplifier	150	230
	Dealer installed accessory.		
—	Transmission: Electronic 4-Speed Automatic (GT/Limited)	722	800
	Includes 4.44 axle ratio.		
—	Trunk Net (Sedan)	17	26
	Dealer installed accessory.		
—	Tweeter Kit (All Except Limited)	58	90
	Dealer installed accessory.		
—	Upgraded Speakers (All Except Limited)	97	150
	Dealer installed accessory.		

LEGACY — SUBARU

CODE	DESCRIPTION	INVOICE	MSRP
—	Wheel Locks	16	24
	Dealer installed accessory.		
—	Wheels: 15" Alloy (L/Brighton)	380	507
	Dealer installed accessory. Includes attachment set.		
—	Woodgrained Patterned Door Switches (All Except Brighton)	45	70
	Dealer installed accessory.		
4AT	Transmission: Electronic 4-Speed Automatic (L/Brighton)	722	800
	Includes 4.11 axle ratio.		
BYA	Gray Carpet Floor Covers	48	74
	Dealer installed accessory.		
DYA	Upgraded Speakers (L/GT)	126	195
DYB	Tweeter Kit (L/GT)	65	100
DYC	Subwoofer/Amplifier	169	260
EYA	CD Player (GT)	264	350
EYB	CD Player (L/Brighton)	264	350
EYC	6-Disc In-Dash CD Changer (GT/Limited)	384	510
FYA	Cross Bars (Wagon - L/GT)	106	170
HWB	Wheels: 15" Alloy (L/Brighton)	413	550
	Includes attachment set.		
IYA	Woodgrained Patterned Door Switches (All Except Brighton)	65	100
IYB	A/T Leather Shift Knob (L/Brighton/GT Wagon)	44	67
	REQUIRES 4AT.		
KYA	Air Filtration System	39	60
L02	Security Group (L)	234	360
	Manufacturer Discount	(15)	NC
	Net Price	219	360
	Includes keyless entry system and security system upgrade.		
L03	Premium Sound Package 1A (L)	624	905
	Manufacturer Discount	(99)	(210)
	Net Price	525	695
	Includes CD player, upgraded speakers, tweeter kit and subwoofer/amplifier. NOT AVAILABLE with CD Player, Subwoofer/Amplifier, Upgraded Speakers, Tweeter Kit.		
L04	Premium Sound Package 1B (GT)	624	905
	Manufacturer Discount	(99)	(210)
	Net Price	525	695
	Includes CD player, upgraded speakers, tweeter kit and subwoofer/amplifier. NOT AVAILABLE with CD Player, Subwoofer/Amplifier, Upgraded Speakers, Tweeter Kit, 6-Disc In-Dash CD Changer.		
L05	Premium Sound Package 2 (GT)	744	1065
	Manufacturer Discount	(144)	(270)
	Net Price	600	795
	Includes 6-disc in-dash CD changer, upgraded speakers, tweeter kit and subwoofer/amplifier. NOT AVAILABLE with 6-Disc In-Dash CD Changer, Subwoofer/Amplifier, Upgraded Speakers, Tweeter Kit, CD Player.		

SUBARU LEGACY

CODE	DESCRIPTION	INVOICE	MSRP
L06	Premium Sound Package 3 (Limited)	553	770
	Manufacturer Discount	(78)	(135)
	Net Price	475	635
	Includes 6-disc in-dash CD changer and subwoofer/amplifier.		
L1A	Popular Equipment Group 1 (L Wagon)	213	334
	Manufacturer Discount	(20)	NC
	Net Price	193	334
	Includes cross bars, splash guards and gray carpet floor covers. NOT AVAILABLE with Cross Bars, Gray Carpet Floor Covers, Splash Guards, Rubber Floor Mats.		
L2A	Popular Equipment Group 2 (L Sedan)	107	164
	Manufacturer Discount	(10)	NC
	Net Price	97	164
	Includes splash guards and gray carpet floor covers.		
L3A	Popular Equipment Group 3 (Wagon - L/GT)	154	244
	Manufacturer Discount	(10)	NC
	Net Price	144	244
	Includes cross bars and gray carpet floor covers.		
LSB	M/T Leather Shift Knob (Brighton/L/GT Wagon)	37	56
LWI	Moon Roof Air Deflector (Sedan - GT/Limited)	41	63
LYA	Rear Gate Bar (Wagon)	42	65
LYC	Rear Window Dust Deflector (Wagon)	65	100
LYD	Multi-Reflector Fog Lights (L/Brighton)	166	255
LYE	Splash Guards (L Sedan)	59	90
LYF	Splash Guards (Wagon - L/Brighton)	59	90
MSV	Wheel Locks	22	34
MYC	Trunk Net (Sedan)	21	32
MYD	Cargo Net (Wagon)	26	40
MYG	Cargo Tray/Mat (Wagon)	48	74
MYK	Gray Illuminated Vanity Visor (L/Brighton)	79	122
NYA	Power Outlet	47	73
	REQUIRES 4AT.		
OYA	Luggage Compartment Cover (Gray) (Brighton)	83	128
PXC	Rear Bumper Corner Molding (2 Pair)	35	54
PYA	Rear Differential Protector	52	80
PYD	Rear Bumper Cover (Wagon)	36	56
RYB	Keyless Entry System (L)	114	175
RYC	Security System Upgrade (All Except Brighton)	120	185
SYK	SD Deep Sapphire Pearl Spoiler (L Sedan)	212	325
SYL	SD Wintergreen Metallic Spoiler (L Sedan)	212	325
SYM	SD Titanium Pearl Spoiler (Sedan - GT/Limited)	212	325
SYN	SD Timberline Green Pearl Spoiler (Sedan)	212	325
SYO	SD Rio Red Spoiler (Sedan - GT/Limited)	212	325
SYP	SD Winestone Pearl Spoiler (L Sedan)	212	325
SYQ	SD Black Granite Spoiler (Sedan - GT/Limited)	212	325
SYR	SD White Birch Spoiler (Sedan)	212	325

2000 LEGACY OUTBACK

2000 Subaru Legacy Outback

What's New?

As with the Legacy platform it's based on, Subaru's hot-selling Outback is completely redesigned for the millennium.

Review

What recipe does an automotive manufacturer use to boost sagging sales? Ask any Subaru executive and she'll tell you to take one part popular Australian movie star and one part advanced all-wheel-drive system. Stir in an undercurrent of SUV backlash with a dash of resurgence in the station wagon market, and behold: The perfect environment for a totally new Subaru Outback.

Available in either wagon or sedan form, the Outback is Subaru's answer to the question: Why would anyone want to drive an ill-handling, gas-guzzling, difficult to park SUV? With 7.3 inches of ground clearance, standard all-wheel drive and a base price in the low 20s, the Outback offers on-road practicality with off-road capability at a bargain price. While no match for the likes of Jeep's Grand Cherokee or Toyota's Land Cruiser in terms of hill climbing, the Outback can hold its own in light to moderate off-road situations without losing an oil pan or cracking a differential.

A Phase II 2.5-liter, 16-valve, 165-horsepower boxer engine powers both Outback models. By reconfiguring the engine's valvetrain, Subaru squeezed a bit more torque from the 2.5-liter, upping the total to 166 foot-pounds @ 4,000 rpm. All models come with either a five-speed manual or four-speed automatic transmission. The Outback Wagon and Outback Limited Sedan come with both the four-speed automatic and Subaru's Active All-Wheel Drive that can transfer power to the wheels that need it even before slippage occurs.

Additionally, all Outbacks receive four-wheel disc brakes, ABS, protective lower body cladding, a heavy-duty four-wheel independent suspension, and 24-hour roadside assistance as standard equipment. Opt for the Outback wagon and you'll also get a 60/40 split folding rear seat, keyless entry, a 12-volt cargo area power outlet, a rear wiper/washer, and breakaway power side-view mirrors. Limited models, in sedan or wagon configuration, get leather upholstery, heated seats, a CD player, and a power moonroof (dual moonroofs on the wagon).

SUBARU
LEGACY OUTBACK

CODE	DESCRIPTION	INVOICE	MSRP

Safety was another area where Subaru refused to skimp. The new Outback models feature a "Ring-Shaped Reinforcement" body structure for maximum protection against frontal, offset, side and rear impacts. Side beams in both the front and rear doors further enhance side-impact protection, but, regrettably, only the Limited models come with side airbags.

These structural enhancements not only boost safety but also improve the Outback's torsional strength by 20 percent. Combined with the new multi-link rear suspension and rubber-isolated subframe, the sedans and wagons offer superior handling and reduced road noise compared to last year's models.

We like the fact that Subaru offers a viable alternative to the SUV. The Outback proves that safety, style and all-weather traction can be had in a non-truck-based vehicle, and at a reasonable price. Now if we could just get one of their turbocharged engines from Japan over here.

Standard Equipment

BASE WAGON (5M): 2.5L H4 SOHC SMPI 16-valve engine; 5-speed OD manual transmission; 430-amp battery; 90-amp alternator; full-time 4.11 axle ratio; steel exhaust; HD ride suspension, front independent strut suspension with anti-roll bar, front coil springs, rear independent multi-link suspension with anti-roll bar, rear coil springs; power rack-and-pinion steering with engine speed-sensing assist; 4-wheel disc brakes with 4-wheel antilock braking system; 16.9 gal. capacity fuel tank; front and rear mud flaps, side impact bars; roof rack; front and rear body-colored bumpers with rear step; black bodyside molding, rocker panel extensions; lower accent two-tone paint; aero-composite halogen auto off headlamps with daytime running lights; additional exterior lights include front fog/driving lights; driver's and passenger's power remote black outside mirrors; front and rear 16" x 6.5" silver alloy wheels; P225/60HR16 M&S RWL front and rear tires; inside under cargo mounted compact steel spare wheel; air conditioning, rear heat ducts; AM/FM stereo, clock, seek-scan, cassette, 4 speakers, and manual retractable antenna; cruise control; power door locks with 2 stage unlock, remote keyless entry, child safety rear door locks, remote fuel release; 2 power accessory outlets, driver's foot rest, smokers' package; instrumentation display includes tachometer, water temperature gauge, trip odometer; warning indicators include oil pressure, battery, key in ignition, low fuel, door ajar, trunk ajar; driver's and passenger's front airbags; tinted windows, power front and rear windows with driver's 1-touch down, fixed 1/4 vent windows; fixed interval front windshield wipers; sun visor strip, fixed interval rear wiper, rear window defroster; seating capacity of 5, front bucket seats, adjustable headrests, center armrest with storage, driver's seat includes 4-way power seat, 6-way direction control, lumbar support, passenger's seat includes 4-way direction control; 60-40 folding rear bench seat with adjustable headrests; front height adjustable seatbelts; cloth seats, cloth door trim insert, full cloth headliner, full carpet floor covering with carpeted floor mats, plastic/rubber gear shift knob; interior lights include dome light, front reading lights; steering wheel with tilt adjustment; passenger's side vanity mirror; day/night rearview mirror; full floor console, mini overhead console with storage, locking glove box with light, front and rear cupholders, instrument panel bin, driver's and passenger's door bins; carpeted cargo floor, plastic trunk lid, cargo cover, cargo tie downs, cargo light, cargo concealed storage; colored grille, black side window moldings, black front windshield molding, black rear window molding and black door handles.

LIMITED WAGON (5M) (in addition to or instead of BASE WAGON (5M) equipment): Engine block heater; viscous limited slip differential; front and rear power sliding and tilting glass sunroof with sunshade; lower accent two-tone paint with badging; driver's and passenger's power remote body-colored heated outside mirrors; AM/FM stereo, clock, seek-scan, cassette, single CD, 8 speakers, and window grid antenna; driver's and front passenger's seat mounted side airbags; deep tinted windows; heated variable intermittent front windshield wipers; heated-cushion front bucket seats; leather seats, leatherette door trim insert, leather-wrapped gear shift knob; interior lights include 2 door curb lights; leather-wrapped steering wheel with tilt adjustment; dual illuminated vanity mirrors; 2 seat back storage pockets and chrome grille.

376   www.edmunds.com   **EDMUND'S® NEW CARS**

LEGACY OUTBACK — SUBARU

CODE	DESCRIPTION	INVOICE	MSRP

LIMITED SEDAN (4A) (in addition to or instead of LIMITED WAGON (5M) equipment): Four-speed electronic OD auto transmission with lock-up; 490-amp battery; 4.44 axle ratio; front and rear body-colored bumpers; body-colored bodyside molding; monotone paint; driver's and passenger's power remote black heated outside mirrors; AM/FM stereo, clock, seek-scan, cassette, single CD, 6 speakers, and window grid antenna; remote hatch/trunk release; tinted windows; rear bench seat with adjustable headrests, center pass-thru armrest and interior lights include dome light, front reading lights.

Base Prices

Code	Description	Invoice	MSRP
YAG	Limited Sedan (4A)	23471	25895
YBQ	Base Wagon (5M)	20588	22695
YBY	Limited Wagon (5M)	23635	26095
	Destination Charge:	495	495

Accessories

Code	Description	Invoice	MSRP
—	6 Pair Ski Attachment (Cross Bars) (Wagon)	81	125
	Dealer installed accessory. Includes ski mounting clamps.		
—	6 Pair Ski Attachment (Round Cross Bars) (Wagon)	81	125
	Dealer installed accessory. Includes ski, kayak and roof basket mounting clamps.		
—	6-Disc In-Dash CD Changer	371	495
	Dealer installed accessory.		
—	Air Filtration System	26	40
	Dealer installed accessory.		
—	All Weather Package (Base Wagon)	451	500
	Dealer installed accessory. Includes viscous limited-slip rear differential, heated front seats, heated exterior mirrors and windshield wiper de-icer.		
—	Anti-Skip Mat	13	20
	Dealer installed accessory.		
—	Battery Warmer	19	30
	Dealer installed accessory.		
—	Beige Illuminated Vanity Visor (Base Wagon)	63	97
	Dealer installed accessory.		
—	Bike Attachment Set (Cross Bars) (Wagon)	84	130
	Dealer installed accessory. Includes bike, kayak and roof basket mounting clamps.		
—	Bike Attachment Set (Cross Bars) (Wagon)	149	230
	Dealer installed accessory. Includes bike, kayak and roof basket mounting clamps.		
—	Bike Attachment Set (Round Cross Bars) (Wagon)	149	230
	Dealer installed accessory. Includes bike mounting clamps.		
—	Bike Attachment Set (Round Cross Bars) (Wagon)	84	130
	Dealer installed accessory. Includes ski, kayak and roof basket mounting clamps.		
—	Bike Carrier (Trailer Hitch) (Wagon)	130	200
	Dealer installed accessory.		
—	CD Player (Wagon)	251	335
	Dealer installed accessory.		
—	Car Cover	65	100
	Dealer installed accessory.		

SUBARU
LEGACY OUTBACK

CODE	DESCRIPTION	INVOICE	MSRP
—	Car Cover Bag	6	10
	Dealer installed accessory.		
—	Cargo Bin (Wagon)	84	130
	Dealer installed accessory.		
—	Cargo Net (Wagon)	23	35
	Dealer installed accessory.		
—	Compartment Sep/Dog Guard (Limited Wagon)	91	140
	Dealer installed accessory.		
—	Compartment Sep/Dog Guard (Wagon)	91	140
	Dealer installed accessory.		
—	Cross Bar Set Round (Wagon)	104	160
	Dealer installed accessory.		
—	Engine Block Heater	19	30
	Dealer installed accessory.		
—	Full Front End Cover	78	120
	Dealer installed accessory.		
—	Gray Illuminated Vanity Visor (Base Wagon)	63	97
	Dealer installed accessory.		
—	Hood Front End Cover	32	50
	Dealer installed accessory.		
—	Integrated Child Safety Seat (Base Wagon)	179	200
	Dealer installed accessory.		
—	Integrated Child Safety Seat (Base Wagon)	180	200
	Dealer installed accessory. REQUIRES AW.		
—	Kayak Carrier Set (Cross Bars) (Wagon)	83	127
	Dealer installed accessory. Includes bike, kayak and roof basket mounting clamps.		
—	Kayak Carrier Set (Round Cross Bars) (Wagon)	83	127
	Dealer installed accessory. Includes bike, kayak and roof basket mounting clamps.		
—	Leather Shift Knob - A/T (Wagon)	38	59
	Dealer installed accessory. REQUIRES 4AT.		
—	Leather Shift Knob - M/T (Wagon)	32	49
	Dealer installed accessory.		
—	Moon Roof Air Deflector (Sedan)	29	45
	Dealer installed accessory.		
—	Power Outlet (Wagon)	32	50
	Dealer installed accessory. REQUIRES 4AT.		
—	Rear Bumper Corner Molding (2 Pair)	38	58
	Dealer installed accessory.		
—	Rear Differential Protector	45	70
	Dealer installed accessory.		
—	Rear Gate Bar (Wagon)	29	45
	Dealer installed accessory.		
—	Rear Window Dust Deflector (Wagon)	46	71
	Dealer installed accessory.		
—	Roof Cargo Carrier (Wagon)	296	395
	Dealer installed accessory.		

LEGACY OUTBACK — SUBARU

CODE	DESCRIPTION	INVOICE	MSRP
—	Rubber Floor Mats	32	50
	Dealer installed accessory.		
—	SD Black Granite Spoiler (Sedan)	185	285
	Dealer installed accessory. NOT AVAILABLE with SD Primed Spoiler, SD Timberline Green Pearl Spoiler, SD White Birch Spoiler, SD Winestone Pearl Spoiler.		
—	SD Primed Spoiler (Sedan)	162	250
	Dealer installed accessory. NOT AVAILABLE with SD Black Granite Spoiler, SD Timberline Green Pearl Spoiler, SD White Birch Spoiler, SD Winestone Pearl Spoiler.		
—	SD Timberline Green Pearl Spoiler (Sedan)	185	285
	Dealer installed accessory. NOT AVAILABLE with SD Black Granite Spoiler, SD Primed Spoiler, SD White Birch Spoiler, SD Winestone Pearl Spoiler.		
—	SD White Birch Spoiler (Sedan)	185	285
	Dealer installed accessory. NOT AVAILABLE with SD Black Granite Spoiler, SD Primed Spoiler, SD Timberline Green Pearl Spoiler, SD Winestone Pearl Spoiler.		
—	SD Winestone Pearl Spoiler (Sedan)	185	285
	Dealer installed accessory. NOT AVAILABLE with SD Black Granite Spoiler, SD Primed Spoiler, SD Timberline Green Pearl Spoiler, SD White Birch Spoiler.		
—	Security System Upgrade	104	160
	Dealer installed accessory.		
—	Stabilizing Brackets (4) (Wagon)	26	40
	Dealer installed accessory.		
—	Subwoofer/Amplifier	150	230
	Dealer installed accessory.		
—	Trailer Hitch (Wagon)	172	265
	Dealer installed accessory.		
—	Trunk Net (Sedan)	17	26
	Dealer installed accessory.		
—	Tweeter Kit (Base Wagon)	58	90
	Dealer installed accessory.		
—	Upgraded Speakers (Base Wagon)	97	150
	Dealer installed accessory.		
—	Wheel Locks	16	24
	Dealer installed accessory.		
—	Woodgrained Patterned Door Switches	45	70
	Dealer installed accessory.		
4AT	Transmission: Electronic 4-Speed Automatic (Wagon)	722	800
	Includes 4.44 axle ratio.		
DYA	Upgraded Speakers (Base Wagon)	126	195
DYB	Tweeter Kit (Base Wagon)	65	100
DYC	Subwoofer/Amplifier	169	260
EYA	CD Player (Base Wagon)	264	350
EYC	6-Disc In-Dash CD Changer	384	510
IYA	Woodgrained Patterned Door Switches	65	100
IYB	A/T Leather Shift Knob (Wagon)	44	67
	REQUIRES 4AT.		
KYA	Air Filtration System	39	60

SUBARU LEGACY OUTBACK

CODE	DESCRIPTION	INVOICE	MSRP
L04	Premium Sound Package 1B (Base Wagon)	624	905
	Manufacturer Discount	(99)	(210)
	Net Price	525	695
	Includes CD player, upgraded speakers, tweeter kit and subwoofer/amplifier. NOT AVAILABLE with CD Player, Subwoofer/Amplifier, Upgraded Speakers, Tweeter Kit, 6-Disc In-Dash CD Changer.		
L05	Premium Sound Package 2 (Base Wagon)	744	1065
	Manufacturer Discount	(144)	(270)
	Net Price	600	795
	Includes 6-disc in-dash CD changer, upgraded speakers, tweeter kit and subwoofer/amplifier. NOT AVAILABLE with 6-Disc In-Dash CD Changer, Subwoofer/Amplifier, Upgraded Speakers, Tweeter Kit, CD Player.		
L06	Premium Sound Package 3 (Limited)	553	770
	Manufacturer Discount	(78)	(135)
	Net Price	475	635
	Includes 6-disc in-dash CD changer and subwoofer/amplifier.		
LSB	M/T Leather Shift Knob (Wagon)	37	56
LWI	Moon Roof Air Deflector (Sedan)	41	63
LYA	Rear Gate Bar (Wagon)	42	65
LYC	Rear Window Dust Deflector (Wagon)	65	100
LYH	Trailer Hitch (Wagon)	188	289
MSV	Wheel Locks	22	34
MYC	Trunk Net (Sedan)	21	32
MYD	Cargo Net (Wagon)	26	40
MYJ	Beige Illuminated Vanity Visor (Base Wagon)	79	122
MYK	Gray Illuminated Vanity Visor (Base Wagon)	79	122
NYA	Power Outlet (Base Wagon)	47	73
	REQUIRES 4AT.		
PXC	Rear Bumper Corner Molding (2 Pair)	35	54
PYA	Rear Differential Protector	52	80
RYC	Security System Upgrade	120	185
SYN	SD Timberline Green Pearl Spoiler (Sedan)	212	325
	NOT AVAILABLE with SD Black Granite Spoiler, SD Primed Spoiler, SD Timberline Green Pearl Spoiler, SD White Birch Spoiler, SD Winestone Pearl Spoiler.		
SYP	SD Winestone Pearl Spoiler (Sedan)	212	325
	NOT AVAILABLE with SD Black Granite Spoiler, SD Primed Spoiler, SD Timberline Green Pearl Spoiler, SD White Birch Spoiler, SD Winestone Pearl Spoiler.		
SYQ	SD Black Granite Spoiler (Sedan)	212	325
	NOT AVAILABLE with SD Black Granite Spoiler, SD Primed Spoiler, SD Timberline Green Pearl Spoiler, SD White Birch Spoiler, SD Winestone Pearl Spoiler.		
SYR	SD White Birch Spoiler (Sedan)	212	325
	NOT AVAILABLE with SD Black Granite Spoiler, SD Primed Spoiler, SD Timberline Green Pearl Spoiler, SD White Birch Spoiler, SD Winestone Pearl Spoiler.		

2000 ESTEEM

2000 Suzuki Esteem

What's New?

The 1.8-liter engine is now standard on all models. GLX and GLX+ models receive 15-inch wheels and tires as standard equipment. Two new paint colors, Bluish Black Pearl and Cassis Red Pearl, replace Mars Red and Midnight Black.

Review

Competing in the subcompact market, the Esteem Sedan and Wagon are available in three equipment levels: GL, GLX and GLX+. The Esteem's styling is better than most of the cars in this class, featuring softly curved lines, a chrome grille, and large, angled multi-reflector headlights.

For 2000, a 1.8-liter, 16-valve, double overhead-cam engine is standard on all models. It generates 122 horsepower at 6,300 rpm and 117 foot-pounds of torque at 3,500 rpm. Acceleration is acceptable with this engine, though it becomes noisy when pushed.

All three of the trim levels come with a long list of standard equipment. The base model GL features items such as a AM/FM/cassette stereo system, an electric rear-window defogger, a fold-down rear seat, a remote trunk release, and 185/60R14 all-season tires. The GLX and GLX+ add upgraded upholstery, keyless entry, power windows and locks, a split-folding rear seat, a tachometer, and larger, all-season radial tires. Air conditioning and power steering are standard on all three trim levels.

The Esteem Sedan and Wagon will seat five. The Wagon holds 61 cubic feet of cargo with the rear seatbacks folded down. Suzuki also says the integrated roof rails can hold up to 100 pounds of cargo. The interior does suffer from seats that lack height or lumbar adjustment and a steering wheel that doesn't tilt. Hard plastic is the predominant interior material used.

We'd like to say that the Esteem is now on equal footing with the rest of the subcompact market. Unfortunately, this is a crowded segment and it takes more than clean styling and a 1.8-liter engine to compete. With the Esteem's lackluster warranty and merely adequate performance, entries from Dodge, Ford, and even Hyundai offer superior value.

SUZUKI ESTEEM

CODE	DESCRIPTION	INVOICE	MSRP

Standard Equipment

GL 1.6 SEDAN (5M): 1.6L I4 SOHC MPI 16-valve engine; 5-speed OD manual transmission; 390-amp battery; engine oil cooler; 70-amp alternator; front-wheel drive; 3.79 axle ratio; stainless steel exhaust; front independent strut suspension with anti-roll bar, front coil springs, rear independent strut suspension with anti-roll bar, rear coil springs; power rack-and-pinion steering; front disc/rear drum brakes; 12.7 gal. capacity fuel tank; side impact bars; front and rear body-colored bumpers; black bodyside molding; monotone paint; aero-composite halogen headlamps with daytime running lights; driver's and passenger's manual black folding outside mirrors; front and rear 14" x 5.5" steel wheels; P185/60SR14 A/S BSW front and rear tires; inside under cargo mounted compact steel spare wheel; air conditioning, rear heat ducts; premium AM/FM stereo, seek-scan, cassette, 4 speakers, and manual retractable antenna; child safety rear door locks, remote hatch/trunk release, remote fuel release; 1power accessory outlet, driver's foot rest; instrumentation display includes water temperature gauge, in-dash clock, trip odometer, warning indicators include oil pressure, battery, lights on, key in ignition; driver's and passenger's front airbags, tinted glass windows, manual front and rear windows; variable intermittent front windshield wipers, rear window defroster; seating capacity of 5, front bucket seats, adjustable headrests, center armrest with storage, driver's seat includes 4-way direction control, passenger's seat includes 4-way direction control; full folding rear bench seat with adjustable headrests; front height adjustable seatbelts; cloth seats, cloth door trim insert, full cloth headliner, full carpet floor covering, plastic/rubber gear shift knob; interior lights include dome light, day/night rearview mirror; full floor console, glove box, front cupholder, instrument panel bin, driver's and passenger's door bins; carpeted cargo floor; chrome grille, chrome side window moldings, black front windshield molding, black rear window molding and black door handles.

GL 1.8 SEDAN (5M) (in addition to or instead of GL 1.6 SEDAN (5M) equipment): 1.8L I4 SOHC MPI 16-valve engine; 3.72 axle ratio.

GLX 1.8 SEDAN (5M) (in addition to or instead of GL 1.8 SEDAN (5M) equipment): Front and rear mud flaps; driver's and passenger's power remote black folding outside mirrors; front and rear 15" x 5.5" silver alloy wheels; P195/55SR15 A/S BSW front and rear tires; power door locks, remote keyless entry; instrumentation display includes tachometer; power front and rear windows with driver's 1-touch down; 60-40 folding rear bench seat with adjustable headrests; passenger's side vanity mirror, 2 seat back storage pockets and cargo light.

GLX+ 1.8 SEDAN (4A) (in addition to or instead of GLX 1.8 SEDAN (4A) equipment): 4-speed electronic OD auto transmission with lock-up; 3.78 axle ratio; front disc/rear drum brakes with 4-wheel antilock braking system and cruise control.

GL/GLX 1.8 WAGON (5M) (in addition to or instead of GL/GLX 1.8 SEDAN (5M) equipment): Fixed 1/4 vent windows, rear window wiper; 60-40 folding rear bench seat with fixed headrests; plastic trunk lid, cargo cover, cargo tie downs and cargo concealed storage.

GLX+ 1.8 WAGON (4A) (in addition to or instead of GLX+ 1.8 SEDAN (4A) equipment): Front power sliding and tilting glass sunroof with sunshade; fixed 1/4 vent windows, rear window wiper; 60-40 folding rear bench seat with fixed headrests; plastic trunk lid, cargo cover, cargo tie downs and cargo concealed storage.

Base Prices

S6L63CV	GL 1.6 Sedan (5M)	11903	12399
S6L77CV	GL 1.8 Sedan (5M)	12383	12899
S6L75Y	GLX 1.8 Sedan (5M)	13343	13899
S6L78GY	GLX+ 1.8 Sedan (4A)	15071	15699
WGN77CV	GL 1.8 Wagon (5M)	12863	13399

ESTEEM / SWIFT — SUZUKI

CODE	DESCRIPTION	INVOICE	MSRP
WGN77EY	GLX 1.8 Wagon (5M)	13823	14399
WGM78FY	GLX+ 1.8 Wagon (4A)	15743	16399
Destination Charge:		450	450

Accessories

—	Sport Package (GLX Sedan)	424	600
	Includes rear spoiler, fog lamps and black body color.		
—	Transmission: 4-Speed Automatic (1.8 GL/1.8 GLX)	960	1000
	Includes 3.78 axle ratio.		
—	Transmission: 4-Speed Automatic (GL 1.6 Sedan)	780	1000
	Includes 3.78 axle ratio.		
—	Two-Tone Paint (GLX+ Wagon)	178	200

2000 SWIFT

2000 Suzuki Swift

What's New?

The 2000 Suzuki Swift remains mechanically unchanged. Two new exterior colors—Brilliant Blue Metallic and Catseye Blue Metallic—are offered.

Review

This is it. This is the car for those of you who need to buy a new vehicle but don't have much more than the lint in your pockets to spend. Suzuki Motor Corp., noted for its mini sport-utility wagons and motorcycles, had you in mind when they developed the Swift.

Calling Suzuki's entry-level hatchback "Swift" borders on false advertising. Fortunately for Suzuki, the Swift has other attributes that keep consumers from filing a class-action lawsuit. The most notable is its price; the Swift comes in at under $10,000. Heck, these days most people

SUZUKI

SWIFT

CODE	DESCRIPTION	INVOICE	MSRP

spend more on used cars without warranties than you'll pay for the Swift with its three year/ 36,000 mile worry-free coverage. What's more, the Swift offers amazing gas mileage: 39 mpg in the city, 43 mpg on the highway. This comes courtesy of a 1.3-liter four-cylinder engine. It generates 79 horsepower and 75 foot-pounds of torque. Yes indeed, the Swift promises to be a cheap set of wheels no matter how you slice it.

Despite the budget price, the Swift does come with standard features such as dual front airbags and daytime running lights. Available accessories include air conditioning and a CD player. The Swift's cousin is the Chevrolet Metro. Both of these cars compete against cars like the Hyundai Accent and the Kia Sephia. True, Hyundai's reliability record is unimpressive, but recent indicators point to improved build quality in the Accent. The Accent also offers a longer list of standard and optional equipment.

Regardless, the Swift is one of the few choices left for Americans who need inexpensive transportation and a warranty. In this category, we feel that the Swift is a car to look at.

Standard Equipment

GA (5M): 1.3L I4 SOHC MPI 16-valve engine; 5-speed OD manual transmission; engine oil cooler; front-wheel drive, 3.79 axle ratio; steel exhaust; front independent strut suspension with anti-roll bar, front coil springs, rear independent strut suspension with anti-roll bar, rear coil springs; manual rack-and-pinion steering; front disc/rear drum brakes; 10.3 gal. capacity fuel tank; side impact bars; front and rear black bumpers; black bodyside molding; monotone paint; aero-composite halogen headlamps with daytime running lights; driver's and passenger's manual black folding outside mirrors; front and rear 13" x 4.5" steel wheels; P155/80SR13 A/ S BSW front and rear tires; inside under cargo mounted compact steel spare wheel; and manual retractable antenna; 1 power accessory outlet, driver's foot rest; instrumentation display includes tachometer, water temperature gauge, trip odometer; warning indicators include oil pressure, battery, lights on, key in ignition; driver's and passenger's front airbags; tinted windows, fixed rear windows; variable interval front windshield wipers, rear window wiper, rear window defroster; seating capacity of 4, front bucket seats, fixed headrests, driver's seat includes 4-way direction control, passenger's seat includes 4-way direction control; full folding rear bench seat; cloth seats, vinyl door trim insert, full cloth headliner, full carpet floor covering, plastic/rubber gear shift knob; interior lights include dome light; passenger's side vanity mirror; day/night rearview mirror; full floor console, glove box, front cupholder, instrument panel bin, driver's and passenger's door bins; carpeted cargo floor, plastic trunk lid, cargo cover; black side window moldings, black front windshield molding, black rear window molding and black door handles.

GL (5M) (in addition to or instead of GA (5M) equipment): Air conditioning; AM/FM stereo, seek-scan, cassette, 2 speakers, and manual retractable antenna.

Base Prices

Code	Description	Invoice	MSRP
HES532Y	GA (5M)	8553	9099
HES533Y	GL (5M)	9493	10099
Destination Charge:		400	400

Accessories

		Invoice	MSRP
—	Transmission: 3-Speed Automatic	611	650
	Includes 3.61 axle ratio.		

384   www.edmunds.com   **EDMUND'S® NEW CARS**

AVALON — TOYOTA

| CODE | DESCRIPTION | INVOICE | MSRP |

2000 AVALON

2000 Toyota Avalon

What's New?

Entering its second generation, the 2000 Avalon is roomier, more powerful and more technically advanced. The Kentucky-built Avalon features new styling inside and out, enhanced safety features, increased engine performance, and more comfort and convenience than its predecessor.

Review

It would seem buyers of full-sized sedans generally aren't too interested in character. Most full-size sedans are dull pieces of machinery to look at and a snooze to drive. The beauty in such a vehicle lies in what it can do for the customer in terms of providing space for people and things without compromising the ride or occupant comfort. It should look upscale, but not gaudy, providing just enough glitz and luxury to let others know you have achieved a degree of success in life. Finally, such a vehicle must also be reliable and able to handle years of daily-driver tasks without so much as a whimper.

Since its introduction in 1995, the Toyota Avalon has fit this description. A little bland, perhaps, but solid, roomy, and dependable. For 2000, the Avalon enters its second generation. Substantial changes have been made to improve its already good traits, as well as add a bit of excitement. There are two models: XL and XLS. The main difference between the two is the level of standard equipment. Both can be ordered with front bucket or bench seats.

Avalon's 3.0-liter V6 engine now features a variable valve timing system (Toyota calls its system VVT-i). The system provides additional horsepower, improved fuel economy and torque, lower emissions and smoother shifting. The previous Avalon was no slouch, so the engine improvements should be just icing on the cake.

Toyota has also updated the styling. A side benefit of this is a reduction in noise, vibration and harshness (NVH). Comfort amenities include a new dual-control air conditioner, an optional JBL premium grade audio (standard on the XLS), and an improved multi-information display. There's also increased trunk volume, grocery bag hooks, and a larger storage tray and cargo net. A universal remote system that can be programmed to open garage doors, gates and doors is standard on XLS models.

TOYOTA   AVALON

| CODE | DESCRIPTION | INVOICE | MSRP |

Safety is enhanced with an optional package on XLS models that includes Vehicle Skid Control (VSC) and traction control. VSC utilizes the braking system to correct understeer or oversteer conditions in a turn. Traction control reduces tire slippage during acceleration. Toyota also added a brake-assist feature that detects emergency braking and applies supplemental line pressure to reduce stopping distance.

Additional new safety features include a stronger body structure that effectively absorbs and diffuses energy along predictable paths, added energy absorbing material to the roof rails, front pillar and center pillar to help reduce potential head injury, and enlarged rearview mirrors. The front seats have been strengthened and a rear center adjustable headrest has been added.

We recommend that potential buyers of a new full-sized sedan take a look at the 2000 Avalon. As before, its price is more than the offerings from Detroit like the Buick LeSabre, Dodge Intrepid and Ford Crown Victoria. But unflappable quality has a price. Want a Lexus but need six-passenger capacity or huge amounts of rear legroom? The Avalon is your car.

Standard Equipment

XL (4A): 3.0L V6 DOHC SMPI 24-valve engine, requires premium unleaded fuel; 4-speed electronic OD auto transmission with lock-up; 582-amp HD battery with run down protection; HD starter; 80-amp HD alternator; front-wheel drive, 3.62 axle ratio; stainless steel exhaust with chrome tip; front independent strut suspension with anti-roll bar, front coil springs, rear independent strut suspension with anti-roll bar, rear coil springs; power rack-and-pinion steering with engine speed-sensing assist; 4-wheel disc brakes with 4-wheel antilock braking system; 18.5 gal. capacity fuel tank; side impact bars; front and rear body-colored bumpers with chrome bumper insert; body-colored bodyside molding with chrome bodyside insert; monotone paint; aero-composite halogen fully auto headlamps with daytime running lights; additional exterior lights include cornering lights; driver's and passenger's power remote body-colored outside mirrors; front and rear 15" x 6" steel wheels; P205/65HR15 A/S BSW front and rear tires; inside under cargo mounted full-size steel spare wheel; air conditioning, rear heat ducts; AM/FM stereo, seek-scan, cassette, single CD, 6 speakers, theft deterrent, and window grid antenna; cruise control; power door locks with 2 stage unlock, child safety rear door locks, remote hatch/trunk release, remote fuel release; driver's foot rest, retained accessory power; instrumentation display includes tachometer, water temperature gauge, in-dash clock, trip odometer; warning indicators include oil pressure, battery, key in ignition, low fuel, bulb failure, door ajar; driver's and passenger's front airbags, driver's and front passenger's seat mounted side airbags; tinted windows, power front and rear windows with driver's 1-touch down; variable intermittent front windshield wipers, electrically heated windshield, sun visor strip, rear window defroster; seating capacity of 5, front bucket seats, adjustable tilt headrests, center armrest with storage, driver's seat includes 6-way direction control, lumbar support, passenger's seat includes 6-way direction control; rear bench seat with fixed headrests, center armrest; front height adjustable seatbelts with front pretensioners; cloth seats, cloth door trim insert, full cloth headliner, full carpet floor covering, plastic/rubber gear shift knob; interior lights include dome light, illuminated entry; steering wheel with tilt adjustment; dual illuminated vanity mirrors; day/night rearview mirror; full floor console, locking glove box with light, front cupholder, driver's and passenger's door bins; carpeted cargo floor, carpeted trunk lid, cargo light; chrome grille, chrome side window moldings, black front windshield molding, black rear window molding and body-colored door handles.

XLS (4A) (in addition to or instead of XL (4A) equipment): Aero-composite halogen fully auto headlamps with washer; additional exterior lights include front fog/driving lights; driver's and passenger's power remote body-colored heated outside mirrors; front and rear 15" x 6" alloy wheels; air conditioning with climate control, air filter; premium AM/FM stereo, seek-scan, cassette, single CD, 7 premium speakers, theft deterrent, and window grid diversity antenna; remote keyless entry, power remote hatch/trunk release, power remote fuel release; instrumentation display includes exterior temp; warning indicators include low washer fluid; ignition disable, panic alarm, security system; driver's seat includes 6-way power seat, lumbar support, passenger's seat includes 6-way power seat; premium cloth seats; simulated wood trim on instrument panel; interior lights include dome light with fade, front and rear reading lights, 2 door curb lights; leather-wrapped steering wheel with tilt adjustment; 2 seat back storage pockets and cargo net.

386   www.edmunds.com   **EDMUND'S® NEW CARS**

AVALON — TOYOTA

CODE	DESCRIPTION	INVOICE	MSRP

Base Prices

3534	Avalon XL (4A)	22058	25195
3544	Avalon XLS (4A)	25742	29755
Destination Charge:		455	455

Accessories

CODE	DESCRIPTION	INVOICE	MSRP
—	Split Bench Seat (XL)	718	820
	Includes power seat package and floor console delete. NOT AVAILABLE with GH, GI, LF.		
—	Split Bench Seat (XLS)	(85)	(100)
	Includes floor console delete. NOT AVAILABLE with LA.		
CF	Carpet/Cargo Mat Set (5-Pc.set)	96	158
DJ	JBL 3 In 1 Premium Combo (XL)	270	360
	Includes AM/FM stereo with cassette, CD and 7 speakers. REQUIRES GH or GI or GK.		
EL	The Elite Package (XL)	199	597
	Includes carpet/cargo mat set (5-pc.set), cargo net and gold package.		
FB	Fabric Seat Trim (XLS)	NC	NC
	REQUIRES Split Bench Seat. NOT AVAILABLE with LA, LB, GL, GU, GV.		
FG	Fabric Seat Trim (XL)	NC	NC
	REQUIRES Split Bench Seat. NOT AVAILABLE with LF, LG, GK.		
GH	Package 1 (XL)	828	1035
	Includes power seat package: power driver's and passenger's seats and keyless entry. NOT AVAILABLE with GI, GK.		
GI	Package 2 (XL)	1136	1420
	Includes power seat package: power driver's and passenger's seats; keyless entry and wheels: 15" alloy. NOT AVAILABLE with GH, GK.		
GJ	Package 3 (XL)	536	670
	Includes keyless entry and wheels: 15" alloy. REQUIRES Split Bench Seat. NOT AVAILABLE with GK.		
GK	Package 4 (XL)	1456	1820
	Includes leather trim package: leather seat trim and leather-wrapped steering wheel; power driver's and passenger's seats, keyless entry and wheels: 15" alloy. REQUIRES Split Bench Seat. NOT AVAILABLE with GJ, FG.		
GK	Package 4 (XL)	2072	2590
	Includes leather trim package: leather seat trim, leather-wrapped shift knob and leather-wrapped steering wheel; power driver's and passenger's seats, keyless entry and wheels: 15" alloy. NOT AVAILABLE with GH, GI, GJ.		
GL	Package 5 (XLS)	1100	1375
	Includes leather trim package with memory: leather seat trim and power driver's seat with memory; wheels: 16" alloy and tires: P205/60R16 A/S. NOT AVAILABLE with GU, GV, GW, FB.		
GN	Cargo Net (XL)	27	42
GP	Gold Package	89	164

TOYOTA
AVALON / CAMRY

CODE	DESCRIPTION	INVOICE	MSRP
GU	**Package 6 (XLS)**	1288	1625
	Includes leather trim package with memory: leather seat trim and power driver's seat with memory: wheels: 16" alloy, tires: P205/60R16 A/S and JBL 3 in 1 premium stereo with in-dash changer. NOT AVAILABLE with GL, GV, GW, FB.		
GV	**Package 7 (XLS)**	1540	1940
	Includes leather trim package with heat and memory: leather seat trim, heated front seats and power driver's seat with memory; wheels: 16" alloy, tires: P205/60R16 A/S and JBL 3 in 1 premium stereo with in-dash changer. NOT AVAILABLE with GL, GU, GW, FB.		
GW	**Package 8 (XLS)**	252	330
	Includes wheels: 16" alloy, tires: P205/60R16 A/S and JBL 3 in 1 premium stereo with in-dash changer. NOT AVAILABLE with GL, GU, GV.		
LA	**Leather Seat Trim (XLS)**	NC	NC
	REQUIRES GL or GU or GV. NOT AVAILABLE with FB, LB.		
LB	**Leather Seat Trim (XLS)**	NC	NC
	REQUIRES Split Bench Seat and (GL or GU or GV). NOT AVAILABLE with FB, LA.		
LF	**Leather Seat Trim (XL)**	NC	NC
	REQUIRES GK. NOT AVAILABLE with FG, LG.		
LG	**Leather Seat Trim (XL)**	NC	NC
	REQUIRES GK and Split Bench Seat. NOT AVAILABLE with FG, LF.		
PC	**Special Color**	187	220
SR	**Power Moonroof**	728	910
	Includes power tilt and slide.		
V2	**Glass Breakage Sensor (GBS) (XLS)**	62	99
V5	**V.I.P. RS3200 Deluxe Security System (XL)**	155	249
VD	**Vehicle Stability Control (XLS)**	680	850
	Includes traction control.		
WL	**Alloy Wheel Locks**	31	52
WS	**Steel Wheel Locks (XL)**	31	52
WZ	**Alloy Wheel Locks (XLS)**	31	52

NOTE: Toyotas sold in Alabama, Florida, Georgia, North Carolina and South Carolina may be equipped with option packages not listed in this guide. You can expect to haggle 25% off the window sticker price on these packages.

2000 CAMRY

What's New?

The Camry sedan receives minor updates for the 2000 model year. The exterior benefits from new front and rear styling. Camry LE models get 15-inch tires with a new wheel-cover design, while the XLE gets standard 16-inch tires. Four-cylinder models make three more horsepower than last year. Interior upgrades include an available JBL premium audio system, automatic climate control, larger buttons on the audio faceplate, imitation wood trim on XLE models, optional leather seats with driver-side power on LE models, and new LE model seat fabric. The hood is now supported with struts and dampers.

388   www.edmunds.com   **EDMUND'S® NEW CARS**

CAMRY — TOYOTA

| CODE | DESCRIPTION | INVOICE | MSRP |

Review

The Toyota Camry is one of America's most-favored mid-size sedans. The reasons are simple. It boasts room for five adults, can be ordered with a powerful and smooth V6, and comes with the reputation of solid Toyota reliability.

The current-generation Camry debuted in 1997 and 2000 marks its first major facelift. The styling of the '97-'99 Camry was generally considered quite plain, so the new nose and tail this year are more than welcome.

The Camry can be equipped for rugged family life, or plush luxury touring. There are plenty of options to choose from, but you'll have to watch what you order if you are on a tight budget. There are three different trims: base-level CE, mid-level LE, and the top-level XLE. Some of the more notable options include side airbags, traction control, a premium sound system, leather interior trim, and a power moonroof. ABS is standard on XLEs and LEs equipped with a V6 engine.

The Camry's 3.0-liter V6 is a fine engine, and it produces 200 horsepower and 214 foot-pounds of torque. Acceleration is solid, and opposed to the Honda Accord or Mitsubishi Galant, the Camry's V6 can be ordered with a manual transmission. Braking is swift and sure with the antilock system, and Camry hangs on well in corners despite rather meek all-season radials.

Inside, controls and gauges are laid-out nicely in a flowing dashboard. The switches and stalks all have a solid and proper feel to them. Storage areas are abundant and feature a deep center console, door bins, and dashboard bins. Front cupholders, the feature by which all cars are truly measured these days, accommodate 20-ounce bottles of your favorite beverage. The only negative is that you might find the seats uncomfortable.

The Camry works exceptionally well as a family sedan. Fully optioned, the Camry is considerably more expensive than its domestic competitors, but given the Camry's sales success, it seems most Americans consider the Camry to be a worthwhile investment.

2000 Toyota Camry

Standard Equipment

CE (5M): 2.2L I4 DOHC MPI 16-valve engine; 5-speed OD manual transmission; 582-amp HD battery; 80-amp HD alternator; front-wheel drive, 3.93 axle ratio; stainless steel exhaust; front independent strut suspension with anti-roll bar, front coil springs, rear independent strut suspension with anti-roll bar, rear coil springs; power rack-and-pinion steering with engine speed-sensing assist; front disc/rear drum brakes; 18.5 gal. capacity fuel tank; front and rear

TOYOTA CAMRY

| CODE | DESCRIPTION | INVOICE | MSRP |

body-colored bumpers; body-colored bodyside molding; monotone paint; aero-composite halogen auto off headlamps; driver's and passenger's manual remote black outside mirrors; front and rear 14" x 5.5" steel wheels; P195/70SR14 A/S BSW front and rear tires; inside under cargo mounted full-size steel spare wheel; rear heat ducts; AM/FM stereo, seek-scan, cassette, single CD, 4 speakers, and window grid antenna; child safety rear door locks; remote hatch/ trunk release, remote fuel release; 2 power accessory outlets; driver's foot rest; instrumentation display includes tachometer, water temperature gauge, in-dash clock, trip odometer; warning indicators include oil pressure, battery, key in ignition, low fuel, bulb failure, door ajar; driver's and passenger's front airbags; tinted windows; manual front and rear windows; fixed interval front windshield wipers, sun visor strip, rear window defroster; seating capacity of 5; front bucket seats, adjustable headrests, driver's seat includes 4-way direction control, passenger's seat includes 60-40 folding rear bench seat with adjustable headrests, center armrest; front height adjustable seatbelts with pretensioners; cloth seats, cloth door trim insert, full cloth headliner, full carpet floor covering, plastic/rubber gear shift knob; interior lights include dome light; steering wheel with tilt adjustment; vanity mirrors, dual auxiliary visors; day/ night rearview mirror; full floor console, mini overhead console with storage, locking glove box with light, front and rear cupholders, instrument panel bin, driver's and passenger's door bins; vinyl cargo floor, cargo light; body-colored grille, chrome side window moldings, black front windshield molding, chrome rear window molding and body-colored door handles.

LE (4A) (in addition to or instead of CE (5M) equipment): Four-speed electronic OD auto transmission with lock-up; driver's and passenger's power remote body-colored outside mirrors; front and rear 15" x 6" steel wheels; P205/65HR15 A/S BSW front and rear tires; air conditioning; AM/FM stereo, seek-scan, cassette, single CD, 6 speakers, and window grid antenna; cruise control; retained accessory power; power front and rear windows with driver's 1-touch down; variable intermittent front windshield wipers; driver's seat includes 6-way direction control and premium cloth seats.

LE V6 (5M) (in addition to or instead of LE (4A) equipment): 3.0L V6 DOHC SMPI 24-valve engine; 5-speed OD manual transmission; 4-wheel disc brakes with 4-wheel antilock braking system and aero-composite halogen auto off headlamps with daytime running lights.

XLE (4A) (in addition to or instead of LE (5M) equipment): 2.2L I4 DOHC MPI 16-valve engine; 4-speed electronic OD auto transmission with lock-up; stainless steel exhaust with chrome tip; front disc/rear drum brakes with 4-wheel antilock braking system; driver's and passenger's power remote body-colored heated outside mirrors; front and rear 15" x 6" aluminum wheels; premium AM/FM stereo, seek-scan, cassette, single CD, 6 premium speakers, and window grid diversity antenna; power door locks with 2 stage unlock, remote keyless entry, ignition disable, panic alarm, security system; driver's seat includes 6-way power seat, lumbar support, passenger's seat includes 6-way power seat; leather-wrapped steering wheel with tilt adjustment; dual illuminated vanity mirrors, dual auxiliary visors and carpeted trunk lid.

XLE V6 (4A) (in addition to or instead of XLE (4A) equipment): 3.0L V6 DOHC SMPI 24-valve engine and 4-wheel disc brakes with 4-wheel antilock braking system.

Base Prices

2525	CE (5M)	15427	17418
2532	LE (4A)	17761	20288
2533	LE V6 (5M)	19486	22258
2540	XLE (4A)	20983	23968
2544	XLE V6 (4A)	22847	26098
	Destination Charge:	455	455

CAMRY — TOYOTA

CODE	DESCRIPTION	INVOICE	MSRP

Accessories

CODE	DESCRIPTION	INVOICE	MSRP
4AT	Transmission: 4-Speed Automatic (CE)	709	800
4AT	Transmission: 4-Speed Automatic (LE V6)	699	800
AB	Antilock Brakes (CE)	521	610
	Includes daytime running lights.		
AW	Wheels: 15" Aluminum (LE/LE V6)	308	385
	Includes P205/65R15 tires.		
BE	Side Airbags	215	250
	REQUIRES HU (CE).		
BN	Black Pearl Emblems (4-Cyl - LE/XLE)	79	149
BN	Black Pearl Emblems (CE/V6)	89	164
CI	Cargo Mat (CE/LE/LE V6)	44	73
CF	Carpet/Cargo Mat Set (5-Pc.set) (XLE/XLE V6)	90	149
CF	Carpeted Floor Mats	55	92
CL	Cruise Control (CE)	200	250
CV	Center Armrest	40	67
DJ	Radio: JBL 3-In-1 Premium Combo (LE/LE V6)	218	290
	Includes AM/FM stereo, cassette, CD, 8 JBL speakers and metal speaker grilles.		
DU	Burlwood Wood Dash	255	499
EL	Elite Package (CE/LE/LE V6)	259	976
	Includes cargo mat and burlwood wood dash.		
ET	Black Elite Package (CE/LE/LE V6)	249	876
	Includes cargo mat and burlwood wood dash.		
GN	Cargo Net	27	42
GP	Gold Package (4-Cyl - LE/XLE)	89	164
GP	Gold Package (CE/V6)	99	179
HJ	Homelink	136	199
HU	Value Package #1 with AC and PO (CE)	807	897
	Includes air conditioning, power package: power door locks, power windows, dual color-keyed power mirrors; variable intermittent windshield wipers and carpeted floor mats.		
HZ	Value Package #2 with Leather (XLE 4-Cyl)	1444	1604
	Includes power driver's seat, seat pocket, leather-wrapped shift knob, AM/FM stereo with cassette and CD, power moonroof and map light. NOT AVAILABLE with P4.		
HZ	Value Package #2 with Leather (XLE V6)	994	1104
	Includes power driver's seat, seat pocket, leather-wrapped shift knob, AM/FM stereo with cassette and CD, power moonroof and map light. NOT AVAILABLE with P4.		
LF	Fog Lights	249	399
M4	Camry Sports Package (LE/LE V6)	949	1193
	Includes black pearl emblems, fog lights, rear spoiler and wheels: alloy.		
M5	Camry Sports Package (LE/LE V6)	949	1193
	Includes black pearl emblems, burlwood wood dash, fog lights, rear spoiler and wheels: alloy.		
MG	Black Mudguards	48	60
P9	6-Disc CD Changer	385	550
	NOT AVAILABLE with P4, P5, P6.		

TOYOTA

CAMRY

CODE	DESCRIPTION	INVOICE	MSRP
RF	Rear Spoiler	329	539
SD	Sunroof Wind Deflector (All Except CE)	33	55
SR	Power Moonroof (LE/LE V6)	800	1000
	Includes map light.		
SS	Wheels: Alloy (CE)	560	755
SS	Wheels: Alloy (LE/LE V6)	440	592
TN	Traction Control (V6)	240	300
	REQUIRES 4AT.		
V2	V.I.P. Glass Break Sensor (GBS) (XLE/XLE V6)	62	99
V3	V.I.P. RS3200 Deluxe Security System (CE/LE/LE V6)	249	399
	NOT AVAILABLE with V4.		
V4	V.I.P. RS3200 Deluxe Security System (CE/LE/LE V6)	334	534
	Includes trunk release. NOT AVAILABLE with V3.		
V5	V.I.P. RS3200 Plus Security System (LE/LE V6)	155	249
	REQUIRES VL or VP or VQ.		
VL	Value Package #5 with Leather (LE 4-Cyl)	1429	1710
	Includes keyless entry, leather seat trim, power driver's seat, seat pocket, leather-wrapped shift knob and leather-wrapped steering wheel. NOT AVAILABLE with VP, VQ.		
VL	Value Package #5 with Leather (LE V6)	880	1100
	Includes 4-wheel ABS with daytime running lights, keyless entry, power driver's seat, seat pocket, leather-wrapped shift knob and leather-wrapped steering wheel. NOT AVAILABLE with VP.		
VP	Value Package #3 (LE 4-Cyl)	549	610
	Includes antilock brakes with daytime running lights, keyless entry, cloth power driver's seat and carpeted floor mats. NOT AVAILABLE with VL, VQ.		
VP	Value Package #3 (LE V6)	NC	NC
	Includes daytime running lights, keyless entry, cloth power driver's seat and carpeted floor mats. NOT AVAILABLE with VL.		
VQ	Value Package #4 with PE and KE (LE 4-Cyl)	NC	NC
	Includes keyless entry, cloth power driver's seat and carpeted floor mats. NOT AVAILABLE with VL, VP.		
WL	Alloy Wheel Locks (All Except CE)	31	52
	REQUIRES AW and VP. NOT AVAILABLE with WS.		
WS	Steel Wheel Locks (CE/LE 4-Cyl)	31	52
	NOT AVAILABLE with WL, WZ.		
WZ	Alloy Wheel Locks (CE/LE/LE V6)	31	52
	REQUIRES SS. NOT AVAILABLE with WS.		

NOTE: Toyotas sold in Alabama, Florida, Georgia, North Carolina and South Carolina may be equipped with option packages not listed in this guide. You can expect to haggle 25% off the window sticker price on these packages.

CAMRY SOLARA — TOYOTA

2000 CAMRY SOLARA

2000 Toyota Camry Solara

What's New?

Solara four-cylinder models will achieve ultra-low-emission vehicle (ULEV) status. The climate control panel has been changed. SLE models get a JBL premium audio system as standard equipment, and a six-disc in-dash CD changer is optional. Two new exterior colors are offered.

Review

With its own sheetmetal, optional V6 power, and a tighter suspension, the Solara is more than just a two-door Camry. OK, so it's based on the Camry platform and uses the same engine and suspension components, but almost every aspect of this sporty coupe has been, how can we say...Solara-ized to give it more fun and less ho-hum.

Available in two basic trim levels, the SE or SLE, Toyota's new sport coupe comes with either a 135-horsepower four-cylinder engine or a 200-horsepower V6. Either engine can be had in the SE model, but the premium-grade SLE comes only with the V6 and automatic transmission. For buyers looking to get the maximum "sport" out of this sport coupe, the V6 and a five-speed manual can be had in the SE model. This V6/manual combination is particularly noteworthy since the Accord Coupe V6 does not offer a manual transmission.

For handling duty, Toyota took the Camry's basic suspension and made it stiffer by increasing the damping rates and adding a brace that joins the front strut towers together. It also reinforced the transom between the trunk and the passenger compartment and stiffened the front and rear suspension mounts for improved overall body rigidity. The Solara also features a steering system that is more sport-oriented than the Camry's. However, the Solara is still geared for comfort. If you're looking for true handling excellence from a coupe, check out the new 2000 Celica.

The interior is typically Toyota, which is to say quiet and full of solid switchgear. The Solara generally contains more standard equipment than the Camry. Safety is always high on Toyota's list of priorities, and the Solara's standard features reflect this philosophy. Included among them are driver and front-passenger airbags, driver and front-passenger seatbelt pre-tensioners, and antilock brakes (optional on four-cylinder models, standard with the V6). Optional side airbags can also be ordered. If you purchase an SLE model, traction control can be checked on the order sheet.

TOYOTA CAMRY SOLARA

| CODE | DESCRIPTION | INVOICE | MSRP |

If you're considering the purchase of a Solara, the main question you need to ask yourself is if the more aggressive styling and minor suspension differences justify the loss of the Camry's two functional rear doors. If so, the Solara will be a fine choice.

Standard Equipment

SE (5M): 2.2L I4 DOHC SMPI 16-valve engine; 5-speed OD manual transmission; 65-amp HD battery with run down protection; HD starter; 80-amp HD alternator; front-wheel drive; 3.93 axle ratio; stainless steel exhaust; front independent strut suspensions with anti-roll bar; front coil springs; rear independent strut suspensions with anti-roll bar, rear coil springs; power rack-and-pinion steering with engine speed-sensing assist; front disc/rear drum brakes; 18.5 gal. capacity fuel tank; side impact bars; front and rear body-colored bumpers; body-colored bodyside molding; monotone paint; aero-composite halogen auto off headlamps with daytime running lights; additional exterior lights include front fog/driving lights; driver's and passenger's power remote body-colored outside mirrors; front and rear 15" x 6" steel wheels; P205/65HR15 A/S BSW front and rear tires; inside under cargo mounted full-size steel spare wheel; air conditioning, rear heat ducts; AM/FM stereo, seek-scan, cassette, single CD, 6 speakers, and window grid antenna; cruise control; power door locks with 2 stage unlock; power remote hatch/trunk release; remote fuel release; 2 power accessory outlets, driver's foot rest, retained accessory power; instrumentation display includes tachometer, water temperature gauge, in-dash clock, trip odometer; warning indicators include oil pressure, battery, key in ignition, low fuel, door ajar; driver's and passenger's front airbags, tinted windows, power windows with driver's 1-touch down; variable intermittent front windshield wipers, sun visor strip, rear window defroster; seating capacity of 5; front bucket seats, adjustable tilt headrests, center armrest with storage, driver's seat includes 6-way direction control, passenger's seat includes 4-way direction control, easy entry; 60-40 folding rear bench seat with fixed headrests, center armrest, front height adjustable seatbelts with pretensioners, premium cloth seats, door trim with full cloth headliner, full carpet floor covering, simulated wood trim on instrument panel, plastic/rubber gear shift knob; interior lights include dome light with fade, illuminated entry; steering wheel with tilt adjustment; dual illuminated vanity mirrors, dual auxiliary visors, day/night rearview mirror; full floor console mini overhead console with storage, locking glove box with light, front and rear cupholders, instrument panel bin, driver's and passenger's door bins, carpeted cargo floor, cargo light; chrome grille, chrome side window moldings, black front windshield molding, black rear window molding and body-colored door handles.

SE V6 (5M) (in addition to or instead of SE (5M) equipment): 3.0L V6 DOHC SMPI 24-valve engine, requires premium unleaded fuel and 4-wheel disc brakes with 4-wheel antilock braking system.

SLE V6 (4A) (in addition to or instead of SE V6 (4A) equipment): Four-speed electronic OD auto transmission with lock-up; body-colored front and rear mud flaps, rear lip spoiler; driver's and passenger's power remote body-colored heated outside mirrors; front and rear 16" x 6" silver alloy wheels; P205/60HR16 A/S BSW front and rear tires; air conditioning with climate control; AM/FM stereo, seek-scan, cassette, single CD, 6 speakers, and window grid diversity antenna; remote keyless entry; garage door opener; instrumentation display includes exterior temp, ignition disable, panic alarm, security system; driver's seat includes 6-way power seat, lumbar support; leather seats, leather-wrapped gear shift knob; leather-wrapped sport steering wheel with tilt adjustment; auto-dimming day/night rearview mirror and 1 seat back storage pocket.

Base Prices

2731	SE (5M)	16774	18938
2733	SE V6 (5M)	19175	21648
2744	SLE V6 (4A)	22887	25838
	Destination Charge:	455	455

CAMRY SOLARA — TOYOTA

CODE	DESCRIPTION	INVOICE	MSRP

Accessories

CODE	DESCRIPTION	INVOICE	MSRP
—	Transmission: 4-Speed Automatic (SE)	709	800
—	Transmission: 4-Speed Automatic (SE V6)	709	800
AB	Antilock Brakes (SE)	521	610
BE	Side Airbags	215	250
CF	Carpet/Cargo Mat Set (5-Pc.set)	100	166
EJ	Radio: JBL 3-In-1 Premium (SLE)	150	200
	Includes AM/FM stereo, cassette, CD, 8 JBL speakers and 6-disc in-dash CD changer. REQUIRES LQ.		
GP	Gold Package (SE)	115	173
GP	Gold Package (SE V6/SLE)	149	224
LQ	SLE Package (SLE)	NC	NC
	Includes standard equipment: perforated leather trimmed seats, power driver's seat with 8-way adjuster, power color keyed heated mirrors, anti-theft, keyless entry, garage opener, auto air conditioning, digital heater control, outside temperature gauge, auto rearview mirror dimmer, P205/60R16 tires with aluminum wheels, rear spoiler and mudguards. REQUIRES EJ.		
MG	Color-Keyed Mudguards (SE/SE V6)	64	80
PC	Special Color	187	220
PE	Cloth Power Driver's Seat (SE/SE V6)	312	390
	Includes 8-way adjustable power. NOT AVAILABLE with SW, SZ.		
SD	Sunroof Wind Deflector	33	55
SL	Upgrade Package #2 (SE/SE V6)	1340	1675
	Includes tires: P205/65R15 A/S, cloth power driver's seat and power moonroof. NOT AVAILABLE with SO, SW, SY, SZ, SX.		
SO	Upgrade Package #1 (SE/SE V6)	620	775
	Includes cloth power driver's seat and tires: P205/65R15 A/S. NOT AVAILABLE with SL, SW, SY, SZ, SX.		
SR	Power Moonroof	720	900
	REQUIRES PE or SO or SX.		
SW	Upgrade Package #3 (SE)	2248	2810
	Includes tires: P205/65R15 A/S, leather and power seat package, leather seats, power moonroof and map light. NOT AVAILABLE with SO, SL, PE.		
SX	Upgrade Package #4 (SE V6)	1368	1730
	Includes tires: P205/60R16 A/S, rear spoiler, perforated leather steering wheel and JBL 3-in-1 premium combo radio. NOT AVAILABLE with SO, SL, SY, SZ.		
SY	Upgrade Package #5 (SE V6)	2088	2630
	Includes tires: P205/60R16 A/S, rear spoiler, perforated leather steering wheel, JBL 3-in-1 premium combo radio and map light. NOT AVAILABLE with SL, SZ, SO, SX.		
SZ	Upgrade Package #6 (SE V6)	2908	3655
	Includes tires: P205/60R16 A/S, rear spoiler, leather and power seat package, perforated leather steering wheel, JBL 3-in-1 premium combo radio and map light. NOT AVAILABLE with PE, SL, SY, SO, SX.		
TN	Traction Control (SLE)	240	300

TOYOTA
CAMRY SOLARA / CELICA

CODE	DESCRIPTION	INVOICE	MSRP
V3	V.I.P. RS3000 Deluxe Security System (SE)	249	399
WL	Alloy Wheel Locks	31	52

NOTE: Toyotas sold in Alabama, Florida, Georgia, North Carolina and South Carolina may be equipped with option packages not listed in this guide. You can expect to haggle 25% off the window sticker price on these packages.

2000 CELICA

2000 Toyota Celica

What's New?

The all-new 2000 Celica is considerably more performance-oriented than the previous model. Highlights include an exciting exterior, a powerful optional engine, and sharp handling.

Review

The 2000 Celica enters its seventh generation considerably leaner and meaner. Styled in the United States by Calty Design Research Inc. in Newport Beach, Calif., the cab-forward design features a high-fashion look with racecar design elements. Sharp-edged panels, dramatic plunging curves, a tall tail and a radically lowered front fascia are stark contrasts. Compared to past models, Celica is shorter in length, but longer in wheelbase.

There are two versions for 2000: a base-level Celica GT, and a more-powerful GT-S. An all-new 1.8-liter, four-cylinder, DOHC all-aluminum engine powers the Celica GT-S. Hitting an impressive mark of 100 horsepower per liter of displacement, the engine generates 180 horsepower at 7,600 rpm and 133 foot-pounds of torque at 6,800 rpm. The GT-S powerplant, co-developed with Yamaha, utilizes Toyota's new VVTL-i engine technology. Similar in concept to Honda's VTEC, the system can adjust both valve timing and lift. The GT model's 1.8-liter, four-cylinder engine produces 140 horsepower and 125 foot-pounds of torque at 6,400 rpm.

The 2000 Celica GT and GT-S are both available with different variations of all-new automatic and manual transmissions. The newly developed four-speed automatic transmission is found in

396   www.edmunds.com   **EDMUND'S® NEW CARS**

CELICA — TOYOTA

both the GT and GT-S models. The GT-S also comes with E-shift steering wheel-mounted buttons, similar to those found in the Lexus GS 400. These allow "manual" shifting of the automatic transmission. As an exclusive feature in this class, the manual transmission in the GT-S features six forward gears.

The suspension and braking systems also have been upgraded. The front suspension is outfitted with MacPherson struts with offset springs and a solid anti-roll bar. The rear suspension is a double-wishbone design with a new camber-control function and a solid anti-roll bar. ABS is optional on both models. The Celica GT rides on 15x6.5-inch steel wheels with 195/60 R15 tires, while the high-grade GT-S features 15x6.5-inch alloy wheels on 205/55 R15 tires. Both models offer optional aluminum alloy wheels.

The 2000 Celica's interior has also been significantly altered. A simple cross-over dash layout, big analog gauges, sporty bucket seats and a purpose-built feel behind the wheel add to Celica's cockpit experience. Both Celica grade levels offer a center console big enough to hold eight CD cases, as well as two oversized cups. The rear seatbacks also can be folded forward, providing additional trunk space. Driver and front-passenger airbags are standard, and side airbags are optional.

The previous-generation Celica was generally considered slow, overweight and expensive. The new 2000 Celica should provide some welcome change to Toyota's sporty-car lineup.

Standard Equipment

GT (5M): 1.8L I4 DOHC MPI with variable valve timing 16-valve engine; 5-speed OD manual transmission; 420-amp battery; engine oil cooler; 70-amp alternator; transmission oil cooler; front-wheel drive, 4.31 axle ratio; stainless steel exhaust with chrome tip; front independent strut suspension with anti-roll bar, front coil springs, rear independent double wishbone suspension with anti-roll bar, rear coil springs; power rack-and-pinion steering with engine speed-sensing assist; 4-wheel disc brakes; 14.5 gal. capacity fuel tank; side impact bars; front and rear body-colored bumpers; rocker panel extensions; monotone paint; aero-composite halogen auto off headlamps; driver's and passenger's power remote body-colored folding outside mirrors; front and rear 15" x 6.5" steel wheels; P195/60HR15 A/S BSW front and rear tires; inside under cargo mounted compact steel spare wheel; air conditioning; AM/FM stereo, seek-scan, cassette, single CD, 6 speakers, and manual retractable diversity antenna; remote hatch/trunk release, remote fuel release; 1 power accessory outlet, driver's foot rest, retained accessory power; instrumentation display includes tachometer, water temperature gauge, in-dash clock, trip odometer; warning indicators include oil pressure, battery, key in ignition, low fuel, door ajar; driver's and passenger's front airbags; tinted windows, manual front windows, fixed rear windows; variable intermittent front windshield wipers; seating capacity of 4, front sports seats, adjustable headrests, center armrest with storage, driver's seat includes 6-way direction control, passenger's seat includes 4-way direction control, easy entry; 50-50 folding rear bench seat; front and rear height adjustable seatbelts with front pretensioners; premium cloth seats, cloth door trim insert, full cloth headliner, full carpet floor covering; interior lights include dome light, front reading lights, 2 door curb lights; steering wheel with tilt adjustment; vanity mirrors; day/night rearview mirror; full floor console, locking glove box with light, front cupholder, driver's and passenger's door bins; carpeted cargo floor, vinyl trunk lid, cargo cover, cargo light; black side window moldings, black front windshield molding, black rear window molding and body-colored door handles.

GTS (6M) (in addition to or instead of GT (5M) equipment): 1.8L I4 DOHC MPI with variable valve timing 16-valve engine, requires premium unleaded fuel; 6-speed OD manual transmission; 420-amp HD battery; 4.53 axle ratio; additional exterior lights include front fog/driving lights; front and rear 15" x 6.5" alloy wheels; P205/55VR15 A/S BSW front and rear tires; rear heat ducts; premium AM/FM stereo, seek-scan, cassette, single CD, 8 speakers, amplifier, and manual retractable diversity antenna; cruise control; power windows with driver's 1-touch down; fixed interval rear wiper, rear window defroster; interior lights include 2 door curb lights, illuminated entry and leather-wrapped steering wheel with tilt adjustment.

TOYOTA — CELICA

CODE	DESCRIPTION	INVOICE	MSRP

Base Prices

2123	Celica GT (5M)	14873	16695
2133	Celica GTS (6M)	18748	21165
	Destination Charge:	455	455

Accessories

—	Transmission: 4-Speed Auto with E-Shift (GT-S)	620	700
—	Transmission: Electronic 4-Speed Auto (GT) *Includes 3.92 axle ratio.*	713	800
AB	Antilock Brakes *Includes 3.12 axle ratio.*	473	550
AW	Wheels: 15" Alloy (GT) *Includes tires: 195/60R15 88H AS Bridgestone/Dunlop brand tires.*	308	385
AW	Wheels: 16" Alloy (GT-S) *Includes tires: 205/50R16 87V.*	48	60
BE	Side Air Bags	215	250
CF	Carpet Floor Mats (4 Piece Set)	45	75
CK	All Weather Guard Package (GT) *Includes cold area package, HD battery, heavy duty rear heater, HD rear window defogger and rear intermittent wiper.*	223	270
DC	Premium 3-In-1 Combo (GT) *Includes premium AM/FM stereo with cassette, 8 speakers and amplifier. REQUIRES UP.*	248	330
GN	Cargo Net	27	42
GP	Gold Package	109	179
LA	Leather Seats (GT-S) *REQUIRES SR.*	496	620
P9	6-Disc CD Changer	385	550
RF	Rear Spoiler (GT)	432	540
RF	Rear Spoiler (GT-S) *Includes fog lamps.*	348	435
SR	Sunroof *Includes tilt and slide moonroof. REQUIRES UP.*	704	880
UP	Upgrade Package (GT) *Includes power windows, locks and cruise control.*	656	820
V3	V.I.P. RS3000 Deluxe Security System	249	399
WL	Alloy Wheel Locks	31	52
WS	Steel Wheel Locks	31	52

NOTE: Toyotas sold in Alabama, Florida, Georgia, North Carolina and South Carolina may be equipped with option packages not listed in this guide. You can expect to haggle 25% off the window sticker price on these packages.

COROLLA — TOYOTA

| CODE | DESCRIPTION | INVOICE | MSRP |

2000 COROLLA

2000 Toyota Corolla

What's New?

The Corolla receives increased performance from VVT-i engine technology. Horsepower jumps from 120 to 125. The Corolla also achieves low-emission vehicle status this year.

Review

The Toyota Corolla has gone through many changes since it was first introduced in 1968. Over the course of its long life, the Corolla has appeared as a hatchback, coupe, wagon and sedan. The world has seen enough people fall in love with this car to make it one of the best-selling vehicles in the history of automobiles.

Now while that's neat and all, we're sure that what's really important to you and your wallet is whether the modern Corolla still has what it takes to stomp out its competitors. The current Corolla platform was introduced in 1998. In those two short years, the Dodge Neon, Ford Focus, Mazda Protege, and Volkswagen Golf have all been substantially redesigned or newly introduced.

To fend them off, the Corolla comes equipped with a 1.8-liter, all-aluminum, DOHC four-cylinder engine that cranks out 125 horsepower. This is five more than last year, thanks to a variable valve timing and lift system that Toyota calls VVT-i. VVT-i employs continuously variable intake valve timing to provide greater engine performance, better fuel economy and reduced pollution over a wide range of rpm.

With the exception of minimal legroom for both the driver and passengers, the Corolla's interior ergonomics are flawless. Toyota also managed to pack a multitude of interior storage compartments into the Corolla, including a small pullout drawer in the dash and a large bin under the HVAC controls.

There is very little road noise and the Corolla handles quite well for a compact sedan.

The Corolla is one of the best compact sedans on the market. Few competitors (with the exception of Honda) can match Toyota's run-forever reputation and high levels of build quality. But the Corolla will certainly have its work cut out for it in 2000. Equipped with options most customers are expecting these days (such as ABS, CD player, and cruise control), the price of a Corolla can quickly jump to more than $18,000.

TOYOTA

COROLLA

CODE	DESCRIPTION	INVOICE	MSRP

Standard Equipment

VE (5M): 1.8L I4 DOHC MPI 16-valve engine; 5-speed OD manual transmission; 80-amp alternator; front-wheel drive, 3.72 axle ratio; stainless steel exhaust; front independent strut suspension, front coil springs, rear independent strut suspension with anti-roll bar, rear coil springs; power rack-and-pinion steering; front disc/rear drum brakes; 13.2 gal. capacity fuel tank; rear lip spoiler, side impact bars; front and rear body-colored bumpers; monotone paint; aero-composite halogen fully auto headlamps with daytime running lights; driver's and passenger's manual black outside mirrors; front and rear 14" x 5.5" silver styled steel wheels; P175/65SR14 A/S BSW front and rear tires; inside under cargo mounted compact steel spare wheel; AM/FM stereo, seek-scan, 4 speakers, and fixed antenna; child safety rear door locks, remote fuel release; 1 power accessory outlet, driver's foot rest; instrumentation display includes water temperature gauge, trip odometer; warning indicators include oil pressure, battery, lights on, low fuel, door ajar; driver's and passenger's front airbags; tinted windows, manual front and rear windows; fixed interval front windshield wipers, rear window defroster; seating capacity of 5, front bucket seats, adjustable headrests, driver's seat includes 4-way direction control, passenger's seat includes 4-way direction control; rear bench seat with adjustable headrests; front height adjustable seatbelts with pretensioners; cloth seats, cloth door trim insert, full cloth headliner, full carpet floor covering, plastic/rubber gear shift knob; interior lights include dome light; vanity mirrors; day/night rearview mirror; full floor console, glove box, front and rear cupholders, instrument panel bin, driver's and passenger's door bins; carpeted cargo floor, cargo light; body-colored grille, black side window moldings, black front windshield molding, black rear window molding and black door handles.

CE (5M) (in addition to or instead of VE (5M) equipment): Rear independent strut suspension with anti-roll bar; front license plate bracket, rear lip spoiler; black bodyside molding; driver's and passenger's manual remote black outside mirrors; AM/FM stereo, seek-scan, cassette, 4 speakers, and fixed antenna; remote hatch/trunk release; instrumentation display includes in-dash clock; variable intermittent front windshield wipers; center armrest with storage; 60-40 folding rear bench seat with adjustable headrests and steering wheel with tilt adjustment.

LE (5M) (in addition to or instead of CE (5M) equipment): Body-colored bodyside molding; driver's and passenger's power remote body-colored outside mirrors; air conditioning; retained accessory power; instrumentation display includes tachometer, exterior temp; power front and rear windows with driver's 1-touch down; rear blind and body-colored door handles.

Base Prices

1714	VE (5M)	11318	12418
1721	CE (5M)	11610	13108
1737	LE (5M)	13346	15068
Destination Charge:		455	455

Accessories

2L	Carpet/Cargo Mat Set (5-Piece)	70	117
4AT	Transmission: 3-Speed Automatic (VE)	456	500
	Includes 3.42 axle ratio.		
4AT	Transmission: 4-Speed Automatic (CE)	709	800
	Includes 2.65 axle ratio.		
4AT	Transmission: 4-Speed Automatic (LE)	708	800
	Includes 2.65 axle ratio.		
AB	Antilock Brakes (CE/LE)	473	550
BE	Side Airbags	215	250

COROLLA — TOYOTA

CODE	DESCRIPTION	INVOICE	MSRP
CI	Cargo Mat	33	55
CF	Carpeted Floor Mats	47	75
	Includes a 4-piece set.		
CK	All Weather Guard Package (CE/LE)	67	80
	Includes heavy duty starter, heavy duty heater and ventilator, heavy duty rear window defogger and rear heat ducts.		
CK	All Weather Guard Package (VE)	223	275
	Includes heavy duty starter, heavy duty heater and ventilator, heavy duty rear window defogger and rear heat ducts. NOT AVAILABLE with DE.		
CL	Cruise Control (CE)	200	250
DA	Burlwood Wood Dash-7 Piece (VE/CE)	165	325
	NOT AVAILABLE with DU.		
DE	Light Duty Rear Window Defogger (VE)	156	195
	NOT AVAILABLE with CK.		
DU	Burlwood Wood Dash-11 Piece (CE/LE)	235	425
	NOT AVAILABLE with DA.		
E6	Special Elite Package (CE/LE)	429	940
	Includes carpet/cargo mat set, burlwood wood dash (11 piece), gold package and rear spoiler. REQUIRES VP.		
EL	Elite Packagea (CE/LE)	239	791
	Includes carpet/cargo mat set, burlwood wood dash (11 piece) and gold package. REQUIRES VP.		
GN	Cargo Net	27	42
GN	Cargo Net	27	42
GP	Gold Package	119	179
MG	Black Mudguards	48	60
	NOT AVAILABLE with TP, TQ.		
P4	Auto Reverse Cassette Deck (VE)	162	231
P5	Compact Disc Deck	235	335
P6	6-Disc In-Dash CD Changer	279	399
P9	6-Disc CD Autochanger	385	550
RF	Rear Spoiler	299	499
SD	Sunroof Wind Deflector (LE)	33	55
	REQUIRES SR.		
SR	Sunroof (LE)	588	735
	Includes map lights.		
SS	Alloy Wheels	375	499
TP	Touring Package (CE)	224	280
	Includes full wheel covers, rear color-keyed mudguards, color-keyed rocker panel extensions, white-faced gauges, tires: P185/65SR14 A/S, tachometer with outside temperature indicator. NOT AVAILABLE with MG.		
TP	Touring Package (LE)	116	145
	Includes full wheel covers, rear color-keyed mudguards, color-keyed rocker panel extensions and white-faced gauges. NOT AVAILABLE with TQ, MG.		

TOYOTA
COROLLA / ECHO

CODE	DESCRIPTION	INVOICE	MSRP
TQ	Touring Package with AW (LE)	408	510
	Includes P185/65SR14 AS tires, wheels: 5.5" aluminum, rear color-keyed		
	mudguards, color-keyed rocker panel extensions and white-faced gauges. NOT		
	AVAILABLE with MG, TP.		
V3	V.I.P. RS3000 Deluxe Security System (CE/LE)	249	399
	REQUIRES VP.		
VP	Value Package (CE)	981	1090
	Includes air conditioner, power package, power windows and power door locks.		
VP	Value Package (LE)	NC	NC
	Includes cruise control.		
VP	Value Package (VE)	657	730
	Includes air conditioner, AM/FM stereo with cassette, 4 speakers and digital clock.		
WC	Painted Wheel Covers (VE)	50	85
WL	Alloy Wheel Locks (LE)	31	52
WS	Steel Wheel Locks	31	52
WZ	Alloy Wheel Locks	31	52
	REQUIRES SS.		

NOTE: Toyotas sold in Alabama, Florida, Georgia, North Carolina and South Carolina may be equipped with option packages not listed in this guide. You can expect to haggle 25% off the window sticker price on these packages.

2000 ECHO

What's New?

The 2000 Toyota Echo brings a new name and a fresh concept to the Toyota lineup. Designed to attract youthful buyers, the Echo features a roomy and comfortable interior, superb gas mileage, and an affordable price.

Review

The Toyota Echo is offered in both two- and four-door models. Price-positioned substantially below the Toyota Corolla, it offers nearly identical passenger volume. This is achieved by combining a tall profile and a cab-forward silhouette. The high roof provides exceptional headroom and allows for more upright seating. The result is reduced driver fatigue and better visibility. This layout also combines the low floor height of a sedan with a high seating position to enhance ingress/egress.

An all-new, 1.5-liter four-cylinder engine features variable valve timing technology (Toyota calls it VVT-i). Tuned to deliver exceptional fuel economy and good power, the engine meets low-emission vehicle status. With output registering 108 horsepower at 6,000 rpm and 105 foot-pounds of torque at 4,200 rpm, Echo's favorable power-to-weight ratio contributes to zero-to-60 acceleration performance on par with key competitors.

Echo will be one of the highest-mileage vehicles ever offered by Toyota in America. Toyota says preliminary tests have resulted in combined city/highway mileage figures over 40 mpg. The engine is linked to either a five-speed manual transmission or four-speed automatic. The automatic has been designed to stay in a lower gear while travelling uphill, minimizing hunting between gears.

ECHO

TOYOTA

CODE	DESCRIPTION	INVOICE	MSRP

The three-box Echo body structure was developed to provide exceptional occupant safety. The front side member, dash cross member, instrument panel support bar and pillar brace form a trapezoidal structure that effectively disperses impact energy from a front-end collision. Standard safety equipment on the Echo includes dual airbags, occupant head impact protection, and seatbelt pre-tensioners with force limiters. ABS and daytime running lights will be optional. Additional safety features include all-new whiplash-reducing front seat frames with fully integrated headrests.

Echo offers audio system choices of exceptionally high quality for this segment. In addition to a standard AM/FM stereo, a deluxe AM/FM receiver with cassette and six speakers will be offered. A 3-in-1 audio system that includes an AM/FM receiver, cassette and CD with six speakers is also available. Echo also features an abundance of storage space that includes large door pockets, seatback pockets, and convenient storage compartments surrounding the audio system.

Clearly styled and appointed to appeal to young buyers, the Echo is priced quite competitively. However, given America's huge appetite for SUVs both large and small, it's unclear at this point on how well the Echo will fare.

2000 Toyota Echo

Standard Equipment

COUPE (5M): 1.5L I4 DOHC SMPI with variable valve timing 16-valve engine; 5-speed OD manual transmission; engine oil cooler; front-wheel drive, 3.53 axle ratio; partial stainless steel exhaust; front independent strut suspension with anti-roll bar, front coil springs, rear semi-independent torsion suspension with rear coil springs; manual rack-and-pinion steering; front disc/rear drum brakes; 11.9 gal. capacity fuel tank; front license plate bracket, side impact bars; front and rear body-colored bumpers; monotone paint; aero-composite halogen headlamps; driver's and passenger's manual black folding outside mirrors; front and rear 14" x 5.5" steel wheels; P175/65SR14 A/S BSW front and rear tires; inside under cargo mounted compact steel spare wheel; rear heat ducts; AM/FM stereo, seek-scan, 4 speakers, and fixed antenna; remote fuel release; 1 power accessory outlet, driver's foot rest; instrumentation display includes water temperature gauge, trip odometer; warning indicators include oil pressure, water temp, battery, lights on, key in ignition, door ajar; driver's and passenger's front airbags; , fixed rear windows; fixed interval front windshield wipers; seating capacity of 5, front bucket seats, adjustable headrests, driver's seat includes 4-way direction control, passenger's seat includes 4-way direction control; rear bench seat with adjustable headrests; front height adjustable

TOYOTA

ECHO

CODE	DESCRIPTION	INVOICE	MSRP

seatbelts with front pretensioners; cloth seats, cloth door trim insert, full cloth headliner, full carpet floor covering, plastic/rubber gear shift knob; interior lights include dome light; steering wheel with tilt adjustment; vanity mirrors; day/night rearview mirror; partial floor console, glove box, front and rear cupholders, 2 seat back storage pockets, driver's and passenger's door bins, front underseat tray; carpeted cargo floor, cargo cover; body-colored grille, black side window moldings, black front windshield molding, black rear window molding and body-colored door handles.

SEDAN (5M) (in addition to or instead of COUPE (5M) equipment): Manual rear windows and child safety rear door locks.

Base Prices

CODE	DESCRIPTION	INVOICE	MSRP
1413	Echo Coupe (5M)	9264	9995
1415	Echo Sedan (5M)	9543	10295
Destination Charge:		455	455

Accessories

CODE	DESCRIPTION	INVOICE	MSRP
—	**Transmission: 4-Speed Automatic (Coupe)**	743	800
	Includes 3.85 axle ratio.		
—	**Transmission: 4-Speed Automatic (Sedan)**	741	800
	Includes 3.85 axle ratio.		
AB	**Antilock Brakes**	505	590
	Includes daytime running lights. REQUIRES GJ and CK.		
AC	**Air Conditioner (PPO)**	740	925
	Port installed option.		
AC	**Air Conditioning**	740	925
	REQUIRES AQ and RC.		
AQ	**Auto Idling Control**	NC	NC
	REQUIRES CK and (PS or GI) and (AC or GJ).		
CF	**Carpet Floor Mats (4 Piece Set)**	39	64
CK	**All Weather Guard Package**	220	275
	Includes cold area package, HD battery, heavy duty rear heater and HD rear window defogger. REQUIRES AQ and RC and (QS or GI).		
DQ	**Digital Clock**	56	70
DZ	**Radio: Deluxe 3-In-1 Combo**	203	270
	Includes AM/FM stereo with cassette, CD, 6 speakers and audio indicator. REQUIRES GI. NOT AVAILABLE with EX.		
EX	**Radio: Deluxe with Cassette**	128	170
	Includes AM/FM stereo with cassette, 6 speakers and audio indicator. REQUIRES GI. NOT AVAILABLE with DZ, GJ.		
GI	**Upgrade Package #1**	832	1020
	Includes power steering, fixed intermittent wipers, dual remote control mirrors, 60/40 split folding rear seat and digital clock. REQUIRES AQ. NOT AVAILABLE with QS.		
GJ	**Upgrade Package #2 (Coupe)**	1123	1420
	Includes air conditioning, deluxe 3-in-1 combo radio and power door locks. REQUIRES GI and AQ and RC. NOT AVAILABLE with QS, EX.		

404　　www.edmunds.com　　**EDMUND'S® NEW CARS**

ECHO — TOYOTA

CODE	DESCRIPTION	INVOICE	MSRP
GJ	Upgrade Package #2 (Sedan)	1159	1465
	Includes air conditioning, deluxe 3-in-1 combo radio and power door locks. REQUIRES GI and AQ and RC. NOT AVAILABLE with QS, EX.		
GN	Cargo Net	27	42
P4	Auto Reverse Cassette Deck	145	207
P5	Compact Disc Deck	185	264
P6	6-Disc In-Dash Changer	400	575
P9	6-Disc CD Changer	385	550
PL	Power Door Locks (Coupe)	180	225
	REQUIRES GI.		
PL	Power Door Locks (Sedan)	216	270
	REQUIRES GI.		
PS	Power Steering	231	270
	REQUIRES AQ.		
QS	Quarter Stone Protector	NC	NC
	REQUIRES AQ and RC and CK. NOT AVAILABLE with GI, GJ.		
RC	Radiator Cover	NC	NC
	REQUIRES CK and AC and GJ.		
RF	Rear Lip Spoiler	80	100
	Available in alpine silver metallic (199), absolutely red (3P0), black sand pearl (209) and super white (040).		
RF	Rear Spoiler (PPO)	80	100
	Port installed option. Available in alpine silver metallic (199), absolutely red (3P0), black sand pearl (209) and super white (040).		
SS	Alloy Wheels	375	499
V3	V.I.P. RS3200 Deluxe Security System	249	399
WS	Steel Wheel Locks	31	52
WZ	Alloy Wheel Locks	31	52

NOTE: Toyotas sold in Alabama, Florida, Georgia, North Carolina and South Carolina may be equipped with option packages not listed in this guide. You can expect to haggle 25% off the window sticker price on these packages.

TO PRICE YOUR TRADE-IN,
PURCHASE EDMUND'S® USED CAR PRICES AND RATINGS.

See page 6 for details.

VOLKSWAGEN

CABRIO

CODE	DESCRIPTION	INVOICE	MSRP

2000 CABRIO

2000 Volkswagen Cabrio

What's New?

Volkswagen's Cabrio gets minor equipment updates for the millennium.

Review

Volkswagen's Cabrio is good fun. A four-seat convertible with simple good looks, spry performance and premium sound, the Golf-based drop top is the perfect summertime cruiser. Road feel is superb, and the thick, four-spoke steering wheel falls readily to hand. At high speeds, the VW feels solid and sure; this is a car that will get you speeding tickets if you're not careful. Handling is excellent, in the Volkswagen tradition. The chassis and suspension communicate clearly with the driver, and Cabrio's multi-adjustable seats are comfortable. All Cabrios come with a fixed, integrated roll bar and a stout top, sporting six layers and latching tightly to the windshield header.

Two trim levels are available for 2000: value-packed GL and high-end GLS. Both come with CFC-free air conditioning, ABS, an eight-speaker cassette stereo with CD capability, a glass rear window with defogger, side airbags and an anti-theft system. GLS models add a power-operated cloth or vinyl convertible top, leather seating and power windows with a one-touch up or down feature to the standard-equipment roster.

For 2000, Cabrios receive sliding sun-visor extenders, improved theft protection, a brake-wear indicator and an optional (dealer-installed) in-dash CD player. A non-smoking package is also available this year.

Both models are powered by the same 115-horsepower, 2.0-liter, four-cylinder engine that powered previous-generation Cabrios. A five-speed manual transmission comes standard and an automatic tranny is optional. Despite its 122 foot-pounds of torque, this inline four is no barnstormer, and will feel downright sluggish underfoot if mated to the automatic. Nonetheless, the latest Cabrio is a solid, refined and comfortable ride, whether cruising at highway speeds or clipping apexes on your favorite mountain road. Capable underpinnings include MacPherson struts and an anti-roll bar that controls front-end movement, while Volkswagen's own "independent track-correcting torsion-beam rear axle" keeps the Cabrio's hindquarters in line. This suspension is complimented by a perfectly weighted, power-assisted rack-and-pinion steering system that

CABRIO — VOLKSWAGEN

offers excellent turn-in and fantastic feedback. This is where the Cabrio makes its leap from cute Barbie-mobile to serious driver's car.

Inside the Cabrio you'll find classy chrome accents and an instrument panel that illuminates in indigo blue and red. Climate and radio controls are within easy reach and have a logical layout. Front seats offer substantial bolstering, firm padding, and a wide range of adjustments to satisfy drivers of all sizes. This is one of the few small cars we've driven recently that had front legroom to spare.

Sure, the Miata may be more fun to drive and some may find the Mustangs more stylish, but the VW Cabrio is no longer the "boy-toy" car it once was. The Cabrio imparts a sense of class and sophistication, and with a conservative price tag, a fantastic two-year/24,000-mile new-vehicle warranty, a 10-year/100,000-mile powertrain warranty, two years of free roadside assistance, and free scheduled maintenance during the first two years or 24,000 miles of ownership, we think this Volkswagen will appeal to those who appreciate a capable drop-top.

Standard Equipment

GL (5M): 2.0L I4 SOHC SMPI 8-valve engine; 5-speed OD manual transmission; engine oil cooler; 90-amp alternator; front-wheel drive, 3.67 axle ratio; stainless steel exhaust; front independent strut suspension with anti-roll bar, front coil springs, rear independent torsion suspension with rear coil springs, gas-pressurized rear shocks; power rack-and-pinion steering; 4-wheel disc brakes with 4-wheel antilock braking system; 13.7 gal. capacity fuel tank; rear lip spoiler, side impact bars; manual convertible roof with lining, glass rear window, roll-over protection; front and rear body-colored bumpers with body-colored rub strip; body-colored bodyside molding; monotone paint; aero-composite halogen headlamps with daytime running lights; driver's and passenger's manual remote body-colored heated folding outside mirrors; front and rear 14" x 6" steel wheels; P195/60HR14 A/S BSW front and rear tires; inside under cargo mounted compact steel spare wheel; air conditioning, air filter, rear heat ducts; premium AM/FM stereo, seek-scan, cassette, CD changer pre-wiring, in-dash CD pre-wiring, 8 speakers, theft deterrent, and fixed antenna; power door locks with 2 stage unlock, remote keyless entry, power remote hatch/trunk release; 1 power accessory outlet, driver's foot rest; instrumentation display includes tachometer, water temperature gauge, in-dash clock, trip odometer; warning indicators include oil pressure, battery, lights on, key in ignition; driver's and passenger's front airbags, driver's and front passenger's seat mounted side airbags; ignition disable, panic alarm, security system; tinted windows, manual front and rear windows; fixed interval front windshield wipers with heated jets, rear window defroster; seating capacity of 4, front bucket seats, adjustable tilt headrests, center armrest with storage, driver's seat includes 6-way direction control, passenger's seat includes 6-way direction control; full folding rear bench seat with fixed headrests; front height adjustable seatbelts; cloth seats, cloth door trim insert, full cloth headliner, full carpet floor covering with carpeted floor mats, plastic/rubber gear shift knob; interior lights include dome light, 2 door curb lights; leather-wrapped steering wheel with tilt adjustment; dual illuminated vanity mirrors; day/night rearview mirror; full floor console, locking glove box with light, front and rear cupholders, 2 seat back storage pockets, driver's and passenger's door bins; carpeted cargo floor, plastic trunk lid, cargo net, cargo light; body-colored grille, black side window moldings, black front windshield molding, black rear window molding and body-colored door handles.

GLS (5M) (in addition to or instead of GL (5M) equipment): Power convertible roof with lining; additional exterior lights include front fog/driving lights; driver's and passenger's power remote body-colored heated folding outside mirrors; front and rear 14" x 6" alloy wheels; cruise control; power front and rear windows with driver's and passenger's 1-touch down; heated-cushion front sports seats; leather seats, leatherette door trim insert and leather-wrapped gear shift knob.

Base Prices

Code	Description	Invoice	MSRP
1V72N4	Cabrio GL (5M)	18301	19990
1V73N4	Cabrio GLS (5M)	21309	23300
	Destination Charge:	525	525

VOLKSWAGEN CABRIO / GOLF

CODE	DESCRIPTION	INVOICE	MSRP
	Accessories		
—	Metallic Paint	NC	NC
—	Transmission: 4-Speed Automatic	864	875
4A3	Cold-Weather Package (GL)	133	150
	Includes heatable front seats. REQUIRES P1V.		
B0W	California Emissions	99	100
	NOT AVAILABLE with NEV.		
NEV	Northeast Emissions	99	100
	States include New Hampshire, New York, Massachusetts, Connecticut, Rhode Island, Pennsylvania, New Jersey, Delaware, Maryland, Virginia, Vermont and District of Columbia. NOT AVAILABLE with B0W.		
P1V	Power Package (GL)	552	625
	Includes power exterior mirrors, power windows and cruise control.		

2000 GOLF

2000 Volkswagen Golf

What's New?

VW's Golf arrives for 2000 with several minor equipment updates.

Review

We've always liked the Golf, a fun-to-drive, chunky-but-spunky hatchback that has been a bestseller in Europe for more than two decades. Here in the States, the fourth-generation Golf does battle against a range of compacts, most of them with far less sporting credentials. Last year, the Golf received a complete redesign, adding smoother exterior styling and more powerful engines. This year, only small changes have been made to the little VW.

GOLF — VOLKSWAGEN

| CODE | DESCRIPTION | INVOICE | MSRP |

The Golf is available as a base two-door GL, an uplevel four-door GLS, or a sporty two-door GTI in either GLS trim or a GLX package. Powertrains include a 2.0-liter, four-cylinder engine with a cross-flow cylinder head, good for 115 horsepower, and a fuel-sipping, 1.9-liter Turbo Direct Injection (TDI) diesel engine. Both are available with a standard five-speed manual or optional four-speed automatic transmission. Opt for the GTI, and the GLX five-speed-only version serves up the torquey 2.8-liter VR6, a narrow-angle V6 with a wide torque band. Horsepower is 174 at 5,800 rpm, while torque is 181 foot-pounds at 3,200 revs. Silky and playful, the GTI with a VR6 makes for high-spirited driving.

Golfs come with a long list of standard features, including side-impact airbags, four-disc ABS, 15-inch wheels and tires, clear halogen headlamps, telescoping steering wheel, anti-theft alarm, remote entry, and a split-folding rear seat with three headrests. Options for the GLS include leather and heated seating, alloy wheels, and power glass sunroof. The GLX adds 16-inch alloys, dark wood decor and cruise control. All have VW's two-year, 24,000-mile limited warranty with free scheduled maintenance for the same period.

For 2000, Golfs also receive standard sliding sun-visor extenders, a brake-wear indicator and an optional, dealer-installed dashboard CD player. The GTI GLX consumer will get a standard eight-speaker sound system (optional on the GLS) while the VR6 buyer receives Anti Slip Regulation.

Consumers will be impressed by Golf's structural rigidity, which not only provides a solid, quiet body with precise gaps between the doors and body panels, but an overall feel of quality. It all rides on the Golf's front MacPherson struts and lower wishbones. The rear suspension employs an independent torsion-beam axle and separate shock and coil-spring mounts to reduce intrusion into the luggage compartment and cut road noise.

Inside, the instrument panel is stylish yet functional, and the dark wood trim in the GLX model blends well with the high-quality fit and finish of the soft-textured surfaces. Like the New Beetle, gauges are backlit in blue with vibrant red pointers. Volkswagen wanted this combination to be marque-specific, noting that they are the same colors used by international air traffic on airfields at night. Seats are firm and supportive, and the back seat folds down for expanded cargo-carrying capacity.

Behind the wheel of the Golf, whether swayed by value or performance, drivers will be racing to start their engines.

Standard Equipment

GL HATCHBACK (5M): 2.0L I4 SOHC SMPI 8-valve engine; 5-speed OD manual transmission; engine oil cooler; 90-amp alternator; front-wheel drive, 4.24 axle ratio; stainless steel exhaust; front independent strut suspension with anti-roll bar, front coil springs, rear independent torsion suspension with anti-roll bar, rear coil springs; power rack-and-pinion steering; 4-wheel disc brakes with 4-wheel antilock braking system; 14.5 gal. capacity fuel tank; front license plate bracket, side impact bars; front and rear body-colored bumpers with body-colored rub strip; body-colored bodyside molding; monotone paint; aero-composite halogen headlamps with daytime running lights; driver's and passenger's manual remote body-colored heated folding outside mirrors; front and rear 15" x 6" steel wheels; P195/65HR15 A/S BSW front and rear tires; inside under cargo mounted full-size steel spare wheel; air conditioning, air filter, rear heat ducts; premium AM/FM stereo, seek-scan, cassette, CD changer pre-wiring, in-dash CD pre-wiring, 8 speakers, theft deterrent, and integrated roof antenna; power door locks with 2 stage unlock, remote keyless entry, power remote hatch/trunk release, power remote fuel release; 2 power accessory outlets, driver's foot rest; instrumentation display includes tachometer, water temperature gauge, in-dash clock, trip odometer; warning indicators include oil pressure, battery, lights on, key in ignition, low fuel, low washer fluid; driver's and passenger's front airbags, driver's and front passenger's seat mounted side airbags; ignition disable, panic alarm, security system; tinted windows; variable intermittent front windshield wipers, sun visor strip, fixed interval rear wiper, rear window defroster; seating capacity of 5, front bucket seats, adjustable tilt headrests, driver's seat includes 6-way direction control, easy entry, passenger's seat includes 6-way direction control, easy entry; 60-40 folding rear bench seat with adjustable headrests; front height adjustable seatbelts with front pretensioners; cloth seats, cloth door trim insert, full cloth headliner, full carpet floor covering with carpeted floor mats, plastic/rubber gear

VOLKSWAGEN

GOLF

| CODE | DESCRIPTION | INVOICE | MSRP |

shift knob; interior lights include dome light with fade, front and rear reading lights, 2 door curb lights; steering wheel with tilt and telescopic adjustment; dual illuminated vanity mirrors, driver's side auxiliary visor; day/night rearview mirror; full floor console, locking glove box with light, front and rear cupholders, driver's and passenger's door bins; carpeted cargo floor, plastic trunk lid, cargo cover, cargo tie downs, cargo light; body-colored grille, black side window moldings, black front windshield molding, black rear window molding and body-colored door handles.

GLS HATCHBACK (5M) (in addition to or instead of GL HATCHBACK (5M) equipment): Driver's and passenger's power remote body-colored heated folding outside mirrors; power door locks with 2 stage unlock, remote keyless entry, child safety rear door locks, power front and rear windows with front and rear 1-touch down; cruise control, driver's seat includes 6-way direction control, passenger's seat includes 6-way direction control; full floor console and 1 seat back storage pocket.

TDI GL/TDI GLS (5M) (in addition to or instead of GL/GLS HATCHBACK (5M) equipment): 1.9L I4 SOHC direct diesel injection intercooled turbo 8-valve engine, requires diesel fuel; 3.39 axle ratio; P195/65HR15 A/S BSW front and rear tires and cruise control (GL).

GTI GLS (5M) (in addition to or instead of GLS HATCHBACK (5M) equipment): 4-wheel disc brakes with 4-wheel antilock braking system; front express open sliding and tilting glass sunroof with sunshade; additional exterior lights include front fog/driving lights; front and rear 15" x 6" silver alloy wheels; front sports seats, adjustable tilt headrests, driver's seat includes 6-way direction control, easy entry, passenger's seat includes 6-way direction control, easy entry and premium cloth seats.

GLX (5M) (in addition to or instead of GTI GLS (5M) equipment): 2.8L V6 SOHC SMPI 12-valve engine; traction control, 3.39 axle ratio; front and rear 16" x 6.5" silver alloy wheels; P205/55HR16 A/S BSW front and rear tires; air conditioning with climate control, instrumentation display includes exterior temp, trip computer; variable intermittent front windshield wipers, heated jets, rain detecting wipers, heated-cushion front sports seats, driver's seat includes 6-way direction control, lumbar support, passenger's seat includes 6-way direction control lumbar support; leather seats, leather door trim insert, genuine wood trim on instrument panel, leather-wrapped gear shift knob; leather-wrapped steering wheel with tilt and telescopic adjustment and auto-dimming day/night rearview mirror.

Base Prices

CODE	DESCRIPTION	INVOICE	MSRP
1J13L4	GL Hatchback (5M)	13904	14900
1J1334	GL TDI Hatchback (5M)	15101	16195
1J1CL4	GLS Hatchback (5M)	15244	16350
1J1C34	GLS TDI Hatchback (5M)	16214	17400
1J16L4	GTI GLS (5M)	16109	17675
1J16X4	GTI GLX (5M)	20576	22620
Destination Charge:		525	525

Accessories

CODE	DESCRIPTION	INVOICE	MSRP
—	Transmission: 4-Speed Automatic (2.0L)	864	875
B0W	California Emissions (2.0L)	99	100
NEV	Northeast Emissions (2.0L)	99	100
	States include New Hampshire, New York, Massachusetts, Connecticut, Rhode Island, Vermont, Pennsylvania, New Jersey, Delaware, Maryland, Virginia and District of Columbia.		

410   www.edmunds.com   **EDMUND'S® NEW CARS**

GOLF / JETTA — VOLKSWAGEN

CODE	DESCRIPTION	INVOICE	MSRP
PLD	Leather Package (GTI GLS)	751	850
	Includes leather-wrapped brake lever, leather seat trim, leather door inserts, leather-wrapped steering wheel, cold weather package, heated seats and heated washer nozzles.		
PLX	Luxury Package (Golf GLS)	1037	1175
	Includes power sunroof and wheels: 15" alloy (Avus).		
PWP	Cold Weather Package (GTI GLS)	133	150
	Includes heated seats and heated washer nozzles.		
RMA	Monsoon Sound System (GLS)	261	295

2000 JETTA

2000 Volkswagen Jetta

What's New?

VW's 2000 Jetta arrives with minor equipment updates.

Review

The Jetta, Volkswagen's sedan version of the Golf, has always been one of our favorites. Like many cars conceived in Germany, the Jetta possesses an uncanny ability to keep the driver in touch with every undulation and irregularity on the road without sacrificing comfort. The fourth-generation of VW's best-selling Jetta rolled off the line with a completely new wrapper for 1999; this year, buyers will see minor equipment changes.

Jetta's entry-level GL model comes with a 2.0-liter, four-cylinder engine that produces 115 horsepower and makes 122 foot-pounds of torque at 2,600 rpm for quick off-the-line acceleration. The GL also has standard side airbags, a cassette stereo, ABS and heated remote mirrors. The next step up the Jetta ladder is the GLS trim level, which can be ordered with an optional V6 powertrain, and offers more standard goodies like cruise control, power windows and mirrors,

VOLKSWAGEN
JETTA

| CODE | DESCRIPTION | INVOICE | MSRP |

and a center armrest. A Turbocharged Direct Injection (TDI) diesel engine is optional on the GL and GLS models. When mated to a manual transmission, the TDI will achieve approximately 49 mpg.

The top-of-the-line Jetta GLX gets you that buttery-smooth, 174-horsepower VR6 engine standard and provides nifty equipment like rain-sensor wipers, automatic climate control, leather seats, self-dimming rearview mirrors and wood trim.

For 2000, Jetta buyers will receive cars with a brake-wear indicator, a sliding sun-visor extension, and an optional (dealer-installed) dashboard CD player. The cold-weather package, eight-speaker stereo system and 16-inch alloy wheels (VR6 only), which are standard on the GLX, are now optional on the GLS model.

The car's exterior is sleek and curvaceous, with big bumpers and wheel arches that house 15-inch wheels. Built with high-tech bonding agents and laser-welding techniques, the Jetta is structurally rigid, which makes for crisp handling and better control.

Jetta has always been a driver's car, providing an enjoyable experience with a modified MacPherson front-suspension strut concept that has more positive caster and a perfected strut layout for improved directional stability. An enhanced track-correcting torsion-beam rear axle, larger stabilizer bars and four-wheel disc brakes with ABS are also standard.

Due to its popularity and subsequent price increases, Jetta is not quite the bargain it used to be. Still, Volkswagen's bread-and-butter sedan competes well with contenders like the Dodge Stratus, Ford Contour and Honda Accord, and the top-level GLX model undercuts other V6-powered German and Japanese sedans by thousands. Sign us up.

Standard Equipment

GL (5M): 2.0L I4 SOHC SMPI 8-valve engine; 5-speed OD manual transmission; 63-amp battery; engine oil cooler; 90-amp alternator; front-wheel drive; 3.39 axle ratio; steel exhaust; front independent strut suspension with anti-roll bar, front coil springs, rear independent torsion suspension with anti-roll bar, rear coil springs; power rack-and-pinion steering; 4-wheel disc brakes with 4-wheel antilock braking system; 14.5 gal. capacity fuel tank; side impact bars; front and rear body-colored bumpers with body-colored rub strip; body-colored bodyside molding; monotone paint; aero-composite halogen headlamps with daytime running lights; driver's and passenger's manual remote body-colored heated folding outside mirrors; front and rear 15" x 6" steel wheels; P195/65HR15 A/S BSW front and rear tires; inside under cargo mounted full-size steel spare wheel; air conditioning, air filter, rear heat ducts; premium AM/FM stereo, seek-scan, cassette, CD changer pre-wiring, in-dash CD pre-wiring, 8 speakers, theft deterrent, and integrated roof antenna; power door locks with 2 stage unlock, remote keyless entry, child safety rear door locks, power remote hatch/trunk release, power remote fuel release; 2 power accessory outlets, front cigar lighter(s), driver's foot rest; instrumentation display includes tachometer, water temperature gauge, in-dash clock, trip odometer; warning indicators include oil pressure, battery, lights in ign., key in ignition, low fuel, low washer fluid, trunk ajar, driver's and passenger's front airbags, driver's and front passenger's seat mounted side airbags, ignition disable, panic alarm, security system; tinted windows, manual front and rear windows; variable intermittent front windshield wipers, rear window defroster, seating capacity of 5, front bucket seats, adjustable tilt headrests, center armrest with storage, driver's seat includes 6-way direction control, passenger's seat includes 6-way direction control; 60-40 folding rear bench seat with adjustable headrests; front height adjustable seatbelts with front pretensioners; cloth seats, cloth door trim insert, full cloth headliner, full carpet floor covering with carpeted floor mats; interior lights include dome light with fade, front and rear reading lights, 4 door curb lights; steering wheel with tilt and telescopic adjustment; dual illuminated vanity mirrors, driver's side auxiliary visor, day/night rearview mirror, full floor console, locking glove box, front and rear cupholders, driver's and passenger's door bins, carpeted cargo floor, carpeted trunk lid, cargo tie downs, cargo light, body-colored grille, black side window moldings, black front windshield molding, black rear window molding and body-colored door handles.

JETTA — VOLKSWAGEN

CODE	DESCRIPTION	INVOICE	MSRP

GLS (5M) (in addition to or instead of GL (5M) equipment): Driver's and passenger's power remote body-colored heated folding outside mirrors; cruise control; power front and rear windows with front and rear 1-touch up and down; premium cloth seats and 1 seat back storage pocket.

TDI GL/TDI GLS (5M) (in addition to or instead of 2.0L (5M) equipment): 1.9L I4 SOHC direct diesel injection intercooled turbo 8-valve engine, requires diesel fuel; 80-amp battery.

GLS VR6 (5M) (in addition to or instead of GLS (5M) equipment): 2.8L V6 SOHC SMPI 12-valve engine; 63-amp battery; traction control, 3.39 axle ratio and sport ride suspension.

GLX (5M) (in addition to or instead of GLS VR6 (5M) equipment): Front power sliding and tilting glass sunroof with sunshade; additional exterior lights include front fog/driving lights; alloy wheels; air conditioning with climate control; instrumentation display includes exterior temp, trip computer; variable intermittent front windshield wipers with heated jets, rear blind; heated-cushion front bucket seats, driver's seat includes 6-way power seat, passenger's seat includes 6-way power seat, lumbar support; leather seats, leather door trim insert, genuine wood trim on instrument panel, leather-wrapped gear shift knob; memory on driver's seat with 2 memory setting(s); leather-wrapped steering wheel with tilt and telescopic adjustment and auto-dimming day/night rearview mirror.

Base Prices

Code	Description	Invoice	MSRP
9M22K4	GL (5M)	15228	16700
9M28K4	GLS (5M)	16087	17650
9M2254	GL TDI (5M)	16764	17995
9M2854	GLS TDI (5M)	17414	18700
9M28W4	GLS VR6 (5M)	18164	19950
9M26W4	GLX (5M)	21976	24170
Destination Charge:		525	525

Accessories

Code	Description	Invoice	MSRP
3FE	Power Sunroof (GLS - TDI/VR6)	764	865
	REQUIRES 4AT (TDI).		
4AT	Transmission: 4-Speed Automatic (All Except TDI)	864	875
4AT	Transmission: 4-Speed Automatic (TDI)	1137	1185
	NOT AVAILABLE with PJ3.		
BOW	California Emissions	99	100
NEV	Northeast Emissions	99	100
	States include New Hampshire, New York, Massachusetts, Connecticut, Rhode Island, Pennsylvania, New Jersey, Delaware, Maryland, Vermont, Virginia and District of Columbia.		
PJ3	Luxury Package (GLS Except VR6)	1037	1175
	Includes wheels: 15" alloy and power sunroof.		
PK1	Cold Weather Package (GLS)	133	150
	Includes heated front seats and heated washer nozzles.		
PL4	Leather Package (GLS)	751	850
	Includes leather-wrapped steering wheel, leather-wrapped shift knob/handbrake, cold weather package, heated front seats and heated washer nozzles. REQUIRES PJ3 or 3FE or PM1.		

VOLKSWAGEN
JETTA / NEW BEETLE

CODE	DESCRIPTION	INVOICE	MSRP
PM1	Luxury Package (GLS VR6)	1214	1375
	Includes wheels: 16" alloy and power sunroof.		
RSM	Monsoon Sound System (GLS)	261	295
	INCLUDED in GLX.		

2000 NEW BEETLE

2000 Volkswagen New Beetle

_____ **What's New?** _____

Several minor equipment upgrades debut on the 2000 New Beetle.

_____ **Review** _____

The New Beetle is a bundle of contradictions. It's a blast from the past and a gateway to the 21st century. It's small but it's safe. It's pretty but it can also be pretty powerful.

Volkswagen's New Beetle debuted at the 1998 North American International Auto Show in Detroit to classic '60s tunes and daisies dotting the dashboards. As a Volkswagen executive said, "It's the birth of a legend, a love affair continued, a dream come true."

The VW folks dubbed it a car that makes people smile. We certainly did. Mixing design elements from the old Beetle of the flower-power era with modern technology and luxuries, the Concept 1 design study that was presented at the same show in 1994 has become a reality. A groovy, cool, or baaaad one depending on your age.

The trademark Beetle body shape is immediately recognizable, though it shares no parts with the old Beetle. It's both larger (161.1 inches in length and 96.3 cubic feet inside) and more powerful than its predecessor and the motor is no longer in the back. Three engines are available today: a turbocharged 150-horsepower, 1.8-liter four-cylinder engine, a 115-horsepower, 2.0-liter four-banger or a high-tech Turbo Direct Injection diesel engine that gets 48 mpg on the highway and has a driving range of 700 miles. With 16-inch wheels and wide tires, cruising in the New Beetle "may remind you of the first time you drove the go-cart around the track," said a company official. Crossing all lines of age, race, and class, the target buyer is men, women, young people or people who are simply young at heart.

NEW BEETLE — VOLKSWAGEN

| CODE | DESCRIPTION | INVOICE | MSRP |

Performance and handling is surprisingly good on all New Beetles, but the 1.8T really shines when pushed to the limit. With 156 foot-pounds of torque available between 2,200 to 4,200 rpm, the New Beetle 1.8T never feels underpowered or overworked. Fun comes both from watching people stare and wave at you and from blasting down the highways or up a canyon road. Steering is responsive and the little car takes corners like a roadrunner, making it easy to rack up speeding tickets if you're not careful.

The safety system features energy-absorbing crush zones, pre-tensioning safety belts, daytime running lights, dual airbags, optional side airbags for front-seat passengers, and excellent bumper crash-test scores. Other standard features include four beverage holders, a remote locking system, anti-theft alarm, a passenger-assist handle above the glove compartment, driver and passenger height adjusters, mesh pockets on the doors, and a bud vase on the dash. Nice touch.

For 2000, the New Beetle gets a brake-wear indicator, improved theft protection, a sliding sun-visor extender, and an optional cold-weather package (GLS models only). Additionally, the 1.8T GLS and GLX versions receive Anti-Slip Regulation as standard equipment this year.

The New Beetle offers a unique combination of safety, fun, practicality and value. There's no denying it: It's Beetle-mania all over again.

Standard Equipment

GL (5M): 2.0L I4 SOHC SMPI 8-valve engine; 5-speed OD manual transmission; 60-amp battery; engine oil cooler; 90-amp alternator; front-wheel drive; stainless steel exhaust; front independent strut suspension with anti-roll bar, front coil springs, rear independent torsion suspension with anti-roll bar, rear coil springs; power rack-and-pinion steering; 4-wheel disc brakes with 4-wheel antilock braking system; 14.5 gal. capacity fuel tank; front and rear body-colored bumpers with rear tow hooks; rocker panel extensions; monotone paint; projector beam halogen headlamps with daytime running lights; driver's and passenger's power remote body-colored heated folding outside mirrors; front and rear 16" x 6.5" steel wheels; P205/55HR16 A/S BSW front and rear tires; inside under cargo mounted full-size steel spare wheel; air conditioning, air filter, rear heat ducts; premium AM/FM stereo, seek-scan, cassette, CD changer pre-wiring, in-dash CD pre-wiring, 6 speakers, theft deterrent, and integrated roof antenna; power door locks with 2 stage unlock, remote keyless entry, power remote hatch/trunk release, power remote fuel release; 3 power accessory outlets, driver's foot rest; instrumentation display includes tachometer, in-dash clock, exterior temp, trip odometer; warning indicators include oil pressure, battery, lights on, key in ignition; driver's and passenger's front airbags, driver's and front passenger's seat mounted side airbags; ignition disable, panic alarm, security system; tinted windows; variable intermittent front windshield wipers, rear window defroster; seating capacity of 4, front bucket seats, adjustable tilt headrests, center armrest with storage, driver's seat includes 6-way direction control, easy entry, passenger's seat includes 6-way direction control, easy entry; full folding rear bench seat with adjustable headrests; front height adjustable seatbelts with front pretensioners; premium cloth seats, leatherette door trim insert, full cloth headliner, front carpet floor covering with carpeted floor mats; interior lights include dome light with fade, front and rear reading lights, 2 door curb lights; steering wheel with tilt and telescopic adjustment; dual illuminated vanity mirrors; day/night rearview mirror; full floor console, mini overhead console with storage, locking glove box with light, front and rear cupholders, 2 seat back storage pockets, driver's and passenger's door bins; carpeted cargo floor, plastic trunk lid, cargo cover, cargo light; black side window moldings, black front windshield molding, black rear window molding and body-colored door handles.

GLS (5M) (in addition to or instead of GL (5M) equipment): Additional exterior lights include front fog/driving lights; cruise control; power windows with driver's 1-touch up and down.

GLS TDI (5M) (in addition to or instead of GLS (5M) equipment): 1.9L I4 SOHC direct diesel injection intercooled turbo 8-valve engine, requires diesel fuel.

VOLKSWAGEN NEW BEETLE / PASSAT

CODE	DESCRIPTION	INVOICE	MSRP

GLS 1.8 (5M) (in addition to or instead of GLS TDI (5M) equipment): 1.8L I4 DOHC SMPI intercooled turbo 20-valve engine, requires premium unleaded fuel; traction control, 3.68 axle ratio and retractable rear lip spoiler.

GLX (5M) (in addition to or instead of GLS 1.8 (5M) equipment): Front power sliding and tilting glass sunroof with sunshade; alloy wheels; variable intermittent front windshield wipers with heated jets, heated-cushion front bucket seats; leather seats, leather-wrapped gear shift knob and leather-wrapped steering wheel with tilt and telescopic adjustment.

Base Prices

Code	Description	Invoice	MSRP
1C13K4	GL (5M)	15151	15900
1C15K4	GLS (5M)	15706	16850
1C1554	GLS TDI (5M)	16675	17900
1C15T4	GLS 1.8T (5M)	17691	19000
1C17T4	GLX (5M)	19608	21075
Destination Charge:		525	525

Accessories

Code	Description	Invoice	MSRP
—	Transmission: 4-Speed Automatic	864	875
B0W	California Emissions	99	100
NEV	Northeast Emissions	99	100
	States include New Hampshire, New York, Massachusetts, Connecticut, Rhode Island, Pennsylvania, New Jersey, Delaware, Maryland, Vermont, Virginia and District of Columbia.		
P1W	Cold Weather Package (GLS)	133	150
	Includes heated front seats and heated washer nozzles. INCLUDED in W2P.		
W1L	Luxury Package (GLS)	1037	1175
	Includes power sunroof and wheels: 16" alloy.		
W2P	Leather Package (GLS)	751	850
	Includes leather seat trim, leather-wrapped steering wheel, leather-wrapped shift knob/handbrake, cold weather package, heated front seats and heated washer nozzles. REQUIRES W1L. NOT AVAILABLE with P1W.		

2000 PASSAT

What's New?

The radio display and anti-theft system have been updated. A brake-wear indicator is now standard on all models.

Review

Volkswagen has been busy in recent years. In between buying up smaller carmakers, designing 12- and 16-cylinder engines, and creating a new line of luxury vehicles, the company has had time to tweak its already excellent Passat sedan and wagon offerings.

The base Passat engine is a 1.8-liter turbocharged four cylinder that makes 150 horsepower and an almost lag-free 155 ft-lbs. of torque. While not a race engine, this powerplant offers

416   www.edmunds.com   **EDMUND'S® NEW CARS**

PASSAT — VOLKSWAGEN

adequate acceleration and contributes more to the Passat's overall grin factor than one might think, especially when mated to the company's excellent five-speed manual transmission.

Stepping up to the 2.8-liter V6 will net you an additional 40 horsepower and 52 more ft-lbs. of torque. The V6 comes standard on Passat GLX models and puts the "fun" back in functional with its broad torque band and responsive acceleration. The GLX package includes Volkswagen's five-speed Tiptronic automatic transmission as standard equipment.

Regardless of drivetrain choice, all Passats come with superb steering, handling and braking characteristics. With ABS four-wheel discs standard on all trim levels, an independent front and rear suspension, and perfectly weighted power rack-and-pinion steering, the Passat is one of the most entertaining sedans (or wagons) in the midsize class. Some drivers note a bit too much body roll during canyon runs, but the pay off comes in its excellent overall ride quality.

In addition to its mechanical pedigree, the Passat offers up an impressive list of standard features. Items like air conditioning, cruise control, one-touch power windows, power locks, remote keyless entry, a remote trunk release, a full-size conventional spare, side airbags and heated exterior mirrors are included on the base GLS models. GLX trim adds the aforementioned V6 engine and automatic transmission, plus a sunroof, heated front seats with driver's seat memory, leather seat coverings and door inserts, variable intermittent wipers with heated jets and an auto-dimming day-night mirror.

A runaway success in Europe, the current Passat is making headway here in North America against heavy-hitters like the Honda Accord, Toyota Camry and Ford Taurus. Based on a stretched Audi A4 platform and using plenty of Audi parts in its construction, the Passat looks, feels, smells and drives like a more substantial car than its price tag would lead you to expect. Its contemporary styling will wear well into the new century and its solid construction should keep the car feeling new as the miles add up.

With Volkswagen expanding into the luxury-sedan, SUV, and exotic sports-car markets over the next few years, they're going to need a solid bread-and-butter model to pay all the upcoming development and marketing bills. We expect the Passat to fill this role and help keep the company afloat during its transitional period. Before rushing out to buy that new Accord, Camry or Taurus, you'd do well to at least test drive a Passat.

2000 Volkswagen Passat

VOLKSWAGEN PASSAT

CODE	DESCRIPTION	INVOICE	MSRP

Standard Equipment

GLS SEDAN (5M): 1.8L I4 DOHC SMPI intercooled turbo 20-valve engine, requires premium unleaded fuel; 5-speed OD manual transmission; engine oil cooler; 90-amp alternator; front-wheel drive; traction control; 3.7 axle ratio; stainless steel exhaust; front independent suspension with anti-roll bar, front coil springs, gas-pressurized front shocks, rear independent suspension with anti-roll bar, rear coil springs, gas-pressurized rear shocks; power rack-and-pinion steering; 4-wheel disc brakes with 4-wheel antilock braking system; 16.4 gal. capacity fuel tank; front license plate bracket, side impact bars, front and rear body-colored bumpers with body-colored rub strip, body-colored bodyside molding, rocker panel extensions, clearcoat monotone paint, aero-composite halogen headlamps with daytime running lights, additional exterior lights include front fog/driving lights, driver's and passenger's power remote body-colored heated folding outside mirrors, front and rear 15" x 6" black steel wheels, P195/65HR15 A/S BSW front and rear tires, inside under cargo mounted full-size steel spare wheel; air conditioning, air filter, rear heat ducts, premium AM/FM stereo, seek-scan, cassette, CD changer pre-wiring, in-dash CD pre-wiring, 8 speakers, theft deterrent, and integrated roof antenna, cruise control, power door locks with 2 stage unlock, remote keyless entry, child safety rear door locks, power remote hatch/trunk release, power remote fuel release, 2 power accessory outlets, driver's foot rest, retained accessory power, smokers' package, instrumentation display includes tachometer, water temperature gauge, in-dash clock, exterior temp, trip computer, trip odometer; warning indicators include oil pressure, battery, lights on, key in ignition, low washer fluid, door ajar, trunk ajar, driver's and passenger's front airbags, driver's and front passenger's seat mounted side airbags, ignition disable, panic alarm, security system, tinted windows, power front and rear windows with driver's and passenger's 1-touch down, variable intermittent front windshield wipers, sun visor strip, rear window defroster, seating capacity of 5, front bucket seats, adjustable tilt headrests, center armrest with storage, driver's seat includes 6-way direction control, passenger's seat includes 6-way direction control, 60-40 folding rear bench seat with adjustable headrests, center armrest, front height adjustable seatbelts with front and rear pretensioners, premium cloth seats, cloth door trim insert, full cloth headliner, front carpet floor covering with carpeted floor mats, plastic/rubber gear shift knob; interior lights include dome light with fade, front and rear reading lights, steering wheel with tilt and telescopic adjustment, dual illuminated vanity mirrors, driver's side auxiliary visor, day/night rearview mirror, full floor console, locking glove box with light, front and rear cupholders, 2 seat back storage pockets, driver's and passenger's door bins, carpeted cargo floor, carpeted trunk lid, cargo tie downs, cargo light, black grille, black side window moldings, black front windshield molding, black rear window molding and body-colored door handles.

GLS V6 SEDAN (5M) (in addition to or instead of GLS SEDAN (5M) equipment): 2.8L V6 DOHC SMPI 30-valve engine, requires premium unleaded fuel.

GLX SEDAN (5M) (in addition to or instead of GLS V6 SEDAN (5M) equipment): Front express open/close sliding and tilting glass sunroof with sunshade; driver's and passenger's power remote body-colored heated electric folding outside mirrors, front and rear 16" x 6.5" silver alloy wheels, P205/55HR16 A/S BSW front and rear tires, inside under cargo mounted full-size alloy spare wheel; air conditioning with climate control, Monsoon premium AM/FM stereo, seek-scan, cassette, CD changer pre-wiring, in-dash CD pre-wiring, 8 premium speakers, amplifier, theft deterrent, and integrated roof antenna, variable intermittent front windshield wipers with heated jets, rain detecting wipers, rear blind, heated-cushion front bucket seats, driver's seat includes 6-way power seat, lumbar support, passenger's seat includes 6-way power seat, lumbar support; leather seats, leatherette door trim insert, genuine wood trim on instrument panel, wood gear shift knob; memory on driver's seat with 3 memory setting(s); leather-wrapped steering wheel with tilt and telescopic adjustment, auto-dimming day/night rearview mirror, and rear door bins.

WAGON (5M) (in addition to or instead of SEDAN (5M) equipment): Fixed 1/4 vent windows; rear window wiper and cargo cover.

418 www.edmunds.com **EDMUND'S® NEW CARS**

PASSAT — VOLKSWAGEN

CODE	DESCRIPTION	INVOICE	MSRP
_____	**Base Prices**	_____	
3B24N5	GLS Sedan (5M)	19293	21200
3B24SR	GLS V6 Sedan (5M)	21642	23800
3B25SR	GLX Sedan (5M)	25124	27655
3B54N5	GLS Wagon (5M)	20016	22000
3B54SR	GLS V6 Wagon (5M)	22365	24600
3B55SR	GLX Wagon (5M)	25847	28455
	Destination Charge:	525	525
	Accessories		
—	Metallic Paint	NC	NC
—	Partial Leather Interior Trim (Sedan - GLS/GLS V6)	1126	1275
	Includes 4-spoke padded leather-wrapped steering wheel, Cold Weather Package: heatable front seats, heated windshield washer nozzles; wood shift knob, driver's and passenger lumbar's support, leather seat trim and leatherette inserts.		
—	Partial Leather Interior Trim (Wagon - GLS/GLS V6)	1126	1275
	Includes 4-spoke padded leather-wrapped steering wheel, Cold Weather Package: heatable front seats, heated windshield washer nozzles; wood shift knob, driver's and passenger lumbar's support, leather seat trim and leatherette inserts.		
5AT	Transmission: 5-Speed Automatic	1073	1075
	Includes Tiptronic feature and 3.73 axle ratio.		
PJ6	Luxury Package (Sedan - GLS/GLS V6)	1325	1500
	Includes wheels: 15"x 6" alloy (Adelaide), power glass sunroof with tilt and slide and manually operated rear sunshade.		
PJ6	Luxury Package (Wagon - GLS/GLS V6)	1223	1385
	Includes wheels: 15"x 6" alloy (Adelaide) and power glass sunroof with tilt and slide.		
RMA	Monsoon Sound System (GLS/GLS V6)	261	295
	Includes amplifier.		
WW1	Cold Weather Package (GLS/GLS V6)	287	325
	Includes heatable front seats and heated windshield washer nozzles.		

TO PRICE YOUR TRADE-IN, PURCHASE EDMUND'S® USED CAR PRICES AND RATINGS.

See page 6 for details.

VOLVO

40-SERIES

CODE	DESCRIPTION	INVOICE	MSRP

2000 40-SERIES

2000 Volvo 40-Series

_____ **What's New?** _____

The S40 is Volvo's completely new entry-level sedan. Along with its wagon variant, the V40, this car rounds out Volvo's vehicle lineup. Safety, styling, and comfort are its main attributes.

_____ **Review** _____

Up to this point, it has been difficult for Volvo to attract younger car buyers. This has been due to both the price of current models and the not-so-hip stereotype that seems to come into play when owning a Volvo. Volvo's elixir comes in the form of the 2000 S40/V40.

Brought over from Europe (the S40 went on sale in 1996 over there), the S40 certainly looks like a Volvo, but the traditional Volvo boxy styling is subdued for a more pleasant shape. The lines are smooth, with a nice integration of the traditional Volvo grille. The V40 Wagon is also softer and kinder than previous "shipping-box-included" Volvo wagons.

All S40/V40s are equipped with a turbocharged, DOHC, 1.9-liter, 16-valve four-cylinder engine. Maximum horsepower is 160 at 5,100 rpm. A more important figure, however, is the 170 ft-lbs. of torque available as low as 1,800 rpm. The low torque peak is due to Volvo's Light-Pressure Turbo system (LPT), which is designed to build boost pressure more quickly than a normal turbo system. The 1.9-liter engine is mated to a four-speed automatic transmission. The transmission offers three modes: Economy, Sport, and Winter. As of now, the automatic transmission is the sole choice.

Inside, the 40 platform doesn't skimp on Volvo's usual strong points of safety and comfort. For safety, there are dual front airbags, side airbags (the S40/V40 uses Volvo's SIPS II side-airbag design, which is said to provide even more protection to the chest and head) and front seatbelts that are adjustable to match the driver's height. The front belts are also equipped with pre-tensioners, which tighten the belts in order to help prevent slack in a frontal collision. The S40/V40 also has Volvo's new Whiplash Protection System (WHIPS) seats that were introduced on the S80 last year. These seats help prevent whiplash in a rear-end collision. The rear seats, including the center, are equipped with three-point belts and headrests. As you would expect, all of these features are standard. Other standard items include automatic climate control, heated rearview mirrors, and an electronic security system.

420   www.edmunds.com   **EDMUND'S® NEW CARS**

40-SERIES VOLVO

| CODE | DESCRIPTION | INVOICE | MSRP |

Volvo has given the 40 platform a fairly taut suspension, though comfort ultimately takes precedence over performance. And the S40/V40's comfort is just one of the strong characteristics that should draw interest from buyers for safety, utility and an improved personality over most other Volvo products. One must be careful when choosing optional equipment, however. A full load of options can bloom the price of a V40 Wagon to around $30,000.

Standard Equipment

S40 A SEDAN (4A): 1.9L I4 DOHC MPI intercooled turbo 16-valve engine; 4-speed electronic OD auto transmission with lock-up; 520-amp battery; 100-amp alternator; driver's selectable multi-mode transmission; front-wheel drive; stainless steel exhaust with chrome tip; front independent strut suspension with anti-roll bar, front coil springs, rear semi-independent multi-link suspension with anti-roll bar, rear coil springs; power rack-and-pinion steering; 4-wheel disc brakes with 4-wheel antilock braking system; 15.8 gal. capacity fuel tank; side impact bars; front and rear body-colored bumpers; body-colored bodyside molding; monotone paint; aero-composite halogen headlamps with daytime running lights, delay-off feature; driver's and passenger's power remote body-colored heated folding outside mirrors; front and rear 15" x 6" silver alloy wheels; P195/60VR15 A/S BSW front and rear tires; inside under cargo mounted compact steel spare wheel; air conditioning with climate control, air filter, rear heat ducts; AM/FM stereo, seek-scan, cassette, CD changer pre-wiring, in-dash CD pre-wiring, 6 speakers, amplifier, theft deterrent, and power retractable antenna; cruise control; power door locks with 2 stage unlock, remote keyless entry, child safety rear door locks, power remote hatch/trunk release; 1 power accessory outlet, driver's foot rest; instrumentation display includes tachometer, water temperature gauge, in-dash clock, exterior temp, trip odometer; warning indicators include oil pressure, battery, low coolant, lights on, key in ignition, low fuel, low washer fluid, bulb failure, service interval; driver's and passenger's front airbags, driver's and front passenger's seat mounted side airbags; ignition disable, panic alarm, security system; tinted windows, power front and rear windows with driver's 1-touch down; fixed interval front windshield wipers, rear window defroster; seating capacity of 5, front bucket seats, fixed headrests, center armrest with storage, driver's seat includes 8-way direction control, lumbar support, passenger's seat includes 4-way direction control; rear bench seat with adjustable headrests, center pass-thru armrest; front height adjustable seatbelts with front pretensioners; cloth seats, cloth door trim insert, full cloth headliner, full color-keyed carpet floor covering with carpeted floor mats, plastic/rubber gear shift knob; interior lights include dome light with fade, front and rear reading lights, 4 door curb lights, illuminated entry; steering wheel with tilt and telescopic adjustment; dual illuminated vanity mirrors; day/night rearview mirror; full floor console, locking glove box with light, front and rear cupholders, instrument panel bin, 2 seat back storage pockets, driver's and passenger's door bins, rear door bins; carpeted cargo floor, carpeted trunk lid, cargo tie downs, cargo light; chrome grille, black side window moldings, black front windshield molding, black rear window molding and black door handles.

V40 A WAGON (4A) (in addition to or instead of S40 A SEDAN (4A) equipment): Front and rear body-colored bumpers with rear step; AM/FM stereo, seek-scan, cassette, CD changer pre-wiring, in-dash CD pre-wiring, 7 speakers, amplifier, theft deterrent, and integrated roof antenna; fixed 1/4 vent windows; fixed interval rear wiper and cargo cover.

Base Prices

644 2502 161 S40 A Sedan (4A)	21329	22900
645 2502 161 V40 A Wagon (4A)	22339	23900
Destination Charge:	575	575

VOLVO
40-SERIES / 70-SERIES

CODE	DESCRIPTION	INVOICE	MSRP

Accessories

CODE	DESCRIPTION	INVOICE	MSRP
—	Child Booster Cushion	255	300
—	Leather-Faced Seating	1032	1200
	Includes seat front storage pockets.		
—	Sport Package (Sedan)	470	550
	Includes rear trunk spoiler, front fog lights and leather-wrapped sport steering wheel.		
—	Sport Package (Wagon)	470	550
	Includes rear spoiler, front fog lights and leather-wrapped sport steering wheel.		
—	Sport-Plus Package	1615	1900
	Includes rear spoiler, front foglights, sport steering wheel, 8-way adjustable power driver's seat, SC-816 stereo with CD, premium speaker system and trip computer.		
—	Sunroof Package	1870	2200
	Includes leather-faced seating, classic red walnut simulated wood dash, simulated wood door trim and simulated wood gear shift.		
—	Touring Package	1275	1500
	Includes 8-way adjustable driver's seat, SC-816 CD radio, premium speaker system, trip computer and leather-wrapped touring steering wheel. NOT AVAILABLE with Sport Package.		
—	Weather Package	725	850
	Includes dynamic stability assistance, heated front seats and headlamp wiper/washer.		
000098	6-Disc CD Changer Pre-Wiring	27	27
PAINT	Metallic Paint	340	400

2000 70-SERIES

What's New?

Volvo introduces a 236-hp HPT convertible and adds to the S70/V70's standard equipment list.

Review

Safe and sturdy describes the Volvo image. To be sure, Volvos are both safe and sturdy, boasting many standard safety features and feeling as though they've been cast from a single block of iron. But, there are other reasons to buy a Volvo.

Turbo power is one. The engine bogs a bit until the turbocharger gets spooled up, but once on boil, a Volvo will rocket forward quickly enough to force your body back into the seat. Brakes are outstanding and steering is firm and linear. All mechanical systems communicate clearly, allowing the driver to understand what the car is doing at all times.

Comfort is another big Volvo advantage. The seats in these Swedish cars are the best the world has to offer. You can drive a Volvo non-stop all day long, and not feel one bit of fatigue, unless of course you and Jose Cuervo visited a bit longer than you should have the night before.

These are the characteristics that keep Volvo buyers returning in droves for new versions of their favorite car, whether it's the C70 Coupe, C70 Convertible, S70 sedan or V70 wagon. They live with the minor ergonomic glitches, trading these blemishes for the comfort, performance and security a Volvo delivers.

70-SERIES — VOLVO

CODE	DESCRIPTION	INVOICE	MSRP

Base S/V70 models have a 2.4-liter, inline five-cylinder engine pumping 162 horsepower through either a five-speed manual or a new five-speed automatic transmission. The engine uses Continuously Variable Valve Timing (CVVT), producing better fuel economy and reducing noise, vibration and harshness levels. GLT sedans, LT coupes and convertibles, and Cross Country AWD wagons are powered by a light-pressure turbocharged (LPT) version of the base engine, good for 190 horsepower. The only transmission available on Volvo cars with LPT engines is the four-speed automatic. T-5 designates the hot-rod front-wheel-drive edition of the sedan, and it comes with a high-pressure turbocharged 2.3-liter, inline five-cylinder engine making 236 horsepower. The AWD R wagon gets this same engine, as do HT editions of the coupe and convertible.

For 2000, all North American models receive standard alloy wheels, a security system and WHIPS seat technology, which minimizes whiplash injuries in a rear-end collision. The seat itself moves back 15 degrees with the occupant after impact, preventing the person's body from snapping forward again. At the same time the headrest moves forward, providing extra support for the head and neck. While the V70 AWD and V70 T-5 have been discontinued, the V70R AWD and S70 T-5 receive Homelink standard. Twin, rear-integrated child-booster cushions are new this year and optional on the V70, Volvo V-Tex Vinyl upholstery is discontinued, and color options Blue/Green, Desert Wind and Sandstone Brown are replaced by Moondust and Venetian Red. All options have been consolidated into packages and are no longer available individually.

These Volvos have a lot more to offer than just safety and security. The C70/S70/V70 models offer fun-to-drive performance, the security of available all-wheel drive, cutting-edge safety technology and, as always, a comfortable ride.

2000 Volvo V70

Standard Equipment

BASE SEDAN (5M): 2.4L I5 DOHC MPI with variable valve timing 20-valve engine, requires premium unleaded fuel; 5-speed OD manual transmission; 520-amp battery; 100-amp alternator; front-wheel drive, 4.0 axle ratio; stainless steel exhaust with chrome tip; front independent strut suspension with anti-roll bar, front coil springs, rear semi-independent multi-link suspension with anti-roll bar, rear coil springs; power rack-and-pinion steering; 4-wheel disc brakes with 4-wheel antilock braking system; 17.9 gal. capacity fuel tank; front mud flaps, side impact bars; front and rear body-colored bumpers; body-colored bodyside molding, rocker panel extensions; monotone paint; aero-composite halogen headlamps with daytime running lights; driver's and passenger's power remote body-colored heated folding outside mirrors; front and rear 15" x 6.5" silver alloy

VOLVO

70-SERIES

| CODE | DESCRIPTION | INVOICE | MSRP |

wheels; P195/60VR15 A/S BSW front and rear tires; inside under cargo mounted compact steel spare wheel; dual zone air conditioning with climate control, air filter, rear heat ducts; premium AM/FM stereo, clock, seek-scan, cassette, CD changer pre-wiring, in-dash CD pre-wiring, 6 speakers, amplifier, theft deterrent, and power retractable antenna; cruise control; power door locks with 2 stage unlock, remote keyless entry, child safety rear door locks, power remote hatch/trunk release, power remote fuel release; 1 power accessory outlet, driver's foot rest; instrumentation display includes tachometer, water temperature gauge, exterior temp, trip odometer; warning indicators include oil pressure, battery, low coolant, lights on, key in ignition, low fuel, low washer fluid, bulb failure, trunk ajar, service interval, brake fluid; driver's and passenger's front airbags, driver's and front passenger's seat mounted side airbags; ignition disable, panic alarm, security system; tinted windows, power front and rear windows with driver's 1-touch down; fixed interval front windshield wipers, sun visor strip, rear window defroster; seating capacity of 5, front bucket seats, fixed headrests, center armrest with storage, driver's seat includes 6-way direction control, lumbar support, passenger's seat includes, 6-way direction control; 60-40 folding rear bench seat with adjustable headrests, center pass-thru armrest; front height adjustable seatbelts with front pretensioners; cloth seats, cloth door trim insert, full cloth headliner, full carpet floor covering with carpeted floor mats; interior lights include dome light with fade, front and rear reading lights, 4 door curb lights, illuminated entry; steering wheel with tilt and telescopic adjustment; dual illuminated vanity mirrors; day/night rearview mirror; full floor console, locking glove box with light, front and rear cupholders, 2 seat back storage pockets, driver's and passenger's door bins; carpeted cargo floor, carpeted trunk lid, cargo tie downs, cargo light; chrome grille, black side window moldings, black front windshield molding, black rear window molding and black door handles.

GLT SEDAN (5A) (in addition to or instead of BASE SEDAN (5A) equipment): 2.4L I5 DOHC MPI intercooled turbo variable valve timing 20-valve engine, requires premium unleaded fuel; 4-speed electronic OD auto transmission with lock-up; driver's selectable multi-mode transmission; premium AM/FM stereo, clock, seek-scan, cassette, CD changer pre-wiring, in-dash CD pre-wiring, 6 speakers, amplifier, theft deterrent, and power retractable diversity antenna; warning indicators include door ajar; driver's seat includes 6-way power seat, lumbar support and memory on driver's seat with 3 memory setting(s).

T5 SEDAN (5M) (in addition to or instead of GLT SEDAN (5M) equipment): 2.3L I5 DOHC MPI intercooled turbo 20-valve engine, requires premium unleaded fuel; 5-speed OD manual transmission; front and rear 16" x 6.5" silver alloy wheels; P205/55VR16 A/S BSW front and rear tires; premium AM/FM stereo, clock, seek-scan, cassette, single CD, 8 speakers, amplifier, theft deterrent, and power retractable diversity antenna; garage door opener; instrumentation display includes trip computer; passenger's seat includes 6-way power seat lumbar support and leather-wrapped steering wheel with tilt and telescopic adjustment.

BASE AWD SEDAN (5A) (in addition to or instead of T5 SEDAN (5A) equipment): 2.4L I5 DOHC MPI intercooled turbo with variable valve timing 20-valve engine, requires premium unleaded fuel; 5-speed electronic OD auto transmission with lock-up; driver's selectable multi-mode transmission; full-time 4 wheel drive, viscous limited slip differential, traction control, 2.49 axle ratio; front independent strut suspension with anti-roll bar, front coil springs, independent multi-link suspension with anti-roll bar, rear coil springs; 17.4 gal. capacity fuel tank; aero-composite halogen headlamps with washer and wiper, daytime running lights, multiple headlamps; front and rear 15" x 6.5" silver alloy wheels; P195/65VR15 A/S BSW front and rear tires; premium AM/FM stereo, clock, seek-scan, cassette, CD changer pre-wiring, in-dash CD pre-wiring, 6 speakers, amplifier, theft deterrent, and power retractable diversity antenna; seating capacity of 5, heated-cushion front bucket seats driver's and passenger's seats fixed headrests, center armrest with storage, driver's seat includes 6-way power seat, lumbar support, passenger's seat includes and 6-way direction control.

BASE WAGON (5M) (in addition to or instead of BASE SEDAN (5M) equipment): 2.8 axle ratio; front and rear body-colored bumpers with rear step; premium AM/FM stereo, clock, seek-

70-SERIES — VOLVO

scan, cassette, CD changer pre-wiring, in-dash CD pre-wiring, 6 speakers, amplifier, theft deterrent, and window grid antenna; fixed 1/4 vent windows; fixed interval rear wiper, rear center armrest and body-colored door handles.

GLT WAGON (4A) (in addition to or instead of BASE WAGON (4A) equipment): 2.4L I5 DOHC MPI intercooled turbo with variable valve timing 20-valve engine, requires premium unleaded fuel; 4-speed electronic OD auto transmission with lock-up; driver's selectable multi-mode transmission; 2.56 axle ratio; driver's seat includes 6-way power seat, lumbar support; memory on driver's seat with 3 memory setting(s).

XC AWD WAGON (4A) (in addition to or instead of GLT WAGON (4A) equipment): Full-time 4 wheel drive, viscous limited slip differential, traction control, 2.49 axle ratio; auto-leveling suspension, 17.4 gal. capacity fuel tank; rear mud flaps; roof rack; front and rear body-colored bumpers with black rub strip; black bodyside molding rocker panel extensions; additional exterior lights include front fog/driving lights; P205/65VR15 A/S BSW front and rear tires; instrumentation trip computer; heated-cushion front bucket seats; leather-wrapped steering wheel with tilt and telescopic adjustment; cargo net and black grille.

R AWD WAGON (4A) (in addition to or instead of XC AWD WAGON (4A) equipment): Sport ride suspension, front independent strut suspension with HD anti-roll bar, HD front shocks, rear independent multi-link suspension with HD anti-roll bar, rear coil springs, HD rear shocks; front power sliding and tilting glass sunroof with sunshade; body-colored bodyside molding, rocker panel extensions; front and rear 16" x 6.5" silver alloy wheels; P205/55VR16 A/S BSW front and rear tires; premium AM/FM stereo, clock, seek-scan, cassette 6-disc CD changer, 8 speakers, premium amplifier, theft deterrent, and window grid diversity antenna; garage door opener; passenger's seat includes 6-way power seat, lumbar support; leather seats, leatherette door trim insert, leather-wrapped gear shift knob; chrome grille and body-colored door handles.

LT COUPE (4A): 2.4L I5 DOHC MPI intercooled turbo with variable valve timing 20-valve engine, requires premium unleaded fuel; 4-speed electronic OD auto transmission with lock-up; 520-amp battery; 80-amp alternator; front-wheel drive, 2.8 axle ratio; stainless steel exhaust with chrome tip; sport ride suspension, front independent strut suspension with anti-roll bar, front coil springs, semi-independent multi-link rear suspension with anti-roll bar, rear coil springs; power rack-and-pinion steering; 4-wheel disc brakes with 4-wheel antilock braking system; 18.5 gal. capacity fuel tank; body-colored front mud flaps, side impact bars; front power sliding and tilting glass sunroof with sunshade; front and rear body-colored bumpers; body-colored bodyside molding; monotone paint; aero-composite halogen auto off headlamps with washer and wiper, daytime running lights; additional exterior lights include front fog/driving lights; driver's and passenger's power remote body-colored heated folding outside mirrors; front and rear 17" x 7" silver alloy wheels; P225/45ZR17 performance A/S BSW front and rear tires; inside under cargo mounted compact steel spare wheel; dual zone front air conditioning with climate control, air filter, rear heat ducts; premium AM/FM stereo, seek-scan, cassette, 3-disc CD changer, 10 speakers, premium amplifier, theft deterrent, and power retractable diversity antenna; cruise control; power door locks with 2 stage unlock, remote keyless entry, power remote hatch/trunk release, power remote fuel release; 2 power accessory outlets, driver's foot rest, garage door opener; instrumentation display includes tachometer, water temperature gauge, in-dash clock, exterior temp, trip computer, trip odometer; warning indicators include oil pressure, battery, low coolant, key in ignition, low fuel, low washer fluid, bulb failure, trunk ajar, service interval, brake fluid; driver's and passenger's front airbags, driver's and front passenger's seat mounted side airbags; panic alarm, security system; tinted windows, power windows with driver's 1-touch down; variable intermittent front windshield wipers, sun visor strip, rear window defroster; seating capacity of 4, front bucket seats, adjustable headrests, center armrest with storage, driver's seat includes 6-way power seat, lumbar support, easy entry, passenger's seat includes 6-way power seat, lumbar support, easy entry; rear bench seat with adjustable headrests, center pass-thru armrest; front height adjustable seatbelts with front pretensioners; leather seats, leatherette door trim insert, full cloth headliner, full carpet floor covering with carpeted

VOLVO
70-SERIES

CODE	DESCRIPTION	INVOICE	MSRP

floor mats, genuine wood trim on instrument panel, leather-wrapped gear shift knob; memory on driver's seat with 3 memory setting(s); interior lights include dome light with fade, front and rear reading lights, 2 door curb lights, illuminated entry; leather-wrapped steering wheel with tilt and telescopic adjustment; dual illuminated vanity mirrors; auto-dimming day/night rearview mirror; full floor console, locking glove box with light, front cupholder, 2 seat back storage pockets, driver's and passenger's door bins; carpeted cargo floor, carpeted trunk lid, cargo light; chrome grille, black side window moldings, black front windshield molding, black rear window molding and body-colored door handles.

HT COUPE (5M) (in addition to or instead of LT COUPE (5M) equipment): 2.3L I5 DOHC MPI intercooled turbo 20-valve engine, requires premium unleaded fuel; 5-speed OD manual transmission; 2.54 axle ratio; front and rear 16" x 7" silver alloy wheels; P225/50SR16 A/S BSW front and rear tires; premium AM/FM stereo, seek-scan, cassette, single CD, 10 speakers, amplifier, theft deterrent, and power retractable diversity antenna and plastic/rubber gear shift knob.

LT CONVERTIBLE (4A) (in addition to or instead of LT COUPE (4A) equipment): Comfort ride suspension; power convertible roof with lining, glass rear window, roll-over protection; P205/55SR16 A/S BSW front and rear tires and power front and rear windows with front and rear 1-touch down.

HT CONVERTIBLE (5M) (in addition to or instead of HT COUPE (5M) equipment): P205/55SR16 A/S BSW front and rear tires; premium AM/FM stereo, seek-scan, cassette, 3-disc CD changer, 14 premium speakers, premium amplifier, theft deterrent, and power retractable diversity antenna and leather-wrapped gear shift knob.

Base Prices

CODE	DESCRIPTION	INVOICE	MSRP
C70LTASR	LT Coupe (4A)	31040	34000
C70HTMSR	HT Coupe (5M)	35090	39000
C70LTACV	LT Convertible (4A)	39635	43500
C70HTMCV	HT Convertible (5M)	41655	45500
S70M	Base Sedan (5M)	25475	27500
S70GLTA	GLT Sedan (4A)	29517	31700
S70AWDA	Base AWD Sedan (5A)	31136	33600
S70T5M	T5 Sedan (5M)	30583	33300
V70M	Base Wagon (5M)	26788	28800
V70GLTA	GLT Wagon (4A)	30830	33000
V70XCAWDASR	XC AWD Wagon (4A)	33411	36100
V70RAWDASR	R AWD Wagon (4A)	37615	41500
Destination Charge:		575	575

Accessories

CODE	DESCRIPTION	INVOICE	MSRP
—	C70 SR Package (LT Coupe)	1520	1900
	Includes leather faced seats and power sunroof.		
—	Full Soft Leather Seating (HT)	1280	1600
—	Leather Upholstery (All Except R Wagon)	960	1200
—	Transmission: 5-Speed Automatic with OD (Base)	1000	1000
	Includes driver's selectable program and 2.76 axle ratio.		

426   www.edmunds.com   **EDMUND'S® NEW CARS**

70-SERIES — VOLVO

CODE	DESCRIPTION	INVOICE	MSRP
000011	Heated Front Seats	200	250
000049	Trip Computer (LT)	200	250
	Includes ambient temperature gauge.		
000156	Wheels: 17" 5-Spoke Alloy (LT)	320	400
	Includes 2 piece Volvo/BBS Hollow Spoke design and tires: P225/45ZR17. NOT AVAILABLE with 000411.		
000162	Wheels: 16" Alloy with All-Season (HT)	NC	NC
	Includes tires: P225/50/VR16 A/S. REQUIRES 4AT. NOT AVAILABLE with 000411.		
000164	Dolby Pro Logic (HT Coupe)	480	600
000164	Premium Audio Upgrade with Dolby Pro Logic (LT Convertible)	1200	1500
	Includes upgrade to SC-90X radio, 4 x 100-amp and rear seat sub-woofers.		
000164	Premium Audio Upgrade with Dolby Pro Logic (LT Coupe)	960	1200
	Includes upgrade to SC-90X radio and 4 x 100 amp.		
000168	Auto Dim Mirror (LT)	80	100
000178	STC Stability/Traction Control System	440	550
000251	Burled Walnut Wood Trim (Red) (LT)	480	600
000281	Soft Top: Sand (Convertible)	NC	NC
	NOT AVAILABLE with 000311.		
000311	Soft Top: Blue (Convertible)	NC	NC
	NOT AVAILABLE with 000281.		
000372	Homelink Remote Garage Door Opener (Coupe)	100	125
000411	Wheels: 17" Multi-Spoke Alloy	1200	1500
	Includes 2 piece Volvo/BBS design and tires: P225/45ZR17. NOT AVAILABLE with 000156, 000162.		
164	Dolby Pro-Logic Surround Sound System (Base)	480	600
303	Wheels: 16" T5 Alloy	NC	NC
	Includes 205/50/16 hi-performance tires (not all season but clearance for snow chains). NOT AVAILABLE with 436.		
322	Integrated Child Booster Cushions (V70)	240	300
436	Wheels: 16" R Dark Graphite Alloy (XC/R)	NC	NC
	Includes 205/55R16 high performance Michelin tires. NOT AVAILABLE with 303.		
4AT	Transmission: 4-Speed Automatic (HT)	1010	1000
	Includes selectable Winter mode.		
COLD	Cold Weather Package (FWD)	680	850
	Includes heated front seats, headlamp wiper/washer and stability traction control (STC).		
PAINT	Metallic Paint (R Wagon)	320	400
SPORT	Sport Package (All Except XC/R Wagon)	360	450
	Includes rear spoiler and front fog lights.		
SUNLTH	Sunroof and Leather Package (All Except R Wagon)	1760	2200
	Includes sunroof, leather upholstery and simulated wood dash and gearshift knob.		
SUNLTH	Sunroof and Leather Package (R Wagon)	NC	NC
	Includes aluminum dash and aluminum shift knob.		
SUNROF	Sunroof	960	1200

VOLVO

70-SERIES / S80

CODE	DESCRIPTION	INVOICE	MSRP
TOUR	Touring Package (Base)	1000	1250
	Includes driver's power seat, memory driver's seat, SC-816 in-dash CD radio, trip computer, Homelink and leather-wrapped steering wheel.		
TOUR	Touring Package (GLT Sedan)	1000	1200
	Includes power passenger's seat, SC-816 in-dash CD radio, trip computer, Homelink and leather-wrapped steering wheel.		
TOUR	Touring Package (GLT Wagon/S70 AWD)	960	1200
	Includes power passenger's seat, SC-816 in-dash CD radio, trip computer, Homelink and leather-wrapped steering wheel.		
TOUR	Touring Package (R Wagon)	NC	NC
	Includes SC-816 in-dash CD radio.		
TOUR	Touring Package (XC)	640	800
	Includes power passenger's seat, SC-816 in-dash CD radio and Homelink.		
XC	XC Outdoor Package (XC)	380	475
	Includes lower body painted grey, roof rail cross bars and rear bumper dirt protector.		

2000 S80

What's New?

The 2.9 and T-6 models go unchanged, save a few new colors and options.

Review

Last year's new S80 ushered the moldy S90/V90 design out to pasture. Volvo public-relations types bragged about the engineering "firsts" that the 1999 S80 showcased, but what really matters to consumers is the way the car looks, drives, coddles and protects.

The S80 certainly represents a departure for Volvo in terms of styling. See that strong character line running up both sides of the hood and forming the lower boundary of the greenhouse? It flows into the rear deck, creating sheetmetal shoulders above the wheels and an interesting ridge in the taillights. The result is a sleeker, more modern-looking vehicle.

For 2000, Volvo carries over the smooth 2.9-liter, 204-horsepower, inline six-cylinder engine in the base trim level. The high-performance version of the S80, called the T-6, has twin-turbochargers tacked onto a 2.8-liter inline six. Horsepower is rated at 268. Available with the world's smallest manual or an automatic transmission, the latter type adapts to the driving style of the driver and includes a winter mode to make acceleration on icy surfaces more surefooted. The S80 T6, when equipped with an automatic, also provides a Geartronic feature, allowing for manual shifting if the driver desires. The car drives like a dream, whether on an ice-covered road or a smooth stretch of highway. While satisfyingly speedy, the S80 is also a handful when the accelerator is mashed to the floor, thanks to prodigious amounts of torque steer that tries to pull the S80 into the curb.

Additions for the millennium include a warm weather package, new Venetian Red Metallic exterior paint color, and a new interior color called Light Sand Beige. The sunroof/leather packages for both trim levels now share a $1,200 price, the full soft leather on the T-6 has been discontinued, and the Blue/Green paint color is no longer available.

Comfort is a Volvo hallmark, and the S80 boasts one of the best interiors we've encountered. It offers excellent climate systems with heat and A/C vents in the B-pillar for rear passengers, cushy seats with thick headrests and an astounding Dolby Pro Logic sound system available with RDS technology. On the down side, we had difficulty sorting out some ergonomic features without the assistance of the owner's manual and the cruise-control activation button is located too close to the horn pad.

Three rear-seat head restraints can be folded down to improve visibility. They fold forward instead of rearward, however, which means that a rear-seat rider must employ them if he expects to be comfortable. Many things might occur in the roomy back seat of an S80, but whiplash isn't one of them. Front-seat occupants are also protected from whiplash, thanks to Volvo's Whiplash Protection System (WHIPS). If some cretin plows into the trunk of the S80 while the car is stopped in traffic, WHIPS allows the backrest and headrest to move backwards in a parallel movement with the passenger's body, thus cushioning the head and upper torso in a more delicate fashion.

Also on the S80 is an Inflatable Curtain (IC), part of the Side Impact Protection System (SIPS) common on Volvos. The IC is essentially an airbag for the head, and it pops out of the headliner to cushion the craniums of both front- and rear-seat riders. Other safety items on the S80 include seatbelt pre-tensioners for all five seating positions and front airbags that measure the force with which they deploy based upon crash severity and whether the seatbelt is in use or not.

There are many other S80 innovations that continue to please, including laminated side-window glass, a multiplex electrical system and a phenomenal full-range traction and stability-control system that all but makes it impossible for the car to careen out of control. Let's just say that the S80 is an incredible automobile that emphasizes safety, style and performance like nothing else on the road.

2000 Volvo S80

Standard Equipment

2.9 (4A): 2.9L I6 DOHC MPI with variable valve timing 24-valve engine, requires premium unleaded fuel; 4-speed electronic overdrive automatic transmission with lock-up; 600-amp battery; 100-amp alternator; driver selectable program transmission; front wheel drive, traction control, 2.8 axle ratio; steel exhaust; front independent strut suspension with anti-roll bar, front coil springs, rear independent multi-link suspension with anti-roll bar, rear coil springs; power rack-and-pinion steering with vehicle speed-sensing assist; 4-wheel disc brakes with 4-wheel antilock braking system; 21.1 gal. capacity fuel tank; front mud flaps, side impact bars; front and rear body-colored bumpers with black rub strip; black bodyside molding; monotone paint; aero-composite halogen headlamps with daytime running lights and delay-off feature; driver's and passenger's power remote body-colored heated folding outside mirrors; front and rear 16" x 7"

VOLVO S80

CODE	DESCRIPTION	INVOICE	MSRP

silver alloy wheels; P215/55SR16 BSW AS front and rear tires; inside under cargo mounted compact steel spare wheel; dual zone front air conditioning with climate control, air filter, rear heat ducts; premium AM/FM stereo with clock, seek-scan, cassette, single CD, 8 speakers, amplifier, theft deterrent, and window grid diversity antenna, radio steering wheel controls; cruise control with steering wheel controls; power door locks with 2 stage unlock, remote keyless entry, child safety rear door locks, power remote hatch/trunk release; 2 power accessory outlets, driver's foot rest; instrumentation display includes tachometer, water temp gauge, exterior temp, trip computer, trip odometer; warning indicators include oil pressure, battery, low coolant, lights on, key in ignition, low fuel, low washer fluid, bulb failure, trunk ajar, service interval, brake fluid; driver's and passenger's front airbags, driver's and front passenger's seat mounted side airbags, front and rear passenger's inflatable overhead curtain airbag; ignition disable, panic alarm, security system; tinted windows, power front windows with driver's and passenger's 1-touch down, power rear windows; fixed interval front windshield wipers, sun visor strip, rear window defroster; seating capacity of 5, front bucket seats with fixed headrests, center armrest with storage, driver's seat includes 6-way power seat with lumbar support, passenger's seat includes 6-way power seat with lumbar support; 60-40 folding rear bench seat with power adjustable headrests, center pass-thru armrest with storage; front height adjustable seatbelts with front and rear pretensioners; premium cloth seats, cloth door trim insert, full cloth headliner, full carpet floor covering with carpeted floor mats; memory on driver's seat with 3 memory setting(s); interior lights include dome light with fade, front and rear reading lights, 4 door curb lights, illuminated entry; leather-wrapped steering wheel with tilt and telescopic adjustment; dual illuminated vanity mirrors; day-night rearview mirror; full floor console, locking glove box with light, front and rear cupholders, 2 seat back storage pockets, driver's and passenger's door bins; carpeted cargo floor, carpeted trunk lid, cargo net, cargo light; chrome grille, black side window moldings, black front windshield molding, black rear window molding and body-colored door handles.

T-6 (4A) (in addition to or instead of 2.9 (4A) equipment): 2.8L I6 DOHC MPI intercooled turbo with variable valve timing 24-valve engine, requires premium unleaded fuel; driver selectable program transmission with manual control; aero-composite halogen headlamps with washer and wiper; additional exterior lights include front fog/driving lights; premium AM/FM stereo with clock, seek-scan, cassette, single CD, 8 performance speakers, premium amplifier, theft deterrent, and window grid diversity antenna; front bucket seats with heated-cushion, genuine wood trim on instrument panel and auto-dimming day-night rearview mirror.

Base Prices

			INVOICE	MSRP
S8029A	2.9 (4A)	....	33060	36000
S80T6A	T-6 (4A)	....	37105	40500
Destination Charge:		....	575	575

Accessories

			INVOICE	MSRP
—	HomeLink Security System	....	508	635
	Manufacturer Discount	....	(28)	(35)
	Net Price	....	480	600
	Includes interior movement sensor, level movement sensor and homelink remote -garage door opener.			
—	Leather Seating	....	960	1200
—	Metallic Paint (2.9)	....	320	400
—	Sunroof and Leather Package	....	1920	2400
	Manufacturer Discount	....	(960)	(1200)
	Net Price	....	960	1200
	Includes power glass sunroof and leather seating.			

430   www.edmunds.com   **EDMUND'S® NEW CARS**

S80 — VOLVO

CODE	DESCRIPTION	INVOICE	MSRP
—	Warm Weather Package	560	700
	Manufacturer Discount	(160)	(2000)
	Net Price	400	(1300)
	Includes infra-red reflective front windshield and rear door side sun curtain.		
000018	Cold Weather Package (2.9)	360	450
	Includes heated front seats and headlamp washer/wiper.		
000142	Volvo Navigation System	2140	2500
	Includes cost of 1 free CD map of the customer's choice and 1 free update.		
000163	Radio: 4 CD In-Dash with Surround Sound (2.9)	800	1000
	Includes Dolby surround 2-way speaker in center of dashboard plus 8 speakers (tweeters and woofers in front doors, coaxial in rear doors and in rear shelf), 4X50W amplifier and diversity function antenna.		
000163	Radio: 4 CD In-Dash with Surround Sound (T-6)	600	750
	Replaces cassette. Includes Dolby surround 2-way speaker in center of dashboard plus 8 speakers (tweeters and woofers in front doors, coaxial in rear doors and in rear shelf), 4X50W amplifier and diversity function antenna.		
000227	Dynamic Stability Traction Control	880	1100
	Automatically counteracts a skid by comparing the vehicle's direction of travel to steering wheel movements. Brakes are applied to each wheel as necessary to help the driver retain control.		
000297	Wheels: 17" Canapus Alloy (2.9)	320	400
	Includes tires: Michelin MXM4 225/50/17 A/S		
000336	Wheels: 17" Alloy (T-6)	320	400
	Includes tires: Michelin MXM4 225/50R17 A/S		

Major Savings On An Extended Warranty

"YOU DESERVE THE BEST"

Call today for your free quote.
Pay up to 50% less than dealership prices!

http://www.edmunds.com/warranty 1-800-580-9889

FREE *for Edmund's readers!*

Buying a New Car just got *more affordable!*

Call 1-800-201-7703 now and save hundreds, even thousands, off the sticker price!

❶ It's easy. Simply provide the make, model, and year of the New Car or Truck you want.

❷ We'll tell you the "Preferred Price" and the dealer nearest you who will honor it!

❸ The "Preferred Price" means you save hundreds, even thousands, off the sticker price without the *hassle of negotiating!*

Call AutoVantage now
1-800-201-7703
(Please refer to Free offer #99940140.)

"Great service saved us $4,000!"
Robert Wilson — Forked River, NJ

Please note: This is a Free consumer service. You are not obligated to visit the dealer or make a purchase.

AutoVantage is a service provided by CUC International Inc., which may modify and improve any part of the service at any time and without prior notice.

© 1997, CUC International Inc.

Specifications and EPA Mileage Ratings

1999 / 2000 New Cars

Contents

Acura	434	Mazda	449
Audi	434	Mercedes-Benz	450
BMW	435	Mercury	452
Buick	437	Mitsubishi	453
Cadillac	437	Nissan	454
Chevrolet	438	Oldsmobile	454
Chrysler	440	Plymouth	455
Daewoo	441	Pontiac	455
Dodge	442	Porsche	457
Ford	443	Saab	458
Honda	445	Saturn	459
Hyundai	446	Subaru	460
Infiniti	447	Suzuki	461
Jaguar	447	Toyota	462
Kia	448	Volkswagen	463
Lexus	448	Volvo	464
Lincoln	449		

specifications

SPECIFICATIONS MILEAGE TABLES

	EPA Hwy (mpg) - Auto	EPA City (mpg) - Auto	EPA Hwy (mpg) - Manual	EPA City (mpg) - Manual	Fuel Capacity	Torque @ RPM	Horsepower @ RPM	Displacement (liters)	Number of Cylinders	Luggage Capacity (cu ft.)	Rear Leg Room (in.)	Front Leg Room (in.)	Rear Hip Room (in.)	Front Hip Room (in.)	Rear Shoulder Room (in.)	Front Shoulder Room (in.)	Rear Head Room (in.)	Front Head Room (in.)	Wheelbase (in.)	Curb Weight (lbs.)	Height (in.)	Width (in.)	Length (in.)
ACURA																							
Integra Coupe - LS-GS	32	24	32	25	13.2	124@5200	140@6300	1.8	4	13.3	28.1	42.7	44.1	50.3	48.8	51.7	35	38.6	101.2	2639	52.6	67.3	172.4
Integra GS-R Coupe	NA	NA	31	25	13.2	128@6200	170@7600	1.8	4	13.3	28.1	42.7	44.1	50.3	48.8	51.7	35	38.6	101.2	2672	52.6	67.3	172.4
Integra GS-R Sedan	NA	NA	31	25	13.2	128@6200	170@7600	1.8	4	13.2	32.7	42.2	49.9	50.7	50.3	51.6	35.9	38.3	103.1	2756	53.9	67.3	178.1
Integra Sedan - LS/GS	32	24	32	25	13.2	124@6200	140@6300	1.8	4	12.3	32.7	42.2	49.9	50.7	50.3	51.6	35.9	38.3	103.1	2712	53.9	67.3	178.1
TL-Series 3.2TL	27	19	NA	NA	17.2	216@3200	225@5600	3.2	6	14.3	35	42.4	50.7	56	55.7	56.2	36.8	39.9	108.1	3493	55.7	70.3	192.9
RL-Series 3.5RL	24	18	NA	NA	18	224@2800	210@5200	3.5	6	14	35.4	42.1	56.5	55.7	56.9	56.9	36.8	38.8	114.6	3840	56.5	71.4	196.6
AUDI																							
A4 1.8T Avant	27	18	29	21	15.9	155@1750	150@5700	1.8	4	31	33.4	41.2	NA	NA	53.4	54.7	37.8	38.1	103	3351	56.7	68.2	176.7
A4 1.8T Sedan	31	21	32	23	16.4	155@1750	150@5700	1.8	4	13.7	33.4	41.3	NA	NA	53.4	54.7	36.8	38.1	103	2987	55.8	68.2	178

specifications

	A4 2.8 Avant	A4 2.8 Sedan	A6 Avant	A6 Sedan	S4 Sedan	TT Coupe		3-Series 323Ci	3-Series 323i	3-Series 328Ci
Length (in.)	176.7	178	192	192	178	159.1		176	176	176
Width (in.)	68.2	68.2	71.3	71.3	68.2	73.1		68.5	68.5	68.5
Height (in.)	56.7	55.8	58.2	57.2	55.8	53		55.7	55.7	55.7
Curb Weight (lbs.)	3494	3164	3858	3560	3585	2655		3153	3153	3197
Wheelbase (in.)	102.6	103	108.6	108.7	102.6	95.4		107.3	107.3	107.3
Front Head Room (in.)	38.1	38.1	39.3	39.3	38.1	37.8		38.4	38.4	38.4
Rear Head Room (in.)	37.8	36.8	38.7	37.9	36.8	32.6		37.5	37.5	37.5
Front Shoulder Room (in.)	54.7	54.7	56.2	56.2	54.7	55.6		54.4	54.4	54.4
Rear Shoulder Room (in.)	53.4	53.4	55.7	55.7	53.4	48.1		54.2	54.2	54.2
Front Hip Room (in.)	NA	NA	NA	NA	NA	NA		NA	NA	NA
Rear Hip Room (in.)	NA	NA	NA	NA	NA	NA		NA	NA	NA
Front Leg Room (in.)	41.2	41.3	41.3	41.3	41.3	41.2		41.4	41.4	41.4
Rear Leg Room (in.)	33.3	33.4	37.3	37.3	33.4	20.2		34.6	34.6	34.6
Luggage Capacity (cu ft.)	31	13.7	36.4	17.2	13.7	10.8		10.7	10.7	10.7
Number of Cylinders	4	4	6	6	6	4		6	6	6
Displacement (liters)	1.8	1.8	2.8	2.8	2.7	1.8		2.5	2.5	2.8
Horsepower @ RPM	150@5700	150@5700	200@6000	200@6000	250@5800	180@5500		170@5500	170@5500	193@5500
Torque @ RPM	155@1750	155@1750	207@3200	207@3200	258@1850	173@1950		181@3500	181@3500	206@3500
Fuel Capacity	15.6	16.4	18.5	18.5	16.4	14.5		16.6	16.6	16.6
EPA City (mpg) - Manual	19	20	NA	NA	20	22		20	20	20
EPA Hwy (mpg) - Manual	27	29	NA	NA	28	31		29	29	29
EPA City (mpg) - Auto	17	18	17	17	NA	NA		19	19	19
EPA Hwy (mpg) - Auto	27	29	26	28	NA	NA		28	28	27

SPECIFICATIONS MILEAGE TABLES

BMW

EDMUND'S® NEW CARS www.edmunds.com

specifications

SPECIFICATIONS MILEAGE TABLES

	EPA Hwy (mpg) - Auto	EPA City (mpg) - Auto	EPA Hwy (mpg) - Manual	EPA City (mpg) - Manual	Fuel Capacity	Torque @ RPM	Horsepower @ RPM	Displacement (liters)	Number of Cylinders	Luggage Capacity (cu ft.)	Rear Leg Room (in.)	Front Leg Room (in.)	Rear Hip Room (in.)	Front Hip Room (in.)	Rear Shoulder Room (in.)	Front Shoulder Room (in.)	Rear Head Room (in.)	Front Head Room (in.)	Wheelbase (in.)	Curb Weight (lbs.)	Height (in.)	Width (in.)	Length (in.)
3-Series 328i	27	19	29	20	16.6	206@3500	193@5500	2.8	6	10.7	34.6	41.7	NA	54.1	54.2	54.4	37.5	38.4	107.3	3197	55.7	68.5	176
5-Series 528i Sedan	26	18	29	20	18.5	206@3500	193@5500	2.8	6	11.1	34.2	41.7	NA	54.1	55.9	56.8	37.8	38.7	111.4	3495	56.1	70.9	188
5-Series 528iT Wagon	26	18	26	18	18.5	206@3500	193@5500	2.8	6	32.7	34.2	41.7	NA	54.1	55.9	56.8	38.5	38.7	111.4	3726	56.1	70.9	189.2
5-Series 540i Sedan	24	18	23	15	18.5	324@3600	282@5400	4.4	8	11.1	34.2	41.7	NA	54.1	55.9	56.8	37.2	37.4	111.4	3748	56.5	70.9	188
5-Series 540iT Wagon	21	15	NA	NA	18.5	324@3600	282@5400	4.4	8	32.1	34.2	41.7	NA	54.1	55.9	56.8	37.4	37.4	111.4	4056	56.7	70.9	189.2
M Coupe	NA	NA	26	19	13.5	236@3800	240@6000	3.2	6	9	34.2	41.7	NA	54.1		51.7		36.7	96.3	3131	50.4	68.5	158.5
M Roadster	NA	NA	26	19	13.5	236@3800	240@6000	3.2	6	5	NA	41.8	NA	54.1	NA	51.7	NA	37.6	96.3	3086	49.8	68.5	158.5
Z3 2.8 Coupe	26	18	26	19	13.5	206@3500	193@5500	2.8	6	9	34.2	41.8	NA	54.1	NA	51.7	NA	36.7	96.3	2943	51.4	68.5	158.5
Z3 2.3 Roadster	26	19	27	20	13.5	181@3500	170@5500	2.5	6	5	NA	41.8	NA	54.1	NA	51.7	NA	37.6	96.3	2899	50.9	68.5	159.4
Z3 2.8 Roadster	26	19	26	19	13.5	206@3500	193@5500	2.8	6	5	NA	41.8	NA	54.1	NA	51.7	NA	37.6	96.3	2910	50.9	68.5	159.4

specifications

	Buick Century Custom/Limited	Buick LeSabre Custom/Limited	Buick Park Avenue Base	Buick Park Avenue Ultra	Buick Regal GS	Buick Regal LS	Cadillac Catera	Cadillac DeVille Base/DHS
Length (in.)	194.6	200.8	206.8	206.8	196.2	196.2	194	207.2
Width (in.)	72.7	74.4	74.7	74.7	72.7	72.7	70.3	74.5
Height (in.)	56.6	55.6	57.4	57.4	56.6	56.6	56.4	56.7
Curb Weight (lbs.)	3368	3443	3778	3884	3543	3438	3770	3978
Wheelbase (in.)	109	110.8	113.8	113.8	109	109	107.5	115.3
Front Head Room (in.)	39.4	38.8	39.8	39.8	39.4	39.4	38.7	39.1
Rear Head Room (in.)	37.4	37.8	38	38	37.4	37.4	38.4	38.4
Front Shoulder Room (in.)	58	59.1	59.2	59.2	58	58	54.6	60.4
Rear Shoulder Room (in.)	57.1	58.9	58.7	58.7	57.1	57.1	55.9	60.1
Front Hip Room (in.)	54.4	54.6	56.4	56.4	54.4	54.4	54.9	56.4
Rear Hip Room (in.)	53.3	54.4	55.7	55.7	53.3	53.3	55.2	56.7
Front Leg Room (in.)	42.4	42.6	42.4	42.4	42.4	42.4	42.2	42.4
Rear Leg Room (in.)	36.9	40.4	41.4	41.4	36.9	36.9	37.5	43.2
Luggage Capacity (cu ft.)	16.7	17	19.1	19.1	16.7	16.7	14.5	19.1
Number of Cylinders	6	6	6	6	6	6	6	8
Displacement (liters)	3.1	3.8	3.8	3.8	3.8	3.8	3	4.6
Horsepower @ RPM	175@5200	205@5200	205@5200	240@5200	240@5200	200@5200	200@6000	275@5600
Torque @ RPM	195@4000	230@4000	230@4000	280@3600	280@3600	225@4000	192@3600	300@4000
Fuel Capacity	17.5	18	18.5	18.5	17.5	17.5	18	18.5
EPA City (mpg) - Manual	NA	NA	NA	NA	NA	NA	NA	NA
EPA Hwy (mpg) - Manual	NA	NA	NA	NA	NA	NA	NA	NA
EPA City (mpg) - Auto	20	19	19	18	18	19	18	17
EPA Hwy (mpg) - Auto	30	30	28	27	27	30	24	26

specifications

SPECIFICATIONS MILEAGE TABLES

	EPA Hwy (mpg) - Auto	EPA City (mpg) - Auto	EPA Hwy (mpg) - Manual	EPA City (mpg) - Manual	Fuel Capacity	Torque @ RPM	Horsepower @ RPM	Displacement (liters)	Number of Cylinders	Luggage Capacity (cu ft.)	Rear Leg Room (in.)	Front Leg Room (in.)	Rear Hip Room (in.)	Front Hip Room (in.)	Rear Shoulder Room (in.)	Front Shoulder Room (in.)	Rear Head Room (in.)	Front Head Room (in.)	Wheelbase (in.)	Curb Weight (lbs.)	Height (in.)	Width (in.)	Length (in.)
DeVille DTS	26	17	NA	NA	18.5	295@4400	300@6000	4.6	8	19.1	43.2	42.4	56.7	56.4	60.1	60.4	38.4	39.1	115.3	4047	56.7	74.5	207.2
Eldorado ESC	26	17	NA	NA	19	300@4000	300@4000	4.6	8	15.3	35.5	42.6	55.7	57.6	57.6	58.2	38.3	37.8	108	3843	53.6	75.5	200.6
Eldorado ETC	26	17	NA	NA	19	295@4000	300@6000	4.6	8	15.3	35.5	42.6	55.7	57.6	57.6	58.2	38.3	37.8	108	3876	53.6	75.5	200.6
Seville SLS	26	17	NA	NA	18.5	275@4000	275@5600	4.6	8	15.7	38.2	42.5	57.5	55.6	58	59.1	38	38.2	112.2	3970	55.7	75	201
Seville STS	26	17	NA	NA	18.5	295@4400	300@6000	4.6	8	15	38.2	42.5	57.5	55.6	58	59.1	38	38.2	112.2	4001	55.4	75	201

CHEVROLET

	EPA Hwy (mpg) - Auto	EPA City (mpg) - Auto	EPA Hwy (mpg) - Manual	EPA City (mpg) - Manual	Fuel Capacity	Torque @ RPM	Horsepower @ RPM	Displacement (liters)	Number of Cylinders	Luggage Capacity (cu ft.)	Rear Leg Room (in.)	Front Leg Room (in.)	Rear Hip Room (in.)	Front Hip Room (in.)	Rear Shoulder Room (in.)	Front Shoulder Room (in.)	Rear Head Room (in.)	Front Head Room (in.)	Wheelbase (in.)	Curb Weight (lbs.)	Height (in.)	Width (in.)	Length (in.)
Camaro Base Coupe	29	19	30	19	16.8	225@4000	200@5200	3.8	6	7.6	26.8	43	43.7	52.8	43.5	57.4	39	38	101.1	3306	51.3	74.1	193.2
Camaro Base Convertible	29	19	30	19	16.8	225@4000	200@5200	3.8	6	12.9	26.8	43	44.4	52.8	55.8	57.4	35.3	37.2	101.1	3500	52	74.1	193.2
Camaro Z28 Coupe	24	17	28	19	16.8	335@4000	305@5200	5.7	8	7.6	26.8	43	43.7	52.8	43.5	57.4	39	38	101.1	3306	51.3	74.1	193.2
Camaro Z28 Convertible	24	17	28	19	16.8	335@4000	305@5200	5.7	8	12.9	26.8	43	44.4	52.8	55.8	57.4	35.3	37.2	101.1	3500	52	74.1	193.2

specifications

	Cavalier Base Coupe	Cavalier Base Sedan	Cavalier LS Sedan	Cavalier Z24 Convertible	Cavalier Z24 Coupe	Corvette Convertible	Corvette Coupe	Corvette Hardtop	Impala Base	Impala LS
Length (in.)	180.7	180.7	180.7	180.7	180.7	179.7	179.7	179.7	200	200
Width (in.)	68.7	67.9	67.9	68.7	68.7	73.6	73.6	73.6	73	73
Height (in.)	53	54.7	54.7	54.1	53	47.7	47.8	47.9	57.5	57.5
Curb Weight (lbs.)	2617	2676	2676	2838	2617	3216	3307	3307	3389	3389
Wheelbase (in.)	104.1	104.1	104.1	104.1	104.1	104.5	104.5	104.5	110.5	110.5
Front Head Room (in.)	37.6	38.9	38.9	38.1	37.6	37.9	37.9	37.9	39.2	39.2
Rear Head Room (in.)	36.6	37.2	37.2	37.6	36.6	NA	NA	NA	36.8	36.8
Front Shoulder Room (in.)	53.9	54.6	54.6	53.9	53.9	55.3	55.3	55.3	59	59
Rear Shoulder Room (in.)	54.9	53.9	53.9	47.1	54.9	NA	NA	NA	58.9	58.9
Front Hip Room (in.)	50	50.8	50.8	50	50	54.2	54.2	54.2	56.5	56.5
Rear Hip Room (in.)	49.5	50.6	50.6	47.8	49.5	NA	NA	NA	55.7	55.7
Front Leg Room (in.)	41.9	41.9	41.9	42.1	41.9	42.7	42.7	42.7	42.2	42.2
Rear Leg Room (in.)	32.7	34.4	34.4	32.6	32.7	NA	NA	NA	38.4	38.4
Luggage Capacity (cu ft.)	13.2	13.6	13.6	10.5	13.2	11.2	24.8	13.3	17.6	17.6
Number of Cylinders	4	4	4	4	4	8	8	8	6	6
Displacement (liters)	2.2	2.2	2.2	2.4	2.4	5.7	5.7	5.7	3.4	3.8
Horsepower @ RPM	115@5000	115@5000	115@5000	150@5600	150@5600	345@5600	345@5600	345@5600	180@5200	200@5200
Torque @ RPM	135@3600	135@3600	135@3600	155@4400	155@4400	350@4400	350@4400	350@4400	205@4000	225@4000
Fuel Capacity	14.3	14.3	14.3	15	14.3	19.1	19.1	19.1	17	17
EPA City (mpg) - Manual	24	24	NA	23	23	18	18	18	NA	NA
EPA Hwy (mpg) - Manual	34	34	NA	33	33	28	28	28	NA	NA
EPA City (mpg) - Auto	23	23	22	22	22	17	17	NA	NA	NA
EPA Hwy (mpg) - Auto	29	29	30	30	30	25	25	NA	NA	NA

SPECIFICATIONS MILEAGE TABLES

specifications

SPECIFICATIONS MILEAGE TABLES

	EPA Hwy (mpg) - Auto	EPA City (mpg) - Auto	EPA Hwy (mpg) - Manual	EPA City (mpg) - Manual	Fuel Capacity	Torque @ RPM	Horsepower @ RPM	Displacement (liters)	Number of Cylinders	Luggage Capacity (cu. ft.)	Rear Leg Room (in.)	Front Leg Room (in.)	Rear Hip Room (in.)	Front Hip Room (in.)	Rear Shoulder Room (in.)	Front Shoulder Room (in.)	Rear Head Room (in.)	Front Head Room (in.)	Wheelbase (in.)	Curb Weight (lbs.)	Height (in.)	Width (in.)	Length (in.)
Lumina	29	20	NA	NA	16.6	185@4000	160@5200	3.1	6	15.5	36.6	42.4	55.3	55.4	58.4	58.4	37.4	38.4	107.5	3330	54.8	72.5	200.9
Malibu Base/LS	29	20	NA	NA	15	190@4000	170@5200	3.1	6	17.1	38	42.2	52	52	55.3	55.5	37.6	39.4	107	3051	56.7	69.4	190.4
Metro Base Coupe	NA	NA	47	41	10.3	58@3300	55@5700	1	3	8.4	32.8	42.2	43.9	47.2	48.9	48.9	36	39.1	93.1	1895	62.6	62.6	149.4
Metro LSi Coupe	34	30	43	39	10.3	75@3000	79@6000	1.3	4	8.4	32.8	42.5	43.9	47.2	48.9	48.9	36	39.1	93.1	1895	62.6	62.6	149.4
Metro LSi Sedan	34	30	43	39	10.3	75@3000	79@6000	1.3	4	10.3	32.2	42.5	42.9	46.9	48.3	49	37.3	39.3	93.1	1984	55.4	62.6	164
Monte Carlo LS	32	20	NA	NA	17	205@4000	180@5200	3.4	6	15.8	35.8	42.4	55.5	55.2	57.8	58.3	36.5	38.1	110.5	3340	55.2	72.7	197.9
Monte Carlo SS	29	20	NA	NA	17	225@4000	200@5200	3.8	6	15.8	35.8	42.4	55.2	55.2	57.8	58.3	36.5	38.1	110.5	3391	55.2	72.7	197.9
Prizm Base/LSi	36	28	37	31	13.2	122@4400	120@5600	1.8	4	12.7	33.2	42.5	51.2	50.5	52.2	52.8	36.9	39.3	97.1	2398	53.7	66.7	174.3

CHRYSLER

	EPA Hwy (mpg) - Auto	EPA City (mpg) - Auto	EPA Hwy (mpg) - Manual	EPA City (mpg) - Manual	Fuel Capacity	Torque @ RPM	Horsepower @ RPM	Displacement (liters)	Number of Cylinders	Luggage Capacity (cu. ft.)	Rear Leg Room (in.)	Front Leg Room (in.)	Rear Hip Room (in.)	Front Hip Room (in.)	Rear Shoulder Room (in.)	Front Shoulder Room (in.)	Rear Head Room (in.)	Front Head Room (in.)	Wheelbase (in.)	Curb Weight (lbs.)	Height (in.)	Width (in.)	Length (in.)
300M	27	18	NA	NA	17	255@3950	253@6400	3.5	6	16.8	39.1	42.2	59.1	57.4	58.7	58.8	37.7	38.3	113	3567	56	74.4	197.8

specifications

	Cirrus LX	Cirrus LXi	Concorde LX	Concorde LXi	LHS	LHS	Sebring Convertible JX/JXi	Sebring Coupe LX/LXi	Lanos Hatchback	Lanos Sedan
Length (in.)	186	186	209.1	209.1	207.7		193	190.9	160.4	166.8
Width (in.)	71	71	74.4	74.4	74.4		69.2	69.7	66.1	66.1
Height (in.)	54.1	54.1	55.8	55.8	56		54.8	53	56.4	56.4
Curb Weight (lbs.)	2911	3168	3452	3532	3589		3332	2967	2447	2522
Wheelbase (in.)	108	108	113	113	113		106	103.7	99.2	99.2
Front Head Room (in.)	38.4	38.4	38.3	38.3	38.3		38.7	39.1	38.9	38.9
Rear Head Room (in.)	36.8	36.8	37.2	37.2	37.2		37	36.5	37.8	37.8
Front Shoulder Room (in.)	55.2	55.2	59.1	59.1	58.8		55	53.1	53.5	53.5
Rear Shoulder Room (in.)	54.7	54.7	58.4	58.4	58.4		49.1	55.1	53.5	53.5
Front Hip Room (in.)	52.8	52.8	56.4	56.4	57.4		52.4	55.1	53.7	53.7
Rear Hip Room (in.)	52.7	52.7	56.8	56.8	59.3		44.7	49.6	53.8	53.8
Front Leg Room (in.)	42.3	42.3	42.2	42.2	42.2		42.4	43.3	42.8	42.8
Rear Leg Room (in.)	38.1	38.1	41.6	41.6	41.6		35.2	35	34.6	34.6
Luggage Capacity (cu ft.)	15.7	15.7	18.7	18.7	18.7		11.3	13.1	8.8	8.8
Number of Cylinders	4	6	6	6	6		6	6	4	4
Displacement (liters)	2	2.5	2.7	3.2	3.5		2.5	2.5	1.6	1.6
Horsepower @ RPM	132@5600	168@5800	200@5800	225@6300	253@6400		168@5800	163@5500	105@5800	105@5800
Torque @ RPM	130@4600	170@4350	190@4850	225@3800	255@3950		170@4350	170@4350	106@3400	106@3400
Fuel Capacity	16	16	17	17	17		16	15.9	12.7	12.7
EPA City (mpg) - Manual	26	NA	NA	NA	NA		NA	NA	26	26
EPA Hwy (mpg) - Manual	37	NA	NA	NA	NA		NA	NA	36	36
EPA City (mpg) - Auto	22	19	21	19	18		19	19	23	23
EPA Hwy (mpg) - Auto	31	27	30	29	27		27	27	34	34

SPECIFICATIONS MILEAGE TABLES

DAEWOO

specifications

SPECIFICATIONS MILEAGE TABLES

	EPA Hwy (mpg) - Auto	EPA City (mpg) - Auto	EPA Hwy (mpg) - Manual	EPA City (mpg) - Manual	Fuel Capacity	Torque @ RPM	Horsepower @ RPM	Displacement (liters)	Number of Cylinders	Luggage Capacity (cu ft.)	Rear Leg Room (in.)	Front Leg Room (in.)	Rear Hip Room (in.)	Front Hip Room (in.)	Rear Shoulder Room (in.)	Front Shoulder Room (in.)	Rear Head Room (in.)	Front Head Room (in.)	Wheelbase (in.)	Curb Weight (lbs.)	Height (in.)	Width (in.)	Length (in.)
Leganza SE	28	20	29	20	17.2	148@2800	131@5200	2.2	4	14.1	38.2	42.3	55.5	53.7	55.9	55.9	37.8	39.3	105.1	3102	56.6	70	183.9
Leganza SX/CDX	28	20	NA	NA	17.2	148@2800	131@5200	2.2	4	14.1	38.2	42.3	55.5	53.7	55.9	55.9	37.8	39.3	105.1	3157	56.6	70	183.9
Nubira Hatchback	30	22	31	22	13.7	136@4400	129@5400	2	4	11.3	34.7	41.9	52.3	51.9	53.6	53.9	38	38.3	101.2	2546	56.1	66.9	167.2
Nubira Sedan	30	22	31	22	13.7	136@4400	129@5400	2	4	13.1	34.7	41.9	52.3	51.9	53.6	53.9	38	38.3	101.2	2566	56.1	66.9	175.4
Nubira Wagon	30	22	31	22	13.7	136@4400	129@5400	2	4	19.4	34.7	41.9	52.3	51.9	53.6	53.9	38	38.3	101.2	2694	56.4	66.9	177.4

DODGE

	EPA Hwy (mpg) - Auto	EPA City (mpg) - Auto	EPA Hwy (mpg) - Manual	EPA City (mpg) - Manual	Fuel Capacity	Torque @ RPM	Horsepower @ RPM	Displacement (liters)	Number of Cylinders	Luggage Capacity (cu ft.)	Rear Leg Room (in.)	Front Leg Room (in.)	Rear Hip Room (in.)	Front Hip Room (in.)	Rear Shoulder Room (in.)	Front Shoulder Room (in.)	Rear Head Room (in.)	Front Head Room (in.)	Wheelbase (in.)	Curb Weight (lbs.)	Height (in.)	Width (in.)	Length (in.)
Avenger Base/ES	27	19	NA	NA	15.9	170@4350	163@5500	2.5	6	13.1	35	43.3	49.6	55.1	55.1	53.1	36.5	39.2	103.7	2879	53	69.1	190.2
Intrepid Base	30	21	NA	NA	17	190@4850	200@5800	2.7	6	18.4	39.1	42.2	56.6	56.2	58.1	59	37.5	38.5	113	3423	55.9	74.7	203.7
Intrepid ES	30	21	NA	NA	17	195@4200	202@5800	2.7	6	18.4	39.1	42.2	56.6	56.2	58.1	59	37.5	38.5	113	3518	55.9	74.7	203.7
Neon Highline	32	23	40	27	12.5	130@4600	132@5600	2	4	13.1	34.8	42.4	52.9	52.4	52.8	53.4	36.8	39.1	105	2567	56	74.4	174.4

specifications

	Stratus ES	Stratus SE	FORD	Contour SE Sport	SVT Contour Base	Crown Victoria Base/LX	Focus LX/SE Sedan	Focus SE Wagon	Focus ZTS Sedan	Focus ZX3 Hatchback
Length (in.)	186	186		184.6	183.9	212	174.8	178	174.8	168.1
Width (in.)	71	71		69.1	69.1	78.2	66.9	66.9	66.9	66.9
Height (in.)	54.1	54.1		54.4	54.5	56.8	56.3	57	56.3	56.3
Curb Weight (lbs.)	2968	2911		2769	3110	3908	2468	2531	2468	NA
Wheelbase (in.)	108	108		106.5	106.5	114.7	103	103	103	103
Front Head Room (in.)	38.1	38.1		39	39	39.4	39.3	39.3	39.3	39.2
Rear Head Room (in.)	36.8	36.8		36.7	36.7	38	38.5	39.9	38.5	38.7
Front Shoulder Room (in.)	55.2	55.2		53.9	53.9	60.8	53.7	53.7	53.7	53.7
Rear Shoulder Room (in.)	54.7	54.7		53.3	53.3	60.3	53.5	53.6	53.5	53.5
Front Hip Room (in.)	52.8	52.8		50.7	50.7	57.1	49.4	49.4	49.4	NA
Rear Hip Room (in.)	52.7	52.7		45.3	45.5	59	49.5	49.5	49.5	NA
Front Leg Room (in.)	42.3	42.3		42.4	42.4	42.5	43.1	43.1	43.1	43.1
Rear Leg Room (in.)	38.1	38.1		34.4	34.3	39.6	37.6	37.6	37.6	NA
Luggage Capacity (cu ft.)	15.7	15.7		13.9	13.9	20.6	12.9	37.5	12.9	18.5
Number of Cylinders	6	4		6	6	8	4	4	4	4
Displacement (liters)	2.5	2		2.5	2.5	4.6	2	2	2	2
Horsepower @ RPM	168@5800	132@5600		170@6250	200@6600	200@4250	107@5000	107@5000	130@5500	130@5500
Torque @ RPM	170@4350	130@4600		165@4250	169@5500	275@3000	122@3750	122@3750	130@4250	130@4250
Fuel Capacity	16	16		15	14.5	19	13.2	13.2	13.2	13.2
EPA City (mpg) - Manual	NA	26		20	20	NA	NA	NA	NA	NA
EPA Hwy (mpg) - Manual	NA	37		28	29	NA	NA	NA	NA	NA
EPA City (mpg) - Auto	19	21		20	NA	17	NA	NA	NA	NA
EPA Hwy (mpg) - Auto	27	30		29	NA	24	NA	NA	NA	NA

specifications

SPECIFICATIONS MILEAGE TABLES

	EPA Hwy (mpg) - Auto	EPA City (mpg) - Auto	EPA Hwy (mpg) - Manual	EPA City (mpg) - Manual	Fuel Capacity	Torque @ RPM	Horsepower @ RPM	Displacement (liters)	Number of Cylinders	Luggage Capacity (cu ft.)	Rear Leg Room (in.)	Front Leg Room (in.)	Rear Hip Room (in.)	Front Hip Room (in.)	Rear Shoulder Room (in.)	Front Shoulder Room (in.)	Rear Head Room (in.)	Front Head Room (in.)	Wheelbase (in.)	Curb Weight (lbs.)	Height (in.)	Width (in.)	Length (in.)
Mustang Base Convertible	27	20	29	20	15.7	220@2750	190@5250	3.8	6	7.7	29.9	42.6	41	52.3	41.4	53.6	35.5	38.1	101.3	3203	53.2	73.1	183.2
Mustang Base Coupe	27	20	29	20	15.7	220@2750	190@5250	3.8	6	10.9	29.9	42.6	47.4	52.3	52.1	53.6	35.5	38.1	101.3	3064	53.1	73.1	183.2
Mustang GT Convertible	23	17	24	17	15.7	302@4000	260@5250	4.6	8	7.7	29.9	42.6	41	52.3	41.4	53.6	35.5	38.1	101.3	3375	53.2	73.1	183.2
Mustang GT Coupe	23	17	24	17	15.7	302@4000	260@5250	4.6	8	10.9	29.9	49.1	47.4	52.3	52.1	53.6	35.5	38.1	101.3	3560	53.1	73.1	183.2
SVT Mustang Cobra Convertible	NA	NA	26	17	15.7	317@4750	320@6000	4.6	8	7.7	29.9	49.1	41	52.3	41.4	53.6	35.8	38.1	101.3	3237	53.5	73.1	183.5
SVT Mustang Cobra Coupe	NA	NA	26	17	15.7	317@4750	320@6000	4.6	8	10.9	29.9	42.6	47.4	52.3	52.1	53.6	35.5	38.1	101.3	3430	53.2	73.1	183.2
Taurus LX/SE-2V Sedan	NA	NA	NA	NA	16	185@3950	155@4900	3	6	17	38.9	42.2	56.3	55.8	56.6	57.4	36.2	39.2	108.5	3331	56.1	73	197.6
Taurus SE Wagon	NA	NA	NA	NA	16	185@3950	155@4900	3	6	38.4	38.5	42.2	56.2	55.8	56.6	57.4	38.9	39.3	108.5	3540	58	73	199.7
Taurus SE-Comfort/SE-SVG Sdn	NA	NA	NA	NA	16	200@4400	200@5650	3	6	17	38.9	42.2	56.3	55.8	56.6	57.4	36.2	39.2	108.5	3333	56.1	73	197.6

specifications

HONDA

	Accord DX Sedan	Accord LX/EX Coupe	Accord LX/EX V6 Sedan	Accord LX/EX V6 Coupe	Accord LX/SE/EX Sedan	Civic CV/DX Hatchback	Civic DX/LX Coupe	Civic DX/LX Sedan	Civic EX Coupe
Length (in.)	188.8	186.8	188.8	186.8	188.8	164.2	175.1	175.1	175.1
Width (in.)	70.3	70.3	70.3	70.3	70.3	67.1	67.1	67.1	67.1
Height (in.)	56.9	55	57.3	55.3	56.9	54.1	54.1	54.7	54.1
Curb Weight (lbs.)	2932	2981	3318	3259	3064	2359	2359	2339	2513
Wheelbase (in.)	106.9	105.1	106.9	105.1	106.9	103.2	103.2	103.2	103.2
Front Head Room (in.)	40	38	38.5	38	38.5	38.8	38.8	39.8	37.4
Rear Head Room (in.)	37.6	36.5	36.5	36.5	36.5	37.2	36.2	37.6	35.4
Front Shoulder Room (in.)	56.9	56	56.9	56	56.9	52.4	52.4	52.4	52.4
Rear Shoulder Room (in.)	56.1	55.4	56.1	55.4	56.1	51.4	51.4	51.8	51.4
Front Hip Room (in.)	54.9	52.1	54.9	52.1	54.9	49.8	49.8	50	49.8
Rear Hip Room (in.)	54.1	46.1	54.1	46.1	54.1	45.6	45.6	49.3	45.6
Front Leg Room (in.)	42.1	42.6	42.1	42.6	42.1	42.7	42.7	42.7	42.7
Rear Leg Room (in.)	37.9	32.4	37.9	32.4	37.9	32.5	32.5	34.1	32.5
Luggage Capacity (cu ft.)	14.1	13.6	14.1	13.6	14.1	13.4	11.9	11.9	11.9
Number of Cylinders	4	4	6	6	4	4	4	4	4
Displacement (liters)	2.3	2.3	3	3	2.3	1.6	1.6	1.6	1.6
Horsepower @ RPM	135@5400	150@5700	200@5500	200@5500	150@5700	106@6200	106@6200	106@6200	127@6600
Torque @ RPM	145@4700	152@4900	195@4700	195@4700	152@4900	103@4600	103@4600	103@4600	107@5500
Fuel Capacity	17.1	17.1	17.1	17.1	17.1	11.9	11.9	11.9	11.9
EPA City (mpg) - Manual	25	25	NA	NA	25	32	32	32	29
EPA Hwy (mpg) - Manual	31	31	NA	NA	31	37	37	37	35
EPA City (mpg) - Auto	23	22	20	20	22	28	28	28	28
EPA Hwy (mpg) - Auto	30	29	28	28	29	35	35	35	35

SPECIFICATIONS MILEAGE TABLES

EDMUND'S® NEW CARS

specifications

SPECIFICATIONS MILEAGE TABLES

	EPA Hwy (mpg) - Auto	EPA City (mpg) - Auto	EPA Hwy (mpg) - Manual	EPA City (mpg) - Manual	Fuel Capacity	Torque @ RPM	Horsepower @ RPM	Displacement (liters)	Number of Cylinders	Luggage Capacity (cu ft.)	Rear Leg Room (in.)	Front Leg Room (in.)	Rear Hip Room (in.)	Front Hip Room (in.)	Rear Shoulder Room (in.)	Front Shoulder Room (in.)	Rear Head Room (in.)	Front Head Room (in.)	Wheelbase (in.)	Curb Weight (lbs.)	Height (in.)	Width (in.)	Length (in.)
Civic EX Sedan	35	28	35	29	11.9	107@5500	127@6600	1.6	4	11.9	34.1	42.7	49.3	50	51.8	52.4	36.2	38.2	103.2	2513	54.7	67.1	175.1
Civic HX Coupe	38	34	43	35	11.9	104@5400	115@6300	1.6	4	11.9	32.5	42.7	45.6	49.8	51.4	52.4	36.2	38.8	103.2	2370	54.1	67.1	175.1
Civic Si Coupe	NA	NA	31	26	11.9	111@7000	160@7600	1.6	4	11.9	32.5	42.7	45.6	49.8	51.4	52.4	35.4	37.4	103.2	2612	54.1	67.1	175.1
Prelude Base/SH	26	21	27	22	15.9	156@5250	200@7000	2.2	4	8.7	28.1	43	41	52.1	50	53.8	35.3	37.9	101.8	2954	51.8	69	178
S2000	NA	NA	NA	NA	13.2	153@7500	240@8300	2	4	5	NA	44.3	NA	49.8	NA	50.2	NA	34.6	94.5	2809	50.6	68.9	162.2

HYUNDAI

	EPA Hwy (mpg) - Auto	EPA City (mpg) - Auto	EPA Hwy (mpg) - Manual	EPA City (mpg) - Manual	Fuel Capacity	Torque @ RPM	Horsepower @ RPM	Displacement (liters)	Number of Cylinders	Luggage Capacity (cu ft.)	Rear Leg Room (in.)	Front Leg Room (in.)	Rear Hip Room (in.)	Front Hip Room (in.)	Rear Shoulder Room (in.)	Front Shoulder Room (in.)	Rear Head Room (in.)	Front Head Room (in.)	Wheelbase (in.)	Curb Weight (lbs.)	Height (in.)	Width (in.)	Length (in.)
Accent Hatchback	36	26	37	28	11.9	97@4000	92@5500	1.5	4	16.1	32.7	42.6	51.8	53.5	52.4	52.8	37.8	38.7	94.5	2132	54.9	63.8	161.5
Accent Sedan	36	26	37	28	11.9	97@4000	92@5500	1.5	4	10.7	32.7	42.6	53.6	53.5	52.2	52.8	38	38.7	94.5	2119	54.9	63.8	162.1
Elantra GLS Sedan	31	22	33	24	14.5	133@4800	140@6000	2	4	11.4	34.6	43.2	54.5	52.4	53.5	54.7	37.6	38.6	100.4	2560	54.9	66.9	174
Elantra GLS Wagon	31	22	33	24	14.5	133@4800	140@6000	2	4	32.3	34.8	43.2	54.5	52.4	53.5	54.7	38.9	38.6	100.4	2648	58.8	66.9	175.2

specifications

	Sonata Base	Sonata GLS V6	Tiburon Base	G20 Luxury/Touring	I30 Luxury/Touring	Q45 Base/Touring	S-Type V6	S-Type V8
Length (in.)	185.4	185.4	170.9	177.5	193.7	199.6	191.3	191.3
Width (in.)	71.6	71.6	68.1	66.7	70.2	71.7	71.6	71.6
Height (in.)	55.5	55.5	51.7	55.1	56.5	56.9	55.7	55.7
Curb Weight (lbs.)	3072	3069	2633	2936	3342	3895	3650	3770
Wheelbase (in.)	106.3	106.3	97.4	102.4	108.3	111.4	114.5	114.5
Front Head Room (in.)	39.3	39.3	38	39.2	40.5	37.6	40.5	38.6
Rear Head Room (in.)	37.6	37.6	34.4	36.8	37.4	36.9	36.9	36.4
Front Shoulder Room (in.)	56.9	56.9	53.5	53.1	56.4	56.7	56.3	56.3
Rear Shoulder Room (in.)	55.7	55.7	49.2	53.2	56.2	56.7	56.7	56.7
Front Hip Room (in.)	55.9	55.9	52.4	52.3	54.3	55.7	NA	NA
Rear Hip Room (in.)	54.3	54.3	47.8	51.9	53	55.7	NA	NA
Front Leg Room (in.)	43.3	43.3	43.1	41.5	43.9	43.6	43.1	43.1
Rear Leg Room (in.)	36.2	36.2	29.9	34.6	36.2	35.9	37.7	37.7
Luggage Capacity (cu ft.)	13	13	12.8	13.5	14.9	12.6	13.1	13.1
Number of Cylinders	4	6	4	4	6	8	6	8
Displacement (liters)	2.4	2.5	2	2	3	4.1	3	4
Horsepower @ RPM	148@5500	163@6000	140@6000	145@6400	227@6400	266@5600	240@6800	281@6100
Torque @ RPM	156@3000	167@4000	133@4800	132@4800	217@4000	278@4000	221@4500	287@4300
Fuel Capacity	17.2	17.2	14.5	15.9	18.5	21.4	18.4	18.4
EPA City (mpg) - Manual	21	20	22	23	NA	NA	NA	NA
EPA Hwy (mpg) - Manual	30	29	31	31	NA	NA	NA	NA
EPA City (mpg) - Auto	21	20	22	22	NA	18	NA	NA
EPA Hwy (mpg) - Auto	28	28	29	28	NA	23	NA	NA

INFINITI: G20, I30, Q45

JAGUAR: S-Type V6, S-Type V8

specifications

SPECIFICATIONS MILEAGE TABLES	EPA Hwy (mpg) - Auto	EPA City (mpg) - Auto	EPA Hwy (mpg) - Manual	EPA City (mpg) - Manual	Fuel Capacity	Torque @ RPM	Horsepower @ RPM	Displacement (liters)	Number of Cylinders	Luggage Capacity (cu ft.)	Rear Leg Room (in.)	Front Leg Room (in.)	Rear Hip Room (in.)	Front Hip Room (in.)	Rear Shoulder Room (in.)	Front Shoulder Room (in.)	Rear Head Room (in.)	Front Head Room (in.)	Wheelbase (in.)	Curb Weight (lbs.)	Height (in.)	Width (in.)	Length (in.)
KIA																							
Sephia Base/LS	31	23	31	24	13.2	108@4500	125@6000	1.8	4	10.4	34.4	43.3	54	52.1	54.2	53.8	37.7	39.6	100.8	2478	55.5	66.9	174.4
LEXUS																							
ES300	26	19	NA	NA	18.5	220@4400	210@5800	3	6	13	34.4	43.5	53.4	53.3	54.1	55.6	36.2	38	105.1	3351	54.9	70.5	190.2
GS 300	25	20	NA	NA	19.8	220@4000	225@6000	3	6	14.8	34.3	44.5	56.1	55	56.6	57.7	37.4	39	110.2	3638	55.9	70.9	189.2
GS 400	24	17	NA	NA	19.8	310@4000	300@6000	4	8	14.8	34.3	44.5	56.1	55	56.6	57.7	37.4	39	110.2	3693	55.9	70.9	189.2
LS400	25	18	NA	NA	22.5	300@4000	290@6000	4	8	13.9	36.9	43.7	56.7	57.1	57.1	57.9	36.9	38.9	112.2	3890	56.5	72	196.7
SC300	24	19	NA	NA	20.6	220@4000	225@6000	3	6	9.3	27.2	44.1	39.2	55.1	52.7	56	36.1	38.3	105.9	3560	53.2	70.9	192.5
SC400	25	18	NA	NA	20.6	300@4000	290@6000	4	8	9.3	27.2	44.1	39.2	55.1	52.7	56	36.1	38.3	105.9	3655	53.2	70.9	192.5

specifications

	Continental	LS V6 Auto	LS V6 Manual	LS V8	Town Car Cartier	Town Car Executive/Signature	626 4-Cyl LX/ES	626 V6 LX/ES
Length (in.)	208.5	193.9	193.9	193.9	215.3	215.3	187.4	187.4
Width (in.)	73.6	73.2	73.2	73.2	78.2	78.2	69.3	69.3
Height (in.)	56	56.1	56.1	56.1	58	58	55.1	55.1
Curb Weight (lbs.)	3868	3593	3546	3692	4015	4015	2864	3023
Wheelbase (in.)	109	114.5	114.5	114.5	117.7	117.7	105.1	105.1
Front Head Room (in.)	39.2	40.4	40.4	40.4	39.2	39.2	39.2	37.8
Rear Head Room (in.)	38	37.5	37.5	37.5	37.5	37.5	37	36.8
Front Shoulder Room (in.)	57.1	57.7	57.7	57.7	60.6	60.6	56.3	56.3
Rear Shoulder Room (in.)	56.6	57	57	57	60.3	60.3	55.9	55.9
Front Hip Room (in.)	55.7	53	53	53	57.3	57.3	NA	NA
Rear Hip Room (in.)	56.5	54.4	54.4	54.4	58	58	NA	NA
Front Leg Room (in.)	41.9	42.6	42.6	52.6	42.6	42.6	43.6	43.6
Rear Leg Room (in.)	38	37.7	37.7	37.7	41.1	41.1	34.6	34.6
Luggage Capacity (cu ft.)	18.4	13.7	13.7	13.7	20.6	20.6	14.2	14.2
Number of Cylinders	8	6	6	8	8	8	4	6
Displacement (liters)	4.6	3	3	3.9	4.6	4.6	2	2.5
Horsepower @ RPM	275@4750	210@6500	210@6500	252@6100	215@4500	200@4250	130@5500	170@6000
Torque @ RPM	275@4750	205@4750	205@4750	267@4300	285@3000	275@3000	130@3000	163@5000
Fuel Capacity	20	18.3	18.3	18.3	19	19	16.9	16.9
EPA City (mpg) - Manual	NA	NA	NA	NA	NA	NA	26	21
EPA Hwy (mpg) - Manual	NA	NA	NA	NA	NA	NA	33	27
EPA City (mpg) - Auto	17	NA	NA	NA	17	17	22	20
EPA Hwy (mpg) - Auto	25	NA	NA	NA	24	24	29	26

LINCOLN / **MAZDA**

SPECIFICATIONS MILEAGE TABLES

EDMUND'S® NEW CARS — www.edmunds.com — 449

specifications

SPECIFICATIONS MILEAGE TABLES

Model	EPA Hwy (mpg) - Auto	EPA City (mpg) - Auto	EPA Hwy (mpg) - Manual	EPA City (mpg) - Manual	Fuel Capacity	Torque @ RPM	Horsepower @ RPM	Displacement (liters)	Number of Cylinders	Luggage Capacity (cu ft.)	Rear Leg Room (in.)	Front Leg Room (in.)	Rear Hip Room (in.)	Front Hip Room (in.)	Rear Shoulder Room (in.)	Front Shoulder Room (in.)	Rear Head Room (in.)	Front Head Room (in.)	Wheelbase (in.)	Curb Weight (lbs.)	Height (in.)	Width (in.)	Length (in.)
MX-5 Miata Base/LS	28	23	29	25	12.7	119@5500	140@6500	1.8	4	5.1	NA	42.8	NA	NA	NA	49.7	NA	37.1	89.2	2332	48.4	66	155.3
Millenia Base	27	20	NA	NA	18	160@4800	170@5800	2.5	6	13.3	34.1	43.3	NA	NA	54.2	55.1	37	39.3	108.3	3241	54.9	69.7	189.8
Millenia S/Millennium	28	20	NA	NA	18	210@3500	210@5300	2.3	6	13.3	34.1	43.3	NA	NA	54.2	55.1	36.5	37.9	108.3	3355	54.9	69.7	189.9
Protege DX/LX	33	26	34	29	13.2	107@4000	105@5500	1.6	4	12.9	35.4	42.2	NA	NA	53.4	53.9	37.4	39.3	102.8	2449	55.5	67.1	174
Protege ES	29	24	30	26	13.2	120@4000	122@6000	1.8	4	12.9	35.4	42.2	NA	NA	53.4	53.9	37.4	39.3	102.8	2537	55.7	67.1	174

MERCEDES-BENZ

Model	EPA Hwy (mpg) - Auto	EPA City (mpg) - Auto	EPA Hwy (mpg) - Manual	EPA City (mpg) - Manual	Fuel Capacity	Torque @ RPM	Horsepower @ RPM	Displacement (liters)	Number of Cylinders	Luggage Capacity (cu ft.)	Rear Leg Room (in.)	Front Leg Room (in.)	Rear Hip Room (in.)	Front Hip Room (in.)	Rear Shoulder Room (in.)	Front Shoulder Room (in.)	Rear Head Room (in.)	Front Head Room (in.)	Wheelbase (in.)	Curb Weight (lbs.)	Height (in.)	Width (in.)	Length (in.)
C-Class C230	29	21	NA	NA	16.4	200@5300	185@5300	2.3	4	12.9	32.8	41.5	53.9	52.8	54.3	54.6	37	37.2	105.9	3250	56.1	67.7	177.4
C-Class C280	27	21	NA	NA	16.4	195@2500	194@5800	2.8	6	12.9	32.8	41.5	53.9	52.8	54.3	54.6	37	37.2	105.9	3316	56.1	67.7	177.4
C-Class C43	23	18	NA	NA	16.4	302@3000	302@5800	4.3	8	12.9	32.8	41.5	53.9	52.8	54.3	54.6	37	37.2	105.9	3448	56.1	67.7	177.4
CLK-Class CLK 320 Conv	29	21	NA	NA	16.4	229@3250 5850	215@5700	3.2	6	9.4	27.4	41.9	44.2	53.7	48	52.9	36.5	37.5	105.9	3650	54.3	67.8	180.3

specifications

	CLK-Class CLK 320 Coupe	CLK-Class CLK 430 Conv	CLK-Class CLK430 Coupe	E-Class E320 AWD Sedan	E-Class E320 AWD Wagon	E-Class E320 RWD Sedan	E-Class E320 RWD Wagon	E-Class E430 AWD Sedan	E-Class E430 RWD Sedan	SLK230
Length (in.)	180.3	180.3	180.3	189.4	190	189.4	190	189.4	189.4	157.3
Width (in.)	67.8	67.8	67.8	70.8	70.8	70.8	70.8	70.8	70.8	67.5
Height (in.)	54	54.3	54	56.7	59.3	56.7	59.3	56.7	56.7	50.7
Curb Weight (lbs.)	3240	3650	3364	3460	3670	3460	3670	3640	3640	2975
Wheelbase (in.)	105.9	105.9	105.9	111.5	111.5	111.5	111.5	111.5	111.5	94.5
Front Head Room (in.)	36.9	37.5	36.9	37.6	37.6	37.6	37.6	37.6	37.6	37.4
Rear Head Room (in.)	35.8	36.5	35.8	37.2	37	37.2	37	37.2	37.2	NA
Front Shoulder Room (in.)	52.9	52.9	52.9	56.3	56.3	56.3	56.3	56.3	56.3	51.7
Rear Shoulder Room (in.)	50.4	48	50.4	57.1	57.1	57.1	57.1	57.1	57.1	NA
Front Hip Room (in.)	53.7	53.7	53.7	54.9	54.9	54.9	54.9	54.9	54.9	54.7
Rear Hip Room (in.)	45.9	44.2	45.9	55.9	55.9	55.9	55.9	55.9	55.9	NA
Front Leg Room (in.)	41.9	41.9	41.9	41.3	41.3	41.3	41.3	41.3	41.3	42.7
Rear Leg Room (in.)	31.2	27.4	31.2	36.1	36.5	36.1	36.5	36.1	36.1	NA
Luggage Capacity (cu ft.)	11	9.4	11	15.3	43.8	15.3	43.8	15.3	15.3	3.6
Number of Cylinders	6	8	8	6	6	6	6	8	8	4
Displacement (liters)	3.2	4.3	4.3	3.2	3.2	3.2	3.2	4.3	4.3	2.3
Horsepower @ RPM	215@5700	275@5750	275@5750	221@5600	221@5600	221@5600	221@5600	275@5750	275@5750	185@5300
Torque @ RPM	229@3000	295@3000	295@3000	232@3000	232@3000	232@3000	232@3000	295@3000	295@3000	200@2500
Fuel Capacity	16.4	16.4	16.4	21.1	18.5	21.1	18.5	21.1	21.1	14
EPA City (mpg) - Manual	NA	NA	NA	NA	NA	NA	NA	NA	NA	21
EPA Hwy (mpg) - Manual	NA	NA	NA	NA	NA	NA	NA	NA	NA	30
EPA City (mpg) - Auto	21	18	18	20	20	21	20	NA	19	22
EPA Hwy (mpg) - Auto	29	25	25	28	26	30	28	NA	26	30

specifications

MERCURY

SPECIFICATIONS MILEAGE TABLES	EPA Hwy (mpg) - Auto	EPA City (mpg) - Auto	EPA Hwy (mpg) - Manual	EPA City (mpg) - Manual	Fuel Capacity	Torque @ RPM	Horsepower @ RPM	Displacement (liters)	Number of Cylinders	Luggage Capacity (cu ft.)	Rear Leg Room (in.)	Front Leg Room (in.)	Rear Hip Room (in.)	Front Hip Room (in.)	Rear Shoulder Room (in.)	Front Shoulder Room (in.)	Rear Head Room (in.)	Front Head Room (in.)	Wheelbase (in.)	Curb Weight (lbs.)	Height (in.)	Width (in.)	Length (in.)
Cougar 4-Cyl.	NA	NA	34	24	16	130@4000	125@5500	2	4	14.5	33.2	42.5	46.1	51.2	51.3	53.9	34.6	37.8	106.4	2892	52.2	69.6	185
Cougar V6	29	20	28	19	16	165@4250	170@6250	2.5	6	14.5	33.2	42.5	46.1	51.2	51.3	53.9	34.6	37.8	106.4	2892	52.2	69.6	185
Grand Marquis GS/LS	24	17	NA	NA	19	275@3000	200@4250	4.6	8	20.6	38.4	42.5	59	58	60.3	60.1	38.1	39.4	114.7	3928	56.8	78.2	212
Mystique GS	31	23	34	24	15	130@4000	125@5500	2	4	13.9	36	42.4	45.3	50.7	53.3	53.9	36.8	39	106.5	2805	54.5	69.1	184.8
Mystique LS	29	20	28	19	15	165@4250	170@6250	2.5	6	13.9	36	42.4	45.3	50.7	53.3	53.9	36.8	39	106.5	2805	54.5	69.1	184.8
Sable GS Wagon	NA	NA	NA	NA	16	182@4000	153@5300	3	6	38.4	36	42.2	56.2	55.8	56.6	57.4	38.9	39.3	108.5	3302	57.6	73	199.1
Sable GS/LS - Sedan	NA	NA	NA	NA	16	182@4000	153@5300	3	6	16	38.9	42.2	56.3	55.8	56.6	57.4	36.6	39.4	108.5	3302	55.4	73	199.7
Sable LS Premium Sedan	NA	NA	NA	NA	16	200@4500	200@5750	3	6	16	38.9	42.2	56.3	55.8	56.6	57.4	36.6	39.4	108.5	3302	55.4	73	199.7
Sable LS Premium Wagon	NA	NA	NA	NA	16	200@4500	200@5750	3	6	38.4	38.5	42.2	56.2	55.8	56.6	57.4	38.9	39.3	108.5	3470	57.6	73	199.1

specifications

MITSUBISHI

	Diamante	Mirage DE Coupe	Mirage DE Sedan	Mirage LS Coupe	Mirage LS Sedan	Eclipse GS	Eclipse GT	Eclipse RS	Galant 4-Cyl DE/ES
Length (in.)	194.1	168.1	173.6	168.1	173.6	175.4	175.4	175.4	187.8
Width (in.)	70.3	66.5	66.5	66.5	66.5	68.9	68.9	68.9	68.5
Height (in.)	53.9	52.4	53.6	52.4	53.5	51.6	51.6	51.6	55.7
Curb Weight (lbs.)	3440	2125	2225	2260	2350	2910	3053	2822	2945
Wheelbase (in.)	107.1	95.1	98.4	95.1	98.4	100.8	100.8	100.8	103.7
Front Head Room (in.)	39.4	38.6	39.8	38.6	39.8	37.9	37.9	37.9	39.9
Rear Head Room (in.)	37.5	35.8	37.4	35.8	37.4	34.9	34.9	34.9	37.7
Front Shoulder Room (in.)	56	53.6	53.6	53.6	53.6	52.2	52.2	52.2	54.5
Rear Shoulder Room (in.)	56.1	53.2	52.8	53.2	52.8	52	52	52	54.2
Front Hip Room (in.)	54.3	53.2	53.2	53.2	53.2	51.9	51.9	51.9	52.4
Rear Hip Room (in.)	55.8	47.6	52.2	47.6	52.2	44.7	44.7	44.7	53.9
Front Leg Room (in.)	43.6	43	43	43	43	42.3	42.3	42.3	43.5
Rear Leg Room (in.)	36.6	31.1	33.5	31.1	33.5	30.2	30.2	30.2	36.3
Luggage Capacity (cu ft.)	14.2	11.5	11.5	11.5	11.5	16.9	16.9	16.9	14
Number of Cylinders	6	4	4	4	4	4	6	4	4
Displacement (liters)	3.5	1.5	1.5	1.8	1.8	2.4	3	2.4	2.4
Horsepower @ RPM	210@5000	92@5500	92@5500	113@5500	113@5500	154@5500	205@5500	154@5500	145@5500
Torque @ RPM	231@4000	93@3000	93@3000	116@4500	116@4500	163@4000	205@4500	163@4000	155@3000
Fuel Capacity	19	13.2	13.2	13.2	13.2	15.9	15.9	15.9	16.3
EPA City (mpg) - Manual	NA	33	33	28	28	23	20	23	NA
EPA Hwy (mpg) - Manual	NA	40	40	37	37	31	28	31	NA
EPA City (mpg) - Auto	18	28	28	26	26	20	20	21	21
EPA Hwy (mpg) - Auto	24	36	36	33	33	27	27	28	28

SPECIFICATIONS MILEAGE TABLES

specifications

SPECIFICATIONS MILEAGE TABLES

NISSAN

	EPA Hwy (mpg) - Auto	EPA City (mpg) - Auto	EPA Hwy (mpg) - Manual	EPA City (mpg) - Manual	Fuel Capacity	Torque @ RPM	Horsepower @ RPM	Displacement (liters)	Number of Cylinders	Luggage Capacity (cu ft.)	Rear Leg Room (in.)	Front Leg Room (in.)	Rear Hip Room (in.)	Front Hip Room (in.)	Rear Shoulder Room (in.)	Front Shoulder Room (in.)	Rear Head Room (in.)	Front Head Room (in.)	Wheelbase (in.)	Curb Weight (lbs.)	Height (in.)	Width (in.)	Length (in.)
Galant V6 ES/LS/GTZ	27	20	NA	NA	16.3	205@4500	195@5500	3	6	14	36.3	43.5	53.9	52.4	54.2	54.5	37.7	39.9	103.7	3140	55.7	68.5	187.8
Sentra GXE/XE	36	27	39	29	13.2	108@4000	115@6000	1.6	4	10.7	32.4	42.3	52.8	50.1	53.1	53.2	36.5	39.1	99.8	2379	54.5	66.6	171.1
Sentra SE Limited	30	23	31	23	13.2	132@4800	140@6400	2	4	10.7	32.4	42.3	52.8	50.1	53.1	53.2	36.5	39.1	99.8	2379	54.5	66.6	171.1
Altima XE/GXE/SE/GLE	30	22	31	24	15.9	154@4400	150@6400	2.4	4	14	33.9	42	52.6	52.5	54.8	55.7	37.1	39.4	103.1	2859	55.9	69.1	183.5
Maxima GXE/SE/GLE	NA	NA	NA	NA	18.5	217@4000	222@6400	3	6	15	34.3	46	55.9	54.3	56.2	56.8	34	36.5	108.3	3320	56.5	70.3	190.5

OLDSMOBILE

Aurora Base	26	17	NA	NA	18.5	260@4400	250@5600	4	8	16.1	38.4	42.6	56.2	55.1	57.9	57.9	36.9	38.4	113.8	3967	55.4	74.4	205.4
Alero Coupe - GL3/GLS	28	20	NA	NA	15	200@4000	170@4800	3.4	6	14.6	35.5	42.2	51.2	50.9	54.6	53.6	36.5	38.4	107	2958	54.5	70.1	186.7
Alero Coupe - GX/GL1/GL2	30	22	NA	NA	15	155@4400	150@5600	2.4	4	14.6	35.5	42.2	51.2	50.9	54.6	53.6	36.5	38.4	107	2958	54.5	70.1	186.7

specifications

SPECIFICATIONS MILEAGE TABLES	Alero Sedan - GL3/GLS	Alero Sedan - GX/GL1/GL2	Intrigue GX/GL/GLS	**PLYMOUTH**	Breeze	Neon Highline	Prowler	**PONTIAC**	Bonneville SE/SLE	Bonneville SSEi
Length (in.)	186.7	186.7	195.9		186.3	174.4	165.4		202.5	202.5
Width (in.)	70.1	70.1	73.6		71	74.4	76.3		72.6	72.6
Height (in.)	54.5	54.5	56.6		54.1	56	50.9		56.7	56.7
Curb Weight (lbs.)	3022	3022	3455		2942	2577	2850		3446	3587
Wheelbase (in.)	107	107	109		108	105	113.3		112.2	112.2
Front Head Room (in.)	38.4	38.4	39.3		38.1	39.1	37.8		38.7	38.7
Rear Head Room (in.)	37	37	37.4		36.8	36.8	NA		37.8	37.8
Front Shoulder Room (in.)	53.6	53.6	58		55.2	53.4	51.6		59	59
Rear Shoulder Room (in.)	52.6	52.6	57		54.7	52.8	NA		58.3	58.3
Front Hip Room (in.)	50.9	50.9	55.6		52.8	52.4	52		55.7	55.7
Rear Hip Room (in.)	51.5	51.5	54.8		52.7	52.9	NA		56.4	56.4
Front Leg Room (in.)	42.2	42.2	42.4		42.3	42.4	43		42.5	42.5
Rear Leg Room (in.)	35.5	35.5	36.9		38.1	34.8	NA		38	38
Luggage Capacity (cu ft.)	14.6	14.6	16.4		15.7	13.1	3		18	18
Number of Cylinders	6	4	6		4	4	6		6	6
Displacement (liters)	3.4	2.4	3.5		2	2	3.5		3.8	3.8
Horsepower @ RPM	170@4800	150@5600	215@5500		132@5600	132@5600	253@6400		205@5200	240@5200
Torque @ RPM	200@4000	155@4400	234@4400		130@4600	130@4600	255@3950		230@4000	280@3200
Fuel Capacity	15	15	18		16	12.5	12		17.5	18.5
EPA City (mpg) - Manual	NA	NA	NA		26	NA	NA		NA	NA
EPA Hwy (mpg) - Manual	NA	NA	NA		37	NA	NA		NA	NA
EPA City (mpg) - Auto	20	22	19		22	NA	17		19	18
EPA Hwy (mpg) - Auto	28	30	27		31	NA	23		28	27

specifications

SPECIFICATIONS MILEAGE TABLES

	EPA Hwy (mpg) - Auto	EPA City (mpg) - Auto	EPA Hwy (mpg) - Manual	EPA City (mpg) - Manual	Fuel Capacity	Torque @ RPM	Horsepower @ RPM	Displacement (liters)	Number of Cylinders	Luggage Capacity (cu ft.)	Rear Leg Room (in.)	Front Leg Room (in.)	Rear Hip Room (in.)	Front Hip Room (in.)	Rear Shoulder Room (in.)	Front Shoulder Room (in.)	Rear Head Room (in.)	Front Head Room (in.)	Wheelbase (in.)	Curb Weight (lbs.)	Height (in.)	Width (in.)	Length (in.)
Firebird Base Convertible	27	19	30	19	16.8	225@4000	200@5200	3.8	6	7.6	28.9	42.9	44.4	52.8	55.8	57.4	35.3	37.2	101.1	3479	52	74.5	193.4
Firebird Base Coupe	29	19	30	19	16.8	225@4000	200@5200	3.8	6	12.9	28.9	42.9	44.4	52.8	55.8	57.4	35.3	37.2	101.1	3323	52	74.5	193.8
Firebird V8 Convertible	24	18	28	19	16.8	335@4000	305@5200	5.7	8	7.6	28.9	42.9	44.4	52.8	55.8	57.4	35.3	37.2	101.1	3613	52	74.5	193.4
Firebird V8 Coupe	24	18	28	19	16.8	335@4000	305@5200	5.7	8	12.9	28.9	42.9	44.4	52.8	55.8	57.4	35.3	37.2	101.1	3446	52	74.5	193.8
Grand Am GT Sedan/SE2 Sedan	28	20	NA	19	15.2	205@4000	175@5200	3.4	6	14.6	35.5	42.1	52.4	52.6	52.8	53.6	37.6	38.3	107	3168	55.1	70.4	186.8
Grand Am GT Coupe/SE2 Coupe	28	20	NA	NA	15.2	205@4000	175@5200	3.4	6	14.6	35.5	42.1	52.4	52.4	55	53.7	37.2	38.3	107	3091	55.1	70.4	186.3
Grand Am SE Coupe/SE1 Coupe	30	22	NA	NA	15.2	155@4400	150@5600	2.4	4	14.6	35.5	42.1	49.3	52.4	55	53.7	37.2	38.3	107	3066	55.1	70.4	186.3
Grand Am SE Sedan/SE1 Sedan	30	22	NA	NA	15.2	155@4400	150@5600	2.4	4	14.6	35.5	42.1	49.3	52.4	52.8	53.6	37.6	38.3	107	3116	55.1	70.4	186.3
Grand Prix GT Coupe	30	19	NA	NA	18	240@3600	195@5200	3.8	6	16	36.1	42.4	54.3	55.7	57.2	58.5	36.5	38.3	110.5	3396	54.7	72.7	196.5
Grand Prix GT Sedan	30	19	NA	NA	18	240@3600	195@5200	3.8	6	16	35.8	42.4	54.3	55.7	57.2	58.5	36.7	38.3	110.5	3414	54.7	72.7	196.5

specifications

SPECIFICATIONS MILEAGE TABLES	Grand Prix GTP Coupe	Grand Prix GTP Sedan	Grand Prix SE Sedan	Sunfire GT Convertible	Sunfire GT Coupe	Sunfire SE Coupe	Sunfire SE Sedan	PORSCHE	Boxster
Length (in.)	196.5	196.5	196.5	181.9	181.9	181.9	181.7		171
Width (in.)	72.7	72.7	72.7	68.4	68.4	68.4	67.9		70.1
Height (in.)	54.7	54.7	54.7	54.1	53	53	54.7		50.8
Curb Weight (lbs.)	3396	3414	3373	2998	2822	2630	2670		2822
Wheelbase (in.)	110.5	110.5	110.5	104.1	104.1	104.1	104.1		95.2
Front Head Room (in.)	38.3	38.3	38.3	34.1	37.6	37.6	38.9		36.5
Rear Head Room (in.)	36.5	36.7	36.7	33.6	36.6	36.6	37.2		NA
Front Shoulder Room (in.)	58.5	58.5	58.5	54.1	54.1	54.1	54.6		NA
Rear Shoulder Room (in.)	57.2	57.2	57.2	47.1	54.8	54.8	53.9		NA
Front Hip Room (in.)	55.7	55.7	55.7	48.7	48.7	48.7	50.9		NA
Rear Hip Room (in.)	54.3	54.3	54.3	47.8	49.5	49.5	51.1		NA
Front Leg Room (in.)	42.4	42.4	42.4	42.1	42.1	42.1	42.1		44
Rear Leg Room (in.)	36.1	35.8	35.8	32.6	32.6	32.6	34.3		NA
Luggage Capacity (cu ft.)	16	16	16	9.9	12.4	12.4	13.1		11.2
Number of Cylinders	6	6	6	4	4	4	4		6
Displacement (liters)	3.8	3.8	3.1	2.4	2.4	2.2	2.2		2.5
Horsepower @ RPM	240@5200	240@5200	175@5200	150@5600	150@5600	115@5000	115@5000		201@6000
Torque @ RPM	280@3600	280@3600	195@4000	155@4400	155@4400	135@3600	135@3600		181@4500
Fuel Capacity	18	18	18	15	15	15	15		17
EPA City (mpg) - Manual	NA	NA	NA	NA	23	24	24		19
EPA Hwy (mpg) - Manual	NA	NA	NA	NA	33	34	34		26
EPA City (mpg) - Auto	18	18	20	22	22	23	23		17
EPA Hwy (mpg) - Auto	28	28	29	30	30	31	31		24

specifications

SPECIFICATIONS MILEAGE TABLES

SAAB

Model	EPA Hwy (mpg) - Auto	EPA City (mpg) - Auto	EPA Hwy (mpg) - Manual	EPA City (mpg) - Manual	Fuel Capacity	Torque @ RPM	Horsepower @ RPM	Displacement (liters)	Number of Cylinders	Luggage Capacity (cu ft.)	Rear Leg Room (in.)	Front Leg Room (in.)	Rear Hip Room (in.)	Front Hip Room (in.)	Rear Shoulder Room (in.)	Front Shoulder Room (in.)	Rear Head Room (in.)	Front Head Room (in.)	Wheelbase (in.)	Curb Weight (lbs.)	Height (in.)	Width (in.)	Length (in.)
9-3 Base 2-Door	25	19	27	20	16.9	194@2100	185@5500	2	4	21.7	34.1	42.3	NA	NA	52.6	52.4	37.9	39.3	102.6	2990	56.2	67.4	182.2
9-3 Base 4-Door	25	19	27	20	16.9	194@2100	185@5500	2	4	21.7	34.1	42.3	NA	NA	52.6	52.4	37.9	39.3	102.6	3030	56	67.4	182.2
9-3 Base Convertible	25	19	27	20	16.9	194@2100	185@5500	2	4	10	33.2	42.3	NA	NA	41.9	52.5	37.8	38.9	102.6	3180	56	67.4	182.2
9-3 SE 4-Door	25	19	27	19	16.9	209@2200	205@5500	2	4	21.7	34.1	42.3	NA	NA	52.6	52.4	37.8	39.3	102.6	3160	56.2	67.4	182.2
9-3 SE Convertible	25	19	27	19	16.9	209@2200	205@5500	2	4	10	33.2	42.3	NA	NA	41.9	52.5	37.8	38.9	102.6	3200	56	67.4	182.2
9-3 Viggen 2-Door	NA	NA	27	NA	16.9	258@2500	230@5500	2.3	4	21.7	34.1	42.3	NA	NA	52.6	52.4	37.9	39.3	102.6	2990	56.2	67.4	182.2
9-3 Viggen 4-Door	NA	NA	27	NA	16.9	258@2500	230@5500	2.3	4	21.7	33.2	42.3	NA	NA	52.6	52.4	37.8	39.3	102.6	3160	56.2	67.4	182.2
9-3 Viggen Convertible	NA	NA	27	NA	16.9	258@2500	230@5500	2.3	4	10	33.2	42.3	NA	NA	41.9	52.5	37.8	38.9	102.6	3200	56	67.4	182.2
9-5 Viggen Convertible	NA	19	NA	NA	16.9	258@2500	170@5500	2.3	4	15.9	36.6	42.3	NA	NA	41.9	52.5	37.8	38.9	106.4	3280	57	67.4	182.2
9-5 2.3i Sedan	26	19	30	21	18.5	207@1800	170@5500	2.3	4	15.9	36.6	42.4	NA	NA	56.5	56.9	37.6	38.7	106.4	3280	57	70.5	189.2

specifications

Specifications / Mileage Tables	9-5 2.3t Wagon	9-5 Aero	9-5 SE V6t Sedan	9-5 SE V6t Wagon	L-Series LS/LS1	L-Series LS2	L-Series LW1	L-Series LW2	S-Series SC1
Length (in.)	189.3	189.2	189.2	189.3	190.4	190.4	190.4	190.4	180
Width (in.)	70.5	70.5	70.5	70.5	69	69	69	69	66.4
Height (in.)	61.1	57	57	61.1	56.4	56.4	57.3	57.3	53
Curb Weight (lbs.)	3640	3410	3410	3760	2910	3153	3075	3230	2367
Wheelbase (in.)	106.4	106.4	106.4	106.4	106.5	106.5	106.5	106.5	102.4
Front Head Room (in.)	38.7	38.7	38.7	38.7	39.3	39.3	39.3	39.3	38.5
Rear Head Room (in.)	37.6	37.6	37.6	37.6	38	38	39.6	39.6	35.7
Front Shoulder Room (in.)	56.9	56.9	56.9	56.9	55.7	55.7	55.7	55.7	54.6
Rear Shoulder Room (in.)	56.5	56.5	56.5	56.5	56.1	56.1	56.1	56.1	50.4
Front Hip Room (in.)	NA	NA	NA	NA	51.7	51.7	51.7	51.7	50
Rear Hip Room (in.)	NA	NA	NA	NA	54	54	54	54	47.7
Front Leg Room (in.)	42.4	42.4	42.4	42.4	42.3	42.3	42.3	42.3	42.6
Rear Leg Room (in.)	36.6	36.6	36.6	36.6	34.4	34.4	34.7	34.7	31
Luggage Capacity (cu ft.)	37	15.9	15.9	37	17.5	17.5	29.4	29.4	11.4
Number of Cylinders	4	4	6	6	4	6	4	6	4
Displacement (liters)	2.3	2.3	3	3	2.2	3	2.2	3	1.9
Horsepower @ RPM	170@5500	230@5500	200@5000	200@5000	137@5800	182@5600	137@5800	182@5600	100@5000
Torque @ RPM	207@1800	258@1900	229@2500	229@2500	147@4400	190@3600	147@4400	190@3600	114@2400
Fuel Capacity	18.5	18.5	18.5	18.5	13.1	13.1	13.1	13.1	12.1
EPA City (mpg) - Manual	21	NA	NA	NA	24	NA	NA	NA	29
EPA Hwy (mpg) - Manual	30	NA	NA	NA	32	NA	NA	NA	40
EPA City (mpg) - Auto	19	18	18	18	20	22	20	20	27
EPA Hwy (mpg) - Auto	26	NA	26	26	NA	26	30	26	37

specifications

SPECIFICATIONS MILEAGE TABLES

SUBARU

	EPA Hwy (mpg) - Auto	EPA City (mpg) - Auto	EPA Hwy (mpg) - Manual	EPA City (mpg) - Manual	Fuel Capacity	Torque @ RPM	Horsepower @ RPM	Displacement (liters)	Number of Cylinders	Luggage Capacity (cu ft.)	Rear Leg Room (in.)	Front Leg Room (in.)	Rear Hip Room (in.)	Front Hip Room (in.)	Rear Shoulder Room (in.)	Front Shoulder Room (in.)	Rear Head Room (in.)	Front Head Room (in.)	Wheelbase (in.)	Curb Weight (lbs.)	Height (in.)	Width (in.)	Length (in.)
S-Series SC2	35	25	38	27	12.1	122@4800	124@5600	1.9	4	11.4	31	42.6	47.7	50	50.4	54.6	35.7	38.5	102.4	2436	53	66.4	180.1
S-Series SL/SL1	37	27	40	29	12.1	114@2400	100@5000	1.9	4	12.1	32.8	42.5	50.2	49.2	53.1	53.9	38	39.3	102.4	2332	55	66.4	176.9
S-Series SL2	35	25	38	27	12.1	122@4800	124@5600	1.9	4	12.1	32.8	42.5	50.2	49.2	53.1	53.9	38	39.3	102.4	2399	55	66.4	176.9
S-Series SW2	35	25	38	27	12.1	122@4800	124@5600	1.9	4	24.9	32.8	42.5	50.2	49.2	53.1	54	38.7	39.3	102.4	2452	55.6	66.4	176.9
Impreza 2.5 RS Coupe	28	22	29	22	15.9	166@4000	165@5600	2.5	4	11.1	32.5	43.1	50.2	49.2	52.2	52.6	36.7	38	99.2	2820	55.5	67.1	172.2
Impreza 2.5 RS Sedan	28	22	29	22	15.9	166@4000	165@5600	2.5	4	11.1	32.5	43.1	50.2	49.2	51.8	52.6	36.7	38	99.2	2825	55.5	67.1	172.2
Impreza L Coupe	29	23	29	22	15.9	149@3600	142@5600	2.2	4	11.1	32.5	43.1	50.2	49.2	52.2	52.6	36.7	39.2	99.2	2730	55.5	67.1	172.2
Impreza L Sedan	29	23	29	22	15.9	149@3600	142@5600	2.2	4	11.1	32.5	43.1	50.2	49.2	51.8	52.6	36.7	39.2	99.2	2735	55.5	67.1	172.2
Impreza L Wagon	29	23	29	22	15.9	149@3600	142@5600	2.2	4	25.5	32.4	43.1	50.2	49.2	51.8	52.6	37.4	39.2	99.2	2835	55.5	67.1	172.2

specifications

SPECIFICATIONS MILEAGE TABLES	Impreza Outback Sport	Legacy Sedan	Legacy Wagon	Outback Limited Sedan	Outback Wagon	**SUZUKI**	Esteem 1.6 Sedan GL	Esteem 1.8 GL/GLX/GLX+	Esteem 1.8 Wagon GL/GLX/GLX+	Swift GA/GL
Length (in.)	172.2	184.4	184.4	184.4	185.8		166.3	166.3	172.2	149.4
Width (in.)	67.1	68.7	67.5	68.7	67.5		66.1	66.1	66.5	62.6
Height (in.)	55.5	55.7	57.1	58.3	63		53.9	53.9	55.9	54.7
Curb Weight (lbs.)	2835	3240	3220	3390	3360		2227	2227	2359	1895
Wheelbase (in.)	99.2	104.3	103.5	104.3	103.5		97.6	97.6	97.6	93.1
Front Head Room (in.)	39.2	38.1	40.2	38.1	40.2		39.1	39.1	38.8	39.1
Rear Head Room (in.)	37.4	36.6	39.1	36.6	39.1		37.2	37.2	38	36
Front Shoulder Room (in.)	52.6	53.9	53.9	53.9	53.9		51.8	51.8	51.8	48.9
Rear Shoulder Room (in.)	51.8	53.6	53.6	53.6	53.6		52.1	52.1	52.1	48.9
Front Hip Room (in.)	1295	51.3	51.3	51.3	51.3		50.8	50.8	50.8	47.2
Rear Hip Room (in.)	1335	51.9	51.9	51.9	51.9		48.2	48.2	48.2	43.9
Front Leg Room (in.)	43.1	43.3	43.3	43.3	43.3		42.3	42.3	42.3	42.5
Rear Leg Room (in.)	32.4	34.2	34.3	34.2	34.3		34.1	34.1	34.1	32.2
Luggage Capacity (cu ft.)	25.5	12.4	34.3	12.4	34.3		12	12	24	8.4
Number of Cylinders	4	4	4	4	4		4	4	4	4
Displacement (liters)	2.2	2.5	2.5	2.5	2.5		1.6	1.8	1.8	1.3
Horsepower @ RPM	142@5600	165@5600	165@5600	165@5600	165@5600		95@6000	122@6300	122@6300	79@6000
Torque @ RPM	149@3600	166@4000	166@4000	166@4000	166@4000		99@3000	117@3500	117@3500	75@3000
Fuel Capacity	13.2	16.9	16.9	16.9	16.9		12.7	12.7	12.7	10.3
EPA City (mpg) - Manual	22	NA	NA	NA	NA		30	NA	NA	39
EPA Hwy (mpg) - Manual	29	NA	NA	NA	NA		37	NA	NA	43
EPA City (mpg) - Auto	23	NA	NA	NA	NA		27	NA	NA	30
EPA Hwy (mpg) - Auto	29	NA	NA	NA	NA		34	NA	NA	34

EDMUND'S® NEW CARS www.edmunds.com

specifications

SPECIFICATIONS MILEAGE TABLES

TOYOTA

	EPA Hwy (mpg) - Auto	EPA City (mpg) - Auto	EPA Hwy (mpg) - Manual	EPA City (mpg) - Manual	Fuel Capacity	Torque @ RPM	Horsepower @ RPM	Displacement (liters)	Number of Cylinders	Luggage Capacity (cu ft.)	Rear Leg Room (in.)	Front Leg Room (in.)	Rear Hip Room (in.)	Front Hip Room (in.)	Rear Shoulder Room (in.)	Front Shoulder Room (in.)	Rear Head Room (in.)	Front Head Room (in.)	Wheelbase (in.)	Curb Weight (lbs.)	Height (in.)	Width (in.)	Length (in.)
Avalon XL/XLS	29	21	NA	NA	18.5	214@4400	200@5200	3	6	15.4	38.3	44.1	57.4	55.8	57.3	57.7	37.8	39.1	107	3340	56.7	70.5	191.9
Camry 4-Cyl	30	23	32	23	18.5	147@4400	133@5200	2.2	4	14.1	35.5	43.5	54.1	54	56.1	56.2	37.6	38.6	105.2	2998	55.4	70.1	188.5
Camry V6	28	20	28	21	18.5	209@4400	194@5200	3	6	14.1	35.5	43.5	54.1	54	56.1	56.2	37.6	38.6	105.2	3175	55.4	70.1	188.5
Camry Solara 4-Cyl.	30	23	32	23	18.5	147@4400	135@5200	2.2	4	14.1	36.3	43.5	54.1	53.6	52.9	55.3	36.3	38.3	105.1	3120	NA	71.1	190
Camry Solara V6	28	20	28	21	18.5	214@4400	200@5200	3	6	14.1	36.3	43.5	54.1	53.6	52.9	55.3	36.3	38.3	105.1	3230	NA	71.1	190
Celica GT	NA	NA	NA	NA	14.5	125@4400	140@6400	1.8	4	16.9	25.4	33	46.8	51.3	50.6	52.6	35	38.4	102.3	2425	51.4	68.3	170.4
Celica GTS	NA	NA	NA	NA	14.5	133@6800	180@7600	1.8	4	16.9	25.4	33	46.8	51.3	50.6	52.6	35	38.4	102.3	2500	51.4	68.3	170.4
Corolla VE/CE/LE	36	28	38	31	13.2	122@4400	120@5600	1.8	4	12.1	33.2	42.5	51.2	50.5	52.2	52.8	36.9	39.3	97	2420	54.5	66.7	174
Echo Coupe	39	32	41	34	11.9	105@4200	108@6000	1.5	4	13.6	35.2	41.1	51	51.1	51	52.3	37.6	38.4	93.3	2020	59.4	65.4	163.2

specifications

	Echo Sedan		Cabrio GL/GLS	Golf GL/GLS	Golf GTI GLS	Golf GTI GLX	Golf TDI GL/GLS	Jetta 2.0L GL/GLS	Jetta TDI GL/GLS	Jetta VR6 GLS/GLX
Length (in.)	163.2		160.4	163.3	163.3	163.3	16.3	172.3	172.3	172.3
Width (in.)	65.4		66.7	68.3	68.3	68.3	68.3	68.3	68.3	68.3
Height (in.)	59.4		56	56.7	56.7	56.7	56.7	56.9	56.9	56.9
Curb Weight (lbs.)	2030		3079	2723	2762	2890	2791	2853	2873	2994
Wheelbase (in.)	93.3		97.4	98.9	98.9	98.9	98.9	98.9	98.9	98.9
Front Head Room (in.)	39.9		38.2	38.5	37.1	37.1	38.5	38.7	38.7	38.7
Rear Head Room (in.)	37.6		36.6	37.7	36.5	36.5	37.7	37.2	37.2	37.2
Front Shoulder Room (in.)	51.8		54.1	53.7	53.7	53.7	53.7	53.7	53.7	53.7
Rear Shoulder Room (in.)	50.7		46.5	52.7	52.7	52.7	52.7	52.9	52.9	52.9
Front Hip Room (in.)	51.1		52.8	NA	NA	NA	NA	NA	NA	NA
Rear Hip Room (in.)	51		51.9	NA	NA	NA	NA	NA	NA	NA
Front Leg Room (in.)	41.1		42.3	41.3	41.3	41.3	41.3	41.3	41.3	41.3
Rear Leg Room (in.)	35.2		31.1	33.3	33.3	33.3	33.3	33.3	33.3	33.3
Luggage Capacity (cu ft.)	13.6		8	18	18	18	18	13	13	13
Number of Cylinders	4		4	4	4	6	4	4	4	6
Displacement (liters)	1.5		2	2	2	2.8	1.9	2	1.9	2.8
Horsepower @ RPM	108@6000		115@5200	115@5200	115@5200	174@5800	90@3750	115@5200	90@3750	174@5800
Torque @ RPM	105@4200		122@2600	122@2600	122@2600	181@3200	155@1900	122@2600	155@1900	181@3200
Fuel Capacity	11.9		13.7	14.5	14.5	14.5	14.5	14.5	14.5	14.5
EPA City (mpg) - Manual	34		24	24	24	20	42	24	42	19
EPA Hwy (mpg) - Manual	41		31	31	31	28	49	31	49	28
EPA City (mpg) - Auto	32		22	22	22	NA	34	22	34	19
EPA Hwy (mpg) - Auto	39		28	28	28	NA	45	28	45	26

VOLKSWAGEN

specifications

SPECIFICATIONS MILEAGE TABLES

	EPA Hwy (mpg) - Auto	EPA City (mpg) - Auto	EPA Hwy (mpg) - Manual	EPA City (mpg) - Manual	Fuel Capacity	Torque @ RPM	Horsepower @ RPM	Displacement (liters)	Number of Cylinders	Luggage Capacity (cu ft.)	Rear Leg Room (in.)	Front Leg Room (in.)	Rear Hip Room (in.)	Front Hip Room (in.)	Rear Shoulder Room (in.)	Front Shoulder Room (in.)	Rear Head Room (in.)	Front Head Room (in.)	Wheelbase (in.)	Curb Weight (lbs.)	Height (in.)	Width (in.)	Length (in.)
New Beetle 1.8T GLS/GLX	NA	NA	NA	NA	14.5	156@2200	150@5800	1.8	4	12	33	39.4	NA	NA	49.4	52.8	36.7	41.3	98.9	2921	59.5	67.9	161.1
New Beetle GL/GLS	28	22	31	24	14.5	122@2600	115@5200	2	4	12	33	39.4	NA	NA	49.4	52.8	36.7	41.3	98.9	2769	59.5	67.9	161.1
New Beetle TDI GLS	45	34	49	42	14.5	155@1900	90@3750	1.9	4	12	33	39.4	NA	NA	49.4	52.8	36.7	41.3	98.9	2867	59.5	67.9	161.1
Passat GLS Sedan	31	21	32	23	16.4	155@1750	150@5700	1.8	4	15	35.3	41.5	NA	NA	54.6	55.8	37.8	39.7	106.4	3122	57.6	68.5	184.1
Passat GLS V6/GLX Sedan	29	18	29	20	16.4	206@3200	190@6000	2.8	6	15	35.3	41.5	NA	NA	54.6	55.8	37.8	39.7	106.4	3245	57.6	68.5	184.1
Passat GLS Wagon	31	21	32	23	16.4	155@1750	150@5700	1.8	4	39	35.3	41.5	NA	NA	54.6	55.8	39.7	39.7	106.4	3201	59	68.5	183.8
Passat GLS V6/GLX Wagon	29	18	29	20	16.4	206@3200	190@6000	2.8	6	39	35.3	41.5	NA	NA	54.6	55.8	39.7	39.7	106.4	3201	59	68.5	183.8

VOLVO

	EPA Hwy (mpg) - Auto	EPA City (mpg) - Auto	EPA Hwy (mpg) - Manual	EPA City (mpg) - Manual	Fuel Capacity	Torque @ RPM	Horsepower @ RPM	Displacement (liters)	Number of Cylinders	Luggage Capacity (cu ft.)	Rear Leg Room (in.)	Front Leg Room (in.)	Rear Hip Room (in.)	Front Hip Room (in.)	Rear Shoulder Room (in.)	Front Shoulder Room (in.)	Rear Head Room (in.)	Front Head Room (in.)	Wheelbase (in.)	Curb Weight (lbs.)	Height (in.)	Width (in.)	Length (in.)
40-Series Sedan	NA	NA	NA	NA	15.8	170@1800	160@5100	1.9	4	14.8	32.7	41.4	51.7	51.7	54.1	54.1	37.2	38.7	100.5	2865	55.6	67.6	176.6
40-Series Wagon	NA	NA	NA	NA	15.8	170@1800	160@5100	1.9	4	33.5	32.7	41.4	51.7	51.7	54.1	54.1	37.2	38.7	100.5	2910	55.7	67.6	176.6

specifications

	70-Series AWD Sedan	70-Series Base Sedan	70-Series Base Wagon	70-Series GLT Sedan	70-Series GLT Wagon	70-Series HT Conv	70-Series HT Coupe	70-Series LT Conv	70-Series LT Coupe	70-Series R AWD Wagon
Length (in.)	185.9	185.9	186.2	185.9	186.2	185.7	185.7	185.7	185.7	186.2
Width (in.)	69.3	69.3	69.3	69.3	69.3	71.5	71.5	71.5	71.5	69.3
Height (in.)	56.5	55.2	56.2	55.2	56.2	56.3	55.7	56.3	55.7	57
Curb Weight (lbs.)	3206	3152	3259	3206	3307	3601	3601	3601	3365	NA
Wheelbase (in.)	104.5	104.9	104.9	104.9	104.9	104.9	104.9	104.9	104.9	104.5
Front Head Room (in.)	39.1	39.1	39.1	39.1	39.1	39	37.4	39	37.4	38.5
Rear Head Room (in.)	37.8	37.8	38	37.8	38	36.6	36.6	36.6	36.6	37.9
Front Shoulder Room (in.)	55.3	55.3	55.3	55.3	55.3	55.5	55.5	55.5	55.3	55.3
Rear Shoulder Room (in.)	57.4	57.2	57.3	57.2	57.3	44.9	52.2	44.9	52.2	57.5
Front Hip Room (in.)	55.2	55.2	55.2	55.2	NA	55.2	55.2	NA	55.2	55.2
Rear Hip Room (in.)	55.2	55.2	55.2	55.2	NA	55.2	55.2	NA	55.2	55.2
Front Leg Room (in.)	41.4	41.4	41.4	41.4	41.4	41.3	41.3	41.3	41.3	41.4
Rear Leg Room (in.)	35.2	35.2	35.2	35.2	35.2	34.6	34.6	34.6	34.6	35.2
Luggage Capacity (cu ft.)	15.1	15.1	37.2	15.1	37.2	7.9	13.1	7.9	13.1	37.2
Number of Cylinders	5	5	5	5	5	5	5	5	5	5
Displacement (liters)	2.4	2.4	2.4	2.4	2.4	2.3	2.3	2.4	2.4	2.3
Horsepower @ RPM	190@5100	168@6100	168@6100	190@5100	190@5100	236@5400	236@5400	190@5100	190@5100	236@5400
Torque @ RPM	199@1800	170@4700	170@4700	199@1800	199@1800	244@2400	244@2400	199@1800	199@1800	244@2400
Fuel Capacity	17.4	17.9	17.9	17.9	17.9	18.5	18.5	18.5	18.5	17.4
EPA City (mpg) - Manual	NA	NA	NA	NA	NA	20	20	NA	NA	NA
EPA Hwy (mpg) - Manual	NA	NA	NA	NA	NA	27	27	NA	NA	NA
EPA City (mpg) - Auto	18	NA	NA	19	19	19	19	19	19	18
EPA Hwy (mpg) - Auto	24	NA	NA	27	27	26	26	27	27	25

specifications

SPECIFICATIONS MILEAGE TABLES

	70-Series T5 Sedan	70-Series XC AWD Wagon	S80 2.9	S80 T6
EPA Hwy (mpg) - Auto	NA	24	27	27
EPA City (mpg) - Auto	NA	18	19	18
EPA Hwy (mpg) - Manual	25	NA	NA	NA
EPA City (mpg) - Manual	19	NA	NA	NA
Fuel Capacity	17.9	17.4	21.1	21.1
Torque @ RPM	244@ 2400	199@ 1800	207@ 4300	280@ 2000
Horsepower @ RPM	236@ 5400	190@ 5100	201 @ 6000	268@ 5400
Displacement (liters)	2.3	2.4	2.9	2.8
Number of Cylinders	5	5	6	6
Luggage Capacity (cu ft.)	15.1	37.2	14.2	14.2
Rear Leg Room (in.)	35.2	35.2	35.9	35.9
Front Leg Room (in.)	41.4	41.4	42.2	42.2
Rear Hip Room (in.)	55.2	55.2	NA	NA
Front Hip Room (in.)	55.2	55.2	NA	NA
Rear Shoulder Room (in.)	57.2	57.5	56.9	56.9
Front Shoulder Room (in.)	55.3	55.3	58	58
Rear Head Room (in.)	37.8	38	37.6	37.6
Front Head Room (in.)	39.1	39.1	38.9	38.9
Wheelbase (in.)	104.9	104.8	109.9	109.9
Curb Weight (lbs.)	3152	NA	3600	3600
Height (in.)	55.2	59.5	57.2	57.2
Width (in.)	69.3	69.3	72.1	72.1
Length (in.)	185.9	186.4	189.8	189.8

CRASH TEST DATA

In 1994, the National Highway Traffic Safety Administration (NHTSA — http://www.nhtsa.dot.gov) changed the way they rate frontal crash-test performances of the cars and trucks they run into a fixed barrier at 35 mph. Instead of the confusing numerical scale that had been in place for years, NHTSA decided to make the data more user-friendly for interested consumers by converting to a five-star rating system. This system is just like the one used by the movie reviewer in your local paper and the lucky folks AAA employs to travel around the world eating and sleeping in the best restaurants and hotels. Boy, they've got it rough, don't they?

For frontal-impact NHTSA crash tests, the scale is as follows:

1 Star	46 percent or better chance of life-threatening injury
2 Stars	a 36-45 percent chance of life-threatening injury
3 Stars	a 21-35 percent chance of life-threatening injury
4 Stars	a 11-20 percent chance of life-threatening injury
5 Stars	10 percent or less chance of life-threatening injury

We convert the NHTSA scale as follows:

1 Star	Very Poor
2 Stars	Poor
3 Stars	Average
4 Stars	Good
5 Stars	Excellent

In 1997, NHTSA began testing side-impact protection as well as frontal-impact protection. For side-impact testing, NHTSA runs a deformable barrier into the side of a car twice, once at the front passenger's level and once at the rear passenger's level. As with frontal-impact testing, the side-impact test is conducted at 5 mph above the federal standard, which means the deformable barrier hits the car at 38 mph.

For side-impact NHTSA crash tests, the scale is as follows:

1 Star	26 percent or better chance of life-threatening injury
2 Stars	a 21-25 percent chance of life-threatening injury
3 Stars	a 11-20 percent chance of life-threatening injury
4 Stars	a 6-10 percent chance of life-threatening injury
5 Stars	5 percent or less chance of life-threatening injury

CRASH TEST DATA

We convert the NHTSA scale as follows:

1 Star	Very Poor
2 Stars	Poor
3 Stars	Average
4 Stars	Good
5 Stars	Excellent

The Insurance Institute for Highway Safety (IIHS — http://www.hwysafety.org) began conducting offset frontal crash tests in 1995. The offset test is conducted at 40 mph, and vehicles crash into a fixed barrier just like in the NHTSA testing, but only half of the front of the vehicle contacts the barrier. The IIHS claims this test, at this speed, more accurately reflects the most deadly real-world crash situations. Offset crash tests do not conform to the scale listed above. Instead, the IIHS rates a vehicle good, acceptable, marginal or poor. There are currently no federally mandated offset crash standards that automakers must meet by law.

The IIHS also conducts bumper-bashing tests. They run cars and trucks into barriers at 5 mph to see how much damage results, in terms of dollars. Front ends are smacked into flat and angled barriers, and they back vehicles into poles and angled barriers. Each vehicle is crashed four times; the lower the total cost for repair after all four tests, the better the vehicle scores. Federal law requires bumpers on passenger cars that can withstand an impact at 2.5 mph. Light trucks are not required to meet bumper-strength standards.

Following are the results of crash testing conducted since 1994, presented in alphabetical order by make and model. All test results are applicable to the 2000 equivalent of the listed model, with one caveat. Most of the models tested before 1998 come equipped with depowered airbags now, and until the vehicle is re-tested by NHTSA, it is unknown how the presence of a depowered airbag will affect occupant safety.

Crash Scores for 2000 Cars and Trucks

Acura Integra

NHTSA Frontal Crash Driver	Good
NHTSA Frontal Crash Passenger	Average
NHTSA Side Crash Front Occupant	Not Tested
NHTSA Side Crash Rear Occupant	Not Tested
IIHS Offset	Not Tested
IIHS Bumper Bash	Not Tested

CRASH TEST DATA

Acura RL
- NHTSA Frontal Crash Driver — Good
- NHTSA Frontal Crash Passenger — Good
- NHTSA Side Crash Front Occupant — Not Tested
- NHTSA Side Crash Rear Occupant — Not Tested
- IIHS Offset — Not Tested
- IIHS Bumper Bash — Not Tested

Audi A4
- NHTSA Frontal Crash Driver — Good
- NHTSA Frontal Crash Passenger — Excellent
- NHTSA Side Crash Front Occupant — Not Tested
- NHTSA Side Crash Rear Occupant — Not Tested
- IIHS Offset — Not Tested
- IIHS Bumper Bash — Not Tested

Audi A8
- NHTSA Frontal Crash Driver — Excellent
- NHTSA Frontal Crash Passenger — Excellent
- NHTSA Side Crash Front Occupant — Not Tested
- NHTSA Side Crash Rear Occupant — Not Tested
- IIHS Offset — Not Tested
- IIHS Bumper Bash — Not Tested

Audi S4
- NHTSA Frontal Crash Driver — Good
- NHTSA Frontal Crash Passenger — Excellent
- NHTSA Side Crash Front Occupant — Not Tested
- NHTSA Side Crash Rear Occupant — Not Tested
- IIHS Offset — Not Tested
- IIHS Bumper Bash — Not Tested

BMW 5 Series
- NHTSA Frontal Crash Driver — Not Tested
- NHTSA Frontal Crash Passenger — Not Tested
- NHTSA Side Crash Front Occupant — Not Tested
- NHTSA Side Crash Rear Occupant — Not Tested
- IIHS Offset — Good
- IIHS Bumper Bash — Poor

BMW X5
- NHTSA Frontal Crash Driver — Excellent
- NHTSA Frontal Crash Passenger — Excellent
- NHTSA Side Crash Front Occupant — Not Tested
- NHTSA Side Crash Rear Occupant — Not Tested
- IIHS Offset — Not Tested
- IIHS Bumper Bash — Not Tested

Buick Century
- NHTSA Frontal Crash Driver — Good
- NHTSA Frontal Crash Passenger — Average

CRASH TEST DATA

NHTSA Side Crash Front Occupant	Average
NHTSA Side Crash Rear Occupant	Average
IIHS Offset	Acceptable
IIHS Bumper Bash	Acceptable
Buick Regal	
NHTSA Frontal Crash Driver	Good
NHTSA Frontal Crash Passenger	Average
NHTSA Side Crash Front Occupant	Average
NHTSA Side Crash Rear Occupant	Average
IIHS Offset	Acceptable
IIHS Bumper Bash	Acceptable
Cadillac Escalade	
NHTSA Frontal Crash Driver	Good
NHTSA Frontal Crash Passenger	Good
NHTSA Side Crash Front Occupant	Not Tested
NHTSA Side Crash Rear Occupant	Not Tested
IIHS Offset	Not Tested
IIHS Bumper Bash	Not Tested
Cadillac Eldorado	
NHTSA Frontal Crash Driver	Good
NHTSA Frontal Crash Passenger	Good
NHTSA Side Crash Front Occupant	Not Tested
NHTSA Side Crash Rear Occupant	Not Tested
IIHS Offset	Not Tested
IIHS Bumper Bash	Not Tested
Chevrolet Astro	
NHTSA Frontal Crash Driver	Average
NHTSA Frontal Crash Passenger	Good
NHTSA Side Crash Front Occupant	Not Tested
NHTSA Side Crash Rear Occupant	Not Tested
IIHS Offset	Poor
IIHS Bumper Bash	Poor
Chevrolet Blazer	
NHTSA Frontal Crash Driver	Average
NHTSA Frontal Crash Passenger	Good
NHTSA Side Crash Front Occupant	Excellent
NHTSA Side Crash Rear Occupant	Excellent
IIHS Offset	Poor
IIHS Bumper Bash	Poor
Chevrolet Camaro	
NHTSA Frontal Crash Driver	Good
NHTSA Frontal Crash Passenger	Excellent
NHTSA Side Crash Front Occupant	Average
NHTSA Side Crash Rear Occupant	Good

CRASH TEST DATA

IIHS Offset	Not Tested
IIHS Bumper Bash	Not Tested

Chevrolet Cavalier

NHTSA Frontal Crash Driver	Average (Cpe.); Good (Sdn.)
NHTSA Frontal Crash Passenger	Good
NHTSA Side Crash Front Occupant	Very Poor
NHTSA Side Crash Rear Occupant	Poor (Cpe.); Average (Sdn.)
IIHS Offset	Poor
IIHS Bumper Bash	Acceptable

Chevrolet Impala

NHTSA Frontal Crash Driver	Excellent
NHTSA Frontal Crash Passenger	Excellent
NHTSA Side Crash Front Occupant	Not Tested
NHTSA Side Crash Rear Occupant	Not Tested
IIHS Offset	Not Tested
IIHS Bumper Bash	Not Tested

Chevrolet Lumina

NHTSA Frontal Crash Driver	Good
NHTSA Frontal Crash Passenger	Excellent
NHTSA Side Crash Front Occupant	Good
NHTSA Side Crash Rear Occupant	Average
IIHS Offset	Good
IIHS Bumper Bash	Marginal

Chevrolet Malibu

NHTSA Frontal Crash Driver	Good
NHTSA Frontal Crash Passenger	Good
NHTSA Side Crash Front Occupant	Very Poor
NHTSA Side Crash Rear Occupant	Average
IIHS Offset	Not Tested
IIHS Bumper Bash	Not Tested

Chevrolet Metro

NHTSA Frontal Crash Driver	Good
NHTSA Frontal Crash Passenger	Good
NHTSA Side Crash Front Occupant	Not Tested
NHTSA Side Crash Rear Occupant	Not Tested
IIHS Offset	Not Tested
IIHS Bumper Bash	Not Tested

Chevrolet Prizm

NHTSA Frontal Crash Driver	Good
NHTSA Frontal Crash Passenger	Good
NHTSA Side Crash Front Occupant	Average (w/o side airbag); Good (w/side airbag)
NHTSA Side Crash Rear Occupant	Average
IIHS Offset	Acceptable
IIHS Bumper Bash	Good

CRASH TEST DATA

Chevrolet S-10 Pickup

NHTSA Frontal Crash Driver	Poor
NHTSA Frontal Crash Passenger	Average
NHTSA Side Crash Front Occupant	Average
NHTSA Side Crash Rear Occupant	Not Applicable
IIHS Offset	Marginal
IIHS Bumper Bash	Marginal

Chevrolet Tahoe (Limited and Z71 only)

NHTSA Frontal Crash Driver	Good
NHTSA Frontal Crash Passenger	Good
NHTSA Side Crash Front Occupant	Not Tested
NHTSA Side Crash Rear Occupant	Not Tested
IIHS Offset	Not Tested
IIHS Bumper Bash	Not Tested

Chevrolet Tracker

NHTSA Frontal Crash Driver	Not Tested
NHTSA Frontal Crash Passenger	Not Tested
NHTSA Side Crash Front Occupant	Not Tested
NHTSA Side Crash Rear Occupant	Not Tested
IIHS Offset	Acceptable (4-door)
IIHS Bumper Bash	Poor

Chevrolet Venture

NHTSA Frontal Crash Driver	Good
NHTSA Frontal Crash Passenger	Average
NHTSA Side Crash Front Occupant	Excellent
NHTSA Side Crash Rear Occupant	Excellent
IIHS Offset	Poor
IIHS Bumper Bash	Poor

Chrysler 300M

NHTSA Frontal Crash Driver	Good
NHTSA Frontal Crash Passenger	Good
NHTSA Side Crash Front Occupant	Good
NHTSA Side Crash Rear Occupant	Average
IIHS Offset	Not Tested
IIHS Bumper Bash	Not Tested

Chrysler Cirrus

NHTSA Frontal Crash Driver	Average
NHTSA Frontal Crash Passenger	Good
NHTSA Side Crash Front Occupant	Average
NHTSA Side Crash Rear Occupant	Poor
IIHS Offset	Poor
IIHS Bumper Bash	Marginal

Chrysler Concorde

NHTSA Frontal Crash Driver	Good
NHTSA Frontal Crash Passenger	Good

CRASH TEST DATA

NHTSA Side Crash Front Occupant	Good
NHTSA Side Crash Rear Occupant	Average
IIHS Offset	Not Tested
IIHS Bumper Bash	Not Tested
Chrysler LHS	
NHTSA Frontal Crash Driver	Good
NHTSA Frontal Crash Passenger	Good
NHTSA Side Crash Front Occupant	Good
NHTSA Side Crash Rear Occupant	Average
IIHS Offset	Not Tested
IIHS Bumper Bash	Not Tested
Chrysler Sebring Convertible	
NHTSA Frontal Crash Driver	Good
NHTSA Frontal Crash Passenger	Good
NHTSA Side Crash Front Occupant	Not Tested
NHTSA Side Crash Rear Occupant	Not Tested
IIHS Offset	Not Tested
IIHS Bumper Bash	Not Tested
Chrysler Sebring Coupe	
NHTSA Frontal Crash Driver	Excellent
NHTSA Frontal Crash Passenger	Excellent
NHTSA Side Crash Front Occupant	Not Tested
NHTSA Side Crash Rear Occupant	Not Tested
IIHS Offset	Not Tested
IIHS Bumper Bash	Not Tested
Chrysler Town and Country	
NHTSA Frontal Crash Driver	Good
NHTSA Frontal Crash Passenger	Good
NHTSA Side Crash Front Occupant	Excellent
NHTSA Side Crash Rear Occupant	Average
IIHS Offset	Marginal
IIHS Bumper Bash	Poor
Dodge Avenger	
NHTSA Frontal Crash Driver	Excellent
NHTSA Frontal Crash Passenger	Excellent
NHTSA Side Crash Front Occupant	Not Tested
NHTSA Side Crash Rear Occupant	Not Tested
IIHS Offset	Not Tested
IIHS Bumper Bash	Not Tested
Dodge Dakota	
NHTSA Frontal Crash Driver	Good
NHTSA Frontal Crash Passenger	Good
NHTSA Side Crash Front Occupant	Excellent
NHTSA Side Crash Rear Occupant	Not Applicable

CRASH TEST DATA

IIHS Offset	Poor
IIHS Bumper Bash	Poor

Dodge Durango

NHTSA Frontal Crash Driver	Poor
NHTSA Frontal Crash Passenger	Good
NHTSA Side Crash Front Occupant	Not Tested
NHTSA Side Crash Rear Occupant	Not Tested
IIHS Offset	Acceptable
IIHS Bumper Bash	Poor

Dodge Grand Caravan

NHTSA Frontal Crash Driver	Good
NHTSA Frontal Crash Passenger	Good
NHTSA Side Crash Front Occupant	Excellent
NHTSA Side Crash Rear Occupant	Average
IIHS Offset	Marginal
IIHS Bumper Bash	Poor

Dodge Intrepid

NHTSA Frontal Crash Driver	Good
NHTSA Frontal Crash Passenger	Good
NHTSA Side Crash Front Occupant	Good
NHTSA Side Crash Rear Occupant	Average
IIHS Offset	Not Tested
IIHS Bumper Bash	Not Tested

Dodge Neon

NHTSA Frontal Crash Driver	Not Tested
NHTSA Frontal Crash Passenger	Not Tested
NHTSA Side Crash Front Occupant	Not Tested
NHTSA Side Crash Rear Occupant	Not Tested
IIHS Offset	Marginal
IIHS Bumper Bash	Acceptable

Dodge Ram Pickup

NHTSA Frontal Crash Driver	Good (X-cab); Avg. (Quad Cab)
NHTSA Frontal Crash Passenger	Good
NHTSA Side Crash Front Occupant	Not Tested
NHTSA Side Crash Rear Occupant	Not Tested
IIHS Offset	Not Tested
IIHS Bumper Bash	Not Tested

Dodge Stratus

NHTSA Frontal Crash Driver	Average
NHTSA Frontal Crash Passenger	Good
NHTSA Side Crash Front Occupant	Average
NHTSA Side Crash Rear Occupant	Poor
IIHS Offset	Poor
IIHS Bumper Bash	Marginal

CRASH TEST DATA

Ford Contour
NHTSA Frontal Crash Driver	Excellent
NHTSA Frontal Crash Passenger	Good
NHTSA Side Crash Front Occupant	Average
NHTSA Side Crash Rear Occupant	Good
IIHS Offset	Poor
IIHS Bumper Bash	Poor

Ford Crown Victoria
NHTSA Frontal Crash Driver	Excellent
NHTSA Frontal Crash Passenger	Excellent
NHTSA Side Crash Front Occupant	Good
NHTSA Side Crash Rear Occupant	Good
IIHS Offset	Not Tested
IIHS Bumper Bash	Not Tested

Ford Econoline
NHTSA Frontal Crash Driver	Good
NHTSA Frontal Crash Passenger	Good
NHTSA Side Crash Front Occupant	Not Tested
NHTSA Side Crash Rear Occupant	Not Tested
IIHS Offset	Not Tested
IIHS Bumper Bash	Not Tested

Ford Escort
NHTSA Frontal Crash Driver	Average
NHTSA Frontal Crash Passenger	Average
NHTSA Side Crash Front Occupant	Average
NHTSA Side Crash Rear Occupant	Average
IIHS Offset	Acceptable
IIHS Bumper Bash	Acceptable

Ford Escort ZX2
NHTSA Frontal Crash Driver	Not Tested
NHTSA Frontal Crash Passenger	Not Tested
NHTSA Side Crash Front Occupant	Very Poor
NHTSA Side Crash Rear Occupant	Good
IIHS Offset	Not Tested
IIHS Bumper Bash	Not Tested

Ford Expedition
NHTSA Frontal Crash Driver	Good
NHTSA Frontal Crash Passenger	Good
NHTSA Side Crash Front Occupant	Not Tested
NHTSA Side Crash Rear Occupant	Not Tested
IIHS Offset	Not Tested
IIHS Bumper Bash	Not Tested

Ford Explorer
NHTSA Frontal Crash Driver	Good
NHTSA Frontal Crash Passenger	Good

CRASH TEST DATA

NHTSA Side Crash Front Occupant	Excellent
NHTSA Side Crash Rear Occupant	Excellent
IIHS Offset	Acceptable
IIHS Bumper Bash	Poor

Ford F-150

NHTSA Frontal Crash Driver	Good
NHTSA Frontal Crash Passenger	Good
NHTSA Side Crash Front Occupant	Excellent
NHTSA Side Crash Rear Occupant	Not Tested
IIHS Offset	Not Tested
IIHS Bumper Bash	Not Tested

Ford Mustang

NHTSA Frontal Crash Driver	Good
NHTSA Frontal Crash Passenger	Good
NHTSA Side Crash Front Occupant	Average
NHTSA Side Crash Rear Occupant	Average
IIHS Offset	Not Tested
IIHS Bumper Bash	Not Tested

Ford Ranger

NHTSA Frontal Crash Driver	Good
NHTSA Frontal Crash Passenger	Good
NHTSA Side Crash Front Occupant	Excellent
NHTSA Side Crash Rear Occupant	Not Applicable
IIHS Offset	Acceptable
IIHS Bumper Bash	Marginal

Ford Taurus

NHTSA Frontal Crash Driver	Excellent
NHTSA Frontal Crash Passenger	Excellent
NHTSA Side Crash Front Occupant	Average
NHTSA Side Crash Rear Occupant	Average
IIHS Offset	Good
IIHS Bumper Bash	Good

Ford Windstar

NHTSA Frontal Crash Driver	Excellent
NHTSA Frontal Crash Passenger	Excellent
NHTSA Side Crash Front Occupant	Excellent
NHTSA Side Crash Rear Occupant	Excellent
IIHS Offset	Good
IIHS Bumper Bash	Acceptable

GMC Envoy

NHTSA Frontal Crash Driver	Average
NHTSA Frontal Crash Passenger	Good
NHTSA Side Crash Front Occupant	Excellent
NHTSA Side Crash Rear Occupant	Excellent

CRASH TEST DATA

IIHS Offset	Poor
IIHS Bumper Bash	Poor

GMC Jimmy

NHTSA Frontal Crash Driver	Average
NHTSA Frontal Crash Passenger	Good
NHTSA Side Crash Front Occupant	Excellent
NHTSA Side Crash Rear Occupant	Excellent
IIHS Offset	Poor
IIHS Bumper Bash	Poor

GMC Safari

NHTSA Frontal Crash Driver	Average
NHTSA Frontal Crash Passenger	Good
NHTSA Side Crash Front Occupant	Not Tested
NHTSA Side Crash Rear Occupant	Not Tested
IIHS Offset	Poor
IIHS Bumper Bash	Poor

GMC Sonoma

NHTSA Frontal Crash Driver	Poor
NHTSA Frontal Crash Passenger	Average
NHTSA Side Crash Front Occupant	Average
NHTSA Side Crash Rear Occupant	Not Applicable
IIHS Offset	Marginal
IIHS Bumper Bash	Marginal

GMC Yukon Denali

NHTSA Frontal Crash Driver	Good
NHTSA Frontal Crash Passenger	Good
NHTSA Side Crash Front Occupant	Not Tested
NHTSA Side Crash Rear Occupant	Not Tested
IIHS Offset	Not Tested
IIHS Bumper Bash	Not Tested

Honda Accord

NHTSA Frontal Crash Driver	Good
NHTSA Frontal Crash Passenger	Good
NHTSA Side Crash Front Occupant	Average (Cpe.); Good (Sdn.)
NHTSA Side Crash Rear Occupant	Good
IIHS Offset	Acceptable
IIHS Bumper Bash	Acceptable

Honda Civic

NHTSA Frontal Crash Driver	Good
NHTSA Frontal Crash Passenger	Good
NHTSA Side Crash Front Occupant	Poor (Coupe); Average (Sedan)
NHTSA Side Crash Rear Occupant	Average
IIHS Offset	Acceptable
IIHS Bumper Bash	Acceptable

CRASH TEST DATA

Honda CR-V

NHTSA Frontal Crash Driver	Good
NHTSA Frontal Crash Passenger	Excellent
NHTSA Side Crash Front Occupant	Excellent*
NHTSA Side Crash Rear Occupant	Excellent*
IIHS Offset	Marginal
IIHS Bumper Bash	Poor

*Note — CR-V rolled one-quarter turn in side-impact testing.

Honda Odyssey

NHTSA Frontal Crash Driver	Excellent
NHTSA Frontal Crash Passenger	Excellent
NHTSA Side Crash Front Occupant	Excellent
NHTSA Side Crash Rear Occupant	Excellent
IIHS Offset	Good
IIHS Bumper Bash	Acceptable

Honda Passport

NHTSA Frontal Crash Driver	Average
NHTSA Frontal Crash Passenger	Good
NHTSA Side Crash Front Occupant	Excellent*
NHTSA Side Crash Rear Occupant	Excellent*
IIHS Offset	Not Tested
IIHS Bumper Bash	Poor

*Note — Passport rolled one-quarter turn in side-impact testing.

Hyundai Elantra

NHTSA Frontal Crash Driver	Average
NHTSA Frontal Crash Passenger	Average
NHTSA Side Crash Front Occupant	Not Tested
NHTSA Side Crash Rear Occupant	Not Tested
IIHS Offset	Acceptable
IIHS Bumper Bash	Poor

Hyundai Sonata

NHTSA Frontal Crash Driver	Not Tested
NHTSA Frontal Crash Passenger	Not Tested
NHTSA Side Crash Front Occupant	Not Tested
NHTSA Side Crash Rear Occupant	Not Tested
IIHS Offset	Acceptable
IIHS Bumper Bash	Marginal

Infiniti Q45

NHTSA Frontal Crash Driver	Not Tested
NHTSA Frontal Crash Passenger	Not Tested
NHTSA Side Crash Front Occupant	Not Tested
NHTSA Side Crash Rear Occupant	Not Tested
IIHS Offset	Marginal
IIHS Bumper Bash	Poor

CRASH TEST DATA

Infiniti QX4
- NHTSA Frontal Crash Driver — Good
- NHTSA Frontal Crash Passenger — Excellent
- NHTSA Side Crash Front Occupant — Excellent
- NHTSA Side Crash Rear Occupant — Excellent
- IIHS Offset — Marginal
- IIHS Bumper Bash — Poor

Isuzu Amigo
- NHTSA Frontal Crash Driver — Not Tested
- NHTSA Frontal Crash Passenger — Not Tested
- NHTSA Side Crash Front Occupant — Not Tested
- NHTSA Side Crash Rear Occupant — Not Tested
- IIHS Offset — Poor
- IIHS Bumper Bash — Poor

Isuzu Hombre
- NHTSA Frontal Crash Driver — Poor
- NHTSA Frontal Crash Passenger — Average
- NHTSA Side Crash Front Occupant — Average
- NHTSA Side Crash Rear Occupant — Not Applicable
- IIHS Offset — Marginal
- IIHS Bumper Bash — Marginal

Isuzu Rodeo
- NHTSA Frontal Crash Driver — Average
- NHTSA Frontal Crash Passenger — Good
- NHTSA Side Crash Front Occupant — Excellent*
- NHTSA Side Crash Rear Occupant — Excellent*
- IIHS Offset — Not Tested
- IIHS Bumper Bash — Poor

*Note — Rodeo rolled one-quarter turn in side-impact testing.

Isuzu Trooper
- NHTSA Frontal Crash Driver — Average
- NHTSA Frontal Crash Passenger — Average
- NHTSA Side Crash Front Occupant — Not Tested
- NHTSA Side Crash Rear Occupant — Not Tested
- IIHS Offset — Not Tested
- IIHS Bumper Bash — Not Tested

Jeep Cherokee
- NHTSA Frontal Crash Driver — Average
- NHTSA Frontal Crash Passenger — Average
- NHTSA Side Crash Front Occupant — Average
- NHTSA Side Crash Rear Occupant — Excellent
- IIHS Offset — Marginal
- IIHS Bumper Bash — Poor

CRASH TEST DATA

Jeep Grand Cherokee
NHTSA Frontal Crash Driver	Average
NHTSA Frontal Crash Passenger	Average
NHTSA Side Crash Front Occupant	Good
NHTSA Side Crash Rear Occupant	Excellent
IIHS Offset	Marginal
IIHS Bumper Bash	Poor

Jeep Wrangler
NHTSA Frontal Crash Driver	Good
NHTSA Frontal Crash Passenger	Good
NHTSA Side Crash Front Occupant	Not Tested
NHTSA Side Crash Rear Occupant	Not Tested
IIHS Offset	Acceptable
IIHS Bumper Bash	Marginal

Kia Sephia
NHTSA Frontal Crash Driver	Not Tested
NHTSA Frontal Crash Passenger	Not Tested
NHTSA Side Crash Front Occupant	Not Tested
NHTSA Side Crash Rear Occupant	Not Tested
IIHS Offset	Poor
IIHS Bumper Bash	Marginal

Kia Sportage
NHTSA Frontal Crash Driver	Average
NHTSA Frontal Crash Passenger	Average
NHTSA Side Crash Front Occupant	Not Tested
NHTSA Side Crash Rear Occupant	Not Tested
IIHS Offset	Marginal (4-door)
IIHS Bumper Bash	Poor

Land Rover Discovery Series II
NHTSA Frontal Crash Driver	Not Tested
NHTSA Frontal Crash Passenger	Not Tested
NHTSA Side Crash Front Occupant	Not Tested
NHTSA Side Crash Rear Occupant	Not Tested
IIHS Offset	Acceptable
IIHS Bumper Bash	Poor

Lexus ES 300
NHTSA Frontal Crash Driver	Good
NHTSA Frontal Crash Passenger	Good
NHTSA Side Crash Front Occupant	Excellent
NHTSA Side Crash Rear Occupant	Good
IIHS Offset	Not Tested
IIHS Bumper Bash	Not Tested

Lexus LS 400
NHTSA Frontal Crash Driver	Not Tested
NHTSA Frontal Crash Passenger	Not Tested

CRASH TEST DATA

NHTSA Side Crash Front Occupant	Not Tested
NHTSA Side Crash Rear Occupant	Not Tested
IIHS Offset	Good
IIHS Bumper Bash	Poor

Lexus RX 300
NHTSA Frontal Crash Driver	Not Tested
NHTSA Frontal Crash Passenger	Not Tested
NHTSA Side Crash Front Occupant	Not Tested
NHTSA Side Crash Rear Occupant	Not Tested
IIHS Offset	Good
IIHS Bumper Bash	Poor

Lincoln Continental
NHTSA Frontal Crash Driver	Not Tested
NHTSA Frontal Crash Passenger	Not Tested
NHTSA Side Crash Front Occupant	Not Tested
NHTSA Side Crash Rear Occupant	Not Tested
IIHS Offset	Acceptable
IIHS Bumper Bash	Good

Lincoln Navigator
NHTSA Frontal Crash Driver	Good
NHTSA Frontal Crash Passenger	Good
NHTSA Side Crash Front Occupant	Not Tested
NHTSA Side Crash Rear Occupant	Not Tested
IIHS Offset	Not Tested
IIHS Bumper Bash	Not Tested

Lincoln Town Car
NHTSA Frontal Crash Driver	Not Tested
NHTSA Frontal Crash Passenger	Not Tested
NHTSA Side Crash Front Occupant	Good
NHTSA Side Crash Rear Occupant	Good
IIHS Offset	Not Tested
IIHS Bumper Bash	Not Tested

Mazda 626
NHTSA Frontal Crash Driver	Good
NHTSA Frontal Crash Passenger	Excellent
NHTSA Side Crash Front Occupant	Average
NHTSA Side Crash Rear Occupant	Average
IIHS Offset	Not Tested
IIHS Bumper Bash	Not Tested

Mazda B-Series Pickup
NHTSA Frontal Crash Driver	Good
NHTSA Frontal Crash Passenger	Good
NHTSA Side Crash Front Occupant	Excellent
NHTSA Side Crash Rear Occupant	Not Applicable

CRASH TEST DATA

IIHS Offset	Acceptable
IIHS Bumper Bash	Marginal
Mazda Millenia	
NHTSA Frontal Crash Driver	Good
NHTSA Frontal Crash Passenger	Excellent
NHTSA Side Crash Front Occupant	Not Tested
NHTSA Side Crash Rear Occupant	Not Tested
IIHS Offset	Acceptable
IIHS Bumper Bash	Marginal
Mazda Protege	
NHTSA Frontal Crash Driver	Good
NHTSA Frontal Crash Passenger	Good
NHTSA Side Crash Front Occupant	Average
NHTSA Side Crash Rear Occupant	Good
IIHS Offset	Acceptable
IIHS Bumper Bash	Poor
Mercedes-Benz C-Class	
NHTSA Frontal Crash Driver	Good
NHTSA Frontal Crash Passenger	Good
NHTSA Side Crash Front Occupant	Average
NHTSA Side Crash Rear Occupant	Good
IIHS Offset	Not Tested
IIHS Bumper Bash	Not Tested
Mercedes-Benz E-Class	
NHTSA Frontal Crash Driver	Not Tested
NHTSA Frontal Crash Passenger	Not Tested
NHTSA Side Crash Front Occupant	Not Tested
NHTSA Side Crash Rear Occupant	Not Tested
IIHS Offset	Acceptable
IIHS Bumper Bash	Poor
Mercedes-Benz M-Class	
NHTSA Frontal Crash Driver	Not Tested
NHTSA Frontal Crash Passenger	Not Tested
NHTSA Side Crash Front Occupant	Not Tested
NHTSA Side Crash Rear Occupant	Not Tested
IIHS Offset	Good
IIHS Bumper Bash	Marginal
Mercury Grand Marquis	
NHTSA Frontal Crash Driver	Excellent
NHTSA Frontal Crash Passenger	Excellent
NHTSA Side Crash Front Occupant	Good
NHTSA Side Crash Rear Occupant	Good
IIHS Offset	Not Tested
IIHS Bumper Bash	Not Tested

CRASH TEST DATA

Mercury Mountaineer
- NHTSA Frontal Crash Driver — Good
- NHTSA Frontal Crash Passenger — Good
- NHTSA Side Crash Front Occupant — Excellent
- NHTSA Side Crash Rear Occupant — Excellent
- IIHS Offset — Acceptable
- IIHS Bumper Bash — Poor

Mercury Mystique
- NHTSA Frontal Crash Driver — Excellent
- NHTSA Frontal Crash Passenger — Good
- NHTSA Side Crash Front Occupant — Average
- NHTSA Side Crash Rear Occupant — Good
- IIHS Offset — Poor
- IIHS Bumper Bash — Poor

Mercury Sable
- NHTSA Frontal Crash Driver — Excellent
- NHTSA Frontal Crash Passenger — Excellent
- NHTSA Side Crash Front Occupant — Average
- NHTSA Side Crash Rear Occupant — Average
- IIHS Offset — Good
- IIHS Bumper Bash — Good

Mercury Villager
- NHTSA Frontal Crash Driver — Not Tested
- NHTSA Frontal Crash Passenger — Not Tested
- NHTSA Side Crash Front Occupant — Not Tested
- NHTSA Side Crash Rear Occupant — Not Tested
- IIHS Offset — Poor
- IIHS Bumper Bash — Good

Mitsubishi Galant
- NHTSA Frontal Crash Driver — Good
- NHTSA Frontal Crash Passenger — Good
- NHTSA Side Crash Front Occupant — Excellent
- NHTSA Side Crash Rear Occupant — Good
- IIHS Offset — Acceptable
- IIHS Bumper Bash — Acceptable

Mitsubishi Mirage
- NHTSA Frontal Crash Driver — Not Tested
- NHTSA Frontal Crash Passenger — Not Tested
- NHTSA Side Crash Front Occupant — Not Tested
- NHTSA Side Crash Rear Occupant — Not Tested
- IIHS Offset — Poor
- IIHS Bumper Bash — Marginal

Mitsubishi Montero
- NHTSA Frontal Crash Driver — Not Tested
- NHTSA Frontal Crash Passenger — Not Tested

CRASH TEST DATA

NHTSA Side Crash Front Occupant	Not Tested
NHTSA Side Crash Rear Occupant	Not Tested
IIHS Offset	Acceptable
IIHS Bumper Bash	Poor
Mitsubishi Montero Sport	
NHTSA Frontal Crash Driver	Average
NHTSA Frontal Crash Passenger	Average
NHTSA Side Crash Front Occupant	Not Tested
NHTSA Side Crash Rear Occupant	Not Tested
IIHS Offset	Poor
IIHS Bumper Bash	Poor
Nissan Altima	
NHTSA Frontal Crash Driver	Average
NHTSA Frontal Crash Passenger	Average
NHTSA Side Crash Front Occupant	Average
NHTSA Side Crash Rear Occupant	Average
IIHS Offset	Not Tested
IIHS Bumper Bash	Not Tested
Nissan Frontier	
NHTSA Frontal Crash Driver	Average
NHTSA Frontal Crash Passenger	Good
NHTSA Side Crash Front Occupant	Good
NHTSA Side Crash Rear Occupant	Not Applicable
IIHS Offset	Poor
IIHS Bumper Bash	Poor
Nissan Pathfinder	
NHTSA Frontal Crash Driver	Good
NHTSA Frontal Crash Passenger	Excellent
NHTSA Side Crash Front Occupant	Excellent
NHTSA Side Crash Rear Occupant	Excellent
IIHS Offset	Marginal
IIHS Bumper Bash	Poor
Nissan Quest	
NHTSA Frontal Crash Driver	Not Tested
NHTSA Frontal Crash Passenger	Not Tested
NHTSA Side Crash Front Occupant	Not Tested
NHTSA Side Crash Rear Occupant	Not Tested
IIHS Offset	Poor
IIHS Bumper Bash	Good
Oldsmobile Alero	
NHTSA Frontal Crash Driver	Good
NHTSA Frontal Crash Passenger	Good
NHTSA Side Crash Front Occupant	Average (Sedan)
NHTSA Side Crash Rear Occupant	Average (Sedan)

484   www.edmunds.com   **EDMUND'S® NEW CARS**

CRASH TEST DATA

IIHS Offset	Not Tested
IIHS Bumper Bash	Not Tested
Oldsmobile Bravada	
NHTSA Frontal Crash Driver	Average
NHTSA Frontal Crash Passenger	Good
NHTSA Side Crash Front Occupant	Excellent
NHTSA Side Crash Rear Occupant	Excellent
IIHS Offset	Poor
IIHS Bumper Bash	Poor
Oldsmobile Intrigue	
NHTSA Frontal Crash Driver	Good
NHTSA Frontal Crash Passenger	Poor
NHTSA Side Crash Front Occupant	Average
NHTSA Side Crash Rear Occupant	Very Poor
IIHS Offset	Acceptable
IIHS Bumper Bash	Acceptable
Oldsmobile Silhouette	
NHTSA Frontal Crash Driver	Good
NHTSA Frontal Crash Passenger	Average
NHTSA Side Crash Front Occupant	Excellent
NHTSA Side Crash Rear Occupant	Excellent
IIHS Offset	Poor
IIHS Bumper Bash	Poor
Plymouth Breeze	
NHTSA Frontal Crash Driver	Average
NHTSA Frontal Crash Passenger	Good
NHTSA Side Crash Front Occupant	Average
NHTSA Side Crash Rear Occupant	Poor
IIHS Offset	Poor
IIHS Bumper Bash	Marginal
Plymouth Grand Voyager	
NHTSA Frontal Crash Driver	Good
NHTSA Frontal Crash Passenger	Good
NHTSA Side Crash Front Occupant	Excellent
NHTSA Side Crash Rear Occupant	Average
IIHS Offset	Marginal
IIHS Bumper Bash	Poor
Plymouth Neon	
NHTSA Frontal Crash Driver	Not Tested
NHTSA Frontal Crash Passenger	Not Tested
NHTSA Side Crash Front Occupant	Not Tested
NHTSA Side Crash Rear Occupant	Not Tested
IIHS Offset	Marginal
IIHS Bumper Bash	Acceptable

EDMUND'S® NEW CARS

CRASH TEST DATA

Pontiac Firebird

NHTSA Frontal Crash Driver	Good
NHTSA Frontal Crash Passenger	Excellent
NHTSA Side Crash Front Occupant	Average
NHTSA Side Crash Rear Occupant	Good
IIHS Offset	Not Tested
IIHS Bumper Bash	Not Tested

Pontiac Grand Am

NHTSA Frontal Crash Driver	Good
NHTSA Frontal Crash Passenger	Good
NHTSA Side Crash Front Occupant	Average (Sedan)
NHTSA Side Crash Rear Occupant	Average (Sedan)
IIHS Offset	Not Tested
IIHS Bumper Bash	Not Tested

Pontiac Grand Prix

NHTSA Frontal Crash Driver	Good
NHTSA Frontal Crash Passenger	Good
NHTSA Side Crash Front Occupant	Not Tested
NHTSA Side Crash Rear Occupant	Not Tested
IIHS Offset	Acceptable
IIHS Bumper Bash	Acceptable

Pontiac Montana

NHTSA Frontal Crash Driver	Good
NHTSA Frontal Crash Passenger	Average
NHTSA Side Crash Front Occupant	Excellent
NHTSA Side Crash Rear Occupant	Excellent
IIHS Offset	Poor
IIHS Bumper Bash	Poor

Pontiac Sunfire

NHTSA Frontal Crash Driver	Average (Cpe.); Good (Sdn.)
NHTSA Frontal Crash Passenger	Good
NHTSA Side Crash Front Occupant	Very Poor
NHTSA Side Crash Rear Occupant	Poor (Coupe); Average (Sedan)
IIHS Offset	Poor
IIHS Bumper Bash	Acceptable

Saab 9-3

NHTSA Frontal Crash Driver	Good
NHTSA Frontal Crash Passenger	Good
NHTSA Side Crash Front Occupant	Not Tested
NHTSA Side Crash Rear Occupant	Not Tested
IIHS Offset	Acceptable
IIHS Bumper Bash	Acceptable

Saturn SL

NHTSA Frontal Crash Driver	Excellent
NHTSA Frontal Crash Passenger	Excellent

CRASH TEST DATA

NHTSA Side Crash Front Occupant	Average
NHTSA Side Crash Rear Occupant	Average
IIHS Offset	Acceptable
IIHS Bumper Bash	Good

Saturn SW

NHTSA Frontal Crash Driver	Excellent
NHTSA Frontal Crash Passenger	Excellent
NHTSA Side Crash Front Occupant	Average
NHTSA Side Crash Rear Occupant	Average
IIHS Offset	Acceptable
IIHS Bumper Bash	Good

Subaru Forester

NHTSA Frontal Crash Driver	Good
NHTSA Frontal Crash Passenger	Good
NHTSA Side Crash Front Occupant	Not Tested
NHTSA Side Crash Rear Occupant	Not Tested
IIHS Offset	Good
IIHS Bumper Bash	Marginal

Subaru Impreza

NHTSA Frontal Crash Driver	Good
NHTSA Frontal Crash Passenger	Good
NHTSA Side Crash Front Occupant	Not Tested
NHTSA Side Crash Rear Occupant	Not Tested
IIHS Offset	Not Tested
IIHS Bumper Bash	Not Tested

Subaru Outback Sport

NHTSA Frontal Crash Driver	Good
NHTSA Frontal Crash Passenger	Good
NHTSA Side Crash Front Occupant	Not Tested
NHTSA Side Crash Rear Occupant	Not Tested
IIHS Offset	Not Tested
IIHS Bumper Bash	Not Tested

Suzuki Grand Vitara

NHTSA Frontal Crash Driver	Not Tested
NHTSA Frontal Crash Passenger	Not Tested
NHTSA Side Crash Front Occupant	Not Tested
NHTSA Side Crash Rear Occupant	Not Tested
IIHS Offset	Acceptable
IIHS Bumper Bash	Poor

Suzuki Swift

NHTSA Frontal Crash Driver	Good
NHTSA Frontal Crash Passenger	Good
NHTSA Side Crash Front Occupant	Not Tested
NHTSA Side Crash Rear Occupant	Not Tested

CRASH TEST DATA

IIHS Offset	Not Tested
IIHS Bumper Bash	Not Tested
Suzuki Vitara	
NHTSA Frontal Crash Driver	Not Tested
NHTSA Frontal Crash Passenger	Not Tested
NHTSA Side Crash Front Occupant	Not Tested
NHTSA Side Crash Rear Occupant	Not Tested
IIHS Offset	Acceptable (4-door)
IIHS Bumper Bash	Poor
Toyota 4Runner	
NHTSA Frontal Crash Driver	Good
NHTSA Frontal Crash Passenger	Excellent
NHTSA Side Crash Front Occupant	Excellent
NHTSA Side Crash Rear Occupant	Excellent
IIHS Offset	Good
IIHS Bumper Bash	Poor
Toyota Camry	
NHTSA Frontal Crash Driver	Good
NHTSA Frontal Crash Passenger	Excellent
NHTSA Side Crash Front Occupant	Average
NHTSA Side Crash Rear Occupant	Average
IIHS Offset	Good
IIHS Bumper Bash	Good
Toyota Camry Solara	
NHTSA Frontal Crash Driver	Not Tested
NHTSA Frontal Crash Passenger	Not Tested
NHTSA Side Crash Front Occupant	Average
NHTSA Side Crash Rear Occupant	Excellent
IIHS Offset	Not Tested
IIHS Bumper Bash	Not Tested
Toyota Corolla	
NHTSA Frontal Crash Driver	Good
NHTSA Frontal Crash Passenger	Good
NHTSA Side Crash Front Occupant	Average (w/o side airbag); Good (w/side airbag)
NHTSA Side Crash Rear Occupant	Average
IIHS Offset	Acceptable
IIHS Bumper Bash	Good
Toyota RAV4	
NHTSA Frontal Crash Driver	Good
NHTSA Frontal Crash Passenger	Good
NHTSA Side Crash Front Occupant	Excellent (4-door)
NHTSA Side Crash Rear Occupant	Excellent (4-door)
IIHS Offset	Marginal (4-door)
IIHS Bumper Bash	Poor

CRASH TEST DATA

Toyota Sienna
- NHTSA Frontal Crash Driver — Excellent
- NHTSA Frontal Crash Passenger — Excellent
- NHTSA Side Crash Front Occupant — Good
- NHTSA Side Crash Rear Occupant — Excellent
- IIHS Offset — Good
- IIHS Bumper Bash — Marginal

Toyota Tacoma
- NHTSA Frontal Crash Driver — Good
- NHTSA Frontal Crash Passenger — Good
- NHTSA Side Crash Front Occupant — Very Poor
- NHTSA Side Crash Rear Occupant — Not Applicable
- IIHS Offset — Acceptable
- IIHS Bumper Bash — Poor

Volkswagen Golf
- NHTSA Frontal Crash Driver — Not Tested
- NHTSA Frontal Crash Passenger — Not Tested
- NHTSA Side Crash Front Occupant — Not Tested
- NHTSA Side Crash Rear Occupant — Not Tested
- IIHS Offset — Acceptable
- IIHS Bumper Bash — Good

Volkswagen Jetta
- NHTSA Frontal Crash Driver — Not Tested
- NHTSA Frontal Crash Passenger — Not Tested
- NHTSA Side Crash Front Occupant — Not Tested
- NHTSA Side Crash Rear Occupant — Not Tested
- IIHS Offset — Acceptable
- IIHS Bumper Bash — Good

Volkswagen New Beetle
- NHTSA Frontal Crash Driver — Good
- NHTSA Frontal Crash Passenger — Good
- NHTSA Side Crash Front Occupant — Excellent
- NHTSA Side Crash Rear Occupant — Average
- IIHS Offset — Good
- IIHS Bumper Bash — Good

Volkswagen Passat
- NHTSA Frontal Crash Driver — Not Tested
- NHTSA Frontal Crash Passenger — Not Tested
- NHTSA Side Crash Front Occupant — Not Tested
- NHTSA Side Crash Rear Occupant — Not Tested
- IIHS Offset — Good
- IIHS Bumper Bash — Good

Volvo S70
- NHTSA Frontal Crash Driver — Excellent
- NHTSA Frontal Crash Passenger — Excellent

CRASH TEST DATA

NHTSA Side Crash Front Occupant	Good
NHTSA Side Crash Rear Occupant	No Data
IIHS Offset	Good
IIHS Bumper Bash	Marginal
Volvo S80	
NHTSA Frontal Crash Driver	Not Tested
NHTSA Frontal Crash Passenger	Not Tested
NHTSA Side Crash Front Occupant	Excellent
NHTSA Side Crash Rear Occupant	Excellent
IIHS Offset	Not Tested
IIHS Bumper Bash	Not Tested
Volvo V70	
NHTSA Frontal Crash Driver	Excellent
NHTSA Frontal Crash Passenger	Excellent
NHTSA Side Crash Front Occupant	Good
NHTSA Side Crash Rear Occupant	No Data
IIHS Offset	Good
IIHS Bumper Bash	Marginal

2000 Volvo S70

WARRANTIES & ROADSIDE ASSISTANCE

All new vehicles sold in America come with at least two warranties, and many include roadside assistance. Described below are the major types of warranties and assistance provided to consumers:

Basic: Your basic warranty covers everything except items subject to wear and tear, such as oil filters, wiper blades, and the like. Tires and batteries often have their own warranty coverage, which will be outlined in your owner's manual. Emissions equipment is required to be covered for five years or 50,000 miles by the federal government.

Drivetrain: Drivetrain coverage takes care of most of the parts that make the car move, like the engine, transmission, drive axles and driveshaft. Like the basic warranty, parts subject to wear and tear like hoses and belts are not covered. However, most of the internal parts of the engine, such as the pistons and bearings, which are subject to wear and tear are covered by the drivetrain warranty. See your owner's manual or local dealer for specific coverage.

Rust or Corrosion: This warranty protects you from rust-through problems with the sheetmetal. Surface rust doesn't count. The rust must make a hole to be covered. Keep your car washed and waxed, and rust shouldn't be a problem.

Roadside Assistance: Most manufacturers provide a service that will rescue you if your car leaves you stranded, even if it's your fault. Lock yourself out of the car? Somebody will come and open it up. Run out of gas? Somebody will deliver some fuel. Flat tire? Somebody will change it for you. See your owner's manual for details, or ask the dealer about specifics.

Make	Basic (yrs/mi)	Drivetrain (yrs/mi)	Rust/Corrosion (yrs/mi)	Roadside Assistance (yrs/mi)
Acura	4/50,000	4/50,000	5/Unlimited	4/50,000
Audi	3/50,000	3/50,000	12/Unlimited	3/Unlimited
BMW	4/50,000	4/50,000	6/Unlimited	4/50,000
Buick	3/36,000	3/36,000	6/100,000	3/36,000

WARRANTIES & ROADSIDE ASSISTANCE

Make	Basic (yrs/mi)	Drivetrain (yrs/mi)	Rust/Corrosion (yrs/mi)	Roadside Assistance (yrs/mi)
Cadillac	4/50,000	4/50,000	6/100,000	4/50,000
Chevrolet	3/36,000	3/36,000	6/100,000	3/36,000
Chrysler	3/36,000	3/36,000	5/100,000	3/36,000
Daewoo	3/36,000	5/60,000	5/Unlimited	3/36,000
Dodge	3/36,000	3/36,000	5/100,000	3/36,000
Ford	3/36,000	3/36,000	5/Unlimited	3/36,000
GMC	3/36,000	3/36,000	6/100,000	3/36,000
Honda	3/36,000	3/36,000	3/36,000	None Available
Hyundai	5/60,000	10/100,000	5/100,000	5/Unlimited
Infiniti	4/60,000	6/70,000	7/Unlimited	4/Unlimited
Isuzu	3/50,000	10/120,000	6/100,000	5/60,000
		(except Hombre)		
Kia	3/36,000	5/60,000	5/100,000	3/36,000
Jeep	3/36,000	3/36,000	5/100,000	3/36,000
Land Rover	4/50,000	4/50,000	6/Unlimited	4/50,000
Lexus	4/50,000	6/70,000	6/Unlimited	4/Unlimited
Lincoln	4/50,000	4/50,000	5/Unlimited	4/50,000
Mazda	3/50,000	3/50,000	5/Unlimited	3/50,000
Mercedes	4/50,000	4/50,000	4/50,000	Unlimited
Mercury	3/36,000	3/36,000	5/Unlimited	3/36,000
Mitsubishi	3/36,000	5/60,000	7/100,000	3/36,000
Nissan	3/36,000	5/60,000	5/60,000	None Available
Oldsmobile	3/36,000	3/36,000	6/100,000	3/36,000
Plymouth	3/36,000	3/36,000	5/100,000	3/36,000
Pontiac	3/36,000	3/36,000	6/100,000	3/36,000
Porsche	4/50,000	4/50,000	10/Unlimited	4/50,000
Saab	4/50,000	4/50,000	6/Unlimited	4/50,000
Saturn	3/36,000	3/36,000	6/100,000	3/36,000
Subaru	3/36,000	5/60,000	5/Unlimited	3/36,000
Suzuki	3/36,000	3/36,000	3/Unlimited	None Available
Toyota	3/36,000	5/60,000	5/Unlimited	None Available
Volkswagen	2/24,000	10/100,000	12/Unlimited	2/Unlimited
			(except Cabrio)	
Volvo	4/50,000	4/50,000	8/Unlimited	4/Unlimited

All data sourced directly from manufacturer customer assistance telephone operatives.

DEALER HOLDBACKS

There's plenty of talk these days about dealer holdback, and we suppose we're to blame for some of the hype over this manufacturer kickback to dealers. We've been reporting holdback data for years. But many consumers don't understand what the dealer holdback is, what it is used for, and what the holdback's role is in the deal-making process. Let's try to clear up some of the confusion.

What is Dealer Holdback?

Dealer holdback is a percentage of the MSRP or invoice of a new vehicle that is paid to the dealer by the manufacturer to assist with the dealership's financing of the vehicle. It is almost always non-negotiable, because it is designed to help the dealer cover some of the extraordinary costs of doing business. However, by knowing about the holdback, you can use it as a negotiating tool in some cases. First, a little more background.

The total invoice cost of the car is due to the manufacturer, payable by the dealership, when the vehicle is ordered, not when it is sold. Since car dealerships (or any retail operation, for that matter) must have an inventory on hand which the consumer can browse and ultimately select a vehicle, they must borrow money from the bank to pay for that inventory. The manufacturer pays for financing and maintenance for the first 90 days the vehicle is on the lot, in the form of a quarterly check called a holdback. After the first 90 days, the dealership dips into its own pocket, and into its own profit, to finance the car. Fortunately, most cars don't stay on the lot for three full months.

This amount is "invisible" to the consumer because, unlike the destination charge, it does not appear as an itemized fee on the window sticker and is included in the invoice cost of the car (except in the case of Mitsubishi, where the manufacturer allows dealers to charge the customer directly for the holdback.) If the car sells within 90 days of arrival on the dealer's lot, he is guaranteed a profit even if the vehicle is sold to you at cost. Because of the holdback, the dealer can advertise a car at $1 over invoice and still make hundreds of dollars on the sale.

For example, let's say you're interested in a Ford with a Manufacturer's Suggested Retail Price (MSRP) of $20,500, including optional equipment and destination charge. Dealer invoice on this hypothetical Ford is $18,000, including optional equipment. The invoice includes a dealer holdback that, in the case of all Ford vehicles, amounts to 3 percent of the total MSRP. (The $500 destination charge should not be included when figuring the holdback.) So, on this particular Ford, the

DEALER HOLDBACKS

true dealer cost is actually $17,400, plus destination charges. Even if the dealer sells you the car for invoice, which is unlikely, he would still be making as much as $600 on the deal when his quarterly check arrived. That is profit to the dealer only; the sales staff doesn't see any of it.

So, if you follow Edmunds.com's advice and offer the dealership 3 percent over invoice for this Ford, or $18,540 plus the destination charge, the dealer and the sales staff are making as much as $1,140 and you're still getting a good deal by paying $1,460 less than the MSRP. (Remember that this price doesn't include destination or advertising charges, additional fees, tax, or license plates.)

However, the true "profit" of holdback money depends on how long the car has been on the lot. If our hypothetical Ford had been sitting there for 45 days before you bought it, the dealer's holdback profit is only half of what it could have been, or only $300, cutting total profit on the deal to $840.

Dealer holdback allows dealers to advertise big sales. Often, ads promise that your new car will cost you just "$1 over/under invoice!" Additionally, the dealer stands to reap further benefits if there is some sort of dealer incentive or customer rebate on the car. Generally, sale prices stipulate that all rebates and incentives go to the dealer. Using the example above, let's see what happens when there is a rebate.

Suppose the car described above has a $1,000 rebate in effect. You need to subtract that $1,000 rebate (remember, the dealer is keeping the rebate) from the dealer invoice of $18,000, which results in a new dealer invoice of just $17,000. Now, you must calculate a fair price. In this example, 3 percent of dealer invoice is $510, which means that the price you should try to buy the car for is $17,510, plus destination, advertising, taxes*, and fees. The dealer is still making as much as $1,110 and you're paying $2,490 less than the MSRP. Remember, the longer the car has been in the dealer's inventory, the less money the dealer is making.

Almost all dealerships consider holdback money sacred, and are unwilling to share any portion of it with the consumer. Don't push the issue. Your best strategy is to avoid mentioning that you know the holdback amount and what it is during negotiations. Mention holdback only if the dealer gives you some song-and-dance about not making any money at 3 percent over invoice.

DEALER HOLDBACKS

So how can you truly benefit from this information? Well, if the dealership doesn't have that pretty green color you're interested in, and they can't find it at another dealership in the area, they have to order it directly from the manufacturer. If that's the case, make sure that they know that you know about the holdback. If a vehicle is special-ordered, holdback money is pure profit, and you will need to factor this into price negotiations.

Domestic manufacturers (Chrysler, Ford and GM) generally offer dealers a holdback equaling 3 percent of the total sticker price, or MSRP, of the car. Import manufacturers (Honda, Nissan, Toyota, etc.) provide varying holdback amounts that are equal to a percentage of total MSRP, base MSRP, total invoice or base invoice.

When calculating a holdback, use the following guidelines.

If a holdback is off the:

- Total MSRP, consumers must include the MSRP price of all options before figuring the holdback.
- Base MSRP, consumers must figure the holdback before adding desired options.
- Total Invoice, consumer must include the invoice price of all options before figuring the holdback.
- Base Invoice, consumers must figure the holdback before adding desired options.

Following is a current list of makes and the amount of the 2000 dealer holdback.

Make	Holdback
Acura	3.5% of the Base MSRP
Audi	No Holdback
BMW	2% of the Base MSRP
Buick	3% of the Total MSRP
Cadillac	3% of the Total MSRP
Chevrolet	3% of the Total MSRP
Chrysler	3% of the Total MSRP
Daewoo	One-price sales. Customer pays MSRP.
Dodge	3% of the Total MSRP
Eagle	3% of the Total MSRP

DEALER HOLDBACKS

Ford	3% of the Total MSRP
GMC	3% of the Total MSRP
Honda	2% of the Base MSRP (except Prelude, which has no holdback)
Hyundai	2% of the Total Invoice
Infiniti	1% of the Base MSRP (holdback) + 2% of the Base Invoice (floorplanning allowance)
Isuzu	3% of the Total MSRP
Jaguar	2% of the Base Invoice
Jeep	3% of the Total MSRP
Kia	3% of the Total Invoice
Land Rover	No Holdback
Lexus	2% of the Base MSRP
Lincoln	3% of the Total MSRP
Mazda	2% of the Base MSRP
Mercedes-Benz	3% of the Total MSRP
Mercury	3% of the Total MSRP
Mitsubishi	2% of the Total MSRP
Nissan	2% + 1.5% of the Total Invoice (holdback + floorplanning allowance)
Oldsmobile	3% of the Total MSRP
Plymouth	3% of the Total MSRP
Pontiac	3% of the Total MSRP
Porsche	No Holdback
Saab	3% of the Base MSRP
Saturn	One-price sales. Customer pays MSRP.
Subaru	2% of the Total MSRP (Amount may differ inNortheastern U.S.)
Suzuki	2% of the Base MSRP
Toyota	2% of the Base Invoice (Amount may differ in Southern U.S.)
Volkswagen	2% of Total MSRP
Volvo	$300 Flat Amount

* Incentives and rebates are actually deducted from the transaction price after Uncle Sam has collected taxes. We have taken editorial license with the process in this example for the sake of keeping it simple.

FREQUENTLY ASKED QUESTIONS

Edmunds.com solicits email queries from consumers who visit our Web site at http://www.edmunds.com. Below are 25 commonly asked questions regarding new cars and the buying process.

1. How do I figure a fair deal?

Use this formula: Dealer Invoice of car and options + 3 percent Fair Profit + Destination Charge + Advertising Fees + Tax - Incentives and/or Rebates = Fair Deal

2. Why won't the dealer accept my offer of 3 percent over dealer cost?

The dealer doesn't have to sell you a car. If demand for the model is high, if supplies are short, or if the dealer enjoys making a healthy profit, you won't be able to buy the car for a fair price. Don't argue the point, just find another dealer. If all the dealers you contact refuse to sell the car at this price, then your offer is too low, and you must start over at a higher value.

3. How can a dealer sell a new car for less than the invoice price Edmunds.com publishes?

Auto manufacturers will often subsidize volume-sellers to keep sales and production up by offering car dealers hefty cash rewards for meeting monthly or quarterly sales goals. In other words, the dealer will take a slight loss on the car in anticipation of larger cash rewards if sales goals are met. It has been our experience that when a dealer sells a vehicle for less than invoice, the manufacturer is in one form or another always subsidizing the deal. In print ads, always look for phrases such as "all incentives and/or rebates assigned to dealer."

Also, since profit can be made on other parts of the deal, a dealer may be willing to take a loss on the price of the car in exchange for profit gleaned from a low-ball trade-in value, high-interest financing, rustproofing, an extended warranty, and aftermarket or dealer-installed accessories. We once met a Plymouth salesman who bragged that he sold a Neon for invoice, but with the undervalued trade-in, high-interest financing and dealer-installed items factored into the deal, the buyer actually paid more than $20,000 for the car. Keep in mind that there is more to a good deal than a low price.

4. How can I find out what customer rebates or dealer incentives are currently available?

Rebates to customers are clearly announced in advertising. Incentives to dealers, commonly known as "back-end monies," are not. Edmunds.com publishes current national and large regional rebate and incentive programs

FREQUENTLY ASKED QUESTIONS

online at http://www.edmunds.com. Local rebate and incentive programs also exist on occasion, but Edmunds.com doesn't have access to this information. Ask your dealer if the local automobile dealer association or advertising association is sponsoring any rebates or incentives in your area. They might actually share this information with you, and it never hurts to ask.

5. Why do some dealer incentives on specific models have a range of values?

Sometimes, the manufacturer will tell the dealer that he must sell a certain number of cars to qualify for an incentive. For example, let's say Nissan offered dealers an incentive of $100-1,000 on the Altima. This is a quota-based incentive. It means that to get the $100 per car, the dealer might have to sell 10 cars before a certain date. To get $500 per car, the dealer might have to sell 50 cars before a certain date. To get $1,000 per car, the dealer might have to sell 100 cars before a certain date. The more cars the dealer sells, the more money he makes, because quota-based rebates are retroactive.

With these types of quota-based incentives, you have leverage. With your sale, the dealer is one car closer to clearing the next hurdle and making more money. We recommend that you request half of the maximum quota-based incentive while negotiating your deal, unless the dealer or salesperson bungles and admits that your sale will put them into the next tier of incentive qualification. In this case, demand the maximum incentive.

6. What is a carryover allowance?

At the beginning of a new model year, some manufacturers provide dealers with a carryover allowance in addition to the dealer holdback. The carryover allowance is applied to cars from the previous model year, and is designed to assist dealers in lowering prices and clearing out old stock. Currently, the only domestic automaker that gives its dealers a carryover allowance is Ford Motor Company. The amounts can vary, but they average 5 percent of the MSRP. General Motors and Chrysler target slow sellers with heavy incentives and rebates. Most import manufacturers subscribe to the incentive and rebate philosophy as well.

7. I want to pay cash for my new car. Do I have an advantage?

Not necessarily. You must remember that no matter how you pay for your car, it's all cash to the dealer. In the old days when dealers carried your note, you could save money by paying cash because there was no risk to the dealer. Today, dealerships finance through one of several lending institutions (banks, credit unions, or the automaker's captive financing division) that pay them cash when the contract is presented. In fact, if dealerships do the financing on your behalf, they tend to make more money on your contract in the form of a reserve; anywhere from ½ to 1 point spread on the interest. For example, if the published rate is 8.75 percent, the lender to dealer rate may be discounted to 8 percent;

FREQUENTLY ASKED QUESTIONS

the .75 percent is the reserve held by the dealer as additional profit. This may not sound like much, but it adds up to hundreds of thousands of dollars a year at larger dealerships. This is the reason you should always arrange financing before going to the dealership, and then ask the dealer if they can beat your pre-approved rate. In most cases, they cannot, because of the reserve.

Paying cash is an advantage if you suffer from poor credit or bankruptcy, because it allows you to avoid the higher interest rates charged on loans to people with past credit problems. The bottom line is that if you think you can invest your money at a higher return than the interest rate of the car loan, you could actually save money by not paying cash.

8. Do factory orders cost more than buying from dealer stock?

All things considered equal, ordered vehicles cost no more than vehicles in dealer stock and, in some cases, may actually cost less. When you buy from dealer stock, you may have to settle for a vehicle with either more or less equipment or your second or third color choice. Moreover, the dealership pays interest on stocked vehicles at a predetermined monthly rate to the manufacturer. This interest is called floor plan, and is subsidized by the dealer holdback. When you factory order, you get exactly what you want, in the color you want, and the dealer should eliminate the floor plan cost. In most cases, the dealer passes the savings on to the customer, and the savings could amount to several hundred dollars.

The downside to ordering is that incentives and rebates are good only on the day of delivery, unless stated otherwise (in writing) by the dealer. If an incentive or rebate plan was in effect when the vehicle was ordered, but not in effect the day of delivery, the customer is usually not eligible for the incentive or rebate. If you order a vehicle, and the delivery date is very close to the expiration date of a rebate or incentive program, beware that the dealer may try to delay delivery until after the rebate or incentive has expired.

From a negotiation standpoint, dealers may be more likely to offer a better price on a vehicle in stock, particularly if the monthly floor plan payments have exceeded the holdback amount and are now chewing into the dealer's profit.

9. Can I order a car directly from the factory?

No you cannot. Dealerships are franchisees of the factory, and are protected as such. However, a few manufacturers are buying large groups of dealerships in some areas to test the idea that a factory-owned store can serve the customer's needs better than individually owned and operated stores. Ford is testing this philosophy in several markets, and Daewoo originally intended to sell cars exclusively through factory owned stores until some states reminded the company that factory dealerships were *verboten.* Even stalwart General Motors is trying to consolidate dealerships in L.A.'s massive San Fernando Valley, but with little success. But signs exist that in the future, factory-owned stores may become commonplace.

FREQUENTLY ASKED QUESTIONS

10. Why are destination charges the same for every dealer around the country?

Auto manufacturers will average the cost to ship a car from the factory to the furthest dealership with the cost to ship a car from the factory to the closest dealership. Some manufacturers do this for each model, others average costs across an entire make. Sometimes, shipping costs to Hawaii and Alaska may be higher than the averaged amount for the contiguous 48 states.

11. Can I avoid paying the destination charge by picking up a car at the factory?

Currently, the only North American factories that allow customers to take delivery the minute a car rolls off the assembly line are the Corvette plant in Bowling Green, Ky., the Dodge Viper plant in Detroit, and the BMW plant in Spartanburg, S.C. Buyers who opt to travel to pick up their new Corvette, Viper or M Roadster still pay the dealer they bought it from the destination charge.

12. Why should I pay advertising fees?

Most vehicles carry a legitimate advertising fee levied by either the manufacturer or by regional dealer groups. National or regional advertising fees, when charged, should not exceed 1.5 percent of the vehicle's MSRP. Because individual dealership advertising is a cost of doing business, you should never pay an advertising fee levied by the dealer rather than a regional dealer association or the manufacturer.

13. Can I negotiate price on a Saturn, Daewoo or at a no-haggle dealership?

You cannot negotiate price on a Saturn, but you can haggle over your trade-in and shop aggressively for the lowest-rate financing to keep costs down. Daewoo dealers also use a one-price philosophy, but the company wants to expand quickly and sell lots of cars, and there are often incentives and rebates available on these models, so the climate is favorable for negotiation.

No-haggle dealerships might wiggle a little on price, but if they're smart, they'll tell you to get lost. If you want to duke it out over $100, why would you shop at a no-haggle dealership wasting their time and yours? Think about this. If the no-haggle dealer caves and drops the price to sell you the car, you're gonna tell your buddies, and they're gonna tell their buddies, and pretty soon the whole town will be haggling over cars with the no-haggle dealer, and the no-haggle dealer isn't a no-haggle dealer anymore. Get it?

FREQUENTLY ASKED QUESTIONS

14. Why won't the dealer give me wholesale value for my trade-in?

When a dealership takes a car in on trade, it is responsible for the car. Before the trade-in can be sold, it must be inspected and often repaired. Sometimes, emissions work is necessary. All this inspection and repair work costs the dealership money. If the trade is in good condition and has low miles, the dealer will put the car on the used-car lot for retail price. When the car sells, it is rarely for retail price, so the profit margin is shaved. The less you accept for the trade-in, the more room the dealer has to make a deal with a prospective buyer, and the more money the dealer will make thanks to increased profit margins.

If the car doesn't sell, if it has high miles, or it is in poor condition, the dealer will have to wholesale it. The dealer will likely sell the car for below wholesale value at the auction, and expects to recoup some of the money spent reconditioning and inspecting the car. If the dealer offered you wholesale price when you traded in the car, he wouldn't make the money back in the event that the trade-in went to auction.

Regardless of the condition of your car, the dealer will anticipate taking the car to auction, and will leave room to make money in that event. Your best bet is to sell your car on your own to a private party, and forget about trading in.

15. Should I buy rustproofing, fabric protection packages, paint sealant, and other dealer-installed items?

Of course not. Most new cars are covered against rust perforation for several years and up to 100,000 miles. Want to protect your fabric? Go to an auto parts store and buy a can or two of Scotchgard. New cars have clearcoat paint, which offers protection from the elements. A little elbow grease and a jar of carnauba wax will keep the finish protected and looking great. By investing a little time and effort into your automobile, you can save hundreds on these highly profitable dealer protection packages.

16. How much does an extended warranty cost the warranty company?

The cost of an extended warranty is based upon the degree of probability that any given vehicle will require repairs during the extended warranty period. Reliability records and repair cost information for a vehicle are evaluated to forecast potential future repair costs, and the extended warranty company will then charge a premium adequate enough to cover the potential cost of repairing the vehicle during the warranty period, while still making a profit. It is important to note that the cost of an extended warranty includes administrative costs for handling paperwork and claims, and insurance to guarantee that claims will be paid.

Extended warranty costs are based on averages, so the cost of applying an extended warranty to any given make and model of car can vary from

FREQUENTLY ASKED QUESTIONS

consumer to consumer. Let's say you bought a $1,000 extended warranty for two identical Brand X vehicles: Car A and Car B. During the extended warranty period, Car A never breaks, so the extended warranty is never used. At the same time, Car B suffers bills amounting to $1,200 for transmission and valve problems. Profit on the warranty sold for Car A will counterbalance the loss suffered on Car B. Extended warranty companies sell thousands of warranties annually, and are able to make a profit when the actual loss experience is lower than the forecast potential for future repair. In other words, when sales exceed overhead the company makes money.

17. Who sets the residual value for a lease?

The financing institution that is handling the lease for the dealership sets the residual value, which can be affected by market forces and vehicle popularity. When shopping leases, it is important to shop different financing institutions for the highest residual value and the lowest interest rate.

18. When I use Edmunds.com's formula to calculate a lease, I get a payment that is substantially higher than what the dealer quoted me. Why is this?

The manufacturer subsidizes most nationally advertised leases. This means that the manufacturer gives the dealer incentive money to lower the capitalized cost (selling price) listed on the lease, or that the financing institution owned by the manufacturer has artificially inflated the residual value to lower the monthly payment, or both. Dealers may not inform you of these adjustments in the numbers.

Another problem with advertised lease payments seen in newspapers and on television is that consumers don't read the terms of the lease carefully. Sometimes, a substantial capitalized cost reduction (down payment) is required. Sometimes hefty deposits and other drive-off fees are involved. Mileage limits may be ridiculously low. Payments may be required for 39, 48 or 60 months rather than the conventional 24- or 36-month term. Read the fine print carefully!

Also, keep in mind that there are more than 250 different lending institutions across the country, and each one sets its own residual values for lease contracts. Don't be surprised if you go to three different dealers and get three different lease payments for the same vehicle over the same term.

19. When is the best time to purchase a car from a dealer?

There's as much advice about when to visit a dealer as there are days in a year. Some say that Mondays are good because business is slower on Monday than on the weekend. Some say holidays like Thanksgiving are good for the same reason: nobody else will be there, and the sales team will be hungry for a sale. Others advise to go when it's raining or snowing; after all, who wants to look at a car and get wet? Then there's the advice that the end of the month is

FREQUENTLY ASKED QUESTIONS

the best time because the dealership needs to make its "quota" of car sales and will be more willing to cut a deal. Still others advise not to buy a car until the end of the model year, or in slow months like August or December when people are busy thinking about going back to school or shopping for Christmas gifts rather than buying a new car.

Our advice is don't buy a car until you're ready. That's usually the best time. By then you have saved enough for a substantial down payment, and you've had plenty of time to do your research for the lowest interest rate, and you know all the current incentives and rebates. There is no way to tell when is the best time to buy other than personal need.

If a dealer has already made his target sales for the month, you're not going to have any advantage by showing up on the 31st of the month. While there may be something to say for going to a dealership on a weekday near the end of the month on Thanksgiving at five o'clock during a raging blizzard, your best bet is to track incentives and rebates, don't buy hot new models, and do your research first.

20. How soon after a price increase does Edmunds.com modify its data?

This depends on how soon our sources are notified. Sometimes, it's a matter of days; other times, it can take longer. Rest assured that we painstakingly attempt to maintain the most up-to-date pricing. If a dealer disputes the accuracy of our pricing, ask them to prove it by showing you the invoice so you can compare. If prices have indeed increased, the amount will not be substantial: the new figures should easily be within a few percentage points of those published in this guide.

21. Why is the car I'm looking at on the West Coast or in the Southern tier of states priced differently than what's listed in this guide?

California, Oregon, Washington and Idaho are the testing grounds for different pricing and option schemes. Because of the popularity of imported makes in this market, domestic manufacturers will often slash dealer profit margins and offer better-equipped cars at lower prices than those available in other parts of the country. This is why some dealer incentives and customer rebates do not apply on the West Coast, and why some option packages available in those states may not be listed in this guide.

In the Southeast, large distributors control Toyota pricing, and take advantage of this monopoly by charging more money for destination and advertising fees. They also front-load many cars with worthless packages of cosmetic items that you don't need. Similarly, in the Northeast, a single distributor, who may charge differently for fees and options than dealers in the rest of the United States, handles Subaru products.

FREQUENTLY ASKED QUESTIONS

22. Why doesn't Edmunds.com list option prices for some makes and models?

Almost all Acura, Honda, and Suzuki options are dealer-installed. Some manufacturers, like Nissan, Subaru, Toyota and Volvo, will offer both factory- and dealer-installed options. Pricing for these items can vary depending on region and dealer. Therefore, it is impossible for Edmunds.com to list an accurate price for these items. Our experience shows that these items often carry a 100 percent markup in dealer profit. We recommend that you avoid buying dealer-installed options if you can help it.

23. When should a car be considered used?

Technically, a vehicle is considered used if it has been titled. However, some dealers can rack up hundreds or thousands of miles on a new car without titling it. In these cases, the ethical definition of a used car should include any car used for extensive demonstration or personal use by dealership staff members. The only miles a new car should have on the odometer when purchased are those put on during previous test drives by prospective buyers (at dealerships where demonstrators are not used), and any miles driven during a dealer trade, within a reasonable limit. If the new car you're considering has more than 300 miles on the odometer, you should question how the car accumulated so many miles, and request a discount for the excessive mileage. We think a discount amounting to a dime a mile is a fair charge for wear and tear inflicted by the dealership.

A car should not be considered used if it is a brand-new leftover from a previous model year. However, it should be discounted, because many manufacturers offer dealers incentives designed to help the dealer lower prices and clear out old stock.

24. What's the difference between a demo car and a program car?

A demo car is one used by the dealership as a demonstrator to potential buyers. Often, dealership personnel will use the car as personal transportation. A program car is a former rental car, purchased at auction by the dealership. Either type of car is more likely to have been abused than a brand-new car or a used car offered for sale by a private owner.

25. Is it fair for a dealer to ask if my trade has ever been wrecked, or damaged in any way?

Certainly. If you were buying a car from a used-car dealer, you'd want to know the same thing, wouldn't you?

LEASING TIPS

You've seen the ads: Honda Civic for $189 a month. Jeep Grand Cherokee for $289 a month. GMC Yukon for $389 a month. Wow! You can't believe your eyes. Visions of shiny new golf clubs in your trunk, a big-screen TV in your living room and two weeks of prime vacationing in Vail release endorphins at twice the Surgeon General's recommended level in anticipation of big savings.

But be careful, because you probably shouldn't believe your eyes when you read such banner ads, not until they're grazing over the fine print. See where it says "Capitalized Cost Reduction"? That's lease-speak for down payment. See where it says "30,000 miles over three-year term"? That's lease-speak for "You're going to the Safeway and back — and that's all folks." Want the car for zero down? That's gonna cost you. You drive someplace more than twice a month? That's gonna cost you, too.

Like most consumers, you want to know how to buy or lease the car of your choice for the best possible price. Buyers are attracted to leasing by low payments and the prospect of driving a new car every two or three years. Many people figure that a car payment is an unavoidable fact of budgetary life, and they might as well drive 'new' rather than 'old.' True, leasing is an attractive alternative, but there are some things you need to understand about leasing before jumping in feet first without a paddle. Whatever. You know what we mean.

How to Lease

Never walk into a dealership and announce that you want to lease a car. Don't talk payment, either. Once a salesperson identifies you as a payment shopper, you're a dead duck. Any competent dealer can find a way to make a car fit your budget while maximizing profit simultaneously. Concentrate on finding a car you like, and know before you go into the dealership what you can afford in terms of sticker price.

Lease payments are based on the capitalized cost, which is the selling price of the car. The residual value is the predicted value of the vehicle at the end of the lease term, and can be expressed as a percentage of the MSRP. Sometimes, the residual value is not the predicted value of the car at the end of the lease, but a number that allows the leasing company to lower the cost of the lease as much as possible without incurring excessive risk when it comes time to sell the off-lease vehicle. A money factor, which is lease-speak for 'interest rate,' is also involved in the calculation of a lease payment. If the money factor is expressed as a percentage, convert the percentage to the money factor by dividing the number by 24 (yes, it's 24 regardless of the term of the lease). For example, a 7 percent (.07) interest rate converts to a .0029 money factor. Then, of course, there are associated taxes and fees that are added. Accept the fact that if the car you want to lease is not a popular model, your lease may be a bit higher than you anticipated.

LEASING TIPS

Calculating an actual lease payment beforehand is nearly impossible, particularly when the lease is subsidized by the automaker, but you can arrive at a ballpark figure by using the following formula, which we will illustrate using a 2000 Honda Accord EX V6 as an example. Remember that if you put any money down, or trade in your old car, you must deduct this amount from the capitalized cost. This deduction is called the capitalized cost reduction. We recommend paying the destination charge, the acquisition fee, the security deposit, and any taxes up front rather than rolling them into the lease.

2000 Honda Accord EX V6

MSRP	$24,550
Capitalized Cost (negotiated fair price)	$22,490
Destination Charge	$415
Acquisition Fee	$450
Security Deposit	$450 (refunded at end of lease)
Capitalized Cost Reduction	$900 (destination charge + acquisition fee)
Total Payment Due at Lease Signing*	$1,350 (security deposit + cap. reduction)
Residual Value after 3 years	(57% of MSRP in this example)
	$24,550 x .57 = $13,993.50
Term Depreciation	(Capitalized Cost - Residual Value)
	$22,490 - $13,993.50 = $8,496.50
Money Factor	(Interest Rate divided by 24)
	7.5% divided by 24 = .0031
Monthly Lease Rate	(Capitalized Cost + Residual Value x .0031)
	($22,490 + $13,993.50) x .0031 = $113.10
Monthly Depreciation	(Term Depreciation divided by Lease Term)
	$8,496.50 divided by 36 = $236.01
State Sales Tax on Payment	([Monthly Depreciation + Monthly Lease Rate] x Sales Tax Rate [6.5% in this ex.)
	$236.01 + $113.10 x .065 = $22.69
State Sales Tax on Cap Reduction	(Cap Cost Reduction x Sales Tax Rate [6.5% in this ex.])
	$900 x .065 = $1.63
Monthly Payment	(Monthly Depreciation + Monthly Lease Rate + State Sales Tax)
	$236.01 + $113.10 + $24.32 = $373.43

* Most leases also require that the first monthly payment be made at lease signing.

For comparison purposes, we used Honda's Web site lease calculator (http://www.honda2000.com/models/calculators/index.html) to see what American Honda Finance Corp. (AHFC) would quote us using as many of the same parameters as possible from our example above. The Web site calculator told us on October 6, 1999, that this sample Accord EX V6 would

LEASING TIPS

run $339.80 per month (including tax), for a 36-month lease with 15,000 miles allowed per year and $1,350 down on a cap cost of $22,490. AHFC reported a residual value at the end of the lease of $14,479.70, which is $486.20 higher than our estimate, and a disclaimer indicated the AHFC quote was based on a net capital cost of $21,590, which is $900 lower than our example. This lower cap cost, according to the disclaimer, is dependent on dealer participation, which tells us Honda is subsidizing Accord leases to the tune of $900 in dealer cash and that it's the dealer's prerogative whether or not the consumer shares in that factory money. The bottom line is that a 2000 Accord EX V6 should run between $340 per month and $375 per month with little money down. If this fits your budget, so does the Accord EX V6.

Keep in mind that every vehicle will have a unique residual value, based on its popularity, its resale value and its reputation for reliability and dependent of the term of the lease. Also remember that the above formula doesn't take the following into account: delivery and handling (D&H fees), documentation fees, the cost of license plates, city or county sales tax (if applicable in your part of the country), or trade-in values. The trade-in value and any cash down payment should be deducted from the capitalized cost before calculating the lease.

If you're upside down on your trade, which means the car is worth less than you owe on the loan, you'll need to add the difference between the balance due on the loan and the trade-in value to the capitalized cost.

The example we illustrated is a straightforward lease with no factory subsidy. This formula will not account for subsidized leases, as evidenced by the subsidized payment the Honda Web site calculated. Subsidized leases allow dealers to lower payments by artificially raising residual values or lowering the capitalized cost through dealer incentives. You can easily recognize a subsidized lease. Any nationally or regionally advertised lease is generally subsidized by the manufacturer to keep lease payments low. The $289 per month Jeep Grand Cherokee popular in TV and newspaper advertising is an example of a subsidized lease payment.

Actual lease payments are affected by negotiation of the sticker price on the vehicle, term of the lease, available incentives, residual values, and layers of financial wizardry that even sales managers can't interpret without divine intervention. Once you find a car you can afford, negotiate the sticker price and then explore leasing based on the negotiated price. Ask what the residual value is and subtract any rebates or incentives from the capitalized cost, and remember that you'll need to pay tax to Uncle Sam for that discount. Use the formula above to calculate a ballpark figure, and if the dealer balks at your conclusion, ask them to explain the error of your ways.

Your best bet when leasing is to choose a model with a subsidized lease. Payments are low, terms are simple to understand, and they are the only true bargain in the world of leasing.

LEASING TIPS

Low Payments

Low payments aren't a fallacy with leasing, when taken in proper context. Let's look at our Honda Accord EX V6 example again. To lease for three years with a minimal capitalized cost reduction (down payment) of $1,350, it'll cost you about $350 per month (plus tax and fees). To buy that Accord, financed for 36 months at a 9 percent annual percentage rate (APR) with $1,350 down, you would pay about $685 per month (plus tax and fees). So you see, leasing is cheaper in terms of a monthly payment when compared to financing for the same term.

There are two flaws here. First, 60-month financing is now the standard, and 72-month financing is becoming more popular. Using the same APR and down payment, the Accord will cost right around $445 per month (plus tax and fees) for 5 years and still be worth a good chunk of change at the end of the loan if cared for properly. Second, ownership is far less restrictive, even if the bank holds the title until 2005. You can drive as far as you want, paint the thing glow-in-the-dark orange with magenta stripes, and spill coffee on the seats without sweating a big wear-and-tear bill down the road. Leasing for three years costs about $13,500 (assuming you get the entire security deposit back), and you don't own the car at lease-end. Financing for three years costs about $26,000, but you own a car worth about $14,000 when the payment book is empty (unless, of course, you've actually painted it orange with magenta stripes and spilled coffee all over the interior), which makes your actual cost close to $12,000. Is leasing cheaper? Monthly payments, when compared to financing over the same term, are lower. But in most cases, leasing is actually more expensive.

Let's compare the longer-term effects of leasing vs. buying, over the same term and under identical conditions. By leasing the Accord in this example for three years, and then buying the car for its $13,993.50 residual value with two-year financing at a higher interest rate than you would have paid new (interest rates rise as the vehicle gets older), you pay thousands more for the car. Assume the interest rate for 24 months on a 3-year-old Accord is 11 percent. Payments for the loan would total about $650 per month, or right around $15,600 for the life of the loan. Added to the cost of the three-year lease, the $23,000 Accord has cost you $29,100 (plus tax) with average payments over 60 months of $500 per month (plus tax). Had you bought the Accord outright, financing for 60 months at 9 percent interest, the Accord would have cost $26,700 (plus tax) with monthly outlays of $445 (plus tax).

But there are several factors that should be kept in mind. When leasing, tax is calculated on the payment; when buying, tax is calculated on the selling price. At a 6.5 percent sales tax rate, the Accord costs the buyer using conventional 60-month financing roughly $300 less in sales tax than the buyer who leases and then purchases the car at the residual value. Other factors, like fluctuating interest rates, down payments, and contractual obligations can

LEASING TIPS

also affect the lease vs. loan scenario. Additionally, vehicle condition can have a tremendous affect on value. A few dents, dings or scratches could easily make a lease the more expensive proposition, with charges for worn tires, excessive mileage and cosmetic repair likely to top $1,000 at the end of the contract.

When trying to determine if leasing or buying is right for you, carefully weigh all the factors that can affect payments over the term of the lease or loan, including the way you drive and maintain a vehicle.

Restrictions

Leasing severely restricts your use of a vehicle. Mileage allowances are limited, modifications to the vehicle can result in hefty fines at the end of the lease, and if the vehicle is not in top condition when it is returned, excessive wear-and-tear charges may be levied. Many dealers and financing institutions will be more lenient if you buy or lease another vehicle from them at the end of your term, but if you drop off the car and walk, prepare yourself for some lease-end misery.

Be sure to define these limitations at the beginning of the lease so that you know what you're getting yourself into. Find out what will be considered excessive in the wear-and-tear department and try to negotiate a higher mileage limit.

Benefits

By leasing, you get to drive a new vehicle every two or three years. This also means that, in most cases, the only time the car will be in the shop is for routine maintenance. And, as long as you lease only for the term of the original manufacturer's warranty, you're not liable for catastrophic repair bills. Additionally, leasing can allow a buyer to make that dream car fit the budget when conventional financing will not. Finally, and perhaps for some people this is the most important benefit, you're never again upside-down on a car loan, unless you try to end the lease early.

Lease-end

Studies show that consumers generally like leases, right up until they end. The reason for their apprehension is rooted in the dark days of open-end leasing, when Joe Lessee was dealt a sucker punch by the lessor on the day Joe returned the car to the leasing agent. Back then, residual values were established at the beginning of the lease, but the lessee was responsible for the difference between the residual value and the fair market value at the end of the lease. The resulting lease-end charges maxed out credit cards and dealers laughed all the way to the bank.

LEASING TIPS

Leasing has evolved, and with today's closed-end leases (the only type of lease you should consider), the lease-end fees are generally reasonable, unless the car has 100,000 miles on it, a busted-up grille and melted chocolate smeared into the upholstery. Dealers and financial institutions want you to buy or lease another car from them, and can be rather lenient regarding excess mileage and abnormal wear. After all, if they hit you with a bunch of trumped up charges you're not going to remain a loyal customer, are you?

Additionally, closed-end leasing establishes a set, non-negotiable residual value for the car in advance, at the beginning of the lease. Also, any fees or charges you may incur at the lease-end are spelled out in detail before you sign the lease. All the worry is removed by the existence of concrete figures. But keep in mind that if you take your business elsewhere, you're going to be facing a bill for items like worn tires, paint chips, door dings, and the like.

Another leasing benefit is the myriad of choices you have at the end of the term. Well, maybe not a myriad, but there are four, which is more than you have after two or three years of financing. They are:

1.) **Return the car to the dealer and walk away from it** after paying any applicable charges like a termination fee, wear-and-tear repairs, or excessive mileage bills. Of course, if you don't plan to buy or lease another car from the dealer, you may get hit for every minor thing, but those are the risks.

2.) **Buy the car** from the dealer for the residual value established at the beginning of the lease. If the car is in good shape, the residual value is probably lower than the true value of the car, making it a bargain, and many leasing companies will guarantee financing at the lowest interest rate available at the time your lease ends. If you've trashed the lease car, compare the lease-end wear-and-tear charges to the devaluation in worth the vehicle has suffered while in your care. You might be surprised to find that it's easier and less expensive to just give the car back and pay the fines.

3.) **Use any equity in the car as leverage in a new deal** with the dealer. Since residual values are sometimes set artificially high, the car is not likely to be worth more than the residual value at lease-end under these circumstances. But a well-maintained, low-mileage lease car might allow the dealer to knock up to a couple of thousand bucks off your next deal.

4.) **Sell the car yourself** and pay off the residual value, pocketing whatever profit you make.

510   www.edmunds.com   **EDMUND'S® NEW CARS**

LEASING TIPS

Conclusion

Closed-end leasing is a win-win situation for everybody except people who want to keep their cars for a good long time. The manufacturer sells more cars, the dealer sells more cars, and you get low payments and a new car every couple of years. However, it is important to stress that you never own the car and leasing can be quite restrictive. If you're a low-mileage driver who maintains cars in perfect condition, don't like tying up capital in down payments and don't mind never-ending car payments, leasing is probably just right for you. If you're on the road all day every day, beat the stuffing out of your wheels, enjoy a 'customized' look or drive your cars until the wheels fall off, buy whatever it is you're considering, because it will be less expensive in the long run.

2000 Honda Accord EX V6 Sedan

Chevrolet IMPALA

The Car You Knew America Would Build

by Ingrid Loeffler Palmer
photos courtesy of General Motors Corporation

The original Impala, which debuted in 1958, was based on the following premise: Build a good-looking car with more performance, amenities and value than the consumer might expect, all at a Chevy price, and success will follow.

And follow success did, with the Impala becoming Chevrolet's best-selling car in its second year of production and one of the most popular cars on the road in years to come. In fact, in 1965 Chevy sold more than one million Impala units in a single year-setting a record that still stands.

At the 1993 SEMA show, a new, retro Impala SS debuted as a high-performance version of the Caprice Classic. The crowds loved it because it was a traditional muscle car. So, Chevy added a bigger engine, slapped some larger wheels on it, and called it good for production in 1994. Unfortunately, this little gem fizzled out two years later when General Motors got rid of it and the Caprice. It figures: they finally get the car just right...and then they kill it.

But that was almost four years ago, and today's Impala is nothing like it used to be. First off, it's built on a front-wheel-drive platform instead of rear-wheel drive. Secondly, the

throbbing V8 of yesteryear is gone; instead, this Impala's most powerful motor is a 3.8-liter, 200-horsepower V6. Finally, it's based on and shares a chassis with the Lumina, which Chevy plans to replace with the Impala during the 2000 model year.

On the outside, the new Impala takes some styling cues from the '60s models, such as the round taillights, and some from the '90s version, like the C-pillar badges found on the SS. We like the styling of the new Impala for the most part, finding it neither too garish nor too boring, though the round taillights remind one editor of beady eyeballs and the rear bumper appears a bit thick.

We took possession of a Torch Red Impala LS during a hot week in August and set out to see how this new take on an old nameplate would fare. The red paint on our test car helped hide the largess of the rear lights and reflector applique, and the deletion of the decklid spoiler kept the Impala's overall shape clean.

Our initial driving impression of the 2000 Impala was that it succeeded as an around-town vehicle. Running errands at moderate speeds proved that the sedan is capable of hauling families to and from the store, school and work. Though the 3800 Series II V6 engine is not underpowered, it certainly isn't going to light anybody's fire with stunning acceleration, either. Making 200 horsepower at 5,200 rpm and 225 foot-pounds of torque at 4,000 rpm, the engine meets low-emission vehicle (LEV) standards. For 2000, Chevy improved this venerable V6 by tuning the throttle body, adding a limp-home mode, increasing the exhaust capacity and putting in a new one-piece flywheel. Happily, there was no whining, engine rumble or revving noises when pushing the Impala to its limits.

No, the noises instead came straight from the road, causing occupants to raise their voices in order to continue conversations. The level of road noise that intruded upon the cabin was unacceptable and annoying. The upgraded stereo in our test car just happened to be equipped with automatic volume compensation, which means that the faster you go, the louder the stereo volume gets. Hmmm, wonder why they installed that feature.

We were smitten with the incredibly smooth automatic transmission (the only kind you can get on the Impala) that shifts precisely when you expect it to under hard acceleration and changes gears imperceptibly under normal cruising situations. We noticed that the shifter had a tendency to

514   www.edmunds.com

stick at times, though, making it difficult to change from "park" to "drive" quickly.

We also found the Impala's seats to be somewhat uncomfortable, feeling both spongy and unsupportive. Visibility, on the other hand, was excellent. We had no problem maneuvering the car around town or on the expressway, thanks in part to the small triangular C-pillar windows designed to enhance the rearward view.

Chevrolet seems to have the suspension sorted pretty well. The front end doesn't exhibit any heaviness and there's little bob or bounce on bumpy roads. The ride, however, is a bit stiff and jiggly on the rough stuff. Overall, Chevy maintained a nice balance between cush-mobile feel and go-kart rumble. Steering is linear and reasonably direct, but somewhat devoid of road feel. Brakes are a strong point for Impala, stopping quickly and without squeal, but the ABS engages easily on rough pavement and the brake pedal doesn't offer enough feedback when depressed. Around corners, we noticed a fair amount of body roll and if you turn the wheel quickly at higher speeds, it feels like the P225/60R-16 tires are considering relinquishing their grip on the pavement. Inside the sedan, we were greeted with a nicely executed interior. The instrument panel and dashboard controls were uncluttered, boasting intelligently placed, ergonomically sound buttons and gauges. We liked the pull on/push off knob for the headlights, the volume dial on the stereo, and the simple dual-zone climate controls. The cockpit offered a huge center console, tall and deep dash

bin and good-sized cupholders that are very American, and very appreciated. The vents worked wonders on scorching days, offering two adjustments per outlet for positioning the air exactly where you want it. Even though the secondary stalk worked a myriad of tasks, it was still easy to use, and the rather large steering wheel came with both stereo and cruise controls mounted right on it. We also appreciated the visor extenders, compass and outside temperature display, and optional sunroof that came on our test vehicle.

Disappointments were limited to the low-rent feel of some interior materials, exposed screw heads in the recesses of the door armrests, the silly-looking AIRBAG notice stamped into the dash in front of the passenger, ugly faux wood strip on the four-color dash, and the overdone cutlines around controls and buttons. In the back seat, we were happy to find a power point, flip-down armrest with cupholders, three 3-point seatbelts for the passengers, and three car-seat tether anchors. Our editor-in-chief found that in this full-size sedan, his knees brushed against the back of the driver's seat-a situation which interestingly does not occur in

Chevy's own midsize Malibu. Chevy claims the Impala has theatre seating in the back; we still felt like we were sitting on the floor. And the backrest is angled so sharply that it causes slouching and makes it impossible for rear-seat passengers to get comfy.

We also noticed that the passenger-side seatbelt adjuster on our test car wasn't working; the harder we pulled on the plastic release button, the more it felt like it was about to break off in our hands. We stopped pulling and let the seatbelt cut across our necks instead. Once, when we had to slam on our brakes to avoid hitting a car that cut us off, both sides of the 60/40 split-folding rear seat came flopping down into the cabin. After inspecting it later, we found that in order to get the seatbacks to latch securely, you must push the cushion back into place with plenty of might. And the latch on the smaller, 40-side of the split seat was jammed. We appreciated Chevy's exceptionally large trunk with cargo net, but wished the luggage lift-in was a bit lower.

Competing in the full-size market, Chevy plans to pit its new sedan against the likes of Ford's Crown Victoria, Toyota's Avalon and Dodge's Intrepid, among others. And that's where the Impala gets into trouble. We like the Buick LeSabre Limited better than the Chevrolet because of its quieter and more comfortable cabin. We'd buy the Chevy Malibu over the Impala for its more comfortable back seat. We'd choose a Chrysler Concorde LX over this car for its beautiful styling and superior interior room. We prefer Dodge's Intrepid ES for its excellent passenger accommodations and sporting nature. Ford's Crown Victoria beats out this vehicle with its kitschy styling, quieter cabin, V8 engine and rear-wheel drive. The 2000 Ford Taurus has suave good looks and a more modern powertrain. Honda's Accord is more sophisticated in feel and simpler in design. Nissan's Maxima is a true driver's car that is available with a stick shift. Toyota's Avalon wins for its superior build quality and better interior materials, as well as its smooth-revving twin-cam V6. The VW Passat has a more comfortable interior, a fun-to-drive nature, and an available manual transmission. The only competitors we would in fact forsake for the new Impala are the Pontiac Bonneville, with a design that only a mother could love, and the Toyota Camry, because it's dull and more uncomfortable than the Chevy.

Able to accommodate six passengers and their gear, the Impala is aimed at 44-year-old family men and women with a household income around $60,000. As Chevrolet's flagship sedan and with Impala's rich history, the company hopes to sell the Impala Sedan and the Impala LS to those with a passion for the "pure American driving experience." Good luck.

When Chevy redesigned the Malibu, the advertising campaign declared: The Car You Knew America Could Build. And they were right on target. Unfortunately, the second time around isn't exactly a charm, and the 2000 Impala may be best described as: The Car You Knew America Would Build. ∎

Vehicle Tested: 2000 Chevrolet Impala LS
Base Price of Vehicle: $22,925 (including destination charge)
Options on Test Vehicle: Rear Spoiler Delete, Electric Sunroof, AM/FM Stereo with Cassette and CD Player (includes seek-scan, digital theft-lock, speed-compensated volume, radio data system and eight speakers), California Emissions, and Preferred Equipment Group (includes driver information center, universal garage door opener, alarm system, electrochromatic rearview mirror, and steering wheel-mounted radio controls).
Price of Test Vehicle: $24,190 (including destination charge)

Muhammad Ali had Joe Louis. Martina Navratilova had Chris Evert. The Lakers had the Celtics. The Bass Master had the Roncho combination Juicer and Nose Picker. Every champion has a foil to prove his or her (or its) greatness. And herein lies the problem facing the new Audi S4.

The reigning champ of midlevel sport sedans— the BMW M3 — has disappeared for 2000. Well, not really disappeared. More of a temporary hiatus. Both a two-door and a four-door version of the M3 were available on the previous-generation 3 Series. But with the current model (it debuted in

Audi
S4

BMW Gets Upstaged

1999), BMW has delayed introducing an M version until 2001. From what our vast network of industry spies tells us, the new 2001 M3 should be quite impressive. But that's next year. Right here, right now, the new Audi S4 is the No. 1 contender.

The S4 is based off Audi's A4 platform. This is a pretty good place to start, as we've liked the current A4 ever since its introduction in 1996. We're impressed by its excellent design, capable handling, good looks, and optional all-wheel drive. All 2000 A4s and S4s also receive subtle improvements to the interior and exterior.

To get an idea of what the S4 represents, picture an A4 with a giant orange "New and Improved!" sticker on it. Under the hood is a 2.7-liter turbocharged V6 engine. It is based on the 200-horsepower, 2.8-liter V6 found in a variety of Audi models. The 100cc reduction of engine displacement is due to slightly smaller cylinder bores. Rather than using one large turbo, Audi has gone with two small turbos to feed the V6. This allows the engine to generate boost pressure much more quickly, resulting in quicker responsiveness. There's a long list of techno-goodies like twin intercoolers, dual-

518   www.edmunds.com   EDMUND'S® NEW CARS

overhead cams, five valves per cylinder, variable valve timing for the intake camshaft, and optimized combustion chambers. It all adds up to 250 horsepower at 5,800 rpm, and 258 foot-pounds of torque at a super-low 1,850 rpm. The torque peak is maintained all the way up to 3,600 rpm. Redline is 6,800 rpm.

Audi A4s can be ordered with either front-wheel drive or all-wheel drive. In the S4's case, the quattro all-wheel-drive system is standard. Quattro comes with a Torsen center differential that distributes up to 66 percent of

by Brent Romans

photos courtesy of Audi USA

the power to whichever axle has the most traction. Both the front and rear differentials also have Electronic Differential Locking (EDL). This feature detects and limits wheel spin and redistributes power from side to side to take advantage of available traction. As any proper sport sedan should have, a six-speed manual transmission is standard equipment. A Tiptronic-controlled five-speed automanual transmission is available as a no-cost option.

Sitting still, the S4 doesn't look all that different from an A4. More moody, maybe. It hunkers down some, thanks to a lowered ride height and special 17-inch six-spoke "Avus" wheels. There are also larger front air-intake openings and various S4 badges scattered about. But given the multitudes of A4s plying American roads, it's going to be tough for an S4 owner to attract jealousy from other German sedan owners. They simply won't know any different. Perhaps that is why Audi is offering two seemingly Slurpee-inspired colors — Imola Yellow and Nogaro Blue. Both of these blazing hues are available on the S4 only.

> *"While certainly perfor-
> mance-oriented, we
> would say the ride is still
> softer than a previous-
> generation BMW M3's."*

Once moving on the road, the S4 is much more capable of capturing attention of both the driver and other cars being passed. The engine rips off a pleasant V6 snarl and mixes it with some soft turbo whooshes and whistles.

Though it lacks some precision in its shifter, we still highly recommend the six-speed manual transmission. It's so rare that a car company recognizes the wants of the enthusiast, so best to take advantage of it. The top cogs are for cruising, of course, but the broad torque band does allow for good acceleration nearly anywhere on the revband. The S4 is quite quick. It will beat any similarly priced 2000-year sedan in acceleration, though it doesn't ultimately have enough steam to outpace big dogs like the Chevrolet Corvette or Porsche 911. Audi says a manual-equipped S4 will go from zero to 60 in 5.9 seconds.

Of course, if a Corvette tried to beat up on an S4 in the wet, it would be a totally different story. Quattro gives the S4 excellent stability on the road, especially in less-than-perfect conditions. Both braking and handling are improved over the standard A4's. The S4 gets larger rotors (12.6 inches in front and 10.1 inches in the rear), high-performance twin-piston front calipers, stiffer springs and shocks, bigger antiroll bars, and 225/45R17 tires. While certainly performance-oriented, we would say the ride is still softer than a previous-generation BMW M3's.

Inside, the S4 gets a livelier interior than those found in A4s. Onyx- or silver-colored leather upholstery is used on power seats that are noticeably more supportive than the A4's. Leather is also used on the rear seat area, the armrest, and the door panels. At no extra cost, buyers can opt for the sport interior package, which adds silver or blue suede inserts to the seats. The

> *"Quattro gives the S4 excellent stability on the road, especially in less-than-perfect conditions."*

main problem here is the lack of legroom for backseat passengers. It's not horrible, mind you, but it's best to take that into consideration if you plan on consistently transporting adults in the backseat.

Pricing for 2000 S4s starts at $37,900. Broken down into individual elements, the car's attributes don't seem all that impressive. Plenty of other cars have all-wheel drive. Japanese manufacturers were bolting two small turbos to six-cylinder engines 10 years ago and getting 300-plus horsepower (Mitsubishi 3000GT VR-4, Nissan 300ZX and Toyota Supra). The idea of a good-handling sedan isn't exactly new, either. But very few carmakers have been able to combine all of this into one complete package, and that's what makes the S4 such an exciting and desirable car. ■

**TO PRICE YOUR TRADE-IN,
PURCHASE EDMUND'S® USED CAR PRICES AND RATINGS.**

See page 6 for details.

Notes

Notes

PAYMENT TABLE

Depicts estimated monthly payment per $1,000 borrowed*

TERM (length of loan)

		12	24	36	48	60
I	4%	85.15	43.40	29.50	22.55	18.45
N	5%	85.60	43.85	29.95	23.00	18.90
T	6%	86.05	44.30	30.40	23.50	19.35
E	7%	86.55	44.75	30.90	23.95	19.80
R	8%	87.00	45.25	31.35	24.40	20.30
E	9%	87.45	45.70	31.80	24.90	20.75
S	10%	87.90	46.15	32.25	25.35	21.25
T	11%	88.40	46.60	32.75	25.85	21.75
	12%	88.85	47.05	33.20	26.35	22.25
R	13%	89.30	47.55	33.70	26.85	22.75
A	14%	89.80	48.00	34.20	27.35	23.25
T	15%	90.25	48.50	34.65	27.85	23.80
E	16%	90.75	48.95	35.15	28.35	24.30

*rounded to nearest nickel

Automobile Manufacturers
Customer Assistance Numbers

Acura	1-800-382-2238
Audi	1-800-822-2834
BMW	1-800-831-1117
Buick	1-800-521-7300
Cadillac	1-800-458-8006
Chevrolet	1-800-222-1020
Chrysler	1-800-992-1997
Daewoo	1-888-643-2396
Dodge	1-800-992-1997
Ford	1-800-392-3673
GMC	1-800-462-8782
Honda	1-800-999-1009
Hyundai	1-800-633-5151
Infiniti	1-800-662-6200
Isuzu	1-800-255-6727
Jeep	1-800-992-1997
Kia	1-800-333-4542
Land Rover	1-800-637-6837
Lexus	1-800-255-3987
Lincoln	1-800-392-3673
Mazda	1-800-222-5500
Mercedes-Benz	1-800-222-0100
Mercury	1-800-392-3673
Mitsubishi	1-800-222-0037
Nissan	1-800-647-7261
Oldsmobile	1-800-442-6537
Plymouth	1-800-992-1997
Pontiac	1-800-762-2737
Porsche	1-800-545-8039
Saab	1-800-955-9007
Saturn	1-800-553-6000
Subaru	1-800-782-2783
Suzuki	1-800-934-0934
Toyota	1-800-331-4331
Volkswagen	1-800-822-8987
Volvo	1-800-458-1552

 edmunds.com
consumer driven

SINGLE COPIES / ORDER FORM

Please send me:

☐ **USED CARS: PRICES & RATINGS** *(includes S&H)* **$13.99**

☐ **NEW CARS**
— American & Import *(includes S&H)* **$13.99**

☐ **NEW TRUCKS [PICKUPS, VANS & SPORT UTILITIES]**
— American & Import *(includes S&H)* **$13.99**

Name _____

Address _____

City, State, Zip _____

Phone _____

PAYMENT: __ MASTERCARD __ VISA __ CHECK or MONEY ORDER $_____

Make check or money order payable to:

Edmund Publications Corporation *P.O. Box 338, Shrub Oaks, NY 10588*

*For more information or to order by phone, call **(914) 962-6297***

Credit Card # _____ Exp. Date: _____

Cardholder Name: _____

Signature _____

Prices above include shipping within the U.S. and Canada only. Other countries, please add $7.00 to the price ($13.99+7.00) per book (via air mail) and $2.00 to the price ($13.99+2.00) per book (surface mail). Please pay through an American Bank or with American Currency. Rates subject to change without notice.

SUBSCRIPTIONS / ORDER FORM
BUYER'S PRICE GUIDES

Please send me a one year subscription for:

☐ **USED CAR PRICES & RATINGS**
AMERICAN & IMPORT (package price includes $10.00 S&H) $34.00
Canada $40.00/Foreign Countries $48.00 (includes air mail S&H)
<u>4 issues/yr</u>

☐ **NEW CARS**
AMERICAN & IMPORT (package price includes $10.00 S&H) $34.00
Canada $40.00/Foreign Countries $48.00 (includes air mail S&H)
<u>4 issues/yr</u>

☐ **NEW TRUCKS [PICKUPS, VANS & SPORT UTILITIES]**
AMERICAN & IMPORT (package price includes $10.00 S&H) $34.00
Canada $40.00/Foreign Countries $48.00 (includes air mail S&H)
<u>4 issues/yr</u>

Name _____

Address _____

City, State, Zip _____

PAYMENT: __ MC __ VISA __ Check or Money Order-Amount $_____   Rates subject to change without notice

Make check or money order payable to:
Edmund Publications Corporation P.O. Box 338, Shrub Oaks, NY 10588
For more information or to order by phone, call **(914) 962-6297**

Credit Card # _____ Exp. Date: _____
Cardholder Name: _____
Signature _____

BUYER'S GUIDES
SCHEDULED RELEASE DATES
FOR 2000 / 2001*

VOL. 34		RELEASE DATE	COVER DATE
U3401	USED CARS & TRUCKS:Prices & Ratings	JAN 00	SPRING 00
N3401	NEW CARS:Prices & Reviews[American & Import]	MAR 00	SPRING 00
S3401	NEW TRUCKS:Prices & Reviews[American & Import]	MAR 00	SPRING 00
U3402	USED CARS & TRUCKS:Prices & Ratings	APR 00	SUMMER 00
N3402	NEW CARS:Prices & Reviews[American & Import]	JUN 00	SUMMER 00
S3402	NEW TRUCKS:Prices & Reviews[American & Import]	JUN 00	SUMMER 00
U3403	USED CARS & TRUCKS:Prices & Ratings	JUL 00	FALL 00
N3403	NEW CARS:Prices & Reviews[American & Import]	SEPT 00	FALL 00
S3403	NEW TRUCKS:Prices & Reviews[American & Import]	SEPT 00	FALL 00
U3404	USED CARS & TRUCKS:Prices & Ratings	OCT 00	WINTER 00
N3404	NEW CARS:Prices & Reviews[American & Import]	DEC 00	WINTER 01
S3404	NEW TRUCKS:Prices & Reviews[American & Import]	DEC 00	WINTER 01

*Subject to Change